Women and Socialism / Socialism and Women

WOMEN AND SOCIALISM
SOCIALISM AND WOMEN

Europe Between the Two World Wars

Edited by

Helmut Gruber & Pamela Graves

Berghahn Books

NEW YORK • OXFORD

First published in 1998 by

Berghahn Books

www.berghahnbooks.com

© 1998 Helmut Gruber and Pamela Graves

Library of Congress Cataloging-in-Publication Data

Women and socialism, socialism and women : Europe between the two World
  Wars / edited by Helmut Gruber and Pamela Graves.
        p.   cm.
    Includes bibliographical references.
    ISBN 978-1-57181-151-6 (hardback: alk. paper) -- ISBN 978-1-57181-152-3
(paperback : alk. paper)
      1. Women and socialism--Europe--History--20th century.
    2. Feminism--Europe--History--20th century.   I. Gruber, Helmut,
    1928–   . II. Graves, Pamela M.   III. Title: Women and socialism,
    socialism and women.
    HX546.W598   1998   98-21339
    335'.0085'094--DC21   CIP
                                                                        Rev.

British Library Cataloguing in Publication Data

A catalogue record for this book is available from the British Library.

Printed on acid-free paper.

CONTENTS

❦

Part II. Grassroots Initiatives

Part III. Political Fractures

Part IV. Prelude to Welfare States

LIST OF PHOTO ESSAYS

⟨⟨⟩⟩

Part II. Activities and Aspirations of British, Dutch, and Belgian Women 176

"Women Will, Can, and Do Vote and Govern!"
- Dutch Socialist Female Parliamentary Election Canvassers, 1922
  Source: International Institute for Social History (IISG), Amsterdam
- Belgian Unenfranchised Wife Asking Husband to Vote Socialist, 1932
  Source: Foto-archiv Archive & Museum of the Socialist Labour Movement
  (AMSAB), Ghent
- LP Members of Parliament, Including Margaret Bonfield,
  First Female Minister
  Source: VGA

*"Women Play an Active Role: in Trade Unions, the Community, and in
Political Manifestations"*
- Labour Councillor Julia Scurr Says "No Surrender" During Rent
  Strike of 1921
  Source: National Museum of Labour History (NMLH), Manchester
- Popular Front Demonstrators, Ostand 1936
  Source: Foto-archiv AMSAB, Ghent
- British National Federation of Women Workers Demonstrate
  Against Unemployment, 1920
  Source: NMLH

"The Future of Women and Socialism Lies in the Next Generation"
- Dutch Socialists and Trade Unions Call Public Meeting on Future
  of Children
  Source: Poster: Fré Cohen, IISG
- Recruitment Poster for the Dutch Socialist Youth: Suggesting
  Gender Equality in Social Commitment
  Source: Poster: Levi Schwarz, IISG

"Women in the Forefront of Disarmament and Anti-Fascism"
- Call for Dutch Women to Vote Socialist under the Slogan
  "Disarmament" 1925
  Source: Poster: Willem Papenhuyzen, IISG
- Belgian Socialist Women Marching against Fascism, 1931
  Source: Foto-archiv AMSAB, Ghent
- Independent Labour Party Demonstration for Peace, 1929
  Source: NMLH

Part III. French, Spanish, Italian Women: Work, Gender Roles, Struggles in Times of National Turmoil 273

"Images of Women's Sphere: Separate or Equal?"
- Vision of Women as Confined to the Domestic Sphere: Poster of
  Conservative Middle-class French Feminists
  Source: Poster: Henri Lebasque, Bibliothèque de Musée Social, Paris

Part IV. Swedish, Norwegian, and Danish Women: Citizenship, Maternity, Selfhood – a Contradiction? 421

"Youth, the Pride of the Ineluctable Socialist Future"

- Danish Socialist Female Youth in Holiday Garb Demonstrating for Peace, 1918
  Source: Danish Workers' Movement Archive & Library (DWMAL), Copenhagen
- Young Danish Female Socialists in Action through Sports, 1931
  Source: DWMAL

"Conflicting Ideals: Housewife, Mother, New Woman"

- One Million Swedish Housewives Demand Higher Wages and Jobs
  Source: Morgonbris, July 1936: Swedish Labor Movement Archives & Library (SLMAL), Stockholm
- Norwegian Workers Party: a Well-run Home and Healthy Children Are Woman's Foremost Responsibility
  Source: Arbeidermagasinet, 1935: Norwegian Labor Movement Archives & Library (NLMAL), Oslo
- Image of the New Swedish Woman: Working, Married, Mother, 1934
  Source: Morgonbris, 1934: SLMAL

"Women Stand up for Their Rights in the World of Work Outside the Home"

- Swedish Domestic Workers Demand Respect and the Eight-Hour Day, 1938
  Source: SLMAL
- Danish Female Metal Workers on Strike, 1930
  Source: DWMAL

"From Projections of Revolution to Practical Politics"

- Norwegian Socialist Banner of 1918: Women and Men as Comrades Fight for a Better World
  Source: NLMAL
- Swedish Election Poster, 1936: "We Women Vote Socialist; We Build the Future"
  Source: Morgonbris, Sept. 1936: SLMAL

List of Acronyms

❦

ADGB	Federation of Trade Unions (Allgemeiner Deutscher Gewerkschaftsbund)
AFSM	Group of Feminist Socialists of Madrid
AIZ	Workers Illustrated Newpaper (Arbeiter Illustrierte Zeitung)
AJC	Labor Youth League
AMA	Popular Front Women's Antifascist Organization (Agrupacion de Mujeres Antifascistas)
ARSO	Working Group of Social Political Organizations (Arbeitsgemeinschaft sozialpolitische Organisationen)
BdF	Federation of German Women's Association (Bund deutscher Frauen)
BDM	League of German Girls (Bund deutscher Mädel)
BWP	Belgian Worker's Party
CGL	General Confederation of Labor (Confederazione Generale Italiana del Lavoro)
CGT	French Trade Union Federation (Confédération Générale du Travail)
CIF	Centro di Iniziativa Femminile
CNAF	National Women's Action Committee (Comité national d'action pour les femmes)
CNFS	National Committee of French Women Socialists (Comité national des femmes socialistes)
CNOC	National Federation of Catholic Workers
CNR	Conseil National de la Résistance
CNT	National Confederation of Labor (Confederación Nacional del Trabajo)

COMINTERN	Communist International
CPGB	Communist Party of Great Britain
Defense	The Defense of Women Workers (La Difesa delle Lavoratrici)
DWS	Danish Women's Society
FNTT	Socialist Agrarian Union
FPS	Provident Socialist Women (Femmes Prévoyantes Socialistes)
GDFS	Group of French Women Socialists (Groupe des femmes socialistes)
GFS	Group of French Feminist Socialists (Groupe féministe socialiste)
IAH	International Workers Aid (Internationale Arbeiter Hilfe)
ILO	International Labor Association
ILP	Independent Labour Party
KJVD	Communist Youth Association (Kommunistische Partei Deutschlands)
KPD	German Communist Party (Kommunistische Partei Deutschlands)
L'Ordine	The New Order
LFDF	French League for the Right of Women (Ligue française du droit des femmes)
LP	Labour Party
LSI	Labour Socialist International
MASCH	Marxist Evening School (Marxistische Arbeiter Schule)
MSPD	Majority Social Democratic Party (Mehrheits Sozialdemokratische Partei Deutschlands)
NEC	National Executive Committee
NLP	Norwegian Labor Party
NSDAP	German National Socialist Party (Nationalsozialistische Deutsche Arbeiterpartei)
OC	Cooperative Office (Office cooperatif)
PCE	Spanish Communist Party (Partida Communista de España)
PCF	French Communist Party (Parti Communiste Français)
PCI	Italian Communist Party (Partito Comunista Italiano)
PSI	Italian Socialist Party
PSOE	Spanish Socialist Workers' Party (Partido Socialista Obrero Español)
PSU	Unitary Socialist Party

RFB	Red Front-Fighters League (Roter Frontkämpfer Bund)
RFMB	Red Women's and Girls' League (Roter Frauen und Mädchen Bund)
RH	Red Aid (Rote Hilfe)
SBZ	Soviet Occupation Zone (Sovjetische Besatzungszone)
SDAP	Dutch Social Democratic Workers Party
SDAP	Austrian Socialist Party
SDWA	Social Democratic Women's Association
SDYA	Social Democratic Youth Association
SED	Socialist Unity Party (Sozialistische Einheitspartei Deutschlands)
SFIO	French Socialist Party (Section française de l'Internationale ouvrière)
SJC	Standing Joint Committee of Industrial Women's Organizations
SPD	German Social Democratic Party (Sozialdemokratische Partei Deutschlands)
SSFA	Soldiers' and Sailors' Families Association
Tribune	Women's Tribune (L'Ordine Nuovo)
UDI	Union of Italian Women (Unione Donne Italiane)
UFSF	French Union for Women's Suffrage (Union française pour le suffrage des femmes)
UGT	General Workers' Union (Unión General de Trabajadores)
USPD	German Independent Social Democratic Party (Unabhängige Sozialdemokratische Partei Deutschlands)
UUWW	Union of Unskilled Women Workers
WCN	Women's Clubs Network
WEA	Workers Education Association
WWA	Working Women's Association
YWCA	Young Women's Christian Association

ACKNOWLEDGMENTS

⤞⤝

The project of which this book is the culmination grew out of my personal interest in the socialist and women's movements in the form of a challenge: How had the two related to each other and could a history of such interactions be written? Personal preference made Europe the terrain of this inquiry; the two decades between the world wars, when both movements had reached a certain maturity, seemed to be the appropriate time. A team of sixteen historians was assembled to pursue this study across eleven national boundaries.

Extensive discussions among members of the group made it clear that we were committed to investigating both the common themes as well as the differences of national experience; that we would attempt to produce a cohesive volume and not simply a collection of essays. A program development grant from the Council for European Studies made it possible to bring the entire team together in planning sessions. We owe a great debt to the Council's Executive Director, Ioannis Sinanoglou, whose support for the project throughout its evolution assured us of its value.

Two workshops were held in Paris at the invitation of the Maison des sciences de l'homme (MSH). At the first in 1996 the common themes addressed by all the authors were established. For the second in 1997 draft chapters had been exchanged and were thoroughly critiqued. We are enormously grateful to the Director of the MSH, Maurice Aymard, for his scholarly and financial support of these workshops.

I especially want to thank Pamela Graves, who joined me as coeditor in 1996 and has fully shared in the complicated task of creating an integral volume from a diverse variety of stylistic challenges. Many thanks are also owed to Guy Baldwin, Managing Editor of International Labor & Working-Class History, for lending his expertise to untangling the Tower of Babel confusion of electronic chapters into a single editable text. Last but not least, I am grateful to Marion Berghahn, publisher of Berghahn Books, for the enthusiasm with which she agreed to publish this rather large volume. Close cooperation with the press's in-house editor, Janine Treves, throughout the various stages of production has helped to make this a better book.

Helmut Gruber
Spring 1998

INTRODUCTION

Socialist Breviary on Women

"Socialism is the hope of the world of women"
"Men and women basically have the same rights and duties"
"Men and women have equal political and civic rights as citizens"
"Men and women are equal but different"
"Men and women represent the rational and emotional side of humanity"

* * *

PART ONE

W*omen and Socialism / Socialism and Women: Europe Between the Two World Wars* is the outgrowth of a cooperative project in compara-tive history begun by sixteen historians in 1993 and brought to a conclu-sion in this volume. The motivation for this project was the realization that until recently pioneering histories of women have generally been segregated from the historical context. This ghettoization (perforce a women's addendum to the history of men)[1] is a natural consequence of the difficulties and resistances encountered by scholars attempting to trace the role of women in societal context through hitherto neglected sources. Such isolation of women, imposed by the necessity of having to establish the legitimacy of this inquiry, has nonetheless resulted in a vast resource of data and created a substantial monographic literature. This first phase of study has been symbolically brought to a close with the publication of the five volume *A History of Women in the West* edited by Georges Duby and Michelle Perrot which, despite significant gaps, has become a benchmark.[2]

We consider our project as part of the next phase of development: the place and role of women *in* history, which raises the central question of power distribution between the genders in specific historical contexts.

Notes for this chapter begin on page 23.

Two problems intrigued the team of participants, all of whom had worked on women or socialism or both (see list of contributors): First, what was the relationship of working-class organizations, which have traditionally laid claim to embody progressive thought and action, to gender and the role of women in their movement and in society in general? The interwar period, when socialist parties and their affiliated trade unions had attained a certain maturity and prominence and when the role of women had perforce become an unavoidable subject of discussion, seemed an ideal and circumscribed time-frame for such a study. Second, how could this problem be formulated so as to allow for a comparison across the national boundaries of western and central Europe? It was clear from the outset that a well defined set of common themes and problems collectively arrived at would need to be at the heart of the enterprise.

A number of premises underlie these approaches: first, that socialism as a national and international movement was more responsive to what was called the "woman question" than other institutions or organizations in interwar society (a claim that was repeated in various programmatic statements throughout the interwar decades); second, that women within the orbit of socialism realized certain gains (even though their experience was frequently negative and their aspirations remained largely unfulfilled); and third, that despite many markedly sharp differences of national expression a common strand of experiences ran across the transnational spectrum.

By highlighting comparative features, restricting the time frame to two decades, and including most of the countries of western and central Europe,[3] we hope to avoid the shortcomings of existing volumes attempting to treat aspects of women's history in a comparative way.[4]

Two Movements in the Interwar Era

We have used the emblematic title *Women and Socialism / Socialism and Women* to highlight the fundamental conception of this volume: that in the interwar decades two great movements grew to prominence, converged, diverged, competed, and cooperated.[5] Each of these movements is viewed as a complex matrix of organized and unorganized participants.[6] In our conception, socialism is shorthand for the many formal and informal activities that made up the working-class movement. The term includes political parties from social democratic to communist and anarchist, with their local and constituent units; youth groups and cultural organizations; trade unions of varying orientations, chambers of labor, and "friends of labor" alliances; cooperative societies and tenants' associations. Supporters of labor also gathered in a variety of professional and reform-oriented groups: sympathizing teachers, social workers, doctors, and lawyers, or members of societies for sexual and civil reform. Finally, the working-class movement consisted of all the men and women who were members as well as those who participated less formally or regularly.

In speaking of women we visualize a movement less structurally organized than the working class but also a blending of very diverse strands. Women organized within political parties and trade unions. They created feminist organizations, civil rights leagues, and community-based reform alliances addressing issues such as abortion and birth control, prices, housing, suffrage, alcohol, public health, and hygiene. Most importantly, it was the shifting memberships and audiences, the spontaneous demonstrations for issues and causes, the constant appearance of new actors and vanguards that made the women's movement appear excitingly new, infinitely varied, and also quite disorganized.

These two significant movements came to fruition between the wars, which were more than mere signposts of their development and relationship. World War I was a defining experience for the European population, particularly for men who served in the armed forces and came in contact with a sophisticated world beyond their limited regional and local origins.[7] For many, living "en masse" led to an awakening to the complex social realities of the time and of their society in general. This raising of consciousness explains such violent outbursts as strikes in the Austrian and German navy, the abandonment of the Dual Monarchy by its nationalities, and the formation of soldiers' and workers' councils at the end of hostilities. Less dramatic but more important was the influx of men into the socialist parties and trade unions, a sign of the personal and group awareness the four years of crisis had produced. Seemingly overnight these became mass institutions called upon to play a political, economic, and social role in every European country and gave unprecedented presence to the popular classes.

World War I was equally defining for the women's movement, because it brought large numbers of women out of a limiting home environment and into the larger world of wage labor, self-sufficiency, family headship, decision making and, most importantly, same-sexed groups and networks providing mutual aid and strength. Bursting upon the larger world raised women's expectations about a future of greater recognition, opportunity for vocations and careers, and more just and equal gender relations. Though this optimism for "true citizenship" was to be dashed soon after the armistice as demobilized soldiers returned to claim their jobs, the controlling functions in societal institutions, and their traditional place at the head of the family, rising expectations among women had been strong enough during the war years to provide the women's movement with a potential mass base as well.

At the other end of the period, as the 1930s drew to a close, another world war loomed large and threatened to overwhelm the two great movements. The promises of socialism made much earlier and often repeated about being the only true proponent of equality and a more just world of universal citizenship, were shelved in view of great national and international uncertainties, especially following the Munich Accord in 1938. Caught between pacifism and patriotism, women were once more made to feel that their needs and their agendas would have to wait; the slow but steady growth of their organizations was brought to a halt as they lost their gendered purpose.

But what about the intervening years between 1919 and 1939? Did they offer great promise or endless turmoil and uncertainty for the relationship of women and socialism? Obviously both. The fact that women had gained the vote in most European countries by the early twenties made them potential and actual political players though, as the following chapters demonstrate, women still lacked the know-how for exploiting this power to extend their citizenship. The relationship between the women's and working-class movements was shaped by dramatic events of the decades: the Bolshevik Revolution, which offered itself to both movements as a counter-model to decadent capitalism; the Popular Fronts; and especially the great strike waves of 1936 in Belgium and France, which brought women into the public sphere.

The coming to power of fascism in Italy and National Socialism in Germany together with the universally destructive impact of the Great Depression became defining and limiting experiences for relations between women and socialists (which at best always were restricted by uncertainties and a lack of mutual trust). These threats could have strengthened the desire for closer, more equal relations but, as the experiences of the eleven countries reveal, they served to harden already fixed and biased positions. Various peace organizations, which initially promised to build bridges between women and socialists, could not sustain their efforts in the light of failure by leading international organizations. The inability of the League of Nations to carry out its primary mission was clearly demonstrated during the Abyssinian crisis and the Spanish Civil War, when the victims of aggression were abandoned to their fate.

The Labour and Socialist International (LSI) and the Communist International (Comintern) also abandoned all attempts by their subordinate Women's Internationals to put a female agenda before the public. The LSI's commitment to internationalism had been feeble from its inception in 1923 (centered on supporting the League of Nations). Despite internationalist clauses in its constitution, the national interests of member parties were paramount. Conflicts of national interest were apparent in the division between a small group of left parties and a right-wing majority over such issues as cooperation with the Comintern in support of the Spanish Republic and, also, in the division between national defensists and neutralists in the final year before the war. The parties of the Comintern were completely bolshevized and the Comintern itself acted as an instrument of Soviet foreign policy (witness Stalin's reversal on conscription and birth control in 1935 and its servile application by member parties). Finally, the Hitler-Stalin Pact negated whatever gains individual communist parties had made during the Popular Front era. By the end of the 1930s it was clear that internationalism simply was not on the agenda, either among the democratic states in the League or for the parties of the left in their internationals. Whatever small opportunities women of the left had been given to fashion a universal women's program were brushed aside in the face of greater exigencies.

For the socialist and women's movements the interwar period was marked by both progress and retreat in the form of challenges for which they were not prepared. The most obvious of these concerned electoral practices and mainstream politics. That led to a division along ideological and class lines for both, and became an obstacle to future collaboration. Equality of suffrage, like Pandora's box contained all the issues that quickly proved divisive: power sharing in the party and access to elective office, equal civil rights, the ambiguities of maternalism, and an underlying redefinition of the qualities of men and women.

A Menu of Comparative Themes and Problems

The actual themes to be pursued in research, which also cut well across national lines, involved an extended round robin of discussions culminating in a workshop.[8] One set of questions dealt with the role accorded to women by the working-class movement in parties, trade unions, and other associations of the generic left. This required a consideration of the representations of women in socialist discourse. What was the relationship between socialist/feminist rhetoric and socialist/feminist realities – between visions and promises in gender relations? It appeared that in these, women's rights challenged privileged male status, and men responded by arguing that women's ties to religion and lack of political understanding made the demand for equality premature.

The women's movement raised another set of questions. By the 1930s European women, in all but three countries, had attained the vote (though only at the municipal level for some). During the heyday of women's suffrage struggles it had been assumed that the vote would be a powerful lever for the realization of a broad women's agenda. Why did the ballot fail to endow women with full citizenship, not to speak of gender equality? The relationship between middle-class feminists and socialist women was an important variable within the women's movement. Can their differences be reduced to the conflict between the primacy of sex or class? Did either one really respond to the most important problems arising from the life cycle of unorganized working-class women? Similarly, to what extent and in which arenas did socialist women present specific female agendas that went beyond the programs of male-dominated parties and trade unions, and how were these received?

By far the most provocative questions dealt with gender relations. Central to these were definitions of femininity and masculinity used as mechanisms of inclusion and exclusion at the workplace, in the home, and in the political arena. What happened to the definitions of "breadwinner" and "homemaker" during critical periods? The mystique of the "new woman" in the 1920s and 1930s presented another challenge to gender identity and relations, not the least of which was the redefinition of the role of men, "new men."

Gender definitions were vital in the discussion of reproduction and family relations. At the root of the discussions between men and women of family planning and child care were the explosive issues of contraception and abortion. Despite their differences, both pro-natalists and neo-Malthusians saw women's role as fundamentally biological. This "essentialist" view raised the question of whether attempts to reform family life and health were steps toward the welfare state or authoritarian means of surveillance and control over women. Underlying the public discussion of "population politics" were masculine fears about changing sexual mores. Within socialist circles sexual proscriptions were directed at women alone and did not challenge the double standard.

Both movements embraced motherhood as the gender-defining condition, though each understood the term differently. By and large, women wanted fewer, healthier, and better-cared-for children and saw birth control as the means. Some women, of course, challenged attempts to use maternity to keep them in the home and to exclude them from party policies and public affairs. The persistence and importance of this subject suggested a transnational consensus among social reformers, repopulationists, and even socialists for "rationalization" of the private sphere.

After a thorough discussion of these wide-ranging questions the team decided upon a list of themes which appeared to be common to the eleven countries. This much narrower focus included: levels of citizenship; social welfare programs; the new woman; maternalism and birth control; sexuality and repopulation; the relationship between socialist and feminist women; the everyday life of women; and the national and international contexts. These themes acted as guidelines for transnational comparisons while the broader questions discussed above allowed national diversity to emerge.

National Similarities

The socialist confrontation with the woman question in the new circumstances after World War I raised an issue that each chapter addresses in some form: the interaction of political ideology with traditional social values. European socialists throughout the interwar years reiterated their commitment to the equality of the sexes, yet they were strikingly unsuccessful in implementing it at almost any level. The major stumbling block in every case was the strength of traditional ideas about appropriate gender roles. Very few men or women were able to accept women's ability and right to share equally in all areas of political life. Most defined women's political roles in terms of their "natural" domestic and maternal interests. There were growing numbers of women who claimed that these interests were just as much a part of socialism as traditional male concerns with the workplace and electoral politics, but they failed to convince their male comrades. No doubt the notion of separate spheres was a deliberate construction to preserve male dominance and female inferiority, and that notion had provided a justification for denying women political power and full civil rights since the early nineteenth century. Socialist men and women rarely acknowledged the contradiction between their shared ideal of gender equality and ingrained notions of gender difference and hierarchy, but it shaped the relations between left-wing parties and women in every country included in this study.

This tension between ideology and social values is a common theme that also demonstrates national difference. In each European society, as socialists set about building their postwar parties and programs, male leaders showed enormous ingenuity in offering rhetorical, theoretical, or potential equality to disguise the reality of continuing male control. Socialist women showed similar ingenuity in using the ideology of separate spheres to break through the barriers to effective policy making. They found that they had more success if they chose issues clearly within their assigned sphere – maternity, women's health and welfare, child care, and protective legislation – than with issues of legal and civil equality. But in each national situation, the contradiction between the ideological goal of equality and the idea of gender difference played out in very different ways. In Holland, for example, socialist women claimed the right to shape party policy in support of peace and disarmament. Their male comrades rejected this claim on the grounds that women supported disarmament not with sound political reasoning (the prerogative of men) but with an emotional "woman's" desire to prevent the deaths of sons and loved ones.

In each country, specific conditions determined how successful left-wing parties were in promoting women's interests in the interwar period. The strength of women's prewar organization in trade unions, cooperatives, socialist or feminist groups was a key variable. Where it existed, it provided a core of experienced, usually middle-class women leaders, bringing their ideas and skills into left-wing parties or staying in separate women's groups to put pressure on the male-dominated organizations. It meant prepared reform agendas based on socialist feminist goals and often with contributions from working-class women. In Britain, for example, the Co-operative Women's Guild and the Women's Labour League had a substantial working-class membership. They lobbied Parliament for the women's vote, divorce law reform, state allowances for mothers, and a national maternity service, and won the first two of these at the end of the war. Prewar socialist women's organizations raised political consciousness among minorities of working-class women, who became local cadres after the war. They raised funds, helped run elections, and sustained the local socialist culture by organizing social events and educating children in socialist values. Where these prewar women's organizations did not exist, they were hard to establish in the formal, class segregated, and male-directed postwar parties.

State institutions and policies also played a significant role in shaping the specific national relationship between socialism and the women's cause. The obvious example is the rise of fascism. When fascist or proto-fascist regimes took power, first in Italy, then in Germany, Austria, and Spain, they banned all left-wing parties, abruptly ending socialist policies relating to women or to anything else. Italian socialists and communists had only the years between 1918 and 1926 to bring women into their parties and to outline their reform agendas. In fact, they made little progress in either direction, and Italian women remained more numerous and active in trade unions than in the socialist parties. German social democrats and communists had by 1933 successfully organized women members and integrated them into distinct socialist cultures. Another institution specific to a group of countries was the Catholic Church. Socialists in Belgium, France, Italy, and Spain were reluctant to support women's suffrage, because they feared that women's votes would go overwhelmingly to the Catholic parties. The Church was a strong influence against divorce, birth control, and abortion and opposed any extension of women's civil or economic rights.

Pro-natalism was the best example of particularities of state policy. Although concern about falling rates of population growth was common to almost all governments in interwar Europe, its impact varied according to national circumstances. Pro-natalist governments were as likely to be fascist or conservative as liberal or socialist. From the point of view of socialist reformers, concerned for the health and welfare of working-class mothers, state pro-natalism could provide a supportive environment for the provision of maternity and child care services. On the other hand, it was often accompanied by punitive measures against abortion or birth control, both of which socialist feminists and many working-class women saw as central to any improvement in their lives. State pro-natalism was very strong in France but in that case, the male-dominated socialist party ignored the issue and French women took matters into their own hands by a tacit refusal to have more children than they felt they could care for. As a result, French population remained at a bare replacement level until after World War II.

The structure of left-wing parties accounted for national differences in the relationship between socialists and women. In countries where social democrats became ruling parties, Sweden for example, the likelihood of legislated reforms in women's interests was clearly greater than where they did not. In the thirties, the Swedish Socialist Party introduced the first comprehensive welfare program in Europe with universal health care and social security. In Austria, particularly in Vienna, the ruling social democrats created the most extensive socialist society and culture in Europe, with housing projects, health centers, and cultural activities intended to take care of every aspect of women's physical health and well-being. The fact that in both Sweden and Austria men designed these comprehensive welfare plans *for* women in accordance with their own ideas, and sometimes missed the mark in meeting women's needs, is further evidence of the persistence of gender hierarchy even in the most progressive parties. Social democrats also came to power in Britain, Belgium, Germany, Holland, Norway, and Denmark but commonly for brief periods as minority governments or coalition partners. Their legislative record on women's issues was slight, not only for lack of power but because they made women-specific reforms a low priority.

Where left-wing parties were unwilling to make women's issues part of their programs, in France for example, socialist women threw themselves wholeheartedly into the class cause without demanding attention to women's needs. Others, notably in Denmark, organized their own socialist groups as allies or auxiliaries of the male-controlled parties. The leaders of these women's groups were usually middle-class socialist feminists, but the members were overwhelmingly working-class housewives. Since they met in the afternoons, younger single working women rarely joined. Many of the women's organizations published their own journals which tended to have a self-consciously educational tone, because their middle-class editors were determined not to assume, as bourgeois journals did, that working-class women were only interested in recipes and knitting patterns.

In each country, the women's groups had very similar programs. They included health care for mothers and children, planned motherhood based on birth control and some form of state endowment for mothers, children, and widows. From the women's clubs in Denmark and the *prévoyante* women in Belgium to the British Labour party's women's sections and Women's Co-operative Guild, these locally based, and primarily urban organizations lobbied local and central governments to support their reform programs. The *prévoyante* women in Belgium, for example, took advantage of the government's pro-natalist policy to set up a network of state-funded mother and baby clinics.

In many countries middle-class feminists organized outside party politics or in Liberal parties had the same reform programs as those of the socialist women's groups. Not infrequently, there was a small cross-membership, a legacy from prewar feminist organizations that had sheltered a range of political points of view beneath the suffrage umbrella. With one or two exceptions, relations between organized socialist women and middle-class feminists grew increasingly hostile in the interwar period despite their common goals. In part, this was a result of the absorption of women into party politics. Except where socialist parties were trying to broaden their electoral base by appealing across party lines, as was the case with the Dutch social democrats, they strongly discouraged their members from alliances with nonparty, bourgeois groups. Their first demand was for class loyalty, and most women socialists were only too glad to comply.

In the broader social context, class relations became increasingly adversarial in interwar Europe. The economic woes of inflation and unemployment had a selective impact, hurting working-class families and those on fixed incomes so much more than the middle-class. Cutbacks and belt-tightening schemes targeted the working-class. As the economic gulf widened, socialist women questioned how "leisured sisters" could understand the problems facing low-income women. Cooperation between socialist women and liberal feminists ended, except in Denmark. There, as liberal feminists moved away from legal equality issues and toward social welfare, socialist club women informally joined with them to fight for birth control and married women's right to work.

All the following chapters pay close attention to the historical context of the time period. While politics may dominate, the material presented here is a powerful reminder of the disruptive social, economic, and cultural changes that underlay the political events pushing Europe towards a second world war. In the older industrialized countries, new forms of economic organization were replacing the old, and the result was widespread dislocation. Older primary industries – coal mining, textiles, and shipbuilding – were in decline and new electrical, chemical, automobile, and food processing industries were taking their place. The new, clean, assembly-line industries, where the work was characterized by repetitive motion, commonly employed young women. They formed a new female industrial workforce, rarely unionized, low paid, and unskilled. Nineteenth century, single industry working-class communities, hard hit by chronic unemployment, slowly gave way to more diffused communities, some in new housing projects. Mass culture, grounded in consumerism, and broadcast through movies, radio, and mass circulation magazines, was replacing the older, localized working-class (popular) culture.

The new consumer culture of the thirties relied on implicit and explicit projections of women's sexuality.[9] The science of sexology, associated with such reformers as Wilhelm Reich, Max Hodann, Dr. Norman Hare, Marie Stopes, and Magnus Hirschfeld, challenged the Victorian denial of women's sexuality and conceded that women were essentially sexual beings. Advertisers discovered the now all-too-familiar use of women's sexuality to sell everything from soup to soap. The tabloids, women's magazines, and the movies all helped to mold the image of the "new woman." She was less class-bound than her twenties predecessor, the middle-class flapper. She was single or newly married, worked in an office, or was a shop assistant; she engaged in sports, went dancing, wore makeup, dressed in mass produced versions of more expensive clothing, and was sexually attractive. She sprang to life everywhere in Europe.

Most socialist and communist parties responded to the "new woman," though the British Labour party was the exception. In Germany, Austria, Norway, Sweden, Belgium, and Holland, the concept was grafted onto the socialist culture. The new woman became the new comrade, still young and healthy, but decidedly working-class, standing beside her male counterpart in a platonic relationship until marriage, when she would give birth to a new generation of socialists. Like the female "Liberty" of the French revolutionary era, the "new comrade" inspired a splendid socialist iconography that appeared in journals and on banners and billboards. Typically standing slightly behind her male comrade and half-turned from him, with her hair flowing, she looks eagerly toward the socialist future with no more resemblance to a real working-class woman than "Liberty" herself. The new socialist female model opened up another space for women in the movement and attracted a new interwar generation of young women to the cause. She helped inspire a sense of gender camaraderie. But she remained symbolic of the equality ideal and did not represent a shift towards gender power sharing.

The main issue addressed in this volume is not how male socialists dealt with the woman question or how women functioned in or outside left-wing parties, but rather how organized socialists, men and women, shaped their parties' policies concerning women and the issues on which they came into conflict. In short, it aims at illustrating the power distribution between the sexes in specific political and cultural contexts.

The cumulative evidence in the fifteen chapters is unambiguous about the lack of change in traditional power between men and women in the two decades between the wars. Equally clear is the growth of women's agency in spaces they created for themselves, formally through organizations and campaigns, and informally in their communities. Women's entry into left-wing parties obliged traditional male-dominated organizations to open up some space to them no matter how limited, to pay attention to women's issues, even if it was only to reject them, to take some account of women constituents and include them in their party programs and manifestoes. All of these developments were groundbreaking. Some issues like birth control and abortion remained explosive; others, such as reform of the civil code, suffrage, and maternity rights forced male leaders to examine their positions even if they did not change them. Despite gender conflict in the working-class movement, areas of gender solidarity remained, notably the shared struggle against the old enemy, capitalism and the new threat of fascism. The Spanish Civil War became the symbol of crisis uniting men and women across class and ideological divisions throughout western and central Europe.

Assessments and Perspectives

Why were the rising expectations in the women's movement in 1914 not realized by 1939? The failings may be attributed to flaws in both the women's and socialist movements. Fragmentation was a constant barrier to the organization of women. The most serious division was based on class, but even within socialist parties there was a gulf between party loyalists and those committed to a feminist orientation. In addition, a myriad of small sects, groups, and loose associations of politically unaffiliated women existed without being able to coalesce, to make alliances with political parties, or to attract larger numbers of women. The differing and conflicting ideas of femininity among the women themselves also subverted the opportunities for collective representation of their concerns and needs. Of these the two most important were supporters of gender equality and integration and those who subscribed to equality in difference based on separate spheres.

Men in the socialist movement had their share of responsibility for women's unrealized expectations. A constant refrain for the postponement of women's agenda within parties and trade unions was that all problems would be solved and goals achieved with the triumph of socialism or that more pressing political and economic issues had priority. Being relegated to the distant future made women's second rate status quite clear, in which their activities were restricted to the domestic, maternal realm. In the short view, the failure of the two movements to coalesce in the form of a gender rapprochement must be laid at the door of the male-dominated, working-class movement, and especially the left parties and their internationals. It was male socialists' fear of sharing or losing power, often rationalized as political necessity, that made them deny women the possibility of equal participation.

Although egalitarianism and democracy already were implicit principles of socialism, anti-democratic practices revealed themselves virtually from the beginning. Most dangerous to democracy in the parties was the growth and entrenchment of bureaucracies, which seemed to arise naturally with the increase of membership, a development which Robert Michels and Max Weber had analyzed and warned about. Bureaucracy gave rise to party practices in direct contradiction to the high, humanitarian goals of socialism: the transformation of the leadership into an oligarchy increasingly distant from the rank and file, in whose name it formulated party programs and controlled the far-flung party enterprises; a growing intolerance of diverse views on tactics, the expression of which was increasingly stifled in the name of party loyalty to majority rule or democratic centralism.

A firm paternalist control was exercised by the revived socialist parties and LSI in the interwar period, despite frequent declarations by their leaders that their democratic practice distinguished them fundamentally from their fraternal opponents. The Trade Union Congresses manipulated the Labour party through the block votes of the largest trade unions to deny any opposition a voice in the party's programs, plans, or actions. In the French SFIO formal factions were permitted, but party congress resolutions masterfully buried dissent in the middle of the broad pronouncements. Socialist leaders in the Scandinavian parties, Holland, and Belgium slipped in and out of ministerial posts, making their demands for loyalty and unanimity all the more compelling. During the Depression vocal dissidents from party policy were unceremoniously expelled: Max Seydewitz and Kurt Rosenfeld from the German SPD in 1931; the left from the Dutch SDAP in 1932; the left-wing Göteburg section from the Swedish party in 1934; *Gauche Révolutionnaire* from the SFIO in 1938; and Stafford Cripps and Aneurin Bevan from the Labour party in 1939. The growing threat of fascism after 1933, the popular fronts, and the Spanish Civil War created a crisis in the LSI, with right-wing parties threatening to split the organization if initiatives to pursue a united antifascist campaign with the Comintern were pursued. By 1934, formal democratic procedures had deteriorated to the point where neither could votes on substantive issues be taken nor could congresses or conferences be held.

Lurking behind the issue of bureaucracy, paternalism, and oligarchical control was the fundamental problem of the relationship of leaders to masses. As the rising of Austrian workers in 1934 and the massive strikes of workers in France and Belgium in 1936 demonstrated, the latter could not always be kept in hand. But aside from such flash points, they could be and were managed. Whether the leadership proclaimed itself as a van-guard or laid claim to power by more representative means, it ultimately exhibited the same distance from the daily life of the rank and file.

In the long run the outcome of the relations between the two move-ments may not have been such a failure if we consider the following achievements: that in every country, and often in the face of brutal restric-tions, women took control over procreation; that the basis for post World War II welfare states was laid by small advances then and by new rising expectations on the part of women, gaining experience and courage even from failed efforts; that a "new woman" had indeed emerged by 1939 – not the artificial being of male socialist reformers or tabloid advertisers, but a person much more conscious of her needs and rights as citizen and human being than her mother had been; and lastly, that the rejuvenation of the working-class movement in Europe after 1945 and the significant role played in it by women was in large measure incubating in the troubled, uncertain, and far from gender-friendly interwar years.

Organization

The national chapters are arranged in geographic and thematic sections. The first groups three left-wing parties in central Europe – the social democrats in Vienna with the German social democratic and communist parties – all of which experimented with building urban socialist cultures that embraced areas of everyday life, from housing to theaters, schools to health clinics, libraries to stadia. The second section brings together social democratic parties in Holland, Belgium, and Great Britain where women developed strong grass-roots organizations and local socialist ini-tiatives were particularly effective. The third section is organized around the theme of Mediterranean political ruptures. Left-wing parties in France, Spain, and Italy faced severe political crises provoked by the rise of fascism. In the three socialist parties and the French communist party, women's issues were marginal and their party membership low. In these patriarchal settings, a handful of women socialists achieved prominence and women were active in some trade unions, but much of women's activity was local and informal. Section four explores the strategies of men and women in the Swedish, Norwegian, and Danish social democratic parties in pursuit of comprehensive social welfare programs.

To further the cohesion of this multinational study, Michelle Perrot, Louise Tilly, and Geoff Eley offer their commentaries and critiques. Michelle Perrot discusses women's expectations on the eve of World War I as a reference point for the national chapters that follow. In the conclusion, Louise Tilly and Geoff Eley comment upon two of the major themes explored in the chapters: the complex relationship between women, citizenship, and power and the connecting path running between the welfare initiatives of interwar socialists, particularly women, and the welfare states of the post-World War II years.

PART TWO

Snapshots of National Singularities

Readers will benefit most if they read the book in its entirety following our organization of chapter groupings with their introductions, thereby getting the full flavor of comparisons. For those who wish to sample parts of the text before plunging in or who are drawn to particular national experiences, the following abstracts should prove useful. But national differences do not obscure the common themes which underlie the encounters of the two great movements.

Austria

The role of women was intrinsically embedded in the Socialist party (SDAP) experiment to create a proletarian culture in Vienna. It was an ambitious enterprise of mass municipal housing, public facilities for health and recreation, transformation of the schools, and creation of "orderly worker families," carried out under the slogan of creating "new men and women." In this largest interwar attempt to create a welfare state environment (at least in the capital) women had a prominent place: as voters, as party and trade union members, and in the myriad cultural organizations of the SDAP. They were also encouraged to become the effective centers of their families – a fearless, open, and relaxed comrade to their husband and friend to their children. Despite the fact that women enjoyed the basic rights of citizenship, planning remained the exclusive privilege of the male party and trade union leadership, and the power relation between the genders (save for the reduction of the birth rate) were affected only slightly. Socialist paternalism, exercised through a large party and municipal bureaucracy, kept women in their place and discouraged independent initiatives.

Germany – SPD

Social Democratic women's attempt to combine class with gender issues had limited success in Germany. While "sisters" from other parties regarded them as "reds" and vice versa as "bourgeois," their male comrades within the Socialist party (SPD) considered them primarily as women and their demands as secondary. Local social projects and organizations concerning welfare, maternity, infant care, and children were the main achievements of SPD women. They also discussed and developed positions on women's employment, family life, and public culture. They welcomed the "new woman," but not the middle-class flapper, combining aspects of modernity with their idea of "cultural socialism" and the "new human being." The latter, as envisioned in the workers' cultural movement, inhabited a more or less socialist, communitarian world in miniature. SPD functionaries supported the rationalization of the worker home and the professionalization of housework – considered a major arena of women's activities. Mass culture received only limited and guarded support from both men and women.

Germany – KPD

Between its founding in December 1918 and its outlawing in February 1933 after the Nazi seizure of power, the KPD developed highly radical and innovative positions on women's rights while still never managing to integrate women into its central revolutionary project. The party waged a powerful campaign to abolish Paragraph #218 of the Penal Code, which criminalized abortion, and to support women's right to control their bodies. Alone among all Weimar parties it supported all women's right to work, even during the mass unemployment crisis of the thirties. Yet, it never fundamentally challenged the gender division of labor in the household, workplace, or public political arena, where men remained responsible for the "real" world of work and policy and women for the world of family and social welfare. The party proclaimed a powerful commitment to women's equality but gained the most female supporters in separate women's and welfare organizations. The KPD continually struggled for the support of the Weimar Republic's new female voters. The KPD's successes and failures in forging a class politics that could include gender, as recounted in this chapter, reveals a great deal about the possibilities and constraints experienced by the interwar European left in confronting the "woman question."

Britain

In the interwar British Labour party, a rhetoric of gender equality failed to overcome traditional ideas of women's difference and inferiority. Most of the quarter million Labour women accepted a distinct female role but struggled hard to win party support for their reform agenda, which included free birth control information for working-class women, family allowances, secondary education, protective legislation, and peace. When male leaders rejected or ignored their program, women socialists concentrated with considerable success on securing government and local initiatives. In the environment of economic depression, class hostility, and the new mass culture of the early thirties, Labour women abandoned their experiment in a women-centered socialism. They adopted a determined opposition to middle-class feminists and joined their male comrades in the struggle against the fascist threat.

Netherlands

In the Dutch SDAP of the mid-thirties a new socialism gained the upper hand. It entailed the transformation from a workers' party into a people's party and proclaimed a humanistic socialist ideology from which the Marxist concept of class struggle was omitted. It also proclaimed democracy as an end in itself rather than a means to other goals. Nevertheless, the party leadership failed to connect the unequal power relations within the family and in society to the practice of democracy. The few women who were in the party's women's organization made the connection, stressing the importance of women's economic independence as a democratic principle. But they were unable to persuade the male leaders that this issue was part and parcel of the new socialism. By narrowing the woman question to rights before the law, the new party program did not transcend liberal thought. Although women had the vote after 1919 and joined the party in increasing numbers in the interwar years, the woman question remained marginal to neorevisionst socialism.

Belgium

Between the two world wars the Belgian socialist women's movement was based on the rank and file female members of the male-dominated socialist political, cooperative, and mutual aid organizations. Although total equality was written in their program, socialists considered their women comrades as second-class citizens, who were to be educated as propagandists in their party's primordial struggle against the domination of the Catholic party and Catholic Church. As women had sworn solidarity with their male comrades, the Belgian Workers' party could nearly always persuade women to put party issues before feminist aspirations. Against the barrage of images of male socialists that women's place was in the home, the women's movement continued to fight for its own program: family allowances, rights for unwed mothers, equality of opportunity in education, equal pay, and birth control. Full female suffrage was their foremost demand.

France – SFIO

The French Socialist party (SFIO) rhetorically supported women's equality but neither took initiatives nor organized campaigns to give women the vote, bring them into the party, improve their position within it, or in other ways to diminish their standing as second-class citizens. The small group of socialist women, committed to the primacy of class over gender, were quite naturally in conflict with middle-class feminists, dedicated to "maternalism" and an "equality of difference" and close to the Radical party; but they also remained isolated from the large number of unorganized women to whom they should have reached out. If the national SFIO was mainly an electoral machine, grass-roots actions by both leading and ordinary women for political and economic rights offer an important insight into the potential for mobilization that neither the working-class party nor the trade unions were prepared to develop; nor should we overlook the independent action of socialist mayors in Paris suburbs and major industrial centers, of some socialist deputies, and of sympathizers from the liberal professions on behalf of women's cause. French women of all classes, despite horrendous laws that threatened them, created the possibility for the improvement of their condition by reducing the birth rate to a replacement level.

France – PCF

From its origins in 1920 to 1939 the French Communist party (PCF) appeared to be the most "feminist" party in France: advocating women's suffrage, promoting women's entry into trade unions and engaging in propaganda among women. A closer look at the PCF's efforts reveals the tiny number of female members. Moreover, during the various stages of its eventful history its policy toward women changed significantly. The PCF supported full citizenship for women including birth control and abortion in the 1920s. Beginning with the antifascist mobilizations of the thirties and reflecting the changed foreign policy perspectives of the USSR and Comintern, the PCF became a national and mass party. As such it abandoned its earlier positions, particularly on birth control, and became conventional, moralistic, pro-natalist, and pro-family.

Spain

Socialist feminism in Spain developed in a male scenario hostile to a feminist agenda. The Socialist party followed a strict labor program that paid little attention to gender issues. A socialist interpretation of feminism was voiced outside of official party structures by a small number of fringe socialists and militant women, who created a heightened awareness of women's issues. Their definition of socialist feminism incorporated Christian humanism, class politics, and modernity but it remained isolated and had little influence on female labor activism. Although the debate on constitutional rights in 1931 forced a redefinition of citizenship based on the paradigm of equality, female enfranchisement still remained contentious for many socialists. Under control of a socialist paternalism a labor welfare maternity scheme was developed that failed to view women as social actors and policymakers. Most socialist women failed to break party conventions by embracing a feminist agenda. Nevertheless, transgressive voices of dissonance by socialist feminists helped to develop independent feminist initiatives and to formulate new gender values and sexual ethics on the left.

Italy

In interwar Italy the "woman question" was largely ignored by both the Italian Socialist and Communist parties. Neither made a serious effort to recruit women, so that female membership remained only 2 to 3 percent of the total. Whereas, the Communist party was willing to include women's demands – like the right to work and equal pay – on its public agenda, neither party made such issues a practical priority. Yet, each party produced capable and well-known leaders, such as the socialist Anna Kuliscioff and the communist Camilla Ravera. Women were more active in trade unions and even unorganized women participated in strike waves during and after World War I. Women's concerns were eclipsed by the fight against fascism after Mussolini's seizure of power in 1922. Following the suppression of both parties by the dictatorship in 1926, women continued to participate in strikes and volunteered for underground activities against the regime. In recognition of their active role in the resistance, women finally received full voting rights in 1946.

Sweden

The twenties were hard times for Swedish working-class women. Although they had participated in the labor market for at least a century, married women's labor rights were questioned by male social democrats in parliament, city councils, and trade unions. As mothers, even single ones, they had no special rights. Women organized networks around those issues across class barriers. But in the thirties the new Social Democratic Welfare State offered women's organizations a certain measure of influence in state committees investigating women's conditions and preparing new laws to deal with them. Through them, mother's insurance, maternity leaves, and support for single mothers were introduced as part of the social welfare program. The dismissal of women on grounds of their being married, engaged, pregnant, or postpartum was prohibited. The sale of contraceptives was legalized and even abortion was permitted based on medical and social criteria. The main reason for these "woman-friendly" improvements was that the emerging welfare state needed women in both production and reproduction. The Social Democratic Women's Federation gained an important role in shaping the People's Home. Although gender relations underwent no basic change, the majority of Swedish women experienced a much better life in the thirties.

Norway

In contrast to the other Scandinavian countries, the Norwegian Labour Party manifested strong revolutionary attitudes. This made class solidarity prevail over gender solidarity. Both men and women within the movement adhered to a dichotomous understanding of gender, seeing women as housewives and mothers and men as providers and public figures. This perception of gender permeated all levels of the movement, from the children's groups upward, and found expression in numerous socialist cultural activities. Nevertheless, social-democratic women, sometimes allied with communist and radical liberal women, succeeded especially on the municipal level in creating important social institutions such as family planning centers. They initiated debates about reproductive practices and health that resulted in reforms at the parliamentary level. Raising the problem of child allowances, they even helped to introduce the principle of universalism, later to become one of the cornerstones of the Scandinavian model of welfare states. Throughout the interwar period social-democratic women rejected cooperation with the bourgeois women's movement. This attitude prevailed even after the Soviet attack on Finland in 1939.

Denmark

Throughout the interwar period the Danish Social Democratic party (DSDP) accepted women members but resisted their demand for a separate organization and voice in policy making. The party's shift from a class to a people's party divided women along class lines and alienated women engaged in workplace activism. Middle-class members of the reorganized party were frustrated with the male leadership's refusal to support independent women's clubs. They joined with organized feminists to fight for married women's right to work, birth control, and kindergartens. Rank and file working-class housewives preferred to focus club agendas around domestic and community issues. Activist women in the labor force rejected the DSDP in favor of their own trade unions and worker organizations. The Association of Women Workers, with a core membership of female iron workers, called for socialist gender equality in wages, hiring practices, and civil rights. Urbanization, changes in women's workforce participation, and the emergence of mass culture provided the backdrop to gender tension and class division. In response to the Depression, the DSDP and its liberal partners laid the foundation of a system of state responsibility for universal social welfare, which reinforced the idea of the male breadwinner and dependent wife. By the end of the thirties, most social-democratic women seemed prepared to accept this traditional view of women's place in the family.

Helmut Gruber and *Pamela Graves*

Notes

1. This ghettoization was driven home to the organizer of this project in trying to establish some kind of gender balance among the participating historians. For reasons best known in graduate history departments, gender history is not a topic of choice among male students. The gender division of our team amounts to thirteen women and three men.

2. The "separatist" approach to women's history still prevails. See, for instance, Olwen Hufton, *The Prospect Before Her: A History of Women in Western Europe*, I: 1500-1800 (New York, 1996). As the contributors to this volume discovered, gender-centered history remains a distant goal. Theorized to the point of tedium in recent years, the field has few empirical practitioners. To paraphrase an old adage: "The point is not to define it, but to do it!"

3. During the planning stage of the project inclusion of East Europe or at least Czechoslovakia, Hungary, and Poland was debated by the team. The final decision to limit the comparison to the eleven countries in this volume was based on: 1) the desire to make a full comparison of western and central European countries going beyond the usual Britain, France, and Germany, which would have to be reduced to make room for the east European sample; 2) the great difficulty in finding historians from these countries who were already engaged in similar work; and 3) the fact that the addition of three chapters would make this volume unmanageable.

4. See *Behind the Lines: Gender & the Two World Wars*, eds. Margaret Randolph Higonnet and Jane Jensen (New Haven, Conn., 1987), which includes a mixture of theory, history, and literature restricted to Britain, France, Germany, and the United States; *Women in Culture and Politics*, eds. Judith Friedlander et al. (Bloomington, 1986) with 26 short pieces encompassing history, biography, & literature with the same geographic restriction; *European Women on the Left*, eds. Jane Slaughter and Robert Kern (Westport, Conn., 1981), which is essentially biographical; and *Maternity & Gender Politics*, eds. Gisela Bock and Pat Thane (London, 1991), which encompasses an unmanageable time frame (1880s to 1950s).

5. It would not be completely far-fetched to see these encounters as gender relations between the male-dominated working-class movement and the female-centered women's movement (with the opposite sex a significant presence in the former and a small group of adherents and sympathizers in the latter).

6. Although inclined to look at women within formal structures, we discovered that women's unorganized activities in rent strikes, price protests, peace marches, and a myriad of other community-based political actions played a central role in bringing larger numbers of women into public life.

7. For a comparative study of the war's impact on families, living standards, women's work, social policy, and ideology, see Richard Wall and Jay Winter, eds., *The Upheaval of War: Family, Work, and Welfare in Europe 1914-1918* (Cambridge, Mass., 1988).

8. It took place in October 1995 at the Maison des sciences de l'homme in Paris and led to the adoption of firm guidelines to be used in the drafting of chapters, which were then to be discussed at a second workshop in January 1996.

9. See Victoria de Grazia with Ellen Furlough, eds., *The Sex of Things: Gender and Consumption in Historical Perspective* (Berkeley, Calif., 1996).

1914 : Great Feminist Expectations

Michelle Perrot
Translated by Colette Pratt

An attempt to encompass the hopes and expectations of European women on the eve of the First World War is a difficult and in many respects artificial enterprise, because of all the aspects which must escape us. Quite a lot of research has been done on women's history at the beginning of the twentieth century and the findings, which make up an immense library, lay claim to our better acquaintance. But many aspects of this history remain buried, perhaps never to come to light, on account of the conventions which bound women to silence, forbidding them either directly or by means of suggestion the expression of their desires, if not desire itself. I am referring to the kind of silence that psychoanalysis, so exact in some of its intuitions if not in its explanations, was then starting to lift about much unspoken suffering. Moreover, regardless of the well-defined position that sexual difference implies for the subordination of women, gender combines with so many other variables – religious, national, ethnic, generational, cultural, social – that even the use of the plural, as in "women" and "some women," may mask a claim to represent women as a single block. A number of illusions influence the pages that follow.

Nevertheless, the noose around women's necks was loosening in the initial years of the century. Women were much more talked about, seen, heard. They seemed troublesome, for they showed signs of rebellion, preferring celibacy to arranged marriages, showing themselves less faithful or merely dreamier, avid readers of serialized novels. They had fewer children, resorting to abortion in proportions that led alarmed demographers to indict them for their selfishness, and accuse them of being the source of the collapse of nations, even of the degeneracy of the "race." Women

Notes for this chapter begin on page 42.

aspired to joining the workforce, not out of an inordinate desire for work, but because paid employment was preferable to unpaid, repetitious, and unrecognized domestic work. They were starting to tire of "this simple life with its boring and easy tasks," as rhapsodized by the poet Verlaine. That included sewing, considered pleasing work, but ill paid and stressful on the eyes. It was better to be employed as a typist or, better yet, as a school-teacher, the model for aspiring working-class girls. But these new service jobs required education. Girls began to want to be educated and a few families welcomed their aspirations.

Signs of impatience were felt in all social strata. Working women, whether sugar refiners or *midinettes* (seamstresses in Parisian dressmaking shops), went on strike more often. Housewives renewed their rioting in the marketplace, which progress in food distribution had made a thing of the past. When in 1910 to 1911, the rise in the price of food broke a long period of economic stability in northern and eastern France, Belgium, Holland, and the German Rhineland, women mobilized, not for bread, which by that time was guaranteed, but for those essential staples of aver-age kitchens: milk, sugar, butter. Some spoke, not without a tinge of irony, of the "international of 15-cent butter," meeting to unite housewives around their food baskets.[1] In these same years, peasant women in the southwest of France complained bitterly about not having access to "worker and peasant" retirement plans, which in principle had just been passed by Parliament (Law of 1910). Often supported by their mayors, who confirmed that in the workplace or on the farm they worked at almost every task, women wrote vehement but respectful letters to their prefects, expressing their astonishment at being counted for nothing in a new social reckoning that made their nonexistence all the more appar-ent.[2] This feeling of dissatisfaction explains, moreover, the exodus of rural women to cities, and the attendant difficulty peasants had finding wives. Rural patriarchy was shaken by the glitter of the city, however false. As another example, when the *Journal,* a Parisian daily, in 1913 surveyed its readership on the question, "Should women be given the right to vote?" it received nearly 500,000 affirmative answers.[3]

More and more women, generally young ones eager to achieve inde-pendence, were whispering, "What about me?" Now that they knew how to read and write and dared speak up somewhat more, they were asking almost everywhere in the towns and in rural areas of Europe, "What about us?" (Research has as yet to quantify the dimensions of this wave of disquiet.) This thrill of hearts and bodies, this awakening of percep-tions and thoughts provided the living tissue on which feminism, coming to a "golden age" in the beginning of the century, was grafted.[4] As such, it was the multiform, but relatively clear and coherent, expression of the "new woman," which the advertising industry and many writers delighted in celebrating, shaming, or excoriating. The workers' movement which based its identity on the exaltation of production and the great virile trades – the brave miner, the physically strong construction worker, the technically clever mechanic, heroes who brought about the second industrial revolution and would change the world – denigrated feminism as "bourgeois." Similarly, the socialists, including the women among them (Clara Zetkin in Germany, or Louise Saumoneau in France), pretended that their own proletarian roots were deep, and that the schoolteachers and postal workers, the lawyers and doctors, who were feminism's agents and organizers were not authentic workers. Socialists glossed over the fact that in the last analysis the enlightenment and socialism were intellectual achievements of this very bourgeoisie whose revolutionary potential Marx himself had extolled. The desire to discredit the women's movement (or movements) tells more about feminism's opponents than about their target. One must bear this in mind as one begins a book devoted to the relationship between women and socialism.

After these less-than-formal preliminaries, let us attempt to apprehend a few of the expectations that outlined a new configuration of the relationship between the sexes.

The Feminine Condition at Issue

"God, why did I get married?" sighed Flaubert's Emma Bovary, the first incarnation of the feminine malaise. Ibsen's Nora would transform this malaise into open revolt by choosing to leave her spouse and family (1879). Perceived as a cornerstone of female subjugation, marriage was more and more openly questioned by women (Olive Schreiner and Sibilla Aleramo) as well as by men (Auguste Bébel and Léon Blum). The rate of celibacy clearly increased for women: in France in 1900 12 percent of women over fifty (compared to 8 percent of men)were celibate; in England, the rate went from 12 percent in 1851 to 16 percent in 1911. "Old maids," these "redundant women," who caused alarm because they disturbed the familial and social scene, the conspicuous *signorine* in Italian towns, whom doctors and confessors found troublesome,[5] were not necessarily wallflowers, deprived of dowry or grace, but women who had shied away from unattractive prospects. The slow transformation that led from marriage to love, and possibly – though in a lesser degree – from heterosexuality to homosexuality or at least to a chosen sexuality, is at work in this history. Women, and particularly young ones, played a great part in the advent of "romantic" marriage, and of the modern couple, the great novelty of the period between the two world wars. As Kafka's *Journal* attests, women more highly defined literary and social personality conveyed to their partners a sense of their distant solitude.

Married women proved themselves more circumspect about mother-hood. Eager to perform motherly tasks better, mothers were required to devote increasing amounts of attention to infants and children.[6] Those who wished to free themselves from such obligations, opted to have fewer children. Almost everywhere in Europe, allowing for some differences between West and East, a "demographic transition" took place, charac-terized by a strong reduction of the death and birth rates. In general, the death rate fell before the birthrate declined (except in France where the reverse was the case), causing excess populations to emigrate in waves both within Europe and to non-European areas. This surplus, increased the industrial labor force and gave impetus to a neo-Malthusianism, that was much more libertarian than its prototype in that it not only advo-cated continence, but also the use of contraceptive methods intended to free the exercise of sexuality from the fetters of procreation. Doctors were the principal supporters of this movement, and England assumed leader-ship of it. Nonetheless, English authorities in 1877 threatened Annie Besant with prison for publishing a tract on birth control. Besant's book, *Law of Population*, sold 175,000 copies. The movement spread to the Low Countries, where Aletta Jacobs opened the first birth control clinic, and to France, where Paul Robin and Jeanne and Eugène Humbert relied on direct action syndicalism and radical feminists like Doctor Madeleine Pel-letier, Nelly Roussel, and Gabrielle Petit to spread the word. "Women, strive to become a mother according to your own wish," urged the stick-ers that activists pasted onto lamp posts and the brochures they distrib-uted outside factories. If, on account of timidity or modesty, women rarely attended their conferences, they seemed to have heeded the message, judging by the coincidence between neo-Malthusian propaganda and lower birthrates in the industrial North, for instance.[7]

In Germany, Helen Stöcker (1869-1943) founded the *Bund für Mut-terschutz* in 1903, which launched a newspaper and opened information centers that by 1914 had advised about 16,000 women. Helen Stöcker advocated a better delivery – "Don't reproduce; produce better" – and insisted that free love is without risk. The audacity of this new ethic contributed to her marginalization within a feminist movement that remained prudish almost everywhere, including in Britain and in the Scandinavian countries. When in 1914 the Women's Labour League, founded in England in 1906, solicited the opinion of its members about the problems they faced, it received letters in which they complained bit-terly about their suffering as wives and mothers. So did the female cor-respondents of Abbé Viollet, founder of the French Association for Christian Marriage.[8] In a remarkable autobiographical novel of the period, *Lise du plat pays*, Lise Vanderwielen berates her husband, a communist activist, for not practicing withdrawal, and she eventually leaves him for a more cautious man.[9]

All this indicates the rudimentary state of contraceptive methods; withdrawal, mostly masculine but feminine as well, remained the primary technique. Hence, the increasingly frequent recourse to abortion, not only on the part of seduced and abandoned girls, but also of married, multiparous women, desirous of limiting the size of their family to a reasonable number of children.[10] (Infanticide, which had by then become abhorrent to most, persisted to some extent in the countryside.) Angus McLaren sees in the desire for smaller families the expression of a "popular feminism." A high rate of female mortality resulted from abortions practiced under questionable medical and sanitary conditions. The rate assumed an almost fantastic magnitude, since clandestinity prevented the collection of any statistics and threw demographers into a panic, particularly in France and Germany where the drop in the birthrate at the beginning of the century was all the more spectacular in view of these countries' tradition of large families. Hence, the alarm on the part of moralists, patriots (Zola in *Fécondité*, 1899), doctors and demographers, who solicited state intervention and helped to introduce the first repressive measures preceding more severe legislations (for instance, the laws of 1920 and 1923 in France).

The concern with birth control, common throughout Europe albeit with strong cultural and religious variations, is undoubtedly the most visible sign of women's refusal to accept their reproductive function as their fate. Of course, birth control is not only women's problem, but that of both partners in a couple. Besides, it is not easy to know which of the partners is responsible for the refusal to have children. The Vichy government blamed men but not women for practicing birth control, as if women had been victims, unable to desert their biological calling.[11] Nonetheless, there are many indications that women sought to take responsibility for contraception. Hence, the relative success of birth control between the two World Wars and, in any case, women's firm refusal to respond to the demographic patriotic mobilization attempted by numerous states. That was the case even in Sweden, and the debate around the Myrdals illustrates this fact. Freely chosen motherhood comes from afar, and foremost from women themselves. At the dawn of the century, this expectation rumbled like muffled thunder.

Must we for that matter speak of sexual liberation? That undoubtedly would be anachronistic. The majority of women professed their desire to be "good mothers"; a few deplored feminism, condemned abortion, and for that reason refused to take a firm stand in favor of contraception. Until very recently this remained a common pattern. However, there is reason to speak of a more demanding sensuality, which led practitioners of the new science of sexology to wonder about women's potential for sexual pleasure. Shouldn't the clitoris, seat of this pleasure, be removed? Some doctors recommended that option for overly passionate young ladies. We know very little about these ablations, which seem to have been more common in the United States than in Europe. In marriage or in adultery, which was beginning to be regarded with greater tolerance, women appreciated the sexual act as the deferred outcome of subtle caresses and not as a brutal act of "possession." Love letters or the indiscretions of legal inquiries reveal to us women who were no strangers to passion or desire.[12]

Lesbian love, the fruit of juvenile passions in girls' boarding schools and high schools, those bastions of sentimental education, blossomed among intellectuals and artists who sometimes contracted more or less accepted "Bostonian" marriages. There existed then a certain indulgence towards "lost women," of whom the Amazons of Paris' Latin Quarter left us a poetic memory. Around Nathalie Clifford Barney, Renée Vivien, Liane de Pougy, Colette, and their friends, a "ladies' paradise" came into being, which was never again so freely asserted. "The most beautiful life is that life which one devotes to self-creation rather than procreation," wrote Nathalie Barney (1910). Renée Vivien (1877-1909) shared her feelings: "Because you love me, I love my body like a garden where you would have been pleased to wander." This woman, who wanted to commit suicide by breathing floral perfumes and died of anorexia at thirty-two, embodies a unique moment of Sapphic innocence repressed by the war.[13] More generally, women evolved towards a discovery of pleasure in love, but also in water, bathing, and sports in the case of the economically privileged, and acquired that consciousness of the body which is the basis of self-awareness.

The Desire for a Better Life

The longing for a better life was widespread in this varied but dynamic Belle Epoque, though variously expressed in different social milieux. For instance, powerful strike movements took place throughout Europe. Women's voices, though muted, were part of this concert. "We are made like you of flesh and bones," declared, the working women of Vienne (Isère) to their bosses in May 1890. "We want our share of happiness."

To live better was to dispose of more money and to have autonomy to manage the family's budget. As administrators of the household's finances – more so, it seems, in France than anywhere else – working-class housewives saw to it that their husbands got paid, and, at the very least, that they themselves received their own wages. As early as 1857 in England and only in 1907 in France, the law would grant them that much, though more for their children's sake than their own. Rarely entitled to a full-time salary, they sought to earn some "extra income" (their pride) through odd jobs integrated into their daily round of activities – errands, housework, babysitting, washing or sewing – and through the homework that a clothing business in full expansion, characterized by rationalization and the division of labor, had been developing everywhere. To own a sewing machine – a Singer or a German make – was the ambition of working-class women, who bought on credit, thus becoming acquainted with installment payments. The endless workdays for miserly wages of this tuberculosis-generating system ended by alarming hygienists and doctors and infuriating feminists, who raised an outcry. Boards of Trades started conducting surveys, and offices for the regulation of women's work sprang up. In 1915, a French law established a minimum wage, the prototype of a collective agreement. More profitable, better paid and better protected, factory war work dealt a fatal blow to home employment. The war accelerated the making of the female factory worker.

A better life meant also to be better fed. Working-class women were chronically undernourished and their diet was poor. In times of shortage, they left the meat, wine, and beer to their husband, the sugar and milk to the children, and made do with cheese and coffee with milk (single women consuming even less). In times of plenty, they compensated with gargantuan meals, gaining weight at a time when new fashions required more slender, youthful bodies.[14]

A better life meant being housed more decently – having access to stable lodgings that did not have to be evacuated furtively when one was down-and-out (the bane of poor people); having more comfortable living space, with a kitchen closet for cooking, a nonsmoking fireplace, separate rooms for parents and children, tap water at the sink (still a rare convenience prior to 1914); painted wallpaper; and curtains to protect an intimacy that from then on became essential for working-class respectability and women's contentment.[15] Nevertheless disparities in working-class housing were considerable; English, Scandinavian, or German housewives and spouses fared better than their Italian or French sisters.[16] The trend towards individual housing, the ambition to own one's home, be it cottage or suburban house, grew in the middle-classes and the upper echelons of the working class. But for the majority of people that dream remained unrealizable.[17]

Men and women began spending more for clothes as the clothing industry developed and made clothes more affordable. Women's magazines, cultural mediators like servants or provincial seamstresses, photographs, and postcards spread the new fashions. Big emporiums, temples of temptation and consumption, contributed to the development of feminine kleptomania, which affected humble housewives, young seamstresses, and bourgeois women on the lookout for trinkets and ready to go into debt to satisfy a whim.[18] To dress better, to make oneself beautiful, bespeaks the desire of women trying to attract admirers. One is struck by the stylishness of working-class women, youngish for the most part, often photographed while coming out of the factory, a custom that became increasingly common at the turn of the century and that recalls the taking of classroom pictures. In the washhouses, on the contrary, photographs featured individual poses against fanciful backgrounds, a sign of the desire to project a beautiful self-image. Even before the war, young women started cutting their hair, daring to put on rouge, shortening their skirts, shedding their corsets, to free and lighten their appearance. They were served or guided in this adventure by famous couturiers such as Poiret and Madeleine Vionnet. The "beautiful woman" of 1900 gave up her plumpness and her bearing for the slenderer silhouette vaunted by advertising and extolled by sports. Modern-style posters represented a supple and serpentine woman.

New ideas about the body and motion were creeping in. As the dancer Isadora Duncan unfolded her veils to "free people from their fetters," young girls practiced rhythmic dance, a type of feminine gymnastic that forbade brusque movements and cultivated harmony. They swam and biked, engaging in sports that justified the wearing of the culotte-skirt and favored family and romantic outings. A modern couple like Pierre and Marie Curie occupied their leisure in this way.

The new woman, particularly young girls, aspired to mobility. To leave one's home, to travel, became more and more the aspiration of those on whom confinement weighed. The city, in spite of its segregated spaces, favored strolling, anonymity, encounters, and those adventures Stefan Zweig later chronicled in *The World of Yesterday*.

Travel opened the world for the privileged: the closed environment of health spas or bathing resorts, cities with an artistic heritage, and museums (according to Baudelaire, the only public places suitable for women). Young women visited museums to contemplate artworks studied in drawing classes. The practice of the "grand tour," the Anglo-Saxon complement to a sound education, became available to girls lucky enough to have been born to broad-minded fathers or to fathers appreciative of their company (for instance Geneviève Bréton or Marguerite Yourcenar). This remained the exception, as did exotic travels to the East or to Africa, or the archeological expeditions of a Jane Dieulafoy who, along with her husband, discovered the frescoes of the Assyrian bowmen, housed today in the Louvre. After the expedition experience Jane Dieulafoy wore only men's clothing, which she and many others associated with freedom of movement and perhaps with creativity.[19]

Leisure time and the ability to dispose of it freely was a common ambition at the turn of the century, and a strong demand of the workers' movement.[20] But it was out of reach for working-class women bound to the triple burden of work-household-children. Even more than salary increases, the shortening of the workday became a major objective of women strikers. Trade union campaigns for the "English week" were more concerned with the advantages of the weekend when women could devote Saturday afternoon to housework and spend Sunday strolling with their families or fishing with their husbands. Contemporary iconography shows them sewing on the river bank while their husband is fishing. This idyllic image of a working-class Sunday reveals the difficulty of representing women's leisure time. Even the bourgeois woman, dubbed a "creature of leisure," was always occupied, notably by her mundane duties. As a counterpart of the right to work, the right to leisure time was conceived in masculine terms. In the same vein, paintings of bourgeois gardens or interiors show women sewing, seated under the lamp beside the man, who most often is reading a newspaper. The newspaper, symbol of entry into the larger world, as denied to women.

Women, by definition, did not have free time; they belonged to others, primarily to their families. They had to steal what time they could from their occupations or household work. Reading was their favorite escape. Travel accounts, edifying literature, and novels nourished an eager feminine imagination. The back pages of daily newspapers were allotted to sentimental intrigues and family sagas that working-class women read surreptitiously with a delicious twinge of remorse.[21] This thirst for reading stimulated the creation of feminine newspapers and magazines, having a large contingent of women assistant editors and writers, particularly in England where 15 to 20 percent of authors in 1900 were women.[22] They gravitated to the novel mostly, building up intrigues in which sexual difference and the question of feminine identity were prominent. At the turn of the twentieth century, women claimed their right to reading, writing, and dreaming.

Towards Independence : Education and Work

In Colette's *La Vagabonde*, the emblematic novel of feminine independence, the protagonist extolls: "Solitude, freedom, my own work ... the new obligation of earning my meals, my clothes, my rent." Education and work, two related themes, paved the road to such independence. Women repeatedly demanded education and training. At the turn of the century, women had for the most part (except in Southern Europe) caught up with men in attaining an elementary education. From then on access to secondary education was the issue. England had led the way as early as 1848 with the founding of second-level colleges, immediately followed in the 1870s by university colleges, which did not award diplomas but which afforded a solid tertiary education. They were, moreover, places of intense feminine sociability; nothing comparable existed on the continent. In this respect, England was far ahead.

Most countries on the continent arranged secondary education for middle-class girls between 1880 and 1920. Germany granted them the *Abitur* in 1891 and counted eleven *gymnasiums* for females by 1906. Austria was not far behind. Most towns in Northern Italy had upper-level girl schools; moreover, young Italian women (20,000 compared to 1,300 young men) attended teaching academies that granted teaching certificates. In France, where in 1861 Julie Daubié had successfully led a hard struggle to be admitted to the baccalaureate, the Camille Sée law of 1880 mandated secondary education for girls. By 1913, forty-one high schools and twenty-nine colleges supervised the education of 35,000 girls (compared with 60,000 boys). But coeducational programs did not come about until 1924, when the baccalaureate became coed. More than mixed schools, comprehensive programs, exams, diplomas, as well as competitive examinations were a favorite ambition of girls and of families aware of the drawbacks of segregation.

Pressure was also put on universities to admit women. Unexpectedly, tsarist Russia was the first country to admit women to universities, particularly in medicine. Their role in populism, even terrorism, was spectacular. Hence, their eventual exclusion which, coupled with anti-Jewish pogroms, obliged many of them to flee to the West in order to complete their studies. They were among the first women students in Zurich and Paris, where their presence aroused male students' hostility, particularly in law schools. Each stage in their conquest of knowledge was an obstacle race. Latin, sacred to the humanities and to law, the foundation of power, were not considered proper subjects of study for women, even less so mathematics, supposedly too abstract for women's brains. The brilliant Russian mathematician Sofia Kowaleskaya had to contract an unconsummated union with a complicitous colleague in order to continue her mathematical work. Art studies presented the same obstacles. Until the 1900 law opened the Beaux-Arts School in Paris to girls, professors and students opposed their admission, under the pretext that nude studies were indecent for young women, who were forced to fall back on private studios like the famous Julian Academy. The diary of Marie Bashkirtseff (1859 to 1884) testifies to the difficulties of becoming a woman painter. Nevertheless, painting was still the most welcoming creative field for women who, at the turn of the century, managed to show their work in salons, and even to make a name for themselves.[23] Sculpture, architecture, music (otherwise than as an accomplishment or teaching) excluded them even more radically. Each one of their advances exposed them to sarcasm, so much did "studying" seemed incompatible with femininity. So-called intellectual women – the *Cervelines* of a pessimistic novel by Colette Yver that depicts the disastrous effects of studies on women – were a favorite target of anti-feminism. On the eve of World War I, Europe counted but a few thousand women students, but these women were already paving new roads.

The trend towards more education for women was irresistible. Women's aspiration coincided with that of a certain number of broad-minded men who wished to find "intelligent companions" and of democrats who saw in the "enlightened" mother and teacher of her children the agent of progress. It also responded to the economic needs of a not so well-to-do lower middle-class, eager to climb the social ladder. Unable to endow their daughters, lower middle-class parents were obliged to afford them the means of earning their living, encouraging them to convert social accomplishments into cash in translation, teaching, and the new service sector.

Indeed, education opened the doors to many professions, particularly teaching. Schoolmistresses and high school and college teachers (university professors would come later) became the new models of professional and even gendered identity. The prestige of schoolmistresses, particularly in France where they incarnated the lay Republic,[24] was very high among the daughters of the urban and rural lower classes. Practically everywhere in Europe, from Greece to Great Britain, women teachers gave feminism its organizers and, in part, its rank and file. In the wake of the war, they acceded to the status of "intellectuals," a recognition so rarely granted to women. Pedagogy was also a privileged area of investigation for them, as the example of the Italian Maria Montessori (1870 to 1952), pioneer in the teaching of maladjusted children, shows. Her round of conferences in 1899 based on the theme of the new woman was a triumph.

Montessori was among the first women doctors in Italy. On the eve of the war, there were only a few hundred women doctors in Europe, whereas nursing care, on the model advocated by Florence Nightingale (1820 to 1910) or the more proletarian one of Doctor Bourneville, the advocate of lay care in Parisian hospitals, was largely in their hands. It was difficult for nurses to obtain high level positions in hospitals, which were devoted to clinical practice controlled by the "big male boss," and to the newer specialties. Madeleine Pelletier, for instance, so proud of her new "doctoress" title, had to struggle to be admitted to the study of psychiatry. The first woman admitted after competitive examination to an internship in an insane asylum, she still did not manage to get the position. It is all the more tragic is the fact that she was declared insane by a court as penalty for performing abortions and confined to an insane asylum where she died in 1939.

Business offices were about to become women's province par excellence. After the sewing machine, the typewriter, it was said, required their "nimble fingers." A learned skill could thus be represented as an innate ability deserving of less pay. As early as 1900, steno typists were to be found in great numbers in government offices and ministries. At the same time post offices became feminized, which often allowed for a reshuffling of male employees. The tertiary sector, services and communications, showed itself more accepting of women than industrial production that, apart from the textile-clothing industry, remained largely masculine. The factory was only minimally a woman's world, even though a few women lived there a great part of their youth (from the age of twelve up to their wedding or the birth of their first or second child), and came back for want of something better in their mature years and solitary old age. The housewife was always a more respected figure than the female factory worker.

In the beginning of the twentieth century, women's employment progressed in general, depending on demographic conditions, levels of industrialization, and standards of living in a given country. The importance of emigration in Italy and the early restriction of births in France created favorable conditions for the employment of women. In 1911, women in Italy were 31 and in France 36 percent of the active work force, with approximately 20 percent of married women in France (the highest number in Europe) bringing home a salary. Married women faced the most obstacles. In Norway, only 2 or 3 percent earned a salary, which was also the case in Spain and Germany. Even in Sweden, where women constituted 19 percent of the industrial workforce and, in England, where the employment rate for women dropped, the idea of the "family wage" prevailed and the principle of equal pay was not accepted until 1907. Wage equality and women's right to work, no matter what their status, were not easily recognized. These themes, which often recurred at international feminist congresses, previewed the fragility of women's employment during the crisis of the 1930s. They revealed the degree to which women as a group had difficulties being recognized as people apart from the family and their maternal role.[25]

For better or worse and not without fiery debates, women's work became, in the manner of children's labor, an experimental sector of social law. Between 1890 and 1914, a whole series of measures limited the workday of women and minor girls and forbade them night work as well as certain types of physical labor. These regulations made the hiring of women and girls more troublesome for employers, thus causing massive layoffs. A number of feminists protested against these perverse results, characterizing the measures as discriminatory.[26] The protection of women about to give birth met with more unanimous approval, for it was intended to protect women's jobs by making sure that they could reintegrate into the factory after their maternity leave.[27] Reconciling the right to work and the bearing of children instead of putting them into conflict was perhaps the best way to promote a higher birthrate. Women in the British Labour party understood that much. They advocated "nursery school education" (Rachel and Margaret McMillan as early as 1894) and, on the local level, women's shelters based on the model of housing for working women. Alva Myrdal, the most ardent apostle of motherhood and salaried work, defended such measures decades later as the only way to halt the decline in the Swedish birthrate. If women wished to work, she argued, they should be helped to do so rather than be dissuaded.

This more democratic idea of motherhood took shape prior to 1914 and reflects women's assertion of their will to join the labor force, not out of love for work but out of a desire for autonomy. To be free of dependence on the wages of one's husband was at once a necessity and a desire that could no longer be satisfied by housework. Many women deemed it better to have access to regular outside employment. Thus, at the turn of the century, wage consciousness became emblematic of women's strong desire for individualization, which war work and the steady development of the tertiary sector was going to fulfill.

Towards Participation in Public Affairs

More and more visible in the public sphere, particularly in an urban, modernizing context, women came to exercise an increasing influence in public life and to contest, either in the silent performance of their daily activities or in the context of open confrontations, the sacrosanct division of public and private. They did this in various ways. Important was the assumption, through charity and philanthropy, of a responsibility which had always depended on them: caring for the weak. Children, prisoners, poor, old and sick people were subjects of their compassion. They sustained numerous associations, and the expanding Salvation Army offers, indeed, an extreme case of the coexistence of women's promotion and power (Kate and Evangeline Booth, the founder's daughters, were respectively "Marshal" of France and General of the organization) with the most ultra traditional model of femininity.[28]

Feminism, for its part, struggled against big social ills such as tuberculosis, alcoholism, and syphilis. It made hygiene something of a virtue. Leaning towards vegetarianism, it defended animals and advocated an ecological city. It protected abandoned children and their unwed mothers, for whom it claimed the right to inquire into the identity of their fathers. It fought against prostitution, representing our "harlot sisters" as the embodiment of feminine alienation. Prison-like hospitals, such as Saint-Lazare in Paris, were the scenes of feminine protests. While most people accepted such control by constituted authorities as a lesser evil, Josephine Butler opposed it, organizing mass meetings under the banner of purity and inciting her "shrieking sisters" to stir up agitation as often as possible. In Hamburg, Lida Gustava Heymann organized and opened public discussions on sexuality and women's rights. Thus, feminism developed a moral and social civic consciousness that some people, notably in Germany, dubbed "maternalism," as if it were a question of duplicating or completing through private action the more political and institutionalized paternalism of the welfare state.

Women thus demonstrated an expertise for which they got recognition, particularly on the local level. In Great Britain, they took over relief work for the poor and managed public assistance. This accounted for their being granted the right to vote in municipal elections as early as 1869. Iceland (1882), Denmark (1883), and Norway (1901) followed suit. In short, women managed to gain a foothold in public affairs primarily through welfare work for the benefit of the poor.

Syndicalism and socialism perforce remained largely closed to them. The following chapters demonstrate this sufficiently well to make more than a few comments superfluous. Both types of association, being masculine provinces, entailed a logic of gender roles: the first presupposed a right to work that the worker's movement was loathe to recognize fully; the second, a right to vote which clearly did not exist (Finland was the first country to grant national suffrage in 1906), and that socialist parties supported half-heartedly. In these dissuasive circumstances, it is understandable that women unionized little; towards 1910, their rate of union activity was 3 percent in France and 11 percent in Sweden. Only a modest number belonged to political parties. The strength of masculine resistance was remarkable, as a few examples will make clear. Take, for instance, the 1913 Couriau affair in which the typesetters of a printing shop in Lyon went on strike to protest the acceptance of a woman colleague in their union; or the difficulties encountered by Adelheid Popp when wishing to speak publicly and to be admitted as a full member of the Austrian Socialist party.[29]

In fact, women could become members of socialist parties but not speak out, much less participate in the leadership or exercise power as delegates to party congresses. The German Socialist party affords us an excellent, if ambiguous, example of this problem. Rosa Luxembourg and Clara Zetkin were recognized as great public speakers; but they both declared themselves hostile to contraception and, particularly in C. Zetkin's case, openly affected an anti-feminist stance. Was that the price they paid in order to rise to the top? Their experience suggests that women's weapons had better be left in the coat room, or at least put to the exclusive service of the class struggle. Another strategy was to form distinct unions or political groups (as in Spain and Austria). Separate factions like these certainly allowed for the discussion of women's issues, but they also marginalized them.

The English situation showed more originality. Women had a higher profile in the Labour party, which was founded on syndicalism. Besides, the distinction between women workers and women intellectuals was much less pronounced in Britain than on the continent. Annie Besant, Eleanor Marx, and Beatrice Webb, for instance, spoke at strike meetings upon the request of women workers who, on their part, petitioned for the right to vote. Around 1900, the strongly unionized women textile workers of Lancashire gathered 30,000 signatures that their delegates presented solemnly to parliament. The English suffrage movement thus came to acquire grass-roots support which, in other countries, proved weak or was nonexistent.

These various obstacles explain the rapid development of feminism, whose name, French in origin and pejorative at first (a medical term designating a pathology of effeminacy), managed to catch on. The same can be said of "feminists," which Hubertine Auclert used in its current meaning for the first time around 1885. From then on, these terms were in vogue and many appropriated them, albeit with qualifications (as in "Christian feminism" for instance). Feminism drew support from "emerging social strata," the educated women of the lower and middle classes, and those men open to modernization and progress. It is difficult to quantify its evolution, since groups fluctuate, but some initiatives involved members by the tens of thousand. At the turn of the century, feminism acquired new dimensions and was about to become, if not a social movement, a mediator and an actor in the public sphere.[30]

Born of the contradictions of a democracy that it meant to realize and prolong while completing it, feminism used democratic practices: petitions, long the only authorized means of protest for women; associations of all sizes and hues (the International Women's Council, founded in the United States in 1888, drew support from 17 national councils in 1914; the International Alliance for Women's Suffrage was founded in Berlin in 1904); and national and international conferences, meetings, and congresses (of which there were twenty-three between 1878 and 1914). Together these made up a framework that served more as a propaedeutic than as a lobby for public action.

Feminist publications and newspapers achieved a wide success in this period. The German *Gleichheit*, the Swedish *Morning Breeze*, the Swiss *Le Mouvement Féministe*, Hubertine Auclert's *La Citoyenne*, Marguerite

Durand's *La Fronde* (1897-1903), and *La Française* (1906-1940) headed, written and put together solely by women, were but a few of the numerous though short-lived titles. This press, which intended to inform, was also a platform and a link between readers, particularly through letters to the editor. It encouraged the development of a new profession, that of the woman journalist, in which Séverine cut a dashing figure in France.

Protest marches were most difficult to manage. Though an essential form of democratic action, they were conducted according to masculine norms. Female demonstrators were tolerated but more in their role of companions or as ornaments. Nevertheless, they dared use that form of action for their own ends. The English suffragettes showed incomparable ingenuity on that score, as much in the matter of slogans, tracts, posters as in the actual marches. They dared resort to violence. They did not hesitate to disturb an official ceremony or celebration to make themselves heard. They broke windowpanes, started a hunger strike, planted bombs, defiled Velasquez' Venus at the National Gallery (which resulted in making museums off-limits to women). On 4 June 1913, Emily Davison killed herself by running under the King's horse during the Derby. On the eve of the Great War, the English suffragettes were proclaiming their aspiration: "Women want to vote."

Women certainly made other claims: civic equality – the right to divorce, the reform of marriage settlements, mail privacy, the right to collect their own salary; economic equality – salarial, professional, educational. These demands recurred like leitmotivs in newspapers and at congresses. British or Scandinavian progresses contrasted with German and Latin stagnation. The German code of 1901 constituted a step backwards; French women nevertheless obtained the right to divorce in 1884, while Italian women would have to wait until 1974. In France, the Napoleonic Code remained in force, but social welfare for mothers and workers improved.

Energies were undeniably focused on the right to vote, as if women considered it the preliminary condition for the obtaining of additional rights. More and more, their exclusion and their lack of representation in elected assemblies seemed to them shameful. They based their claim to representation sometimes on equality, other times on difference. According to some historians, French women used the equality argument more often and English women the latter.[31] In fact, both availed themselves of both arguments. They maintained that their know-how could be useful in the big household of the state. Have the Scandinavian countries, where politics is more practical and less sacred than elsewhere, been more responsive to this way of seeing things? They were in any case the first ones to grant women the right to vote: Finland in 1906 (in 1910, ten women were seated in Parliament), Norway in 1912.

But whatever the arguments and the political philosophies at issue, the admission of women to full citizenship was circumspect business. Most countries adopted step-by-step solutions, granting women the vote initially at the local level (Great Britain, 1869, Iceland, 1882, Denmark, 1883), then at the national level (Denmark, 1915, Great Britain, 1918); or yet again distinguishing the right to qualify for the vote (Sweden, 1909) from actual suffrage (Sweden, 1924), as if it were preferable to open the door to capable women than to allow them the freedom to choose for themselves. Elsewhere, age became a factor: in Britain in 1918, only women over thirty years old were considered eligible to vote; younger women had to wait until 1928 for the same right. In any case, the question of women's suffrage was widely considered and debated in Europe on the eve of the war, and public opinion, at least in the North and the West, proved more and more favorable to a positive outcome. Nevertheless, political and institutional opposition remained strong. No political party made that issue a priority. Jurists continued to quibble and political assemblies to waver. In France in 1914, women's suffrage was approved by a majority in the Chamber of Deputies but rejected by the Senate, and this scenario recurred six times between the two World Wars. Politics, this masculine sanctuary, remained closed to women.

In general, feminism in this period stressed equality more than freedom. Confronted by widespread misogyny and its attendant anti-feminist reactions, the movement focused on women's status as mothers, more than on their rights. On the issues of sex and contraception, it showed a timidity well short of private practices.

Feminism grew into a constellation of diverse religious and philosophical currents: Catholic, Protestant, free-thinking, libertarian. Some feminists dreamed of masculinity (Madeleine Pelletier, for instance). Others sang the praises of a salvational feminism, like that of the French Louise Kopp or the Swedish Ellen Key, apostle of "female heart power," rooted in the nature and ferment of feminine culture. Advocate of a strict separation of masculine and feminine spheres, roles, and spaces, Key demanded a salary for housewives and with reluctance joined a suffrage movement, which seemed to her a useless incursion into the male world of politics.

At the beginning of the twentieth century, the debate on sexual difference was revived and formulated anew. The issue was not only biological but psychical, and it became particularly intense in the Germanic world. It ran through the heart of Nietzsche's work; Freud, too, was entirely taken up with it. He hoped to found a science of sexuality through psychoanalytical practice. Matriarchy, an anthropological question addressed in the past by Morgan and Bachofen, fascinated intellectual coteries from Vienna to Berlin and Paris. To such circles belonged the

Van Richtofen sisters, associates of Max Weber and D. H. Lawrence, who set the "New Eve" against a decrepit "Old Adam."[32]

Faced with women's dazzling progress, some men (and likewise some women who feared change) felt the earth crumble under their feet. An important crisis in sexual identity developed, that found expression sometimes in a virulent anti-feminism, other times in serious thought.[33] In 1903, Otto Weininger published *Geschlecht und Charakter,* in which he gave credence to the idea of two separate genders, presented as cultural and symbolic constructs apart from biological sex, but hierarchical, with the masculine being absolutely superior to the feminine. Did he feel himself unable to attain virile power? He committed suicide shortly after having given voice to the sexual anguish haunting his generation.[34] Lou Andreas Salomé answered him, though in a quiet manner. She too believed in irreducible sexual differences, but, by turning things on their head, she extolled women's ability to find fulfillment in their specificity. She celebrated the joy of being a woman, of assuming one's body as well as one's relationship to time and things. World War I brought this nascent quest to an abrupt halt by confining each sex to its place.

The sections and chapters that follow will weave together the strands of events through which women's aspiration to be their own persons affirmed itself so forcibly in the interwar years.

Notes

1. Jean-Marie Flonneau, "Crise de vie chère et mouvement syndical (1910-1914)," *Le Mouvement social* (July-Sept.,1970).
2. Elise Feller, "Vieillissement et société dans la France du premier 20e siècle, 1905-1953" (Ph.D. diss., University of Paris VII, 1997), pp. 436-470.
3. Laurence Klejman and Florence Rochefort, *L'égalité en marche. Le féminisme sous la Troisième République* (Paris, 1969).
4. Florence Rochefort, "Du droit des femmes au féminisme en Europe, 1860-1914," in *Encyclopédie politique et historique des femmes (Europe, Amérique du Nord),* ed. Christine Fauré (Paris, 1997), pp. 551-570.
5. On the emergence of young women as a specific category, see "Le temps des jeunes filles," presented by Gabrielle Houbre, *Clio. Histoire, femmes et sociétés* 4 (1996), particularly the studies of Michela De Giorgio on the *signorine* and of Carole Lécuyer on the first women students.
6. Yvonne Knibiehler and Catherine Marand-Fouquet, *Histoire des mères* (Paris, 1982); Catherine Rollet, *La politique à l'égard de la petite enfance sous la Troisième République* (Paris, 1990).

7.   Angus McLaren, *A History of Contraception from Antiquity to the Present Day* (London, 1990); Francis Ronsin, *La grève des ventres: propagande néo-malthusienne et baisse de la natalité en France, 19e-20e siècles* (Paris, 1980).
8.   Richard J. Evans, *The Feminists: Women's Emancipation Movement in Europe, America, and Australia, 1840-1920* (London, 1977), and *The Feminist Movements in Germany 1894-1944* (London, 1976); Martine Sèvegrand, *Les enfants du Bon Dieu, Les Catholiques français et la contraception* (Paris, 1995), and *L'amour en toutes lettres* (Paris, 1996).
9.   Lise Vanderwielen, *Lise du plat pays* (Lille, 1983).
10. Denise Fuchs, *Poor and Pregnant in Paris: Strategies for Survival in the Nineteenth Century* (New Brunswick, N.J., 1992).
11. Francine Muel-Dreyfus, *Vichy et l'éternel féminin* (Paris, 1996).
12. Anne-Marie Sohn, *Chrysalides. Femmes dans la vie privée 19e-20e siècles* (Paris, 1996).
13. Florence Montreynaud, ed., *Le XXe siècle des femmes* (Paris, 1996) – a remarkable work that gives the main events concerning women worldwide year by year; Shari Benstock, *Femmes de la Rive Gauche, Paris 1900-1914* (Paris, 1987); Judith Walkowitz, "Sexualités dangereuses," *Histoire des femmes en Occident, vol. 4, Le XIXe siècle*, eds. Geneviève Fraisse and Michelle Perrot (Paris, 1991), pp. 389-419.
14. Joan W. Scott and Louise Tilly, *Women, Work, and Family* (London and New York, 1978); Victoria de Grazia and Ellen Furlough (eds.), *The Sex of Things. Gender and Consumption in Historical Perspective* (Berkeley, Calif., 1996).
15. Michelle Perrot, ed., *De la Révolution à la Grande Guerre, Histoire de la vie privée*, eds. Philippe Ariès and George Duby, IV (Paris, 1987).
16. Lion Murard and Patrick Zylberman, *L'hygiène de la République* (Paris, 1996).
17. Maurice Halbwachs, *La classe ouvrière et les niveaux de vie. Recherches sur la hiérarchie des besoins dans les sociétés industrielles contemporaines* (Paris, 1912).
18. Leora Auslander, "The Gendering of Consumer Practices in 19th-century France," and Erika Rappaport, "'A Husband and His Wife's Dresses': Consumer Credit and the Debtor Family in England, 1864-1914," in Victoria de Grazia, *The Sex of Things. Gender and Consumption in Historical Perspective* (Berkeley, 1996), pp. 163-88.
19. Michelle Perrot, "Sortir," in *Histoire des femmes*, pp. 468-94; Dea Birkett, *Spinsters Abroad: Victorian Lady Explorers* (Oxford, 1989).
20. Gary Cross, *A Quest for Time. The Reduction of Work in Britain and France, 1840-1940* (Berkeley, Calif., 1989); Alain Corbin, ed., *L'avènement des loisirs, 1850-1960* (Paris, 1995).
21. Anne-Marie Thiesse, *Le roman du quotidien. Lecteurs et lectures populaires à la Belle Epoque* (Paris, 1984).
22. Christophe Charle, *La République des universitaires* (Paris, 1994), and *Les intellectuels en Europe au 19e siècle* (Paris, 1996).
23. Denise Noël, Ph.D. diss. about women painters (1880-1914) in Paris, University of Paris VII, in progress.
24. Jacques and Mona Ozouf, *La République des instituteurs* (Paris, 1992).
25. Scott and Tilly, *Women, Work, Family*; Laura L. Frader and Sonya O. Rose, eds., *Gender and Class in Modern Europe* (Ithaca, N.Y., 1996).
26. Leora Auslander and Michelle Zancarini-Fournel, *Différence des sexes et protection sociale (XIXe-XXe siècles)* (Saint-Denis, 1995); Mary John Stewart, *Women, Work, and The French State. Labor Protection and Social Patriarchy, 1879-1919* (Kingston, 1989).

27. Gisela Bock and Pat Thane, eds., *Maternity and Gender Policies. Women and the Rise of the European Welfare States, 1880's-1950's* (London and New York, 1991); Anna Cova, *Maternité et droit des femmes en France (XIXe-XXe siècles)* (Paris, 1997).

28. Michel Allner, "L'Armée du Salut. Grande-Bretagne, Etats-Unis, France, 1880-1980," (Ph.D. diss., University of Paris VII, 1994).

29. Adelheid Popp, *Die Jugendgeschichte einer Arbeiterin* (Munich, 1909); on the Couriau Affair, see Charles Sowerwine, "Workers and Women in France before 1914: the Debate over the Couriau Affair," *The Journal of Modern History* 55, 3 (September 1983), and *Les Femmes et le socialisme* (Paris, 1978; English translation, 1982).

30. Numerous works on feminism are available. See particularly R. Evans, *Feminists*; Anne-Marie Käppeli, "Scènes féministes," in *Histoire des femmes*, 495-525 (bibliography); Florence Rochefort in Christine Fauré, *Encyclopédie*; and Bonnie Smith, *Changing Lives. Women in European History since 1700* (Lexington and Toronto: 1987).

31. Pierre Rosanvallon, *Le sacré du citoyen. Histoire du suffrage universel en France* (Paris, 1992).

32. Martin Green, *The Von Richtofen Sisters* (New York, 1974).

33. Annelise Maugue, *L'identité masculine en crise au tournant du siècle* (Paris, 1987), and "L'Ère nouvelle et le vieil Adam," *Histoire des femmes*, vol. 4, pp. 527-547.

34. Jacques Le Rider, *Le cas Otto Weininger. Racines de l'antiféminisme et de l'antisémitisme* (Paris, 1987), and *Modernité viennoise et crise d'identité* (Paris, 1990).

Part I

Part I

SOCIAL EXPERIMENTS

Introduction

Atina Grossmann

Germany and Austria emerged from World War I with new democratic republics, novel plans for experiments in social welfare, and a newly enfranchised female electorate. The Social Democratic and Communist parties, newly formed or newly reconstituted in the wake of the Russian Revolution and the defeat of old empires, laid special claim to shaping modern and progressive welfare states. Their language and programs were saturated with visions of the "new": new human beings (the *Neue Menschen* of Red Vienna's social laboratory), new women, new housing, new lifestyles. Central to this celebration of newness was the promise of equality between men and women. At the same time, the utopian commitment to comprehensive social welfare and the improvement of living and laboring conditions for the working class spurred a continuing attention to gender differences, especially the particular role of women as mothers and guardians of the family. The three chapters in this section trace the common tensions that accompanied this equality/difference dilemma while also addressing the unique situations in Austria and Germany and the divisions between communists and socialists.

The challenge of incorporating and defining women as citizens of the postwar republics was particularly sharp for the working-class parties that historically aspired to include women as partners in the workplace and in politics. Moreover, the problems associated with establishing women as citizens, political agents, and workers as well as housewives and mothers took on particular resonance in the interwar years. Then, economic, political, and social relations ranging from the workplace to the parliament to the kitchen and bedroom were reshaped by what the historian Detlef Peukert has called a "crisis of classical modernity." The old-fashioned nineteenth-century European state faced highly varied options as it confronted this crisis: Americanism or Bolshevism; social welfare state or fascist racial state. The intensity of economic and political crisis that hit Germany and Austria in the interwar years seemed to create political opportunities as well as extreme restrictions. This was especially true for women whose relegation to the motherhood/social welfare corner of their parties took on new significance at times when the workplace and the public sphere in general were in a precarious state. Socialists and communists struggled with an ultimately insoluble conundrum: how to attract women by addressing their special concerns as mothers, household managers, and young workers, while also asserting the primacy of the general class struggle.

Germany and Austria in particular were shaken by political upheaval, extreme political polarization, severe economic crisis, and the need to modernize a work force into a new world of assembly-line industrial production and an expanding white-collar sector. A successful reconciliation of maternity and modernity was crucial to this allegedly new and modern project. With their willing and remarkably non-nostalgic embrace of the new world of science, technology, and mass politics, the working-class parties created a kind of social and cultural laboratory of modernity in the interwar years. Thus, they confronted regularly the contradictions of integrating women – so often viewed, as Adelheid von Saldern notes in her discussion of German Social Democracy, as aliens in the class struggle – into their organizing and governing tasks.

Former comrades in the pre-1917 Second International, communists and social democrats in Central Europe were bitterly, indeed fatally, divided in their political views 1) of the Bolshevik Revolution and the viability of the Soviet Union as a model workers' paradise, and 2) of the efficacy of joining governing coalitions. Yet, on basic issues relating to women and gender – encapsulated in the sphere of the social (rather than the directly political) – they were united by some remarkably similar assumptions. As Gruber, von Saldern, and Grossmann outline here, communists and social democrats in Austria and Germany shared a consensus about the importance of healthy motherhood and eugenic hygiene for the production of a fit new generation. They shared also a rather breathtakingly hopeful faith in the ability of science, medicine, and technology to promote a healthy, sturdy, and orderly working-class family capable of hard work in the workplace and for the party. In particular, they all adopted a language of "rationalization" that promised a more efficient, regular, and streamlined organization not only of work processes but also of everyday life. This meant that communists and socialists both were interested in population policy and social welfare; in maternal and infant health, in birth control and sex education, in household organization and housing reform – in *Lebensreform*, the reform of life, or in today's parlance, new lifestyles.

Gruber and von Saldern both stress that for the social democrats, especially with their central place in municipal politics, housing policy and architecture were key, offering a laboratory for modern scientific

notions about health, hygiene, population policy, and family. The fascination with rationalization as a means of equalizing and ordering daily life
extended not only from the assembly line to the kitchen and the bedroom
but even to language itself. Witness the socialist flirtation with Esperanto,
the ultimate perhaps in standardization.

Helmut Gruber's discussion of the Austrian social democratic "counter-
model" to the Soviet Union in Red Vienna poses most sharply the
contradictions and ambivalences of reform raised by the socialist commitment to the creation of a new breed of healthy and orderly men and
women in well-structured communities. He presents a world in which
maternalism – a program of improving the lives of mothers and children –
overrode other commitments to female equality in politics and the workplace. This was a world in which the emphasis on discipline and surveillance of the working-class family, especially of the working-class woman,
consistently overrode the emancipatory promise of expanding public
health and social welfare facilities. He questions the number of workers
that actually benefitted from the famed Vienna housing projects and suggests that even the most successful innovations depended on locating
women primarily as mothers rather than as equal partners in work, family,
political, and indeed, sexual life. He notes that the attention to birth control and sex education, certainly radical in terms of Austria's dominant
clerical culture, was couched in terms of eugenic hygiene rather than sexual pleasure. Red Vienna most clearly, but also the housing projects of the
German trade unions and the welfare organizations of the German Communist party (KPD), present a familiar irony: interventionist social welfare
and hygiene projects both aided and disciplined; both invaded working-
class women's space and provided opportunity for middle-class women
reformers; both set problematic norms of fitness and decency and provided overworked women with concrete aid and advice.

Gruber stresses, as do von Saldern and Grossmann for Germany, the
socialists' anxious relationship to the very new women they celebrated and
aimed to organize. They honored the modern mother, attentive to all the latest innovations in nutrition and hygiene, adept juggler of the double burden
of domestic and work responsibilities, committed to party women's activities.
But they were highly suspicious of other kinds of models of the new woman,
like the flighty garçonne-like white-collar workers, or the sexually emancipated woman in the metropolis. They did not know how to respond to the
expansion of mass commercial popular culture after World War I, with its
unlimited opportunities for propaganda and publicity but also its temptations
and distractions from the more traditional solidarities of working-class association. Here, too, women were of particular concern since, less grounded in
the discipline of the workplace, they were deemed to be particularly suscep-
tible to, indeed in the vanguard of, the distractions and temptations of com-

mercial entertainment, especially the illustrated magazine and the cinema. Trash and kitsch were considered the domain of the female. In all three cases discussed in this section, party leaders and activists contended with this tension between the homogenizing force of popular culture and the particular appeal of a separate class-conscious subculture, trying simultaneously to counter mass culture and deploy or mirror it. The working-class movement, in its films, clubs, and journals, wanted to mirror mainstream culture while also subverting it; they were never comfortable with the overlaps, especially for women and youth, two categories both desirable and disruptive for socialist and communist organizing. Party leaders also shared an ambivalence about the "traditional" working-class woman; they valorized the long-suffering, hard-working proletarian mother, but they also chastised her for politically backward allegiances, attachments to unhygienic child rearing and housekeeping practices, and mistrust of the clean new housing projects, in which intrusive but well-meaning social workers wanted to install her. Women's organizers interested in reform also continually negotiated problematic relationships with bourgeois feminist and welfare organizations, who offered gender solidarity while preaching class hierarchy.

All three parties clung to a rhetoric of class equality while sanctioning gender separate organizations that proved in practice to be more hospitable to women. In a familiar conundrum, they offered women a "room of their own" in which to develop their own leadership, journals, conferences, and issues, but a room always located somewhere in the back of the party's house. This arrangement, in which a rhetoric of integration coexisted with a practice of separatism, seemed to suit many women as much as it did male activists. All three parties presented new visions of comradeship and companionate heterosexual relationships while still not fundamentally questioning the gender division of labor (material and emotional) within the household. All three parties professed demands for equal pay for equal work and women's right to work, but they also worried about gender competition at the workplace, especially under conditions of mass unemployment, and insisted on women's all-important maternal role. Indeed, it was one measure of the comparative radicalism and risk-taking of the KPD discussed by Grossmann that it alone was willing to firmly defend married women's right to work during the crisis of the Great Depression. Moreover, the KPD most clearly distinguished itself from the socialists in Germany and Austria on the vexed issue of sexuality and women's right to control their own bodies. While socialists also supported birth control and sex counseling and education, only the KPD was willing to take a clear position in favor of abolishing laws criminalizing abortion.

All three parties contended with a gender gap – the gap between their apparently pro-woman program and the notable reluctance of women to flock to socialist or communist parties. They shared dissatisfaction with electoral results among women; having supported female suffrage, they did not gain as much from it as they thought they deserved. All contended with the distance between leadership and rank and file, between the ambition to organize the working class and the realities of middle-class leadership. When it came to organizing women, the additional irony was that parties dedicated to the working class did much better at mobilizing housewives than harried female wage earners. Social democrats in Germany especially, with their significant role on the national governing level, but also socialists in Austria and communists in Germany, who participated powerfully in politics on the municipal level, faced the dilemma of how to represent a working class in crisis and simultaneously carry out the responsibilities of a mass party that could win elections and participate in governments.

What emerges most clearly, perhaps, in these three chapters are the immense difficulties of constituting notions of citizenship for women in the interwar period, not only at the state level but also within political parties and trade unions. Determining what gets defined as political and what is coded as welfare was the problem. Whether communist or socialist, women were assigned to the social space, which expansive as it might appear – encompassing an impressive array of housing, health, and welfare innovations – never quite counted as politically central. The KPD experiments with sex reform and youth organizations, as well as the defense of married women's right to work and the right to abortion, pushed the hardest at the parameters of a politics that tried to reconcile commitment to political, social, and economic equality with insistence on the primacy of motherhood, and thus revealed the limits of left-wing women's politics most clearly.

The successes in Austria and Germany were circumscribed, in some ways as potentially coercive as liberating. In any case, they were brutally cut off by the triumph of fascism in Germany and Austria. Still, these chapters do describe brave new efforts at creating new ways of living; they alert us to ways in which participation in socialist and communist movements offered practical entries into modernity for women. At the same time, they reflected the ambivalence always present in rationalizing strategies that control and empower, divide and discipline women while also providing a basis for claiming entitlements and citizenship. Working-class parties in Germany and Austria did attempt to address this new electorate in their multiple, overlapping, and often clashing roles as mother, worker, voter, citizen, and comrade. A measure of how far these experiments in new life (*Neues Leben*) tried to reach is that they were so thoroughly dismantled by the fascist regimes that followed the republican experiments in Austria and Germany.

The "New" Proletarian Woman in Austria and Germany

"A Body Made Supple and Disciplined by Sports"

Socialist Athletes, International Worker Olympics, Vienna 1931
Source: Verein für Geschichte der Arbeiterbewegung (VGA), Vienna

Workers' Gymnastic Club, Dortmund 1923
Source: Fritz-Hüser-Institut, Dortmund

"As Wage Earners in Workshop and Factory"

Baby-Carriage Workshop/Factory in Vienna, 1920s
Source: VGA

Plant Producing Shampoo, Germany, 1930
Source: Schwarzkopf GmbH, Hamburg, Germany

"Politically Engaged in the Ranks and as Leaders"

Socialist Youth
Celebrating
Founding of the
Austrian Republic,
1931
Source: VGA

German
Communist
Women
Demonstrating
for Women's
Rights, 1927
Source: Stiftung
der Parteien und
Massenorgan-
isazionen der DDR
im Bundesarchiv
Berlin

Marie Juchacz of the SPD Executive
Addressing Party Meeting
Source: Friedrich-Ebert-Stiftung, Bonn

"The Future New Woman and Some Current Obstacles"

Unequal Vision of Ability, Labor,
and Activity
Source: Arbeiter Kalender, January
1932: Bundesarchiv Koblenz (BARCHK)

Bobbed Hair, Sensible Clothes, Goal
Directed, Equal, and in Control
Source: Arbeiter-Illustrierte-Zeitung,
22 (1931)

Victim of the Anti-abortion Law
Source: Arbeiter Kalender, February 1932:
BARCHK

Chapter 1

The "New Woman"
Realities and Illusions of Gender Equality in Red Vienna

Helmut Gruber

The Austrian socialists' Vienna experiment, from 1919 to 1934, was the largest and most successful attempt by a socialist party in inter-war Europe to create a comprehensive proletarian counter culture.[1] The vast array of initiatives and reforms undertaken in Red Vienna were closely related to innovations of social democracy in Germany and the Scandinavian countries but offered a larger vision, which served as a counter model to the Bolshevik's cultural project in Soviet Russia. Before turning to the place of women – the "women question" in the formulations of party spokesmen – in the Viennese cultural experiment, it would be useful I think to set the stage by giving an overview of the commanding position of the Austrian Socialist Party (SDAP) in the city and province of Vienna and to highlight some of the aspects of the cultural program they aspired to and were actually able to carry out.[2]

Proletarian Cultural Experiment

The socialist leaders believed that Austromarxism, unlike other versions of Marxism, could fulfill the promised foretaste of the socialist utopia in the present. When Otto Bauer spoke of "a revolution in the soul of man," he implied much more than the elevation of oppressed and deprived pro-letarians through *Bildung* (civilizing education) in order to make them conscious actors in the dialectical unfolding of history.[3] His aphorism sug-

---

gested as well a sea change in the behavior and mentality of workers through invasion of their private and intimate spheres leading to the creation of *neue Menschen* (a new proletarian humanity).[4]

What were the accomplishments of municipal socialism that prompted the socialists to advertise Vienna as the "Mecca" of social innovation? The centerpiece was the 64,000 apartments housing some 200,000 Viennese in over 300 projects of which the largest had the monumental quality of "peoples' palaces." The latter were serviced by a host of communal facilities: mechanized laundries, bathhouses, kindergartens, playgrounds and swimming pools, medical and dental clinics, libraries and lecture halls, and youth and mothers' consultation bureaus.[5] An aggressive public health program sought to combat disease; the Public Welfare Office undertook to uplift the moral climate in Vienna by aiming at the creation of the *ordentliche* worker family – a term connoting not only orderliness but also decency, respectability, and discipline.[6] Strongly eugenic in orientation, the Welfare Office proceeded in various ways to intervene in the lives of worker families to assure that children were raised properly, but was less forthcoming on the problems of birth control and abortion, for which it offered admonitions and restrictions rather than constructive assistance.

What was the socialists' plan of action for transforming Viennese workers into self-conscious, willful actors in their own liberation as *neue Menschen*? At its high point the Socialist Party directed more than forty cultural organizations with an aggregate of some 400,000 members.[7] The party sought to include and sponsor the most diverse interests through a network of cultural enterprises running the gamut from the popular workers' libraries; lecture bureaus; theater, singing, art, film, and radio societies; an association for sports and body culture; and a department sponsoring events ranging from mass festivals to more esoteric clubs for chess players, animal lovers, and Esperanto enthusiasts. The numerical success of some of these enterprises was remarkable: 6,500 lecture evenings in 1932 drew an audience of 160,000; book borrowing from the fifty-three worker libraries reached 2.4 million in the same year; two million theater and concert tickets were distributed by the art center between 1922 and 1926; membership in sport clubs reached 110,000 in 1931; and a mass festival at that time drew an audience of 260,000 over four days.[8]

Impressive as such an array of cultural organizations and number of participants may appear, they are deceptive. For reasons which cannot be pursued here the great majority of Viennese workers experienced few of the benefits of municipal socialism and party culture directly. At the same time the symbolic effect of the socialists' experiment should not be overlooked, for the workers perceived a sea change in the daily life of Vienna where the mayor and most officials who counted were socialists, where the fortress-like Peoples' Palaces (such as the kilometer-long art deco Karl-Marx-Hof) suggested proletarian power as well as a more decent form of habitation, and where the ensemble of socialist initiatives signaled an entirely new dignity for the status of worker. But the symbols, too, were deceptive. In the Austromarxists' vision culture would play the role of a weapon in the armory of the class struggle.[9] Increasingly, however, the cultural experiment in Vienna became a surrogate for political action in the national arena where the real exercise of power by the Catholic-conservative camp was to sweep the cultural experiment from the stage of history.

Most interwar socialist parties put the legal and political equality of women in their long-range programs, calling for a gender-neutral citizenship. SDAP leaders sought to realize that goal at once by guaranteeing women's republican rights but also aimed higher toward making the citizenship of men and women social and cultural as well. Their attempts to solve the "woman question," limited from the outset by a traditional masculine psychology and world view in conflict with the reality of women's lives, aspirations, and agendas, form the substance of this chapter.

Female Citizenship: In the Party & Trade Union

The emergence of Republican Austria – a German-speaking enclave of 6.2 million – from the former multi-national empire of 52 million in November 1918 brought a virtual silent revolution regarding the condition of women in its wake. The long-standing demand for women's suffrage and right to stand for public office on the part of both SDAP and feminist organizations became a fundamental principle of the constitution.[10] A practical consequence of female suffrage was the election of twelve women to the Viennese Municipal Council in December 1918 and the election of ten women to the Provisional National Assembly in March 1919. Men had voted to give women these rights. Had they suddenly freed themselves of all the common prejudices by which women's disenfranchisement had been justified? In declarations for public consumption women were to be rewarded for their efforts and sacrifices during the war. Behind the scenes both socialists and Catholics (in the Christian Social party) were prepared to gamble on their ability to attract and keep a majority of women voters.

Equally important in the official empowerment of women was the abolition of paragraph 30 of the Law of Association of 1867, which had denied women the right to join political organizations. This cleared the way for working-class women, who had been organized in "apolitical" auxiliaries to the SDAP, to finally join the party. In a similar vein the Civil Code was reformed to reflect the principle that all citizens were equal before the law, with all privileges based on birth, rank, class, confession, and sex annulled. All of the above reforms, though dramatic on paper, were contested in practice. Armed with such legality and supported by shifting male allies, Austrian women entered the struggle for full equality which remained illusive.[11] By the late 1920s, to meet these problems, the socialist Viennese municipal administration provided legal aid to women through Women's Legal Advice Centers in virtually all districts. These played an adversarial and protective role for women especially on questions of family rights, marriage, and divorce.[12]

Although the SDAP benefitted from hardships experienced by women during the war in the election for parliament in 1919, by the next year the women's vote moved to the right under the influence of Catholic propaganda. With fewer women than men voting for the SDAP, the fears of those in the party who opposed female suffrage on the grounds that women would be putty in the hands of priests seemed to be substantiated. But by 1927 the municipal election in Vienna (using different colored envelopes for the two sexes) recorded an equal number of male and female votes for the party. Municipal maintenance of rent control and a dedicated program of political education among women had turned the tide guaranteeing safe socialist majorities in municipal government until 1934.[13]

The proportion of women among SDAP members grew throughout the period, reaching 34 percent nationally and 36 percent in Vienna by the early 1930s.[14] Of these 51.6 percent were employed, with 51.5 percent of them active as blue and white collar workers. Women constituted about 20 percent of party leadership at the grass roots level – the unsalaried cadres (21,500 in Vienna alone). But the higher levels of the party bureaucracy, especially the editorship of publications (included those for women) and direction of the forty-odd cultural enterprises, and especially the party executive, remained essentially a protected male preserve. Of the twenty members and alternates in the latter there were three aging women – Adelheid Popp, Gabriele Proft, and Therese Schlesinger – participating in a leadership inured to change and outside (younger, more activist) influences.

Women's interests within the party were debated and formulated by SDAP Women's Conferences preceding party congresses at which general guidelines and programs were put forward and approved. The Women's Conference of 1923, for instance, tabled and adopted the following demands: abolition of the Church's control of marriage for Catholics; equal pay for equal work; recognition of motherhood as a social function; and the repeal of paragraph 144 of the Penal Code making abortion a crime.[15] Some of these conferences were far from routine, as that before the important Linz party conference of 1926, to be discussed later, reveals. There, differences were not only fundamental but sharp between women delegates and between them and the party's leading men who were accustomed to have the first and last word.[16]

Socialist women were clearly visible in the SDAP delegations to the *Nationalrat* (Parliament), accounting for some 13 percent at their high point of participation.[17] Socialist women were better represented in the Viennese municipal government where they accounted for nearly 20 percent of SDAP councillors by the early 1930s. Although there were many more new faces here than in the delegation to the *Nationalrat*, the average age was still 50 to 55, with the age group of women with children from 25 to 40 not represented at all (in a party whose members were considerably younger than the general population). Only one female city councillor came from the established women's leadership elite; two-thirds had a working-class background or occupation; and all had spent more than twenty years in party work at the district, social, and cultural level.

As we shall see, the percentage of women SDAP members and voters in national and municipal elections as well as their selective representation in parliament and the Viennese City Council were symbolic of their political citizenship. Their official status as equals was not translated into practice; at the decision-making level women and women's aspirations and goals were at best of tertiary concern to be identified, screened, censored, and even dictated by the male leadership. A search through the protocols of SDAP Executive Committee meetings reveals virtual silence on the subject of women from 1922 to 1927. The minutes report a continuous attempt from 1928 to 1930 to reduce the financing of the extremely popular women's weekly, *Die Unzufriedene*, addressed to nonparty women, with a circulation of 154,600 and announce that in view of the deepening national political crisis from 1932 to 1933 the annual National Women's Conference will be canceled.[18]

The opportunity for rank and file socialist women to participate in activities sponsored by the party was considerable, including the renters' association, consumers' union, friends of nature, song societies, lecture series, and workers' libraries, with the broad array of sports clubs and athletic activities most popular among young, unmarried women workers.[19] All of these auxiliary creations of the SDAP served its members first of all, but also were the means by which non-party women and men could be attracted to vote for and eventually join the party. They made the SDAP permeable and welcoming to women with a limited range of sociability, who would have kept their distance from meetings of a party cell, where male social norms of behavior were generally dominant. They also emphasized the tertiary sector of party life distant from the primary political decisions and activities. The majority of female socialist party members were from the working class, and for them membership in a trade union was the most common other form of engagement.

By 1934, the percentage of women in full employment in Austria and Vienna was 38.1 and 41.5 respectively, a proportion greater than in most other countries.[20] The situation of women workers was substantially more insecure and less rewarding than that of working men. According to the realities of the labor market women were given the most menial positions, were the first to be fired, and received wages reaching only 50 to 65 percent of male wages for equal work.[21] Although women were protected by law from night shifts, heavy physical labor, and dangerous occupations, labor inspectors' reported frequent breaches of the rules. The condition of female home workers was far worse: their wages were 50 percent less than those of women in industry; they had no collective wage contracts; they suffered from intermittent unemployment; their living quarters were among the smallest and most densely populated and served as workrooms in addition to their many other functions. Domestic servants were the most exploited and least protected. Although a law of 1920 regulated hours of work, wages, time off, and vacations, working conditions remained largely unsupervised.

National membership in the SDAP-allied Free Trade Unions declined drastically from 896,763 in 1923 to 520,162 in 1932, due largely to the constantly accelerating unemployment. But, the percentage of women union members remained a stable 22.8 throughout the period. From surveys at the time it appears that women who joined their shop's trade union did so because they were SDAP members or their father or sibling was either in the party, union, or both, or because it was an expected part of female sociability at the workplace.[22] The trade unions did little to alter the impression that women were an unwanted presence at the workplace. Lip service was given to equal pay for equal work at trade union congresses, but on the shop floor the attitude prevailed that women took away men's jobs. As in most other countries, there was a widespread attack on married working women as "double earners," which the trade unions appear to have abetted. This lack of support is astounding when one considers that the working women of Vienna supplied 26.4 percent of the trade union membership.

That the trade unions made little effort to integrate women workers or to accord them positions in their organizations commensurate with their numbers can be adduced from the low percentage of female shop stewards,[23] the male orientation of trade union papers, and the under representation of women trade unionists at general congresses.[24] It is small wonder then that trade unionism for women workers remained a formality, something expected of them, and that only 21.7 percent of the women trade unionists in Leichter's study ever attended union meetings and only 3 percent read the union papers.[25]

It is imperative that we correct this gloomy picture of working conditions one receives from the marketplace and self-serving protectionism of the trade unions. Economic legislation passed by the first socialist-led national coalition government included unemployment and sickness insurance, restrictions on female and child labor, the eight-hour day,[26] and one to two weeks of paid vacation. The most important law passed – especially regarding the condition and welfare of working women – created the Chamber of Workers and Employees, with the function of overseeing collective contracts between trade unions and employers, supervising the execution of labor laws, and advising the parliament on labor legislation.[27]

In 1925 the headquarters of the Chamber in Vienna created the post of Official Advisor on Women Workers and appointed Käthe Leichter, a committed socialist from the left wing of the SDAP with a doctorate in sociology from the University of Heidelberg.[28] For the next seven years Leichter made her office into a remarkable instrument of working women's interests and demands. In three excellent large surveys – of domestic workers, home workers, and industrial workers – she exposed the conditions of women at the workplace and in the private sphere. She worked closely with female factory inspectors to investigate whether the protective laws and mandatory pregnancy leaves were being enforced. In addition to editing the collective volume *Handbuch der Frauenarbeit* (1930), which surveyed ten years of working women's activities, she created a special women's supplement for the Chamber's monthly *Arbeit und Wirtschaft*, and gave a series of evening lectures on "socialism for women."[29] This remarkable effort gave the conditions and problems of women's work and, most importantly, the triple burden when household and child rearing were included for many women, a favorable public exposure.

From the moment the socialists gained control of Vienna, they began to experiment with means of improving the quality of workers' lives through welfare measures directed at the worker family and centered on the working-class wife and mother.

The Orderly Worker Family: Public Health, Hygiene, and Social Welfare

When the socialists assumed control over the administration of the city in the summer of 1919 the ravages of war were everywhere apparent: the virtual breakdown of public sanitation; a generally weakened population due to four years of malnutrition; the danger of epidemics; a sharp increase in the traditional killer disease of tuberculosis and in venereal diseases; overcrowding of less than adequate hospital facilities; a sharp growth in the number of indigent and homeless; and a general shortage of fuel and food stuffs needed for a return to public health. The socialist municipal government moved quickly to arrest and reverse these adverse conditions mainly by investing more public resources in the expansion of clinics, family assistance programs, and aid to children. Closely associated with measures to arrest the deterioration of public health and welfare was a drive for cleanliness and hygiene in public places, made possible by the introduction of sprinkler trucks and a new method of mechanized garbage collection.[30]

Socialist approaches to these problems remained piecemeal and lacked a focus until the summer of 1920, when Dr. Julius Tandler became city councillor for welfare. He came to his office with the experience gained in public service as Under Secretary for Public Health in the short-lived coalition national governments. Tandler was a distinguished anatomist, one of the few Jewish chaired professors on the medical faculty of the university, and a man with strong socialist and scientific beliefs.[31] With an enlarged budget at his disposal, made possible by new luxury taxes, Tandler proceeded to alter the perspective and practice of public health and social welfare.[32] In place of the notion that health and welfare were matters for Christian Karitas or other private charitable organizations, the socialists in the city council adopted Tandler's view that health and welfare were the right of every citizen.[33]

Although this view seems in many ways exemplary and humanitarian at first glance, its explication both as theory and practice aroused considerable resistance not simply from the Church or the Christian Social party, where one might expect it, but also from the workers in whose interest it was developed. Tandler went to great lengths in subsequent publications to explain and justify his approach in order to allay what he believed (and quite correctly) was suspicion among the workers.[34] What emerged from these explications was a number of advertised principles underlying the Viennese welfare system: that society is committed to assist all those in need; that individual welfare assistance can be administered rationally only within the context of family welfare; that constructive welfare aid is preventive welfare care; and that the organization of welfare must remain a closed system.[35]

What were the practical accomplishments to which the city council pointed with great pride? The decline of the death rate by 25 percent and of infant mortality by 50 percent from prewar levels stood high on the list.[36] The incidence of tuberculosis, which had been rampant particularly in the working class, was only somewhat reduced and continued to be the major threat to health among school children. A comprehensive system of aid to children was put in force. It included school lunches, school medical and dental examinations, provisions for publicly sponsored vacations and summer camps, and newly created after-school centers. The number of kindergartens increased significantly from 20 in 1913 to 113 with almost 10,000 children in 1931. Municipal bathing facilities including swimming pools, with some nine million visitors in 1927, were also high on the list of attainments in public hygiene. Prophylactic medical examinations for adults and children in municipal clinics reached 123,000 in 1932 and welfare workers carried out 91,000 home visits in the same year. No doubt this was a commendable record of accomplishment for the municipal administration, but it was by no means so unique as the socialists claimed. If we compare it to a number of contemporary German cities, Düsseldorf for instance, we find an almost identical roster of health and welfare measures and achievements.[37]

Like other aspects of Viennese municipal socialism, it was the instrumental role of the health and welfare programs to be played in the lives of the workers that gave them a special character. In part these municipal interventions were a compensation for the limited national provisions for maternity leave, for instance.[38] Under the forceful direction of Tandler, the welfare department pursued an overall policy of population politics and assumed the responsibility for improving the quantity and quality of the population. This mission was predicated on the duty and power of the public authority to intervene in the life of the family to produce these ends. Population politics, particularly the concern about the steady decline in population and the need to add not only to the number of workers but also to improve their biological qualities, was a major concern among leading socialists in the party and municipal government.[39]

Tandler's own version combined elements of neo-Lamarkian and social Darwinist ideas: that changes in the human environment could be transmitted through the germ plasm and that "natural selection" carried out by responsible officials would enhance and improve the genetic pool of future generations.[40] At times Tandler slipped into eugenic phantasies of sterilization and other means of reproductive control by society quite frightening in their implications. Finding no contradiction between these ideas and his commitment to socialism, he set out to fashion a powerful organization of social intervention to put population politics into practice.

Under the auspices of the Public Welfare Office a number of institutions were created to assist the family in its task of rearing the next generation. Where the family failed to provide optimal conditions, the Public Welfare Office was to provide temporary or alternative care. The municipality thus empowered itself to remove children from their parents if it judged them deficient in their nurturing capability and responsibility. Tandler was attacked repeatedly in the City Council by Christian Social members who accused him of alienating children from their parents in order to indoctrinate them with socialist ideas. His stock reply was that he considered the family sacred but only if it was capable of performing its vital function. Under Tandler's direction the Public Welfare Office proceeded to put the population under surveillance with the argument that preventive welfare, aimed at raising the moral climate of families, necessitated that it act in a supervisory capacity. The methods employed combined persuasion with compulsion, voluntary cooperation with juridical force.

The realm of municipal family supervision was organized in lock step virtually from conception to adulthood, when the cycle continued as the former child became a parent. The most original and controversial agency was a marriage consultation center created in 1922. Its function was to advise couples intent on marriage about their sexual health, genetic deficits, hereditary weaknesses, and prospects for producing normal and healthy children.[41] The center offered to issue certificates to prospective conjugal sexual partners that they were free of disabilities such as syphilis and tuberculosis and hoped, thereby, to improve the quality of the population. But very few individuals were prepared for such intrusions into their private lives, and after ten years the venture was admitted to be a failure. Throughout its existence the center met with violent opposition from the Church and the Christian Social party ("the Jews are touching the holy state of Christian matrimony"). Tandler's true intention in founding the center, of using marriage consultation for weeding out those "eugenically unfit for reproduction" and the possible legal misuse of the case records, no doubt did not escape the general public. The center made a point of refusing to have anything to do with sex counseling or birth control advice, subjects which might have made it attractive and useful.

The marriage consultation center was the only failure; all other agencies of the Public Welfare Office concerned with the life cycle of the Viennese family were successful in promoting its aims. At the beginning of family control were the municipal hospitals, in which 83 percent of all births took place.[42] Social workers in the maternity wards registered the newborn infants, arranged for a subsequent home visit, and recommended that mother and child regularly attend a Mothers' Consultation Center for further assistance in infant care. By 1927 there were thirty-four of these centers concerned with infant and child care to the age of six distributed throughout the city. In Denmark, Britain, Norway, Belgium, Germany, and Catalonia such mothers' clinics also offered birth control instruction and sex consultation. Doctors advised mothers on breast feeding and infant and child care and hygiene, and resident social workers followed up these instructions with home visits to see that consulting mothers had carried them out. This was but one way in which the Public Welfare Office found entry into the home in order to observe and judge the quality (adequacy or insufficiency) of family nurture for the children. The right to regular inspections of families receiving any kind of municipal assistance was statutory and, as we shall see, gave the welfare machinery tremendous power not only over individual cases but in setting the norms of family health and behavior.

In 1927 Tandler proposed to the Municipal Council that the Public Welfare Office be granted the right to distribute, regardless of need, infant layettes to all newborns as a "birthday present" from the municipality. After an extended and heated debate, in which the socialists were accused once more of using city hall to make political propaganda, the measure was forced through by the socialist majority. These gifts were packed in attractive red cartons with a reproduction of a famous mother-and-child image by the sculptor Anton Hanak on the cover and a listing of the thirty-four mothers' consultation centers with addresses on the inside. Before long, some 13,000 of these municipal caring parcels were distributed annually. Without diminishing the virtue of such "need-blind" distributions, it is necessary to also consider the "Trojan horse" aspects of these gifts. Their distribution by social workers made it possible for the Public Welfare Office to have insight into homes which were otherwise outside its purview.

By and large, however, the welfare authorities did not depend on invitations to pass judgement on family life. The Municipal Council as early as 1921 claimed guardianship over children born out of wedlock, foster children, and those in institutional care.[43] After this group, subject to the most intense form of control, came all those who received public assistance in any form. Such families were subject to regular visits by social workers who kept close watch on the standard of housekeeping, especially cleanliness, the condition of beds and clothing, food preparation, and family relations. Adolescents with problems were referred to or expected to seek assistance at Youth Consultation Centers throughout the city. Families also came to the attention of the welfare authorities and thus subject to home visits because the school doctor had reported some health problem of their children or because court proceedings, for eviction for instance, drew attention to the family as being "troubled."[44] Kindergartens and after-school youth centers worked hand-in-hand with welfare efforts to produce the orderly family. Special attention was paid to the professional training of social workers.[45] They were exclusively women, because Tandler and most leading socialists believed that a special "female empathy" was necessary for the often emotional demands on welfare workers.

Finally, we come to the question implicit in all of the welfare activities: What happened when the social worker making a home visit concluded that the family did not meet the municipalities' norms of the orderly family? A report was made to the Childrens' Diagnostic Service, a modern observation center under the direction of the child psychologist Charlotte Bühler, charged with deciding the fate of the child from problematic environments. A court order was issued requiring the parents to surrender the child to the diagnostic service, which in the course of some four weeks would make a recommendation that had the force of law.[46] The decisions reached included: being put in the care of foster parents, being sent to a childrens' home or correctional institution, being admitted to a hospital, or being returned to the parents. Of the various reasons given for being remanded to the diagnostic center, relatives admitted to a hospital, poverty, and homelessness ranked highest, neglect and delinquency were frequent, but endangered morals and parental conflict were rarely mentioned.[47]

How working-class communities reacted to the municipality's attempts to transform them into the orderly families of its definition is not easy to discern. Contemporary means of grass roots communication among workers were virtually non-existent. We have only a scattering of local communist newsletters which, despite their expected political line, throw some light on how the welfare system worked and was perceived from below. In these, complaints are all centered on the behavior of social workers and other municipal officials: their treatment of the needy, their arrogance in dealing with sick workers needing medical and pharmaceutical referrals, their tendency to treat workers like children, and the poor functioning of kindergartens.[48] There are also claims that welfare payments to families are being cut on spurious grounds such as that a family has "gained property" in the form of a bag of apples and needs less support. More directly aimed at the subjective judgements of the welfare department was the charge that a social worker took a child to the police rather than dealing with the mother who was estranged from her husband.[49]

Oral histories of working-class families and social workers of the First Republic depict public welfare as a coercive system. The judgment of what was respectable, orderly, and decent on the part of social workers was arbitrary.[50] Very often being poor – a condition becoming ever more widespread after the impact of the Depression and further growth of unemployment – was sufficient cause to put a family on notice for further investigation or to threaten the mother with sending her children to the diagnostic center if she did not improve the general appearance of her domicile, the condition of the beds and childrens' clothes, or the nourishment of the family meals. But in the world of increasing poverty among Viennese workers it was necessary to pawn household objects and bedding, cut corners on food offered to children by serving *Schmalzbrot* (bread spread with lard),[51] and repair all clothing items to the point where they were ragged. The tendency of the welfare system to look upon the poor, the unemployed, those evicted, or those who consumed a glass too many as deviants or at best marginal families needing the full measure of social control to bring them to the standard of normalcy made welfare

workers appear as hostile agents of the government in working-class communities. Indeed the removal of children to the diagnostic center, as
described by one social worker, resembled a police raid, with social worker
and bailiff arriving unexpectedly to reduce the amount of parental resistance to what they considered a violation of their rights.[52]

The socialists had put their health and welfare program into effect
against the vociferous objection and condemnation of the Christian
Social party in the Municipal Council. It is interesting to observe that the
whole *Kulturkampf* being waged did not arise from differences about the
right or necessity of higher authorities to intervene in the life of the family. The nature of the intervener lay at the heart of the struggle: whether
it should be the state acting through the agency of a socialist municipal
government or the Church acting through its apostolic spokesmen. Neither side paid much attention to the similarity of positions; only the differences were fought over.

The Worker Family as Context

The SDAP attempted to create a climate in the public sphere of Vienna
conducive to the implantation and acceptance of its cultural program.
The worker family received particular attention as the most fundamental
agency for influencing and shaping changes in behavior and consciousness. It was not well understood that the family, as a center of private life
and repository of accepted habits and practices, commanded powers to
resist intrusions into its realm of activity and control.[53] The nuclear family model became pervasive in Vienna and other European cities only
between the late nineteenth century and the early 1920s as an adaptation
to changing productive techniques of high industrial capitalism, which
demanded a stable worker existence and assured reproduction of labor.
This "closed" form of family socialization gradually replaced previous
"open" forms such as concubinage and other types of unregulated associations with a high degree of illegitimate births.[54] The emerging disciplined and orderly worker family approximated the model proposed by
middle-class social reformers of the late-nineteenth century. They had
hoped to integrate the worker family into the norms of bourgeois life and,
thereby, to assure stability and peace in the social order. Whether the stable and orderly worker family would provide the basis of proletarian
embourgeoisement or for greater class consciousness and participation in
working-class organizations remained an open question.[55]

The Austrian socialist leaders clearly aimed at the second of these two
possibilities and sought to strengthen the formal structure and shape the
values of the nuclear working-class family.[56] In following this strategy, the
Austromarxists appeared to reject the accepted Marxist canon, which

anticipated the dissolution of the family under capitalism and its replacement by communal forms of social organization.[57] In the Viennese context after 1919 their embracing of the nuclear family model was pragmatic; it also brought them dangerously close to the interventionist position of their bourgeois and clerical opponents. The former regarded the family as the foundation of social stability; the latter considered it the primary spiritual unit of Christian morality. As we shall see, the socialists' intervention into the workers' private sphere, like the presumption of their opponents, assumed that the worker family was a passive entity. That view yielded a paternalism with a social purpose, as one recent commentator characterized it: "Whilst the old order and its father figures had fallen from power, the social democratic leaders came forward in the chaos of the first postwar years as new father-figures."[58]

Men were not a direct subject of the SDAP's attempt to transform the working-class family. They were, however, always in the background as beneficiaries of the more orderly, relaxing, and peaceful home environment to be created. The task of building this domestic haven was placed on the shoulders of women, whose nature, appearance, and responsibilities were to be altered and enhanced and whose role as wives and mothers was to be redefined.

The "New Woman" – Symbol & Reality

What actual place was accorded to women in the cultural experiment to transform working-class life? Socialist party publications were silent or at best obtuse on the subject of women per se or of female consciousness and identity. The women's role was generally subsumed under various higher social goals: the creation of orderly worker families; the need for rational and controlled reproduction, leading to a "healthy" new generation; and the desire to make a varied party life central to the lives of workers. Since female workers accounted for about 40 percent of the labor force and because 80 percent of married women were in some way employed,[59] the party literature devoted considerable space to the plight of women compelled to bear the triple burden of work, household, and child rearing.[60] In attempting to rescue working-class women from this plight, the socialist reformers hypostatized "the new woman" as the female part of the *neue Menschen* they were in the process of creating in the class struggle on the cultural front.

What picture of the "new woman" did the socialist literature project for its readers? Her physical appearance was youthful, with a slender *garçon*-figure made supple by sports, with bobbed hair and unrestraining garments bespeaking an active life; her temperament was fearless, open, and relaxed. To her husband she was a comrade; for her children she was a friend.[61] The working- class woman of yesterday – careworn in appearance, imprisoned by her clothes, unapproachable by those who needed her – was to be abolished by waving a magic wand. This image, like many other aspects of the socialists' program, was adapted from middle-class attempts to redefine the role of females in society. A seminal work in this liberation movement was the widely translated and somewhat scandalous *La garçonne* by Victor Margueritte of 1922, which featured an independent, self-assured, and worldly woman, who fought against the double standard and demanded the right to sexual experimentation. In the 1920s the *garçonne*/flapper became a widespread female role model in the industrialized world.

How was the transformation envisaged by the SDAP to be accomplished? One standard answer was the equalization of female and male wages, making it possible for women to turn over housework and child care to paid, trained help.[62] The most common advice for reducing the triple burden was the rationalization of housework. This fascination with rationalization in the domestic sphere echoed the latest developments in the scientific management of industrial production and reflected the emphasis on science and efficiency of the home economics movement in the United States. It went hand-in-hand with house proudness exemplified by cleanliness and neatness, an aesthetic of simplicity and functionality, and the demand for formal training in efficient housework.[63] The SDAP's conception of domestic rationalization sought mainly to lighten the burden of each woman in her home, thereby contradicting the demand for professionalization of housework.

The party offered working-class women a variety of practical advice. They were encouraged to provide themselves with electric hot plates and irons, sewing machines, and vacuum cleaners.[64] When the costliness of these implements was remembered, the party suggested that women forgo the "luxury of personal presents such as jewelry and dresses" in favor of these labor-saving devices. Otherwise, women were advised to purchase and use these machines collectively. Rationalization of the household was the keynote, and the popular weeklies such as *Der Kuckuck* and *Die Unzufriedene* provided a steady stream of labor- and money-saving tips for the simplification of housework.[65] One of the most influential pamphleteers of the period turned her ingenuity to simplifying the elaborate Sunday lunch – the bane of working-class women. According to her formula soup was to be abandoned in favor of cold canapés (with sardines, capers, or olives!); preparation of the main dish and baked dessert were to take place on the previous afternoon; and the accumulated mound of dishes, if neither husband nor children were inclined to wash them, should be left for Monday. Thus, the harassed housewife was "liberated" on Sunday afternoon.

On occasion, the subject of the sexual division of labor in the household was raised but never really explored.[66] Instead, the socialist reformers offered the by now familiar nostrums: equal pay, the shortened work day, extension of the social support system (nurseries, kindergartens, youth centers) and collective facilities, and the use of trained paid houseworkers. The apparent object of these measures was to reduce the triple burden of working women and to make it possible for them to "participate in the working-class movement and to remain intellectually sharp by reading 'sensible' periodicals and books."[67] But reformers set other goals for the appropriate use of the free time to be won for women. Repeatedly, the literature applauded the opportunity thus created for women to devote themselves emotionally to husband and children.[68]

Time gained by women through the rationalization of housework was not to be at their own disposal. The socialist reformers had already allocated it: husbands ground down by conditions at work were to be weaned from the *Gasthaus* and tied to the home with tenderness and understanding. Marriage itself was to be altered by these opportunities for freedom. Helene Bauer saw that old institution being transformed into "an erotic-comradely relationship of equals," as women gained status through their work.[69] Her excessive optimism about the liberating power of work for women led to a sharp critique. Bauer's notion, it was argued, might apply to a few bourgeois women, but for proletarian women work remained a burden rather than a sign of progress in status. However, the visions of the "new woman" were formulated and no matter how many new creative attributes became associated with the image, the emphasis in the end was always on woman's role as mother. The sculptures of women selected for public places such as municipal housing by the city fathers invariably depicted the static, ample, and nurturing mother rather than the dynamic, *garçon*-figured new woman. Repeatedly motherhood was invoked as woman's "most noble" calling. The whole subject was subsumed under the rubric "population politics," denoting a eugenic approach to the creation of a healthy and supportable new generation (see below).

SDAP publications laid great stress on the healthy female body as the means to a so-called natural beauty. Central to good personal hygiene was the daily bath and rub down including those parts below the navel.[70] The use of cosmetics was discouraged, save for homeopathic remedies for less than glowing facial skin. After 1930, with the onset of the economic crisis and increased competition for jobs, periodicals made concessions to the use of commercial cosmetics to enhance the appearance of female job seekers. In addition to personal hygiene, fresh air and, especially, physical exercise were obligatory for the new woman. Working women of childbearing age were encouraged to participate in the SDAP sports program or at the very least to do ten minutes of calisthenics on their own before going to work.

What was the everyday life of Viennese working-class women really like? To what extent were they in a position to be transformed into the new woman, which the SDAP proffered both as ideal and attainable goal? It seems reasonable to look for answers to these questions among workers in industry, where the larger context, contact with trade union and party, and accessibility to new ideas were most likely to lead to the conflict and gradual blending of traditional values and changing circumstances.[71]

As we follow the industrial working woman through her normal day and extrapolate her experience for the week, month, and year, it becomes apparent that the socialist reformers' rendition of the triple burden treated it far too lightly and schematically. When working hours, travel time, and household obligations were totaled, most women had a work-day of sixteen to eighteen hours. Almost half of the women and three-quarters of those married did all the housework; those receiving assistance relied overwhelmingly on mothers and mothers-in-law.[72] Conditions in the homes of these female workers were not more promising for the rationalization of housework. For managing their households 18 percent had gas, electricity, and running water; but an equal number had none of these (though more than a third had both electricity and water). Almost half of the women workers, and even a quarter of those married, did not have a home of their own but lived with parents (36.6 percent) or as sub-tenants. Bedrooms were shared with two or more persons by more than half and with three or more persons by more than a third of the women. Even those who were fortunate enough to live in the new municipal housing (10.8 percent) generally shared their bedrooms with husbands and children because of the limited space (38 to 48 square meters) in these apartments. Latter-day oral histories have added interesting details to this picture of crowding. It was common for young married couples to wait five to six years for an apartment of their own and to live with parents and younger siblings in cheek-by-jowl conditions. It was not uncommon for children to share their parents' bed or the bed of the same-sexed parent.

The triple burden of many working women included child care, which further occupied their time and drained their energy. Some mothers complained about available kindergartens because all accepted children only at age four, many only opened their doors at 8 a.m. (one hour after the adult workday had begun), some served no lunchtime meal, and most had long and frequent holiday periods or closed abruptly because of childhood diseases. In many cases the small fees charged by kindergartens and after-school centers were beyond the means of the family. Was the triple bur-den lightened on weekends? Three-quarters of the sample and four-fifths of the married women devoted Saturday afternoon (the morning was a workday) to housework. Only Sunday afternoon was available as a time for rest and/or recreation to a majority of women; one-third of those married and two-thirds of those single had Sunday morning free.

Why, then, did women work in factories? Leichter concludes that it was out of pure economic necessity.[73] Would they have continued to work if that were not so, if their husbands or fathers had been able to support them? Eighty-five percent answered no.[74] The imperatives for such a choice are not difficult to understand. A retreat from work into the household was the only way open for women workers to reduce the triple burden. Neither the city fathers nor the socialist reformers had been able to create sufficient and appropriate social services to reduce their labor in the domestic sphere nor had they seriously broached the traditional sexual division of labor there, which would have made a greater difference than all the labor saving devices and rationalization schemes. And, yet, there are indications that women derived certain psychological benefits from work outside the home in the form of female solidarity.[75]

If we look at the bare facts offered in Leichter's study, we need hardly wonder that working women were light years removed from that attractive image of the "new woman" projected in the socialist literature. How could a working woman transform her body into the figure of a *garçon* when her diet consisted largely of bread, starchy grains, and fat, coffee was her mainstay morning, noon, and night, and sugar was the cheapest source of calories?[76] What time or energy was there in the working woman's day for sports, meetings, cinema, concerts, theaters, or even reading?[77] Given the stress of meeting her daily responsibilities, what opportunity was there for her to be "fear less, open, and relaxed," to become "a comrade to her husband and friend to her children?"

At this point one may ask whom these socialist messages might have reached and served. In Vienna, certainly, the principal audiences consisted of SDAP functionaries and cadres, of whom there were more than 20,000 by 1931, and functionaries in the trade unions and Chamber of Labor.[78] Beyond them, workers in safe and well-paid employment in the public and municipal sectors, who had already reached a lower middle-class living standard, could be reached.[79] But the rank-and-file female worker in industry and especially the home workers and domestics were by and large beyond the wavelength.

Surely the socialist reformers were well-meaning, especially in the light of their many initiatives in bettering the lives of Austrian workers. Why, then, were their transformational plans for women so unrealistic, so blind to the actual life styles and deprivations of working women? In the cultural laboratory of Vienna a fundamental and perhaps unbridgeable distance between leaders and masses came to light. The average worker and the higher functionary inhabited two different worlds between which there was little contact. Female leaders in parliament all belonged to an older generation, whose age in 1930 ranged from fifty-one to sixty-seven. But even younger female leaders, who had professions outside politics and were more perceptive about social realities in general, such as Käthe Leichter or Marianne Pollak, were distant middle-class analysts of the working-class world. It was all well and good for Therese Schlesinger, Anna Boschek, Adelheid Popp, Gabriele Proft, and even Marianne Pollak and Käthe Leichter to exhort working-class women to rationalize housework. These leaders knew next to nothing about a burden they were able to turn over to hired help.[80] The same applies to the other nostrums they offered to their readers. Most spoke in imperatives – "society should," "the municipality is obligated" – and often neglected what actually might have been done in their self-congratulatory formulations. The socialist reformers' attempts to superimpose the "new woman" over working-class reality may have appealed to an elite of functionaries and privileged workers, but they could not find resonance among ordinary proletarian women.

Socialist Population Politics – Sex, Maternity, and Birth Control

What place was accorded to sexuality in the transformation of working-class life?[81] From the beginning of the Viennese experiment, sexuality received considerable attention from the socialist reformers. But with very few exceptions they were primarily concerned with the social effect of sexuality on the party, on the worker family, and particularly on the next generation, which was expected as *neue Menschen* to make socialist culture a reality. As one typical programmatic statement put it: "Sexual relations meet a physiological and psychological need, whose satisfaction has social consequences. For that reason sexual activity is not simply a private matter."[82] Sexuality was viewed as having a social utility, especially in uplifting the moral standards of worker families. The end product was to be the orderly family; sexuality as a means of attaining it would have to be shaped and constrained to accomplish that end. Sexuality played a similar socially practical role in the extensive discussions of "population politics," from which the need for rational and controlled reproduction leading to a healthy new generation emerged.

But sexuality was not only viewed as a means to social ends. Much of the socialists' concern with the subject centered on its possible negative powers, which threatened to distract workers from the programs, organizations, and activities being created by the SDAP and to lead them into private spheres that were at best neutral in relation to collective culture. Seen in that light, sexuality was to be sublimated to make the workers' "marriage" to the party possible. The socialist reformers showed little concern for sex as a source of pleasure and as a normal and important part of everyday life. In its "raw" form sex was an embarrassment and treated obliquely. Most frequently party publications dealt with it as a problem of social control in which women and youth were the primary subjects.

Socialist periodical and pamphlet literature was obsessed with the dangers of prostitution to which it claimed working-class females were exposed. In part these fears were only a continuation of a major preoccupation of middle-class reformers of the 1880s and 1890s.[83] They also reflected the popular and totally unreliable tracts on the dangers and evils of prostitution and pervasiveness of venereal disease circulating in the 1920s. But even the increase of prostitution during wartime and the immediate postwar period, a further source of socialist anxiety, seems to have been exaggerated. In 1920 there were eight thousand arrests for prostitution in Vienna, and 40 percent of those arrested were from the middle class.[84] A later survey of venerologists, gynecologists, and alienists pointed to the marked decline of prostitution in postwar Vienna.[85] Attempts to replace the construct of decadence and to situate sexual waywardness within the context of social neglect in general were rare and reached only a select audience of specialists. For popular consumption the socialists provided cautionary and moralizing articles and tracts.

Socialist party sermonizing against sexual decadence began early. An article of November 1919, in the bi-weekly for female SDAP members, took the reader rapidly through the general evils of capitalism to the dangers of female promiscuity leading, ultimately, to prostitution.[86] The two, although sequential, the anonymous author insisted, were different. Promiscuous women engaged in sexual intercourse for its own sake because they desired men. Prostitutes sold themselves for money. But "mothers" did neither, because they desired only one specific man and engaged in intercourse only for the purpose of procreation. Far more influential were the marriage pamphlets of Johann Ferch, a popular socialist writer of romantic fiction and founder of the Union against Forced Motherhood. One of his frequently reprinted pamphlets is a treasure trove of male, middle-class attitudes on marriage and sexuality, ending with the advice that women be on their guard against sexual desire, which generally stems from men.[87]

Such patronizing warnings are reminiscent of nineteenth-century moralizing in all of the countries in this study. A greater irony lies in the fact that these socialist sermons – restricting the conjugal act to procreation by married women and denouncing premarital sex as the act of fallen angels – might have come directly from the pages of the pastoral letters of Austrian bishops in 1919 and virtually every year thereafter.[88]

The above examples are typical of the verbal sublimation served up in the party literature. One further illustration is necessary to demonstrate the predominant eugenic strain in virtually all discussions of the sexual question. A physician writing in *Die Unzufriedene*, the SDAP's popular weekly aimed at unaffiliated women, praised the virtues of marriage and building a home but strongly urged women not to succumb to the prevalent notion of love without marriage.[89] Sexual relations before the age of twenty were particularly dangerous, the doctor insisted, because the as yet immature female sexual organs would be permanently damaged and future offspring might be harmed. Moreover, no woman should enter the state of matrimony without obtaining a certificate of health from her prospective spouse, considering that the well-being of the next generation was at stake. In a later attack on sexual abstinence literature, Wilhelm Reich singled out the harmfulness of designating an arbitrary age – twenty or even twenty-four – as medically appropriate for the onset of sexual intercourse. In his experience as a sex counselor, he maintained, those who had not made the transition from masturbation to intercourse by the age of twenty experienced difficulties in doing so later.[90]

The subject of sexual promiscuity was also aired in the more scientific setting of an international congress of the World League for Sexual Reform held in Vienna in 1931. There, Tandler, who was a socialist member of the Municipal Council and head of its Public Welfare Office, presented the official SDAP view.[91] Sexual problems arising from sexual pathology, he asserted, were one of the principal sources of moral decay and social disintegration. The chief cause of this misery, he insisted, was the overcrowding of habitations; therefore, the basis of sexual reform must be a public program to create new housing for the working class. In the ensuing discussion, dominated by Viennese socialist physicians, Tandler was criticized for linking sexuality essentially with procreation, for failing to recognize it as a special condition of human existence, and for avoiding the reality that promiscuity in the working class had its origins in the repression of women by men. A further interpellation challenged the right of society to punish the sexual transgressions of youth so long as no one assumed responsibility for sex education.

The most pointed attack on Tandler's traditionalist position came from Wilhelm Reich. In the average Viennese worker domicile, he claimed, four persons share a single room, and as a consequence the sexual act is performed fully clothed, in fear of disturbance, or with an indifference to others present. This condition, he added, leads not to promiscuity but to the general impoverishment of sexuality in the working class. Youth, who cohabit in the woods during fair weather, are driven into dark doorways in other seasons. Therefore, it was the sexual repression (created and maintained by capitalism) of the workers and not their license which was the true problem to be confronted.

Although Tandler and Reich (and other critics) agreed that decent housing would have a positive effect on the sexual life of workers, the two sides disagreed fundamentally about the essence of worker sexuality. For Tandler it was reproduction in the stable surroundings of municipal housing and under the influence of the party's institutions, which would guard against moral decay and assure the creation of respectable worker families. Reich argued for a sexual expressiveness, even for youth and those unmarried, that in the eyes of the party leadership bordered on anarchic permissiveness and rationalized the very license the party hoped to stamp out. SDAP leaders opted for Tandler's more orderly position, and the pages of party publications, particularly those meant for mass circulation, generally remained closed to opposing points of view.

The most personally and socially dangerous aspect of sexuality was not promiscuity (an arbitrary designation at best) but its consequences in illegitimate children, unwanted births, and illegally terminated pregnancies. Abortion, according to paragraph 144 of the penal code, was punishable by substantial prison terms.[92] It was also, in the absence of sex education in the schools and readily available and inexpensive contraceptives (both of which were fought vigorously by the Catholic Church), a prevalent form of birth control in the working class. How widespread the practice actually was is difficult to say. One medical source estimates an abortion rate of 20 to 40 percent of all pregnancies.[93] Considering that abortion was illegal and therefore excluded from official statistics, the upward reaches of that range seem appropriate for the working class. At any rate, the incidence of abortion was high enough to make it a major issue of controversy in the social and political arena.

Throughout the period the SDAP occupied a series of ambiguous positions on the abortion question. In 1920 a National Conference of SDAP Women demanded the revision of paragraph 144 to allow for abortion in the first trimester of pregnancy. At the end of the year Adelheid Popp presented that proposal for reform to parliament, where the Christian Social Party prevented it from being formally considered.[94] In internal party discussions during the following years, the trimester model was maintained but arguments in its support were largely eugenic. The demand by the gynecologist Karl Kautsky, Jr. that each medical intervention be duly reported to the police to underline the seriousness of the act undertaken raised doubts about the conviction of the reformers. Socialist reservations about the trimester plan or, more specifically, about allowing women a major say in determining the need for abortion, became clear at a conference of SDAP physicians on abortion and population politics held in May 1924. The conference adopted the position of Tandler, popularly called "the medical Pope of social democracy," that under no circumstances could abortion be performed on demand because society had to keep control of sexual reproduction and could not become dependent on the needs of individuals. In his influential writings Tandler had insisted that life is created at the moment of conception and that society and not the mother has juridical control over the embryo. Tandler proposed three criteria to determine the justification for abortion: medical, eugenic, and social. The first two were to be determined by a panel of physicians. As concerns the social criteria, a panel consisting of a judge, a physician, a woman, a lawyer representing the embryo, and a representative of society were to determine each case on its merits.

The SDAP program of 1926, which outlined the party's position on a variety of social and cultural questions, also included a special section on birth control. Although the party refused to adopt Tandler's complicated and restrictive plan, the determination of the need for abortion was implicitly left in the hands of experts. The program recommended the carrying out of abortion by public hospitals if the birth might affect the health of the mother, produce an abnormal child, or endanger the mother's economic existence or that of her children. In the years that followed, the SDAP never went beyond this position.

The abortion platform at the Linz party congress of 1926 had been managed by the male leaders without apparent opposition.[95] But at the National Women's Conference preceding the congress there had been a broader spectrum of views, mainly because more radically feminist delegates from Styria, led by the prominent socialist politician Martha Tausk, challenged the conservative positions of the party doyennes.[96] The radical Styrians rejected the right of men to place limitations on the need or right to abortions and argued for women's right to control their own bodies. This challenge to the official SDAP position was easily voted down by female leaders, whose views on abortion were of a piece. They ranged from Therese Schlesinger, who favored Tandler's plan of determining social criteria through panels, to Adelheid Popp and Gabriele Proft, who cautioned against going too far beyond the present mentality of working-class women, to Emmy Freundlich, who insisted that childbearing was a female duty and proposed that men should have a say on prospective abortions.[97] The common ground among leading female socialists appears to have been the fear of bearing the eugenically unfit, who would become a burden to society.[98] On the subject of eugenics the socialists had unexpected bedfellows among racists, anti-Semites, and National Socialists, who demanded that paragraph 144 be used to weed out the unfit and to promote the motherhood of healthy women.[99]

Female party leaders continued to argue for reform of the law in public and in print but usually did so by invoking the importance of motherhood in allowing pregnancies to be terminated for social reasons.[100] It is difficult to explain why the position of prominent female socialists on the abortion question, though more differentiated than that of male leaders, should have failed to go much beyond the official party view. Schlesinger offers some insights into the difficulties experienced by female socialists within the inner precincts of the SDAP, in Parliament, and in the Municipal Council. In order to function in a party of men, she suggests, women had to accept the view that female oppression was a condition of capitalism, had to be on the defensive against charges of putting gender issues before the "important" questions of the party, and ultimately had to internalize what was expected of them.[101] Younger socialist women leaders, as well as the old guard, also found a certain amount of distrust for being bourgeois (in lifestyle) and intellectual from rank-and-file women.

The SDAP's equivocation on paragraph 144 can in part be explained by its principled stand on birth control. It called for the creation of public birth control clinics and the dispensing of contraceptives through the public health service.[102] These demands had been made repeatedly in the past, especially by socialist women, who regarded these measures as essential in reducing the need for abortion and in making the separation of pleasure from procreation in intercourse.[103] But neither the SDAP nor the municipality developed a strong and comprehensive plan to turn such programmatic exhortations into reality. This is not to say that scattered attempts were not made by or with the blessing of the above institutions, but they lacked the single-minded commitment with which programs in housing, welfare, and health were undertaken. The municipality did create thirty-six mothers' consultation clinics throughout Vienna, but their emphasis was on the problems of childbirth, female prenatal and postpartum health, and infant care.[104]

The problem of inadequate information about birth control and the inaccessibility of contraceptives remained largely unsolved. A few consultation clinics were created for married couples and the Association for Birth Control did sponsor lectures on sexuality as did women's groups of the party's cultural associations. But such efforts touched a very small proportion of the working class. Discussions about and advertisements for contraception did creep into party publications. This was particularly true of *Die Unzufriedene*, which took up women's issues most seriously. But for every article touching on sexual questions there were scores dealing with proletarian motherhood in the party literature. The latter was equated with a healthy sex life in which erotic pleasure appeared to play no role. Instead, the negative consequences of sexuality in unwanted births and abortions ran as a danger signal through the popular party publications.[105]

The important beginning made by Wilhelm Reich in opening six sexual consultation clinics for workers and employees in 1929 received no support from the party or municipality. The clinics were staffed by pschoanalysts and midwives and were open two hours a day for consultation by youth as well as married and unmarried clients.[106] Reich's extremely sober pamphlets on sexuality, written in a style understandable by the average

reader and dealing with coitus and contraception in a clear and supportive manner, were not published by the party publishing house.[107] Nor did
the party make printed material on birth control or sexual practices available to the working-class public. Neither Max Hodan's popular *Bub und
Mädel* for proletarian youth, nor the middle-class sex manual *Die voll-
komene Ehe* by Th. H. Van de Velde, nor the numerous more popular
versions of the same available in Germany were published by the SDAP
or otherwise made available at prices affordable by workers.[108] Various
marginal petitioners for party or municipal action were too dispersed to
make the public health service carry out the frequently demanded and
promised free dispensing of pessaries and other contraceptives.

In looking back on the SDAP's efforts regarding abortion reform and
birth control, one cannot escape the impression that the party gave lip
service to the second in order to avoid having to confront the first. Both
of these issues were of great importance to workers, especially to women.
The party failed to provide assistance in this aspect of private life not
because it shunned intervention there but because it feared the emotionally charged atmosphere surrounding sexuality as a public issue.

The SDAP does deserve credit for having made the issues of birth control and abortion part of its official program, unlike the socialist parties of
Belgium, Britain, and Spain which considered birth control a private matter and not a party issue. At the same time it raises the question of why
the SDAP was so cautious in its proposals. The leaders explained their
moderate approach as a means of disarming the political opposition in
parliament. The Christian Socials had no program of their own save the
absolute rejection of any modification of paragraph 144 and the support
of steady population growth. They used this simple negative weapon to
ward off all socialist attempts from 1920 to 1932 to restructure the abortion law.[109] In the face of such determined and successful opposition in
parliament, was moderation the best course and was Parliament the only
or primary arena for waging a campaign for reform? By keeping the struggle confined within strict legislative bounds, the SDAP prevented any
expression of public sentiment, any mobilization of action from below by
diverse groups in society among whom abortion was practiced in constant
fear. In Germany, in 1931, a massive mobilization of the public attempted
to abolish the restrictive antiabortion laws.[110] Nothing comparable took
place in Austria.

This failure to encourage initiatives from below points to one of the
cardinal weaknesses of the SDAP. The highly bureaucratized and paternalist party saw no need for rank and file initiatives other than symbolic
mass celebrations which it organized and controlled. The fear of losing
control appears to have been uppermost in the minds of the leaders;
mass mobilization threatened the legality to which they were committed

above all else. The socialist workers' culture, which the party was attempting to implant in Vienna, also served to enhance the passivity of the rank and file. After all, what need was there for popular expression on abortion (or on other issues) when the party claimed to be taking care of all of the workers' needs and problems through its network of social and cultural organizations?

Such criticism must not overlook the fact that the SDAP had genuine reasons for fearing the opposition of the Christian Socials on the abortion and birth control issues. In no European country did the Catholic Church advance more conservative views or play a more direct political role.[111] Every attempt by the socialists to reduce the public influence of the Church, such as the abolition of compulsory religious instruction in the schools, resulted in a bitter struggle in Parliament with the Christian Socials and in the streets with a host of Catholic action groups.[112] Since the Church equated morality with Christianity, of which it was the sole guardian and only spokesman, it fought most vigorously any attempts to tamper with what it defined loosely as moral conduct. It equated abortion with murder and threatened transgressors with excommunication, denounced the artificial restriction of the number of children in families as blasphemy, opposed co-education and sex education in the schools as invitations to lust, and blamed all of these "signs of modern degeneracy" on socialist immorality.[113]

Intimate Life of Women Workers

What clues are there to the sex life of adult Viennese workers? In view of the early sexual maturation and onset of adult responsibilities, it is not surprising that sexual intercourse and cohabitation before marriage (often for many years) seems to have been widely practiced.[114] From the point of view of socialist reformers, this behavior was exemplary of the "disorderly living" among workers they aimed to correct. In working-class neighborhoods it was accepted as part of the courtship pattern leading to marriage. A number of oral history subjects reported that their parents gave their tacit consent to their sexual relationship by allowing the couple to live on the premises. The choice of marriage partners was largely in the hands of the young people. Among the desirable characteristics looked for in their prospective mate, women often mentioned safe employment and fidelity. It was customary for courting couples to get married when the woman became pregnant. The ceremony itself and the wedding night seldom attained the importance given to them by the middle class.

The best source of indirect information about sexuality can be found in studies of the birth rate in the working class. In the generation of women born after 1900, the majority had only one child and virtually none more than two. This feat was accomplished without the assistance of the municipality or socialist reformers by the couples and especially by the women themselves. It stemmed from the recognition by workers that their aspirations to, or maintainance of, a higher standard of living depended on a smaller family size. Moreover, Viennese proletarian women, most of whom were employed for wages, apparently recognized that the only possible reduction in the triple burden of work, housework, and child care could be achieved through reducing the number of children.

It is in the domain of birth control, where proletarian couples needed the most assistance, that the SDAP failed them most abysmally. The methods of contraception available to workers were primitive, unreliable, impoverishing of the coital act, and dangerous. Workers who had served in the army experienced commercial sex and became acquainted with condoms. But there is little evidence that these or other rubber contraceptives were widely used, partly because of inconvenience (the absence of privacy to apply these devices) but mainly because of cost.[115] Coitus interruptus is the formal technique most frequently mentioned in memoirs and oral histories. Not only was this form of prevention unreliable, it also depended on the skill and good will of the male partner. Control and reduction of births probably depended at least as much on abortions resorted to by women regardless of the danger to their health and of falling foul of the law. It was a method totally controlled by the women themselves. In a number of court cases involving abortions by married women, the procedure had been carried out without the husband knowing that his wife was pregnant.[116]

Though abortion was practiced widely as a form of birth control, it was a threat to women's health and a breach of the law. But there are indications that the abominable paragraph 144 was fully subscribed to mainly by the Catholic clergy and diehard leaders of the Christian Social party. Both the number and notoriety of abortion trials appear to have declined sharply in the fifteen years after the war.[117] In the sixteen case files for 1921 to 1932 I found in the municipal archive, none of the women was actually punished for having attempted or carried out abortions. In all of them actual sentences were reduced by the judges (employing a provision for leniency) to one year of probation, giving child care, health, work, and family obligations as the reasons.[118] Only midwives with prior arrest or conviction records were given prison terms of two to nine months. The Viennese judges seem to have balked at punishing women who had undertaken these desperate acts. Juridical leniency toward women found guilty of abortion was also the rule in France, Belgium, and even Italy. The humane considerations of these pillars of society suggest that the SDAP missed an important opportunity to launch a broad-based campaign against paragraph 144.

Virtually every feature of the SDAP and municipal leaders' attempt to harness sexuality to a new socialist workers' culture was centered on controling and redefining the role of girls and women. In their view of females as creatures of instinct, these leaders mirrored the attitudes of middle-class reformers and moralists of previous generations. The main function assigned to women in the desired orderly worker families was to act as affective centers. As Otto Bauer put it, she was to organize the home in such a way that her husband would find it a place of peace, privacy, and comfort.[119] The role assigned to women within the SDAP was equally circumscribed and tertiary. With the exception of a small number of very visible functionaries, the typical female activist was relegated to social welfare activities closely resembling middle-class sociability but at a tangent to the real (political) life of the party.[120] To a large extent, the working-class woman's "marriage to the party" was a means of reinforcing and enhancing the role she was expected to play in the family.

What explanation is there for such a restricted role assignment – for the apprehensions expressed by male leaders about female sexuality in a constant harping on promiscuity and for their failure to deal with actual problems of women such as birth control? In part the answer may be found in the middle-class values and attitudes of the principal male socialist leaders, which at times bordered on misogyny.[121] Their narrow-mindedness regarding sexuality and birth control needs to be viewed from another perspective and a larger context. From the beginning of the Republic the SDAP engaged in the class struggle on the political *and* cultural front. After 1927, as the extra-parliamentary intentions of the political opposition became more apparent, the SDAP increasingly retreated to the cultural realm in the enclave of Vienna. Even when the signs of a final political confrontation became unavoidable, Bauer and other leaders refused to confront their enemies. The rising in February 1934 was a tragic postscript in which the workers suddenly became their own leaders in a doomed resistance.

The same paralysis of will on the cultural front may help to explain the socialists' timid position on matters like birth control and abortion. To have taken a forceful stand in the Municipal Council on these issues, or simply to have distributed contraceptives free of charge through the health service, would have led to a confrontation with the Catholic Church, which was also the power behind the political opposition. The party was not prepared to mobilize the larger public on issues that clearly had wide appeal. No doubt the leaders were correct in assuming that going beyond the "legal" ground of parliamentary and party action would bring on a civil war on the cultural front leading to a final showdown. That risk the socialists were not prepared to take.

Recapitulations and Reflections

The collapse of the Austro-Hungarian monarchy and creation of the First Austrian Republic in 1919 brought universal suffrage in its wake. Prewar socialist demands for suffrage had been concentrated on men, with women's rights relegated to some distant future. Suddenly, the vote made women visible and important in the public sphere: Catholics and Socialists both vied to incorporate them into their ranks. A growing male awareness emerged that there were women's perspectives and issues. But such male insights were grudgingly expressed as constituting the "woman question." Women were as yet unprepared to exploit the value of their citizenship status in other domains. The Socialist party at any rate did its best to subordinate female citizenship to what it held as central for all workers: membership in an exploited class. The party made every effort to integrate female citizens into its complex network of cultural organizations, many of which served women specifically.

The orderly, stable worker family, long considered by the industrial bourgeoisie as essential in building a stable workforce, became a prominent goal of the Socialist party as well. The main function assigned to women in these ideal worker families was to act as affective centers: fearless, open, and relaxed; a comrade to her husband and friend to her children. To attain this goal, women's role would have to be redefined: norms of behavior had to be made consistent with socialist goals; instruments of supervision and control had to be created. Thus, the Socialist party viewed working-class women as the natural maternal executors of the party's transformational vision. Planning was to remain the exclusive privilege of the male party leadership.

The influential members of the Association of Viennese Socialist Physicians, under the leadership of Municipal Councillor for Social Welfare and Health Dr. Julius Tandler, dedicated itself to a eugenically inspired program for the improvement of the quality of the worker family. Central to all such efforts was the working-class woman in her function as mother, whose health had to be supervised and improved, whose knowledge of nutrition and hygiene would have to be enhanced, and whose gender-determined nurturing skills would have to be supplemented by an array of instituions provided either by the municipality or the Socialist party. Social workers, law courts, physicians, and party bureaucrats – the supervising experts – were charged with assuring that women, seen as creatures of instinct within the party hierarchy, would behave in the rational ways expected of them.

A major conflict between party reformers and working-class women involved family planning. Party physicians and doyens not only balked at fighting for a real reform of the punitive anti-abortion law; they also

dragged their feet about promoting the sexual consultation centers introduced by Wilhelm Reich or making the distribution of condoms and pessaries a normal function of the public health service. As in other
countries, Austrian women took the issue of family planning into their
own hands at great cost to their personal and sexual well being, reducing
the birth rate to a replacement level by the early 1930s. Lurking behind
population politics was the subject of sexuality about which the rather
puritanical socialist leaders had views similar to bourgeois attitudes and
the male hysteria of the Catholic clergy.

The representation of women as objects in Austrian society ran the
gamut from the high art of Secessionist painting to advertising copy on
billboards and in the press to socialist projections of the female family
nurturer and Catholic sanctifications of unblemished motherhood.
Socialist reform conceptions, therefore, emanated from a matrix of male
misconceptions about the nature of women, their needs and wants. The
important studies of Käthe Leichter or publication of the Chamber of
Labor failed to alter the conventional wisdom about women pervasive
among the party leadership. Female party leaders did not differ greatly
from their male confreres in the generally negative view of women's
capacities. A small minority in a very masculine world, they were constantly on trial and ultimately forced to accept the protective coloration
of a masculine world view in order to function at all.

Unlike the French Socialist party, in which women played such a
minor role in such small numbers, women were well represented in the
SDAP at all levels. Yet, the leadership, both male and female, was very
distant from the actual lives of worker families and the life cycle of
women in particular. An army of party functionaries insulated leaders
and their initiatives from the rank and file's daily needs and larger aspirations. This led to rotten compromises to be carried out on such vital
issues as abortion or led to the party's sloganizing of demands for the
"rationalization of the household" or the constant refrain that female
workers transform themselves into "new women."

Despite the fact that women enjoyed the basic rights of citizenship, the
power relations between the genders were at best affected only slightly.
Socialist party and trade unions were happy to include women as dues-
paying members but did everything in their power to protect male control. If one stood the much touted cultural achievements of Red Vienna
on their head, one might view them as a further attempt to reduce the
power of women in the private sphere by the introduction of experts and
bureaucrats ever prepared to direct and control. Despite such socialist
paternalism, women did gain a stronger sense of self in two domains: as
breadwinners during the height of the depression and in the management of the small family leading to zero growth by the census of 1934.

The Viennese experiment was swept away by Dollfusses coup d'état: the SDAP was outlawed, free trade unions were dissolved, and the great cultural network was dismantled. Austrofascism's singular success was to hollow out and prepare the country for Hitler's annexation in 1938 and ultimately for complicity with the Third Reich. Public opinion prevailing in Austria's reemergence as an independent republic in 1955 was not receptive to a resumption of the socialists' prewar experiment. But the Austrian socialists' project had been implanted in the cultural memory of workers as aspirations, wants, and rights that were to shape the contemporary welfare state. As we have seen the route followed by Red Vienna differed markedly from paths taken in other countries of this study in arriving at the welfare goal. Austromarxism survives only in the historical literature and in the memory of elderly survivors. And the "new woman?" Looking back from today one could say that she exists but is still incomplete, and more than ever conscious that the quest for gender balance is a perpetual struggle.

Notes

1. The experiment was brought to an abrupt and brutal end in February 1934 with an abortive rising of workers against the destruction of parliamentary government by Chancellor Dollfuss. See Anson Rabinbach, *The Crisis of Austrian Socialism: From Red Vienna to Civil War 1927-1934* (New York, 1983), chs. 8-9.

2. Virtually all of the Austrian socialists' efforts to create a working-class counter-culture were concentrated in Vienna (with nearly a third of the country's population) which they controlled from 1919 to 1934, with electoral majorities of 58 to 60 percent. See Helmut Gruber, *Red Vienna: Experiment in Working-Class Culture 1919-1934* (New York, 1991).

3. Otto Bauer, *Der Weg zum Sozialismus* (Vienna, 1919), and *Die österreichische Revolution* (Vienna, 1923).

4. Max Adler, *Neue Menschen: Gedanken über sozialistische Erziehung* (Berlin, 1924).

5. Gruber, *Red Vienna*, pp. 46-65; and Helmut Weihsmann, *Das rote Wien: Sozialdemokratische Architektur und Kommunalpolitik 1919-1934* (Vienna, 1985).

6. See Joseph Ehmer, "Familie und Klasse: Zur Entstehung der Arbeiterfamilie in Wien," in *Historische Familienforschung*, eds. Michael Mitterauer and Reinhard Sieder (Frankfurt/Main, 1982).

7. See Dieter Langewiesche, *Zur Freizeit des Arbeiters: Bildungsbestrebungen und Freizeitgestaltungen österreichischer Arbeiter im Kaiserreich und in der Ersten Republik* (Stuttgart, 1979) and Joseph Weidenholzer, *Auf dem Weg zum "Neuen Menschen": Bildungs-und Kulturarbeit der österreichischen Sozialdemokratie in der Ersten Republik* (Vienna, 1981).

8. See Reinhard Krammer, *Arbeitersport in Österreich* (Vienna, 1981); and Béla Rasky, *Arbeiterfesttage: Die Fest-und Feiernkultur der sozialdemokratischen Bewegung in der Ersten Republik Österreich 1918-1934* (Vienna, 1992).

9. For discussions of the new symbolic appearance of the worker's body, see Dietmar Petzina, ed., *Fahnen, Fäuste, Körper, Symbolik und Kultur der Arbeiterbewegung* (Essen, 1986).

10. For the following, see Stefanie Braun and Carla Zaglitz, *Frauenbewegung, Frauenbildung und Frauenarbeit in Österreich* (Vienna, 1930); and, especially, Harriet Anderson, *Utopian Feminism: Women's Movements in fin-de-siècle Vienna* (New Haven, Conn., 1992). The first street demonstration in Vienna for women's suffrage organized by the socialists in March 1911 drew 20,000 female and male marchers. Sizeable demonstrations followed in 1912 and 1913.

11. Although both feminist and socialist women had fought for these rights before the war, they had never been able to overcome mutual suspicions necessary for a real alliance. Anderson, *Utopian Feminism*, pp. 88-89, 249.

12. See Elizabeth Schilder, "Frauenrechtsschutzstelle Ottakring," *Die Arbeiterzeitung,* 22 September 1930, p. 5, and 15 August 1933, p. 8; and "Was soll die Frau vom Recht wissen?," *Die Bildungsarbeit,* October-November 1933.

13. *Frauenbeilage der "Internationalen Information,"* May 1927, pp. 228-29. The SDAPs appealed to men and women who were not party members or even workers.

14. For the following, see Afred Georg Frei, *Die Arbeiterbewegung und die "Grasswurzeln" am Beispiel Wiener Wohnungspolitik 1919-1934* (Vienna, 1991), pp. 51, 212-13; Käthe Leichter, "Wer sind die weiblichen Parteimitglieder?," *Die Arbeiterzeitung,* 6 June 1932; *10 Jahre gemeinsame Organisation* (Vienna, 1930), pp. 30-35; and Peter Kuhlmann, *Am Beispiel des Austromarxismus: Sozialdemokratische Arbeiterbewegung in Österreich von Hainfeld bis zur Dollfuss-Diktatur* (Hamburg, 1979), pp. 309-18.

15. Frauenzentralkomitee, *Die Forderung der Frauen an Parlament und Verwaltung: Verhandlungen der dritten deutschösterreichischen Frauenkonferenz,* 13 and 14 November 1923 (Vienna, 1923), pp. 6-25.

16. The leading young socialist Käthe Leichter criticized these conferences for being insufficiently political and for endorsing the subordinate position of women in the party, shortcomings for which she blamed the men. See Gabriella Hauch, "Käthe Leichter, geb. Pick: Spuren eines Frauenlebens," *Archiv: Jahrbuch des Vereins für Geschichte der Arbeiterbewegung* 8 (1992): 115-16.

17. For the following, see "9 Sozialdemokratinen im Parlament," *Die Unzufriedene* 48 (29 November 1930): 3; "Die sozialdemo kratischen Gemeinderätinen von Wien," ibid.: 23-24 (11 and 18 June 1932); and Brigitta Zaar, "Frauen und Politik in Österreich, 1890-1934: Ziele und Visionen," in *Frauen in Österreich: Beiträge zu ihrer Situation im 20. Jahrhundert,* eds. David F. Good et al (Vienna, 1994).

18. SDAP Partei Vorstand, *Sitzungsprotokolle,* 1921-1933, Mappen pp. 3-6, Verein für Geschichte der Arbeiterbewegung (VGA), Vienna.

19. *Mit uns zieht die neue Zeit: Arbeiterkultur in Österreich 1918-1934* (Vienna, 1981), pp. 187 and passim.

20. Ehmer, "Familie und Klasse," p. 470, table 1. The census figures left out home workers who were employed less than full time.

21. For the following, see Käthe Leichter, "Die Entwicklung der Frauenarbeit nach dem Krieg," *Handbuch der Frauenarbeit,* pp. 40 and 42; and Edith Riegler, *Frauenleitbild und Frauenarbeit in Österreich* (Vienna, 1976), p. 132; Käthe Leichter, "Vom Frauenberuf: Das schwache Geschlecht bei der Arbeit," *Das kleine Blatt,* 19

October 1927, and *So leben die Wiener Heimarbeiter* (Vienna,1928), pp. 11, 13, 19, 25, 37, 41, 45; and Gabriele Czachay, "Die soziale Situation der Hausgehilfinnen Wiens in der Zwischenkriegszeit" (M.A. thesis, University of Vienna, 1985), pp. 143-48.

22. For the following, see Leichter, *So leben wir...1320 Industriearbeiterinnen berichten über ihr Leben* (Vienna, 1932), 114; Wilhelmine Moik, "Die Freien Gewerkschaften und die Frauen," *Handbuch der Frauenarbeit*, p. 581; Peter Stiefel, *Arbeitslosigkeit: Soziale, politische und wirtschaftliche Auswirkungen am Beispiel Österreich* (Berlin, 1979), pp. 200-202; "Frauenarbeit," *Arbeit und Wirtschaft* 7, 15 (1 August 1929): 698; and "Doppelverdiener," *Die Arbeiterin*, 7, 4/5 (April-May 1930): 5; and "Frauenarbeit," *Jahrbuch 1932 des Bundes der Freien Gewerkschaften Österreichs* (Vienna, 1933), p. 115.

23. "Frauenarbeit," *Arbeit und Wirtschaft*, p. 702.

24. At the Trade Union Congress of 1931 the number of female delegates reached 11.3 percent. But female union membership was twice as high. See Heinz Renner, "Die Frau in den Freien Gewerkschaften Österreichs 1901-1932," *ITH Tagungsbericht 13* (Vienna, 1980), 1: 322, 329.

25. Leichter, *So leben wir*, pp. 116 and 122. But 73.3 percent of her sample were trade union members.

26. It was a euphemism for the 48-hour week usually involving five full days and a Saturday of half-day work. Women's weekly hours under the law were reduced to 44.

27. From the outset, the socialist trade unions won more than 80 percent of the seats on the Chambers of Workers and Employees.

28. See Herbert Steiner, ed., *Käthe Leichter: Leben und Werk* (Vienna, 1973).

29. See Käthe Leichter, "Entstehung und Aufbau der Arbeiterkammern," *Handbuch für Frauenarbeit*, pp. 542-57 and *Bildungsarbeit* (Vienna, 1926), p. 2.

30. See Gottfried Pirhofer, "Wirtschaftspolitik," and "Politik am Körper," *Ausstellungskatalog Zwischenkriegszeit – Wiener Kommunalpolitik 1918-1938* (Vienna, 1980), pp. 21, 65-67.

31. See Karl Sablik, *Julius Tandler: Mediziner und Sozialreformer: Eine Biography* (Vienna, 1983).

32. See Felix Czeike, *Wirtschafts und Sozialpolitik der Gemeinde Wien, 1919-1934* (Vienna, 1959), pp. 159-65 and Franz Patzer, "Zeittafel sämtlicher Sitzungen des Wiener Gemeinderates von 1918 bis 1934," *Streiflichter auf die Wiener Kommunalpolitik, 1919-1934* (Vienna, 1978), pp. 61-123.

33. Julius Tandler, "Gemeinde und Gesundheitswesen," *Die Gemeinde: Halbmonatschrift für sozialdemokratische Kommunalpolitik* 8 (1920), pp. 165-69.

34. See Julius Tandler, *Wohltätigkeit oder Fürsorge?* (Vienna, 1925).

35. See Franz Karner, *Aufbau der Wohlfahrtspflege der Stadt Wien* (Vienna, 1926).

36. For the following, see *Das neue Wien: Städtewerk* I: 602-5; Hermann Hartmann, *Die Wohlfahrtspflege Wiens* (Jena, 1929), pp. 98-100; Wolfgang Speiser, *Paul Speiser und das Rote Wien* (Vienna, 1979), pp. 49-50; Felix Czeike, *Liberale, Christlichsoziale und Sozialdemokratische Kommunalpolitik (1861-1934): Dargestellt am Beispiel der Gemeinde Wien* (Vienna, 1962), pp. 99-101, 107-110; and Philipp Frankowski and Dr. Karl Gottlieb, *Die Kindergärten der Gemeinde Wien* (Vienna, 1927), pp. 9, 11, 46-48.

37. See David Crew, "German Socialism, the State and Family Policy, 1918-1933," *Continuity and Change* 1, 2 (1986).

38. See Gerda Neyer, "Sozialpolitik von, für und gegen Frauen: Am Beispiel der historischen Entwicklung der Mutterschutzgesetzgebung in Österreich," *Österreichische Zeitschrift für Politikwissenschaft* 4 (1984): 430-34.

39. See Frauenzentralkomitee, *Frauenarbeit und Bevölkerungs politik: Verhandlungen der sozialdemokratischen Frauenreichskonferenz, Oktober 29-30, 1926 in Linz* (Vienna, 1926) and Dr. Margarete Hilferding, *Geburtenregelung* (Vienna, 1926). The decline of the birthrate and quality of future generations preoccupied most national governments, racists, imperialists, as well as social reformers of every stripe. See Michael Teitelbaum and Jay Winter, *Fear of Population Decline* (Orlando, Fla., 1985). In interwar France it led to family allowances based on the number of children. See Cicely Watson, "Population Policy in France: Family Allowances and other Benefits: I," *Population Studies* 7 (1953-54): 263-86.

40. For the following, see Doris Beyer, "Sexualität – Macht – Wohlfahrt: Zeitgemässe Erinnerungen an das 'Rote Wien'," *Zeit Geschichte* 14, 11/12 (August/September 1987): 453; Julius Tandler, "Die Gefahren der Minderwertigkeit," *Das Wiener Jugendhilfswerk*, 1928, pp. 3-6, and *Ehe und Bevölkerungspolitik* (Vienna, 1924), pp. 20-22; Reinhard Sieder, "Housing Policy, Social Welfare and Family Life in 'Red Vienna,' 1919-1934" *Oral History: Journal of the Oral History Society* 13, 2 (1985): 13; *Stenographischer Bericht über die Sitzung des Gemeinderates*, 18 December 1928; and Dr. Karl Kautsky Jr., "Die Eheberatung im Dienste der Wohlfahrtspflege," *Blätter für das Wohlfahrtswesen der Stadt Wien* 24 (1925): 26-28.

41. For the following see, ibid., p. 26; Sabler, *Tandler*, pp. 278-80; and Beyer, "Sexualität Macht Wohlfahrt," pp. 454-55.

42. For the following, see Gertraud Ratzenböck, "Mutterliebe: Bemerkungen zur gesellschaftlich konstruierten Verknüpfung von Mutterliebe und Familie," in *Familie: Arbeitsplatz oder Ort des Glücks?* ed. Monika Berold et al. (Vienna, 1990), pp. 37-40; *Das neue Wien: Städtewerk* 3 (Vienna, 1928): 214; Gottfried Pirhofer and Reinhard Sieder, "Zur Konstitution der Arbeiterfamilie im Roten Wien: Familienpolitik, Kulturreform, Alltag und Ästhetik," in *Familienforschung*, eds. Michael Mitterauer and Reinhard Sieder (Vienna, 1982), p. 332; Beyer, "Sexualität – Macht – Wohlfahrt," p. 457; Sablik, *Tandler*, pp. 283-85; Pirhofer and Sieder, "Konstitution der Arbeiterfamilie," p. 332; and *Das neue Wien* 3: 215-18.

43. By 1927 almost 20,000 children were wards of Vienna. Sieder, "Housing Policy, Social Welfare," n 50.

44. See Czeike, *Wirtschafts/Sozialpolitik*, pp. 165-71.

45. By 1927 Vienna already had more than 6,000 social workers. See Sablik, *Tandler*, p.290.

46. See Beyer, "Sexualität – Macht – Wohlfahrt," p. 457; Sablik, *Tandler*, pp. 224-25.

47. Sieder, "Housing Policy, Social Welfare," p. 15, offers figures for 1925 to 1927.

48. See *Der Kaisermühlner Prolet* 5 (1932) and 6 (1933), and *Döblinger Echo* 1 (1929).

49. See *Rund um die Friedrich-Kaiser-Gasse* 1 (February 1933); and *Der rote Beobachter von Mödling* 1 (October 1932) and 2 (April 1933).

50. See Pirhofer and Sieder, "Konstitution der Arbeiterfamilie," 332-34; and Sieder, "Housing Policy, Social Welfare," 16-20.

51. See Robert J. Wegs, *Growing Up Working Class: Continuity and Change Among Viennese Youth, 1890-1938* (Philadelphia, 1989), pp. 63-64.

52. There was a close relationship between the Public Welfare Office and the municipal police, which acted as a source of information and enforcement. See Beyer, "Sexualität – Macht – Wohlfahrt," p. 459.

53. See Richard J. Evans, "Introduction: the Sociological Interpretation of German Labour History," in Wegs, *The German Working Class 1888-1933: The Politics of Everyday Life* (London, 1982), pp. 40-41.

54. See Joseph Ehmer, *Familienstruktur und Arbeitsorganisation im frühindustriellen Wien* (Vienna, 1980), pp. 208-36.

55. See Joseph Ehmer, "Vaterlandslose Gesellen und respektable Familienväter: Entwicklungsformen der Arbeiterfamilie im internationalen Vergleich, 1850-1930," in Helmut Konrad, ed., *Die deutsche und die österreichische Arbeiterbewegung zur Zeit der Zweiten Internationale* (Vienna, 1982), pp. 136-38.

56. See, particularly, Otto Bauer, *Mieterschutz, Volkskultur und Alkoholismus: Rede im Arbeiter-Abstinentenbund am 20. März 1928* (Vienna, 1929).

57. This development had been presumed by Marx and Engels and, more recently, by August Bebel, Klara Zetkin, and Lilly Braun.

58. Reinhard Sieder, "Behind the Lines: Working-Class Family Life in Wartime Vienna," in Richard Wall and Jay Winter, eds., *The Upheaval of War: Work and Welfare in Europe 1914-1918* (Cambridge, Mass., 1988), p. 134.

59. See Joseph Ehmer, "Frauenarbeit und Arbeiterfamilie in Wien: Vom Vormärz bis 1934," *Geschichte und Gesellschaft* 7, 3/4 (1981), pp. 451, 470, tables 1 and 2. A total of 41.3 percent of all women were married.

60. The subject quite naturally received extensive and repeated coverage in publications intended for women: *Die Frau, Die Un zufriedene, Die Mutter,* and *Einheit.* But it was also a major concern of *Die sozialistische Erziehung, Der Vertrauensmann, Bildungsarbeit, Das kleine Blatt, Der Kuckuck,* and *Der Kampf.* See, also, Erna Appelt, *Von Landenmädchen, Schreib-fräulein und Gouvernanten: Die weiblichen Angestellten Wiens zwischen 1900 und 1934* (Vienna, 1985), pp. 169-78.

61. For the following, See Gottfried Pirhofer, "Politik am Körper: Fürsorge und Gesundheitswesen," *Ausstellungskatalog Zwischenkriegszeit – Wiener Kommunalpolitik* (Vienna, 1980), p. 69; Marianne Pollak, "Die Unnahbarkeit der Frau," *Der Kampf* 20, 9 (September 1927), pp. 435-37; and Marianne Pollak, *Frauenleben von Gestern und Heute* (Vienna, 1928), pp. 23-24.

62. See Therese Schlesinger, *Die Frau im sozialdemokratischen Parteiprogramm* (Vienna, 1928), pp. 5-9.

63. See Reinhard Sieder, "Hausarbeit oder die andere Seite der Lohnarbeit," *15. österreichischer Historikertag, Salzburg 1981* (Salzburg, 1984), pp. 159-61 and Joseph Ehmer, "Frauenarbeit und Arbeiterfamilie," p. 459.

64. For the following, See Emmy Freundlich, "Zur Frage Einküchenhaus," *Die Frau* 34, 7 (1 July 1925): 5-6; Marianne Pollak, "Wie kommt die berufstätige Frau zu ihrem Achtstundentag?" *Arbeit und Wirtschaft* 1 (1 January 1929): 44-46; Irena Hift- Schnierer, "Die neue Frau im neuen Haushalt," *Die Mutter* 1, 12 (May 1925): 16-17; and Pollak, *Frauenleben,* pp. 37-43.

65. "Hilf dir selbst," *Der Kuckuck* 2, 4 (26 January 1930).

66. See Therese Schlesinger, "Proletarisches Spiessbürgertum," *Der Jugendliche Arbeiter* 23, 3 (March 1924): 10-11; Marianne Pollak, "Beruf und Haushalt," *Handbuch der Frauenarbeit in Österreich* (Vienna, 1930), pp. 413-19; and Otto Felix Kanitz, "Vortrag auf dem 2. Kongress für Sozialismus und Individualpsychologie," *Die sozialistische Erziehung* 7, 11 (November 1927).

67. See Robert Danneberg, *Die neue Frau* (Vienna, 1924), p. 9. The stated aim of this pamphlet was an "exchange of views" between the party and its female members. It is difficult to imagine what the mechanism for such an exchange might have been.

68. Pollak, *Frauenleben*, p. 45. For Danneberg, the model for such emotionalization was the bourgeois woman. See *Neue Frau*, p. 9.

69. For the following, see Helene Bauer, "Ehe und soziale Schichtung," *Der Kampf* 20, 7 (July 1927): 319-22; Neschy Fischer, "Ehe als soziales Problem, *Der Kampf* 20, 8 (August 1927), pp. 387-89; Pirhofer, "Politik am Körper," pp. 48 and 69; and Fedora Ausländer, "Frauenarbeit und Rationalisierung," *Handbuch der Frauenarbeit*, p. 30.

70. For the following, see Martha Eckl, "Körperkultur und 'proletarische Weiblichkeit' 1918-1934" (Diplomarbeit, Vienna University, 1986), pp. 54-55; Veronika Kaiser, "Österreichs Frauen 1918-1938: Studien zu Alltag und Rollenverständnis in politischen Frauenblättern" (Ph.D. diss., University of Vienna, 1986), 87; and Pollak, *Frauenleben*, pp. 24-25.

71. See Leichter, *So leben wir*. This study was based on one-third return of 4,000 questionnaires distributed in 1931 by shop stewards at the workplace, supplemented by interviews and written communications from the workers. The sample was drawn from all the leading industrial sectors in which women were employed.

72. For the following, see Leichter, *So leben wir*, pp. 73-74, 81- 83, 94-97, 109-110; Reinhard Sieder, "Housing Policy, Social Welfare and Family Life in 'Red Vienna' 1919-1934," *Oral History: Journal of the Oral History Society* 13, 2 (1985): 39; and Pirhofer and Sieder, "Zur Konstitution der Arbeiterfamilie," pp. 342-43.

73. 42.2 percent of the husbands or life companions of these women were unemployed; 82.3 percent of the women supported others or at least themselves. Leichter, *So leben wir*, pp. 13, 103, 107.

74. Ibid., p. 54. Leichter exaggerates the importance of the fact that 31.9 percent of the single women said they would continue working in any case. She overlooks that these women had as yet only limited household and child care responsibilities.

75. See Marie Jahoda, Paul Lazersfeld, and Hans Zeisel, *Die Arbeitslosen von Marienthal: Ein soziographischer Versuch* (Bonn, 1980 [1933]), pp. 91-92 and Ehmer, "Frauenarbeit," pp. 466-69. In the female network of factory labor information about birth control and abortion was traded freely.

76. See "Der Lebensstandard von Wiener Arbeiterfamilien im Lichte langfristiger Familienbudgetuntersuchungen," *Arbeit und Wirtschaft* 13,12 (December 1959), supplement 8, 10; and Roman Sandgruber, *Bittersüsse Genüsse: Kulturgeschichte der Genussmittel* (Vienna, 1986), pp. 81, 182.

77. Leichter reports, in *So leben wir*, pp. 108-15, that 78.7 percent spent evenings at home doing housework. Meetings were attended by a mere 4.4 percent. Entertainment outside the cinema were virtually unknown. Only the radio (aside from the press) offered a steady contact with the wider world, but only for 36.1 percent of the sample. See also Monika Bernold, "Kino(t)raum: Über dem Zusammenhang von Familie, Freizeit und Konsum," in *Familie Arbeitsplatz*.

78. Helene Maimann, ed., *Die ersten 100 Jahre: Österreichische Sozialdemokratie 1888-1988* (Vienna, 1988), p. 351.

79. Women were grossly under represented in the public sector except for social welfare where 2,884 of them were employed. Anna Grünwald, "Die Frau in der Gemeindeverwaltung der Gemeinde Wien," *Handbuch der Frauenarbeit*, p. 653.

80. For a suggestive complaint about socialist female employers who exploited their domestics, see Helene Goller, "Klassenkampf im Haushalt," *Die Frau* 37,3 (1 March 1928): 5.

81. For the problems of writing the history of sexuality in everyday life, see Dorothee
     Wierling, "Alltagsgeschichte und Geschichte der Geschlechtsbeziehungen: Über
     historische und historiographische Verhältnisse," in *Alltagsgeschichte: Zur Rekon-
     struktion historischer Erfahrungen und Lebensweisen*, ed. Alf Lüdtke (Frankfurt/
     Main, 1989).
82. "Leitsätze für sexuelle Aufklärung der Jugend," *Bildungsarbeit* 19 (1932).
83. See Anna Hauer, "Sexualität und Sexualmoral in Österreich um 1900: Theo-
     retische und literarische Texte von Frauen," in *Die Un geschriebene Geschichte:
     Historische Frauenforschung* (Vienna, 1985), pp. 143-47. For parallel expressions
     in Victorian England, see Judith Walkowitz, *Prostitution and Victorian Society:
     Women, Class, and the State* (Cambridge, Mass., 1980), chaps. 4-7; in Germany,
     see Regina Schulte, *Speerbezirke: Tugendhaftigkeit und Prostitution* (Frankfurt,
     1979), pp. 11-56.
84. See Alfred Pfoser, "Verstörte Männer und emanzipierte Frauen: Zur Sitten-und
     Literaturgeschichte der Ersten Republik," in *Aufbruch und Untergang: Österre-
     ichische Kultur zwischen 1918 und 1938*, ed. Franz Kadrnoska (Vienna, 1981),
     p. 206.
85. "Erhebung über Sexualmoral," *Studien über Autorität und Familie: Forschungs-
     bericht aus dem Institut für Sozialforschung* (Paris, 1936), pp. 279-80.
86. "Prostitution und Gesellschaftsordnung," *Die Arbeiterinnen- Zeitung* 22 (18
     November 1919): 3-4.
87. *Glückliche und unglückliche Ehe?: Ein Mahnwort an junge Ehe und Brautleute*
     (Vienna, 1922), pp. 5-9. His novels bore such titles as *Küsse die Leben werden; Die
     nicht Mütter werden dürfen* and *Am Kreuzweg der Liebe*.
88. For instance, *St. Pöltner Diözesanblatt* 1 (1919).
89. Dr. Gertrud Ceranke, "Willst du Heiraten?" *Die Unzufriedene* 6 (7 August 1926):
     7. This journal ran advertisements for contraceptive devices, gave tips on health,
     beauty, clothing, and cooking in an uncommercial fashion, offered a column on
     "Women Speak from the Heart," and a personal column for marriage seekers. By
     1933 it reached a circulation of 160,000 and was mentioned as the preferred
     weekly of female industrial workers. See Leichter, *So leben wir*, p. 116.
90. "Erfahrungen und Probleme der Sexualberatungsstellen für Arbeiter und
     Angestellte in Wien," *Der Sozialistische Arzt* 5 (1929): 99.
91. For the following, see "Wohnungsnot und Sexualreform," in Weltliga für Sexual-
     reform, *Sexualnot und Sexualreform: Verhandlungen* (Vienna, 1931), pp. 5-14, 39-
     42, 74-75, 80-83.
92. An attempted abortion was punishable by a term from six months to one year; a
     successful abortion from one to five years; and midwives and physicians impli-
     cated were subject to the same terms. A law of leniency, however, was at the dis-
     posal of the judges to reduce or cancel prison sentences. See Dr. W. Gleisback,
     "Das Verbrechen gegen das keimende Leben im geltenden und Künftigen
     Strafrechte," *Zeitschrift für Kinderschutz Familien-und Berufsführsorge* 20, 1 (Janu-
     ary 1928): 2.
93. See W. Latzko, *Wiener Medizinische Wochenschrift*, 26 (1924), p. 1387.
94. For the following, see Karin Lehner, "Reformbestrebungen der Sozialdemokratie
     zum Paragraph 144 in Österreich in der 1. Republik," *Ungeschriebene Geschichte*,
     pp. 298-303, and, *Verpönte Eingriffe: Sozialdemokratische Reformbestrebungen zu
     den Abtreibungsbestimmungen in der Zwischenkriegszeit* (Vienna, 1989), chap. 3;
     Benno Wutti, "Die Stellung der Sozialdemokratischen Partei Österreichs zur
     Frauenfrage" (Ph.D. diss. Vienna University, 1975), pp. 102-11; "Die Schwanger-
     schaftsunterbrechung: Eine Tagung der sozialdemokratischen Ärzte," *Arbeiter-

Zeitung, 144 (25 May 1924); Julius Tandler, "Ehe und Bevölkerungspolitik," *Wiener Medizinische Wochenschrift*, 74 (1924); Sablik, *Tandler*, pp. 281-82; and Therese Schlesinger, *Die Frau im sozialdemokratischen Parteiprogramm* (Vienna, 1928). The pertinent paragraphs were reprinted in the journals aimed at women.

95. Otto Bauer was chairman; the commission included most of the male notables. The sole woman was Adelheid Popp, who had made it clear at the prior women's conference that she supported the position of the socialist physicians (i.e., party loyalty). See Lehner, "Reformbestrebungen," pp. 146-47.

96. For the following, see Frauenzentralkomitee, *Frauenarbeit und Bevölkerungs-politik: Verhandlungen der sozialdemokratischen Frauenreichskonferenz, Oktober 29-30, 1926 in Linz* (Vienna, 1926), pp. 15-50 and Lehner, *Verpönte Eingriffe*, pp. 137-50.

97. Leopoldine Glöckel summed up the position of the majority that women could not have the right to control their own bodies until they had been completely enlightened.

98. See Dr. Margarete Hilferding, *Geburtenregelung* (Vienna, 1926), pp. 14-15 and Gertrud Ceranke, "Willst du Heiraten."

99. See, for instance, Herwig Hartner, *Erotic und Rasse: Eine Untersuching über gesellschftliche, sittliche und geschlechtliche Fragen* (Munich, 1925), pp. 52-53 and Robert Hofstädter, *Arbeitende Frau: Ihre wirtschaftliche Lage, Gesundheit, Ehe und Mutterschaft* (Vienna, 1924).

100. For instance Adelheid Popp, "Geburtenregelung und Menschenökonomie," Weltliga, *Sexualnot*, p. 503.

101. "Zur Psychologie der Geschlechter," *Der Kampf* 18 (June 1925): 25-27.

102. See "Geburtenregelung und Kinderschutz," *Die Unzufriedene* 35 (28 August 1926): 1.

103. For instance, Dr. Margarete Hilferding, "Probleme der Geburtenregelung," *Die Mutter*, 1 (April 1925): 6.

104. The first of these was created in 1917. After 1924, they were spread throughout Vienna by the Municipal Council in response to Tandler's campaign against syphilis. The clinics gave advice but no treatment so as not to conflict with private physicians. See Sablik, *Tandler*, p. 283. See, also, Gertraud Ratzenböck, "Mutterliebe," in *Familie: Arbeitsplatz*.

105. Eckl, "Körperkultur und proletarische Weiblichkeit," pp 91-92.

106. See Karl Fallend, "Wilhelm Reich: Dozent der Psycho-analyse, Sexualberater und Rebellischer Parteigenosse" (Ph.D. diss., Salzburg University, 1987), pp. 169-74; and Reich, "Erfahrungen und Probleme," p. 98.

107. For instance *Sexualerregung und Sexualbefriedigung* (Vienna, 1929) and *Geschlechtsreife, Enthaltsamkeit, Ehemoral* (Vienna, 1930). Both were published by the Münster Verlag and appeared in four or more printings. The former discussed the safety and use of condoms, pessaries, antispermatic pills, recommended the best brands, and quoted the approximate price.

108. See Grossmann, "New Woman and Rationalization of Sexuality," pp. 159-62. Publications on sexuality and birth control were also readily available in the Scandinavian countries, Britain, Holland, and even Italy until 1926.

109. See Andrea Schurian, "Der Agitationswert der Abtreibungsfrage in den sozialdemokratischen Medien der Ersten österreichischen Republik" (Ph.D. diss., Vienna University, 1982), pp. 252-53.

110. See the chapter by Atina Grossmann in this section.

111. See Ferdinand Klostermann et al., *Kirche in Österreich 1918-1965* (Vienna, 1965), pp. 241-71.

112. See Wolfgang Maderthaner, "Die Schule der Freiheit – Otto Glöckel und der Wiener Schulreform," *Archiv: Mittteilungsblatt des Vereins für Geschichte der Arbeiterbewegung* 24 (July-September 1984): 9-10.

113. All bishops' pastoral letters can be found in *Wiener Diözesanblatt* and/or *St. Pölten Diözesanblatt* by year of proclamation.

114. For the following, see Pirhofer and Sieder, "Konstitution der Arbeiterfamilie," pp. 346-48; Eva Viethen, "Wiener Arbeiterinnen: Leben zwischen Familie, Lohnarbeit und politischen Engagement" Ph.D. diss., University of Vienna, 1984), pp. 309 and 357; Ehmer, "Frauenarbeit," pp. 438-73; and Elizabeth Maresch, *Ehefrau im Haushalt und Beruf: Eine statistische Darstellung für Wien auf Grund der Volkszählung vom 22. März 1934* (Vienna, 1938), pp. 13 and 36.

115. See *Sexualerregung*, pp. 24-26 and Bendikt Kautsky, *Die Haushaltstatistik der Wiener Arbeiterkammer 1925-1934*, supplement of *International Review of Social History* 2 (1935): 245-46.

116. Ehmer, "Frauenarbeit," 468-69.

117. In the period from 1851-1920 seventy case files were deposited in the Vienna archives, including the notorious Mittermayer file. See Katharina Riese, *In wessen Garten wächst die Leibesfrucht?: Das Abtreibungsverbot und andere Bevormundungen Gedanken über die Widersprüche im Zeugungsgeschäft* (Vienna, 1983), pp. 49, 89-119.

118. See "Strafprozessakte zum Paragraph 144," Archiv der Stadt und Landes Wien.

119. *Mieterschutz, Volkskultur und Alkoholismus* (Vienna, 1929), pp. 8-9.

120. See Appelt, *Ladenmädchen*, pp. 124-25; Krammer, *Arbeitersport*, p. 181.

121. See Doris Beyer, "Die Strategien des Lebens: Rassenhygiene und Wohlfahrtswesen – Zur Entstehung eines sozialdemokratischen Machtdispositivs in Österreich bis 1934" (Ph.D. diss., University of Vienna, 1986), pp. 238-55.

Chapter 2

Modernization as Challenge
Perceptions and Reactions of German Social Democratic Women

Adelheid von Saldern

Introduction

A t the end of World War I and the beginning of the Weimar Republic, the German Social Democratic party (SPD) and the trade
unions (ADGB) looked at their own history with some pride. The hated
Empire had been abolished, and the party as well as the unions received
official recognition. At the time, party and union activists remembered
their history and especially the anti-socialist law of 1878, which had
outlawed their movement up to 1890. During the remainder of the
Wilhelmine period the party and the unions, although officially legalized, were confronted politically by the major bourgeois parties and the
governments. The majority of the working-class movement lived in the
certainty, or at least in the hope, that only large working-class organizations were the means of gaining control over the political system by winning a majority in the *Reichstag* election. In that event, bourgeoisie
opponents were expected to revolt against the electoral results, which,
in turn, would lead to a successful revolution by the working class. The
final victory envisaged the introduction of socialism by the will of the
majority of the people.[1]

This anticipated development – and some other visions, which must
be neglected here – "allowed" only one view of gender: women were

---

respected as potential militants, because they had had the right since 1908 to join a party and, moreover, as influential educators of the next generation of (male) activists. The interest in women did not include an interest in women's affairs. These were seen as secondary concerns which basically could be solved only in a socialist society. The majority of active socialist women shared this perspective, which meant that serious gender-related conflicts could be avoided.

In these Social Democratic visions the complex reality of the 'Weimar Republic' was not foreseen. Political decision making became much more complicated. The working-class movement split in 1917 and the (Majority) Social Democratic party (MSPD), although it retained the bulk of members, did not attract the desired number of votes. In the revolution of November/December 1918 the MSPD decided to cooperate with bourgeois parties and even with former leaders in the military and administration. Furthermore, the (M)SPD declared the Communist party (KPD) to be the main threat to society, and even refused to cooperate in future with the Independent Social Democratic party (USPD), which had a brief existence as a halfway house between socialism and communism. No matter how much effort the MSPD put into the many elections held during the Republic, its success was always limited, with the highest percentage of 28.7 percent reached in the *Reichstag* election of 1928.

The first part of this chapter focuses on party and politics. Modernization of the political system and the introduction of women's suffrage in 1919 challenged women to use the many new opportunities and to overcome the remaining traditional structures in party and politics. What the (M)SPD women thought of the party, in which areas they were active, and how the (M)SPD men considered gender issues will be discussed. The relationship of SPD women to parliament, to the bourgeois women's movement, to communist women, and to the Nazis will also be considered. In the second part three important spheres of society are analyzed: employment, home, and public culture. Modernization changed each of these spheres in a particular way, and with it came the challenge of the "role of gender" in modern times. The central question addressed below is, how did the Social Democratic party in general and SPD women in particular deal with these challenges?

I. Party and Politics

Although every female SPD member had her own biography, some collective characteristics, which can be represented by two main types, are striking. These types indirectly give insight into the worlds in which active SPD women functioned.

The dominant type was a dissident, middle-aged or relatively old woman, who was not gainfully employed – a housewife and mother whose children no longer attended school.[2] A second less numerous type was gainfully employed and unmarried (or divorced).[3] Of the one-third of the Berlin female functionaries who were gainfully employed, 40 percent were white-collar workers (social workers, municipal employees, and teachers), and one third were ordinary workers (with 12 percent in the textile industry). These two main types were again split into two subtypes: female functionaries with or without a relatively good formal education. Most of the women delegates in the *Reichstag* and Prussian *Landtag* came from working-class families and had no higher education.

Within Social Democratic Organizations

The SPD as well as the other parties had no way of knowing how women's suffrage and the constitution would alter politics. It was uncertain whether women would fight together, across party lines, for women's causes or whether they could be integrated into the various parties.

For male SPD functionaries in general a large number of members was the most important party goal. But the number of female Social Democrats remained relatively limited, comprising 15.8 percent of SPD members in 1924 and 23 percent in 1930.[4] Compared with Social Democracy in other countries (e.g., France, Spain, Belgium, Italy, Sweden, Norway and England) and compared with other parties in Germany, this percentage was, however, not low. Even so, women were strongly under represented in the leadership of the party, among delegates to congresses, and in the local branches, and they never attained the percentage of representatives that corresponded to their percentage share in the party.[5] Although there was a special Office for Women's Concerns within the party executive, headed by Marie Juchacz,[6] women were not able to gain influence within the party via this office,[7] because their issues were subordinated to the party's main concerns.

The general disadvantages of women did not mean, however, that there were no improvements. At the party congress in 1925, for instance, the SPD accepted a motion to reduce the number of female members needed for a female seat on the Party Committee. Some also claimed that in the second half of the twenties the party provided many opportunities "to educate women systematically for political life."[8] But many complaints remained, especially among rank-and-file women. Younger functionaries, who came from the USPD, strove for a basic change in gender relationships and emphasized the "special class situation of women." In the mid-twenties they described their discrimination within the party and discussed the reasons which were, among others, clearly seen as competition between men and women.[9] As a consequence of the frequent neglect of their demands, women discussed them at their own women's conferences, which took place after each party congress. On the whole women were seen as an alien element in the party, and although women themselves clearly recognized their situation, there never was one united women's front against male domination.

Marie Juchacz basically avoided controversies and attempted to stress views and interests shared by women and men. In general, her analysis and that of most other SPD women "was based on a division of society according to class rather than to sex."[10] Juchacz was typical of visible women leaders in most social democratic parties (e.g., Austria and France) in playing according to the rules laid down by SPD male leaders, which made her position as a woman difficult and distanced her from the female rank and file. Together with their male colleagues, they were concerned with general social problems of the working class and attempted to attain improvements through politics: reforms of social security during times of unemployment and illness; amelioration of the bad living conditions through a public building program; better education and training; and more recreational facilities. Gender issues generally remained in the background,[11] and thus disadvantages for women in such matters as insurance and training were not considered or were given a very low priority in discussions of official party policy.

The SPD social reform profile was supported by the creation of its own welfare organization. A common view was that the running of the Workers' Welfare Organization was the women's central task and domain, especially at the local level. Nonetheless, the top positions of its executive were occupied by men. During World War I women had involved themselves more than previously in welfare work; as the living conditions of working-class families deteriorated rapidly, many women became aware of their important role in social and community work. This concentration on social work was, however, ambiguous.

> Though the wartime emphasis on social welfare work was in itself not negative, it later became a convenient way to channel the energies of socially conscious women and to divert them from pressing their own claims for more rights and greater participation in the Social Democratic party and German society.[12]

This channeling was facilitated by the fact that many Social Democratic women themselves more or less accepted the view of a gender-determined division of labor, retaining the concept of motherhood as a social welfare profession and defining this task in a positive way. Women were to be committed to women's concerns, that is, to education and welfare activities, which, compared with the prewar period, became more extensive and diverse. Moreover, SPD women regarded their welfare work as a successful strategy for convincing male comrades that women could perform well in public affairs. No wonder that in Berlin 4,000 to 5,000 women, (i.e., about half of the female SPD membership), did voluntary work as aides in the local Workers' Welfare Organization.[13] Thus, many local branches (1,914 in 1926 and 2,600 in 1933) with 150,000 helpers in 1926 and 135,000 helpers in 1933 developed into social and cultural centers similar to the consumer union stores in workers' neighborhoods.[14] With a female membership of 60 percent, the Workers' Welfare Organization was the principal arena for SPD women's activities. Although women's welfare activities impressed the male membership, such work was not acknowledged as political activity. Thus, social welfare did not provide an entrance to other areas of politics for SPD women.[15] As an alternative they tried to become professional social workers, but their progress was slow, numbering only 600 female professionals in Germany by 1929. The competition between SPD and bourgeois women for such jobs was great, and even a Social Democratic social work school failed to improve SPD women's chances.[16]

SPD Women's Periodicals

Different views regarding the focus of women's periodicals led to serious discussions and conflicts among SPD women on how to reach women workers. To be decided was whether women's situation was to be interpreted as being defined more by class than by sex. The periodical *Gleichheit*, which in the Empire period was concerned with theoretical issues under the supervision of the left Marxist theorist Clara Zetkin, changed its editorial policy after 1919 under the management of the editors Marie Juchacz and later Clara Bohm-Schuch.[17] The new editors wanted to appeal to a wider audience through reports and information on practical questions and problems. Although the politically moderate party leaders were relieved that Zetkin's leftist theoretical approach had been dropped, they stopped financing the journal during the height of the inflation. Thereafter the publication of *Genossin. Information for Female Functionaries* replaced the former *Gleichheit*. This periodical reported on reform issues concerning women, such as health, child rearing, and the maintenance of industrial health and safety standards. It contained information on women's position within the party and in public office as well as on the international women's movement.

While the *Genossin* was a periodical especially for female party functionaries and other politically committed women and had a circulation of about 40,000, the women's magazine *Frauenwelt* (Women's World) was addressed to potential SPD voters or members. *Frauenwelt*, which was comparable to the Austrian *Unzufriedene* and cost thirty pfennigs, had its highest circulation of 100,000 in 1926 and was edited by a man until 1927.[18] It treated many of the subjects which could be found in contemporary bourgeois magazines – fashion, household tasks, health, art, sex and morals, birth control, housewives' rights within the family, short stories and reports on nontraditional women and their lives – in general with infusions of socialist morality.[19] Topics such as the strenuous daily routine of female workers at their workplaces and critical reports or literature were not included; instead household chores made up a large part of the contents. Practical advice on how to save money and about self-help evidently met with widespread approval.[20]

Frauenwelt was expected to inform and entertain. Its popularity was in part determined by readers' acceptance or rejection of the new popular culture, which obviously already had altered people's habits and taste and of the journalists' reporting of political and societal affairs.[21] The success of *Frauenwelt* also depended on its references to the actual experience of women. The politically conscious minority of leftist female Social Democrats critically pointed out that socialist ideas at best were camouflaged. Theoretically oriented SPD women longed for the return of the "good old" periodical *Gleichheit*. By contrast, the proponents of *Frauenwelt* wanted to slowly further a step-by-step improved understanding of socialism among ordinary women.[22] Although the periodical was aimed at unorganized women, it was in fact female party members (40 to 60 percent of them), who read it regularly.[23]

Frauenwelt has to be considered as a parallel phenomenon not only to the bourgeois women's magazines but also to the Social Democratic newspapers' women's supplements, which could be found in 63 out of 170 SPD daily newspapers.[24] In Hamburg, for instance, 80 to 90 percent of the social democratic households read the social democratic *Hamburger Echo* which also had a women's supplement. Such supplements "were filled with fiction, which were matters of no importance" in the eyes of female SPD leaders.[25] They mainly contained stories, poems, and reviews on books and films, with secondary articles on education, health, work, equality, social policy, domestic science, prostitution, sexuality, and abortion. Furthermore, in every issue one could enjoy humor and satire, look at fashion, read columns for children, and pick up naive tips on health and daily life.[26] The women's supplements were usually edited by men, a fact that was criticized, for example, by Clara Bohm-Schuch in 1926. That political topics were usually excluded also angered politically aware SPD women. In 1924, Juchacz complained that nothing was published on women's role in the election. Other SPD women criticized the inferior quality of these supplements.[27]

An independent women's press did not exist in Weimar Germany,[28] although it is not clear whether and in which way contents and layout of the periodicals and the supplements would then really have changed. Moreover, SPD women faced working-class women's widespread lack of interest in politically oriented articles and their preference for entertaining stories and daily-life subjects.[29]

Women's Causes Viewed from a Male Socialist Perspective

Evidently, Social Democratic men, fearing competition, were reluctant to allow women to have influential positions.[30] The SPD men ignored women's disadvantages in the party and in the public sphere. They basically accepted a woman's commitment to public and party affairs only if her activity did not interfere with her family life, retaining the traditional view that housework and child care were female tasks.[31] Many SPD men looked at women's causes from the perspective of polarized genders and regarded women as the "other pole," but of "equal value" to men (equal, but different – *gleichwertig, nicht gleichartig*). In their view the value of women consisted in balancing the nonsensual, rational male world with the human and emotional female world.[32] In the eyes of party officials women's problems were seen as "peculiarities" that could only be handled by the women themselves. Therefore, on the whole, the party did not discuss women's concerns, except at the Magdeburg party congress in 1929. There, a female delegate demanded that the SPD should stop relying on the socialist analysis of women's oppression as spelled out by Friedrich Engels or August Bebel. But the congress ignored this demand and continued to support only the economic side of women's right to work and clung to "the old analysis that women's plight in the family was a result not of biological or sexual dependency but purely an outcome of their subordinate economic status."[33] Another tactical procedure by SPD men to assure their domination was to demand equality for women, in the Civil Code for instance, or by acknowledging the right of women to earn money, without, however, taking appropriate action and without giving up the idea of women as "special beings."[34] This two-faced view on women's causes was widespread.

A further strategy was to voice the party's disappointment in women's voting behavior. Since the revolution of 1918/19 the male SPD leadership credited itself with the introduction of women's right to vote and expected appreciation and gratitude. In fact election results put SPD women on the defensive, especially since male party members charged that too many women voted for the conservatives, especially for the Catholic Center party, and thereby disadvantaged the SPD.[35] The male Social Democrats used this argument to justify the marginalization of women's causes.[36] They placed the responsibility for the allegedly relative low number of female votes for socialist candidates on the poorly run women's organization within the party. According to research done in and about Hamburg, voting behavior of female workers must be differentiated. In traditional SPD milieus the number of women who voted for the SPD was almost as high as those of the male voters or even higher, whereas in bourgeois neighborhoods fewer women than men voted for the SPD. Consequently, social milieu can be said to have influenced the voting behavior of women.[37]

The modes of neglecting women's concerns were becoming more contradictory, more subtle, and more refined than they had been in the prewar period. A reason for this change was that the SPD had more power and responsibility for making policy decisions after World War I and, as a consequence, could no longer safely place the blame for neglecting women's causes on the political system as a whole.

SPD Women's Work within the Parliaments and Local Authorities

In 1919, women's suffrage and the Weimar Constitution expanded the public sphere and rights of women. From then on women could enter legislative bodies at all levels.

In the National Assembly of 1919 to 1920 eighteen (10.9 percent) of the (M)SPD's 165 delegates were women. The percentage of SPD women deputies in the *Reichstag* (1920 to 1933) oscillated between 9 and 13 percent.[38] Although the female delegates had joined the party many years before, they were not trained in public speaking, in contrast to those women who had left the SPD and joined the USPD or the KPD, especially such leaders as Luise Zietz (USPD), Clara Zetkin (KPD), and Rosa Luxemburg (KPD). Many of the female Social Democratic politicians regarded their political work as the necessary means for preventing society from becoming impersonal and dehumanized. With that mission in mind Juchacz promised that the new women who entered the *Reichstag* politics would not lose their femininity.[39] A lot of projects were considered achievable especially with the help of women.[40] Social Democratic women viewed such a male-defined role as a two-edged sword; on the one hand was the achievement of recognition, on the other the continuation of the attitude that particular attributes and capacities were associated with gender.

In general, the female SPD *Reichstag* deputies did not speak on the "major" topics of foreign policy and the economy.[41] They contributed, however, to the discussions on what was seen as women's issues: social policy (above all protection of mothers), housing, public health, social programs for youth, demographic policy, and women's civil rights.[42] Evidently, SPD women made many proposals on activities and projects for which they felt responsible. During the first years after the revolution, when the welfare state was an important issue, SPD women had a little more influence in the *Reichstag* than later on. Their greatest success concerned maternity leave. In 1927 a law entitled mothers to six weeks' leave before and six weeks leave after childbirth with partial compensation. By 1929 the compensation for mothers was raised from 50 to 75 percent of their normal pay. Other social improvements for women were, however, rejected because, it was argued, they would be too costly or for other reasons. Thus, the success of SPD women's work in the *Reichstag* was ultimately very limited.[43]

With their role in the national parliament marginalized, SPD women assumed that local parliaments offered an opportunity for women to enter politics more easily. Women elected to local government resembled socialist women in Britain, Austria, Sweden, and Denmark in their commitment and dedication, especially on the commissions for health, school, youth, and social work. But local politics was no more hospitable than the national arena, as the small number of female municipal councillors made clear.[44] In the municipal councils only 4 percent of the SPD councillors were women and in rural regions female representatives were even rarer.[45] In Berlin, where female deputies at least ranged between 11 and 15 percent, women wanted to be considered on equal terms with men when candidates were chosen, but they hoped in vain.[46] Juchacz interpreted this as a consequence of the strong competition between men and women, but she also presumed that, in many cases, women did not project themselves effectively. She deplored the fact that the list of women candidates was badly prepared, because the names of the nominees were not accompanied by well-founded arguments concerning their abilities and programs. This could have given the impression, she concluded, that women were nominated only because they were women.

Clearly, women were not able to obtain influence within the parliaments. In Germany, as in other countries (e.g., Norway and even in Austria where women were well represented at the national and municipal level) women were welcomed but marginalized. They could only have gained more parliamentary influence if they had had more influence within the party and its policymaking centers. Women, however, apparently always remained an alien element in such inner circles and were excluded "from all of the behind-the-scenes politics so intrinsic to parliamentary politics and so essential for attaining positions of power and influence within the system."[47]

Relationship to the Bourgeois Women's Movement, the Communists, and Nazis

The key question of whether class or gender interests should determine the political attitude of SPD women was answered in "one voice" in favor of class. This decision stemmed from the tradition of the prewar SPD when socialist women and the bourgeois women's movement were locked into their separate spheres. During World War I the distance between socialist and bourgeois women activists diminished, when they cooperated in welfare work for the first time. But that cooperation was due to the special challenges of the war and did not mean that the split between bourgeois and proletarian women had been resolved. During the Weimar Republic politically active women argued and acted more in the spirit of their parties on the whole than according to the general interests of women. Moreover, in the view of SPD women the bourgeois women's movement was more directed against (bourgeois) men than allegedly was the case between socialist women and men. In the eyes of SPD women the common class situation of the proletariat regardless of gender was their common basis of cooperation. This point of view demonstrates that the SPD women themselves relativized their inner party struggles when they compared their own situation with that of bourgeois women.

One of the main problems for SPD women when dealing with the bourgeois women's movement was the influence of conservative associations, such as the association of housewives on the Federation of German Women's Associations (BdF).[48] On political and cultural issues the bourgeois women's movement came close to the views of these conservatives and lost their relatively radical prewar profile.[49] Thus, the Weimar configuration of the bourgeois women's movement was not well suited to improving the position of women within and outside the family. In fact, there were many fundamental differences between bourgeois and socialist women, especially on the issues of abortion and the status of unmarried mothers.[50]

Only a small group of radical bourgeois feminists, such as Anita Augspurg, Lida Gustava Heyman, and Helene Stöcker, all three of whom had supported pacifism and feminist causes and had been expelled from the BdF during the World War I, were political partners of the SPD women. Helene Stöcker's League for the Protection of Motherhood and Sexual Reform in particular in many aspects shared the views of Social Democratic women.[51] The main problem of that supposedly radical bourgeois organization was that it had no chance of influencing the BdF or bourgeois parties.

Conflicts with the bourgeois women's movement were complemented by those with the Communist women's movement. Social Democratic and Communist women held many views in common, but in the *Reichstag* they maintained their distance and remained true to their own party line.[52] This was also the case at the Federation of Trade Unions (ADGB) general meetings, which were always an occasion for communist and socialist women and men to meet.[53]

At the Trade Union Congress of 1922, for example, a series of demands aimed at improving women's situation was presented by four women and supported by forty-six other delegates, mostly men, who presumably were members or supporters of the Communist party. Theodor Leipart (SPD), head of the ADGB, rejected the proposals, arguing that they were based on insubstantial arguments, and he was supported by the majority of delegates. Later, the leader of female unionists, Gertrud Hanna, interpreted the proposals as stemming from a specific political camp.[54] In her view important demands were intertwined with impossible ones and, as a consequence, she likewise distanced herself from all of them.[55] Whether this was Hanna's own opinion or whether she was put under pressure by the male union leadership (SPD), remains unknown, but, in any case, this was an example of SPD female unionists integrating themselves into the party line and by doing so helping to confirm the split between the two working-class parties. Since many of the active Communist and Social Democratic women were housewives, common experiences at the workplace were lacking. This and the separate welfare organizations minimalized the connections and increased the split between Social Democratic and Communist women. There were, however, some important exceptions. In proletarian working-class districts women from the two parties lived as neighbors sharing local lifestyles and problems. Thus, it is not an accident that at the neighborhood level leftist Social Democratic women occasionally cooperated with their communist sisters in subsistence-oriented street protests, in commissions investigating food profiteers, and in the campaign against the antiabortion law (Paragraph 218 of the criminal code) in 1931.

While a part of the SPD female rank and file cooperated with their communist sisters in some situations at least on the local level or pursued similar interests, every sixth former SPD-voter voted for the NSDAP between September 1930 and July 1932.[56] Most of these, it appears, were not anchored in the social democratic milieu and presumably were accustomed to changing party loyalties.[57] Former Social Democratic women were also among the new NSDAP voters; there is, however, no evidence that more female than male SPD voters shifted their support to the Nazis. Although not all SPD male and female voters remained loyal to their party, the SPD nevertheless lost far fewer male and female voters to the NSDAP than did the bourgeois parties.[58] According to the few gender statistics in the *Reichstag* election of 1930, approximately half of NSDAP voters were male, half female.[59]

In contrast to the some of the former SPD voters, female SPD activists clearly politicized their work again in the early 1930s, fearing the National Socialists in general and their anti-feminism in particular.[60] Not until the end of the Weimar Republic did "the female segment" of the body politic expand its protests by organizing women's street demonstrations, in a bid for broader and deeper political influence in a male-dominated society.[61] Many of these protests demanded the abolition of the antiabortion law. The International Women's Day, whose yearly celebration was already a tradition among socialist and pacifist women, was opened in 1931 with the slogan "Against war and Nazi terror, for socialism and peace." Even in the generally apolitical *Frauenwelt* there were articles intended to enlighten the readers about Nazi goals.

After 1933 the political life of all Social Democrats, male and female, ceased to exist. But the gender asymmetry was maintained nonetheless among the persecuted; women made up "only" 15 percent of the politically persecuted.[62] Several of the most active female and male Social Democrats were sent to prison or concentration camp. During the Third Reich, Toni Pfülf, Minna Bollmann, and Gertrud Hanna, all well-known female Social Democrats, committed suicide. Others, such as Marie Kunert and Anna Siemsen, Mathilde Wurm, Toni Sender, and Marie Juchacz emigrated or lived abroad for a long period.[63] A number of Social Democratic women who stayed in Germany participated in circles which attempted to maintain an informal cultural resistance against the Nazis. Finally, many former female and male SPD voters survived by coming to terms in varying degrees with the Third Reich.

In conclusion, SPD women were mainly concerned with social policy and reform, and for this purpose they developed a well-functioning welfare organization. Thus SPD women were active, above all, in arenas that corresponded to their traditional role. Their participation in the Workers' Welfare Organization was not seen by male colleagues as a stepping stone into politics, but rather as a publicly praised sidetrack, based on the traditional view of gender roles. Women did not have enough elbowroom to develop an independent female policy. Moreover, it is striking that women were more active at the beginning of the Republic than in the following years.[64] This leads to the conclusion that in the period immediately following the end of the war, much energy was expended by the SPD in encouraging women's expectations of gender equality in the party – hopes that were soon dashed.

In the twenties, SPD women, ready for compromises, attempted to strike a balance between a class-oriented solidarity, which appeared important to them, and a female-orientated policy. The established female leaders of the SPD were prepared to compromise with their male colleagues to such an extent that they were in danger of losing the support of younger women both in and out of party. The fact that only a few women in the party and in politics – and these mainly middle-aged or older – held responsible positions led to a generation gap. But there was no overt struggle between representatives of the various generations and no collective generational grass-roots protest. Although the SPD female leaders were relatively open-minded on female sexuality and procreative function, they could not count on the support of women in bourgeois parties. Official cooperation with communist women was not possible for ideological reasons, except for some local initiatives between rank-and-file members.

During the Weimar Republic, SPD women were not concerned only with party and politics in the narrow sense. They became involved in numerous activities in the social and cultural arena, which for them always meant politics in the sense of shaping society.

II. Employment, Home, and the Public Culture

In 1919, women received not only the right to vote, but were also given comprehensive equal rights in Article 109 of the Weimar Constitution, which stated "that men and women have basically the same rights and duties." The question is whether and, if so, how this legal guarantee was put into practice.

The following analysis is organized around three important "nonpolitical" spheres: first, the arena of employment, combined with a critical glimpse at the ADGB; second, the private domain of motherhood, family and home; and third, the public cultural terrain, which was about to transform society and which already challenged the gender balance at the time. These three central arenas of society, which stood under the sign of modernization, will be examined closely. The focus here is on how female SPD and trade union members understood the changes and reacted to them.

Employment and Unions

As World War I opened the labor market to women, the number of them who were gainfully employed increased sharply.[65] Women entered formerly exclusively male industries. Many of them became self-confident as a result of their new work experience, although they did not receive equal wages. After the war, competition in the job market took a new turn. Male workers, wishing to return to prewar "normality," successfully ousted women from the job market in the period immediately after the war.[66] The ADGB congress formally proclaimed equal rights for men and women. This resolution, however, was not accepted by the newly established Workers' Councils, which made their own decisions within the individual companies in which they were a presence.

As a consequence of the demobilization phase and up to 1923 to 1924, the job market posed many problems for women, since the rate of unemployment among them was greater than among men. Thereafter, the chances for women of finding a job improved. By 1925, the census showed that 35 percent of all women (i.e., 11.5 million) were employed. This was an increase of 5 percent over 1907,[67] which approached the high percentage of women workers in Austria and France. In addition, many women worked in agriculture and in small family-owned businesses and handicrafts as "helping family members" as they had done before. But there were also some spectacular shifts in the labor force that provoked discussions of female work. The manner in which women "took over" certain types of jobs, especially in the strongly expanding sector of distribution, presented a danger to SPD women leaders.[68] Juchacz believed that young female shop assistants, who often came from proletarian families, were influenced by their professional surroundings against Social Democracy. Even though they come from the poorest milieus they imagine that they are something "better," while they themselves can hardly earn enough money to buy the cheap clothes with which they adorn themselves."[69]

Women in this service sector were in general more visible to the public than those in other jobs and therefore became symbols of the frequently criticized excessively modernized Weimar society. Moreover, some of these new jobs were connected with the projection of sexual attractiveness – especially those of sales personnel in shops and secretaries in offices. Although sexualization of jobs was more often represented in advertising, films, pictures, and in fantasy than in reality, cultural conservatives in all bourgeois parties regarded these trends, often called "new woman," as a deterioration of mores. This type of young, gainfully employed woman, who was regarded as economically independent through her employment, raised the fear that her kind might neglect their "real destiny" of motherhood and family.[70]

Beyond the invasion of low-wage jobs by young women in the expanding sector of distribution, rationalization, and mechanization in industry changed the configuration of the workforce. This change was symbolic of the ambiguous impact of rationalization and Fordism.[71] Instead of employing highly paid, skilled male workers, in many cases not only male semi-skilled workers but also unskilled female workers were hired, especially in engineering and in the textile and food processing industries.[72] Usually females received only 60 to 70 percent of the men's wages, even if they did the same work.[73]

New opportunities for women on the job market also included higher positions. Some women could be found in ministries, schools, and hospitals; they could become lawyers, doctors, teachers, and university professors. But, in fact, in this sector of the job market an "invisible hand" usually worked against women, especially with respect to top positions. Article 129 of the Weimar Constitution gave women equal opportunities in the civil service, but there were some exceptions: women could not become civil assessors or magistrates. In 1921 the *Reichsrat* rejected the decision of the *Reichstag* to admit women to such posts with the officially stated reason that women were too emotional.[74] Continuity and change on the job market for women were tightly interwoven and made the position of the unions difficult.

After full formal legitimation of the unions was achieved in the revolution of 1918/1919, more female workers joined the ADGB than in the prewar period. In 1920, 22 percent of union members were women, while the percentage in the years between 1905 and 1914 had been between 5 and 8 percent. After 1920, however, the percentage fell again, presumably because the unions did not fulfill women's expectations. Finally, in 1931 14 percent of ADGB members were females and around 20 percent of the female workforce belonged to the unions.[75] Not only did women's interest in union membership decline, but also their interest in participation in strikes. In the Hamburg area, where many strikes took place in the early Weimar years, between 1919 and 1923 the proportion of women among strikers fell from 35 to 5 percent.[76] The decrease in female members and strikers could mean that female workers assessed the time immediately after the war and the beginning of the Weimar period as a phase with relatively open structures and new opportunities for them.

Within the unions women were greatly under represented among the national delegates to annual ADGB congresses. In 1928, for instance, there were only two females among the 282 delegates. Moreover, no woman was ever elected to the executive committee of the ADGB during the Weimar Republic. Its congress in 1919 was the only one to have women's work on the agenda. Women usually were treated as though they formed a small minority within society and, therefore, little interest was shown for their concerns. The manner in which the unions dealt with female apprentices was typical of their attitude toward women; they only occasionally mentioned the necessity of improving professional training for women; they did not protest the small number of female apprentices or act to increase it.[77] Some active female unionists made great efforts themselves to further the education of young women. They established a special young women's group within the unions' youth organization, which organized separate meetings, whose success was reflected in the increase of female union members. This gender-specific program was important because the youth organization within the unions was dominated by young males, whose prejudices against females was expressed in the youth periodical with observations such as: "In general women do not seem to be very amenable to rational education."[78] This judgment was, of course, rejected by others, who pointed out the low level of self-confidence most of the young women had, but it nonetheless revealed what many unionists really thought about women and girls.

Compared to the female SPD functionaries, women trade unionists were reluctant to voice their opinions and avoided challenging their male colleagues. The union leader Gertrud Hanna always sought compromises with the male unionists,[79] as can be seen in the pages of the *Gewerk-schaftliche Frauenzeitung* (1916 to 1933) for which she was responsible. This periodical focused on female employment, hygiene in industry, laws protecting mothers and young people, the job market, welfare, insurance, education, and nutrition. While information was presented in a rather dry fashion, the series served as entertainment. Avoiding critical descriptions of contemporary society, many articles dealt with distant periods such as ancient history ("The status of women in ancient Greece") or offered stories about far-away countries ("From Turkish life"). In 1922 the periodical had a circulation of 460,000, but this number dropped to 70,000 by 1928,[80] a sign that it did not cater to the interests of trade union women and that it was probably too defensive in character.

New problems facing the unions arose from the challenges of Fordism, especially from the introduction of gendered job descriptions in industry. Although the German unions were attracted to Fordism because in the future they expected fewer strikes and higher wages for workers in general, they were eager to minimalize the disadvantages of Fordism for male workers. The unions evidently regarded the above-mentioned "feminization" of jobs through rationalization, especially so far as male branches were concerned, as problematical for the maintenance of traditional hierarchical gender lines. Therefore, it is not by accident that progress in protecting female workers was used to (re)gender the work place. The unions officially fought for equal pay for equal work, but not for equal pay for equivalent work. Moreover, protective labor laws for women were seen as a compensation for lower pay.[81]

Both the unions and male workers considered turning a lathe a purely male domain without explaining why such work was more harmful to women than to men. Union functionaries' hidden interests in a hierarchy of wages corresponded to those of the employers; it concerned not only skilled, semi-skilled, and unskilled workers but also male and female wages. Because unskilled female workers were the cheapest employees, they were often preferred to men. By the same male consensus women were regarded as being physically less able to do strenuous work, as being absent from their jobs more often than men, and as less interested in their work. It was a self-serving belief that women considered their jobs only temporary and were not as well-trained for work as men and, ultimately, were less interested in a permanent job.

The unions' restricted view of gender with respect to work and family determined their attitude about work-related gender issues. The ideal of a family, combined with the idea of the natural (biological) hierarchy of the sexes, explains the unions' lack of interest in the issue of equal pay. Many male unionists viewed marriage, motherhood, and home as the natural destiny of women. This attitude stemmed from the culturally conventional view of many unionists that the employment of women was merely temporary before marriage, or at most, before motherhood. That such narrow views prevailed in the unions can be explained by the fact that these were presumably dominated by more highly skilled and better paid workers, who subscribed to the cliché model of a family with a full-time mother.[82] Men were considered potential heads of families who were supposed to earn enough to support these without a gainfully employed wife.

Among the Social Democratic women unionists there were differing opinions on the relationship of women to work. Many considered financial necessity as the reason why mothers would seek employment, whereas a minority included other motives such as the desire for equality and economic independence.[83] The *Gewerkschaftliche Frauen-Zeitung*, for example, did not reject the idea behind traditional gender roles that considered the primary task of husbands to be support of the family and the primary task of women was to maintain it.[84]

By contrast, Juchacz argued that work had become a life-defining task for many women, especially insofar as they performed skilled work.[85] The unionist Wally Barnick went a step further and wanted young women to regard their jobs as their "life's goal."[86] The very active SPD leftist politician Mathilde Wurm argued for class interests in criticizing the consequences of the existing gender-divided labor force. The weaker segment, consisting of branches that could be considered the domain of women, she argued, were more exploited by employers.[87] She endorsed the traditional position of female socialist theory that only such a woman "can be won to socialism who through her occupation becomes a full member of society."[88]

The issue of women's right to work gained much publicity during the Great Depression when unemployment was high during the last years of the Weimar Republic. The unions officially argued like the SPD: "of course" women had the right to work, but in cases of double-income one of the two was expected to make room on the job market, if one paycheck was enough to support the family.[89] This demand did not address women only, as the unions claimed, but in fact it applied only to women.[90] Unions officially rejected the campaign against "double-earners" that automatically regarded wives as "expendable." They stressed the importance of economic independence for women, while simultaneously arguing in favor of higher social recognition of housework and motherhood.[91] Most of the gainfully employed women, however, worked because of economic necessity.[92] There were relatively few married women in positions which men also desired or were able to fill.

Notwithstanding the economic facts, "double-earners" became a symbol that challenged the traditional view of the gender order in modern society. A survey revealed the proportion between pro and con positions: the right of married women to be gainfully employed was only accepted by one-third of blue- and white-collar workers.[93] There are no statistics on how many female breadwinners there were at that time, but this is less significant than the psychological implications: the paternalist hierarchy of the family was threatened, and male identities based on skill and their role as breadwinners were put into question. Tensions and conflicts within families were widespread, as well as depression and apathy among the unemployed husbands and fathers.[94] Like other issues, that of the "double-earner" did not lead to a clear confrontation between unionist men and women, because there were married female unionists who only accepted work if there was a serious economic necessity.[95] In their opinion, it was the married women's duty to make room for the many unemployed male workers.[96]

In conclusion, the attitude of many male unionists towards women was shaped by a traditional view of the family and the role of wives and mothers as well as by the gender-related division of the job market. Despite the term "comrades," which was used to suggest equality in the relationship between the sexes, male-dominated unions did not address the gendered division of labor, the disadvantages of female apprenticeship, and the gendered hierarchy with respect to wages and jobs. They played a double game with respect to the "double-earners" issue. Masculinity continued to mean providing for the family.

At Home – Motherhood and Family

In the Weimar Republic motherhood and family were issues that produced a great variety of conflicting discourses. Demographers argued that every family had to have at least three children in order to reproduce the population. In fact, many people were concerned about the declining birthrate in Germany from the turn of the century and especially during World War I. Neo-Malthusians feared proletarianization and therefore promoted birth control, while eugenicists, concerned with the quality of population, were eager to establish birth control in order to stop "degeneration." Among the latter there were some Social Democrats, such as the professor of medicine Alfred Grotjahn, who promoted so-called practical eugenics.[97] His and other social democratic sexual and marriage counseling services enlightened and educated workers, especially women, about contraception and abortion. Condoms and diaphragms, the latter to be fitted by a physician, were the recommended contraceptives, alongside coitus interruptus, which was widely practiced, because condoms were too expensive for many workers and they were not accustomed to using them. Waiting rooms in counseling offices were important communication centers.[98] Social Democrats – both men and women – were much more committed to birth control than their bourgeois counterparts.[99]

These, especially the cultural conservatives, fearing that the perceived "decline of morals" would damage the ideals of motherhood and family and threaten the basis of state and society, rejected liberal reforms. Such a fear was also shared by the BdF, which declined to put pressure on the public for more liberal reforms. Only the already mentioned radical feminists gathered around Anita Augspurg and the League for the Protection of Motherhood and Sexual Reform were committed to change. They argued that society had to liberalize its view of motherhood and family to preserve the family as an institution. "New ethics" and "new sexual morals" were the key words, which interested these feminists as well as some of the younger Social Democrats and Communists.

The status of illegitimate children, closely related to motherhood and family, was a very controversial topic. The war seemed to have changed public attitudes toward illegitimate children, because the declining birth rate and the high losses sustained by the troops made every child valuable. In the Weimar Republic illegitimate children had – according to the Constitution – the right by law to the same physical, psychological, and social conditions necessary for their development as legitimate children. In 1926 the illegitimacy rate was 12.6 percent.[100] The SPD, however, was not able to carry out reforms such as equal rights to inheritance and the right to use the father's name.[101] As inheritance was not a significant issue for workers' families, the reform strivings of the SPD female functionaries had an intraclass perspective. With respect to illegitimate children, one of the most bitter differences between bourgeois and Social Democratic women was the automatic firing of unmarried female civil servants who became pregnant. The Social Democratic women, who defended the unmarried mothers, were however defeated in the parliament, not least by their bourgeois sisters.

The most divisive issue was abortion. The abortion rate was incredibly high, estimates rising to one million in 1928.[102] While the majority of the politicians, as well as the BdF, supported the existing strict law forbidding abortion, a minority, especially the already mentioned bourgeois League for the Protection of Motherhood and Sexual Reform and the Communists wanted a liberalization of the law. Although in 1920 the USPD and a minority of the (M)SPD in the parliament supported a bill proposing that termination of pregnancy be allowed without restriction within the first trimester of pregnancy, the SPD later officially rejected this radical reform. By 1927 the only SPD progress in this matter was a law providing that women sentenced for abortion were no longer sent to the peniten-

tiary but only to prison. But many leftist Social Democratic women supported the reform of Paragraph 218, especially toward the end of the
Weimar Republic, and even supported the communist-sponsored campaign against the antiabortion law.

One of the interesting aspects of the family policy of the twenties was
the maintenance of the conservative regulations of the Civil Code.
Although it had been introduced in 1900, it regulated family law according to premodern principles. Astonishingly, during the Weimar Republic
the legal status of women did not improve. Legal inequality in family law
and property rights continued to exist. Clause 1354 of this code gave the
husband the "ultimate right to decide on all matters concerning their
joint marital life."[103] Although Article 119 of the Constitution declared
that "marriage is based on the equal rights of both sexes," the Civil Code
was not amended to translate this statement into reality. Thus, women
were caught in the contradiction between a progressive Constitution and
a traditional Civil Code. The Social Democrats were not strong enough
to alter the situation. Although property – of which workers had little or
none – played an unimportant role in the working class, the SPD sought
to reform inheritance laws. More relevant for workers was the reform of
divorce,[104] which was also supported by the SPD, in particular by SPD
female deputies. But despite all attempts, the legal grounds for divorce
remained inflexible, and no progress was made to include incompatibility. The latter was finally introduced in the Third Reich as part of Nazi
racial population policy.

Finally, we need to ask what Weimar social policy did for mothers and
families. In the Constitution mothers were granted the right to the care
and protection of the state.[105] One of the reforms carried out in the 1920s
concerned maternity leave. The already mentioned 1927 law improved
the protection of pregnant women and mothers at work, except for rural
and domestic workers. SPD women objected to these exceptions but
were not able to attain a majority in their favor. Nevertheless, the German program for mother protection ranked high in comparison with
most European countries.[106]

More reforms took place in welfare, which lost its bad name of poor
relief from the previous century. Social work was professionalized and
bureaucratized, and the pool of subsidized persons was enlarged by
including veterans and their families or the widows of veterans. More
objective classifications of welfare recipients and their inspection by professional social workers were also considered a sign of modernization.
Workers who were on long-term support were visited by social workers of
the local community, who had to report on how the family lived, how
"orderly" it was, and whether it should receive special support by the
local welfare office.[107] The youth law of 1922 demanded that local

authorities establish facilities for young people and erect a special local office for youth matters. This law also regulated the cases and procedures of compulsory education. Considerable progress was made in establishing consultation clinics for infant care, whose number increased from 1,000 in 1920 to 5,000 in 1928.[108]

The combination of progress in both welfare and surveillance, inspired by modern principles of reform pedagogy and social engineering, was somehow characteristic for the Weimar period and reveals the ambiguity of modernity. Since the extension of welfare programs was always limited by economic and financial problems of the state and by local authorities, the SPD, viewed as the party of social reform, was threatened by loss of support from worker families. Although some reforms respecting mother-hood and the much discussed and debated family were introduced, the anticipated breakthrough in modernizing motherhood and the family did not occur. Social policy was not as much centered around families as one might have expected from the many discussions about them. This obser-vation must be relativized, because of the large subsidized housing pro-gram that was intended to transform family life.

Home and Housework

With the concept of "new living" that was to be realized through a subsi-dized housing program, the roles of women and men were redefined in a modern context. "New living" meant better and healthier homes as well as attempts to rationalize housework through the introduction of electric appliances and the use of professional domestics. Within such improved environments a more intensive and conscious care for children by their mothers was anticipated. An SPD parliamentary delegate, Nanny Kur-fürst, hoped that in the new housing estates "which are far away from the center of the city, families will associate closely and have a much better opportunity of using their influence than in the centers of towns with their cinemas and other superficial temptations."[109] The new housing estates were supposed to function as the means to improve family life. Various "upgraded domestic tasks" were expected to enrich the private sphere and the everyday life of housewives. The new subsidized mass housing program, which created models of such a modernized private sphere between 1924 and 1931, clearly adhered to the traditional view of gender tasks. Some 7.7 million people, most of them white-collar work-ers, officials, and the upper strata of workers, participated in this experi-ment, which served as a model for the present and future.[110]

The rationalization of the working-class household in the old neigh-borhoods was also attempted, for instance, by the social democratic Hanover *Volkswille*,[111] but this project met with little success mainly because of the very poor quality of existing workers' habitation. Most working-class families lived in badly ventilated, sunless, two-room apartments consisting of a livingroom-kitchen and a small bedroom, often with a view only of dark alleys. The greatest problem was overcrowding, as workers' families were on the average larger than those of white-collar workers and civil servants.[112] Six percent of the workers' families had lodgers to supplement their income.[113] The newly constructed apartments, although subsidized by the state, were too expensive for them.

Male trade union leaders regarded the upgrading of the "private sphere" through better housing as an important task for many reasons, including giving the men better opportunities for relaxation and pleasure at home after the strenuous Taylorized work day.[114] New working conditions demanded new homes. The unions themselves started an extensive housing program organized and in part financed by their own companies.[115] Except for some cooperatives, the concept supported by the SPD and the unions was that of private, self-contained family apartments and did not extend to forms of communal living on housing estates such as community rooms or collective kitchens and participation of the tenants in the housing administration.[116] On the whole the Soviet model of community kitchens was rejected in Germany as a negative and unwanted development of "improved" living.[117]

In general, "new living" was considered women's domain: "The woman clearly has a great interest in creating living conditions fit for human beings, because the home is her workplace, the area of her activity as mother of a family."[118] At the National Women's Conference of 1927 Social Democratic women discussed the new public housing. They favored greater standardization of the new housing estates: rationalized floor plans, modern kitchens, and sensible mass-produced furniture. In their view, millions of women were very conservative about their households. The task of women as visualized by their leaders involved "revolutionizing their own egos" – a search for a style of living "in which the socialist human being can develop and the socialist community will be created." Young people, it was felt, would be able to practice the new style of living most fully.[119] All the same, the trade union housing estate periodical *Einfa* tried to motivate existing tenants, especially SPD women, to modernize their lives. "As I am a human being of today my rooms are not allowed to exude the old scent of past times."[120] People who were uninterested in the new rationality at home were deeply resented, and the still widespread practice of setting aside a *gute Stube* (front room) in cramped worker apartments was regarded with contempt.[121] From the many recorded complaints it can be concluded that a great number of housewives did not heed the reformers' advice.

Social Democratic and trade union women as well as bourgeois reformers collaborated on modernization and rationalization of the home and housework. Politically committed reformers of all parties may have hoped that the rationalization of housework would give housewives more time "to commit themselves to public life."[122] Aside from adult and continuing education, some political work seemed better suited to home and family than the gainful employment of the mother.

Some active Social Democratic women complained about the attitude of their male "comrades" at home. At the National Women's Conference in 1925 a delegate received lively applause, when she pointed out that even within the working-class movement men did not act "in the interest of socialism, because they do not yet know how to introduce socialism to family life as the first step."[123] The trade unionist Wally Barnick charged that many men in the movement were petty bourgeois at home, devoted to coziness and their own comforts. In her view women were not accepted as comrades in the true meaning of the word.[124] At the 1929 Magdeburg SPD congress, Anna Geyer proposed a radical alteration of the private sphere: housework was to be shared by husbands and wives; motherhood was to be regarded as a concern of society; and child rearing should become a task of the community. In the Hanover *Volkswille* Martha Henkel demanded communal kitchens, central laundries, and more nursery schools for women who were gainfully employed.[125] She argued that building cooperatives were to provide these novel facilities with the financial support of local authorities.[126] Even the SPD unionist Käte Lindenberg, who held the pessimistic view that the gainful employment of women would lead "to a dissolution of the family and to a change in the marital state, rejected the solution that women should return to their homes, because this would foster the gender division of labor."[127]

New housing provided new opportunities to rethink the meaning of home, family, housework, and gender. While the majority of Social Democratic women more or less accepted the gender divisions at home, some active Social Democratic and trade union women severely criticized this attitude and wanted far-reaching reforms in the so-called private sphere.

Public Culture

Cultural debates were strongly marked by popular culture which was gender-based from its beginnings. To some extent it was personified and symbolized by the "new woman," who was considered to have conquered the public sphere. The new woman image had various facets. Her basic characteristics included economic independence, antipaternalism, self-confidence, activities in the public sphere, and, to a degree, openness to modern views and lifestyles (fashion and bobbed hair, for example). These characteristics were welcomed in the bourgeois women's movement as well as among active SPD women. Other more controversial facets of the new woman included association with the youth cult, Americanization, superficiality, trashy mass culture, provocative fashion, and cosmetics as well as "crazy Negro-song-dancing" and premature sexuality.

The latter aspects of the new woman met with disapproval within the bourgeois women's movement as well as among SPD women. The Social Democratic *Reichstag* deputy Anna Stegmann considered "premature sexual maturity [of women] an evil."[128] However, whether premature sexuality was widespread is difficult to say. Prewar sources indicate that young female workers usually had a boyfriend (*Schatz*) at sixteen, and in the 1920s young male workers had their first sexual experiences at seventeen or eighteen.[129] The age of sexual initiation presumably depended not least on working-class strata: the lower the stratum the more sexual freedom at an early age. No solid evidence shows that in the lower strata of the working class there was a great shift in premature sexual behavior in the 1920s compared with the Empire. Sexual intercourse often was the natural consequence of working together in factories. This type of sexual activity was to a certain extent matter-of-course, although it was kept secret. Women were almost as sexually liberated as men, and sex between unmarried partners was not a reason for social ostracism among workers. In the event of pregnancy, however, marriage was usual; otherwise the expectant mother faced great material hardships and reproaches and moral condemnation from parents, friends, and relatives.[130] Then, abortion was the only possible solution.

The biggest change regarding sexuality from the *Kaiserreich* to Weimar was that sexuality became a subject of public debate among young people and gained increased visibility in the mass media and the public domain. This debate also included sexual education, abortion, and sexual satisfaction (within marriage). Based on this extensive public awareness and concern with sexuality, some have presumed that an impact on actual sexual practices resulted.[131] Indeed, sexuality and reproduction were increasingly separated from each other. Despite the increase of extramarital sex, the number of illegitimate children decreased in big cities during the 1920s, more than legitimate birth rates.[132] Although there were public discussions about sex education in the 1920s, a continuity existed between the Empire and Weimar Republic in the working class regarding sex education in the family. The subject was taboo, even in Social Democratic families.[133]

Many Social Democrats accepted the bourgeois reformers' lamentation about the "crisis of the family," which basically meant the crisis of women, of young people, and of sexual mores – all allegedly created primarily by exposure to popular culture. Juchacz remarked critically that married women and mothers went to the movies "even when their income is relatively low and when they often have to live in want."[134] While Juchacz transformed her critical view on popular culture into an active reform strategy of her own, Marie Kunert (first USPD, then SPD) remained fixated on a wholesale rejection of popular culture. She exposed a new destructive agent: the influence of the *nouveau riche* with ostentatious taste. "Art is increasingly being dominated by his perverse instincts. Kitsch governs." The mental health of the people was being "damaged by trashy art."[135]

Modernity was only accepted selectively. Social Democrats and unionists worked together with the symbol of modernity, the Bauhaus, but Marie Kunert argued that not everything modern was acceptable. The selection of what was good and bad in modern culture also included Americanization, which she accepted as a rationalization of the economy and society, but she considered its cultural aspects ambiguous. The widespread cultural struggle against the Americanization of German culture was supported even by some Social Democratic women, such as Meta Corssen. The issue was the correct modernization of women, which in her view was not the case in the United States.[136] She believed that American women were too superficial and far removed from the goal of a "free and honest comradeship between the sexes."[137] In particular she criticized the so-called girl-culture, which she saw as an integral part of mass culture superficiality – cheap amusement, revues, and so on. There was general agreement that workers (among them many women), in addition to lower level white-collar employees, formed the majority of film audiences.[138] Notwithstanding the many agreements between bourgeois critics and Social Democrats with respect to popular culture and the new woman there was one point of difference: Social Democrats did not accept the bourgeois view that moral and cultural crises only or primarily affected the working class.[139] Social Democrats made it clear that bad living conditions influenced morals more than did mass culture.[140]

How the public cultural sphere was to be defined was also an issue when SPD women attempted to recruit new members. The official male view within the party considered political work with nonorganized women a female task and, in general, SPD women accepted this view. At first they tried to attract nonorganized women through meetings concerned with general political issues. When such meetings turned out to be failures, others with a broader program were organized, including "worthwhile" films or more specialized political female concerns. Finally, the strategy was adopted of combining topics such as women's movements and women's concerns with discussions of more individual matters. Whether such women's evenings were the right way to address the unorganized or whether they were too apolitical remained a burning issue among Social Democratic women.[141] As a matter of fact, both types of meeting only had a limited success, especially among housewives, because they generally centered their daily lives around household, family, and the social networks in their own neighborhoods. They were, therefore, neither interested in politics nor did they need the women's evenings to create social ties.[142]

Reformers had difficulty convincing not only "mere" housewives to join the party, but also gainfully employed women, even those in industry.[143] Among the many reasons why this was so, three should be stressed. First, gainfully employed women in particular lacked time and energy – if they had a double or triple burden or if there were other "bad" circumstances.[144] Second, based on their socialization, women thought it enough that their husbands were committed to the party or the unions. Politics was generally considered a male matter and that was often also their husband's opinion.[145] Third, an increasing number of women, especially young female workers, were evidently more attracted to kitsch movies and "worthless" magazines than to the SPD or ADGB including their cultural organizations. One SPD women lamented, "many of these girls see their pleasure in enjoying the good things in life together with a well-heeled boyfriend in a highly depraved manner on Sundays after a six-day week."[146] The expression "enjoying the good things," although used in a critical manner, reveals the aspiration for a good life in which all the misery and poverty of workers' daily existence are forgotten. A Social Democratic woman reported on her attempts to convince girls to accept the working-class leisure-time programs with their, as she put it, cheerful and joyful culture: "We hike and play and sing, do sports and dance in order to harden our bodies to make them strong for the struggle of life. We also act in plays and speak in choruses ...."[147] We know nothing about the reception of these strivings, but seen as a whole, the organization of young people had limited success. In 1926, the number of the members under 21 of the socialist youth organization in Germany was 368,800 (among them 94,300 females), which represented 8.5 percent of all youth organizations' members and 3.6 percent of all German youth.[148]

There were two positions prevalent at that time about the leisure of young workers. The first considered organized or spontaneous leisure as mutually exclusive alternatives. According to that position a social worker dealing with youth recognized a split among young female workers: Some of them went to the club organized by the church; others were dress-up and pleasure addicts, went to dances and the movies, and hung around.[149] A recent study of workers' culture confirms this division.

Many [working-class] youngsters were entirely "privatized" in their spare time, neither belonging to nor identifying with a political or religious movement. And this even in socialist or communist or otherwise politically involved households …. Gymnastics, swimming, bathing, going for walks and hikes were frequently, but far from universally, linked to membership in and activities of labor movement organizations. They were often just family-centered, or undertaken in an informally organized group of friends, or even alone.[150]

The other position is based on the assumption that many workers partook, presumably asymmetrically, of the cultural offerings both inside and outside the organizations. "For the majority of young people membership in clubs was completely reconcilable with the consumption of commercial offers."[151] The easiest way to reconcile the two was through "valuable" commercialized products; great international films such as *The Blue Angel* or *Metropolis*, and socially critical films such as *Kuhle Wampe*, were seen by organized as well as unorganized workers. The range of practices is perhaps best revealed by assuming that there were three types of leisure attitudes: the two described above – inside and outside the organizations – and the alternating use of both. But it must also be kept in mind that in 1925, out of sixteen million male and female workers, perhaps only 10 to 12 percent were organized in the workers' cultural associations.[152]

Among the members, women were a minority in a male-dominated club culture, especially in the sport clubs. In the workers' gymnastic and sport organizations only 17 percent of the members were female, in the club Friends of Nature the female rate was about one-third, while in the singing club and the club for public health every fourth member was female.[153] Instead of joining a male-dominated workers' club, young women often tended to gravitate to commercialized popular culture. Recent feminist research suggests that many women from all social strata recognized the new opportunities commercialized popular culture offered them, especially the movies, light novels, and magazines. In films and even "trashy" stories they often envisioned the good life – in contrast to their real lives. Entertainment not only enabled them to escape reality, but also stimulated their social and gender-specific fantasies and desires.[154]

Similar to the Austrian Socialists,[155] German SPD men and women did not accept the breakthrough of 'modernity' in general and commercialized popular culture in particular without reservations. For them the problem was that commercialized popular culture offered many more "trashy" products, which were to be rejected, than products of good quality, which were accepted or desired.[156] In their view, workers' cultural clubs were considered an alternative to commercialized popular culture, but they had difficulty attracting young female workers who had not grown up in social democratic milieus or wanted to escape from them.

Because commercialized popular culture was open to everyone and offered many new, evidently attractive experiences, this enemy could not be defeated either by high-brow culture or the workers' cultural movement. The number of social democrats who absolutely rejected mass culture was estimated at only 200,000.[157] With respect to the cinema, the SPD as well as the KPD attempted, by and large ineffectively, to develop leftist alternatives:

> Although leftist intellectuals and artists, including Anna Siemsen, Heinz Lüdecke, Erwin Piscator, Franz Jung, Hanns Eisler, and Bertolt Brecht, had promoted and experimented with such alternatives at various times throughout the period, they received little support and were often criticized by the political parties of the left. For the most part they developed and practiced their models of artistic production and reception independent of the SPD's and KPD's cultural programs.[158]

In summary, social democratic female politicians were not only involved in improving the situation of working-class women. They also concerned themselves with the liberalization and equality of bourgeois women's condition. This became clear when SPD women committed themselves to the reform of family law which, particularly in the matter of property rights, was of little or no importance to workers. Here political strategies, which crossed classes, are recognizable. They were certainly more assertive, at least in retrospect, than female trade unionists, whose actions against pay discrimination of women were very limited. Presumably the latter regarded efforts in this direction as futile, because both male unionists and entrepreneurs opposed reforms and because women themselves recognized that their chances on the labor market were dependent on low pay.

In other areas a generational conflict between the older female functionaries and young female workers emerged. In the view of many female functionaries, mothers were supposed to work only because of financial need. Moreover, many young workers of both sexes were not interested in being integrated into the organization and cultural boundaries of cultural socialism. Therefore, socialist youth organizations had a relatively low membership. Mass culture offered numerous possibilities of self-organized leisure activities, insofar as free time was available, after a forty-eight-hour work week (plus overtime). The efforts to rationalize homes were defeated by the reality of bad housing conditions for many working-class families. The extreme crises during inflation (1923) and the Great Depression (1930-1933) undermined many socialist cultural plans and efforts. The increasing harshness of discussions about cultural policies during the Great Depression suggests that there was not only an economic crisis, but also a cultural one. In other words, as in the conflict between social policy and the national constitution, the economic crisis offered the opportunity to delay new cultural initiatives. Since the SPD appeared powerless after 1930, the Nazis saw their chance. The conservatives' fear about whether the "two sphere society" of sexes and its traditional hierarchy could be maintained was exploited by the Nazis during the Great Depression. They promised order and security in response to the threat of a changing hierarchy of sexes exemplified by women's representation in the public sphere, popular culture, and Americanization, as well as through the many unemployed men at home. As a solution they presented a modernized, professionalized, and scientist private sphere as the new, racially contained German-Aryan women's world and declared it to be a higher stage of society – the German *Volk* community. Although in many respects the gender-polarized two-sphere society had been sustained during the Weimar Republic, the backlash after 1933 marked a return to male domination in the public domain.[159] This regression was accepted by the majority in the bourgeois women's movement in some respects and was more or less tolerated by women, including those from the working-class, who voted for the Nazis.[160]

Conclusion

Social Democratic women's attempts to combine class with gender issues had limited success. While "sisters" from other parties regarded them as "reds" and vice versa as "bourgeois," their male partners within their own party considered them primarily as women (the "second" sex). Among the range of topics considered important by the male-dominated SPD women's issues were clearly secondary. This attitude did not differ from that of other European countries at that time, such as Belgium and Britain. In fact, in all of the eleven countries of this volume party work and political issues were intensely gendered. In Germany, as in most other European countries, local social projects and social organizations concerning welfare, maternity, infant care, and children were the main achievements of SPD women. There was not, however, always a completely consistent gendering of views, a strict demarcation between male and female opinions, as for example with respect to the right of married women to work. Moreover, a number of common class-related interests were shared by women and men, which relativized controversies on gender issues and led to some cooperation. In addition, Social Democratic women in Germany, as elsewhere, themselves often used gendered arguments either for tactical reasons or because they believed in them. In Germany, as well as in Norway and Britain, some younger women did protest against the gendering of party work, but a long-range opposition by young women could not develop within the SPD, because it was destroyed by the Nazis.

Fundamental changes in the three important spheres of employment, home, and public culture in the 1920s led to extensive debates among reformers in all parties.

For female workers jobs and workplaces in the Weimar period meant a fluctuation of opportunities, characterized by demobilization, Fordism, crises, and enlargement of the distribution sector. Women became more "visible" at their workplace, in particular as sales clerks or as secretaries, but such modernization at the workplace often meant "regendering." With respect to gainful employment, firing, wages, and professional training for young girls, the prejudicial practice of the ADGB differed greatly from its high-minded program, a contradiction which existed to varying degrees in all the countries of this study. Women themselves evaluated their work in various ways, depending on their age and family status, the quality of their job, and their view of gender roles. Many men and women thought that mothers with small children should not be gainfully employed except in cases of real need.

Socialist women – in Germany as in Norway or Denmark – welcomed the new woman, but only a particular variant as described above. They combined segments of modernity with their idea of cultural socialism and the "new human being." Their ideas of culture were similar to those of their socialist sisters in Austria, and the Netherlands for instance. In Germany, the socialist "new human being," as envisioned in the workers' cultural movement, inhabited a more or less socialist, communitarian world in miniature, while the bourgeois reformers clung more to traditional or moderately modern views in their own cultural projections.

Many reformers, regardless of party and gender, agreed on the need for rationalization of the home, professionalization of housework, and the social engineering of human beings, strivings which could also be found in Britain, Austria, and Sweden, for instance. Although women did everything but follow the good advice on how to handle domestic chores and furnish their rooms, the iconography of the modern home in the media, advertisings and exhibitions reinforced the traditional gender division; women remained responsible for their homes and this message legitimized existing reality in a new way.

In Germany large differences existed between female Social Democratic women and the majority of politically active middle-class women regarding abortion and unmarried mothers. The only exception was the already mentioned League for the Protection of Motherhood and Sexual Reform. The majority of middle-class women, especially the cultural conservatives, clung to a traditional views on morals and mores and tried to maintain the "gender order" in its conventional pattern notwithstanding the modernization of other aspects of society.

For socialist women in Germany as in other countries, sex education, maternalism, family planning, and welfare were crucial topics of interest and commitment. Achievements, however, remained limited. Many workers' wives lived under strained circumstances as they had before. Economic crises, unemployment, and housing shortages squashed hopes for the future. The words of the Constitution giving women "basically the same rights and duties" were continuously undermined by various interpretations of the word "basically," thus hindering progress in women's issues. In most European countries including Germany, and except for Sweden, Belgium, and Norway, very limited progress – if any – was made in changing the family law.

More than in other countries, except for France, the German socialist women's movement was in a difficult position because it was not the sole representative of female workers. Both the Communist party and the Center party had strong women's organizations of their own. SPD women also found it hard to develop a distinctive identity on some cultural problems in the face of the bourgeois feminist movement.

Male Social Democrats and the male unionists believed that they were in the forefront of the reformers of gender divisions and women's concerns during the Weimar Republic but, in retrospect, this "forefront" was not very near the front.[161] They never seriously addressed the issue of the gender division of labor and the hierarchy of gender within the party, at the workplace, in the home, and in the public cultural sphere. Comradeship ended at the kitchen door in Germany as elsewhere. The decade of social planning, social rationalization, and popular culture tended to alter the everyday lives of both men and women, but did not, in general, change the crucial balance of gender roles.[162]

It has been suggested "that the prevailing attitudes in Weimar Germany presaged the practices of the Third Reich."[163] After 1933 gender struggles as well as class struggles of the Weimar period were compulsorily stopped and the relations between the sexes and the classes transferred into the idea of a *Volksgemeinschaft*. That was an invented community of an imagined harmonized people, destined to live in a new social order. Therein, men and women, workers and the middle-class knew exactly what their tasks and roles were to be – a community from which "the others," especially the Jews, were to be excluded (and later eliminated). In general, active Social Democratic women were also excluded, which is what most of them wanted facing the terrorist regime.

SPD female politicians of the Weimar period, insofar as they had survived the Third Reich, were again active after 1945. They concentrated their activities in particular on the social state, which they had already wanted to develop in the Weimar period. Their postwar values with respect to family and society reflect a continuity with Weimar, but these were increasingly challenged by the new women's movement of the 1970s. Although it emerged outside of the SPD and the unions, in due course it increasingly influenced these organizations. In contrast to the old female functionaries of the SPD the new women's movement demanded the equality of women not only in the economy, politics, and society, but also between men and women through a redistribution of housework and the daily responsibility for children.

Notes

1. This projection was developed by the late Friedrich Engels and Karl Kautsky. See Erich Matthias, "Kautsky und der Kautskyanismus. Die Funktion der Ideologie in der deutschen Sozialdemokratie vor dem ersten Weltkriege," in *Marxismus-Studien*, ed. Iring Fetscher (Tübingen, 1957), p.190. I thank Jutta Schwarzkopf, Helmut Gruber, and Gisela Johnson for advice and criticism and for help with respect to the translation. I also thank Hans Peter Riesche and Claudia Renken who assisted my search for documents.

2. In 1930, 67 percent of female party members were non-income earning housewives, a percentage which roughly corresponded to the proportion of non-income earning housewives in the female population. Karen Hagemann, "Equal but Not the Same: The Social Democratic Women's Movement in the Weimar Republic," in *Bernstein to Brandt: A Short History of German Social Democracy*, ed. Roger Fletcher (London, 1987), p. 137; see also *Protokoll über die Verhandlungen des Parteitages der Sozialdemokratischen Partei Deutschlands* (Berlin, 1927), Reichsfrauenkonferenz, p. 328. (In the following abbreviated: *Sozialdemokratischer Parteitag.*)

3. Only 10 percent of the functionaries were married *and* gainfully employed. Christl Wickert, "Von der Hausarbeit zur Sozialarbeit. Sozialdemokratische Frauenpolitik und 'Arbeiterwohlfahrt' in Berlin 1919-1933," in *Studien zur Arbeiterbewegung und Arbeiterkultur in Berlin*, ed. Gert-Joachim Gläessner et al. (Berlin, 1989), p. 119.

4. Renate Bridenthal and Claudia Koontz, "Beyond Kinder, Küche, Kirche: Weimar Women in Politics and Work," in *When Biology Became Destiny: Women in Weimar and Nazi Germany*, ed. Renate Bridenthal et al., (New York, 1984), p. 39.

5. Among the 21 members of the party executive one woman, Marie Juchacz, was a voting member. In addition, two other women belonged to that institution as observers. Women were excluded especially in commissions where political strategies were conceptualized. And the average participation of female delegates in National party congresses was only between 12 and 13 percent. Furthermore, on the party candidates' lists for the *Reichstag* elections only women who already had secure positions in their constituencies were nominated for a safe position on

the list – and those were few. Moreover, in 1932 only 22 percent of all SPD local branches had a female in an executive position. Hagemann, "Equal," p. 142. Compared with other Weimar parties, however, the percentage of women within the party leadership of the SPD was highest.

6. Marie Juchacz (1879 to 1956) came from a working-class background with little formal education. She became active in the party in 1905. During the Weimar Republic she held many positions in the party, in Parliament, and in the Social Democratic Workers Welfare Organization (*Arbeiterwohlfahrt*). After the Nazis came to power she emigrated first to the Saarland, then to Alsace, afterwards to southern France, and finally to the United States. After 1945 she came back to Germany, (re)organized the *Arbeiterwohlfahrt* and the American "Care-package" campaign. Renate Pore, *A Conflict of Interest: Women in German Social Democracy* (Westport, Conn., 1981), p. 33. With respect to this biography and also those which follow, see Christl Wickert, *Unsere Erwählten: Sozialdemokratische Frauen im Deutschen Reichstag und im Preussischen Landtag 1919 bis 1933* (Göttingen, 1986).

7. The women's bureau was founded before World War I. For its activities, see Christl Wickert, "Frauen im Parlament: Lebensläufe sozialdemokratischer Parlamentarierinnen in der Weimarer Republik," in *Lebenslauf und Gesellschaft. Zum Einsatz von kollektiven Biographien in der historischen Sozialforschung*, ed. Wilhelm Heinz Schröder (Stuttgart, 1985), p. 237.

8. Marie Juchacz, *Sozialdemokratischer Parteitag* (Berlin, 1931), p. 249. For an opposite view, see Hagemann, "Equal," p. 142.

9. Hagemann, "Equal," p. 142.

10. Pore, *Conflict*, p. 51.

11. For instance, women received lower unemployment benefits than men.

12. Pore, *Conflict*, p. 38.

13. Wickert, "Hausarbeit," pp. 124 and 126.

14. Christiane Eifert, *Frauenpolitik und Wohlfahrtspflege. Zur Geschichte der sozialdemokratischen "Arbeiterwohlfahrt"* (Frankfurt and New York, 1993), p. 34. The consumer union shops were centers of the social network of women in the neighborhoods. Detlef Schmiechen-Ackermann, *Nationalsozialismus und Arbeitermilieus. Der nationalsozialistische Angriffe auf die proletarischen Wohnquartiere und die Reaktion in den sozialistischen Vereinen* (Bonn, 1998), p. 633.

15. Eifert, *Frauenpolitik*, p. 231, see also pp. 129-30.

16. Adele Schreiber, "Die Sozialdemokratin als Staatsbürgerin," in *Die Frauenfrage im Lichte des Sozialismus*, ed. Anna Blos (Dresden, 1930), p. 133.

17. Clara Bohm-Schuch (1879 to 1936) was born in Stechow/Westhavelland and grew up in a worker's family together with five sisters and brothers. She attended the elementary school in her village and then a commercial school in Berlin. Later she worked in several offices and also wrote articles. In 1906 she married, became a housewife and gave birth to a daughter. She worked for the party and the unions from 1904 onward, organized a women's group and was committed to social welfare. In 1918 she became a party delegate, a member of the National Assembly (1919/20) and the Reichstag (1924 to 1933). After 1933 she was in prison for some weeks and as a consequence of her treatment there died in 1936. Her burial became a significant anti-Nazi demonstration with 5,000 participants.

18. The editor was Richard Lohmann, who was replaced by Toni Sender in 1928. It comes as no surprise that among the 400 to 500 editors in the party there were only one or two females. *Sozialdemokratischer Parteitag* (Berlin, 1929), p. 50.

19. Pore, *Conflict*, pp. 62-64. For the following see Elisabeth Vormschlag, *Inhalte, Leitbilder und Funktionen politischer Frauenzeitschriften der SPD, der USPD, der*

KPD in den Jahren 1890-1933 und der NSDAP in den Jahren 1932-1945 (Göttingen, 1970), pp. 154-56.

20. Karen Hagemann, *Frauenalltag und Männerpolitik. Alltagsleben und gesellschaftliches Handeln von Arbeiterfrauen in der Weimarer Republik* (Bonn, 1990), p. 46.

21. Eve Rosenhaft convincingly analyzed this shift in "Lesewut, Kinosucht, Radiotismus. Zur (geschlechter-)politischen Relevanz neuer Massenmedien in den 1920er Jahren," in *Amerikanisierung: Traum oder Alptraum im Deutschland des 20. Jahrhunderts,* ed. Alf Lüdtke, Inge Marssolek, and Adelheid von Saldern (Stuttgart, 1996).

22. Juchacz, *Sozialdemokratischer Parteitag* (Berlin, 1929), Frauenkonferenz, pp. 333-4. Juchacz felt that popular culture had to be accepted as a fact and that *Frauenwelt* should consider such needs. She regarded *Frauenwelt* as a means of freeing women from the influence of middle class magazines. The SPD changed its position on laws against "trash" and "dirt" in commercialized popular culture. In 1920 the prohibition of "harmful" movies by law, ("*Reichsfilmgesetz*") was still supported by the SPD. In 1926, when the bill for protecting young people against "trash and dirt" ("*Schund und Schmutz*") was discussed in parliament, the SPD rejected the motion (as did the Communists) because it was afraid that the law could be misused.

23. For example, one of the readers was an unmarried female textile-worker and active unionist, who read the journal *Textilarbeiter* as well as the *Frauenwelt* and "sometimes a good book." Hagemann, *Frauenalltag*, p. 537; *"Mein Arbeitstag – mein Wochenende". Arbeiterinnen berichten von ihrem Alltag 1928,* newly ed. Alf Lüdtke (Hamburg, 1991), p. 74.

24. Schreiber, "Sozialdemokratin," p. 144. According to textile union members' reports, reading of the social democratic newspaper was mentioned several times. *"Mein Arbeitstag,"* pp. 69, 73, 74, 86, 99, 106.

25. *Sozialdemokratischer Parteitag* (Berlin, 1924), Frauenkonferenz, p. 244.

26. Wickert, *Unsere Erwählten* 1: 156. This is an analysis of the *Vorwärts* supplements.

27. Schreiber, "Sozialdemokratin," p. 144.

28. The Hanover *Volkswille,* which has been analyzed with the help of Karen Heinze, confirmed this opinion.

29. See Walter Hofmann, *Die Lektüre der Frau. Ein Beitrag zur Leserkunde und zur Leserführung* (Leipzig, 1931), pp. 28, 66, 194; see also Hagemann, *Frauenalltag,* pp. 561-62.

30. Pore, *Conflict,* p. 57.

31. *Sozialdemokratischer Parteitag* (Berlin, 1925), p. 168. A contrary example is Dora Fabian's demand for community kitchens; see: Dora Fabian, "Frau und Technik," *Kulturwille* 3, 9 (1926): 180.

32. Hagemann, "Equal," p. 134.

33. Pore, *Conflict,* p. 53.

34. See, for instance, the periodical *Vorwärts*. Christoph Rülcker, "Arbeiterkultur und Kulturpolitik im Blickwinkel des 'Vorwärts' 1918-1928," in *Archiv für Sozialgeschichte* 14 (1974), p. 131.

35. Exact statistics are not available because only a few local authorities counted the votes according to gender. Male SPD voters outnumbered female voters by 5 to 10 percent in one third of the elections in which votes were recorded by gender but the difference declined during the 1920s. Gabriele Bremme, *Die politische Rolle der Frau in Deutschland* (Göttingen, 1956), p. 71. The male party leadership

regarded the difference between male and female votes as "too" high, although in retrospect the difference was slight.

36. Bridenthal and Koontz, "Beyond," p. 39.
37. Hagemann, *Frauenalltag*, p. 559.
38. Wickert, *Unsere Erwählten*, 2: 64-5.
39. Pore, *Conflict*, p. 41.
40. Report by Dr Schöfer, *Sozialdemokratischer Parteitag* (Berlin, 1920/21), pp. 11-12.
41. As did Luise Zietz from the USPD before 1922. Another exception was Toni Sender. Anette Hild-Berg, *Toni Sender. Ein Leben im Namen der Freiheit und der sozialen Gerechtigkeit* (Cologne, 1994), pp. 146-59.
42. Wickert, *Unsere Erwählten* 1: 183, 185.
43. Compared with SPD women in the *Reichstag*, SPD women in the Prussian Parliament were even less influential because of the rigid rules within the SPD delegation. There were only a few discussions on women's concerns. SPD women succeeded only in regard to the midwives law of 1922. This law laid down the tasks of the midwives, secured their financial situation and upgraded their profession. At the same time their training and their work were precisely regulated and observed. Their tasks consisted of helping during birth, taking care of mothers and their newly born babies during the first weeks after birth, diet suggestions, and the care of infants. Wickert, *Unsere Erwählten* 1: 206, 216.
44. And this small number decreased even further during the later years of the Republic.
45. *Sozialdemokratischer Parteitag* (Berlin, 1925), Reichsfrauenkonferenz, p. 333. In 1929 it was 5.6 percent. *Jahrbuch der SPD 1929*, ed. Parteivorstand (Berlin, 1930), p. 183.
46. Wickert, "Hausarbeit," p. 130.
47. Pore, *Conflict*, p. 67.
48. See Renate Bridenthal, "Class Struggle around the Hearth: Women and Domestic Service in the Weimar Republic," in *Towards the Holocaust. The Social and Economic Collapse of the Weimar Republic*, ed. Michael N. Dobkowski and Isidor Wallimann (Westport, Conn., 1983), pp. 243-65.
49. Richard J. Evans, *The Feminist Movement in Germany 1894-1933* (London and Beverly Hills, 1976), p. 243.
50. See Atina Grossman's chapter in this volume.
51. Christl Wickert, "Helene Stöcker and the Bund für Mutterschutz," *Women's Studies International Forum* 5,6 (1982): 618; Pore, *Conflict*, p. 44.
52. See examples in Hans Jürgen Arendt, "Zur Frauenpolitik der KPD und zur Rolle der Frauen in der kommunistischen Arbeiterbewegung Deutschlands," in *Arbeiterbewegung und Feminismus*, ed. Ernest Bornemann (Frankfurt, 1982), p. 50.
53. In 1929 the communists left the ADGB and created their own unions affiliated to Moscow.
54. Gertrud Hanna (1876 to 1944), dissident, was born into a Berlin worker family. She attended elementary school and afterwards was an unskilled worker in a printing company. In 1907 she was employed by her union and joined the SPD one year later. In 1915 she began editing the union women's periodical (*Gewerkschaftliche Frauenzeitung*); in 1918 she became a member of the executive of the ADGB and leader of its women members. After 1933 she was interrogated by the *Gestapo* several times and eked out a pitiful existence by mending clothes together with her sister. They committed suicide together in 1944.
55. Gisela Losseff-Tillmanns, *Frauenemanzipation und Gewerkschaften (1800 to 1975)*, (Ph.D. diss., Bochum, 1975), pp. 526, 529.

56. Jürgen W. Falter, "Warum die deutschen Arbeiter während des "Dritten Reiches" zu Hitler standen," in _Geschichte und Gesellschaft_ 13, 2 (1987): 228.

57. Jürgen W. Falter and Dirk Hänisch, "Die Anfälligkeit von Arbeitern gegenüber der NSDAP bei den Reichstagswahlen 1928-1933," in _Archiv für Sozialgeschichte_ 26 (1986): 206 and Jürgen W. Falter, _Hitlers Wähler_ (Munich, 1991).

58. Except the Catholic Center party.

59. Wickert, "Hausarbeit," p. 130. In the following elections, however, the percentage of women decreased.

60. Hagemann, "Equal," p. 142.

61. Karen Hagemann, "Men's Demonstrations and Women's Protest: Gender in Collective Action in the Urban Working-Class Milieu during the Weimar Republic," in _Gender and History_ 5 (spring 1993): 115.

62. Christl Wickert, "Widerstand und Dissens von Frauen – ein Überblick," in _Frauen gegen die Diktatur – Widerstand und Verfolgung im nationalsozialistischen Deutschland_, ed. Christl Wickert (Berlin, 1995), p. 18.

63. For the fate of the various women see Wickert, _Unsere Erwählten_, 1: 231-83; Pore, _Conflict_, p. 35.

64. This does not mean that women as a rule participated in the revolutionary organizations, the workers' councils, or were pushed to the fore during revolutionary events. No doubt, Rosa Luxemburg and Clara Zetkin were exceptions. Helga Grebing, _Frauen in der deutschen Revolution 1918/19_, (Heidelberg, 1994), p. 25.

65. Pore, _Conflict_, p. 90.

66. Ibid., p. 94. The SPD was pressured by SPD women at the time and demanded equal rights in employment for women. Hagemann, "Equal," p. 136.

67. Bridenthal and Koontz, "Beyond" p. 44. An additional three million women and four million men entered the labor market. That was a great increase of gainfully employed women compared to men. Ibid., p. 45.

68. Besides the new jobs, young poorly paid women replaced older and better-paid male white-color workers and "feminized" previously "male" jobs in shops and offices. The number of women in the sectors of commerce and transportation increased by 82.3 percent. Pore, _Conflict_, p. 97.

69. Juchacz, _Sozialdemokratischer Parteitag_ (Berlin, 1925), Reichsfrauenkonferenz, p. 370. Such fears were also expressed about domestic servants.

70. See for instance, _Die Neue Frau. Herausforderungen für die Bildmedien der Zwanziger Jahre_, ed. Katharina Sykora et al. (Marburg, 1993).

71. For more see Mary Nolan, _Visions of Modernity. American Business and the Modernization of Germany_, (New York and Oxford, 1994).

72. _Volkswille_, 21 August 1928.

73. Pore, _Conflict_, p. 101; compare Losseff-Tillmanns, _Frauenemanzipation_, p. 492.

74. Evans, _Feminist Movement_, p. 246.

75. Hagemann, "Men's Demonstrations," p. 113 and Hagemann, "Equal," p. 136.

76. Hagemann, "Men's Demonstrations," pp. 113-4.

77. For example Anna Geyer. Losseff-Tillmanns, _Frauenemanzipation_, pp. 506, 594, 516.

78. Manfred Rexin, "Die Freigewerkschaftliche Jugendzentrale in Berlin," in _Gewerkschaftsjugend im Weimarer Staat_, ed. Detlef Prinz and Manfred Rexin (Cologne, 1983), pp. 94-6, 100, 102, 109-10. The citation is on page 95.

79. Losseff-Tillmanns, _Frauenemanzipation_, p. 523.

80. Hagemann, _Frauenalltag_, p. 493. The periodical was subscribed to by women who entered the unions. Vormschlag, _Inhalte_, p. 118.

81. Willy Albrecht et al., "Frauenfrage und deutsche Sozialdemokratie vom Ende des 19. Jahrhunderts bis zum Beginn der zwanziger Jahre," in *Archiv für Sozialgeschichte* 19 (1979), p. 509.
82. Compare Hagemann, "Equal," p. 137.
83. For example Hannover *Volkswille*, 27 March 1928, supplement; *Volkswille*, 29 February 1928, supplement.
84. Apparently Hanna also accepted the "gendering of jobs." Losseff-Tillmanns, *Frauenemanzipation*, pp. 514-6; see also Vormschlag, *Inhalte*, p. 114.
85. *Sozialdemokratischer Parteitag* (Berlin, 1929), p. 244.
86. See Prinz and Rexin, *Gewerkschaftsjugend*, p. 106.
87. Pore, *Conflict*, p. 95.
88. Cited in ibid.
89. For the debates within the SPD see for instance, *Sozialdemokratischer Parteitag* (Berlin, 1925), pp. 54, 168; (Berlin, 1931), p. 284; similar statements in: Pore, *Conflict*, p. 52.
90. Ibid., p. 99.
91. Hagemann, "Equal," p. 143.
92. Moreover, the majority of (married) female workers could be found doing undesirable, unskilled work and poorly paid jobs. 2.3 million married women were employed in agriculture and only 730,000 married women in industry, and 427,000 in commerce and transportation – primarily in retail sales. Pore, *Conflict*, p. 98. Moreover, women in certain jobs could not automatically be replaced by men, for instance in the textile industry where special skills were required. *Sozialdemokratischer Parteitag* (Berlin, 1927), Reichsfrauenkonferenz, p. 331.
93. Helgard Kramer, "Veränderungen der Frauenrollen in der Weimarer Republik," in *Beiträge zur feministischen Theorie und Praxis* 5 (1981), p. 24.
94. See Marie Jahoda et al., *Die Arbeitslosen von Marienthal. Ein soziographischer Versuch über die Wirkungen langandauernder Arbeitslosigkeit* (Frankfurt, 1980 [first ed. 1933]).
95. Mathilde Wurm deplored this at *Sozialdemokratischer Parteitag* (Berlin, 1927), Reichsfrauenkonferenz, p. 316.
96. Stated by Susanne Jacobson at *Sozialdemokratischer Parteitag*, (Berlin, 1927), Reichsfrauenkonferenz, p. 327.
97. Alfred Grotjahn, *Die Hygiene der menschlichen Fortpflanzung. Versuch einer praktischen Eugenik* (Berlin, 1926).
98. Cornelie Usborne, *Frauenkörper – Volkskörper: Geburtenkontrolle und Bevölkerungspolitik in der Weimarer Republik* (Münster, 1994), pp. 158-9; Atina Grossman, *Reforming Sex. The German Movement for Birth Control & Abortion 1920-1950* (Oxford, 1995).
99. In 1928, there were several hundred private and municipal marriage and sexual counseling services, although women clearly preferred the private ones. For more details see Atina Grossman's chapter in this volume.
100. Pore, *Conflict*, p. 83.
101. Ibid., p. 43. The SPD had had similar strivings already in the prewar period. Annette Mühlberg, Arbeiterbewegung und Sexualität im deutschen Kaiserreich," in *Mitteilungen aus der kulturwissenschaftlichen Forschung* 15 (1992) 31: 163.
102. Usborne, *Frauenkörper*, p. 137.
103. Hagemann, "Equal," p. 137.
104. Twenty-one out of 1,000 marriages ended in divorce in 1901 to 1905, compared to sixty-two divorces out of 1,000 marriages in 1921 to 1925. Unfortunately, there is no information available on the number of divorces among workers. Ute

Frevert, *Frauen-Geschichte zwischen bürgerlicher Verbesserung und neuer Weiblichkeit* (Frankfurt, 1986), p. 188.

105. Pore, *Conflict*, p. 43 *(Artikel 119)*.
106. Wickert, *Unsere Erwählten*, 1: 188-9; Usborne, *Frauenkörper*, p. 74.
107. For details see David Crew, *Germans on Welfare* (Oxford, 1998).
108. Usborne, *Frauenkörper*, p. 74.
109. Nanny Kurfürst, *Sozialdemokratischer Parteitag*, (Berlin, 1927), Reichsfrauenkonferenz, p. 358. In general see Adelheid von Saldern, *Häuserleben. Zur Geschichte städtischen Arbeiterwohnens vom Kaiserreich bis heute* (Bonn, 1995), pp. 153-93.
110. Between 1919 and 1932 newly created and remodeled apartments accounted for 16 percent of national domiciles. Josef Mooser, *Arbeiterleben in Deutschland 1900-1970. Klassenlagen, Kultur und Politik* (Frankfurt, 1984), p. 146.
111. Hanover *Volkswille*, 29 February 1928.
112. Reinhard Sieder, *Sozialgeschichte der Familie* (Frankfurt 1987), p. 209. Figures are related to marriages from different years which still existed in 1939. Workers' marriages stemming from the years before 1905 had 4.67 children, workers' marriages of 1910/14 had 3.27 children and those of 1920/24 only 2.39. The corresponding figures for middle class employers: 2.98; 2.02; 1.48. Ute Frevert, "Tradition und Veränderung im Geschlechterverhältnis," in Funkkolleg *Jahrhundertwende. Die Entstehung der modernen Gesellschaft 1880-1930* (Weinheim and Basel, 1989) 9: 96.
113. Hanover *Volkswille*, 29 February 1928.
114. Compare Kramer, "Veränderungen," p. 24.
115. Dirk Schubert, *Stadtplanung als Ideologie* (Berlin, 1984), p. 121.
116. A comparison between German housing estates with those in Red Vienna reveals that in both cases the self-supporting individual family was the basic structure in the housing blocks. But in contrast to German settlements there were more community rooms, such as meeting halls and the reading rooms in Red Vienna. See Helmut Gruber's article in this volume.
117. There were few reports on the achievements of equality for women in Soviet Union, but these were rather positive. See Valtin Hartig, "Von Frauen in Russland," in *Kulturwille* 3, 1 (1926): 11.
118. Hanover *Volkswille*, 8 December 1927. The author's sex is unknown.
119. Juchacz at *Sozialdemokratischer Parteitag* (Berlin, 1927), Reichsfrauenkonferenz, pp. 367-8, 363-4.
120. *Einfa* 2 (1931): 10.
121. They ignored the cultural meaning of this "irrationality." Skilled workers wanted to show that they were as "cultured" as the bourgeoisie. Moreover, the front room served as a status symbol within the working class.
122. *Sozialdemokratischer Parteitag* (Berlin, 1927), Reichsfrauenkonferenz, p. 359.
123. Ibid. (Berlin, 1925), p. 345.
124. See Prinz and Rexin, *Gewerkschaftsjugend*, p. 104.
125. Hanover *Volkswille*, 29 February 1928 (supplement); see also 8 February 1928 (supplement). Only the 1928 issues of the Hanover *Volkswille* have been examined.
126. Similar ideas were presented at the Reichsfrauenkonferenz of 1927, p. 353; see also "Hauswirtschaft," in *Der Kulturwille* 2,1 (1925): 12.
127. Cited in Prinz and Rexin, *Gewerkschaftsjugend*, p. 98.
128. *Sozialdemokratischer Parteitag* (Berlin, 1927), Reichsfrauenkonferenz, p. 362.
129. See Detlev J.K. Peukert, *Jugend zwischen Krieg und Krise. Lebenswelten von Arbeiterjungen in der Weimarer Republik* (Cologne, 1987), p. 241.

130. Otto Rühle, *Illustrierte Kultur-und Sittengeschichte des Proletariats* (Lahn-Giessen, 1977 [first ed. 1930]), pp. 18-25. Rühle's account is based on contemporary investigations.

131. See Dietrich Mühlberg, "Modernisierung in der proletarischen Lebensweise," in *Mitteilungen aus der kulturwissenschaftlichen Forschung* 15, 30 (1992): 54-57.

132. Hagemann, *Frauenalltag*, p. 185.

133. Heidi Rosenbaum, *Formen der Familie. Untersuchungen zum Zusammenhang von Familienverhältnissen, Sozialstruktur und sozialem Wandel in der deutschen Gesellschaft des 19. Jahrhunderts* (Frankfurt, 1982), p. 426; Hagemann, *Frauenalltag*, pp. 225-31; interview with Heidi Rosenbaum on 13 July 1996. See also Usborne, *Frauenkörper*, p. 118; Peukert, *Krieg und Krise*, p. 241.

134. Juchacz, *Sozialdemokratischer Parteitag* (Berlin, 1924), Reichsfrauenkonferenz, p. 227.

135. *Prussian Landtag*, vol. 12, 244th session, 14 May 1923, pp. 17 and 361.

136. The unions more or less accepted Americanization (Fordism) in production and the home.

137. *Sozialistische Monatshefte* 34 (67), II (July 1928), p. 619.

138. See, for instance, the articles in *Kulturwille* 2, 11 (1925) : 217.

139. See, for instance, party secretary Wilhelm Krüger, *Preussischer Landtag*, vol. 4, 75th session, 25 November 1921, p. 4,986. For the cultural crisis see: Sollmann, *Reichstag*, vol. 428, 176th session, 16 June 1930, p. 5458.

140. See, for instance, *Reichstag*, vol. 391, 245th session, 3 December 1926, pp. 8 and 378.

141. *Sozialdemokratischer Parteitag* (Berlin, 1927), Reichsfrauenkonferenz, p. 329.

142. Compare Hagemann, "Equal," p. 137.

143. Juchacz, *Sozialdemokratischer Parteitag* (Berlin, 1931), p. 250.

144. See the many reports in *"Mein Arbeitstag."*

145. See, for instance, Caroline J. in Hagemann, *Frauenalltag*, p. 561.

146. The lack of young women in the women's movement was repeatedly deplored. *Sozialdemokratischer Parteitag* (Berlin, 1929), Reichsfrauenkonferenz, p. 350, and (Berlin, 1927), p. 311 (citation).

147. Hanover *Volkswille*, 24 March 1928, supplement. Kitchy movies were also severely criticized by Marie Juchacz, *Sozialdemokratischer Parteitag* (Berlin, 1927), p. 335.

148. Detlev J.K. Peukert, "Jugend zwischen Disziplinierung und Revolte" in Funkkolleg *Jahrhundertwende. Die Entstehung der modernen Gesellschaft 1880-1930* (Weinheim/Basel, 1988) 3:82.

149. In Lydia Lueb, *Die Freizeit der Textilarbeiterinnen. Eine Untersuchung über die Verwendung der Freizeit der Arbeiterinnen des christlichen Textilarbeiterverbandes Bezirk Westfalen* (Ph.D. diss., Münster, 1929), p. 37.

150. W. L. Guttsman, *Workers' Culture in Weimar Germany. Between Tradition and Commitment* (New York, 1990), pp. 118 and 120; see also the reports in *Mein Arbeitstag*.

151. Mühlberg, "Modernisierung," p. 49.

152. There are no overall statistics of the workers' clubs and the figures do not identify double and triple membership. There has been a controversy over the evaluation of the *quantative* importance of the workers' cultural movement for the workers' strata. See Franz Nitsch and Lorenz Peiffer eds., *Die roten Turnbrüder. 100 Jahre Arbeitersport* (Marburg, 1993), pp. 63-75 with further literature.

153. For further data see, Peter Lösche and Franz Walter, "Die Organisationskultur der sozialdemokratischen Arbeiterbewegung in der Weimarer Republik," in *Geschichte und Gesellschaft* 15, 4 (1989): 526.

154. Patrice Petro, *Joyless Streets. Women and Melodramatic Representation in Weimar Germany* (Princeton, 1989); and for the earlier period: Miriam Hansen, "Early Silent Cinema: Whose Public Sphere?" in *New German Critique* 29 (spring/summer 1983).

155. For Austria see also Helmut Gruber, *Red Vienna. Experiment in Working-class Culture 1919-1934* (Oxford, 1991).

156. There is no place to discuss the shift in acceptance/rejection during the course of the Weimar period.

157. Lösche and Walter, "Organisationskultur," p. 536.

158. Bruce Murray, *Film and the Weimar Left in the Weimar Republic. From Caligari to Kuhle Wampe* (Austin, 1990), p. 237; see also Adelheid von Saldern, "Massenfreizeitkultur im Visier. Ein Beitrag zu den Deutungs-und Einwirkungsversuchen während der Weimarer Republik," in *Archiv für Sozialgeschichte* 33 (1993): 45-51.

159. Compare Kramer, "Veränderungen," p. 24; Bridenthal and Koontz, "Beyond," p. 55.

160. See Richard J. Evans, *Comrades and Sisters. Feminism, Socialism, and Pacifism in Europe 1870-1945* (Brighton, 1987), pp. 168-70.

161. See Albrecht et al., "Frauenfrage," p. 510.

162. Gender experiments among socialists remained limited to small circles.

163. Bridenthal and Koontz, "Beyond," p. 56.

Chapter 3

German Communism and New Women
Dilemmas and Contradictions

Atina Grossmann

The gender politics of the Communist Party (KPD) in the Weimar Republic present a series of paradoxes unsurprising to any student of "women and the European left." Proclaiming the most militant positions on women's rights, the party also had the least female support. Boasting the highest proportion of female legislators of any Weimar party, it also had the smallest percentage of female voters. Theoretically fixated on the industrial workplace, it found its most enthusiastic adherents among housewives, intellectuals, and female white-collar workers. Supporting a radical politics of woman's right to control her own body (*Dein Körper Gehört Dir*, "Your Body Belongs to You" was the slogan), it also embraced medicalization of reproduction, maternalism, and eugenic hygiene. Dedicated to creating "new" women and men and new relations between female and male comrades, it profoundly mistrusted the Weimar "New Woman" and her association with Americanism and the "distraction" of mass consumer culture. Pressing beyond the familialist and maternalist proclivities of both Social Democracy and middle-class feminism, the KPD achieved its greatest popular success among women on the cross-class and potentially divisive issue of abortion.[1]

Revolution and Republic

The German Communist Party (KPD) was established in December 1918, one month after the end of a devastating lost war, the collapse of the Wilhelmine Empire, and the precarious birth of a new republic. Its early development was marked both by the utopian enthusiasms stirred by the October Revolution in Russia and the bloodshed of the failed Spartacus uprising in January 1919 when party leaders Karl Liebknecht and Rosa Luxemburg were murdered by *Freikorps* units supported by their former comrades, the Social Democrats now in power.

In keeping with this tense beginning, party policy on women's role was rife with both possibility and contradiction from the outset. The founding congress of the Communist International in March 1919 – itself a signal of the post-World War I divisions in the working class movement – dutifully proclaimed, "The dictatorship of the proletariat can only be achieved and maintained with the intensive and active participation of working class women."[2] Already in 1920, the KPD's "Guidelines for the Communist Women's Movement" limited the scope of women's organizing. They insisted on strict separation between the bourgeois and the proletarian women's movement and clearly relegated women's issues to only a subordinate position in the general class struggle. At the same time, however, the guidelines reluctantly affirmed the necessity for separate women's organizing.[3] Throughout the Weimar years, the party's central committee and women's and social welfare organizations repeatedly stumbled, both practically and theoretically, as they tried simultaneously to organize women as a distinct constituency and contain their issues within the "primary contradiction" of class politics.

World War I had introduced many women to rationalized semiskilled labor in factories and offices, providing glimpses of higher wages and union organization along with the deprivations of scarcity and rationing. Demobilization brought declines in the relatively high wartime levels of women's activism and trade union and socialist party membership. Splits among Majority and Independent Social Democrats and Communists as well as the bitter conflicts unleashed by the twenty-one conditions imposed by Moscow for membership in the Third International also contributed to a waning of female support.[4] The inflation crisis of 1923 with its dramatic impact on prices and consumption re-radicalized some women but also pushed the young KPD into militant adventurism and failed uprisings, resulting in a temporary ban on the party.

Rationalization and Bolshevization

In the mid 1920s, economic stabilization and industrial rationalization posed new challenges for women's organizing. The KPD aimed both to endorse the technological modernity of mass production and to critique what it called the capitalist Americanized conditions under which the rapid transformation of the German economy was being conducted. The introduction of scientific management and assembly lines, new standards of speed, efficiency, and productivity, and the explosive growth in consumer manufacture particularly affected women for whom the twin pressures of nerve-wracking new work processes and the traditional wage differential between male and female workers were now added to the burden of endless unpaid labor at home. According to the 1925 German census, almost 11.5 million female wage earners constituted 35.8 percent of the total labor force. About a third were married; many had young children or were of childbearing age. Women's share of the insured workforce rose from 35.3 percent in 1928 to 36 percent in 1930 and 37.3 percent in 1931; the increase in single white-collar workers was paralleled by the rise in percentage of married women workers.[5] The growth of the service sector increased job opportunities for the young and unmarried, while the introduction of the assembly line in light industry required the long-term industrial labor of married women. Women were now located in such traditional sectors as agriculture and the home and in the most advanced sectors of assembly-line production and the new white-collar occupations. Even if most German women, in fact, still worked at tasks defined as traditional, either as unpaid workers within the family and household or within family enterprises, wage labor had for many women ceased to be a way station before marriage and children, or an expedient in times of family crisis. It had become a permanent fixture of a modern sex-segregated labor force. While not significantly increasing the proportion of women in the labor force or precipitating a female invasion of male labor preserves, rationalization reorganized the economy in such a way that women stood at the forefront in assembly-line factories, in mechanized offices with typewriters, filing cabinets and switchboards, behind the sales counters of chain stores, and in the expanded social service bureaucracies of a welfare state.[6]

Responding to the obvious failure of KPD revolutionary strategy, a bolshevization program pushed by the Comintern at the 1925 party congress in Frankfurt only partially addressed these new political and economic circumstances. The party's focus on "point of production" organizing tended to neglect or isolate potential women recruits, most of whom were working-class housewives or earned their wages in areas unlikely to attract the attention of KPD organizers, such as consumer industry, white-collar jobs, domestic service, and agriculture.[7] But Bolshevization also encouraged the development of mass organizations that gave increased importance and visibility to women's and social welfare issues, even as they retained the language of proletarian solidarity and opposition to separatist, bourgeois women's groups. The KPD's first separate women's organization, the Red Women's and Girls' League (*Rote*

Frauen und Mädchen Bund, or RFMB), was established in Berlin in November 1925 as a counterpart or auxiliary to the self-defense organization Red Front-Fighters League (*Rote Frontkämpfer Bund*, or RFB), which wanted to preserve its paramilitary image from increasing infiltration by young female militants. Some women resisted relinquishing the uniformed glamour of the RFB but rather ironically, given its distrust of bourgeois separatism, the party insisted on all-female groups to facilitate using personal issues such as motherhood, sexuality, abortion, and food prices to draw unorganized women into general (and always primary) class politics. Eventually, the strategy promised, they would be diverted from the immediate concerns that had first mobilized them.[8]

In many ways, the omnipresent tensions between class and gender politics and the twists and turns of KPD demands on women supporters are well illustrated by the shifting fortunes and convictions of the RFMB's leader Helene Overlach. A protegé of Ernst Thälmann, the party's chairman and 1925 presidential candidate, Overlach initially rejected "the formation of a women's movement since women belonged in the party on equal terms." She resented her new assignment for pulling her away from the "real" politics of wages and work conditions, war and peace. Yet she yielded to party discipline and dutifully organized women's and children's meetings where previously indifferent women sang, read poems and stories and were gently introduced to political themes in thirty-minute question and discussion periods, while their youngsters ate sweets and were entertained by a "red marionette puppet." Still, she remained frustrated in the women and children's realm, complaining that it would be more important to organize the large numbers of women working in the crucial chemical and electro-technical industries.[9] Virtually all female KPD activists reported this conflict between their desire to organize women and their fear of being shunted into the woman question corner.

A Woman's Place: The Delegate and Conference Movement

In 1928, with the Social Democrats (SPD) briefly in power under Chancellor Hermann Müller and the momentarily stable republic engaged in a host of social welfare innovations, the Sixth Comintern Congress declared Social Democracy "social fascist" but also urged alliances with the SPD's working-class base. This "United Front from Below" strategy offered Willi Münzenberg, head of the mass organization International Workers Aid (IAH) and the KPD's master coalition builder, the opportunity to build noncadre organizations in which women, chronically under represented among Communist voters, would play an important role.[10] Female membership or electoral support was actually not as low as one might expect either from historical accounts or from the persistent complaints by Communists themselves. In 1928, 17 percent of 130,000 KPD members (and 21 percent of 867,671 SPD members) were women; in large cities, the figure was closer to 25 percent.[11] Eric Weitz has pointed out that the model Soviet Communist Party had only 13.7 percent female membership in 1929.[12] However, the KPD was engaged in a continual competition with the Social Democratic and Catholic Center parties for female voters, especially those related to men who voted Communist. The SPD tended to have a more equal gender balance among its voters while the socially conservative Catholic Center counted a preponderance of women supporters. As Helen Boak has observed, "The party that gained least from female suffrage – the KPD – was the one party that had the most radical platform on women's issues."[13] In the moderate 1928 elections which brought the SPD back to national power after the period of relative stabilization, the KPD counted a paltry 5.8 percent of male and 3.1 percent of female voters, presenting the party with a huge organizing challenge among both women and men (Table 3.1).[14]

Table 3.1 Distribution of Male and Female Voters across the Political Parties (in percentages)

Party	1924 election		1928 election		1930 election	
	male	female	male	female	male	female
KPD	17.1	11.2	5.8	3.1	12.5	7.3
SPD	24.4	22.2	36.5	28.4	29.0	23.8
Center	13.5	20.7	23.9	38.1	21.8	35.8
NSDAP	25.7	26.3	8.7	6.2	18.9	14.2

Source: Maurice Duverger, *The Political Role of Women* (Paris, 1955), p. 54.

In keeping with the party's newly ordained mass strategy (*Heran an die Massen*), Helene Overlach, elected as a Reichstag deputy in 1928, was again ordered to build a women's movement, this time based on working-class housewives' soup kitchen activism during the great Ruhr and Silesian strike wave of 1927 to 1929. Following the Bolshevik model of organizing women as delegates to local, regional, and national conferences, committees of working women largely replaced the wilting, still mostly cadre-oriented RFMB. This Delegate and Conference Movement endeavored to track unorganized, indifferent or Social Democratic women into the KPD – or at least into one of Münzenberg's mass organizations such as the International Workers Aid (IAH) or the Red Aid (*Rote Hilfe*) for political prisoners and their families. The KPD liked to highlight its success at attracting the unorganized or SPD apostates and to downplay its own leading role; nonetheless, like the RFMB, the Delegate and Conference Movement probably drew women who were themselves, or whose family members were, already close to the party. This was a particularly important task in regions with a predominantly Catholic or religiously mixed population where men were much more likely to vote KPD. Party officials hoped that attention to women's "personal" problems might neutralize opposition, especially from housewives and white-collar workers, who were deemed likely to imagine Communists as godless barbarian cannibals. (*Menschenfresser*).[15]

The party aimed for at least 50 percent participation from female industrial workers at the congresses, of whom 80 percent were to be partyless, with a 20 percent representation from bourgeois and trade union women. Nonetheless, a large number of delegates described themselves as housewives; the most militant female strike participants had not been, as Marxist-Leninist theory prescribed, striking female textile workers, but rather the wives of striking Ruhr workers organized under the auspices of the IAH. Their personal concerns about birth control and abortion and family survival rather than workplace issues dominated the numerous local and regional conferences held from 1929 on. While always affirming that "Without the women, any revolution can be only half a revolution," KPD leaders soon complained that the delegate and conference movement actually only diverted members of the IAH and RH into autonomous women's groups rather than broadening the party's base of support.

A women's program that simultaneously promised "women's liberation from pots and pans" (*Befreiung der Frau vom Kochtopf*) and "protection for mother and child" proved difficult to negotiate. KPD women's organizers strove to maintain a principled commitment to industrial workers while struggling to include working-class housewives and women in less central occupations. They acknowledged that in those areas, such as the Ruhr, where mostly male heavy industries dominated, it was crucial to gain the support of wives and daughters. Moreover, participants at the regular meetings repeatedly noted that women working in the expanding service sector were in many ways a vanguard of the new rationalized labor force. They complained of a killing work pace and low wages, and argued that the lot of young saleswomen and clerical workers was not different, and in some ways worse, than that of the classical industrial worker. Organizers tried to appeal to white-collar workers at large department stores (90 percent of whose employees were female) and even turned their attention to the large category of domestic servants who remained excluded from the republic's growing social insurance programs.

The women's committees published their own journal, *Die Kämpferin* (the woman fighter), which interspersed attacks on the reactionary positions of all other parties and trade unions with reports on women's working conditions, a *Mutter und Kind* section, and inspirational accounts of life in the Soviet workers paradise. The movement's regular conferences offered delegates a rare opportunity to escape workplace and domestic obligations and develop a sense of community and leadership skills, whether debating resolutions, touring the big city of Berlin (and in some cases the Soviet Union), or hiking in the woods.[16] The commitment to all female congresses also helped develop significant national female leadership. Overlach was only one among the proportionately highest number of female delegates to the Reichstag; 17.1 percent versus the SPD's 11.1 percent in 1930. Given that in a system of proportional representation, election depended on a high enough placement on the candidates' list, the relatively high number of women delegates to the national parliament does suggest some significant party support for women's political participation, at least on the level of public representation.[17] The KPD tried to field a broad spectrum of women candidates, carefully identifying them as fitting a whole palette of categories to be organized: housewives, mothers of large families, agricultural laborers, white-collar workers, or unemployed.[18]

Communist appeals to women were also based in large measure on incessant invocation of the heroic Soviet Union and its pioneering family legislation of the late teens and early 1920s.[19] In a kind of revolutionary tourism, German women delegates traveled to a struggling Soviet state, which they presented at their conferences and in their journals as a paragon of hygienic and scientific modernity. Delegates visited children's homes where the workers wore white coats and cared for children in white beds with white sheets, assuring "painstaking cleanliness," and fathers were not allowed to visit their wives and babies in state-run maternity hospitals lest they transmit germs. Eager to disprove stories about hunger and social breakdown, Soviet hosts proudly showed off a factory canteen feeding 35,000 people daily, or the former Singer sewing machine plant in Moscow, where 7,800 workers, including 2,000 women, toiled to fulfill a five-year plan in three or four years, while enjoying a cinema, theater, library, and chess club, not to mention a seven-hour workday (in three shifts) and equal pay for men and women. Women toured exemplary programs to treat venereal disease (not as an embarrassment but as a treatable misfortune), and ingenious night sanatoriums where workers could go for diagnosis, treatment, and rest, after a full day's work, thereby better preserving their fragile labor power. They visited centers for the rehabilitation of prostitutes and prisons where women inmates worked in an adjoining textile factory that even granted breaks for nursing infants. In the former villas of the wealthy, delegates were treated to children singing "Grandfather Lenin shows us the way" and they departed with tears in their eyes, "filled with an iron will to fight in Germany so that our children can also have such homes." In one highly publicized women's tour, the delegates were specifically invited to witness the validity and fairness of one of the first great sabotage trials leading to the purges of the 1930s.[20]

Social Welfare, Sex Reform, and the Abortion Campaign

In propaganda addressed to women, the Soviet Union was especially touted as the first modern nation to legalize safe medical abortions as well as provide comprehensive benefits for the protection of mother and child. Indeed, in many ways, the story of the KPD and the woman question is the story of its uneasy relationship to sexual politics and the call for women's right to control their own bodies. The abolition of Paragraph 218 of the penal code banning most abortions had been raised as a major demand since the party's founding in 1919; it emerged as a central issue for broad organizing among both women and men of all classes. The Women's Commission in party headquarters formulated what would be the standard KPD position throughout the Weimar period: "a society not able to provide women with the material means for motherhood" also had "no right to demand that women take on the cares and burdens derived from motherhood."[21] Sexual politics provided a way for the KPD, always in thrall to Comintern directives from Moscow, both to develop a popular mass strategy (especially in its social welfare organizations) and to propagandize the virtues of the Soviet Union.

Having launched a new and distinct women's movement, and faced with SPD strength during the period of relative stabilization, the KPD was poised in 1928 for further new initiatives that could broaden its appeal and distinguish it from a reformist SPD. The KPD proceeded to follow a dual policy of, on the one hand, separate organization of activist women (such as the RFMB and the Delegate and Conference Movement) and, on the other hand, mixed mass (i.e., front) organizations such as the IAH. The latter specifically focused on social welfare, did not try to identify as workers' groups, and therefore attracted many women as well as progressive professionals and intellectuals of both sexes otherwise skeptical of rigid party dogma. Links to groups such as Helene Stöcker's League for the Protection of Motherhood and Sex Reform and various popular leagues campaigning for birth control and sex education also connected Communist activists to eclectic initiatives for lifestyle reform, (*Lebensreform*) ranging from food reform, anti-immunization and graphology, to natural health, athletics, and modernist housing projects.

At the same moment, therefore, that the party was encouraging the Women's Delegate and Conference Movement, it also actively joined the ranks of the Sex Reform movement and its calls for legal abortion and broad popular access to birth control and sex education. The Working Group of Social Political Organizations (*Arbeitsgemeinschaft sozialpolitischer Organisationen*, ARSO), another brainchild of the KPD's mass organizing genius Willi Münzenberg, was a subgroup (with partially overlapping membership) of the IAH. Under Münzenberg's charismatic leadership, the IAH functioned as a kind of KPD auxiliary for intellectuals and a broad range of women unwilling to join the party and uncomfortable with party discipline, but eager to support causes as diverse as freedom for the "Scottsboro boys" jailed on lynching charges in the American South, sex and birth control counseling centers, and the drive against Paragraph 218. Composed primarily of professionals and intellectuals and led by two KPD Reichstag deputies, Martha Arendsee and Siegfried Rädel, ARSO became the primary KPD representative in social welfare and abortion reform campaigns.[22]

Arendsee (1885 to 1953), like many female party stalwarts, was a veteran of the working-class movement. The daughter of a Social Democratic printer, the young Arendsee devoured August Bebel's 1879 book on women in socialism and other modern and pseudo-scientific classics such as Ernst Haeckel's eugenic tracts. At age fourteen, she went to work as a bookkeeper in a factory, a quintessentially female occupation (and one that would be frequently represented in Weimar proletarian literature and film). But when she officially joined the socialist cause at age twenty-one in December 1906 and subscribed to the SPD women's paper, *Die Gleichheit* (Equality), she kept her serious involvement secret from her committed socialist father who did not believe women should be politically active. Many of her female KPD comrades, hardened in the distinctly woman-unfriendly smoky tavern culture of the imperial SPD, would tell similar stories. For these *Kaiserreich* veterans, the lifting of the Prussian Law on Association in 1908 marked a crucial opening to the public world of party and trade union politics.

Further radicalized by the carnage of World War I, Arendsee was arrested in 1915 for her antiwar activities. In 1919 she was elected to the Prussian Landtag and from then on she defined herself as a professional politician, a calling that obviously suited her much better than all her previous white-collar positions (where she had been victimized, as she later remembered, by sexual harassment). As a Reichstag deputy from 1924 to 1930, she led the KPD's unsuccessful efforts to expand maternal protection and abolish Paragraph 218. From 1930 until 1933 she served as editor of the ARSO journal and on the central committee of the IAH. Following a typical trajectory, she fled to Moscow in 1934.[23]

With the advent of extreme economic crisis in 1929, the KPD was reluctantly forced to recognize that much of its core constituency was now unemployed, spending more time waiting on line at welfare and unemployment offices than working on the production line, the proper site of organizing according to Communist theory. Indeed, mass unemployment and social despair fed Communist organizing.[24] By the fateful Reichstag elections of September 1930, which catapulted the National Socialists into political prominence, KPD vote totals were rising again (77 delegates), as they would continue to through the last free November 1932 elections (100 delegates). Communists gained 12.5 percent of male and 7.3 percent of female voters, compared to 21.8 percent male and 35.8 percent women for the Center, and 29 percent male and 23.8 percent women for the SPD. All three parties were now severely challenged by the National Socialists and their share of about 18.9 percent of the male and 14.2 percent of the female electorate. These figures were highly variable by region as well as by age: In Red Berlin's 1930 Reichstag elections, the Nazis collected 15.2 percent of the male vote and 14.1 percent of the female vote; the SPD 26.8 percent of men and 27.7 percent of women, with a large chunk of especially young men and women voting for the KPD, 31 and 24 percent respectively.[25] While the KPD clearly benefitted from male working class disillusionment with the SPD, it continued to be frustrated by a persistent gender differential at the polls, which was considerably higher than for other parties and sometimes over 20 percent.[26]

The February 1931 arrest of two physicians, Else Kienle and the playwright and KPD member Friedrich Wolf, on charges of violating Paragraph 218 offered the party – with a membership still at only about 200,000 – a situation tailor-made for Münzenberg's "Alliance Politics" of collaboration with special interest groups, such as intellectuals, youth, or women, who were understood to be theoretically and organizationally marginal to the class struggle, but electorally useful. By unequivocally calling for abolition of Paragraph 218, the KPD presented itself as ethical and principled and scored propaganda points over the waffling SPD, which sanctioned all kinds of exceptions and extenuating circumstances but insisted on keeping an abortion ban on the books – if only to protect women against irresponsible men trying to escape their paternal obligations.[27]

The militance and momentum of the anti-218 campaign, the attention from the media, and the broad appeal to women of all classes provided a space for highly public and pointedly feminist interventions unique in the history of the Weimar left. A politics of *Dein Körper Gehört Dir* had not been a standard part of political, medical, or eugenic arguments for abortion, but it slipped into the Communist-led struggle in 1931 and managed temporarily to disrupt, if not displace, the dominance of class struggle politics and a consensus on the importance of eugenic health and responsible motherhood. Thus, the KPD rather inadvertently found itself in the vanguard of a movement that linked woman's economic and political emancipation with the right to control her own body and that spoke for all women, not just the most oppressed and downtrodden.

The anti-218 campaign also allowed the party to combine a broad appeal to women with the militarization of imagery and rhetoric generally characteristic of left-wing working-class politics in the interwar period. In the huge anti-218 rallies, women could partially claim and partially counter-balance the KPD's infatuation with militant spectacle.[28] While women did not participate in the street-fighting culture of some young KPD toughs, they did appropriate the language of struggle, for example in the title of the cadre paper, *Die Kämpferin*, or in the array of "battle" or "action" committees formed to fight for the doctors' release and against Paragraph 218.

The initial successes of the Women's Delegate and Conference Movement and the anti-218 campaign only highlighted the contradictions of KPD women's and reproductive politics. By raising the slogan, "Your Body Belongs to You" and by waging a lonely battle in the Reichstag for complete decriminalization of abortion, the KPD broke the bounds of its own class analysis. Implicitly, if rather nervously, it defended even a bourgeois woman's right to choose abortion for personal reasons not directly connected to dire material need. Rather astounded by the militant women's movement it had encouraged, and clearly discomfited by the recurrent challenges to the primacy of its economic analysis, the KPD trod a delicate line between feminist and class politics, trying desperately both to sustain a commitment to abortion rights and to subsume that commitment within the principal working-class struggle.

Yet, ideological ambivalence notwithstanding, it remains a noteworthy political fact that the one instance in its history when the KPD successfully attracted and mobilized masses of usually skeptical women came with a campaign for abortion rights – the topic that so many communist and socialist parties and reform groups have been wary of, for fear of alienating the masses.[29] Abortion politics also offered female leadership an opportunity to gain importance and visibility beyond the confines of the separate women's conference movement. Helene Overlach, the veteran party organizer, who had first complained that, "Again and again, for weeks, months, years, until it made us retch, we did the abortion paragraph," experienced some of her proudest moments during the 1931 campaign. Five months pregnant, she fought for the right to be the party's main speaker at a huge rally in April. "This is, after all, a women's question; I can do this better than a male comrade," she insisted, and won her point.[30] Orthodox cadres worried about possible dilution of class politics soon reasserted their power, but in the winter of 1931, the majority seized the chance to humanize the party by addressing women both as mothers and as "new women."

New Women, Proletarian Mothers, and the
Sexual Struggle of Youth

The KPD's representational politics on gender, as conveyed most dra-
matically in the 1931 abortion campaign, can be read as both intriguingly
flexible and hopelessly contradictory. The Soviet-style tractor driver
heroine of labor coexisted with the oppressed but stoic and loving mother
displayed in posters by Käthe Kollwitz and the fresh faced, physically fit
young girl in sports outfit with bobbed hair but no makeup. In Münzenberg's illustrated press, especially the *AIZ* (Workers Illustrated News magazine), and films, Soviet women generally appeared as tough soldiers or
industrial laborers; Germans were more likely to surface as oppressed
mothers or flighty white-collar workers who needed, like the protagonists
in the films *Kuhle Wampe* or *Mutter Krause's Fahrt ins Glück*, to be seduced
and properly disciplined by class-conscious male workers. Communist
cultural products therefore proffered a diverse array of images and connotations: the valorization of the long suffering mother alongside distrust
of the housewife as backward and politically unreliable; calls for women
to move out from the isolating slavery of domestic drudgery; fearful contempt for women who succumbed to the temptations of commercial
entertainment and consumption.[31]

Especially Münzenberg's alternative popular culture empire of publishing houses, newspapers, and the Prometheus film company, which
produced *Kuhle Wampe* in the summer of 1931, appealed to (and tried to
discipline) an audience of new women white-collar workers as well as
harassed mothers and housewives – both groups presumed to be immersed
in mass, rather than class, culture, impressed more by Americanism than
Bolshevism, and vulnerable to the so-called distractions of commercial
consumer culture such as the cinema.[32] Illustrated journals offered consumer and fashion news as well as serialized novels like Franz Krey's lurid
anti-218 melodrama about the consequences of a stenotypist's botched
abortion, *Maria und der Paragraph*, directed at female readers presumably
accustomed to a mass circulation literary diet of romance, crime, and
tragedy. That the KPD was ambivalent about these appeals is clear; the
"petty bourgeois romanticism" of young white-collar workers was
described as " … Salesgirls, seamstresses, spinning / golden fairy tales of
luck and the wages of true love / … Beautiful girls ceaselessly follow the
pictures and swallow in the lies."[33] Hortatory images of Soviet women on
tractors, fit sportswomen, and competent rationalized jugglers of the double burden, competed for space with victims of the "shameful paragraph"
and pert white-collar workers at the movies.

With party journals divided into those designed for cadre (*Die
Kämpferin* for women) and for mass circulation, Münzenberg's *Arbeiter*

Illustrierte Zeitung (Workers Illustrated Newspaper, *AIZ*) and its little sister, *Der Weg der Frau* (launched during the 218 campaign in 1931) offered recipes for nutritious and economical meals, medical advice, patterns for sewing one's own clothes, tips on home repairs ("The woman as electrician – practical help for the household")[34] and how to do housework without expensive appliances. These columns were accompanied by the inevitable comparisons with happy workers' families in the Soviet Union.[35] The communist press propagandized the modern rationalized woman, nimble and cost-effective at both home and the workplace. The "triple reproductive burden" of childbearing, child rearing, and housework would be lightened by a technological solution to the "petty slavery of housework" in communal kitchens or laundries, or at least by greater efficiency in individual housework.

Mass unemployment during the Depression forced new attention to gender roles; Communist journals chastised chauvinistic comrades for being philistines only superficially covered in red (*rotangestrichene Spiesser*) in their private lives and prodded husbands with time on their hands to pitch in with the housework so their wives would also have some time for political activity. Such comradely help did not, however, fundamentally alter the sexual division of labor within the family, as illustrated in a typical plot line for "A Day in the Life" of a proletarian Berlin family, as portrayed in an IAH film strip. The husband leaves home for meetings of the Communist trade union opposition, while his wife's political involvement begins when, after "mending everybody's stockings ... she has a short hour's rest and is glad that she can finally sit still a little after all the day's drudgery," and read "the great women's magazine *Weg der Frau*, which every working-class woman must read." If, the text adds, she later "talks to the other tenants about a way out of the misery of the proletarian life, she too contributes her share in the struggle against the oppressors."[36] Another classic example of Communist notions of companionate marriage was an entry in the 1932 *Workers Calendar*: "Common Life, Common Struggle" captioned a photo of a man sitting at a kitchen table reading the KPD daily *Rote Fahne* (Red Flag), while a woman wearing an apron stands at the stove, stirring a pot, and glancing over at him and his newspaper![37]

Such examples from working-class movements have by now been documented and commented on so often as to become trite and predictable.[38] Nevertheless, they provide context for KPD gender and sexual politics. Communists perceived the political implications of the double burden and women's heavy responsibility for family survival. But they resisted any basic reconceptualization of the family or gender relations. The KPD's primary target was not the family or the sexual division of labor within the family but the hypocrisy of bourgeois morality and the social and economic conditions that threatened the well-being of the proletarian family. As with plans for reformed sexual relations which, depended on improved contraception and medical abortions, the proposed solution was mechanistic. The alternative to the double day was not to push women out of the workforce and "back into the home" but to "liberate them from the cooking pot" and ease their "burden as housewife and mother by shifting to communal and technically advanced living and household conditions." Especially necessary, of course, was "rational birth control."[39] The party never retreated from defending women's right to work, but it also never questioned women's primary responsibility as mother and housewife. The new Bolshevik woman presented in the play *Nora 1932* would be "A new type … that will have nothing in common with either the emancipated woman or the comely little housewife," and who could appreciate technology's potential to lighten traditional tasks and stabilize daily life.[40]

In contrast to their intended constituents, prominent party women's leaders led the privileged lives of Weimar new women, often in companionate marriages with male leaders. The elite of the Communist movement enjoyed a comfortable lifestyle in the avant garde milieu of large cities. They knew each other, often lived in comfortable "red" apartment blocks, and earned their living as intellectuals or white-collar workers (editors, journalists, translators, secretaries) for the party. Some, like Martha Arendsee, had been socialized into the working-class movement through the tight SPD subculture of the *Kaiserreich*. Others grew up in the Jewish bourgeoisie (*Bildungsbürgertum*), and reported being radicalized by personal struggles for autonomy, education, and professional advancement. Their sense of social outrage was initially driven by direct contacts with the lower classes, whether with the servants in their own families or their engagement as doctors, teachers, or social workers in proletarian neighborhoods. If working-class women were likely to have grown up in the social democratic labor movement, rebellious middle-class daughters turned Communist often credited the bourgeois women's movement and the openings it provided for education and work; several took advantage of pioneering high school courses in Berlin which prepared women for the graduation exams (*Abitur*) and opened the door to university and especially medical study. Unlike their less radical bourgeois sisters, many of these women gave up full-time studies (often in medicine or pedagogy) in favor of professional political work in party bureaucracy and propaganda.

Frieda Düwell, daughter of an orthodox Jewish family, described in her party memoir how, chafing at religious and sex discrimination, she came to prefer international communism to the parochialism of bourgeois feminism: "Now she belonged to a cause that advocated for all to whom injustice was done: women, Jews, Negroes, workers. That was much simpler ... than belonging to lots of different associations." After the war, she remembered her "lovely four-room apartment with garden at the corner of Kurfürstendamm near Halensee, a long way from the Rosenthaler Strasse," where she worked in the central party offices in the dilapidated eastern Berlin Scheunenviertel district.[41]

Women and girls integrated into the urban Communist subculture were able to live a life quite different from the downtrodden proletarian *Alltag* they protested. They later remembered with nostalgia happy weeks spent in a relaxed atmosphere at a party training camp in the Berlin suburb of Fichtenau, swimming in the nearby Müggelsee, studying and playing. (A favorite game was role playing where one character had to impersonate the SA.) As the artist Lea Gründig reported in her memoir, such seminars, even where women were in the minority, were a wonderful antidote to the grind of living on the dole while doing party work. In the morning one studied Marxism-Leninism, sometimes with much admired Soviet comrades; in the afternoon one did one's assignments and practiced public argument and speaking; and in the evening, "One got together, put together the relief pennies, and celebrated modest orgies with cheap *Schnaps* and a gramophone."[42]

As part of its effort to reach beyond its primary constituency of workers, the KPD experimented with both new sexual ethics and utopian visions of new women and new men. Contending with the vaunted Weimar generation gap as well as working-class attraction to mass consumer culture, Communist youth groups sought support by engaging "the sexual struggle of youth." Assisted by doctor and lawyer advisers (including but certainly not limited to Wilhelm Reich) they worked to meet urban young people's concrete needs for sex advice, contraceptives, abortion, and protection from repressive parents and state agencies. Like bourgeois and clerical critics of modern mass culture, leftist reformers professed disapproval of sexual licentiousness, but they did so in different terms (on which they hardly agreed). Far from seeing in organized youth groups a haven for immorality, they welcomed their emphasis on physical fitness and comradely relations between the sexes as an antidote to the "wild cliques" of unorganized urban youth culture and the turmoil of adolescence.

The official KPD position was influenced by Lenin's famous conversation with Clara Zetkin, in which he urged her to use the maternal influence of the women's movement to assure that communist youth spent their time swimming, hiking, and doing gymnastics rather than expending energy discussing or engaging in sex, thereby falling victim to what he saw as a fad being pushed by bourgeois party intellectuals trying to justify their own "overheated sexuality." In a 1926 leaflet, "Lenin Calls All

Working Women," the KPD recirculated the discussion in which Lenin professed astonishment upon hearing that Communist women in Hamburg had taken up organizing prostitutes and asked plaintively, "Are there in Germany really no female industrial workers whom one could organize?" In a further sign of anxiety about the appeal of sex reform journals with their exotic and illicit themes, Lenin complained: "There must really be more prominent problems than the marriage forms of the Australian aborigines or incest in ancient times.[43]

By the early 1930s, however, sex reformers in, or close to, the KPD were stretching the definitions of healthy and natural to include adolescent sexual activity as preferable to masturbation or initiation by prostitutes, and indeed as useful for building satisfying companionate adult relationships.[44] The film *Kuhle Wampe*, produced in 1931 at the height of anti-218 agitation, juxtaposed images of the working-class father, hanging on to petty bourgeois morality and threatening his daughter, newly in love with a handsome young worker, ("If anything happens, I'll beat your brains out") even as he himself reads aloud from semipornographic trash literature. And when Anni is helped by comrades in the local Communist youth group, the message is clear: the party will not only undertake campaigns against Paragraph 218 but will also provide concrete, illegal aid in case of unwanted pregnancy.[45] For young activists like Anni, the IAH offered birth control counseling as well as instruction in "proper proletarian behavior" designed to help achieve a balance between personal desire and party discipline (and how to handle problems like jealousy).[46]

Young women were more likely to join the coeducational Communist youth movement (KJVD) than the social welfare oriented women's groups. They gathered in sports associations and for evening classes at the MASCH (Marxist school), where by 1930/31, 4,000 students worked with 160 instructors, including Wilhelm Reich, in a kind of family atmosphere that provided social as well as educational and political experiences.[47] Children of Communist leaders attended the progressive Karl Marx private school established in 1919 in Neukölln, which like the experimental boarding school Odenwaldschule, offered a core curriculum based on experiential learning featuring open discussion, student self-government, no formal examinations, cooperative work and much outdoors activity. Youth activist Erna Nelki who remembered going to "sex doctor" Max Hodann for advice and a diaphragm when she and her comrade boyfriend wanted to consummate their relationship, described the collapse of their world when the Communist schools and community centers were forcibly closed and the students who rallied to protest were beaten and chased away by the SA: "For us, this was incomprehensible. We had lived in a world in which we had believed that the revolution and a socialist community was realizable in the foreseeable future ..."[48]

Members of Communist youth groups and female KPD leadership as well as the spouses of male leaders lived therefore in a world of multiple contradictions. Women faced the continued strict sexual division of labor within the household and the difficulties of nurturing relationships and raising children while maintaining a primary commitment to political work that frequently necessitated prolonged family separations. Sometimes they skirmished with their Social Democratic domestic servants. Female activists also confronted the gap between women's assignment to the "social" sphere and the party's valorization of militance and even street fighting, especially in the early and late periods of the republic. Finally, they had to face the drastic break between an essentially secure if hectic life in the German republic and the horror of repression and exile that followed.

Communist Radicalism and the Crisis of Late Weimar

Paradoxically, the breakdown of traditional working-class and family structures and the extreme precariousness of the welfare state in late Weimar created space for radical innovation by the left, especially in the sexual struggles of youth and women. Conventional politics seemed increasingly out of control and a bitterly divided left saw the Nazis exploit a virtually unbroken stream of public exposure and activity. Yet, in the face of spiraling unemployment and with some urban neighborhoods settling into a state of virtual civil war between Nazis and Communists, Berlin became more "red." By the last Weimar election in November 1932, nearly one third of the Berlin electorate voted Communist, and the KPD gained a majority in nine proletarian districts; the Communists were the strongest party in the capital.[49] Even in Catholic Cologne the 1932 elections brought the KPD 29.0 percent of the male and 20.0 percent of the female voters compared with 18.6 percent and 16.4 percent respectively for the SPD.[50]

With the release of Wolf and Kienle from prison and the waning of the abortion struggle in early summer 1931, the KPD began to search for new recruits among the restless lost generation of Depression youth, especially youngsters in foster care or reformatories or in trouble with youth welfare authorities. The party tried to appeal to young people (especially male) on the wrong side of the law, in the cliques that competed with organized youth groups, even to those with ties to the underworld, and to the street fighters associated with the SA and the Communist Red Front.[51] Unlike the SPD, the KPD was willing to engage in illegal acts such as forcible prevention of evictions, armed self-defense, the protection of runaway adolescents and referrals for illegal abortions. At the same time that cadre politics became more rigid and defensive, ever more tightly committed to attacking Social Democrats as well as Nazis, Münzenberg's front organizations appealed to antifascist intellectuals and professionals and fostered a vibrant communist counterculture.

The intensified focus on youth and sexuality followed the collapse of the 218 campaign, in certain ways substituting for further mass organizing of women. Unable (and unwilling) to sustain the momentum and promise of the movement to free Wolf and Kienle, the KPD was nonetheless still impressed by the continuing appeal of the lay leagues and the powerful resonance of the abortion issue. Moreover, the campaign's demonstrated potential for a powerful mass women's movement posed a fundamental and ultimately insoluble problem for the KPD. Always leery of women's separatism and its association with bourgeois feminism, the party leadership feared losing control over the strong, broad-based, and potentially autonomous women's movement that its support of alliance politics had helped to create.

Communist activists like Helene Overlach had set into motion masses of women with no long-term strategy for organizing them and no structures into which they could be absorbed. Overlach had slowly developed into an ardent advocate of separate organizing for women within the party. She defended the coffee and cake afternoons, where women talked, sang, or read poetry, against party leaders who mistrusted such get-togethers as petty bourgeois, SPD deviationism, or simply a waste of time. Carrying her guitar, she canvassed the dark courtyards of working-class Berlin with homemade brochures because she considered the official ones unsatisfactory. Overlach was keenly aware of the tension between the tactics useful for first attracting women and those required for the more difficult job of organizing them and containing their energy once they had been mobilized. "One has to hang on to them, after all," she fretted, as she confronted the dilemma of simultaneously taking women's daily struggles seriously and suggesting they were not really so important. She could pull masses of women to an abortion rights or International Women's Day demonstration, but the move into party cadre, where reproductive and social welfare issues were again subordinated, was too long a leap for most new recruits. Wilhelm Pieck, her direct superior, criticized her nonauthoritarian approach as indecisive.

Organizer Overlach was herself hard-pressed to resolve the contradictions between the personal and the political in her own life. Determined to have a child, she finally became pregnant at age thirty-seven, just as the abortion campaign was heating up. Unmarried and deeply involved in her political work, she was nonetheless convinced that as a mother she would be better able to reach the constituency of working-class women she wanted to organize. But she became so ill during her difficult pregnancy that she was forced to withdraw from her leadership position in the mass campaign. Later, Overlach blamed the dissipation of the anti-218 movement on her illness: "Unfortunately, because I had a baby, the work did not progress," she remembered, barely aware of the irony implied by her words. It was surely no accident that the Central Committee packed this most visible women's leader off to Moscow to work for the Comintern in the summer of 1931 just when the women's committees might have invigorated the faltering abortion campaign. Loyal as always, Overlach went to the Soviet Union, still recovering from her pregnancy, with a two-month-old infant, and speaking not a word of Russian.[52] Without strong leadership and party support, the Women's Delegate and Conference Movement, which had been so central to the anti-218 campaign and might have provided a political home for women politicized by the abortion struggle, gradually disintegrated, a victim of anxiety about separatism and women's lack of solid connection to the industrial proletariat.

The Delegate and Conference movement's apparent success in reaching housewives, in raising personal consciousness and fostering community, was also its downfall. In a familiar repetitive pattern of self-criticism at insufficient organizing successes followed by exhortations to do better at fulfilling dictates of party policy, KPD leaders excoriated the Delegate and Conference Movement for defying the principles of democratic centralism, for not attending enough to female workers, for building a movement that was simply too broad! Worst of all, the movement intended to organize the unorganized had grown so quickly that leadership was being entrusted to women who had not yet themselves joined the party and hence were more likely to build autonomous women's groups rather than the desirable workplace cells. KPD leaders feared that they might have spawned a separatist movement vulnerable to the seductive blandishments of bourgeois feminism.[53]

Any considerable success at mobilizing women, especially nonworkers, provoked ambivalence in the KPD leadership. The "Criticism Corner" of *Die Kämpferin* pointedly published a letter complaining, "What should I do with this paper? There's always only stuff about the workplace in it and after all, I don't have anything to do with that anymore. And on the other hand, there's nothing about household matters ...." But it also warned that "it is precisely these women [housewives] who are first of all themselves most alienated from all activity, and who secondly also hinder the man in his party work."[54] Rosa Meyer-Leviné, the wife of a central committee member, recalled:

> Once I was carried away by the sight of a large demonstration. "Too many housewives, women, youngsters," Ernst coolly remarked. "What is wrong with women and youngsters," I asked slightly piqued. "Nothing. But for the revolution we need factory workers, organized in a party or at least in trade unions."[55]

In a retreat from the coalition organizing so successful in the anti-218 campaign, and in defiance of all previous experience, the KPD rigidly tried to reinstate the workplace as the center of organizing efforts. The collapse of the KPD anti-218 women's movement must therefore be understood in the context of the party's ambivalence toward women's politics. Despite the repeated exhortations to organize them, women, especially housewives, were distrusted as unreliable voters and conservative influences on their Communist husbands. Somewhat like the *Lumpenproletariat*, women were suspect as an overly spontaneous, undisciplined, potentially dangerous anarchic mass that had to be organized and disciplined. They were considered a dormant mass, ready to be awakened, which however, once roused, needed to be channeled into proper and appropriate paths; their energies harnessed and disciplined. In the party's view, women like men, should be organized at the point of production; even if concessions were made to the peculiarities of women's situation, it was still expected that women workers would best understand and respond to KPD analysis of the double burden. In fact, however, working-class housewives had proved easier to organize than women workers, a circumstance that should not have surprised anyone familiar with the hectic and exhausting daily life of a married woman worker.[56]

In October 1931, at the height of Depression retrenchments, the KPD Reichstag faction had introduced an ambitious but utterly unrealistic "Protective Program for the Working Woman," which sought to combine its maternalist and women's rights agenda. Radically extending the demands of the abortion campaign, it called for women's complete economic, social, cultural, and political equality; equal pay for equal work; no employment discrimination against married women or mothers; full social insurance for all working women; no dismissals up to one year after childbirth; full legal rights for married women, with equal parental control over children; equal rights for illegitimate children and unwed mothers; the right to be called *Frau*, regardless of marital status; and finally, state funding for medical abortions and the abolition of Paragraph 218 with amnesty for all those previously convicted.

While the program was nominally aimed at working women, it contained numerous demands that applied to all women, thus acknowledging their special status as social glue and casual breadwinners at a time of skyrocketing unemployment. In its calls for protection of women's employment and insurance rights, the KPD also recognized that women, especially married "double earners," were particularly victimized by employer and state responses to the economic crisis. Communists understood quite clearly that futile attempts to combat male unemployment by pushing women out of a tightly sex-segregated labor market worked not so much to eliminate women workers but to deny them the benefits accorded "full" workers. They remained responsible for maintaining a precarious family sub-economy that might include "off the books" casual labor, taking in boarders, raising rabbits on the roof and foodstuffs in the family garden, negotiating the welfare system, and finding bargains through community gossip networks.[57]

By February 1932, over six million people were officially counted as unemployed; there was barely a working-class family that was not somehow affected. The KPD was the only party that staunchly defended married women's right to work. In the pages of *Die Kämpferin*, the party attacked the SPD and the trade unions for selling out women workers and insisted on women's right to their jobs. Significantly, the justification was not only the expected stress on the necessity of women's wage labor during hard times, but a ringing defense of women's basic claim to independence and self-fulfillment in employment:

> The proletarian woman is gradually freeing herself from bourgeois notions about the family in which the woman is supposed to be dependant on and subject to the husband, and coming to the healthy insight that she must be man's equal in every respect, in order to be independent economically and as a human being.[58]

The article went on to berate majority socialist trade union officials for not taking the promise of "equal pay for equal work" seriously enough and for yielding to the spurious argument that women were stealing men's jobs. Sarcastically, *Die Kämpferin* asked whether they "wanted to organize the struggle of men against women. After all, that would be the first struggle that they ever bothered to organize – but it's certainly not one that is in the interest of the working class." As with the call for "Your Body Belongs to You," the KPD floated calls for women's liberation that transcended its own more hesitant practice.

After the successes of 1931, female membership declined, even as party strength in general was gaining, probably in response to the shift in focus back to cadre issues as well as escalating militarization and valorization of street fighting culture. The mass organization IAH, with a total membership of 55,635 in 1931 (many of them women), became an even more important site for women's organizing.[59] Indeed, a disillusioned Clara Zetkin, still an important figurehead for the KPD, wrote from Moscow to her young protegée Maria Reese (that prized commodity, a convert from the SPD), urging her to join the Women's Committee (*Frauenrat*) of the IAH as a more congenial alternative to the party itself.[60] The IAH, therefore, simultaneously offered women a "room of their own" within the KPD, and contributed to their continuing marginalization – only briefly challenged by the anti-218 campaign – into social welfare and domestic arenas. At the same time, central party directives continually entreated women's organizers to improve efforts at the work-place and among the unemployed.

Total party membership in 1923 was supposedly 267,000, down to 120,000 in September 1930, and then up again to about 200,000 in 1931. Still, these figures need to be kept in relative perspective; in red Berlin-Brandenburg the percentage of female party members grew from 18 per-cent to 20 percent between September and November 1932, even as the party scored impressive (but, of course, insufficient compared to the National Socialist juggernaught) totals of over five million votes in the July 1932 presidential election and almost six million in the November 1932 Reichstag election.

Sensing renewed opportunity in the deep crisis of 1932, the KPD lead-ership called for a campaign to recruit 100,000 new members, of whom 30 percent were to be women, including 33 percent industrial workers. The continual admonitions from the top to increase propaganda and organizing work among women and to intensify efforts to run them for party office did not, however, seem to have had much effect on the ground. The repetitive Leninist incantation that "a revolution without women is only half a revolution" could not conceal that the most effec-tive tactics around issues of daily reproduction were being discredited and abandoned. Nonetheless, the very call, unyielding and unrealistic as it was, for a quota of one-third female representation in the party, was indeed a revolutionary vision, certainly when compared to the rest of the political spectrum.[61]

National Socialist Triumph and Communist Resistance

In the last stages of the Weimar Republic, neither the KPD nor SPD nor the working-class movement in general were able to defend their own culture or the existing social welfare state. The party insisted that major attention be paid to industrial workers and the male unemployed at the very time that more and more women, even those previously employed, had been excluded from the restrictive unemployment compensation sys-tem and were identifying again as harassed housewives.[62] Party activists were never able to maneuver properly the tensions between a rigid ideo-logical commitment to workplace organizing and the primacy of the industrial proletariat with the Weimar realities of mass unemployment and a burgeoning white-collar sector. Nor were they able to reconcile the dual demands of building a united front against fascism while keeping up angry attacks on the SPD. The non-street fighting social welfare branches of the party were reduced to documenting and minimally alle-viating social misery and the emergency decrees that only exacerbated its impact. The third and last Congress of Working Women met in Berlin in the spring of 1932; under the banner "Against Hunger, Fascism, War," the party offered half-hearted directives to mobilize proletarian housewives in the markets, department stores, and welfare agencies.[63] Women were recruited with calls for peace, but in keeping with the ongoing militarization of party activity in the last years of the Republic, they were encouraged to participate in decidedly unpacific activities such as weapons training, the better to help protect the Soviet Union in a projected imperialist war.

At the very last minute, in a militant return to neighborhood organizing, women were organized as vigilantes to monitor Nazi activity or to help resist evictions in working-class communities. Women organizers were instructed to exploit every misfortune, eviction, death after abortion, suicide, occupational accident, pensions cut, and tax increase on necessities such as salt as propaganda opportunities. They were finally called on to focus on the Nazi threat rather than the "social fascist" one by seeking to expose the hollowness of Nazi pledges to "save the family" even as severe cutbacks under Chancellors Papen and Schleicher all further undermined family welfare. Faced with the all-important 1932 presidential elections, KPD women demanded "Work, Bread, Freedom, and Equality," and tried to position Hindenburg as the inevitable trailblazer for, rather than alternative to, Adolf Hitler.[64]

This hectic activity notwithstanding, a divided left and a demoralized working class could not stop the Nazi onslaught. After Hitler's triumph as Chancellor in late January 1933, the Reichstag fire the night of 27 February 1933, led to the outlawing of the KPD, and arrest or swift moves into the underground for many activists. Others headed for the borders of France and Czechoslovakia and to the Soviet Union. Welfare organizations such as the IAH and the *Rote Hilfe*, which helped prisoners of the Nazis and their families, and underground Communist sports groups initially tried to carry on, taking directives from exile leadership in Paris. At least through 1934, women also continued to gather in small informal groups to hear lectures on birth control and to distribute contraceptives.[65] KPD operatives tried to maintain control over distribution and prevent "inexperienced" women from taking over the leadership. At the same time, missives from exile criticized the lack of effort devoted to infiltrating mass Nazi women's organizations and the inability to exploit purportedly widespread outrage – especially among women – over sexual excesses in youth organizations, such as the large number of pregnancies among girls who attended League of German Girls (BDM) camps. Communists who had been attacked for their sexual Bolshevism now fulminated against heterosexual licentiousness in the girls' organizations and against homosexual perversion "under the whip of sadistic and homosexual youth leaders" in the Hitler Youth. Communist freethinkers who had been attacked as godless propagators of promiscuity now dreamt of organizing women against the Nazi "subversion of the family."[66] But these efforts could not be sustained as the Communist underground organization was systematically rounded up and incarcerated.

Repression, Exile, and Resistance

Leading Communists, including those most prominently associated with sex reform or women's politics such as Friedrich Wolf and Martha Arendsee, fled to the Soviet Union or went underground. Despite their increasing unease at the ongoing trials and purges in the 1930s, many still looked to the Soviet Union as the source of the great social and political experiment that had inspired them to envision a new "race" of sexually and socially healthy women and men, and as the last best hope for defeating a murderous fascism that was ravaging Germany, Italy, and Spain.

Helene Overlach, the former leader of the KPD women's movement against Paragraph 218, returned to Germany in 1933 from her Comintern assignment in Moscow to join underground resistance efforts. In her memoirs, she poignantly described her toddler's reaction to the young woman at the train station who was to pose as her mother on the journey across the border to safety with comrades in Switzerland. The little girl began to weep when told, "This is now your Mutti; after all, in a situation typical of the conspiratorial life shared by the young children of resisters, this was already her third or fourth mother." Overlach moved in and out of Nazi jails; mother and child were briefly reunited in 1942 when the by then ten-year-old returned to Germany only to witness her mother's transport to the women's concentration camp, Ravensbrück; the child had to inform comrades and make sure that money and contraband material were hidden. The girl was placed in a children's home, and Overlach, who had been so insistent on bearing a child despite all the obstacles presented by party work, did not see her until after the war had ended.[67]

This separation from children and family was a fate she shared with many of her comrades in the KPD and sex reform movement, especially as they faced imprisonment and exile. Party activist Franziska Rubens remembered the conflicts KPD women experienced in relation to their own mothering even as they fought in and out of parliament for the protection of women and children and women's right to resist "coercive motherhood." She cited a conversation she had with the revered Socialist and Communist women's leader Clara Zetkin about another period of exile when the SPD was temporarily banned in Second Empire Germany:

So one day I asked her [Zetkin] a question that very much occupied not only me but many of the female comrades: do revolutionaries have the right to have children? With her response she freed me once and for all from all doubts. "Of course they have not only the right but even the duty. Do you know that it was Rosa (Luxemburg's) greatest sorrow that she could not have children? But one thing is decisive, you must raise them to total independence." And then Clara told me of the difficult years she spent in exile in Paris, and how she had lived there, despite the greatest difficulties, with her children. I thought about this advice from comrade Zetkin at many times in my life, I followed it, and it helped me to endure with my own children, the difficult years of illegality, emigration and evacuation [from Moscow during the war].[68]

German Communists fleeing Nazi terror faced increasing disillusionment and repression in the Soviet Union. Arrests had begun after the assassination of Kirov, the moderate and popular Leningrad party chief in December 1934, and culminated in the terror of the show trials beginning in August 1936. Despite revived hopes tied to the new Soviet constitution, repression intensified, and "the first large wave of arrests of Germans" came in the summer and fall of 1936; they coincided with Stalin's recriminalization of abortion.[69] For many Communists committed to sex reform and women's emancipation, the recriminalization of abortion in the USSR in 1936, via the decree "In Defense of Mother and Child," produced shock and confusion similar to that which the Nazi-Soviet Pact brought their comrades three years later. The most noted KPD campaigner for abortion rights, Martha Ruben-Wolf, committed suicide in 1939 in the Soviet Union she had so zealously propagandized. She had unsuccessfully protested the 1936 abortion decree, and in 1938 her husband Dr. Lothar Wolf (among many other of her German comrades) had been purged and sentenced as an anti-Soviet spy.[70] Reporting on the death of Martha Ruben-Wolf, Susanne Leonhard, a Communist activist who spent long years in Stalin's Gulag, bitterly remembered her dismay at what she perceived as the Soviet about-face:

> Friedrich's Wolf's [anti-218 drama] *Cyankali* was our propaganda piece with which we won over not only working class women but women from all classes and groups for the idea of the liberation of women from the captivity of Paragraph 218. We boasted everywhere about the Soviet Union, the most progressive state in the world in which abortion was permitted.[71]

Franziska Rubens, who lived with her two children and surgeon husband in the Comintern Hotel Lux, noted carefully in her official memoir for the Communist Party of the German Democratic Republic (SED), "It is not easy to write about the memories from that time, to write about them honestly." But she did remember the fear and mistrust that colored the years of supposed safety in the Soviet Union, the convoluted attempts to explain the mass disappearances as honest errors or the result of sabotage by the fascist class enemy, and her own complicity when trusted comrades disappeared because it was "better to arrest one too many than one too few," and those remaining free crossed the street in order to avoid contact with those who might be under suspicion. Later, she wrote, "The psychological pressure was incredible .... Our faith in the party and the immutable correctness of its directives, its politics, was so strong that even the quietest doubts, the possibility of its being wrong, of errors or indeed of crimes on the part of leading functionaries, was for us completely taboo."[72]

KPD women in exile from the Nazis watched in horror and confusion as their comrades, not infrequently their husbands or companions, even their children, were dragged away on trumped up charges, noting forlornly in their official memoirs that the accused had now long since been rehabilitated. It fell to the women, working again as office workers, translators, journalists, and secretaries, to support their families and those of comrades who had been arrested. They had to handle the burdens of harsh everyday life in wartime Russia, and the anxieties of their children coping with unfamiliar Russian schools after the dissolution of the German Karl Liebknecht School and the Ernst Thälmann summer camp, as well as fears for their parents and themselves. Children were removed from those under suspicion and placed in orphanages where some died of malnutrition or typhus. Others were alienated from their families and identified completely with their new "Vaterland" as Soviet citizens and patriots, no longer wanting to have anything to do with their German background. "At least the children were not spoiled under these conditions," Rubens remarked, not without irony. [73]

Despite the terror, women exiles such as Rubens or Martha Arendsee welcomed the opportunity to participate in the war effort against the Nazis. The lingering pain of the Soviet exile experience is only suggested in the guarded language, the crossed out words, the scribbled asides, in the official and highly programmed (but still very moving and revealing) "memory reports" (*Erinnerungsberichte*) commissioned by the SED in the 1950s and 1960s from its honored party veterans, and preserved in the party archives.[74] Martha Arendsee, together with Friedrich Wolf, Frieda Rubiner, and Franziska Rubens, with whom she had worked closely during the anti-218 campaign, became one of the organizers of the National Committee for a Free Germany, which tried, with little success, to promote communist and antifascist propaganda among German troops and prisoners of war. She also broadcast radio programs directed toward German women. Arendsee returned to Eastern Germany, where as an honored party veteran she was appointed to the presidium of the Communist trade union organization FDGB.[75]

Other Communist activists remained in Germany, enduring a seesaw existence of underground illegal work, attempted normality, and incarceration in jails and concentration camps, until the arrival of the Red Army in spring 1945 allowed a return to activist careers in the Soviet zone and the German Democratic Republic. Hanna Himmler, for example, a working-class daughter born in 1894 who worked as a white-collar employee (and then organizer) in department stores and served as KPD Berlin City Council and Reichstag delegate during the Republic, went underground after the Reichstag fire, was arrested and then released, found work with a Jewish businessman until he emigrated, found another white-collar job until she was arrested again in 1939, was released again to work in a business owned by KPD sympathizers, only to be rearrested after the failed attempt to assassinate Hitler on 20 July 1944 and taken to Ravensbrück where she was liberated in May 1945. She was able to rejoin her husband and daughter and become active again in Thuringia.[76] There were also communist resisters like Elfriede Paul, who followed a typical career path for a woman doctor in Nazi Germany, working for the League of German Girls (BDM), in a hereditary and racial welfare counseling center and as a school physician. By 1936, she was also heavily involved in the conspiratorial resistance activities of the Communist Red Orchestra group. Her waiting room hosted meetings; her car, normally used for house calls, was made available for actions and for summer excursions to campsites on the Baltic where cadre relaxed and planned strategy. Arrested in 1942, Paul was one of the few members of the group to survive imprisonment. She became an important figure in the formulation of postwar population policy in the German Democratic Republic (GDR), bringing to her tasks a curious but not unusual melange of Weimar, Soviet, and Nazi notions about social health.[77]

By the early 1950s most of the Weimar KPD women activists who had returned to the Soviet zone to build a new socialist Germany had been shunted aside as honored relics. The one exception perhaps was Hilde Benjamin, the Red Hilde, who had always resisted any identification with women's issues. Her rage at the Nazis who had murdered her physician husband Georg Benjamin, and her closest friend, the Jewish poet Gertrud Kolmar, and driven her brother-in-law, Walter Benjamin, to suicide in exile, seemed to nourish her doctrinaire rigidity as a feared and hated prosecutor and later Minister of Justice in the SBZ/GDR.[78] The old KPD lived on only in ritualized celebrations of party veterans or antifascist resistance fighters. The heritage of a party that had been both more innovative and varied, and more disastrously smashed than all other European Communist parties, was lost, permanently destroyed by the temporary triumph of National Socialism and the ongoing shocks of Stalinism.

Notes

1. For extensive discussion of the KPD and the sex reform movement, see Atina Grossmann, *Reforming Sex: The German Movement for Birth Control and Abortion Reform 1920-1950* (New York, 1995).
2. Robert F. Wheeler, "German Women and the Communist International: The Case of the Independent Social Democrats," *Central European History* 8, 2 (June 1975): 114.
3. Stiftung Archiv der Partein und Massenorganisationen der DDR im Bundesarchiv Berlin Lichterfelde West [hereafter BArch(Sapmo)], Central Committee (ZK) of the KPD, I 2/701/28, Abt. Frauen.
4. On SPD/USPD/KPD splits see Wheeler, "German Women." According to Wheeler, women in the USPD and the left working-class movement were more likely to oppose acceptance of the Comintern's twenty-one conditions during the great split of 1920, but those who were won over (including veteran activists Anna Geyer, Anna Nemitz, and Toni Sender, who later changed her mind) were moved by admiration for the Soviet Union's social welfare projects. In the spring of 1920, the ECCI (the Third International) appointed the 62-year-old grand dame of socialism, Clara Zetkin, as International Secretary for Communist Women. On World War I and demobilization, see Ute Daniel, "Women's Work in Industry and Family: Germany 1914-1918," in *The Upheaval of War: Family, Work and Welfare in Europe, 1914-1918*, eds. Richard Wall and Jay Winter (Cambridge, 1988), and Richard Bessel, *Germany after the First World War* (Oxford, 1993). On women's wartime militance around issues of consumption, see Belinda Davis, "Food Scarcity and the Empowerment of the Female Consumer in World War I Germany," in *The Sex of Things: Gender and Consumption in Historical Perspective*, ed. Victoria de Grazia with Ellen Furlough (Berkeley, Calif., 1996).
5. Helen Boak, "Women in Weimar Germany: The Frauenfrage and the Female Vote," in *Social Change and Political Development in Weimar Germany*, Richard Bessel and E.J. Feuchtwanger, eds. (Totowa, N.J., 1981), p. 163.
6. On rationalization see Mary Nolan, *Visions of Modernity: American Business and the Modernization of Germany* (New York, 1994) and Detlev J.K. Peukert, *The Weimar Republic: The Crisis of Classical Modernity* (New York, 1989). On rationalization and women's wage labor see Renate Bridenthal, "Beyond 'Kinder, Küche, Kirche: Weimar Women at Work," *Central European History* 6, 2 (1973):148-66; Renate Bridenthal and Claudia Koonz, "Beyond *Kinder, Küche, Kirche*: Weimar Women in Politics and Work," in *When Biology Became Destiny. Women in Weimar and Nazi Germany*, eds. Renate Bridenthal, Atina Grossmann, and Marion Kaplan (New York, 1984), pp. 33-65; Annemarie Tröger, "The Creation of a Female Assembly-Line Proletariat," in *When Biology Became Destiny*, pp. 237-70; the remarkable contemporary articles, Marguerite Thibert, "The Economic Depression and the Employment of Women," *International Labor Review* 27, 4 (April 1933):443-70 and 5 (May 1933):620-30; and Judith Grunfeld, "Rationalization and the Employment and Wages of Women in Germany," *International Labor Review* 29, 5 (May 1934):605-32.
7. On the history of the KPD see Eric Weitz, *Creating German Communism, 1890-1990: From Popular Protests to Socialist State* (Princeton, N.J., 1996). On the politics of Bolshevization, see Hermann Weber, *Die Wandlung der KPD in der Weimarer Republik* (Frankfurt, 1969); Ossip Flechtheim, *Die KPD in der Weimarer Republik* (Frankfurt, 1969). With the exception of Weitz's fine chapter on the "Gendering of German Communism," pp. 188-232, there is remarkably little

work on women and the KPD; what there is dates mostly from the 1970s and bears the marks of its time. See Sylvia Kontos, *Die Partei kämpft wie ein Mann* (Basel and Frankfurt, 1979), especially pp. 25-91; and Michael Rohrwasser, *Saubere Mädchen, Starke Genossen, Proletarische Massenliteratur?* (Frankfurt, 1975). See three fact-filled if necessarily limited GDR dissertations: Hans-Jürgen Arendt, "Der Kampf der Kommunistischen Partei Deutschlands um die Erziehung der werktätigen Frauen in der revolutionären deutschen Arbeiterbewegung in der Periode der Weltwirtschaftskrise (1929 bis 1932)" (Ph.D. diss., Leipzig, 1970); Leopoldine Auerswald, "Zum Kampf der Kommunistischen Partei Deutschlands um die Einbeziehung der proletarischen Frauen in die revolutionäredeutsche Arbeiterbewegung in der Zeit der revolutionären Nachkriegszeit (1919-1923)" (Ph.D. diss., Hochschule Clara Zetkin, Leipzig, 1976); and Werner Freigang, "Die Frauenpolitik der Kommunistischen Partei Deutschlands in den Jahren der relativen Stabilisierung des Kapitalismus (unter besonderer Berücksichtigung der Zeit vom II.Parteitag 1924 bis zum XI.Parteitag 1927)" (Ph.D. diss., Karl Marx University, Leipzig, 1971). See also the document collection *Arbeiterinnen kämpfen um ihr Recht. Autobiographische Texte rechtloser und entrechteter "Frauenpersonen" in Deutschland, Oesterreich und der Schweiz des 19. und 20.Jahrhunderts,* Richard Klucsarits and Friedrich G. Kuerbisch, eds. (Wuppertal, n.d.), pp. 101-44, 159-78.

8. The newly formed RFMB gained 4,000 members in six weeks. See BArch ([Koblenz]) R134/30 (Reichskommission für die Überwachung öffentlicher Ordnung, Nachrichtensammelstelle im Reichsministerium des Innern), p. 21. See also R134/30/33/37, and R58/757 (Reichssicherheitshauptamt). Police records provide excellent source material for the RFMB and all KPD organizations dealt with here, since they consist to a large extent of material produced by the organizations themselves: internal reports, memoranda, annual programs, and leaflets.

9. Helene Overlach memoirs, BArch(Sapmo) EA 1053.

10. See Helmut Gruber, "Willi Münzenberg's German Communist Propaganda Empire 1921-1933," *The Journal of Modern History* 38, 3 (September 1966): 278-97 and Babette Gross, *Willi Münzenberg: A Political Biography* (East Lansing, Mich., 1974).

11. See Karen Hagemann, "Men's Demonstrations and Women's Protest: Gender in Collective Action in the Urban Working-Class Milieu during the Weimar Republic," *Gender and History* 5, 1 (spring 1993): 105-06.

12. Eric Weitz, "The Heroic Man and the Ever-Changing Woman: Gender and Politics in European Communism 1917-1950," paper presented at North American Labor History Conference (October 1994), p. 1.

13. Boak, "Die Frauenfrage," p. 59.

14. Maurice Duverger, *The Political Role of Women,* (Paris, 1955), p. 54.

15. Personal interview, Manes Sperber, Paris, 1 February 1978.

16. On the Delegate and Conference Movement, see its journal *Die Kämpferin, Organ der Gesamtinteressen der arbeitenden Frauen,* 1927-1932, 1929-1931, and police reports in BArch(K) R 134/60, 61, 62, 66, 70, 71. The KPD acknowledged that membership was "quite catastrophic" in smaller and rural areas, and the party did not even try very hard to recruit rural workers or peasants. At the Berlin Congress in November 1930, over half the delegates identified as housewives. Police reports counted 918 delegates including 476 industrial workers, 287 working-class housewives, fifty-one white-collar workers, nine rural laborers, one peasant, nine domestic servants, fourteen professionals, fifteen servers, thirteen domestic workers, and 167 unemployed. KPD members numbered 214 (of

which 184 had just recently joined), 499 were partyless (the preferred category for such events) and another 103 joined the party during the congress. See BAK R 134/70, 140. See also *Die Kämpferin* 14 (1931): 4, for discussion of housewives at conferences in 1931. See also Brian Peterson, "The Politics of Working-Class Women in the Weimar Republic," *Central European History* 10, 2 (June 1977): 87-111.

17. Already in 1920, thirteen KPD delegates were women, 17.1 percent versus sixteen (11.1 percent) for the SPD and four (5.5 percent) for the Center Party. Ironically, "the women in the Reichstag provide us with a dramatic case of 'tokenism,'" because higher percentages of women were elected at the national level than at local or municipal levels, where one would expect to find evidence of genuine grass-roots activity. See Claudia Koonz, "Conflicting Allegiances: Weimar Women Legislators," *Signs* 3 (1976): 667-68.

18. See for example, *Die Kämpferin* 13/14 (1930):8-9.

19. On Soviet family and welfare policy see Wendy Z. Goldman, *Women, the State, and Revolution: Soviet Family Policy and Social Life, 1917-1936* (Cambridge, Mass. and New York, 1993).

20. BArch(K) R 134/70. Report, 9 March 1931, on delegates' journey to the Soviet Union in January 1931 after second congress of working women in November 1930.

21. BArch(Sapmo) I 2/701/28, ZK KPD, Abt. *Frauen, Kampagne gegen die Par.218/219.*

22. On ARSO generally see, Elfriede Foelster, "Die Arbeitsgemeinschaft sozialpolitischer Organisationen (ARSO) von 1927-1929. Zur Geschichte der Sozialpolitik der KPD," *Beiträge zur Geschichte der Arbeiterbewegung* 20:2 (1978):222-36. For detailed information collected by the police and government, see Geheimes Staatsarchiv Preussischer Kulturbesitz Dahlem (GStA) Landeskriminalamt Berlin, Rep. 219/56-59. See also BArch(K) R58/336 (10,11,13), 548 (5-13), 757, 775 (14-17), 776; R58/700 on other mass cultural organizations; BA R 134/67, 70, 73, 40; R86/2306, 2369(1); and for KPD material BArch(S) I 4/11/2.

23. Martha Arendsee memoir, BArch(Sapmo) EA 0017.

24. See Eve Rosenhaft, *Beating the Fascists? The German Communists and Political Violence 1929-1933* (Cambridge, Mass., 1983).

25. In local Berlin municipal elections, the figures were similarly high (1928, 28.2 percent male, 21.4 percent female for KPD); in Frankfurt, too, 17.3 percent of male voters and 12.7 percent of females voted KPD in the 1930 parliamentary elections. But even in Catholic Cologne, in 1930, the KPD was able to show 20.7 percent for men and 13.2 percent for women versus 18.1 percent and 31.8 percent respectively for the Center. See Duverger, *Political Role of Women,* pp. 54-58.

26. See BArch(K) NS 26/810 for KPD membership statistics. See also Gabrielle Bremme, *Die politische Rolle der Frau in Deutschland. Eine Untersuchung über den Einfluss der Frauen bei Wahlen und ihre Teilnahme an Partei und Parlament* (Göttingen, 1956), p. 73; Duverger, *Political Role of Women,* pp. 54-65; and Peterson, "Politics of Working-Class Women."

27. See, for example, Käte Frankenthal, *PP 218 streichen – nicht ändern* (Berlin, 1931). On the SPD, see also Renate Pore, *A Conflict of Interest. Women in German Social Democracy 1919-1933* (Westport, Conn., 1981), pp. 78-80; Alfred Grotjahn, *Erlebtes und Erstrebtes. Erinnerungen eines sozialistischen Arztes* (Berlin, 1932); Werner Thoennessen, *The Emancipation of Women. The Rise and Decline of the Women's Movement in German Social Democracy 1863-1933* (London, 1973),

and most comprehensively, Karen Hagemann, *Frauenalltag und Männerpolitik. Alltagsleben und gesellschaftliches Handeln von Arbeiterfrauen in der Weimarer Republik* (Bonn, 1990). For a more favorable view of the SPD, see Cornelie Usborne, *The Politics of the Body in Weimar Germany: Women's Reproductive Rights and Duties* (Ann Arbor, Mich., 1992).

28. On militarization of action and imagery see Hagemann, "Men's Demonstrations and Women's Protest" and Eric Weitz, "The Heroic Man and the Ever-Changing Woman: Gender and Politics in European Communism, 1917-1950," in *Gender and Class in Modern Europe*, eds. Laura L. Frader and Sonya O. Rose (Ithaca, N.Y., 1996), especially pp. 312-28.

29. For a comparative perspective that highlights the KPD's radicalism, see the other articles in this volume. See also Weitz, "Heroic Man."

30. Overlach memoir, BArch(Sapmo) EA 1053, and personal interview, Berlin, GDR, 11 January 1977.

31. See also Eric Weitz's perceptive discussion in "Heroic Man" and in *Creating German Communism*, pp. 188-232.

32. Among numerous texts on new women and mass culture in Weimar, see, for example, Patrice Petro, *Joyless Streets: Women and Melodramatic Representation in Weimar Germany* (Princeton, N.J., 1989) and Atina Grossmann, "Girlkultur or Thoroughly Rationalized Female: A New Woman in Weimar Germany?" in *Women in Culture and Politics: A Century of Change*, eds. Friedlander, Cook, Kessler-Harris, and Smith-Rosenberg (Bloomington, Ind., 1986), pp. 62-80.

33. Brian Peterson, quoting the poet Bruno Schönlank, in "Politics of Working-Class Women," p. 98.

34. *AIZ* 9, 20 (1930):386.

35. See issues of *AIZ*, 1929-1933, and *Weg der Frau*, 1931-1933. For the Soviet-German comparison, see "24 Stunden aus dem Leben einer Moskauer Arbeiterfamilie," *AIZ* 10, 38 (1931). The Russian Filipows were compared to the "Bauarbeiterfamilie Fournes in der Kösliner Strasse" and "Mutter Fournes Arbeitstag" *AIZ* 10, 48 (1931), p. 968. See also police reports on IAH film strip, Berlin, 27 September 1932, and 3 June 1932, BArch(K) R58/614. For views of housework, see the comic stories about Frau Gründlich and Frau Grämlich in *Weg der Frau*.

36. Text of IAH film strip, *Neue Deutsche Lichtbildstelle*, in BArch(K) R58/614. The RGO (Red Trade Union Opposition) set up housewives' groups in 1932. See R134/81, pp. 219-220.

37. *Arbeiter Kalender*, January 1932, in BArch(K) ZSg 1, 61/5(5).

38. Similar, or more benighted, stories have been told for the SPD. See Hagemann's study of the Hamburg SPD, *Frauenalltag und Männerpolitik*; also her "Men's Demonstrations and Women's Protest," and Helmut Gruber, *Red Vienna. Experiment in Working Class Culture 1919-1934* (New York, 1991).

39. Käthe Duncker, "Die Familie im Wandel der Zeiten," *Proletarische Sozialpolitik* 4, 6 (June 1931): 176.

40. Hilde Wirsch on her play *Nora 1932*, performed by *Junge Volksbühne*, 26 December 1932, in BArch(K) R58/613. See Nolan, *Visions of Modernity* for discussion of the left's infatuation with technology and rationalization.

41. BArch(Sapmo), EA 0173, Frieda Düwell, story told on 3 March and 9 March 1951. See also Margarete Buber-Neumann's memoir, *Von Potsdam nach Moskau. Stationen eines Irrweges* (Stuttgart, 1957). This desire to escape particularistic and burdensome identities into the universalism of mass movements is a theme for many Communist Jews and women. See for example, Barbara Einhorn, "Anna

Seghers: GDR Literature and German-Jewish Commitment to Communism," in
Yale Handbook of Jewish Writing in Germany, eds. Sander L. Gilman and Jack
Zipes (New Haven, Conn., 1995).

42. Lea Gründig memoir, BArch(Sapmo), EA 1658; see also Luise Dornemann memoir, EA 1653.

43. *Lenin ruft die werktätigen Frauen*, (KPD, 1926) in BArch(K) ZSg 1/61/28(5).
    See also Clara Zetkin, "My Recollections of Lenin: An Interview on the Woman
    Question," in *Feminism. The Essential Historical Writings*, ed. Miriam Schneir
    (New York, 1972), pp. 335-43. Zetkin later went to some pains to reassure an
    obviously distressed associate of Magnus Hirschfeld's Institute for Sexual Science
    that Lenin had not intended to imply that Communist youth organizations
    should tabooize sexuality. She insisted that comrades Zinoviev and Krupskaya
    (Lenin's wife) both checked her recollections before publication and would have
    rejected an anti-sex position as "un-Leninist." Zetkin, for her part, affirmed that
    Lenin saw "sexual enlightenment and education on the basis of reliable scientific
    findings, as well as coeducation, as social necessities that should not have to wait
    until after the revolution." Clara Zetkin Correspondence, BArch(Sapmo), NL
    5/83, letter to Richard Linsert, 27 September 1930.

44. See *Arbeiterjugendbewegung in Frankfurt 1904-1945. Materialien zu einer verschütteten Kulturgeschichte*, eds. Holtmann, Pokorny, and Werner, (Lahn-Giessen,
    1978); Gerhard Roger, *Die Pädagogische Bedetung der Proletarischen Jugendbewegung Deutschlands* (Frankfurt, 1971), pp. 97-99.

45. Bertolt Brecht, *Kuhle Wampe. Protokoll des Filmes und Materialien*, eds. Wolfgang
    Gersch and Werner Hecht (Frankfurt, 1969).

46. See also reports by Erna Gysi on *Jugendberatungsstelle* in Nos. 8 (August 1932):
    244-48 and 9 (September 1932): 266. The potential appeal of IAH centers is
    indicated by the fact that in 1931, *Die Welt am Abend*, a Münzenberg "mass"
    organ had a circulation of 229,000; see Helmut Gruber, "Münzenberg's German
    Communist Propaganda Empire," p. 288, n. 31. See also "Richtlinien für Jugendberatungsstellen," in BArch(K) R 58/685.

47. See Gabriele Gerhard-Sonnenberg, MASCH. Of course, there were also those
    party women's leaders who came from working-class families and themselves
    started as factory workers. See for example Roberta Gropper's story of working in
    a cigarette factory, BArch(Sapmo) EA0307.

48. In *Eine Stumme Generation berichtet. Frauen der dreisiger und vierziger Jahre* (Frankfurt, 1982), p. 42.

49. Rosenhaft, *Beating the Fascists*, pp. 13-14.

50. Boak, "Die Frauenfrage," p. 169 n. 21. In the 1930 Cologne Reichstag elections,
    the KPD counted 20.9 percent of male voters and 18.0 percent of female voters.
    In Leipzig in 1930, 34.5 percent of male and 35.3 percent of female voters went
    SPD; 22.0 percent of males and 16.0 percent of females for the KPD.

51. See Detlev Peukert,"The Lost Generation: Youth Unemployment at the End of the
    Weimar Republic," pp. 172-193; and Elizabeth Harvey, "Youth Unemployment
    and the State: Public Policies towards Unemployed Youth in Hamburg during the
    World Economic Crisis," pp. 142-171, both in *The German Unemployed: Experiences and Consequences of Mass Unemployment from the Weimar Republic to the Third
    Reich*, eds. Richard Evans and Dick Geary (London, 1987); Eve Rosenhaft, "Organizing the 'Lumpenproletariat.' Cliques and Communists in Berlin during the
    Weimar Republic," in *Social Change and Political Development in Weimar Germany*,
    eds. Richard Bessel and E.J. Feuchtwanger (Totowa, N.J., 1981), pp. 207-240.

52. Overlach's memories are from a personal interview, Berlin-GDR, 11 January 1977 and her unpublished memoir, BArch(Sapmo) EA 1053.

53. See for example internal party critiques of the Conference Delegate Movement in BArch(K) R 134/67, pp. 231-236. The conflict between establishing a broad popular base and creating cadre among the designated vanguard of the industrial working class clearly repeated itself after World War II in the Soviet zone when the officially nonpartisan women's councils (*Frauenausschüsse*) were abolished – to much protest – in 1947 in favor of workplace groups and the tightly party controlled mass organization Democratic Women's League of Germany (*Demokratischer Frauenbund Deutschlands*, DFD).

54. *Die Kämpferin* 8 (1930):8.

55. Rosa Meyer-Leviné, *Inside German Communism. Memoirs of Party Life in the Weimar Republic* (London, 1977), pp. 142-43. See also her collected papers, BArch(K).

56. See the extraordinary reports by women textile workers in *Mein Arbeitstag, Mein Wochenende*, ed. Deutscher Textilarbeiterverband (Berlin, 1930).

57. *Stenographische Berichte der Verhandlungen des Reichstages* vol. 451, KPD-Antrag # 1201, 16 October 1931, and *Die Kämpferin* No.15 (1931): 4. See also Richtlinien: Frauen and Mädchen Staffeln Gegen den Faschismus, police report October 26, 1932, in BArch(K) R134/75, pp. 159-174.

58. *Die Kämpferin* No. 5 (1929): 7.

59. BArch(K) NS26/10. See also R58/684, 674, 504, 401 and R134/10 as well as the journals *Die Frauenwacht*, *Frauen in Front*, and *Der Vormarsch*.

60. Maria Reese papers, Kleine Erwerbungen 379/1, BArch(K).

61. See BArch(K) 134/71, pp. 196-223.

62. See BArchK R45/IV/1524 for further documents on KPD frustrations with women's organizing.

63. See *Die Kämpferin* No. 7 (1932), and BArch(K) R134/71, pp. 196-233; R134/67, pp. 231-236. KPD membership reached unprecedented heights in 1931; in December 1931, 2,768 women had been recruited: 13.4 percent of total new members. But by 1932, with the anti-218 euphoria gone, the membership picture was gloomy again. See BArch(K) NS26/810, p. 4.

64. Barch (K), R134/66, 66/74; R134/69, pp. 68-73; R134/81, p. 160. See also Rosenhaft, *Beating the Fascists*.

65. BArch(Sapmo) KPD ZK Politburo I/2/3/252.

66. "Bericht über die Arbeit der Bezirksleitung der Berliner Roten Kulturfront," 26 August 1935. BArch(Sapmo) KPD ZK Politburo. I/2/3/252.

67. BArch(Sapmo) EA 1053. Interview, Berlin GDR, 11 January 1977.

68. Franziska Rubens Memoir, BArch(Sapmo), EA 0787.

69. David Pike, *German Writers in Soviet Exile 1933-1945* (Chapel Hill, N.C., 1982), pp. 355-56.

70. Dr. Lothar Wolf was "driven to his death" on 9 September 1940. *Internationales Ärztliches Bulletin* , eds. Tennstedt, Pross, Leibfried, p. xi. On Martha Ruben-Wolf, see also Susanne Leonhard, *Gestohlenes Leben. Schicksal einer Politischen Emigrantin in der Sowjetunion* (Frankfurt, 1956), pp. 48-49.

71. Susanne Leonhard, *Gestohlenes Leben*, p. 48. See also the extraordinary memoirs of her son, Wolfgang Leonhard, *Child of the Revolution* (Chicago, 1958).

72. Rubens memoir, BArch(Sapmo), EA 0787. On the horrors of life in the Hotel Lux during the purges, see Ruth von Mayenburg, *Hotel Lux: Das Absteigequartier der Weltrevolution* (Munich, 1991). See also Margarete Buber-Neumann, *Als Gefangene bei Stalin und Hitler* (Seewald, 1968).

73. Rubens EA 0787; Markus Wolf, *Die Troika: Geschichte eines nichtgedrehten Films. Nach einer Idee von Konrad Wolf* (Berlin, 1989); Konrad Wolf's moving film, *Ich war neunzehn* (DEFA, 1968).

74. The SED officially solicited these memoirs from party veterans in the 1950s and 1960s. However distorted, these memoirs collected in the SED Archives now housed in the Bundesarchiv, Berlin Lichterfelde West, are a valuable source.

75. Martha Arendsee memoir, BArch(Sapmo), EA 0017.

76. Hanna Himmler memoir, BArch(Sapmo), EA 1365.

77. See Elfriede Paul Papers, BArch(Sapmo), NL 229/10, and her memoir, Elfriede Paul, *Ein Sprechzimmer der Roten Kapelle*, ed. Vera Küchenmeister (Berlin, DDR, 1981).

78. Hilde Benjamin memoir, BArch(Sapmo), EA 0053.

Part II

Part II

***

GRASSROOTS INITIATIVES

Introduction

Pamela Graves

E ffective grassroots organization of women was the most remarkable characteristic of Social Democratic parties in interwar Belgium, Britain, and The Netherlands. In each country, mostly middle-class women leaders built a national network of women's sections, clubs or mutual aid societies. In each case, working-class housewives were the majority of the thousands of rank-and-file members who sustained these local groups over the interwar period. With limited education and low incomes, homes to run and children to raise, they were unlikely political activists. Yet, in a period when the national parties made only halting progress towards social welfare, these women demonstrated socialism at work in their communities through a broad range of practical reforms. Working inside and outside municipal councils, they fought for better housing and sanitation, mother and baby clinics, preschool education, school meals, and equal educational opportunities for girls. They were the proud sponsors of municipal parks and playgrounds, libraries and community laundries. They raised money for the party, helped get out the vote on election day, marched for peace, and organized social events that were central to the local socialist culture.

How this vigorous grassroots organization emerged in parties with different structures and programs, and in countries with significant political and cultural differences, is not easy to pinpoint. Evidence from the following chapters suggests a number of possible explanations. In every case, the interwar organization was able to build on a prewar foundation. The Dutch Federation of Social Democratic Women's Clubs was founded in 1908. By the time the party gave it official status in 1925, it already had a significant membership, organized in clubs throughout the country and educated in citizenship and socialism. The Federation had taken part in the successful fight for women's suffrage and put together programs for maternity care and better working conditions for women wage earners. It was the same in Britain. The Labour party's women's sections took over the national branch network of the prewar Women's Labour League formed in 1906. The League had a history of political activity in suffrage and welfare reform, similar to that of the Dutch Federation. In Belgium, there had been autonomous women's groups attached to the Belgian Workers' party (BWP) since its foundation in 1900. Some were political, others consumer cooperatives and mutual aid societies. When the party organized the Provident Socialist Women in 1922, a cadre of women was on hand to pass organizing skills and reform agendas on to the new generation.

The evidence also implies that women in each country turned to local organization and activism because of the barriers raised against their participation at the national level. In Britain, the barriers were constitutional. The party was organized in such a way as to guarantee male trade union dominance and to shut women out from power and policy making. Labour women tilted at these barriers for over a decade without success. In Belgium, male leaders of the BWP clearly felt that women's lack of voting rights in national elections relieved them of any obligation to share power or implement women's policy proposals. Dutch social democratic leaders held a similar view. Men represented the political mainstream and women were outside and "other." Office holding at the national level remained a male preserve, and women were expected to confine their activities to organizing the female vote.

Firm convictions of gender difference barred women from full integration into the national parties, though they were rarely acknowledged. Official party rhetoric uniformly endorsed gender equality. The BWP and the British Labour party spoke of men and women as comrades destined for equality under socialism. Party leaders in The Netherlands congratulated themselves for including a clause in support of "equal rights … for all members of the community, irrespective of sex or race" in their 1936 constitution. But these socialist and democratic ideals of inclusion and equality were nowhere translated into political practice. Assumptions about gender difference and female inferiority dictated strategies that kept women's activities within boundaries deemed appropriate to their gender. Whenever socialist women demanded an extension to their narrow sphere, they were reminded of the need for party solidarity. In all three countries, male party leaders marginalized women's organizations to deny them power, then made them responsible for supposedly women's issues, with the result that the issues were similarly marginalized.

Each chapter contains an example of the frustration socialist women experienced in their efforts to shape national party policy. In The Netherlands, the issue was disarmament. Dutch social democratic women united in support of international peace and urged their party to make a clear commitment to disarmament. Party leaders, struggling to get into power, determined to win middle-class electoral support with an unequivocal statement favoring national defense. Because women were a "bloc," the leaders interpreted their different point of view in purely gender terms. They accused party women of responding to disarmament with a woman's emotional and short-sighted desire to prevent suffering and death. Male rationality called for national self-assertion, and this was the correct political response; women had no power to resist such an argument.

In Britain, the issue was birth control. In the 1920s, Labour women passed resolution after resolution calling on the party to allow local mother and baby clinics to offer birth control advice to women who wanted it. They saw birth control as the key that would open the door to better conditions of life for working-class women and their families. Year after year, party leaders refused to consider the issue, arguing that birth control was a matter of private conscience outside the realm of politics. As in The Netherlands, women had no power to resist. In Belgium, the women's vote was the cause of gender tension. Fearing that the Catholic party would be the major beneficiary of female suffrage, BWP leaders backed down from an earlier endorsement. Antagonism towards Catholics, rather than a desire to promote women's activism, motivated their support for the Provident Women's groups. They shared the view of their Dutch counterparts, that women's natural propensity for "caring" disqualified them for serious politics.

Trade unionism among women wage workers in all three countries was too weak to offer activist women an alternative arena for their reforming socialism. In Britain and The Netherlands, the strong prewar female unions disintegrated during and after World War I, and in German-occupied Belgium, women's high rate of unemployment produced a similar result. During the interwar years, women's overall trade union membership declined everywhere. Male unionists were unwilling to organize them, and women were moving into nonunionized employment in shops and offices. The inability of trade unions to protect women wage workers, especially married women, who came under attack in each country as unemployment grew, left social democratic women to take up their cause. In Belgium and Britain, they formed brief alliances with feminists and other women's groups to protest the injustice of the firing of married women civil servants and teachers.

Confined to a narrow sphere of activity in the national parties and without a trade union base, social democratic women might have been tempted to renew their prewar cooperation with reform-minded feminist groups on a wide range of issues, not just married women's right to work. The reasons why this did not happen seem to be different for each country. Ulla Jansz argues that feminism in The Netherlands was driven onto

the defensive in the interwar years in a backlash against women's new citizenship and political participation. In Belgium, World War I shattered the
prewar feminist movement. An attempt at rebuilding it after the war in the
form of a coordinating National Women's Action Committee failed to
unify the disparate women's groups. Socialists and feminists in Belgium
and Britain pursued similar goals along separate paths. Belgian feminists
attacked the Napoleonic Code that denied married women control over
their own property, while women socialists demanded that separated
women be allowed to dispose of their own belongings. British feminists and
Labour women campaigned separately for family allowances and clashed
over protective legislation for women workers. In each country individual
socialist feminists were prominent in social democratic politics and in
some cases maintained their ties to independent feminist organizations.

   Two other interwar developments offered social democratic women in
these countries an opportunity for promoting their women-centered
socialism. One was state-sponsored social welfare and the other, the
changes in women's sexuality and image associated with the "new
woman." When they failed to find support in their national parties, social
democratic women appealed to the state to take responsibility for the care
of working-class mothers and children. They argued that the state owed
mothers the same financial support given to the armed forces because
mothers, like soldiers, performed a vital service for their country. State
pro-natalism was insignificant in the Netherlands and Britain, but in Belgium, Provident Women were able to take advantage of this policy to
open mother and baby clinics and offer cash payments at marriage and
childbirth. The impact of the new woman idea was similarly disparate.
Youth movements were the most likely to adapt the liberated woman
with her dangerous overtones of sexuality and materialism to a more puritanical and less threatening comrade-woman. This was true for The
Netherlands and Belgium. In Britain, the Labour party ignored the image
of the new woman, and its influence was greatest on the younger generation of party women who rejected feminism as old-fashioned, left the
separate women's sections to the now aging housewives, and went to regular party meetings with the men.

   Neither the State nor the new woman culture, however, offered social
democratic women in Belgium, Britain, and The Netherlands the space
to pursue their reform agenda that the national parties all denied them.
Only local community politics did that. At the local level, gender worked
for and not against them. Voters were willing to concede that certain
political issues were best left to women. Mothers, babies, young children,
unmarried mothers, the sick, and the elderly fell within women's natural
sphere, meaning that women were allowed a voice in planning and implementing local social welfare programs. In the interwar years, such pro-

grams were in their developmental phase, and it was socialist women who shaped them in ways that influenced, to varying degrees, the postwar welfare states. Their programs had remarkable similarities. They all insisted on state benefits for pregnant women, married or not, for local midwifery and lying-in hospitals. They argued for slum clearance and state-subsidized housing with indoor plumbing. They demanded that girls have the same opportunities for education at all levels as boys. Because they were only minimally represented in the postwar governments that passed welfare legislation, their contribution has been forgotten. The following chapters suggest it ought not to be.

Activities and Aspirations of British, Dutch, and Belgian Women

"Women Will, Can, and Do Vote and Govern!"

Dutch Socialist Female Parliamentary Election Canvassers, 1922
Source: International Institute for Social History (IISG), Amsterdam

Belgian Unenfranchised Wife
Asking Husband to Vote
Socialist, 1932
Source: Foto-archiv Archive &
Museum of the Socialist
Labour Movement (AMSAB),
Ghent

LP Members of Parliament, Including Margaret
Bonfield, First Female Minister
Source: VGA

"Women Play an Active Role: in Trade Unions, the Community, and in Political Manifestations"

Labour Councillor Julia Scurr Says "No Surrender" During Rent Strike of 1921
Source: National Museum of Labour History (NMLH), Manchester

Popular Front Demonstrators, Ostand 1936
Source: Foto-archiv AMSAB, Ghent

British National Federation of Women Workers Demonstrate Against Unemployment, 1920
Source: NMLH

"The Future of Women and Socialism Lies in the Next Generation"

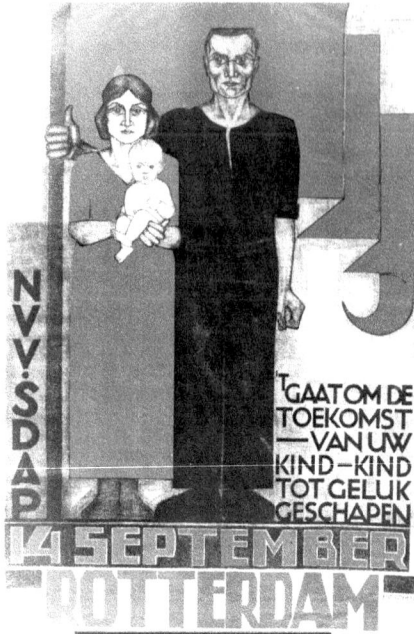

Dutch Socialists and Trade
Unions Call Public Meeting on
Future of Children
Source: Poster: Fré Cohen, IISG

Recruitment Poster for the
Dutch Socialist Youth:
Suggesting Gender Equality
in Social Commitment
Source: Poster: Levi Schwarz,
IISG

"Women in the Forefront of Disarmament and Anti-Fascism"

Call for Dutch Women to Vote Socialist
under the Slogan "Disarmament" 1925
Source: Poster: Willem Papenhuyzen, IISG

Belgian Socialist Women Marching
against Fascism, 1931
Source: Foto-archiv AMSAB, Ghent

Independent Labour Party Demonstration for Peace, 1929
Source: NMLH

Chapter 4

An Experiment in
Women-Centered Socialism
Labour Women in Britain

Pamela Graves

Introduction

In Britain, the socialist and women's movements grew up together. Between 1880 and 1914, the two groups fought their way onto the national political agenda in militant campaigns calling for civil and economic rights.[1] Both were umbrella movements for a wide range of opinions that were in each case more pragmatic than ideological, more reforming than revolutionary. Both sought to build a solid foundation of organization among the working class. For the most part their paths ran parallel, but there was a point of convergence. A minority of socialists and women's rights activists became convinced that capitalist relations oppressed women in the home as much as they oppressed men and women in the workplace and that both forms of exploitation would disappear once socialism was achieved. Socialist feminists founded the Women's Co-operative Guild in 1883 and the Women's Labour League in 1906 as companion organizations to the mostly male Co-operative Union and Labour party. In 1918, when the war ended and women over thirty won the right to vote, the Labour party, opened its doors to women members and invited the League to merge with the mainstream body.

Notes for this chapter begin on page 212.

The merger was something less than an alliance between socialists and feminists. Most working-class women, socialists and suffragists, joined the Labour party but the Women's Co-operative Guild, with a similar membership, remained independent. The majority of middle-class feminists also rejected affiliation with the Labour party, preferring to remain outside party politics.[2] Despite this organizational split, popular opinion inside and outside the party strongly identified Labour with the woman question in the immediate postwar years. Labour had been the only political party to support women's suffrage before the war, and its 1918 manifesto, *Labour and the New Social Order*, included a lengthy section entitled "The Emancipation of Women" promising them equal rights as citizens and workers. The Party Secretary, Arthur Henderson, invited women to join the party on terms of complete equality and stand shoulder to shoulder with the men in the struggle for socialism. Between 1918 and 1939 a quarter of a million working-class women, most of them housewives and mothers, responded to his call. Lily Watson was among the pioneer generation. Explaining her reasons for joining in 1920, she wrote: "The Labour party, I believe, stands for the comradeship of the sexes whether it be in our social life or in industry.[3]

Such was the auspicious beginning of the interwar relationship between the majority socialist party in Britain and the cause of women. But, by 1933 at the latest, the relationship had collapsed. Women had become a large but mostly silent minority in the national Labour Party.[4] Photographs of annual party conferences where Labour made its policy decisions show only a handful of women in a sea of male faces. The party had refused to adopt a number of welfare reforms its women members fought for year after year, and in two short periods in office, it left unfulfilled the 1918 promise to extend women's rights as citizens. In just over a decade, Labour lost its postwar reputation as the party that supported women's social and economic emancipation. British feminists who had seen Labour as their best parliamentary hope in 1918, had come to see it as an enemy, not an ally. Socialism and feminism were effectively divorced.

Labour Women in the Interwar Years

Any assessment of the socialist record on women's issues in the interwar period has to come to terms with Labour's glaring defection. But the national party's backsliding is only part of the story. The Labour party was not a monolith. It had a number of constituent parts in addition to the male trade unionist majority that controlled policy making. After 1918, Labour developed a national network of local parties for individual members of either sex and separate women's sections to accommodate the majority of female members who preferred their own meetings. Local party members and section women, together with small affiliated socialist organizations like the Independent Labour Party (ILP), frequently disagreed with the dominant trade union perspective. Their ideas and policy proposals deserve consideration as part of the socialist response to women's issues even though they rarely prevailed in national party policy.

Among these other voices in the ranks of the Labour party, women's were the loudest and most persistent in their demands that the movement address the needs of working-class women and their families. They took responsibility for women's issues because they felt this was their area of expertise and because the male majority discouraged their participation in other areas of socialist politics. Labour men quickly acquired the habit of shunting any issue traditionally associated with women over to the so-called women's side of the movement. As a result, Labour women set the agenda for party debates on women's issues in the interwar period, pushing hard for equal rights in the franchise, wages, and unemployment benefits and for such special needs as free birth control advice for poor women, maternal and infant care, protection for women industrial workers and family allowances. When the national party either passed over or rejected many of these proposals, Labour women turned to their local parties and municipal government where they had more success in arguing that the welfare of working-class women and children was part of the female sphere in socialist politics.

The socialist response to the woman question in interwar Britain was therefore overwhelmingly Labour women's response and one that was more effective locally than nationally. In either context, socialist feminists had more to contend with than the indifference or hostility of their own party. In the interwar period, neither the economy nor the government gave much encouragement to progressive reform in the interests of working-class women. Although Britain avoided the descent into fascism, it had its share of the problems that caused such crises elsewhere in Europe. From 1921, unemployment was a dreary constant in the distressed areas of the declining textile, shipbuilding, coal, and steel industries, spreading to newer industries during the depression of the early-1930s. Chronic unemployment made jobs a contentious gender issue taking the form of a bitter dispute over married women's right to work.

The political climate was equally unsympathetic. The Conservatives were in power for all but five of the interwar years, on their own or as the dominant party in national coalitions. Their remedy for economic problems was to cut already inadequate social welfare programs. To make matters worse, when the Conservatives set out to punish the unions for their temerity in calling a General Strike in 1926, Labour dropped its own reform initiatives to concentrate on defending trade unionists. Nor did

British Conservatives offset their harsh economic policies with the pro-natalism that induced many of their European counterparts to support maternalist reforms. Despite some concern over falling birth rates in the 1930s, they seemed satisfied that the Empire would make up for a man-power shortfall as it had done in World War I. Of much more concern to them was the danger of social disruption from any increase in the size of an unruly – and in this case, a potentially Bolshevik – working class. As it turned out, the united and militant working class they feared was becoming an anachronism in the interwar years. Uneven economic development created a sharp division between working-class families dependent on declining heavy industries in the North and those with work opportunities in the new electrical, automobile, and food-processing industries of the Southeast. Subsidized housing estates built away from traditional working-class neighborhoods undermined the prewar cohe-siveness of working-class communities. A mass culture based on the cin-ema, radio, and popular magazines helped bridge the cultural gap between classes and spread new ideas about women's sexuality and gender rela-tions. Many younger women, both middle and working class, felt suffi-ciently emancipated to reject feminism as old-fashioned and unnecessary. By the 1930s, the number of Lily Watsons had declined, and those who did join the party preferred to go to mixed sex meetings rather than women's sections. The overall impact of these changes was to discourage class-wide and gender-specific reforms.

Labour women, of course, did not perceive these obstacles all at once or in anything like the same light as they appear in hindsight. How they saw them and found the space in which to promote their women-centered reform agenda is the subject of this chapter. Their story falls into three dis-tinct periods, corresponding to changes inside the Labour party, in national and international politics, in the economy, and in working-class communi-ties. The first is the two-year period of postwar economic boom when women entered the mainstream party in large numbers and socialists of both sexes pledged their support for women's civil rights. The second is the decade of recession from 1921 to 1931, when Labour women fought a los-ing battle with male leaders for social welfare reforms to halt the decline in working-class living standards. The last section covers the 1930s when Labour women set aside their women-centered agenda to support their class and party in the struggle against reactionary government and fascism.

Less Than Equal: Women Join the Labour Party 1918 to 1920

The concurrence of the ending of World War I and the first suffrage grant to British women (restricted to women thirty and older to avoid a

female voting majority) made organized socialists more aware of women
as potential comrades and fellow citizens than ever before. For the first
time, Labour party men included women in their rhetoric about a socialist future. As Labour's newspaper, the *Daily Herald*, stated proudly: " We
believe in the unity of interest between the workers and the soldiers, …
between men and women and … between nations.[5] The long association
of the prewar socialist women's organizations – the Co-operative Guild
and the Labour League – with social welfare and peace, acquired a new
relevance in the aftermath of the war. Determined never to return to a
world of profiteers, warmongers, and slum landlords, socialist men and
women were united in demanding fundamental social change as the only
justification for working people's wartime sacrifice. Labour women's
ardent affirmation that they would bring a new morality to socialist politics and help build a "better world in which workers' children would
have a fair chance in life"[6] fit the Labour party's goal of socialist transformation. Arthur Henderson, party leader in 1918, made this clear
when he spoke to Labour women at their first conference: "We are at one
with you in the resolve to establish a new social order in which the very
young and the very old will be protected and cherished and in which the
welfare of all will be the paramount consideration. The dominant issues
are human and moral."[7]

    Even with this recognition of shared goals it is doubtful whether the
Labour party would have admitted women members without the franchise grant of 1918. Labour leaders made no overtures to the League
until the franchise was assured. Women's ethical socialism was clearly of
less interest to them than the prospect of gaining five million new working-class voters just when the party was poised to challenge the Liberals
for the position of second party. Against all the evidence of previous
extensions of the franchise, they were convinced that the power of the
women's vote would make it impossible for Labour or any other party to
ignore women's voices or their interests. They agreed to change Labour's
constitution to accommodate women's membership and launched a pamphlet campaign to win their support. The period of months in 1918 when
Labour and League leaders negotiated the terms of women's entry was
crucial to future gender relations in the party and to how the majority
socialists would respond to the women's agenda in the next twenty years.

    The issue raised in these negotiations was one that many European
socialist women faced as they joined male-dominated parties. Should
women become party members on equal terms with men or as a distinct
group with special interests and responsibilities? In the British case, both
sides came to the negotiations stating their commitment to the ill-defined
gender equality of postwar socialist rhetoric. But both sides also brought
with them an unacknowledged, deeply ingrained assumption of separate

gender spheres. Labour and even League leaders accepted as axiomatic that men belonged to the world of work and public life and women to domesticity and maternity. Agreement on distinct gender roles neverthe-less produced very different visions of women's place in the party. For Labour men, equality meant something like their ideal of working-class marriage – a partnership in which women would provide support services while men continued the real work of political struggle. For women, equality meant separate but equal policy-making power. They expected women to be responsible for a socialist agenda of traditional women's concerns – maternity, housing, education, the care of children and the elderly – and the male majority to give as much attention to these issues as they gave to hours of work and trade union rights. The arrangements that resulted from the talks showed the contradiction between the expressed goal of equality and the underlying assumption of difference. Inevitably it also demonstrated the imbalance of power between the men and women negotiators.

The Labour party's 1918 constitution offered women members inte-gration and equality in theory but separation and marginality in practice. Officially, women could join the party as members of affiliated trade unions or as individual members of local parties. They could compete on equal terms with male trade unionists or local party members for the all-important slots as delegates to the annual party conferences that decided policy. They were eligible for nomination and election to the party's National Executive Committee (NEC) and to seats on local government councils or in Parliament. According to these terms, men and women in the Labour party had equal rights, but in reality women had no power base from which to take advantage of their on-paper equality. They were either barred from membership in the large industrial unions or so under represented as rarely, if ever, to be chosen as union delegates. Since the trade union delegates controlled party conferences with their powerful block votes, women's chances of influencing conference decisions or being elected to the NEC were slim to nonexistent. Margaret Llewelyn Davies, the leader of the Women's Co-operative Guild, saw the situation clearly: "It is always said," she wrote, "that there is equality for men and women in the movement. Certainly most of the doors are open. But the seats are full and possession is nine-tenths of the law so that in reality the opportunity is not equal and seats are hard to win."[8]

Pursuing their goal of separate but equal power, League leaders won the right to hold their own annual women's conference "to express col-lectively the woman's point of view" and to representation on an advisory body with the cumbersome title of Standing Joint Committee of Indus-trial Women's Organizations (SJC), consisting of prominent women from the trade unions, the Co-operative Guild, and the party. But neither the

SJC nor the women's conference had any direct policy-making power. There was no mechanism by which women's resolutions could be passed on to the annual (men's) conference to be considered as party policy. No matter how strongly women supported a particular social reform, unless they won NEC endorsement, the male majority was under no obligation even to discuss it.

The 1918 constitution also deprived Labour women of leaders who would be directly responsible to them. It allowed for a Chief Woman Officer but made clear that as a party appointee, her first loyalty was to the party leadership, which was overwhelmingly male. Marion Phillips, who had been prominent in the Women's Labour League, held that office from 1918 until 1931. She consistently supported the party line, and worked hard to discourage "dissident" women.[9] Throughout the protracted birth control debate of the 1920s, she stood with the male leadership and opposed the will of the vast majority of women members. The handful of Labour women elected to Parliament in the interwar period, and the even smaller number – only two – who held government office, took a similar position. They answered to the party's National Executive, their Parliamentary colleagues and their constituents, not to Labour women. To get elected and have any credibility in the party, they had to play by male rules and could not afford to identify themselves solely with the women's side of the movement. Margaret Bondfield is a good example. As a young working-class shop assistant, she had succeeded almost single-handedly in organizing a union for women in the retail and distributive trades. But when she became Employment Minister in the 1929 Labour Government, she pushed through the Anomalies Act that discriminated against unemployed married women, as if determined to show that she was not "soft" on women.

The constitution left Labour women only one clear area in which to practice their socialism and make a contribution to their chosen party – in their local parties. But even here, segregation could marginalize their efforts. Most new members, when they found that men did all the talking at local party meetings and elected men to attend conferences, chose to join the separate women's sections. Separate meetings helped women overcome some of their shyness in public speaking and encouraged them to develop a women-centered socialism but all too often the separation encouraged party men to treat women comrades as socialist housewives who would raise funds, run elections and make the tea while they did the actual political work. The gender division of power and responsibility among British socialists limited the chances of the national party making a strong response to the woman question in the interwar period.

Why did Labour women allow themselves and their women-centered agendas to be marginalized under the false colors of comradeship? And why did Labour party leaders indulge in the hypocrisy of declaring equality to exist where it could not? The women had little power to resist. Their only alternative was to stay outside the mainstream organization, but the records indicate no support for such a move. A number of older, politically-seasoned League women objected to the terms of the 1918 constitution, but new members seemed to feel that their lack of political experience justified an initial inequality. They were eager to prove their loyalty to their class and the socialist cause, to put to rest traditional male complaints that women were strike-breakers or workers who undercut male wage-rates. The men's guiding principle seems to have been to avoid at all costs a sectionalism based on what they called "sex antagonism" – hostility or competition between the sexes. Like their male comrades in Belgium and Denmark, Labour leaders who tolerated divisive challenges from the left and the right among male members, blanched at the thought of gender discord. Throughout the interwar period, Labour men returned to the theme of the dangers of sex antagonism whenever party women challenged their authority or asked for equal access to policy-making power.

Creating a Woman-Centered Socialism: Labour Women and Reform 1918 to 1921

The terms on which women became party members and the assumptions about gender roles that shaped them clearly narrowed the space in which they could work for reforms in the interests of working-class women. But in the immediate postwar years, new women members did not seem to recognize their limitations. They found the space they needed by accepting and pushing out the boundaries of their separate political sphere. With all the enthusiasm of the newly converted, they put together a socialist program to improve the lives of working-class women, continuing prewar campaigns and beginning new ones in response to the problems the end of the war brought working women. In these immediate postwar years, they were able to take advantage of the reforming and collectivist mood among British socialists and of their own rapid growth that made them a majority in some of the newly established local parties.

One way Labour women created space was by taking key ideas in the national party's program and reconstructing them to fit a women-centered agenda. Their postwar interpretation of citizenship is a good example. In *Labour and the New Social Order*, the party confined its policy on the woman question to issues of citizenship defined as equal civil rights. They promised to secure for women an equal franchise, seats in Parliament, on municipal councils, and on juries, and equal access to all jobs within their physical capacity. Their social reform pledges in the areas of education, health, and welfare, made no mention of the particular needs of women or girls. Before the war, League and Guild women also distinguished between citizenship and social reform issues, seeing the first as a necessary prerequisite for the second. After 1918, they blurred the distinction. Though still supporting an extension of civil rights, Labour women leaders argued that women's citizenship embraced their roles as housewives and mothers. In a series of classes in citizenship for new members, the topics were home life, maternity and infancy, housing, education, and child welfare.[10] These issues they claimed were "not fully understood by men or by women of other classes and therefore cannot be properly dealt with unless working women take them up."[11] By this shift of emphasis, Labour women achieved two goals. They broadened their party's limited definition of what women could expect from a socialist government, and they staked their claim to a larger area of party policy.

They adopted a similar strategy in reconstructing collectivism. *Labour and the New Social Order* called for the nationalization of key industries as the basis for the collectivist state. Labour women chose to focus instead on collective responsibility for social welfare – the welfare state. Labour women had a long tradition of addressing their reform demands directly to national and local government officials. Before 1918, with only minimal representation in any branch of organized labor and still outside the political system, they had no other avenue of effective political action. The war validated this strategy and vastly increased their faith in the state's capacity to finance and run large-scale welfare programs. Guild and League women argued that if the government could pay a weekly separation allowance to the wives and dependents of servicemen in wartime, it could pay poor mothers a weekly allowance in peacetime. Similarly, if the government could control rents and food profiteering in times of national crisis, it could do so even more easily when that crisis passed. Even after they won the vote and joined the party, Labour women continued to call directly on the state to fulfill its obligations to women. In the postwar years, they expected the state to pay either in cash or in services for women's performance of the essential national task of restoring population levels. As one Labour woman pointed out, "The loss of men in war, makes clear the value of every baby to the nation."[12]

Between 1918 and 1920, Labour women outlined a reform program that was in many ways a model of the post-World War II welfare state but with a much greater emphasis on the needs of working-class women. Arguing that women were the "custodians of the nation's health," they demanded an all-woman consultative committee to serve under the Minister of Health. The first task of the committee would be to ensure that any national health service would provide free medical care to working-class women regardless of their employment or marital status. They pressed the government to implement and extend the provisions of the Maternal and Infant Welfare Act of 1918 for which they had campaigned before and during World War I. They wanted state-funded local clinics, professional midwifery services, and lying-in hospitals available to working-class mothers everywhere. They persuaded the party to adopt non-contributory old-age, widows' and mothers' pensions – the last for women bringing up children alone or with husbands who were incapacitated, of whom there were a great many after the war. They discussed at length another prewar plan for some kind of state endowment of motherhood, which they later formalized as family allowances paid in cash directly to working-class mothers.

In education, Labour women campaigned for nursery schools, not with working mothers in mind (they hoped that poverty would no longer drive working-class mothers into the labor market) but to provide very young children with the space, fresh air, and play equipment unavailable in most working-class homes. The pioneers of nursery school education in Britain were Rachel and Margaret McMillan, both active socialists and founding members in 1894 of the Bradford branch of the Independent Labour Party. By insisting that the proper care of working-class infants and children was a vital foundation for a socialist society, the McMillans convinced Labour women that they had an important job to do in the socialist movement. They provided the model for Labour women's postwar plans for the education, feeding, and health care of the pre-school child, plans that called for local government responsibility and state financing. Nationally, in local sections and as borough councillors, party women made this cause their own. They were among the party's most vocal supporters of municipal nursery schools, school meals programs, and universal, free secondary education to age fifteen years, for girls equally with boys.

Labour women's postwar reform plans differed from those of most other European socialist parties not so much in content but in the level of grass-roots participation. Instead of a party elite drawing up and executing reforms for the good of the working-class, as they did in Austria, for example, Labour women leaders inherited from their prewar organizations the practice of asking their local members to submit ideas and using them to create social welfare policies. A good example of this approach was Labour women's postwar housing policy. In 1918, immediately before it merged with the Labour party, the Women's Labour League asked its members to submit plans for their ideal "working woman's house." At the end of the war, the housing stock, particularly in Britain's older cities (London, Glasgow, Leeds, and Manchester) was woefully inadequate, overcrowded, unsanitary and ramshackle. The Labour party made new housing a priority in *Labour and the New Social Order* and the League wanted to be sure that the women who would clean, cook, and raise children in the new houses would have a say in their design. In letters and questionnaire responses, they gave their views on the number of bedrooms, where to put the kitchen range (in a separate scullery or in the living room) the location of the bathtub, upstairs or down, and whether or not to keep the "parlor," which working-class families lucky enough to have one traditionally used only for formal occasions. League leaders sifted through the responses and produced a working paper entitled, "The Working Woman's House," which the party, still in its reforming phase, published as a pamphlet in 1919 and accepted as a policy commitment.[13]

Unemployment was the most immediate and serious problem for many working-class women at the end of the war. Women war workers who had been encouraged to take previously all-male jobs and praised for sustaining the country's wartime production were shocked by their abrupt dismissal as soon as the war was over. By early 1919, close to half a million women and 26,700 girls under the age of eighteen were officially unemployed.[14] The coalition government's decision to pay no unemployment benefit to women who refused domestic service, that most unpopular of jobs, aroused working women's fury, and they took to the streets in protest marches. Labour women were eager to support them, but while they denounced the government's policy, they hesitated over an alternative. Middle-class feminist groups were insisting on women's right to be considered for all jobs on the basis of merit, but the Labour party stood firmly for a restoration of the prewar status quo. Most Labour women seem to have accepted returning servicemen's priority right to jobs, but there were some who warned of the danger of conceding the principle that "no woman has a right to earn her bread while any man is out of work."[15] The outcome was a compromise for socialist women, a defeat for feminists. Labour women drew up a *Domestic Workers' Charter* calling for the organization of domestic workers into a union as a means of improving their conditions of work.

From the historian's point of view, this issue would seem to have been a clear instance of conflict between socialist women's class and gender loyalties. But all the evidence suggests that most Labour women did not see it that way in the immediate postwar years. They did not recognize the conflict because they thought of the needs of working-class women as integral to the overall class cause. Only a handful of middle-class, educated women who had been leading suffragists in the prewar struggles were aware of the tension and resented the male majority's willingness to sacrifice women's interests for men's, whether as wage workers or party members. The rank and file seem to have accepted their party's equality rhetoric and worked hard to prove their own worthiness. Most knew little about what went on at the decision-making level of the national party. As housewives and mothers, they were obliged to stay close to home. Their arena for socialist reforms was local and it was there that they made their greatest impact on the welfare of working-class women.

Labour Women and Municipal Socialism 1918 to 1921

Among the civil rights working-class women won with the national franchise was the right to serve on local municipal and county councils and on the boards of guardians that oversaw the workhouses for the indigent poor.[16] Local Labour parties selected candidates for these offices, and since women in the early postwar years were a majority in a number of local parties, they made an impressive initial entry into this new field of elective office.[17] They soon recognized that their chances of election were directly related to their gender. Local voters took the view that it was natural for women to be Poor Law Guardians because their work involved such traditional female responsibilities as care of the sick, the elderly, and the very young. To a lesser degree they found it appropriate for women to serve on municipal councils though only on the committees that dealt with maternal and child welfare, education, and civic amenities.

Labour women's municipal election manifestos played both the gender and class cards. They claimed that their gender and class background gave them a clear advantage in understanding the needs of those most likely to be clients of guardians and local magistrates or recipients of municipal and national welfare services. Knowing at first hand how hard it was for working-class housewives and mothers to make ends meet and bring up children on low, irregular, or nonexistent wages, they understood the suffering unemployment caused. They promised that, if elected guardians, they would allow outdoor relief (cash allowances) to the long-term unemployed, contrasting their attitude with that of middle-class guardians who denied it on the grounds that direct payments sapped unemployed workers' initiative and deterred them from seeking work.[18] They argued for their financial skills on the grounds that as working-class household managers, they knew precisely what food, rent, and children's shoes cost and how to balance a budget down to the last farthing.

In these practical, everyday terms local Labour women addressed the woman question in the immediate postwar years. As Poor Law guardians, they tried to bring a new spirit of humanity to their relations with workhouse inmates, who were, they insisted, "unfortunate, not blameworthy." They worked to remove babies and young children from the "sordid surroundings" of the workhouse and into home like environments. A Mrs. Fawcett of York persuaded the Board of Guardians to purchase a babies home for that purpose and arranged small group homes for older children.[19] Labour women guardians demanded an end to the punitive attitude toward unmarried mothers and what they regarded as male guardians' salacious inquiries into their "fall." As municipal councillors, they wanted to take advantage of the full range of permissive powers granted to local councils, including free milk for pregnant women, nursing mothers, babies and school children, maternal and infant clinics, direct labor subsidized housing, and secondary school scholarships. They chose special projects that would bring immediate and practical relief to overburdened housewives. A favorite was to open a public washhouse where women could do their laundry with the benefits of hot water and steam driers and thus avoid days of damp sheets and clothing hanging up in the scullery and over the cooking range.

In the optimism of postwar reconstruction, the Labour party routinely praised the achievements of its women members, noting their remarkable growth in numbers, their fund-raising contribution, and municipal successes. The party adopted several measures from the women's agenda, including equal franchise, municipal housing, and noncontributory widows' and mothers' pensions. When Labour's bill for the Complete Emancipation of Women was defeated in the House of Lords in favor of an ineffectual Conservative measure entitled the Sex Disqualification (Removal) Act, the party introduced two more – unsuccessful – bills to extend the female franchise. Despite the disappointment of a poor showing in the 1918 general election, Labour's leaders expressed their continuing confidence that working women's votes would help bring them to power. In their turn, Labour women maintained an undiminished enthusiasm for their party, accepting, at least for a time, the constitutional barriers that denied them access to policy making. However, it remained to be seen whether the party would sustain its interest in the woman question under the more challenging circumstances following the collapse of the postwar economic boom.

Socialist Conflict over Women's Issues 1921 to 1931

The recession that began in late 1920, dragging on for the entire decade in some areas and then deepening into the Depression in 1930, forced a shift in the socialist response to the woman question. Alarmed by the threat of a return to prewar poverty levels and a drastic decline in trade union strength, Labour party socialists put aside their plan of social reconstruction in favor of defensive strategies. After 1920, they talked less about making working-class women equal citizens and partners in a new socialist state and more about protecting them as workers, wives, and mothers from capitalist greed and reactionary government. While Labour women generally supported the shift towards protection, they had a different view of what this meant in policy terms. After 1924, when Labour became an elected minority government for the first time, the men argued that women's problems would all be solved when the party won a big enough majority to legislate socialism. Labour women, on the other hand, were unwilling to allow working-class women to suffer while the party awaited its electoral opportunity. They wanted to do all in their power to help the women of their class before they slid further down into the well of poverty.

The recession took a heavy toll on working-class women and their families. Among the lowest paid workers, the "weak link in the industrial army," women were the first to feel the impact of wage reductions and the withdrawal of government support from the trade boards that maintained wage levels in the sweated trades. Women in these trades, lace, glove, and chain makers, for example, as well as agricultural workers and domestic servants were not covered by unemployment insurance, and if they fell below the poverty line, *Labour Woman* warned ominously, "the streets may offer the only profession." [20] The recession affected skilled workers in the cotton industry as severely as their so-called unskilled sisters. After 1920, they faced chronic unemployment with the additional aggravation of gender discrimination. As women, they lost unemployment benefits if they refused domestic service and for "not genuinely seeking work" if they lived at home with their families while waiting to be rehired.[21]

Rising unemployment and falling wages encouraged government agencies and the popular press to make scapegoats of married women workers, accusing them of taking jobs from family providers, assumed to be men. The government gave credence to this distorted view of the labor market by announcing that women teachers and civil servants must resign on marriage no matter what their circumstances. Despite a strong commitment to the male breadwinner, the Labour party stood firmly for married women's right to work. Male trade unionists did not want employment reduced to the level of relief work nor did they want government officials interfering in workers' private lives. In contrast, Labour women had divided opinions. While most agreed that dismissing married women workers was "an unjustified interference with the freedom of employees who should be judged not by their private circumstances but by the value of their work,"[22] others argued that if jobs were scarce, it was only fair to limit each family to a single breadwinner. The Women Clerks and Secretaries Union, thinking of their own mostly unmarried members, introduced a resolution at the 1925 Labour Women's Conference stating that "preference in employment should normally be given to those entirely dependent on their wages over married women whose husbands can afford to support them ...." The conference unanimously demanded the withdrawal of this reactionary resolution but there is no doubt that the Women Clerks were not its only supporters among Labour women outside the conference.[23]

At the same time as unemployment and declining wages threatened working-class living standards, the Conservative chancellor, Sir Eric Geddes, decided to cut unemployment benefit and social services in order to reduce the deficit and return the pound to its prewar value. The Geddes Axe, like unemployment, had a more deleterious affect on working-class women and their young children than on other sectors of the population. Cuts in free or subsidized milk for pregnant women, nursing mothers, and young children and similar cuts in school meals, were a very real threat to health for those already undernourished. Poor mothers knew they could not replace the food value of the free milk and school meals from the family's diminishing budget. Many women would have attested the truth of the adage that "a reduction of wages is felt by the head of the family as a shortage of money, by the mother as a shortage of food."[24]

Labour women responded early and vigorously to the crisis. In their journal, *Labour Woman*, and in conference resolutions, they accused the government of being "the employers' government" and castigated it for "abandoning the infant population at the beginning of a winter when unemployment is unprecedented ... in order to save a few thousand pounds."[25] To protect wage levels, Labour women and women trade unionists began a campaign to bring unorganized and still voteless young working women into the trade union movement. "Get that union feeling!" urged *Labour Woman*. Women's sections arranged deputations to local authorities and Members of Parliament, demanding a restoration of free milk, school meals, and medical inspections. While pursuing these efforts, Labour women launched three new reform campaigns which they felt would give working-class women their best chance of defending themselves against unemployment and welfare cuts – free birth control advice, family allowances, and protective legislation for women industrial workers.

Gender Struggles over Birth Control and Family Allowances 1923 to 1929

Before World War I, birth control was a taboo subject for most working-class women, something hinted at but rarely named. In 1914, when the League and its sister organization, the Women's Co-operative Guild were campaigning for a national maternity service, two hundred or so of their members wrote letters describing their experience of childbirth. The three or four who implied that they had used birth control assumed that their readers would judge them harshly for indulging in an immoral and unnatural practice. Yet the *Maternity Letters* showed with painful clarity why Labour women became so united and determined in their support of birth control after the war. Many of the correspondents described chronic and debilitating health problems, miscarriages, and infant deaths that had come from too frequent pregnancies and inadequate medical attention. Others wrote as movingly of the day-to-day struggle to bring up a large family on low and irregular earnings, knowing that they could not give their children a good enough start in life to enable them to escape the treadmill of poverty.[26]

Two influences transformed birth control from a moral taboo to the political issue that dominated Labour women's agenda in the 1920s. The first was World War I. In the early years of mass mobilization, official anxiety about an increase in illegitimate births and the spread of venereal disease brought birth control into public discourse and onto the shelves of the corner shop in the form of condoms. Wartime disruption of working-class family life also helped break down traditional taboos related to sexuality and birth control. Men in the armed forces were issued condoms as prophylactics but just as significant in changing their sexual behavior no doubt was the knowledge that life expectancy at the front was pitifully short. Young working-class women knew this too. Their education in matters of sex and birth control owed much to the fact that so many of them were living and working away from home for the first time.[27]

More open public discussion of birth control and sexuality may explain how individual socialist women overcame their earlier reticence on the subject but not how they came to make the issue the primary focus of their reform program. The impetus for this came from a small group of middle-class socialist feminists, party members but not national leaders, who saw birth control as a key issue in the class struggle. They argued that deliberate limitation of family size was as much responsible for the comfortable living standards of the middle class as their higher incomes. They wanted the same advantages for working-class families and aware that no working-class wife could afford to seek advice from a private doctor as middle-class women did, they proposed that local maternal and child welfare clinics be allowed to offer free birth control information to any married woman who wanted it. Led by Dora Russell, they called upon other Labour women to support their campaign.

To say that Labour women leapt at this chance to become a socialist lobby for birth control would be an understatement. Dora Russell's initiative released all the strong feelings expressed in the Maternity Letters. Rank-and-file Labour women poured out their condemnation of unlimited childbirth, arguing that it maimed women's bodies, created marital disharmony, placed impossible strains on the family budget and limited the ability of working-class mothers to give their children a chance in life. Their vehemence against the conventional view of motherhood as woman's greatest joy shocked Dora Russell.[28] Russell's message that birth control was a matter of class justice came to them with all the force of a revelation. They asked with some bitterness why working women had to suffer through endless pregnancies while the knowledge that would save them remained a middle-class secret, because only the middle-class could afford to pay for it. Mrs. Jones of Greenwich, speaking at the National Conference of Labour Women in 1924 said: "The wealthy woman says how many children she can afford to have because she can afford to pay for the knowledge and we say that the working mother should be able to get the knowledge although she has no money."[29]

Labour women rapidly transformed a modest demand that working-class women should be allowed access to birth control advice at their local clinics into a socialist crusade. When Dora Russell, Frieda Laski, and others formed the Workers' Birth Control Group, many Labour women set up branches in their sections where they discussed works by Margaret Sanger and Marie Stopes and put pressure on their local parties and Medical Officers of Health to support the cause. Before long, a great many were convinced that birth control was the socialist answer to the woman question. It would bring class justice by raising the standard of living of working-class families for generations to come. It would save working women's lives and give them the time and energy to raise healthy socialist children. At present, one woman argued, "when their children went into schools at five years of age, 42 percent were under-nourished and sickly."[30] Some Labour women went even further in their claims. A Mrs. Palmer described birth control as "an essential factor in the abolition of poverty, the civilized substitute for war, for famine, for pestilence, for disease."[31]

Labour women launched their birth control campaign at the 1923 Labour Women's Conference. With few dissenters, they passed the first of many resolutions calling on the party to introduce a bill that would allow state-funded mother and baby clinics to offer free birth control advice to married women. It seemed to come as a surprise to them when Labour party leaders, including the Chief Woman Officer, opposed their resolutions while refusing to discuss the matter. When the NEC finally acknowledged the issue in 1925, it took the position that "the subject of birth control is in its nature not one that should be made a political party issue but should remain a matter on which the members of the party should be free to hold and promote their individual convictions."[32] Over the next four years, the leadership, concerned about organized resistance from Roman Catholic members, restated this view as its only response to women members' annual barrage of resolutions. In 1926, the NEC imposed a three-year moratorium on discussion of the issue. Dora Russell came back with a direct appeal to the miners who had the power to sway the conference. She asked them to think of birth control as a job safety issue and to support the women's cause as the women had supported theirs in the General Strike. The miners acknowledged their obligation and voted to suspend the moratorium, but the victory was a mere stay of execution. By 1928, it was all over and Labour women had to acknowledge that they had no power beyond persuasion to influence party policy.

The birth control struggle and its outcome were a direct result of gender segregation in the Labour party and indeed in the rest of the labor movement. Segregation encouraged Labour women to choose birth control as the cornerstone of their socialist policy while also making it impossible for them to turn it into party policy. While Labour women were throwing so much of their energy into this campaign, Labour men were absorbed with a completely different set of problems from which women were virtually excluded. Between 1921 and 1925, the men spent hours of debating time on whether to allow the British Communist party to affiliate. No women took part in those debates. During the General Strike, Labour men were deeply involved in discussions with trade union leaders over strategy, while women set up local relief committees to feed the needy. When the strike ended in defeat, followed by one of the longest and most brutal lock-outs in mining history, party leaders gave their attention to getting back into power so as to reverse anti-union legislation, while the women raised money and arranged temporary adoptions of miners' children. With this segregation of roles, an issue like birth control that seemed to Labour women the answer to all the social and economic problems of their class appeared to Labour men jarringly inappropriate and a threat to their electoral chances.

The Issue of Family Allowances 1924 to 1928

The second welfare reform Labour women fought for in the 1920s was family allowances. League women had discussed different ways of endowing motherhood before the war, some arguing for payment in kind – free milk, school meals, children's boots, etc. – and others for a state-paid mother's wage. When it became clear in 1922 that poverty was growing worse, they revived their discussions and by 1925 were agreed upon a monetary allowance, using their earlier argument that the State had an obligation to pay mothers for the important national task of raising children. They thought it would benefit workers generally if women and children were removed from "the battlefield between employers and workers." Their party ignored the subject as long as family allowances was just a women's issue, but it took action when the Independent Labour Party included it in its *Living Wage* policy. The ILP proposed a statutory minimum wage for all workers, supplemented by children's allowances paid out of direct taxation as a means of raising working-class living standards and redistributing wealth from the rich to the poor.[33] The Labour Party set up a joint committee of party and trade union representatives (no women were invited to participate) to discuss the matter and make a policy recommendation. The committee tried for three years to reach an agreement but while the party members came to support the ILP's position, trade union members remained opposed. They argued that if the state paid mothers for children, trade union negotiators could no longer bargain for a family wage for male providers and employers would feel free to lower male wages to the level of women's. Rather than divide the two wings of the movement, the Labour party backed down. Once again, Labour women and minority socialists had to accept their powerlessness in the face of the male trade union majority.

Labour men's rejection of the two reforms that dominated the women's agenda for most of the decade had deeper roots than a mere difference of opinion over political strategy. It is clear that many male socialists regarded family allowances and birth control as threats to traditional working-class male control over the family income and marital sex. This gender tension broke the political surface on several occasions. Comrade Rhys Davies, a delegate to the party's 1930 annual conference complained that family allowances would mean that, "instead of a working man getting his wages at the factory pay office, his wife would draw his wages for him at the post office."[34] The Labour MP for Reading, Somerville Hastings, expressed male resentment of family allowances by suggesting that "working-class women don't have the requisite knowledge to spend an allowance in the right way. They would spend the money in free enterprise shops on adulterated food."[35] Fighting words indeed! Labour women were incensed by this charge and responded with a series of letters to *Labour Woman* putting Hastings firmly in his place, arguing that as a man in comfortable circumstances, he was in no position to criticize working women's hard-earned skill at feeding their families out of limited resources. The evidence that gender tension existed over birth control was the unbroken male silence on the issue. In contrast to other European socialists in this period, the Dutch for example, British Labour party leaders were reluctant to make anything pertaining to sexuality a political issue. Neither the NEC nor the party in conference ever discussed the merits of birth control as a social welfare reform. They merely repeated the formula that it was a private not a political matter. If Labour women had reached the conclusion that the private was the political, most Labour men had not.

Socialists against Feminists:
The Issue of Protective Legislation

Protective legislation for women workers was Labour women's third major campaign to solve the woman question in the 1920s. Here they were on safer ground than with either birth control or family allowances. Since it was in no way a threat to trade union authority, Labour men were prepared to endorse protective legislation as a legitimate women's concern and leave it to the women's side of the movement to pursue. Immediately after the war in which women had taken on jobs previously seen as well beyond their capacity, Labour women leaders questioned the need for special legislation to protect women workers. They argued that sex-based regulations limited women's job opportunities while perpetuating low wages and gender-segregation in the workforce. By the late 1920s, they had changed their minds. Working women's pay and conditions had markedly deteriorated. Employers' efforts to boost profits had gone beyond wage reductions to include layoffs, assembly-line speed-up and longer working hours. A favorite device was the two shift system. Women workers had to leave home as early as four in the morning for the first shift. After a few useless spare hours in the middle of the day, they went back for the second shift and often did not get home until ten at night. The 1918 Washington Convention restricted shift work for women but the British government disregarded the international ruling and allowed shift work in "essential trades," a sufficiently loose term to encourage widespread abuse. Working women had little power to resist these pressures. Since 1919, their trade union membership had declined by a third and efforts to raise the numbers failed to stop the slide.[36] Labour women leaders recognized that protective legislation was not the ideal way of solving women's long-term problems in the labor force but they argued that it was a vital first step in improving working conditions that threatened women's health as workers and future mothers.

Labour women drafted a factory act which outlawed the two shift system and night work, limited women's working week to forty-eight hours, provided them with protection against dangerous substances like lead in the workplace, mandated toilet facilities and rest periods, proper ventilation, and temperature control. The party promised to implement this reform as soon as they were in a position to do so, but opposition to the proposals came from another quarter. Middle-class "equality" feminists organized as *The Open Door Council* subjected Labour women's factory act to loud and scathing criticism. They challenged Labour's Chief Woman Officer, Marion Phillips, to a public debate on the BBC and argued against protective legislation in some of the same terms Labour women themselves had used just after the war. Labour women translated this very public dispute over what was good policy for working women into the language of class. Not for the first time, but with greater vehemence than before, socialist women criticized middle-class, leisured women for making pronouncements on subjects outside their experience. What did these privileged women know about factory labor – the heat, dust, noise, accidents, and abuse? By the end of the decade, the criticism of middle-class women had turned into a general critique of feminism. At the National Labour Women's Conference in 1928, Marie James pointed out that feminism was a middle-class philosophy with no relevance to working women: "The feminist problem was how to rescue women from their degrading dependence on a good man's love ... It was not concerned with the more degrading dependence of women on employers who exploited their labor in the interests of large profits."[37]

The rift between socialist women and middle-class feminists ended an informal alliance forged in the prewar decades that had been responsible for the Maternity and Child Welfare Act of 1918, Divorce Law Reform and, in large measure, women's suffrage. From the moment that they admitted women as members, the Labour Party warned them against joining nonparty women's organizations, presumably to prevent feminist sirens luring them away. Party leaders came within a few votes of an outright ban on such associations in 1925. Labour women who had strong ties with feminist groups before 1918 and those who became local or Parliamentary candidates ignored the warnings. The largest feminist organization, the National Union of Societies for Equal Citizenship, gave financial and canvassing support to women candidates from all parties, and since Labour women rarely had trade union funds at their disposal, they were grateful for this support. But Labour women who maintained their connections with middle-class feminist organizations were a tiny minority. Most working-class members became increasingly suspicious of feminism as the economic and political environment that raised the level of class tension.

In 1929, as Labour women looked back over a decade of struggling to save working-class women and children from attacks on their health and welfare, a minority recognized the party constitution as the major obstacle to their political effectiveness. They felt as a Mrs. Bevan put it, that they "did not want to be in the nursery any longer." They were ready for the full equality that party leaders had promised in 1918. At their 1928 and 1930 conferences, they passed resolutions calling for constitutional changes to give women policy-making power.[38] They wanted to elect their own representatives to the NEC, make the women's conference an autonomous body or have just three of their resolutions appear each year on the Annual Party Conference agenda. Male leaders rejected all the resolutions, urging women members to be content with their supposed influence over party decisions. Labour women expressed scepticism at this suggestion, especially when the Party proceeded to change the constitution in a way that left women with even less power than before. To reduce the size of the annual conference, party leaders decided to cut the number of trade union delegates. Trade unions responded that they would only accept the loss of representation if proportional cuts were made in the socialist organizations and local parties. Under the new terms, a local party could only send a second delegate if it had more than 2,500 women members. Very few local parties could meet the requirement. Limited to one delegate, most local parties chose a man. As a result, women's representation was reduced from small to almost nonexistent.

After this, Labour women's space for political action on the woman question narrowed considerably at the national level. Not only were they further removed than ever from policy making, but their party suffered a series of shattering reverses that pushed the woman question entirely out of the picture. In 1929, the party came to power for the second time and with a record nine women members of Parliament, but its minority status prevented the passage of anything reassembling socialist legislation. By late 1930, the Labour government was engulfed in the financial crisis stemming from the collapse of the U.S. stock market. Unable to resist the pressure from the financial community, the party leader, Ramsey MacDonald and his chancellor, Phillip Snowden, made drastic cuts in unemployment benefits and instituted a harsh means test. Appalled by this betrayal, the rest of the Labour government resigned, the ILP disaffiliated, and Labour was soundly beaten in the general election that followed.

In legislative terms, Labour women's decade-long struggle to keep women's issues in the forefront of the national party's attention had few positive results. Ironically, Labour's record compared unfavorably with that of the Conservatives. Labour passed two housing acts providing state subsidies for local councils to build low rent houses and an unemployment insurance act which offered small increases in benefits while maintaining unfair treatment of married women workers. Conservatives were responsible for divorce law reform, widows' pensions, extension of old age pensions, and the equalization of the franchise in 1928. Labour had the excuse of being in power for much shorter periods and then as a minority government, but party programs after 1920 offered little to meet women's specific social welfare needs. Labour women had been unable to persuade the dominant male majority that women could not wait for socialism but needed help right away, or that birth control and family allowances were just as much socialist concerns as relations with the Communist party or the right to work or maintenance.

Labour Women's Reform Initiatives in
Local Politics 1921 to 1931

In contrast to this disappointing outcome in the national party, Labour
women could point to a much better record in their local parties and
municipalities. Persistent neighborhood campaigning on the birth control
issue bore fruit in some areas when local government funding was converted to a block grant system in 1930. Recognizing that he could no
longer control how local councils allocated funds, the Labour Minister of
Health sent a discreet memorandum to local health authorities giving the
Maternal and Child Welfare committees the right to offer birth control
advice to married women "in cases of medical necessity."[39] Where Labour
women had been most active and health officials supportive, working-
class women gained access to free birth control advice.[40] Just how many
clinics provided this service is hard to determine. As it was entirely at the
discretion of local councils, one can assume that they interpreted the
phrase "in cases of medical necessity" as narrowly or broadly as they saw
fit. Certainly the service was not advertised and the subject of birth control remained officially and publicly taboo. Yet, Labour women's meetings
and discussions undoubtedly helped demystify the subject, spreading the
idea that something could be done to prevent unwanted pregnancies to
a widening circle of working-class women.

Labour women's local initiatives were successful in other areas of working-class women's welfare. Unable to secure state-paid cash allowances for
mothers, Labour women pressured local councils into providing allowances
in kind – free milk for mothers and young children, school meals, and
medical services. In the distressed areas, worst hit by the Depression, they
set up and ran communal kitchens to provide free meals for hungry mothers and children. During the eight-month miners' lock out following the
General Strike of 1926, local Labour women raised the astonishing sum of
three hundred thousand pounds by collecting at movie theaters, auction-
ing donated rings and watches, organizing concerts of Welsh miners'
choirs, and selling miniature miners' lamps. The money went to miners'
wives to enable them to buy food, boots, and clothing for their families.

Labour women became a visible presence in their communities when
they took to the streets in protest marches, held public rallies, and street
corner meetings. Peace became one of their major crusades. Many local
sections vociferously opposed the military marches held on Empire Day
and the tradition of sending orphaned boys into the navy. When the York
Labour Party proposed sending representatives to a "Military Sunday"
demonstration (Labour had supported the war and many Labour men
were veterans), the women's section told them in no uncertain terms
that their attendance was "contrary to the desire of the party to work for

the abolition of the loathsome business of war."[41] They kept a close eye on their local schools and protested any attempt to glorify militarism and war to the children. Unemployment was another issue that brought Labour women into the streets. Local sections organized pickets outside the Labour Exchanges to advise women on how to avoid the pitfalls of the "not genuinely seeking work" clause and anomalies provisions in unemployment benefit regulations. The Jarrow section successfully insisted that the Council provide women waiting in lines outside the Labour Exchange with shelter, seating, and toilet facilities.[42]

The minutes of local women's sections suggest that in the 1920s, British Labour women created an effective grass roots socialist movement which like the *Prévoyante* women's groups in Belgium, aimed at improving the welfare of working-class women and their families. Local section women worked in cooperation with socialist women's national and international organizations including the Women's International League for Peace and Freedom and the Workers' Birth Control Group. Many had a strong enough sense of the value of their contribution to challenge local male control over party policy and office holding. However, in the early-1930s, this movement went into precipitous decline. In section after section, average weekly attendance fell from around fifty or sixty in 1925 to 1929 into the teens by 1931. Members no longer asserted their rights as women in sharply worded letters of protest. As the economic, political, and cultural environment changed, so did Labour women's approach to the woman question.

Class Loyalty before Women's Issues 1932 to 1939

After 1931, women ceased to be a political concern for Labour party socialists. Inside the party, women members almost dropped out of sight. National party records and conference debates give the impression of an all-male club with only the occasional woman speaker. There were no more women's campaigns to stir up "sex antagonism" and distract the trade unionist majority from its own agenda. Outside the party, working-class women lost their distinct identity as equal partners in the brave new socialist world or as special targets of capitalist exploitation. Women's issues faded into insignificance as the party became absorbed in the struggle against fascists and reactionary government to the right of them and communists to the left. Party leaders demanded unity and conformity in response to the crisis and, with few exceptions, Labour women were willing to comply. They turned away from their crusade on behalf of working-class women and threw all their energies into defending their class. Looking back, socialist women as well as men recalled the strong sense of comradeship they shared in these years. Only a minority reflected that the price of comradeship for women was the sacrifice of their own agendas and the women's cause.

Labour women signaled a move away from their decade-long struggle on behalf of the women of their class when they stopped asking for separate but equal status and accepted the limitations of the 1918 constitution. On at least two occasions in the decade, Labour women had the chance to renew the struggle for greater autonomy. In 1933 and again in 1936, the Labour party made changes to its constitution but Labour women let both opportunities go by without comment. Furthermore, they did not raise a single complaint when the party announced that of the four constituent groups in the party, trade unionists, socialist party affiliates, local constituency parties, and women, women were the only ones who would not be able to elect their own representatives on the National Executive. Neither the SJC nor Labour women in conference even discussed the matter. The contrast with 1929 when women fought hard for just three of their resolutions to go to the Annual Conference could not be more striking. The same indifference to the equality issue appeared when Labour women leaders asked the sections in 1935 if they would be willing to contribute a small sum annually to socialist women's parliamentary campaigns. Only 165 of the 2,045 sections bothered to return the questionnaires, and not all of those supported the levy. Labour women leaders were obliged to drop the scheme.[43]

Labour women's change of direction is revealed even more strikingly by their lack of interest in the abortion issue. As they did with birth control in the 1920s, a small group of middle-class socialist feminists organized the Abortion Law Reform Association (ALRA) in 1936 to promote working-class women's right to safe, legal abortion. The leaders, who included Dora Russell and other veterans of the Workers' Birth Control Group, supported their cause with a class argument similar to the one they used so effectively on behalf of birth control. They argued that while middle-class women could afford to pay private doctors or go to private clinics for illegal abortions, working women had to resort to unqualified neighborhood abortionists to "help them out" or to pills and potions heavily advertised in working-class newspapers. As a result, working-class women were more likely to suffer severe infections or death following an abortion than middle-class women. The two campaigns were also directly linked in that many working-class women still relied on abortion as a last resort means of birth control. Despite these links, Labour women paid no attention whatsoever to the abortion campaign at the national or local level. Whether this was because they felt it was useless to try again after the failure of their birth control struggle or because they were involved in mainstream class issues is hard to say.[44]

If further evidence were needed of a shift of direction, the change in rhetoric is decisive. In the 1920s, Labour women, including the rank and file used a socialist feminist rhetoric. They spoke directly to the needs of working-class women as housewives, mothers, and workers. Whether they were discussing housing, education, health, industry, pensions, rent, the cost of living, or peace, they consciously put forth the woman's point of view. Their housing plan was the "Working Woman's House"; their health concerns centered on maternal and child welfare, maternal nutrition, and birth control; in education, they stood up for the equal rights of girls; in industry, protective legislation for women workers; pensions were for mothers, abandoned wives and widows; rents and the cost of living were part of the housewife's budget and peace an aspect of maternalism. Labour women hardly ever gave a speech or wrote a letter without mentioning women. A good example of this self-conscious socialist feminism is this extract from a speech by a Mrs. Hood at the 1927 national women's conference: "Women are consumed with an holy discontent – men have failed them with regard to housing, education, employment, pensions, and war. Even the laws of the country are most unjust to its women citizens who are rising in revolt."[45]

In the 1930s, Labour women discussed many of these same issues but now their comments drew attention to class not gender injustice. Instead of designing the working woman's house, Labour women attacked the government for removing rent controls and allowing private contractors to build substandard housing for workers. When they spoke of education, they no longer called for equal opportunity for girls but accused the government of denying all working-class children educational opportunities. They were particularly incensed with the Conservatives' 1935 Education Act which extended the school leaving age to fifteen without providing maintenance grants and included a clause allowing children to leave for "beneficial employment" or "home duties." These provisions clearly discriminated against working-class children and Labour women responded with anger. Dorothy Elliott remarked: "They [the Tories] wanted to keep the workers' children in the mines and feeding machines instead of having an opportunity for a proper education."[46]

Even when they made women the subject of a special campaign, which was not often in the 1930s, Labour women were less interested in securing welfare reforms than in placing the responsibility for women's problems firmly with the "employers' government." In the maternal mortality campaign, for example, they argued that by cutting unemployment benefits and imposing the means test, the national government had pushed nutrition levels among unemployed families so low as to endanger the lives of pregnant women. Despite the evidence of (Dr.) Edith Summerskill, a Labour woman herself, that medical malpractice and inadequate antenatal care were more likely causes of maternal mortality, Labour women persisted in the malnutrition argument because it gave them ammunition against the class enemy. They were no longer trying to empower women by providing them with the resources to help themselves as they did in their birth control and family allowance campaigns. Rather, they made women's problems the sticks with which to beat reactionary government. This is not to suggest that they no longer cared about the sufferings of working-class women, only that they had moved closer to the male socialist position on the way to alleviate them. They were more ready to accept the Labour party's view that the woman question would only be solved under a socialist government. Mrs. Eleanor Barton put it this way: "We know well we can best fight the battle for the welfare of our children and our homes by standing side-by-side with our men folk in the struggle to lay the foundation of a new and better order of society."[47]

The shift from a gender to class-based focus brought Labour women much closer into line with the goals and strategies of the national party than they were in the 1920s. For the first time since the party opened its doors to them, women divided ideologically along the lines of their male comrades instead of forming a single women's interest group. There were women who supported the Popular Front and those who were opposed and both sides argued for their point of view in the same terms as the men in the party. Men and women opposed to the Front objected to an alliance with the capitalist Liberal party as much as they objected to the Communists. Supporters argued that if British socialists did not fight fascism with every means available to them then the whole society would fall prey to fascist dictatorship. Labour women also divided along the same lines as male socialists over the disarmament question. In the 1920s they had made peace a women's issue, arguing that if women had had the vote in 1914 there would have been no war and that working-class mothers would never again allow their sons to become cannon fodder. In the 1930s, those who favored peace joined the men who argued for unilateral disarmament, while others moved closer to the men for whom the fascist threat justified rearmament.

This realignment represented a profound change for women in the Labour party. Within three or four years, they had moved from segregation and women-centered programs to much greater integration and shared agendas. The whys and the wherefores of this change are significant since they explain the demise of a valiant attempt at creating a British socialist party which would give as much attention to women's concerns as to men's. What made Labour women abandon the attempt after a decade of struggle? Was it because, as a second generation, they had different ideas about gender and socialist politics from the pioneers? Did they reconstruct their policies to reflect the economic and social changes affecting women and the working-class in the 1930s? Or were they following an earlier pattern of going where they were most needed, this time to the aid of their class?

Labour party organizers noted as early as 1931 that the new women members were different from those who had joined in the early-1920s. The pioneers had come from large working-class families. They had left school at fourteen or earlier and worked mostly as domestic servants or in the sewing trades. The majority were housewives and mothers. A significant percentage had been involved in the women's movement through a variety of prewar organizations – the League, the Women's Co-operative Guild, the National Federation of Women Workers, or the Railway Women's Guild. Nineteenth century socialist feminists had shaped their political sensibilities around the needs and interests of the women of their class. In contrast, the second generation came from smaller families, had often been in school longer and were likely to work in offices or as teachers. They were young and usually single when they joined. The act of 1928 equalized the suffrage so that women voted at twenty-one, not thirty, and this no doubt explains the age difference. If they had any previous political experience it was likely to have been in the Labour League of Youth or a mixed trade union rather than a women's group. The Labour Party organizer approved of the change. He commented: "The new generation of young women, lacking the background of the suffrage agitation is not swayed to anything like the same extent by sex antagonism or mere sex interest."[48]

The new generation was responsible for breaking down gender segregation in the party. Since many of them worked during the day, they could not attend women's sections in the afternoons but went to regular party meetings with the men in the evening. The number of sections declined from 1,704 in 1932 to 1,601 in 1938 while membership rose from 160,000 to 178,000.[49] The new generation disapproved of the separation of the sexes and felt themselves to have more in common with the young men in the local constituency parties than with the older generation of women. Indeed the tensions in the Labour Party after 1931 were about generation, not gender. The Labour League of Youth took the women's place as the thorn in the side of the male leadership. It was the young of both sexes who took up the demand for greater autonomy and decision-making power and forced the NEC to devise strategies to keep them in line.

The Labour party organizer seems to have been right in his assessment that the new generation of Labour women were less "sex-conscious" than their predecessors.

By the 1930s, socialists generally scorned feminism as a middle-class ideology inimical to the interests of working-women. On the rare occasions when Labour women used the word "feminism" they explained their reasons and apologized for it. In part this was a response to the bitter words exchanged between the Open Door Council and Labour women over the protective legislation issue. But it was also a reflection of the growing class hostility stimulated by the Depression and entrenched Conservative government. Labour women as members of the working-class deeply resented being "reformed" – told what they ought to do by middle-class do-gooders with no understanding of their circumstances. But at another level, anti-feminism was prevalent in the Labour party because it was prevalent in the working-class and in popular culture. One of the products of the social, economic and intellectual changes in Britain in the mid-1930s was the "new woman" who did not need feminism or any other special treatment because she was sexually attractive, athletic, capable, and independent. Feminists suffered the fate of witches in an earlier age. They were portrayed as unattractive and fanatical old maids.

In the 1930s, Britain had become two nations, to use Disraeli's apt term. The division was economic, cultural, and to some degree generational. At all these levels it affected the working-class and women in particular. One "nation" lived in the North and West of the country, where the old industries – textiles, mining, and ship building – were in chronic decline. Working-class communities there clung to prewar patterns of mutual exchange of goods and services, voluntary associations and limited contact with the mainstream culture. Though few actually starved, many suffered a want of the basic necessities of life. The means test added insult to injury, driving secondary wage earners from the home and bringing inspectors to snoop into every cupboard and cooking pot. Unemployment was endemic with groups of hopeless men on street corners while women at home struggled to put food on the table. Labour women's sections declined in these areas not because of new members who preferred evening meetings but because of poverty. As Mrs. A.G. Bennett from Pennydarren in South Wales explained in her letter to the Chief Woman Officer, the section could not compete with charitable organizations that offered women food and clothing. She asked for a donation of clothes so that she might lure her members back from the Quakers.[50]

The other "nation" lived in the South and East of Britain. In this region, the Depression was over by late 1931 and a mass consumer culture in full swing by 1933. New housing estates, some privately built and others put up by the local council, sprang up like mushrooms throughout the Home Counties. The magic of "hire purchase" (installment buying) enabled working families to buy new furniture. Closed working-class communities opened up as working people moved into the wider culture. Working families joined the middle-class at the cinema, read the same mass circulation magazines, and began to take annual seaside holidays. They listened to the BBC, which despite its stiff, middle-class didacticism, was a formidable power in the creation of a national culture. New factories, faced with shiny chrome and a far cry from the dirty brick and chimney structures of the North, lined the circular roads around London, producing everything from pickles and jams to mops and carpet sweepers. Cars rolled off the assembly lines in Dagenham, and pharmaceuticals poured out of Dartford. These new industries meant an expansion of job opportunities in manufacturing and clerical work and more of them went to women, proportionally, than to men. Women did not appear disadvantaged in this part of the country. On the contrary, they were an integral part of the new labor force exemplified by young office girls with marcel-waved hair, wearing cheap copies of expensive clothing, cosmetics, and high-heeled shoes.

As this image suggests, young women in the South, workers, and young marrieds, were at the center of the economic and cultural reconstruction of the working class. Sexologists, sociologists, mass market surveyors, and above all the producers of consumer goods pushed them this way and that until they came up with a product – the so-called new woman. Women's magazines were the medium most responsible for shaping and popularizing the new woman. In its first issue, in June 1937, *Woman* describing itself as the "National Home Weekly" identified its typical reader as "a cool, efficient, determinedly attractive person, doing her utmost to fill both places [home and work] at once." This new woman had "come a long way in the last two-hundred years." She did not belong to the old order when the home was women's only sphere, but she was equally uncomfortable with the "newer order" when women "fought like tigresses for the vote, for education, for many things." According to *Woman*'s editor this order had gone too. In her opinion – one that she clearly felt fit the ideas and expectations of her readers – "The fierce feminist is an old-fashioned figure, unsympathetically remembered by all but a very few." So there it was, feminism was out of date. The new woman did not need it. She was "an independent worker, a good citizen, a charmer, a sportswoman, a housewife, a mother." She had discovered fashion, which meant that she wore clothes that made it "impossible to tell whether she came from Batter Sea or Belgravia."[51]

What were socialist women – and men for that matter – to do with such a divided constituency? How could they represent the women of Pennydarren who could not go to meetings because they did not have shoes or clothes fit to go out in and the women of the London working-class suburbs who preferred to spend their spare time at the cinema, riding a bike, or shopping for some of the products they helped to make? Older Labour women tended to identify with the women of Pennydarren.

Many had grown up in similar conditions of poverty, and the desire to change these conditions, especially for women and children had provided their motivation for becoming socialists. The new generation included some women with similar direct experiences of poverty but more who had seen poverty from outside. As socialists, they had a strong sense of social justice and a desire to improve the conditions of the working class, but they were less likely than the earlier generation to see women as especially victimized or to want to identify themselves politically with the women's cause.

The majority socialists in Britain ignored the new woman as they ignored women generally after 1932, nor did the party adapt its policies to accommodate the new working class in the South and East. Most of its members were still drawn from the older industries, and their block votes remained decisive in policy decisions. The divided working-class culture seems to have brought more pluralism into the party among women as well as men. The difficulties of reaching a consensus on social policy was no doubt one reason for party leaders to focus their attention on the external class enemy. Class struggle became the natural and almost the only focus of the party after 1933, and it unified members across the divisions of gender and generation. Women shared with men the exhilaration of what seemed so clearly a fight of good against evil, of workers against their real or potential oppressors, and many felt as if they were equal partners in this struggle.

Few British socialists, women or men, perceived what had been lost in the 1930s. One woman who recognized Labour women's frustrated hopes in 1936 blamed societal values, not her own party. She wrote: "In our own sections, there are many women who are ready for a better system, who have suppressed their own aspirations for freedom and equality because they are tied by custom and sentiment to the idea of inferiority."[52] But socialists did have a responsibility. The price women paid for greater integration and comradeship was political anonymity and powerlessness. When Labour women abandoned their specific concern with social welfare for working-class women, there was no one else in the party to take it up. As a result, when Labour leaders created the welfare state after World War II, they turned not to Labour women for their programs but to the Liberal intellectuals William Beveridge and Eleanor Rathbone, neither of whom spoke for the interests of working-class women as they themselves might have defined them. Working-class women had to settle for welfare based on traditional paternalism. Labour men had their share of responsibility too. When they allowed women socialists only theoretical equality, they almost ensured that women's issues would not become a focus of party policy. In effect, they turned their backs on half of the working-class citizens they claimed to represent.

Conclusion

The British Labour Party, like so many other European socialist parties, failed to advance the cause of women in the interwar period. Despite repeated promises of support for gender equality and women's issues, the party marginalized its women members, neglected women's civil rights, and refused to endorse social welfare reforms to improve working-class women's health and well-being. To offset this defection, Labour party women assumed responsibility for women's concerns and their achievements were more specific to the British case. They built strong grassroots socialist organizations in their neighborhoods and effectively represented working-class women's interests in their local parties and municipal government. The reasons for this pattern were complex, but traditional ideas about gender roles, a hostile political and economic environment, and changes in working-class culture all contributed to Labour's response to the women's concerns.

The ingrained notion that men and women naturally differed in their abilities and interests, that politics was a male concern and domesticity a woman's, played a much bigger role in determining gender relations in the party than Labour men in particular ever openly acknowledged. The assumption of separate gender spheres undermined the trumpeted socialist ideal of equality of the sexes and resulted in an unequal distribution of power and policy making within the party, which paralyzed women's reform efforts at the national level. Yet the same idea worked to their benefit in local politics. They were elected to local government office simply because they were women and therefore best suited to those aspects of the job traditionally associated with their gender – the care of mothers and infants, school children, the elderly, the sick, and the insane. Labour women took full advantage of this opening to give themselves and their party a reputation for the humane treatment of those in trouble and for civic amenities to meet the practical needs of working-class women and children.

An economic and political environment that was hostile to working people in general and to trade unions in particular also lessened the chances of Labour leaders taking up and sustaining an interest in women's issues. Mass unemployment, declining trade union membership, and a failed general strike put the unions into a crisis that distracted Labour's attention from social welfare programs. The gender division of responsibility in the party meant that men and women responded differently to this crisis. While the men focused on winning political power to right Labour's wrongs, Labour women called for state-sponsored welfare programs to protect the health of mothers and their children and asked their party to support the right of working-class women to control their fertility. From the male trade unionist point of view, women's welfare programs, especially the controversial subject of birth control, could only undermine a delicate system of wage bargaining and electoral power. The two approaches proved irreconcilable, and women's lack of power made them the losers.

In the 1930s, Labour women also abandoned their women-centered agendas and the struggle for equal rights in the party. Cultural as well as political and economic changes were responsible for this abrupt shift. The new generation of Labour women were part of the new woman phenomenon, which emphasized women's independence but not their solidarity, their sexuality but not their gender interests. They found feminism old-fashioned and associated it with the middle-class, leisured women now suspect as a class enemy. They moved away from a women-centered isolation and towards integration around the defense of their class against reactionary government and the threat of international fascism. The new spirit of comradeship obscured, though it did not change, women's second-class status in the party and ended what had been a brave experiment in a new kind of socialist politics in which women were to count as much as men as policy makers and constituents.

Notes

1. The Women's Social and Political Union led by the Pankhursts surpassed the trade unions in shock tactics and set an example of anti-property terrorism that other European suffragists admired if they did not imitate. It was however, the minority women's suffrage group.
2. The largest feminist organization was the National Union for Equal Citizenship led by Eleanor Rathbone.
3. Lily Watson, "Why I support the Labour Party," in Essay for Workers' Education Course (unpub.).
4. Membership in the Labour party was divided into "individual" and "trade-union" categories. In 1933 (the first year the party published women's membership) there were 154,790 individual women members to 211,223 men. Total party membership was 2,305,030 (a big decline from 4,359,807 in 1920), most of these were male trade unionists. See G.D.H. Cole: *History of the Labour Party Since 1914*, (New York, 1969), p. 480.
5. *The Daily Herald*, (31 March 1919), 1.
6. Margaret Mitchell, interviewed by *Tottenham People's History* (1 May 1980).
7. Arthur Henderson, speech to National Conference of Labour Women, June 1919, reported in *Labour Woman* (July 1919): 27.

8. Women's Co-operative Guild, *Annual Report* (London and Manchester, 1919 to 1920): 1.

9. Dora Russell who led the birth control campaign reported that Marion Phillips ordered her to withdraw her section's resolution calling for party support on this issue and said, "Sex should not be dragged into politics. You will split the party from top to bottom." Dora Russell, *The Tamarask Tree*, vol.1 (London 1977), p. 172.

10. *Labour Woman* (June 1918): 14.

11. Ibid.: 15.

12. Ibid. (February 1918): 261.

13. *Labour Woman* (December 1919 to July 1919). Sections submitted their plans for the Working Woman's house and decided to keep the parlor but not as an "occasional" room.

14. *Labour Woman* (March 1919): 30.

15. Winifred More in a letter to *Labour Woman* (November 1920): 178.

16. Middle-class women who paid local taxes had these rights earlier, from 1894 for Poor Law Boards and from 1907 for municipal councils.

17. *Labour Woman* (May 1920): 217 gave the figures for Labour Women in local government. There were 206 guardians, seventy municipal councillors and seven county councillors.

18. Labour women competed successfully with middle-class Liberal women for jobs as guardians, on schools boards, and in local government. In working-class constituency Labour women were much more successful in elections as Poor Law guardians than to school boards.

19. *Labour Woman* (December 1919): 142-3.

20. "Women In and Out of Work," *Labour Woman* (March 1923): 23.

21. *Labour Woman* (July 1925): 123. Unemployed married women cotton operatives who had worked all their lives were considered to have given up their employment if they lived with their families and were not immediately rehired.

22. *Labour Woman* (March 1923): 52.

23. "Report of the National Women's Conference," *Labour Woman*, (July 1925): 126.

24. "The Mother Suffers First," *Labour Woman* (November 1924): 174.

25. *Labour Woman*, (October 1921): 160.

26. M. Llewelyn Davies, ed., *Maternity: Letters from Working Women* (London, 1978).

27. Jeffrey Weeks, *Sex, Politics, and Society* (London, 1981), p. 88.

28. Dora Russell, *The Tamarisk Tree*, vol. 1.(London, 1977), p. 17.

29. Mrs. Jones, speech to the NCLW, reported in *Labour Woman* (June 1924): 96.

30. *Labour Woman* (October 1924): 31.

31. Mrs. Palmer from Southampton, speech to the NCLW, reported in *Labour Woman* (June 1924): 96.

32. *Report of the Annual Conference of the Labour Party* (Liverpool, 1925): 44.

33. HN Brailsford, *Socialism for Today* (London, 1925), pp. 76-83.

34. Rhys Davies, speech at the Labour Party Conference in 1930, *Labour Party Report* (1930): 177.

35. Somerville Hastings, MP, letter to *Labour Woman* (August 1930): 121.

36. "Women in the Labour Force" reported that there were three million women in the workforce in 1924, and of those only 500,000 were unionized (17 percent). Between 1921 and 1924, the percentage of unionized women had fallen by 45 percent. *Labour Woman* (October 1924): 153.

37. Marie James, speech to the NCLW in June 1926, reported in *Labour Woman* (July 1926): 12.

38. A prominent ILP woman, Dorothy Jewson, argued for the three resolutions to go forward to the party conference, and sections from Norwich, Manchester, Leeds, Durham, Birmingham, and elsewhere sent resolutions of support for allowing women to elect their own NEC members.

39. Linda Ward, *The Right to Choose, a Study of Women's Fight for Birth Control Provisions*" (Ph.D. diss., University of Bristol, 1981), p. 326.

40. *The Bradford Pioneer* (9 January 1935) contained an article about councillor Marjorie McIntosh who spoke at the Council meeting on the subject of birth control advice facilities at public health clinics and "turned what looked like impending defeat into victory for the proposal."

41. York Labour Party, Women's Section Minutes (April, 1924).

42. Jarrow Divisional Labor Party (Hebburn Division) Labour Party and Trades Council Minutes (17 March 1925).

43. Standing Joint Committee Minutes (11 April 1935).

44. None of the local women's section minutes contain any references to abortion. Perhaps the lack of interest had something to do with the fact that by the mid-1930s, most section members were beyond the childbearing years.

45. Mrs. E. Hood, speech to the NCLW of 1927. Report in *Labour Woman* (June 1927): 3.

46. Dorothy Elliott, speech to the NCLW of 1936 in the *Report of the NCLW* (1936): 47.

47. Mrs Eleanor Barton, letter to *Labour Woman* (May 1934): 57.

48. JS. Middleton, B. Ayrton Gould, G.R.Shepard: *Report on the Chief Woman Officer's Dept.* presented at a meeting of the Organization Sub-committee (20 April 1932): 262-68.

49. Membership and section figures were given in the *National Organizers' Report* to the Annual Labour Party Conference (1932): 41; (1935): 40; (1939): 77.

50. Elizabeth Andrews (Wales) forwarded the letter from Mrs. A.G. Bennett from Pennydarren, dated 17 October 1937. *Organizers' Reports* (Labour Party Archives, File 489)

51. "Woman – Where She Stands Today" in *Woman* 1(5 June 1937): 7-8.

52. Hilda Hallworth, letter to *Labour Woman* (May 1936): 75.

Chapter 5

Gender and Democratic Socialism in the Netherlands

Ulla Jansz

At its 1937 party conference, the Social Democratic Workers' Party (SDAP) in the Netherlands accepted a new party program that marked its transition from a workers' party into a people's party. Other western European Social Democratic parties followed a similar pattern but not until after World War II.[1] The new program stated a humanistic socialist ideology from which the Marxist concept of class struggle was omitted, and marked an ideological shift from economics to ethics and culture. This neorevisionism emphasized democracy as an end in itself, rather than as a means toward other goals.

The adoption of the new program meant the victory of a new generation of party leaders over the old, many of whom had been around from the founding of the party in 1894. It followed more than a decade of fierce debate on the direction party politics should take. This debate originated in the mid-1920s when it became clear that the party was unable to win more than 25 percent of the vote under universal suffrage and was destined to remain in opposition. The final decision to change the party's platform came in the wake of two disasters – a crushing defeat in 1933 and the events in Germany in the same year. The German SPD had been the model for the Dutch SDAP, and its destruction by Hitler had a devastating impact on Dutch socialists.[2]

The great source of inspiration for the neorevisionists was the Belgian socialist Hendrik de Man's book *The Psychology of Socialism* (1926.)[3] In his

Notes for this chapter begin on page 234.

critique of Marxism, de Man stressed the importance of democracy for socialism. He argued that Marxism equated political democracy with capitalism, where it functioned only as one means of helping to bring about the victory of the working class. In his own view, however, democracy was a mental precondition for socialism, a root of the tree of socialism. In this context, de Man also rejected the traditional Marxist condemnation of women's aspirations to equality and self-determination, scornfully labeled "bourgeois feminism." De Man saw these aspirations as part and parcel of the development towards democracy.[4]

Despite de Man's theory, the shift in emphasis from class struggle to democracy does not seem to have had a significant effect on party attitudes toward the woman question. As of old, in the SDAP the category "working-class" had an exclusively male construction. In the early years of the century for instance, universal manhood suffrage was seen as a matter of class struggle, while women's suffrage was quite a different matter, inferior to the working-class vote and therefore to be postponed to a later date.[5] Another explicit statement of this gendered definition of the working class can be found in a 1913 discussion on the possible introduction of a regular women's column in the party newspaper *The People*. Editor Willem Vliegen, on that occasion, dismissed the proposal with the words: "Men don't read a women's column. And they are the masses."[6]

In this respect, the interwar period brought nothing new. Both the concept "people" and the new groups the party turned to – small farmers and retailers, white collar employees, and intellectuals – appeared as male as the old categories "worker" and "working class."

Women in the Party

Since its foundation in 1908, the Dutch Federation of Social Democratic Women's Clubs had been striving toward a better position for women within the party, and for more attention to women's rights issues in party politics. The relationship between the SDAP and its women's organization had been a difficult one. Many prominent party members were not convinced of its right to exist and feared a party within the party. Among them were Willem Vliegen, party chairman from 1906 to 1926, and Suze Groeneweg, the first woman elected to the Dutch parliament, in 1918, the year when women won that right. From 1914 to 1936, she was the only female member of the party executive.[7] Only after women's suffrage had been introduced in the Netherlands in 1919 did the executive recognize the need for special propaganda among potential female voters. As a result, the relationship between the party and the Federation was finally settled in 1925. The party executive then appointed the jurist Liesbeth Ribbius Peletier as a salaried secretary for women's propaganda, and she simultaneously became a member of the Federation's executive.

The main activity of the Federation of Social Democratic Women's Clubs in the interwar period, apart from special party propaganda directed at women, was the education of Club members in citizenship through classes and reading groups. From its beginnings, it had aimed at introducing working-class women to the socialist program through issues of concern to them such as women's suffrage, maternity care and benefits, a better position for women in the labor market, and disarmament. After women had won the vote, local politics became an important area for socialist women to attempt to realize their aims. Nationally, the SDAP remained in opposition during the interwar period, and it was unable to implement its reform program, but in the municipalities the party often participated in coalition governments. In 1939, there were 179 SDAP aldermen in 156 municipal councils.[8] Through these local councils, socialist women attempted more or less successfully to obtain better facilities in the field of education, maternity and child care, school meals, and clothing. Unfortunately, so far, very little is known about the general extent to which these attempts succeeded.[9]

The share of women in party membership increased from 20 percent in 1920 to 33 percent in 1938. This was no doubt partly due to the activities of the Social Democratic Women's Clubs. The total membership of their Federation, however, never comprised more than half of the number of female party members.[10] Thus, many women belonged to the party without being organized in the Social Democratic Women's Clubs. Moreover, the results of one of the scarce in-depth local studies indicate that as much as three-quarters of the woman members were wives of male party members. The authors of that study suggest that the rise in female membership in the interwar period can be explained to a large extent by recruitment among the members' own families.[11]

The Women's Clubs consisted mainly of housewives. They did not appeal to young unmarried women, who made up the vast majority of women in the paid workforce but were probably also under represented in the SDAP as a whole. The rank and file of the Clubs was nevertheless predominantly working class. Many had been domestic servants before marriage, as this was the occupation of the largest part of the female workforce in that period. The majority of them had very little education, probably less than the average male party member.[12] The leadership on the other hand was middle class and usually well educated (teachers, social workers, and the like). They had joined the women's organization primarily to further the educational and welfare interests of working-class women, not women of their own class.

After the vote was won, the Federation did its best to promote women for election in parliament and in provincial and municipal councils, but this proved to be a difficult task. Male party officials were often reluctant to pay explicit attention to gender, with the result that the ideal candidate all too often was male, with the one exception of the token woman on the list. Throughout the interwar period, the number of socialist women in representative bodies did not exceed 5 to 10 percent of the total of SDAP representatives. Contrary to what might be expected, the percentage in municipal councils (5 percent) did not exceed that on the national level, nor did it rise during the interwar period.[13]

Little is known about the female party members who chose not to join the women's organization. But there are indications that in the interwar period, these party members did not feel attracted to the Women's Clubs. This is the impression one gets from a discussion in 1930 between two young women, Mien Olree and Lena Bleeker, in the left socialist newspaper, *The Socialist*. They were discussing the adoption of separate girls' meetings within the youth movement, analogous to the women's organization and its reading clubs. Mien Olree described separatism as out of date and much less desirable than working side-by-side with men in the socialist movement. Nevertheless, she agreed with her opponent that the position of women in the party left much to be desired. The prevailing theory on equality between the sexes notwithstanding, the practice was that women hardly ever raised their voices at meetings and seldom held office.[14] The few women who participated in the political debate raging in the party in the early thirties do not seem to have been active in the Social Democratic Women's Clubs either.[15] Ironically, it was not these younger women, but seventy-five-year-old Mathilde Wibaut, the grand old lady of the Federation of Social Democratic Women's Clubs, who had to intervene in 1937 to ensure that women's rights had a place in the new party program.

Neorevisionism

Three strands of neorevisionism emerged in the SDAP in the late 1920s: religious socialism, the ideology of the Labor Youth League (AJC), and the group usually called "the young socialists."[16] Each one took a position on the woman question to which the leaders of the women's organization responded in an effort to exert some influence over the new party program.

Religious socialists became much more influential in Dutch socialism between the wars than their numbers would suggest. They formed a small but very active faction led by the theologian Willem Banning, an admirer of the work of Jean Jaurès, the French socialist who had also been an important source of inspiration for Hendrik de Man.[17] Banning together with Koos Vorrink, the Labor Youth leader and later party chairman, led the party to its renewal in the 1930s – a process completed in 1946 with the founding of the Labor party, in which the SDAP merged with two smaller parties. While Vorrink was the organizer and orator, Banning was the thinker. Tirelessly, he propagated de Man's anti-materialist, ethical conception of socialism until finally in 1935, he succeeded in convincing the party executive that a new program was necessary.[18]

De Man's influence was already clear in Banning's first book, *For the Sake of the Community's Growth* (1926) in which he attacked the "bourgeois" character of the Dutch socialist movement.[19] According to Banning, socialism meant a new cultural ideal. He complained that the majority of the proletariat did not concern itself with true culture, but spent its leisure time in the cinema, at the soccer field, or reading pulp fiction. Regrettably, few socialist workers deviated from this pattern. It was no wonder, wrote Banning, as it was impossible for a socialist culture to flourish under capitalism.[20] Capitalism and with it, bourgeois culture, had destroyed ethics. Not only had it nothing more to offer for the inner emptiness of the urban workers than the pub and the cinema, it had also disrupted marriage and family life. But the labor movement had neglected this type of ethical question.[21] Banning did not specify the direction of the socialist ethics he found so necessary. Therefore, his book leaves an impression of conservatism in matters of mass culture, sexuality, and domestic life – the more so as he did not follow de Man in his application of democracy to relations within the family.

Banning's friend Koos Vorrink, a former schoolteacher, had more to offer in this respect. Less of a theoretician, he derived his inspiration for the way in which to build the Labor Youth League from the German Socialist Worker Youth. After two visits to Germany in 1921, he described with admiration the attitude to drink, the cinema, and pulp fiction he had encountered there: they did not fight it; they simply laughed at it. Vorrink envisioned the youth movement's new style as the socialist response to bourgeois culture. In the propaganda pamphlets for Labor Youth he published in the 1920s, he too stressed the banality of mass culture. Pubs, cinemas, cabarets, dance halls, exciting music, gaudy colors, and fashionable clothes all figure on his list of the manifestations of this evil.[22]

On sex and gender, however, Vorrink was more explicit than Banning. Often mentioned in this context is *Storm Tide* (1924), a sex education booklet for the young. The central message in it is that the young should learn to control their growing inclinations and passions. For this, Vorrink wrote, the best environment was the socialist youth movement with its natural, free, and easy companionship between young men and women. He contrasted it with the streets, pubs, cinemas, and dance halls, which encouraged young men and women into relationships and marriages devoid of any "higher consecration."

In *Storm Tide*, Vorrink scorned the double standard that allowed young men what it forbade young women. He reminded readers that they lived in a world where laws were still mostly made by men. But capitalism had prepared for the liberation of women by driving them from the home into the factory, and now, gradually, better-paid jobs were opening up to them in teaching, office work, and management.[23] As a result, wrote Vorrink, a growing number of women did not have to marry out of financial need and therefore could take a more free and independent position vis-à-vis men. Thus, times were changing, even if, admittedly, traditional relations between husband and wife still existed in many families.[24]

This progress had its darker side, however; according to Vorrink, the "free" working girl lacked a sense of responsibility:

> "Without inner attitude, she abuses the newly acquired freedom to give rein to an evil coquetry in dress and manners, by which she degrades herself to a mere sex creature that consciously or unconsciously wants to seduce the male animal, and by which she debases her full humanity."[25]

There was no corresponding paragraph describing how "free" young men tried to seduce women. Perhaps for Vorrink, this was already a thing of the past, not worth worrying about.[26]

Former members remember the relations between the sexes in the Labor Youth League as very egalitarian, very modern in accordance with the image Koos Vorrink painted time and again. "In the AJC, we didn't speak about women's emancipation. We simply were emancipated."[27] Historians of the AJC, however, have established that responsibilities were clearly segregated along gender lines. For instance, when camping, the boys did the heavy work and the girls the cooking and the flower arrangements. Moreover, in the movement's administration, the men dominated, while the much lower paid clerical staff was all female. Also, many salaried administrators' wives participated in the AJC work as a matter of course, by giving dance lessons, for example, or doing numerous organizational chores, all unpaid. Thus, the general principle of egalitarianism, coeducation and companionship between boys and girls, as it was propagated in the Youth League, coexisted with a practice of sex segregation in both administration and chores.[28]

Vorrink himself recognized the existence of a gender tension in the youth movement that contradicted the propaganda. When he became chair of the Socialist Youth International, he wrote a manual for youth leaders, *Creating the New Community's Free Human Being* (1933), in which he noted that even the coeducational youth movement was aware of the sexual problem. But he attributed it to the fact that the majority of members had had the wrong kind of sex education. The right education should be directed at preventing an early fixation on sexual matters. The longer this fixation could be postponed, the better it would be for the development of "unrestrained mental activity."[29] In this text, mass entertainment is not used as a scapegoat. Nor is the personification of the darker side of women's emancipation, the seductive, independent young woman.

Vorrink had a section on homosexuality in this manual, presumably because it was aimed at adult readers, whereas *Storm Tide* was for the young. He assured the reader that one could find as many high-minded individuals among homosexuals as among heterosexuals. Still, according to Vorrink, homosexuals were a greater danger, because seduction by them could "bend the normal sexual direction" in young people.[30] He made no mention of the possibility that the young themselves could display homosexual tendencies without being seduced by an adult.

In a number of passages throughout the book, Vorrink applied the principle of democracy to relations between the sexes as de Man had done in *Psychology of Socialism*, the work he admired so much. Vorrink described the development from autocracy to democracy in family life as well as in the political system and industry. He argued that because this process was incomplete, socialists ought to support women in their struggle for equal rights, not only in law, but first and foremost in everyday life. According to Vorrink, coeducation in the youth movement offered the opportunity to learn how to live as equals and thus to realize the democratic principle in the relation between the sexes.[31]

Starting in 1934, Vorrink had ample opportunity to push the same ideas in the SDAP, as he had been appointed party chairman. However, no evidence shows that he made any effort to put them into effect within the party or its policies. Democracy in the family did not figure in the debate on the new program. This was equally true of issues related to sexuality, including birth control. Outside the Labor Youth League, matters related to sex were hardly ever discussed publicly in the SDAP. Individual party members might be proponents of birth control, might practice it themselves, might even belong to the Neo-Malthusian League. But the leaders took care to avoid giving the impression that the party adhered to such views. For instance, at a 1934 party executive meeting, Suze Groeneweg aired her concern about a booklet written by physician and prominent party member, Agnes de Vries-Bruins, on women's reproduction, because it implied that social democrats favored birth control. None of her colleagues on the executive contradicted her.[32]

Meanwhile, family planning seems to have been a common practice among socialists. A family of four children was regarded as the ideal, and by the interwar period, thanks to the activities of the Neo-Malthusian League, the means were available to achieve that goal for those who knew how to acquire and use them. Many in the movement, including the women's organization, frowned upon sex before marriage and rejected abortion. The dominance of these views came to light in 1932, when the elderly couple, Mathilde and Floor Wibaut, respected long-time party members, dared to publish their views on marriage. In their book, *Changing Marriage*, they argued not only for women's self-determination in sexual relations and birth control, but also for sex before marriage, and even, under certain circumstances, marital triangles. This did not go down well with their own socialist movement! The daily newspaper, *The People*, found it necessary to stress that the book did not reflect the opinion of organized social democracy but of two individual members. Another veteran couple, S.J. Pothuis and Carry Pothuis-Smit, responded with their own book which affirmed accepted socialist sexual morality and denounced the Wibauts' ideas as bourgeois.[33]

The third group of neorevisionists, the young socialists, were just as conservative in their views on sex and gender as the Labor Youth League. They consisted mainly of intellectuals who had been active in the socialist student movement and became a separate group in the SDAP around 1930. Inspired by the English socialist H.N. Brailsford's book title, they united behind the slogan, "Socialism Now."[34] They had much in common with both religious socialism and the AJC ideology, such as the aversion to contemporary mass culture. Thus, even these young revisionists placed themselves "in an exterior relationship to the everyday working-class," to borrow Geoff Eley's phrase.[35] For instance, the Romanist and teacher Henk Brugmans fulminated against that "opium of the people," the popular film. His main point of criticism was the way in which, from motives of gain, movies depicted love, marriage, and the family. In the cinema, he wrote, he had never seen a faithful, happy young couple as he would wish it to be in his own life. On the contrary, capitalist films preached that attractiveness was everything and that it was legitimate to look for sexual comfort elsewhere when your wife no longer attracted you. And this filth was shown to the working masses, in whose lives the family was the only place of rest and happiness![36]

In response to a left-wing critic, Brugmans in a second article denied that the movement for the further emancipation of women was a specifically revolutionary socialist phenomenon. Like Vorrink, Brugmans thought that capitalism itself, because it needed female labor power, would put an end to the traditional husband-breadwinner as owner of his dependent, subordinate wife. The job of socialism was to accelerate this capitalist development to ensure a harmonious outcome. Brugmans thought he could already perceive the contours of the coming "socialist family style."[37] When Henk Brugmans, like Vorrink, became a member of the committee appointed in 1936 to draft the new party program, a position where he could show whether his professed support for women's emancipation was serious, he also failed to take advantage of his position to promote progressive policies on women's issues.

According to the young socialists, the socialist movement was dragging its feet because the party leadership was happy with the SDAP as it was. They, on the other hand, were in a hurry for change. That was why they were initially attracted to the political radicalism of the party's left wing, which found expression in the weekly paper, *The Socialist*. But the young socialists' critique of Marxism was precisely the opposite of the leftists' demands. Therefore, after their mediatory efforts had failed, the majority of young socialists declined to follow the left wing when it was expelled from the party in 1932.[38] Instead of the banned *Socialist*, the SDAP executive founded a new weekly, *The Social Democrat,* as a forum for debate on party strategy and principles. It became the young socialists' new platform.

In contrast to the other two neorevisionist groups, the young socialists distinguished themselves by having at least a few women members who took part in the political debate. Two of them, Fie Eggink and Matty Vigelius, were not prominent party members, then or later.[39] Both published decidedly feminist articles on women's rights in *The Socialist* and *The Social Democrat*. Their topics included Alexandra Kollontai and differences between the situation of working-class women in Russia and Western Europe.[40] Eggink and Vigelius received very little response to their articles. Apparently these questions did not interest party members who were concerned with the course the party should take in the near future.

The same was true even for the only woman among the young socialists to become a member of several important party committees, the sociologist, Hilda Verwey-Jonker. She was the daughter of an ardent feminist Lena Westerveld, the first woman to study mathematics at the University of Amsterdam.[41] The daughter, however, kept aloof from the woman question. In the many articles on party strategy and principles Hilda Verwey-Jonker published in the 1930s, she failed to mention the subject even once. In the same period, she lectured for Social Democratic Women's Clubs but without connecting the existence of these clubs to the woman question. In her view, the members were most in need of general knowledge on politics in society, which she (and others with her level of education) could provide. Looking back in her memoirs, Verwey-Jonker wrote that through her lecture tours she learned a great deal about the conditions under which working-class women lived. According to her, things were not too bad in the late-1920s. Unemployment was low, more and more good working-class housing was being built, and the eight-hour day had been introduced.[42] From 1930 onwards, circumstances deteriorated rapidly due to the rising unemployment rate and the subsequent national budget cuts intended to combat the deep economic crisis.

There are no indications that as the only woman on the committee to draw up the new party program, Hilda Verwey-Jonker saw the woman question as a political problem worth discussing in the context of the new party strategy. The contrast with the publications by Matty Vigelius are striking. In 1932, the latter wrote an article in *The Social Democrat* on why so few women played an active role at party branch meetings. Her explanation was working-class women's household drudgery. According to Vigelius, housework was so tiring that women preferred to go to the movies in their scarce leisure time than to a dull party meeting. In contrast to other revisionist socialists, Vigelius did not condemn the cinema. She stated as a matter of fact that it demanded nothing of the woman's mind and therefore was an agreeable pastime. Vigelius envisioned the solution to the burden of domestic labor in collective living arrangements which would make housework easier, she mentioned housing projects in Vienna as an example. And of course, men and children should also lend a hand. Why not? This was the only way women would have the time and energy to educate themselves and to work together with the men in the party.[43]

This type of argument is reminiscent of the dominant view in the Federation prior to the mid-1920s. These early feminist socialists had argued that women should have equal rights in the labor market. Their triple burden should be alleviated by making their household tasks easier. Federation women opposed restricting or banning married women's wage work. This position put them at odds with many prominent male and female socialists (and moderate nonsocialist feminists) who in the 1930s won the party over to such a ban when unemployment soared.[44] According to Vigelius, women's emancipation had hitherto only referred to bourgeois women. It was, however, a question of democracy that working-class women be liberated also. Socialism should not tolerate oppression of any individual, women included. The spirit of socialism ought to extend to the family as well.[45]

These were not the issues Hilda Verwey-Jonker addressed. She appeared to share the prevailing masculine view that the woman question was unrelated to the party's political agenda, which by the 1930s centered on the fascist threat to Dutch democracy. She wrote a series of articles on this topic, arguing that anti-democratic thought was most likely to appeal to professedly politically neutral groups. In the present situation, the "neutral" person was an easy prey for the capitalist amusement culture. According to Verwey-Jonker, the nonpolitical person needed to be educated and given a set of sound ideas to hang onto – socialist ideas.[46] In these publications, no reference to gender issues can be found. Even where one would expect it, in her 1937 pamphlet on Woman and National Socialism, the text is ambiguous concerning the attraction of national socialism for German women. Her conclusion that national socialism had succeeded in mobilizing women for politics where other political movements had failed referred to middle-class women. She reassured the reader that working-class women had not fallen for Nazi propaganda. According to Verwey-Jonker, the resistance to national socialism among German feminists was not specifically "womanly." These women protested because of their democratic or pacifist persuasion.[47]

Apparently, Hilda Verwey-Jonker did not care for the gender-focused analysis of the German history of the time, which circulated in the SDAP women's organization. An example of such feminist analysis is an article entitled "Women in Germany" published anonymously in 1934 in the Federation's monthly periodical. The author argued that Weimar had brought women political equality with men but not an equal economic or social position. The overwhelming majority of women had the less well paid, unskilled jobs with no decision-making power. They were required to be obedient and often had the double burden of wagework and housework which tended to keep them out of politics. They were the subject of political decisions without having any influence over them. Equal political rights had been granted them without the social preconditions necessary for actual political participation. The educational work by the socialist movement had only reached a small minority of politically active women.[48] The obvious parallels with the Dutch situation were not drawn in this article.

Verwey-Jonker stuck to her focus on the middle-class. In the 1937 pamphlet, she repeated her opinion that socialist propaganda had failed to reach both sexes of that class.[49] All this is consistent with her work for the program committee the previous year. There, Verwey-Jonker had not shown any interest in the issue of political participation of women.[50]

Disarmament or National Defense?

Before turning to the history of the new party program, the positions and activities of the SDAP women's organization need some clarification. After the vote was won in 1919, among all the issues that stayed on the Federation's agenda – maternity care and benefits, women's position in the labor market, and disarmament – the last was the only one that the SDAP considered important. The others were special women's interests with which male party members hardly ever concerned themselves. But in the early 1920s, socialism, and national and international disarmament were still closely connected. Consequently, the Federation was in line with official party policy with its strong anti-militarist propaganda appealing to women as mothers of possible future soldiers.

The situation changed, however, when Hitler came to power in Germany. Some party members began to doubt whether it was wise to keep striving for national disarmament. The result was a deep division of opinion in the party that was to last for several years and cause endless emotional discussions. One group, to which the new party chairman, Koos Vorrink, and the party leader Albarda belonged, was of the opinion that national disarmament could not be kept on the party program under the new circumstances. The second group chose the middle road. They wanted to hang on to national and international disarmament, but thought the SDAP should not resist a mobilization for an impending war. This position, the official party policy as of the spring of 1934, meant that going to war with the aim of defending the country became acceptable. The third group was opposed to this last option, and the Women's Clubs shared its position, arguing that women's nature and motherhood made it impossible for them to endorse war in any form. Some spokeswomen, including the influential Carry Pothuis-Smit, editor of the Federation's weekly, *The Proletarian Woman*, even went so far as to reject protective measures against air attacks, because this would be the first step towards accepting a defensive war.[51]

The Federation's position on the extreme wing resulted in a series of struggles with the party executive. This happened when the Women's Clubs went against official party policy as they did when they joined peace demonstrations organized by the nonsocialist women's peace movement. The party executive refused to give permission for such activities.[52] In 1934, the Federation wanted to propose a motion to the party congress in favor of maintaining its position on disarmament. The executive was alarmed by what it regarded as attempts by the Federation to go against the rules by interfering in party tactics. These confrontations ended with Liesbeth Ribbius Peletier giving in, but only after party secretary Kees Woudenberg had reminded her that she was accountable to the party and not first and foremost to the Federation of Women's Clubs.[53]

Two years later, against the backdrop of the League of Nations' failure regarding Abyssinia and Germany's reoccupation of the Rhineland, the SDAP leadership decided that finally the time for a change of course had come. Now a possible majority for national defense could be discerned in the party. But a group of diehards remained: a few Marxists, many of the religious socialist group under Banning's leadership, and the Federation of Social Democratic Women's Clubs. Some prominent party women made a stand against national defense: Carry Pothuis-Smit, Hilda Verwey-Jonker, and Agnes de Vries-Bruins, who was an MP and the Federation's new chair after Mathilde Wibaut resigned.[54]

At first glance, disarmament is one of those general political questions that have nothing in particular to do with women or with relations between the sexes. Nevertheless, many women felt very strongly about the issue, so gender apparently did make a difference. To understand the meanings women and men attributed to sexual difference in the politics of war and peace, it is necessary to study the language used in the disarmament debate.[55] However, such a study would require much more in-depth research into the disarmament question as it figured in the SDAP and its women's clubs than has been done so far. An indication of the possible direction it would take comes from a discussion in *The Social Democrat*, the biweekly that was used as a forum to forge a party majority for national defense. Early in 1936, the paper featured a series of articles by a spokesperson for the views of the party leadership, the pedagogue G. van Veen. Van Veen was not prominent in the party hierarchy himself. He was very active in the Religious Socialist League.[56] But his articles and the reactions they provoked reveal the gender content of the disarmament debate in the SDAP.

Because women formed a bloc in the party, gender differences came to the surface instead of remaining implicit. This comes through in an article by van Veen on the dilemma the party leadership faced. If it decided to support national defense, then the party might split. Van Veen examined the seriousness of this danger for both wings of the party. He concluded that losses on the left would never be serious, as even Soviet politics had become extremely patriotic, but the loss of votes on what he dubbed the "ethicist" wing was another matter. Nevertheless, he concluded that this price should be paid in order to win thousands of bourgeois democratic votes. Once the party took a strong and unequivocal position on this issue, it would be eligible for a place in a national coalition, which in turn would enable it to influence government policy on unemployment.

The most interesting point from a gender perspective was that van Veen told readers why they should not bother about one section of the ethicist wing: women's opposition to national defense. He explained that the circumstances were now such that women's opinions could have no bearing on the matter, directly or indirectly. The sentiment that drove the women to reject all preparation for violence was praiseworthy but short-sighted. "If we men let the women tie our hands, we would plunge our wives and children into a sea of misery, which they can scarcely comprehend."[57] In other words, "we men" are far wiser in these matters than women could ever be.

Not surprisingly, Carry Pothuis-Smit could not tolerate women being called short-sighted by a male member of her own party and protested immediately.[58] Thereupon van Veen took time to explain what he had meant. Of course he did not want to deny women any rights. But women and men were different. Men had the creative powers, they could accept sacrifices in the present to save the future; they had foresight. Women on the other hand had a much narrower vision; they cared for life in the pre-sent in accordance with their first and foremost task, childbearing and child rearing. In tense situations, real men would always act as men, and real women would always resist male views until they understood that men could not act against their nature. In this particular case, men nat-urally would not let an enemy who threatened their country's culture overrun it. Women, on the other hand, would shrink from the danger to individuals in such a struggle. In the male view, a national culture that lacked the will to self-assertion gave up its right and chance to live. A democracy that went under after a vigorous struggle had the hope of res-urrection. Van Veen concluded his article with an appeal to SDAP women pacifists to join a different party – he mentioned the Christian Democrat Union (CDU) – and "allow the SDAP, out of a manly sense of responsibility, to accept reality and perform its manly democratic duty."[59]

The significance of this essay is not only the explicit connection that is made between fighting, manliness, and democracy, but also the minimal response to it. As with the first essay, the only reaction to appear was the one by Carry Pothuis-Smit, the grand old lady of pro-disarmament women socialists. Sarcastically, she reassured van Veen that "the manly men" would win the debate, as nearly all the other political parties in the Netherlands shared this point of view. But neither she nor other promi-nent SDAP women (or men, for that matter), within or outside the Fed-eration, accepted the challenge to counter the argument about women's alleged nature or the interpretation of democracy which justified exclud-ing pacifist women from the party. No one stood up to say that such an exclusion, advocated with the professed aim of saving democracy, in fact sacrificed the essence of democracy, which is inclusion.

That van Veen's statements reflected a general opinion in the party about the status of women members was confirmed on the eve of the 1937 SDAP congress, where the report of the Committee for the Study of the Military Question was on the agenda. A minority of that committee, consisting of Banning, Verwey-Jonker, Pothuis-Smit, and de Vries-Bruins, had voted against national defense. The party leadership feared that this minority would have some success at the congress, and therefore the SDAP newspaper, *The People*, wrote deprecatingly about the minority viewpoint as one held by only "three women and a clergyman." Party leader Albarda, in his address to the party congress, went so far as to stress that it was pure coincidence that the three female members of the committee all adhered to the minority viewpoint.[60] In the end, everything went well for him: the vote was 1,509 to 328, and the SDAP changed its course on the defense issue.

This whole episode might very well be called symptomatic of the power relations in the party at the time. The party leadership tolerated and even encouraged the Federation of Women's Clubs as long as it kept to specific tasks, such as recruiting new women members. But controversies could easily arise when the Federation voiced opinions on party policy, which party leaders called "interference with party strategy." Thus, women organizing *as women* in the party were contained within very narrow limits. Attempts to mobilize the little influence and power they had were easily thwarted. Consequently, the party remained as male-dominated as it had always been. This domination was legitimized by an implicit suggestion that the really important issues were male and universal, while women's issues were secondary and specific to them. Sadly, the Federation leaders had no response to the "difference" argument. How could they? Especially in their disarmament propaganda, they had made their case on the basis of women's different nature and their special role as mothers.

The New Party Program

At the same party congress where the disarmament issue was settled, the party endorsed the new program. A committee of eighteen had drafted it in the winter and spring of 1935/36. All the different tendencies in the party, Marxists, religious socialists, other neorevisionists, and those in between had had some input, but of the eighteen drafters, only one, Hilda Verwey-Jonker was a woman, and she did not support a separate women's agenda.

In July 1936, the committee published the final draft in order to provoke a discussion in the socialist press. In contrast with the old 1912 program, it no longer started with a description of socioeconomic developments, from which the aim of the movement followed. Instead, the draft began with the aim of democratic socialism: a society based on collective ownership of the main means of production and collective administration of trade and industry; one that guaranteed spiritual and political freedom with prosperity and social security for all, while creating the social conditions necessary to the full development of the individual and the community. Another major change from the old program was a paragraph on the inseparability of socialism and democracy and the incompatibility of socialism and dictatorship. Democracy was now the principle that determined all socialist activities. The new program stipulated that state intervention in socioeconomic life would not be at the expense of equality before the law.[61] Hilda Verwey-Jonker insisted on the inclusion of this proviso. In her view, equal rights of all citizens before the law was essential, but in all the deliberations, she never mentioned the importance of a specific statement about women's equality as citizens. Indeed, she did not address women's issues at all. Neither did Koos Vorrink or Henk Brugmans, committee members, who, as we have seen, had written about the importance of democracy in the family and new relations between the sexes.[62]

Initially, Carry Pothuis-Smit was the only woman to react to the draft, and she appeared content with it.[63] Hilda Verwey-Jonker herself published a series of articles in the monthly leaflet for Federation cadre, but again without paying any special attention to the woman question.[64] This was consistent with the overall policy of the periodical, in which the scant space given to the debate on the new socialism, omitted comments on gender aspects.[65] The message here was that women ought to be interested in and learn about party policy, but not challenge it. Nor should they try to apply the overall gender-neutral principles of equality before the law and equal access to prosperity and social security to the day-to-day realities of their lives.

However, in October 1936, the Federation's executive finally stirred. It proposed an insertion in the program that would make clear that the party supported women in their struggle for economic independence.[66] Probably this was done at the prompting of Mathilde Wibaut, former president of the Federation and seventy-four years old at the time.[67] She was one of the few socialist women who had continued to write feminist articles on the question of women's labor, stressing the importance of their economic independence even at a time when this was no longer popular in the party – if it had ever been. Moreover, she connected these issues to the question of democracy. An example of this was an article in the Federation weekly, *Proletarian Woman*, in April 1934, which began by pointing out that The Netherlands was a complete democracy in the sense that female citizens had full political rights, in contrast to such so-called democracies as France and Switzerland. But, Wibaut wrote, even Dutch women had not attained full democratic freedom on the same level as men, legally or economically. For instance, democracy was absent from Dutch marital law, since it still made the husband the head of the family. Nor did Dutch women enjoy equal opportunities in the workplace, since many occupations were formally or informally closed to them. The current high unemployment rate impaired women's opportunities to earn a living even more. As for wages, it was universally accepted as a law of nature that women's should be lower than men's. After this description of the state of Dutch democracy, Wibaut turned to Dutch women's compliance with attempts to violate the few rights they had, for example the dismissal of married women workers. Even if circumstances were such that women had difficulty upholding the rights they had struggled so long to obtain, it was of the utmost importance that they stand firm. Otherwise the society social democracy aimed to create, the society in which democracy would reign throughout, would never materialize.[68]

The circumstances Mathilde Wibaut described were bleak indeed. The Depression crisis hit The Netherlands hard, and at that moment, in 1934, there were no signs of improvement. The high unemployment rate (30 percent in 1934)[69] tempted many socialists, including socialist women, to support the idea that married and even unmarried women should forfeit their jobs to unemployed men. Where dismissals were necessary, married women should be the first to go. This was the official SDAP position.

Earlier in the interwar period, the party had supported the right to work for men and women alike.[70] In this, the SDAP opposed its competitors for working-class votes, the confessional parties, which strove to ban married women's employment even before the onset of mass unemployment. In contrast to neighboring countries, pro-natalism was not a major issue in this debate, perhaps because the birthrate in The Netherlands was comparatively high. The confessional parties had gained strength and power with the introduction of general suffrage, and consequently in 1924 the government had been able to introduce the marriage bar for female civil servants as a first step. From 1925 onward, women teachers could legally be dismissed upon marriage. In the 1930s, attempts followed to remove all women from jobs not specifically female and even from factory labor.[71] Although these last attempts failed in the end, the attitude was clear: paid work ought to be exclusively reserved for males.

The socialist rank and file were often sympathetic to the idea of reserving employment for men, despite official party policy. They subscribed to the traditional idea of gender roles: men should be the breadwinners, women should be housewives. This ideology was closer to actual facts in The Netherlands than in neighboring countries. In 1930, for instance, 24 percent of the Dutch labor force was female, compared to 31 percent in Great Britain, 36 percent in Germany, and 37 percent in France. In the same year, only 6 percent of married women in The Netherlands was gainfully employed.[72]

Socialist opinions on working women did not differ from those current in trade unions. Women's trade union membership was low. Even in the clothing industry, where women made up two-thirds of the workforce, only 4 percent of women were organized in 1930 compared to 12 percent of the men. Around 1900, there had been attempts at separate women's unions, but by World War I they had disappeared or merged into mixed organizations. Trade union officials – of whom an overwhelming majority were men – complained about women's low membership, but they blamed the women workers instead of their own policy for this. Therefore, they made no special effort to organize women by appealing to their concerns or addressing their needs in the workplace. In the trade unions as in the party, women were first and foremost future housewives and mothers, not workers.[73]

These were the adverse conditions in which Mathilde Wibaut and her allies on the Federation executive tried to keep feminist principles alive in the SDAP women's organization and in the party leadership. Reacting to the draft for the new party program, Wibaut wrote a short piece in the *Social Democrat* under the title, "Something is Missing in the Party Program."[74] Here she once again made a connection between the democratic principles stressed in the draft program and the attempts by the bourgeois parties to drive women away from the labor market. She proposed to make explicit in the program that "the acknowledgment of the value of the human personality" entailed "the acknowledgment of the equivalence of the sexes." She stated that a true social democratic state could never be realized without the abolition of the dominance of one group over another.

Wibaut's next step was to ensure support in the program committee, which she did by contacting Hilda Verwey-Jonker. The latter replied that in her view, the right place in the program for the principle of equal rights for men and women was not in the paragraph on democracy, but next to the fundamental freedoms of religion, speech, the press, and assembly, and equality before the law. This was the draft paragraph on the state to which Verwey-Jonker had added the equality principle. However, she wrote to Wibaut, she was willing to defend the Federation's proposal.[75] Here the differences between the two women's views became clear. In contrast to Wibaut, who saw the woman question in its social and economic context, Verwey-Jonker, in the classical liberal tradition, reduced it to a question of equal rights before the law.[76]

The Federation executive ultimately proposed that the party program include the phrase, "the equivalence of the sexes, both economically and politically," and state the party's support for women in "their struggle for economic independence" in the paragraph on democracy.[77] The latter sentence apparently was not to the committee's liking. It decided, however, to include the acknowledgment of "equal rights in the political and the economic sphere for all members of the community, irrespective of sex or race" in the paragraph on democracy. This decision was a victory for the Federation executive, the more so as it was the only alteration of any importance that the committee allowed in response to suggestions made after the publication of the draft. One the other hand, the victory was a limited one, as the added sentence referred to "rights" only. The feminist issues of economic independence and democracy within the family were left out.

Conclusion

The most striking aspect of this history of the new SDAP program is that none of the members of the committee, even those who had previously voiced sympathy for women's position in family and society – Koos Vorrink, Henk Brugmans, and Hilda Verwey-Jonker – considered the woman question important enough for a passage in the new party program. Here too, there was a deep division between stated principles and party policy on the woman question, which was seen as outside mainstream party concerns. The old socialist and feminist party member Mathilde Wibaut had to take the initiative to change this, however marginally. Apparently, no other influential socialist, male or female, associated the principles of democratic socialism with the unequal position of women, at least in the official formulation of party principles. Even when this was corrected, it was done in the most minimal way by mentioning equal rights only. By thus narrowing the woman question down to a question of rights before the law, the SDAP failed to transcend liberal thought.

All in all, the sources leave an impression of self-congratulation, of socialists comparing the SDAP stand on women's rights with other parties and concluding that little in their own party left much to be desired. Despite the low number of female party members, conditions were steadily improving. That women's participation in the work of the party and in politics generally was far from equal to men's seems to have worried only a very small minority of Dutch socialists. They occasionally mentioned unequal power relations within the family in connection with democracy in the social sphere, but eventually this too disappeared from the party's priorities. A group of feminist socialist women defended women's right to work in the adverse conditions of the interwar years, but they did not succeed in connecting this issue firmly to the questions of democracy that were at stake in the general debate on the renewal of socialism. Their lack of success shows how much feminism was driven onto the defensive in this period. The sad fate of women's opposition to national defense makes clear that contrary to conventional wisdom on the equality of the sexes in the party, women were regarded as second-class citizens after all. They had the vote, they joined the party in increasing numbers, but they did not gain power or even influence.

Notes

1. Dietrich Orlow, "The Paradoxes of Success: Dutch Social Democracy and Its Historiography," *Bijdragen en Mededelingen betreffende de Geschiedenis der Nederlanden* 110 (1995): 43.
2. Peter Jan Knegtmans, *Socialisme en democratie. De SDAP tussen klasse en natie, 1929-1939* (Amsterdam, 1989). See also: Orlow, "Paradoxes of Success."
3. First published in German as *Zur Psychologie des Sozialismus*, and soon translated into several European languages. See Peter Dodge, *Beyond Marxism: The Faith and Works of Hendrik de Man* (The Hague, 1966) p. 68. In Dutch: Hendrik de Man, *De psychologie van het socialisme* (Arnhem, 1927); in English: Henry de Man, *The Psychology of Socialism* (New York, 1928).
4. De Man, *Psychology of Socialism*, pp. 111-18.
5. Ulla Jansz, *Vrouwen ontwaakt. Driekwart eeuw Sociaal-democratische vrouwenorganisatie tussen solidariteit en verzet* (Amsterdam, 1983), p. 46; Tom van der Meer, "Kiesrecht zonder onderscheid van sekse. De SDAP en de strijd voor het vrouwenkiesrecht (1899-1908)," in *Jaarboek voor vrouwengeschiedenis 1981*, eds. Josine Blok et al. (Nijmegen, 1981), p. 150.
6. *Verslag 19e congres SDAP, maart 1913*: 11-12. On Vliegen, see also: Jos Perry, *De voorman. Een biografie van Willem Hubert Vliegen 1862-1947* (Amsterdam 1994), p. 88. For an analysis of the construction of the "working class" as masculine, see Carole Pateman, *The Sexual Contract* (Cambridge, Mass., 1988), pp. 125-42; and Joan Scott, *Gender and the Politics of History* (New York, 1988), pp. 53-163.
7. Perry, *De voorman*, pp. 298-99.
8. Jos Perry, "Aanpakken wat nodig is. De SDAP en haar gemeentepolitiek," in *Het negende jaarboek voor het democratisch socialisme*, eds. Marnix Krop et al. (Amsterdam, 1988), p. 16.
9. The only overview to date is the very summary C. Pothuis-Smit, "De Sociaal-Democratische Vrouwen," in *Wat deden de vrouwen met haar kiesrecht? Het algemeen vrouwenkiesrecht in de practijk*, ed. C. Pothuis-Smit (Arnhem, 1946), pp. 13-64. The subject deserves further scholarly research.
10. The party doubled in size from 1925 (41,200) to 1933 (87,000), after which there was a slight decline. In 1920, party membership was 37,400 of which 7,600 were women; Federation membership was 4,100. In 1938, party membership was 82,100 of which 26,900 were women; Federation membership was 12,000. See Jansz, *Vrouwen, ontwaakt*, pp. 209-10.
11. Corrie van Eijl et al., "Het vergeten voetvolk. Een onderzoek naar de leefwereld van SDAP'ers in de Utrechtse wijk Ondiep 1920-1940," *Tijdschrift voor sociale geschiedenis* 11 (1985): 7-8. See also Jos Perry and Annet Schoot Uiterkamp, "Herkomst, gezindte en beroep van SDAP-leden in Maastricht," *Tijdschrift voor sociale geschiedenis* 14 (1988): 251-61.
12. Heili Both, "Socialisme beteekent geluk voor de vrouw," *Tijdschrift voor vrouwenstudies* 22 (1985): 211.
13. Jacqueline C. Schokking, *De vrouw in de Nederlandse politiek. Emancipatie tot actief burgerschap* (Assen, 1957), pp. 141-42; Jansz, *Vrouwen ontwaakt*, pp. 75-83.
14. Mien Olree, "Een Meisjesconferentie. Samen – in de beweging," *De Socialist* 74 (28 February 1930):5; Lena Bleeker, "Samen in de Beweging," *De Socialist* 76 (14 March 1930): 9-10; Mien Olree, "Nogmaals: Samen in de Beweging!," *De Socialist* 77 (21 March 1930): 10-11
15. Fie Eggink, "De vrouw geweldloos van nature?" *De Socialist. Links socialistisch weekblad* 5 (3 November 1928): 3.

16. For this tripartite grouping, see Rob Hartmans, "Van 'wetenschappelijk socialisme' naar wetenschap en socialisme. De ideologische heroriëntering van de SDAP in de jaren dertig," in *Het twaalfde jaarboek voor het democratisch socialisme*, eds. Marnix Krop et al. (Amsterdam, 1991), pp. 17-45

17. Ibid., pp. 27-28.

18. Knegtmans, *Socialisme en democratie*, pp. 189-90.

19. Rob Hartmans, "Het socialisme van Willem Banning. Bij de honderdste geboortedag van een 'vergeten' ideoloog," *Socialisme en Democratie* 45 (1988): 8-14.

20. W. Banning, *Om de groei der gemeenschap* (Arnhem, 1926), pp. 36-37.

21. Ibid., pp. 191-93.

22. Koos Vorrink, *Een nieuwe jeugd, een nieuwe taak* (Amsterdam, s.a. [1922]), p. 4; also Leo Hartveld, Frits de Jong Edz., and Dries Kuperus, *De Arbeiders Jeugd Centrale AJC 1981-1940/1945-1959* (Amsterdam, 1982), pp. 40-47.

23. Official statistics confirm these occupational changes. Of one hundred gainfully employed women, in 1909 only ten were white-collar workers; in 1920, nineteen, and in 1930, twenty-one. Corrie van Eijl, *Het werkzame verschil: Vrouwen in de slag om arbeid, 1898-1940* (Hilversum, 1994), p. 371.

24. Koos Vorrink, *Stormtij* (Amsterdam, s.a. [1924]), pp. 11-22.

25. Ibid., pp. 23-24.

26. The recent historical study of sex education literature by H.Q. Röling, *Gevreesde vragen: Geschiedenis van de seksuele opvoeding in Nederland* (Amsterdam, 1994) does not mention either Vorrink's ideas or those current in the AJC (Labor Youth League) in general. More research is required to establish how progressive he exactly was in the context of his own time.

27. Hartveld et al., *Arbeiders Jeugd Centrale*, p. 62. Also Vorrink, *Nieuwe jeugd*, p. 6.

28. Hartveld et al., *Arbeiders Jeugd Centrale*, pp. 60-64.

29. Koos Vorrink, *Om de vrije mens der nieuwe gemeenschap. Opvoeding tot het demokratiese socialisme. Handboek ten dienste van de vrije jeugdvorming*, vol. I (Amsterdam, 1933), pp. 241-48.

30. Vorrink, *Vrije mens*, 248-51. Here Vorrink did not deviate from what was usual in the Netherlands prior to World War II. See Röling, *Gevreesde vragen*, pp. 207-9.

31. Vorrink, *Vrije mens*, pp. 61, 191, 243.

32. Notulen Partijbestuursvergadering, 2 June 1934, *Archief SDAP, International Institute for Social History*, Amsterdam (hereafter cited as SDAP-archive).

33. Jan de Bruijn, *Geschiedenis van de abortus in Nederland: Een analyse van opvattingen en discusssies 1600-1979* (Amsterdam, 1979), pp. 134-44.

34. H.N. Brailsford, *Het socialisme-nu!* (Amsterdam, 1927).

35. Geoff Eley, "Cultural Socialism, the Public Sphere, and the Mass Form: Popular Culture and the Democratic Project, 1900-1934," in *Between Reform and Revolution: Studies in the History of German Socialism and Communism from 1840 to 1990*, eds. David E. Barclay and Eric D. Weitz (Providence and Oxford, 1998).

36. Henk Brugmans, "Socialisme en censuur, " *De Socialist* 129 (20 March 1931): 8-9.

37. Henk Brugmans, "Gezin, Revolutie en Partij," *De Socialist* 143 (26 June 1931): 11-12.

38. Knegtmans, *Socialisme en democratie*, pp. 52-60.

39. I deduce this from the lack of biographical data on both of them – nothing on Eggink and a few newspaper cuttings recording Vigelius' death in January 1936 at age 48. Vigelius seems to have been a freelance journalist active in several nonsocialist women's organizations. (Biographical Press Cuttings, Folder 3929, International Information Center and Archives for the Women's Movement [IIAV], Amsterdam.)

40. Matty Vigelius, "Alexandra Kollontai: Een leven gewijd aan de vrijmaking der vrouw," *De Socialist* 6 (10 November 1928): 6-7 and 7 (17 November 1928): 6; Fie Eggink, "Een ongelijke strijd: Toekomst der Russische vrouw, " *Sociaal-Democraat* 1,12 (19 December 1931): 6-7.

41. Anneke Ribberink, "Radicalisering of integratie van de SDAP in de jaren dertig: de levensgeschiedenis van Hilda Verwey-Jonker," in *Het tweede jaarboek voor het democratisch socialisme*, ed. Jan Bank et al. (Amsterdam, 1988), p. 112.

42. Hilda Verwey-Jonker, *Er moet een vrouw in. Herinneringen in een kentering van de tijd*, (Amsterdam, 1988), pp. 57-64.

43. Matty Vigelius, "De vrouw en het socialisme. Strijd naast den man," *De Sociaal Democraat* 1, 43 (23 July 1932): 4-5

44. Jansz, *Vrouwen ontwaakt*, 83-99; see also Ulla Jansz, "Women or Workers? The 1889 Labor Law and the Debate on Protective Legislation in the Netherlands," in *Protecting Women: Labor Legislation in Europe, the United States, and Australia, 1880-1920*, eds. Ulla Wikander, Alice Kessler-Harris, and Jane Lewis (Urbana and Chicago, 1995), pp. 197-205.

45. A similar argument can be found in Jac.a E. de Jonge, "Democratie in het gezin," *De Proletarische Vrouw* 958 (10 January 1934): 7.

46. Hilda Verwey-Jonker, "Fascisme in Nederland. Het is latent aanwezig," *De Sociaal-Democraat* 2, 27 (1 April 1933):1-2; and "Fascisme in Nederland. Wat kunnen we er tegen doen?" *De Sociaal- Democraat* 2, 28 (15 April 1933): 2-3.

47. H. Verwey -Jonker, *De vrouw en het nationaalsocialisme* (Assen, 1937), pp. 21-25.

48. "Vrouwen in Duitschland," *Mededeelingen voor de propaganda onder de vrouwen*, 1933/34 (March 1934), pp. 53-64.

49. Verwey-Jonker, *Vrouw en het Nationaalsocialisme*, pp. 31-32.

50. Notulen Programcommissie, folder Beginselprogramcommissie, box 16, Archive Boekman, International Institute for Social History, Amsterdam (hereafter Archive Boekman 16).

51. Knegtmans, *Socialisme en democratie*, p. 103.

52. Notulen PB 3.31.1934, SDAP archive; Notulen DB 1.21.1936.

53. Congresverslag SDAP 1934, 31-32; notulen PB 4.7.1934, (SDAP Archive); notulen DB 4.30.1934; notulen PB 10.6.1934. See also Knegtmans, *Socialisme en democratie*, pp. 103-10.

54. Knegtmans, *Socialisme en democratie*, pp. 203-11.

55. Joan W. Scott, "Rewriting History," *Behind the Lines: Gender and the Two World Wars*, eds. Margaret Randolph Higonnet and Jane Jenson (New Haven and London, 1987), pp. 25-26.

56. H.F. Cohen, *Om de vernieuwing van het socialisme. De politieke oriëntatie van de Nederlandse sociaal-democratie 1919-1930* (Leiden, 1974), p. 208.

57. G. van Veen, "Moeilijk maar onafwijsbaar dilemma," *De Sociaal-Democraat* 5, 11 (29 February 1936): 1-2.

58. C. Pothuis-Smit, "Moeilijk, maar onafwijsbaar dilemma? Beschouwingen naar aanleiding van G. van Veen's artikel," *De Sociaal-Democraat* 5, 12 (14 March 1936): 3-4.

59. G. van Veen, "Van vooroordeel en werkelijkheidsbesef III," *De Sociaal-Democraat* 6, 16 (9 May 1936): 5-6.

60. Congresverslag SDAP 1937, pp. 61-62, 85-90.

61. "Het ontwerp-beginselprogram der SDAP," *De Sociaal-Democraat* 5, 21 (18 July 1936): 4-5.

62. Notulen Programcommissie, 8 June 1936, Boekman Archive 16.

63. C. Pothuis-Smit, "Ons nieuw program," *De Sociaal-Democraat* 5, 25 (12 September 1936): 4.

64. Hilda Verwey-Jonker, "Het Beginsel-program der SDAP," *Mededelingen voor de propaganda onder de vrouwen* 1936/7 (October 1936), pp. 7-8; "Het uiteindelijk doel van het socialisme," (November 1936), pp. 9-10; "Het nieuwe partijprogram verder besproken," (January 1937), pp. 38-40.

65. W. Ploegsma-Bentum, "Het rapport van de herzieningscommissie der SDAP," *Mededeelingen voor de propaganda onder de vrouwen,* 1933/4 (February 1934), pp. 37-51, and the series by F. Polak-Leverpoll on Democracy, in 1935/36, pp. 6-8, 22-24, 25-28, 36-37, 41-43, 54-56.

66. E. Ribbius Peletier, "Verslag van de Hoofdbestuursvergadering," *De Proletarische Vrouw* 1101 (14 October 1936): 2

67. That she had not reacted earlier might be explained by the fact that her husband, Floor Wibaut, had died of cancer in April of that year. See G.W.B. Borrie, *F.M.Wibaut: Mens en magistraat* (Amsterdam and Assen, 1968), p. 223.

68. M. Wibaut-B v.B., "De Vrouw en de democratie," *De Proletarische Vrouw* 973 (25 April 1934): 5.

69. Erik Hansen and Peter A. Prosper, "Political Economy and Political Action: The Programmatic Response of Dutch Social Democracy to the Depression Crisis, 1929-1939," *Journal of Contemporary History* 29 (1994): 133-34. There are no figures for unemployed women.

70. Jansz, *Vrouwen ontwaakt,* pp. 91-96.

71. Van Eijl, *Het werkzame verschil,* 271-88.

72. Ibid., pp. 373-74.

73. Corrie van Eijl and Gertjan de Groot, "'Zij besteden hun geld liever aan een strik in het haar': Vrouwen en vakbonden (1890-1940)," in *De Kracht der Zwakken. Studies over arbeid en arbeidersbeweging in het verleden,* eds. Boudien de Vries et al. (Amsterdam, 1922), pp. 363-90.

74. M. Wibaut-B. v. Berlekom, "Leemte in het Partijprogram," *De Sociaal-Democraat* 6, 2 (October 24 1936): 5.

75. Hilda Verwey-Jonker to M. Wibaut, November 5 1936, M.Wibaut Archive, International Institute for Social History, Amsterdam.

76. See Mary Dietz, "Context is all: Feminism and theories of Citizenship," *Dimensions of Radical Democracy: Pluralism, Citizenship, Community,* ed. Chantal Mouffe (London and New York, 1992), p. 68.

77. Brugmans' memo to Program Committee, 18 November 1936, Boekman Archive, p. 16.

Chapter 6

Bread and Roses
Pragmatic Women in the Belgium Workers' Party

Denise De Weerdt

The Socialist-Catholic political rivalry which was so central to Belgian politics began with the formation of the Belgian Workers' Party (BWP) in 1886. The details of this rivalry are critical for understanding aspects of both the woman question in general and the position of the socialist women's movement between the wars.

The BWP was very strongly opposed to the Catholic church and its stronghold in the Catholic party. In this period, the influence of the church and priests on women was still considerable in small towns and rural communities, especially in Flanders. Consequently, the socialist women's movement was characterized by an aversion to any and all things that suggested Catholicism.

Socialists vs. Catholics in Belgian Politics

The Belgian Workers Party had followed a social democratic course since 1886, with the goal of winning the political and economic emancipation of the working class through progressive reform of the existing capitalist regime. This was to be achieved by electing a socialist parliamentary majority through universal male suffrage. Party leaders wanted the working class to act as an organic entity, channeling its hopes and grievances into unions, health services, and buyers' cooperatives as well as

---

Notes for this chapter begin on page 263.

political and cultural organizations, to prepare the way for the ultimate seizure of the state. The party drew its strength from this organizational "stacking" – the vertical structuring of party institutions and constituent parts on an ideological base.

The BWP was at its peak membership during the interwar years. In this period, it moved from marxist revolutionary strategies to integration into Belgium's political system. It became the second biggest political formation, just behind the Catholic party. In several short periods, the party participated in coalition governments; more often, it played the role of loyal opposition. Just before the end of the First World War the majority of the socialist leaders had agreed that the BWP should participate in the National government. In return, the government conceded universal male suffrage. This brought the first break in the Catholic party's absolute majority. From then on, it had to depend on coalitions with nonconfessional but preferably conservative partners.

In the early postwar period, the BWP joined the governing coalition in an effort to hasten Belgium's economic recovery and guarantee social peace. The 1919 elections for Parliament, the first conducted under universal male suffrage, produced some electoral shifts, but no socialist majority. Nevertheless, the coalition passed into law a significant part of the socialist program: the right of workers to organize, the eight-hour day, old age pensions, unemployment compensation, and compulsory contributions to social security. As a result, membership in unions and other socialist organizations rose sharply.

In the 1925 elections, a dynamic Socialist party scored a substantial success, obtaining its highest vote ever (35 percent). It formed a left-oriented government together with the Christian-Democratic wing of the Catholic party. The Vandervelde (Socialist)-Poullet (Catholic) government, in which socialists occupied important ministerial posts, had been elected largely on the basis of the 1894 Socialist electoral program, known as the Quaregnon Charter, after the city in which the Socialist congress met that year. The Christian-Democrats collaborated with the socialist program, in part because they had no full-scale electoral program of their own (the first Catholic program was not passed until 1945).[1] This first Socialist experiment in coalition rule was short-lived. The other parties combined to defeat the government by provoking a financial panic. Out of fear of inflation, which could undermine the party's own organizations, the BWP agreed to cooperate with a Conservative government. Many militants, even traditional reformists, opposed this surrender to an old tactical trick in order to save Belgian capitalism. In 1927, the BWP returned to the opposition.

The Conservative "cure" lasted seven years, for the party was unable to regain the dynamism it had enjoyed in the early-1920s. The economic boom favored the parties that supported capitalism. The BWP had not amended its Quaregnon program in ways that would attract other social groups; in the same period, it began to lose its close connections with the working class, which resented party leaders' readiness to preserve the capitalist order. The number of party members declined; in the elections of 1929 the socialist vote fell to its 1921 level.

Hostility to Women's Political Organization

The feminist movement in Belgium had minimal influence before the war. Its only achievements were minor changes in the civil code, which applied more to bourgeois women than to proletarian, as they concerned mostly property matters. Unlike other countries in which women's labor during World War I contributed to the passage of women's suffrage laws, extremely high unemployment was the pattern during German occupation of the country. Belgian women's wartime contributions had been in espionage and the resistance, as prison camp inmates, in nursing, child care and philanthropy; nevertheless, they continued to be denied full voting rights.

The BWP had sponsored women's political groups since it was founded; indeed, autonomous groups existed in most of the industrial cities. In a first attempt at unification they joined together in 1900 to form a nationwide socialist women's movement. From its beginning, members of the national political women's organization opted to cooperate closely with the party. In theory, Belgian socialists considered women as equal to men, but male leaders and rank and file were inconsistent in their treatment of the women as a movement. The socialist women's organization never achieved the rank of other special-mission party organizations such as the socialist youth movement, or the Workers' Education Center. Male socialists perceived working-class women as sharing the same interests as male workers and thought they should struggle together for better wages and women's enfranchisement. This idea of combining class and gender struggles was very often difficult to realize.

World War I shattered the existing feminist and women's movements. As soon as the war was over, both feminist and nonfeminist women reestablished their organizations; however, the first municipal elections after the war showed that socialist women lacked a constituency. At the municipal level, Conservative voters were more numerous (or more conscientious) than those in parliamentary elections, from which women were still excluded. As they did in France, Socialist party leaders blamed the influence of the Catholic church on women and their lack of education. Henceforward, leaders tolerated specifically political activities for women only under the strict control of the party. Again as in France, Socialist women's main task was to disseminate propaganda for the party program among working class women, a job essential to win women's votes.

Socialist women could choose to organize themselves in separate political groups but were not obliged to do so; each female member of a socialist union, a cooperative league, or mutual benefit society was automatically counted as a member of the party. Since the party's political organization for women failed to attract members, the BWP after 1922 put all its efforts into the organization of women in a mutual benefit society, called the Provident Woman, later changed to Provident Socialist Women (FPS). These organizations were conceived as competitors for similar Catholic women's groups, which were class-based: one for middle-class women, one for women peasants, one for working-class women. The latter, the Catholic Women Workers' Movement, was based on parish leagues, which sponsored family-centered activities, home economics courses, and religious education. This group prepared its first program for the municipal elections of 1932, emphasizing housing, public sanitation, and the defense of public morality.

The socialists hoped to attract the hard-to-organize category of housewives through the FPS. The mutualist women's groups became the most important socialist women's organizations, with more members and impact than the political groups and cooperatives. There were no separate socialist women's trade unions. Unlike the women's groups in the French Section of the Workers' International (SFIO), Belgian women's organizations were linked in a loosely co-ordinated National Women's Action Committee (CNAF), especially during electoral periods. In 1935, women's socialist organizations of all varieties had 110,000 members. On the local level, it was often difficult to distinguish among the various socialist women's organizations. More often than not, attempts at unification and reorganization failed. This became an ongoing subject of debate, and sometimes of contention, during party congresses, and continued until very recently.

Although in theory men and women party members were equal, women members were never given substantial financial and material help, nor did their leaders demand it. Socialist women usually subordinated their feminist claims to the party's definition of their political role. As in the British party, female socialist leaders often acted as the mouthpiece of their male "patrons"; in this, they were not much different from ordinary male comrades and militants.

The Belgian party feared that too much focus on feminist issues could lead to gender division that would endanger class solidarity. Class issues had to come first. After all, the party was not made to champion women, but to fight capitalism and its abuses. Like the British Labour party, the BWP frequently postponed women's issues. Most Belgian socialist women apparently shared the party's belief that "the women's question would automatically be solved in the future socialist society." During the 1920s, family issues were more important than questions of women's political rights. This change of direction, already apparent in the priority the party gave to the FPS, is reflected in socialist imagery. The wartime image of "Marianne," the comrade-worker, disappeared, replaced by the working-class mother with her children and strong male provider.

A latent hostility, indifference, and sometimes jealousy, broke through in the heated debates on women's total enfranchisement. Male socialist militants and workers were still strongly influenced by prejudices against women. On the one hand, they argued that women "are guided by their feelings," "are less educated, and less able than men to understand complicated economic and political matters," and "have deep religious feelings." On the other hand, women were thought to have greater spirituality than men, and to place greater value on humanitarian causes.

Socialist women as well as men associated feminist concepts with bourgeois women. Further, the ideal of equality between comrades made many men dubious about separate women's groups within the party. The pleas of prominent women for greater responsibility and input rarely received much support from the party. Socialist women struggled for political and legal equality, the right to work and equal wages, and the expansion of educational opportunity for girls and women. On some issues, they acted independently of the party. Isabelle Blume ignored the party's nonintervention position during the Spanish Civil War to rescue the children of republicans,[2] but never were women permitted meaningful participation either inside the party, or in the larger political arena.

Very few women held elected political office, and they were merely tolerated in decision-making councils. The rare women who managed to gain elective office were given responsibility for gender-role-affirming matters, such as infant welfare, maternal and child care, housing, and other social matters, such as education.[3] Like their counterparts in the British Labour party, Belgian Socialists made issues connected with women's traditional activities the responsibility of the women's side of the movement. Women were considered to be novices, who had yet to learn the first principles of the political alphabet. Regular activities in local women's groups tended to be practical, not political. They included holiday camps, exhibitions of handicraft, children's parties, needlework and cooking courses, or household design. It was mainly thanks to the influence of emancipated middle-class or educated women like Marie Spaak, Alice Pels, Alice Heyman, and Isabelle Blume who joined the cause of the working class, that the socialist women's movement matured.[4]

Neither the social and cultural climate of the working class, nor the mentality of BWP leaders was ready for feminism. The tendency of the popular press to portray middle-class values and norms as the ideal for the working class irritated socialists, confirming their socialist ideals and encouraging their rejection of anything associated with prewar "bourgeois capitalist" feminists. Even when they had common agendas, class prejudice made cooperation between the middle-class and working-class women's movements impossible. Socialist women found difficulty in overcoming the class prejudice they learned from their mothers and grandmothers, who had often expressed horror at the idea of becoming dependent on middle-class charity. There was a similar split along class lines in France, whereas women's movements in Sweden and Denmark found it much easier to cooperate across the class divide.

The political and intellectual roots of middle-class feminists lay in the progressive wing of the Liberal party, the free-thinkers' movement, and freemasonry. Their organizations, the National Women's Council, for instance, and the peace and women's suffrage movements were considered politically liberal. There was only one case of cross-class cooperation among organized women in the interwar period; middle-class feminists and socialist and communist women campaigned together against the government's proposal in 1935 to ban married women's right to work.[5] In contrast, there was no cooperation at all between socialist women and the Catholic women's movement. These powerful rivals remained each other's worst enemies throughout the interwar period.

Second-Class Citizens

During the interwar years, socialist women were able to win the support of party leaders for some of their women-centered reforms. In 1923, they outlined a program, which in many ways prefigured – as was the case in the United Kingdom – the post-World War II welfare state. The party enthusiastically endorsed those sections of the program that concerned social issues such as maternal and child health, or the protection of women's labor.

When it came to women's suffrage, the party's response was far less supportive. It showed how wide was the gap between its assertions of gender equality and the reality of women's inferior status in the party and society. The bitter struggle for Belgian women's right to vote illustrated what happened when a political issue became entangled with gender interests. Despite the "higher moral quality" and "common sense" ascribed to women, women lost out in the opportunistic horse trading between the Liberals and Socialists, both of whom feared that the likely outcome of general elections with women voting would be more votes for Catholic and other conservative parties.

Party debate about this issue began as early as 1902. At the annual Socialist Women's congress, many delegates spoke out for the immediate realization of universal suffrage. However, the general congress of the BWP rejected the women's demand for a simultaneous grant of political rights to both sexes. The men argued that women could better spend their efforts in the fight for peace, since this was closer to their nature. This set the course for the party's stance on women's suffrage until after World War II.

Adult suffrage was granted only to men in 1918, out of fear that "women's strong religious feeling" would help the Catholics retain their absolute majority in Parliament. After lengthy debates on the suffrage question, women received only the municipal vote.[6] The socialist promise to give them access to provincial elections went unfulfilled. The BWP justified its decisions with the same old arguments: women lacked education and were not fit to participate in higher governmental matters. Women had to prove they were really interested in political rights by joining socialist women's groups; they could then practice their art in "the primary school," meaning the municipal councils.

In 1921, working-class women won the right to serve in local government. Familiar with the problems faced by working-class families, the women elected to municipal office were more capable than expected, as they applied their domestic experience and skills in a public context. In the case of parliamentary elections, women MPs were in an absurd situation; they could run for office, they were eligible for office, but they could not vote for themselves. One is finally led to suspect that socialist men found an altogether too easy alibi in the alleged influence of the Catholic church on women. Could it be that they feared that their patriarchal authority was at risk?

Male status was even more directly threatened when Belgian feminists began to attack the civil superiority and privileges of men, based on the still unrevised Napoleonic Code. Starting in the last decades of the nineteenth century, they had stubbornly, but with much patience and tact, tried to force through an equal rights program. They used none of the violent tactics of the British suffragettes, but politely and firmly appealed to public opinion through pamphlets, and bombarded governing bodies with endless petitions. Gradually, small inroads were made in that bastion of male supremacy, the Civil Code. Several legal aspects of financial relations between husband and wife were modified. In the struggle against married women's civil incapacity, socialist women chose to fight for a different set of legal reforms than those middle-class feminists demanded. They were especially anxious to secure a woman's right to withdraw small sums from a savings account without her husband's approval (even a working wife had to request his authorization to spend her own earnings). They proposed to give separated wives complete authority to dispose of their belongings. The law of 1927 went only part of the way; a separated woman was permitted to control only her moveable property (not real estate, for which she still needed marital approval).

The first substantial change in the inferior legal status of married women, one which opened the path to equality between spouses, was achieved in the 1932 marriage law. This accorded some rights to married women, especially over their personal possessions, but the consent of the husband was still needed in many cases.[7] Full civil capacity of married women was only achieved decades later, in 1958. What a difference from Sweden, where a 1919 marriage law gave the same rights and responsibilities to husbands and wives!

Population Politics: Promoting Births

Belgian women were denied full political and civil equality in the interwar period simply because of their perceived shortcomings as women. But one female quality – and a highly rated one at that – was not to be overlooked: women's reproductive function. After World War I, mothers were badly needed for the repopulation of the *patrie*. Like other European countries, Belgium undertook a campaign to reverse population decline, convinced that the nation's vitality, its economic revival, the security of its borders, all depended on large numbers of children. Belgium's birthrate had fallen precipitously during the war, but fertility decline had already begun by about 1900.[8] Moreover, all efforts to raise the birthrate had failed.

The Socialist party generally supported postwar government mother and infant-care programs without recognizing the contradiction between its denial of civil rights to women, and its effort to create better social conditions for mothers and children. The BWP decided to work for these reforms through the FPS (the Provident Socialist Women) which had proved so much more successful in recruiting working-class women members than the political organization. The FPS was linked to socialist mutual benefit societies and was very much involved in providing its members with cash payments at marriage and births, aid in case of illness and/or widowhood, an infant's layette, and other amenities.

Belgian infant and child mortality rates were high, especially in working-class families. The government had taken measures to promote reproduction; now it sought to persuade couples to produce children who were strong and healthy. Many working-class parents realized that poverty and unsanitary conditions caused sickly children. Party

propaganda discussed eugenic measures to prevent the unfit from repro-
ducing (the Norwegian party took a similar view). These were echoes
from the late-1890s, however. References to neo-Malthusian theory or
practice disappeared during the interwar years.[9] In the 1920s, socialist
efforts to lower child mortality focused on improving living conditions.
They delegated the task of providing decent housing to *female* members
of city councils.

The housing problem was made a priority immediately after the
Armistice when efforts were made to clear the worst of the nineteenth
century slums. In the textile city of Ghent, for example, a special commission of the local administration sought out houses deemed uninhabit-
able, based on sanitary criteria. The commission began by condemning
cellar dwellings, gypsy caravans, and houseboats. Local authorities,
Catholic housing associations and the Socialist Co-operative Building
society, which had its own construction crew, planned and built new
workers' homes. Together they produced a total of 2,349 affordable
houses, mainly in suburban workers' neighborhoods. This was far from
sufficient; many people remained on waiting lists. In the same period,
6,588 new middle-class homes were built in the private sector.[10]

To promote healthy children, various agencies set up well-baby clinics
offering prenatal and infant care, and centers for the treatment of female
and venereal diseases. The socialist mutual benefit societies created modern clinics at which women and future couples were welcomed. Doctors
and nurses, and the socialist women's press as well, tried to counter working-class mothers' practices and prejudices about child care, which they
agreed were unhygienic.

The FPS established baby welfare centers in popular neighborhoods.
This put them in competition with the until-then unchallenged Catholic
supremacy on the board of the National Child Welfare Council. The welfare centers received state funds on a per crib basis, on the condition that
the mother join the center voluntarily. With the help of the board of the
CNAF, Marie Spaak introduced a bill in 1933 calling for the revision of
the law on child protection, the extension of baby and child day care centers, and the replacement of the free subsidy by compulsory insurance.
Under the subsidy system, she complained, "Mothers are virtually being
bought. Whoever refuses to sympathize with one or the other group risks
being thrown out." Her bill was not passed.[11] Nevertheless, the collective
efforts for mother and child care attracted more mothers and their children to the baby-clinics in the 1930s. The number of children subsidized
by the National Child Welfare Council rose from 68,137 in 1930 to
105,548 in 1939.

The notion of improving people's health through a system of public
subsidies inspired the women's movement to make claims for social legis-

lation based on their procreative function or, as they put it, on "the possession of a womb." In so doing, they followed the example of the
women's movement in Sweden where "the population question became a
platform for feminist demands." Belgian women used the same claim of
protecting mothers to call for maternity leave for all working women,
based on the 1919 Washington Convention which specified up to six
weeks before delivery and six weeks after. Mothers were to be compensated with maternity insurance to cover the loss of wages during that
period. The principle had already been adopted by the 1910 International Conference of Socialist Women, in Copenhagen. In Belgium, a bill
introduced by Marie Spaak in 1923 laid out the various steps to be taken
in the matter of health politics "within the limits of our knowledge of the
female body." State intervention for motherhood insurance was in everybody's interest, for, as the socialist women's movement put it, it was "a
community service." They described the nine months of pregnancy as a
national service comparable to male military service. This would not do
for Marie Spaak, who commented: "A soldier does not have to stay on the
job like the pregnant working woman does. She is at the same time a
mother, a wet-nurse, a housewife, and a working woman."

Some years later socialist women went a step further and included all
women in the motherhood insurance scheme, with the argument "that
the work of a housewife has an economic value." Nonworking mothers
should be assisted by paid help during the first week after birth, or in case
of illness, for "husbands are the first to appreciate the fact that the
household keeps going, when the wives are absent or ill."[12] However,
they never went as far as Swedish social democrats, whose plan paid
maternity insurance directly to the mother, and not the father as head of
the family. The "right of the womb" was not fully recognized in Belgium
until after World War II.

Socialist women's plans for the protection of mothers and children
included encouraging smaller families. They thought that a family with at
most four children was the ideal. In Norway, socialist women also calculated that limiting the number of children would benefit the family budget and would eventually allow working-class families to provide an
education to their children. Belgian socialist posters and illustrations portrayed an ideal family consisting of two children, usually a boy and a
girl.[13] One of the government's policies to counter population decline was
a supplement to workers' wages based on the number of children in the
household (family allowance). Originally employers paid these allowances, but the public law passed later applied to all wage earners. This
program was not very popular in the socialist women's movement because
it favored the creation of large families. The allowance increased with
each consecutive birth. Working-class women preferred the larger

allowance to be paid at the first birth, which, they argued, incurred greater expense and more changes in family life than subsequent births.[14]

The desire to restrict the number of children was linked to the knowledge and practice of birth control. The concept was never openly admitted; nor was it discussed in socialist texts. Belgian criminal law banned the sale or distribution of contraceptives, which were believed to encourage abortion. Indeed, even advertising contraceptives or publishing information about contraception was a criminal offense as specified in title VII of the criminal code along with abortion, infanticide, kidnaping, bigamy, adultery, pornography, prostitution, and rape. The Napoleonic Code introduced legislation forbidding abortion into Belgium in 1810. In 1867, it was incorporated into articles 348 to 353 of the Penal Law as a crime against family order and public morality. There were relatively few convictions for abortion, and little is known about its incidence before the 1970s.

Belgians practiced abstinence and withdrawal (*coitus interruptus*) to prevent birth. Ron Lesthaeghe speculates that the French-speaking bourgeoisie introduced withdrawal from France and it spread gradually to rural Catholic and Flemish couples. The 1966 national fertility survey reported that 40.7 percent of all married couples were still practicing withdrawal (43.7 percent in Flanders, 32.3 percent in Wallonia, and 34.1 percent in Brussels). These percentages were roughly comparable to those found in the UK and the United States in the 1920s and the 1930s.

The Catholic Church's strong opposition to the use of all contraceptives was the main reason for Belgian conservatism in this matter. Before 1914, when middle-class couples were already practicing fertility control, Cardinal Mercier and the Belgian bishops had issued instructions for the parish clergy to counteract the "plague of onanism." However, the Church could only slow, not stop, the diffusion of contraceptive practices among its parishioners. For its own reasons, the BWP also was not eager for liberalization of the use of contraceptives. The fact that population growth was considerably higher in predominantly Catholic Flanders made Walloon socialists fear demographic decline in their region. Emile Vandervelde was silent in the 1920s about population matters, possibly because his male comrades, like French Socialists, considered birth control a private matter.

Nevertheless, socialist women made their first, timid efforts to introduce family planning and sexual reform before World War I.[15] They circumvented the law by introducing the notion of voluntary motherhood, which they called "conscious motherhood." They supported the prevention of unwanted pregnancy, on the grounds that its consequences, such as dangerous abortion practices or infanticide, were tragic. In the newspapers of the early-1920s articles appeared almost weekly about abortion related deaths or the murder of newborns. Despite potential criminal prosecution, young women risked both their personal freedom and their lives out of sheer desperation, and abortion was the surest after-the-fact contraceptive.

Socialist women protested against the toughening of the existing law on contraceptives in 1923, the same year in which France amended its law. They planned a "mother protection" program offering birth control information and counseling services, and for those women who wished to have children, an expansion of birth clinics, prenatal counseling, postnatal nursing services and mother care, and rest homes for working mothers. In the premarital counseling section, doctors hired by the socialist mutualities informed couples on the facts of life. At first young people were reluctant to go, for they were shy about the gynecological examination, given to predict and treat difficult deliveries, and the general examination for traces of venereal diseases, but growing numbers eventually accepted the services.[16] In the meantime, the practice of abortion – never openly discussed – continued.

Only in the late 1930s was the notion of conscious motherhood mentioned in the socialist women's press. At that time, writing about such matters required considerable courage. The family planning movement did not achieve a breakthrough until 1956, when the Dutch Association for Sexual Reform established a Belgian branch with the help of the FPS; it quickly recruited 630,000 members. The infamous articles of the criminal law against the sale or distribution of contraceptives were revised only in 1990, half a century later than in Norway.

For a Better Quality of Life

Belgian socialist women shared the view of German feminist Lily Braun that it was not enough to fight for fundamental changes in the conditions of wage labor and in the legal and political status of women. Full emancipation meant radical changes in family life and a solution to the difficulties arising from women's double burden as workers and housewives.[17] Women's contributions in World War I did little to change patriarchal attitudes. Women came forward to serve wherever they were needed, but men were by no means convinced that this should continue after the war. On the contrary, soldiers returning from the deadly trench warfare, wanted their wives waiting at home to help them forget the hardships of war. As soon as the war ended, the government and political leaders – including the newly installed socialist ministers – were ready to promise a comfortable domestic life for workers.[18] What better means was there of restoring social stability than the nuclear family, in which women, by remaining in their traditional role, could create a haven for men's physical and psychological recovery?

Leaders of the Socialist party and trade unions understood that this meant continuing the double burden for women. Their answer was to fight for better wages for men, so that women could stay at home to occupy themselves with household tasks, child rearing, and making the home attractive for their husbands. This was the classic response to male fears that women workers, because of their lower wages, were a threat to working men. The socialist women's press presented a different point of view; working-class women knew that a second income was needed in most households to make ends meet. Nevertheless, both male workers and trade union members believed that better wages for themselves that allowed them to support stay-at-home wives was the best solution to the problem of low family incomes.

Given the BWP's endorsement of "equal pay for equal work" constantly cited in women's and trade union programs, this attitude was both contradictory and ambiguous. It may be that socialist women thought "equal pay" referred to the entire female working population, whereas men understood it to apply only to unmarried and young married women. Women often continued wage work outside the home during the first years of their marriage, and stayed home only after the birth of the first child. Instead of the family wage, socialist women preferred state-funded social insurance. They called for municipal community services such as laundries, kitchens, and kindergartens or day care centers, which would enable them to cope with their double burden. A female factory worker and socialist militant wrote: "The inadequate wage of the father should be supplemented by social insurance, in order to enable our mothers to devote their full attention to the education of the children, and to the preservation of a real home for the family ... Our female companions must help us realize this as soon as possible." [19] At the same time, however, a minority of socialist women stressed the importance of female wage labor as contributing to women's independence.

What about women who wished to take on a third burden, the political one? During the 1923 women's week at the Labor College, Marie Spaak lectured about women's political role. She argued against the long-standing opinion that a woman doing political work necessarily neglected her family; instead, she declared that the better-educated a woman, the more capable she was of running a household. Municipal politics were the chosen domain for women, On their town councils, women representatives could turn their understanding of the needs of working-class women and their families to good account. They would be in a position to establish kindergartens and day care centers, and expand professional and technical education for girls.[20]

In the 1930s, both the popular press and state education attempted to raise the standards of domesticity, propagating an ever more demanding and complex middle-class model of home economics. Home economics schools and courses taught girls how to do household tasks. Often these courses enunciated Taylorist principles: planning, timing, efficient storage, labor-saving machinery. Taylorism applied to housekeeping risked bringing about a sixteen-hour day for wage-earning women! Together with the higher standards of child care, it made the double burden even heavier, for men did little to help in the kitchen, or elsewhere.

Socialist women's magazines reflected these changes in domestic economy. In 1935, they were advertising electric appliances like vacuum cleaners and refrigerators, despite the fact that such purchases were beyond the means of the vast majority of their readers. Working-class women were generally proud of their homes, even when they were overcrowded slum houses or apartments in public housing projects. They kept everything very clean and liked to boast that, "in our home, one can eat off the floor."[21] But most had to make do with only a two-burner gas stove and an oven, and perhaps a semiautomatic wooden washing machine. Daily shopping for food increased the time they spent on household tasks.

In an effort to respond to this heavy burden, the socialist women's movement promoted shared gender responsibility for domestic tasks. During a debate, Alice Heyman remarked that a father should participate in household activities. "The direction of the home should rest on two heads. Husband and wife should share responsibility for a smoothly functioning home life as they do for the education of their children." In the early 1930s, this notion of shared responsibility and division of household tasks came to be called "marital democracy."[22]

Gender sharing of domestic tasks made little progress in most working-class homes. More practical help came from the socialist consumer cooperatives with their network of bakeries, groceries, pharmacies, coal-delivery services, lingerie and dress shops. Members received help in budget planning and shared in the profits of the cooperative, paying lower prices on purchases throughout the year. The aims of the Cooperative Office, (OC) were not simply materialist, however. The cooperatives taught members to become aware consumers. During the 1920s, the OC created the Socialist Women's Cooperative League in order to reach more working-class women and housewives. The League's sections held monthly meetings where the women, while enjoying social contact and refreshments, were taught to appreciate and buy the cooperative's products, and not to be lured by flashy inferior ware.[23] In periods of inflation, socialist women organized marches to protest rising prices. They also demonstrated in support of the BWP's rent control proposal, which would protect tenants against exploitation by their landlords.

Educating Women Socialists

Immediately after World War I, the Socialist party sought to attract educated women, who would become the core of the women's organization
and train as propagandists. The party could rely only on a small number
of schooled middle-class women who, unlike their working-class sisters,
had leisure time in which to disseminate its propaganda.[24] However,
when the core of middle-class women organizers began their work, they
found that their efforts met with a very limited response from working-
class women. In 1923, the organizers complained about the small number
of women attending socialist courses and expressed the view that working-class women had minimal interest in matters beyond their homes and
families. During the congress held the same year at the Workers' Education Center, a male speaker declared: "Women's lives are central to the
society as a whole, since most of the incongruities of the capitalist system
can be explained with reference to the condition of women." But what
solution did he and his fellow comrades offer? They organized courses
which focused on women's traditional responsibilities as housewives and
mothers, with topics such as "population policies and child care" and
"the ethical duties of wives and mothers in the family circle!" [25]
    The Labor College did its part in the education of women socialists by
holding a women's week once a year. In 1923, the executive of the CNAF
prepared a program for fifty-five participants, although many more
women from all over the country were eager to come. The week was
devoted to finding some guiding principles for initiating socialist women's
action. The pupils were warned not to imitate men: "our strong language
must be softened by our finer female feelings. We must not become too
outspoken, or too flamboyant in the way we dress. The women's movement must still overcome ill will and prejudice."[26] Alice Pels and Isabelle
Blume presented the pupils with what was called "a simple program."
Lectures on national and international socialist politics, syndicalism and
cooperatives were given for two hours each morning. Lecturers strongly
emphasized the value of mutual benefit societies and the protection they
provided to women. The courses centered on education as a necessary
instrument of women's emancipation. Both leaders warned their students
that a woman had to work twice as hard as a man to achieve and keep
whatever position she sought.
    Because the women's week was directed mainly towards working-class
women, presenters tried to speak and write simply. The pamphlets were
brief and written in simple language. Isabelle Blume provided short, easy-
to-read biographies of ten famous women who had devoted their lives to
the workers' movement and the emancipation of women.[27] Nevertheless,
in the 1920s, the socialist women's press had little impact on women, and

Isabelle Blume blamed this on a lack of publicity. However, ordinary women preferred to read popular romances rather than the nonfiction recommended by the Workers' Education Center. The center tried to persuade women to read militant literature, such as the anti-militarist works of Barbusse and Andreas Latzko, biographies of Jaurès, or histories of the French Revolution. Women were encouraged to read Bebel's *Women and Socialism* and Lily Braun's *Frauenfrage*, as well as the biography of Olympe de Gouges by Clara Zetkin. Both men and women, however, preferred Emile Zola's novels, especially *Germinal* and *Nana*. They recognized themselves and their world in these grittily realistic works. The results of a survey by the socialist newspaper *Vooruit* of its female readers were even more discouraging: they preferred the love stories of Courths-Mahler and Ruby M. Ayres. In these penny novels they found the things they missed in day-to-day life: kindness, true and passionate love, comfort, and wealth.

Socialist cultural politics failed because the mass of the population was more attracted to leisure possibilities than to serious reading. Both men's and women's cultural interests could be found in the world of music and theater. On Saturday evenings people went to the popular socialist People's House, their cultural temple, where they could see skits performed, listen to music, or join in singing their favorite romantic and militant songs. In the *Feestlokaal* an orchestra played dance music, while the socialist harmonic orchestra contributed light classical music or opera. In the 1930s, the radio brought this music into the home; there, listeners were introduced to British culture through BBC broadcasts. A huge movie theater was built next door to the *Feestlokaal*, and in working-class neighborhoods smaller theaters provided a weekly opportunity to spend a dime to see favorite film stars. The path to mass culture lay ahead.

Modern Women?

During the interwar period, the working-class standard of living improved markedly. In the decade of the 1920s, economic growth was followed by higher wages and full employment. Budget studies show that Belgian workers' families began to consume more and better food.[28] How did working-class women deal with these changes in lifestyle? To what extent did they cope easily with the radically changing image of women, or was it difficult for them to break with old traditions? The new woman image affected fashion in the working class, as elsewhere, but was this outward change accompanied by inner changes? Answers are partially provided by looking at reactions in the press and at the representation of women in socialist publications.

Legislators, political parties, and the Church might well try to restrict women to the role of mothers and homemakers, but they were unable to halt the advance of modernism. The image of the modern woman was implanted in society, thanks to the growing influence of the new communications media, radio and film. Although working-class women did not adopt the more extravagant modern styles, their appearance was very different from that of their mothers. Better food gave them a fresh complexion, and they began to wear neat, brightly colored clothes. Dresses of mid-calf length replaced the long, wide skirts and aprons. Sensible leather or suede shoes, fastened with a buckle, replaced the wooden clogs that had made walking clumsy and noisy. They wore a modest touch of face powder, and very daring young women sometimes used a little lipstick. On Sunday, a hat and a fur collar on their coat offered the older women middle-class respectability. Women cut their hair short, and some went to the hairdresser for a perm. Women who smoked, however, were strongly criticized.

The changing appearance of women and girls aroused suspicion in conservative circles. Was this perhaps a dangerous sign of too much female sexual freedom? The popular success of the novel *La Garçonne* confirmed the worst fears of the Catholic Church, conservative newspapers, women's and girls' groups, and moralists who warned about the dangers of modern fashion. To adopt the *garçonne*-look could only lead to one outcome – "a life of depravity." On the other hand, the modern woman image found supporters in socialist cultural circles. Newspapers and journals editorialized in favor of Victor Margueritte's creation, mainly because of censorship of the film version. They drew the line at immorality and "perversion," however, which they identified with the upper bourgeoisie. Moreover, they insisted that women should be moderate in fashion and not adopt extremes of the new look. A socialist woman ought not to adopt barbaric customs, such as pierced ears or skirts that showed her knees.

Working-class women's mental outlook in these years is far more difficult to fathom than changes in their outward appearance. The claim of the 1920s for the right of women and youth to live a full sexual life remained the strict privilege of the artistic avant-garde, and of wealthy "golden youth." Neither working-class men nor women seemed to have acquired more sexual freedom, which was beyond imagining for both middle- and working-class women, if one can believe the 1990s interviews of some twenty people, who were in their teens and twenties in the interwar years. Those interviewed all said, however, that even at that time they had believed a woman ought to speak up for herself in marriage, and not settle for being an obedient wife.[29]

Workers sought dignity and respect as morally upright citizens, but they seem to have been willing to bend the rules in their judgment of social behavior. For example, while they clearly understood that alcoholism and violence against women were undesirable, they viewed them as unavoidable traits in men. Working people generally accepted unmarried mothers. Socialist women's programs for mother and child care and maternity insurance included unmarried mothers. Natural children were as welcome as legitimate children, but it was expected that the father legitimate his child when he married the mother. Very often illegitimate children by previous liaisons were adopted by the man who married their mother.

Male and female approaches to sexual issues, particularly birth control, differed significantly. Men were willing to say that they had practiced a limited range of birth control techniques, while women claimed to have had no sexual knowledge at all before marriage. Effective contraceptive methods were barely known, even in non-Catholic families. Some married women eventually figured out that their husbands used condoms. But the daily ads in newspapers for remedies to bring on "late menstruation" suggest that contraception was more often used after than before the act. Women were held responsible for avoiding unwanted births. They took pills that produced severe cramps and diarrhea but that were not certain to induce an abortion. My mother tucked away somewhere a little rubber syringe, and a douche can. Even she, however, took the notorious "Doctor Dupuis' red pills" when she feared she was pregnant. In socialist cooperative People's Pharmacies one could buy remedies that promised "excellent results, without danger."[30]

But were working-class people prudish? One has only to listen to vernacular songs, with their crude and direct allusions to sex and married life, to be convinced that the facts of life were very well known to men at least. They could express themselves through this language, which was often too crude to be used at home. They would not normally speak about sexual matters; but when they did, they depended upon obscene language to allude to sexuality because they knew no other words to express it. Among themselves, men boasted about women and sex. Women, however, even those with a secondary school education, were astonishingly ignorant and shy about the facts of life.

Socialists were publicly prudish to the extent of refusing to sponsor and organize sexual education courses, despite discussing their necessity in their publications. In 1921, the socialist teachers' union, and the socialist school leagues proposed adding a course on "sexual life and reproduction, the illnesses and dangers that threaten the health of the couple, to be given to a mixed public of men and women" to adult education programs. The careful avoidance of any mention of the content of the course is typical for the period. The socialist women's movement hoped "with all its heart" that the proposed course would be given "because of the big gap in women's knowledge on the matter." They feared fierce resistance from official bodies, which had veto power in educational matters, "against the expansion of sexual knowledge among the people."[31] Such an addition to the adult educational program remained only a proposal in the interwar period. The BWP was contemptuous of Catholic bigotry, but at the same time it distrusted the so-called "unbridled sexuality" of the working class and sought to discipline the social interactions of the urban masses.

One of the socialist youth movements, the Workers' Youth League, broke this pattern of reticence. It taught and practiced the ethics of physical health and sexual morality. This group adopted the ideal of a sane mind in a healthy body, and the love of nature and camping, from the German socialist youth movement. They incorporated socialist population politics and ethics into lessons on healthy behavior and character building. Marriage was to be based on comradeship and the practice of a disciplined sexual life. Sex should never serve exclusively for the satisfaction of the body. Not lust, but friendship and cooperation between men and women ranked high in socialist gender ideology. Genuine comradeship between boys and girls, and between husband and wife, was the sign of an important change in the traditional ideas about the male and female role in marriage and society. Several women I interviewed stressed the comradeship on which their marriage was based, for then, "sex was not so important as it is nowadays."[32]

One reason for socialist concerns about gender relations was a rejection, on psychological and ethical grounds, of women's physical submissiveness. Emile Vandervelde had made an appeal to "his women" to help him rectify the evil that certain male behavior had engendered in society. The allegedly female "higher moral quality" and "understanding of human values" made women the best warriors against the consequences of alcoholism, prostitution, and war. In short, women were to be the moral vanguard of the socialist movement.

Vandervelde himself was well-known for his opposition to alcohol abuse. A law that bore his name was passed in 1919 to control the sale of spirits in pubs and liquor stores. The Vandervelde law helped reduce the heavy consumption of alcohol. Through the interwar period, Vandervelde and the Socialists opposed Liberal party attempts to amend the law in favor of free enterprise. Pub owners organized demonstrations for the return of a free market in alcohol in public places. The government even went so far as to establish a special commission to evaluate the claims of this important group of voters. In the heat of the battle, socialist women marched in a crusade against the "social scourges that have brought nothing but misery into women's lives," for which they held men responsible. Socialist MP Lucie Dejardin gave an emotional speech about her drunken father who spent the family income on beer and alcohol, causing misery and poverty, and more often than not, inflicting violence on his wife and children. A drunken husband was a constant source of anxiety and stress, with lifelong consequences for the physical and psychological health of his family.[33]

Although one finds daily newspaper accounts of beaten women, maltreated children, and rape, there was seldom collective protest against violence and cruelty, with two exceptions. The public reserved its deepest condemnation for the rape or murder of children. Most cases of violence and public acts of indecency were attributed to the effects of heavy drinking.

Socialist women launched a crusade in the interwar years to eliminate prostitution, which was not considered immoral or the fault of the prostitute. Socialists considered it a symptom of the depravity of capitalist society, an example of the abuse of poor girls and women by the rich and powerful, and the solution offered was more jobs for women. Socialist women argued that women prostituted themselves out of economic need, and indeed most prostitutes came from the working class. Prostitution was legal, but regulated through police registration and compulsory gynecological examinations. However, many prostitutes did not register and thus escaped control. To the socialist women's movement the legalization of prostitution simply perpetuated the unjust system, so it had to be abolished. At the same time, these women recognized that realistically, clandestine prostitution would continue, so they called for prophylactic measures to be taken against the spread of venereal diseases. They wanted a special unit of policewomen to oversee the transition.

In the 1930s, socialist women joined the revival of the international movement against the white slave trade. In this campaign the psychological undertone of protest against bodily subservience was much more evident than in the condemnation of prostitution. In a sense, the prostitute made her own decision about her situation, although it was difficult for her to escape once she moved into a brothel. White slaves were entirely forced. Abolitionist texts demonstrate strong feeling about the total bodily submission of the white slave, using terms such as "slavery," " victims," "traffic in human flesh," "abominations," and " cancer of our civilization."[34]

The Onslaught against Female Labor

The economic crisis and the move to the right in politics forced the BWP into a defensive position in the 1930s. The pursuit of day-to-day politics to the exclusion of all initiatives was a sign of a deep malaise in the party. It was unprepared to cope with either the Depression or the political reaction. During the Great Depression, one out of three work-

ers was unemployed; real wages dropped 50 percent; and consumer pur-
chasing power declined by 10 percent. In 1932, disillusioned workers
resorted to wildcat strikes. In this time of crisis, the new generation of
BWP men was eager to assume command and challenged Vandevelde.
The left wing led by Paul-Henri Spaak emerged the winner, leading to
the recall of Hendrik de Man.

Women workers were the first victims of the economic slowdown.
They were vulnerable, as were their sisters in France, Sweden, and Norway, to the charge of being responsible for male unemployment and
declining wages. Over the interwar period, the proportion of women in
the manufacturing labor force declined (especially in the textile and
clothing industries, including lace making), while their proportion in public service doubled. Also on the increase was women's employment in
commerce and health care, while the number of female domestic servants was more than halved. In general, the crisis moved unskilled female
labor from the industrial to the commercial sector; while the expansion of
government services in response to the economic crisis provided jobs for
skilled female labor in public service and administration.[35]

Married female workers were the first targets of the economic retrench-
ment. The government was quick to deny them unemployment pay. Then
the Catholic party introduced a bill which threatened to replace married
women in certain job categories with male workers. The wages of married
female civil servants were cut. In the heat of the crisis, socialist women
allied with liberal feminist organizations and with Communist women to
oppose the government's decision to ban married women from the labor
market. After this unified, and successful, defense of women's economic
rights, some socialist women turned to antiwar activities; others joined
socialist militias, fighting against rising fascist movements.

The BWP's proposed response to the economic crisis was a project based
on the new ideas of a planned economy called the Works Plan. Its author
was Hendrik de Man, soon to be the party leader. Without a parliamentary
majority, the BWP was unable to implement the project, so de Man formed
a coalition government with the Christian Democrat, Van Zeeland. That
government's attempt, with BWP support, to solve the unemployment
problem did not satisfy voters or reduce their attraction to Belgian anti-
democratic forces. Votes for the fascist Rex party increased substantially in
the elections of 1936. The limited implementation of the Works Plan frustrated workers who launched a wave of strikes inspired by France's Popular
Front strikes. To quell this social unrest, a second Van Zeeland government
reached an agreement with employers, winning new social concessions,
including a weekly minimum wage, a six-day annual paid leave, freedom to
organize, a gradual transition to a forty-hour week, joint industrial committees, and direct negotiations between the social partners.

The relative weakness of the BWP's response to the economic and political crisis of the early 1930s exacerbated the generational conflict in the party. The older generation, including Emile Vandervelde, argued for international class solidarity and the creation of a Popular Front as in France. Hendrik de Man and Paul-Henri Spaak, on the other hand, believed it was time to change the party from its working-class base into a broader people's party, which would include intellectual workers. The last years before World War II were characterized by a political crisis that produced a series of unstable governments in which socialists participated.[36]

A Passion for Peace

In this climate socialist women pursued their efforts to preserve world peace. Before World War I, few of the socialist women who strongly opposed war had joined international peace organizations. Belgian pacifism was limited to disseminating antiwar propaganda among schoolchildren through courses that emphasized the evils of militarism and the benefits of peace. Patriotism returned with the outbreak of World War I. Many pacifists were ardent defenders of the fatherland, but few of these were socialists. Although international socialist solidarity received a hard blow in the assassination of Jean Jaurès, it still prevailed over this petty patriotism. Here again the difference between socialist and middle-class women, who defended nationalist interests, was evident: socialist women continued to believe in international pacifism.

Throughout the interwar period, Belgian women socialists organized an antiwar day (11 November) each year, in remembrance of the armistice. It was their response to the appeal of Marion Philips, secretary of the women's sections of the British Labour Party, to celebrate a "war on the war" day. They rephrased Marx's slogan to read: "The international solidarity of the workers of the world is now the mothers' cause." They appealed to women as mothers to prevent their sons from going to war. To make its point, the socialist women's press made extensive use of Käthe Kolwitz's drawings of mourning mothers. The sorrow was sometimes transformed into appeals to rebellion. "Mothers shouldn't decorate departing soldiers and trains with flowers, they should throw themselves before the engine, and break the rails to prevent the organized murder of brothers and sons."[37]

In the 1930s, socialist women worked in a variety of ways to safeguard world peace. One group produced a position paper on disarmament, to be presented by the Belgian delegates to the World Conference for Disarmament. In 1934, some formed a Women's Committee against War and Fascism, under the auspices of the Paris International Women's Congress against War and Fascism. In November 1935, others organized a public meeting to discuss their demands for disarmament, controls on the private weapons industry and trade, and strengthening the League of Nations.[38]

Socialist women also mobilized to help the victims of fascism. During the Spanish Civil War, women expressed their opposition to the party's position of neutrality. Isabelle Blume went to Spain several times to bring practical help to the freedom fighters. This involved sending convoys of food, clothing, and even weapons through the connections of the Transport Workers' union. Socialist women's groups organized the evacuation of Spanish children relying on the network of socialist children's homes. The first convoy of 450 Basque children arrived in Belgium at the end of March 1937, after the bombing of Guernica. With the cooperation of the Belgian Red Cross and the Communist party's "Red Help," socialist women provided shelter in Belgium for a total of 4,000 Spanish refugees. In a second phase, women from the left parties contacted socialist families who were prepared to take in a little Spaniard. By the end of December, 5,000 families had answered the appeal: 1,100 children were placed. Socialist help for Red Spain amounted to five million francs in cash, two million in food, 1.5 million in medical supplies.[39]

Apart from being the tireless leader of socialist women's activities, Isabelle Blume also spoke on several occasions in Parliament on behalf of German refugees from Nazism, and on the fate of Jews held in the prison camp of Merksplas. In November, 1936, she condemned Italian and German help to Franco, spoke in favor of the International Brigades, and expressed her increasing concern about the possibility of war in Europe. In his answer, socialist minister for exterior affairs Paul-Henri Spaak reproached her for being overly guided by passion.[40]

Conclusion

Belgian socialists made limited progress in their periodic attempts to address the woman question in the interwar years. Socialist women remained without a consistent voice in the party's national decision making and achieved few of the changes in civil rights and social welfare that they struggled to achieve. They and Belgian women generally had to wait for significant reforms until after 1945.

After the armistice of 1918 the Socialist party participated in several coalition governments. At two crucial moments, 1919 and 1936, it was able to realize some of its program for ameliorating the condition of the working class. However, its party line on class solidarity among all workers, men and women, usually produced results that ignored women's interests. The party focused its struggle against the Catholic party, and sought to win over the new male working-class voters who were granted suffrage only in 1918. In the process, the Socialists moderated their more radical electoral politics, including demands for women's general suffrage.

A powerful tension developed between the highly idealistic vision of women's total equality in the future socialist society, and the ambivalent attitude towards women in day-to-day politics. Vandervelde assigned women an important moral and humanitarian mission against men's tendency to brutal actions, but at the same time denied them equal opportunities in the youth movement or the educational center, both led by men. There, as in the political arena, women were only second-class comrades and citizens. The voices of socialist women in their congress counted for little against those of men in the general party congress.

Hampered by male militants' nineteenth-century prejudices about "women's nature," and by their wish to eliminate the Catholic party's absolute majority, socialists mistrusted women's political sense. The few who managed to construct a career in the party or in politics were regarded with a certain hostility. Socialist women had to be loyal to their male comrades; they were not to fight for women's suffrage until all men had secured the vote. They were not to fight for equal wages for themselves but for better wages for men, who ought to be the family wage earners. Nevertheless, socialist women proclaimed women's right to choose to combine the life of a housewife with that of a working woman.

Although the BWP treated its women as second-class citizens, it gave them a distinct place in the fight for a better quality of life for the working class. In the social domain, women could enjoy the privileges linked to their respected function as mothers. During the 1920s the BWP launched several important programs which eased working-class wives' burdens. No universal social security program was yet in place, but the social benefits and insurance offered by the socialist mutual aid societies and cooperatives were a welcome supplement to the family budget. The party created two special women's organizations to win female members and voters from among housewives. The cooperatives filled working-class consumers' shopping baskets, while the FPS appealed to women and housewives through benefits and social advantages. They contributed to the fight against child mortality through their own infant care centers, prenatal services, and treatment of female and venereal diseases. These organizations were more popular than women's political groups, and in 1945, they became the only officially recognized socialist women's movement.

Population policies – no matter how modest they may seem today – were the most long-lasting legacy of the socialist women's movement, not only during the interwar years, but long after 1945. The movement, through its periodicals, informed its readers about the social value of family planning. Socialist women campaigned hard for mother and child care provisions and contraception, and although the party supported these issues primarily to prevent any decline of working-class voters, it incorporated them into electoral and party programs, especially at the municipal level. Elected socialist women were expected to "devote themselves" to matters affecting mothers and children, the realization of a healthy family, and building comfortable housing with affordable rents.

Trade unions fought for better, gender-specific, conditions for women in the workplace. They were the advocates of maternity leaves and family allowances, and supported bills introduced by female members of parliament to provide these benefits. Socialist welfare bills had a distinctive imprint, differentiating them from Catholic efforts to maintain or encourage large families. In this way, women had the opportunity to connect their private motherhood function to responsibilities in the public sphere, thus achieving a measure of social citizenship. The 1930s ended, however, without a social security system and with the welfare state unrealized. A good many provisions of the women's program were included in the "Charter of Social Security" drawn up during World War II and legislated immediately after the war by the socialist government of Achille Van Acker.

During the interwar period, the BWP launched an extensive program of popular cultural and educational projects. Under the direction of Hendrik de Man, the educational center was a model for socialist cultural politics, and the Labor College became an efficient instrument for training militants. Emile Vandervelde, Hendrik de Man, and other leaders acted as supportive "fathers," or "brothers," towards women. They wanted to educate them, and make them full-fledged militants by means of the special women's week at the Labor College. Courses especially for women were included in the program of socialist evening classes. The socialist youth movement, as well as the women's movement became propagandists for a new ethics of marriage: spouses were to be comrades, and in the family men and women were expected to share household duties.

The socialist women's movement also educated its members, mainly through the written word. It is difficult to estimate the impact of the distribution of its brochures, sometimes as many as 80,000, on its members, or to know which articles in the socialist women's press caught its readers' attention. In fact, the magazines, and women's pages in socialist newspapers, were made attractive through articles on cooking, fashion, knitting, and sometimes poetry and nursery rhymes. Women, however, often preferred popular romances about princes and dream houses, or realistic descriptions of the hard life the older generation had endured.

The real center of cultural life remained the People's House, where people could relax, go to meetings, chat, eat and drink, and celebrate festive occasions such as May Day or electoral victories. There, socialists could find concerts performed by their own harmonic orchestra, often including female singers from their ranks. In its theater, they attended performances of works by socially engaged playwrights, and movies, ranging from light comedies to Eisenstein. On its upper floor, socialist youngsters folk danced, wearing their red and blue uniforms. Most of all, however, people liked singing songs celebrating the hard lives of factory workers and their united struggle against capitalists. The worker's heroine, Marianne, figured in many of their songs. Socialists believed that she would lead them to the future socialist society in which everyone would be equal.

Notes

1. Els Witte and Jan Craeybeckx, *Politieke geschiedenis van België sinds 1830* (Antwerpen, 1981), pp. 168-69; B.S. Chlepner, *Cent ans d'histoire sociale en Belgique* (Bruxelles, 1956); Luc Huyse and Kris Hoflack, *De democratie heruitgevonden* (Leuven, 1995), pp. 172-175.

2. Isabelle Blume (1883 to 1975). Teacher; national secretary of the FPS, 1924; national secretary of the CNAF, 1928; councilwoman in Uccle (Brussels), 1932; member of Parliament, 1936 to 1954. Expelled from the BWP for disagreement about politics of the Cold War, she joined the Belgian Communist party.

3. There were three women MPs in the interbellum: Marie Spaak was appointed Senator in 1921; Lucie Dejardin, elected in 1929, served until 1936; and Isabelle Blume.

4. Marie Spaak (1873 to 1960). Progressive liberal, then socialist; teacher; councilwoman in Saint-Gilles (Brussels), 1921; Senator, 1921 to 1958; author of various bills; first woman in the Belgian Parliament. Alice Heyman (1883-1954). Secretary of the socialist women's section of Gent, 1918; editor of *De Stem der Vrouw*; councilwoman in Ghent, 1921; alder woman for Social Works in Ledeberg (Ghent), 1921; member of the CNAF. Alice 'Lily' Pels (1882 to 1964). Editor of *La Voix de la Femme* until World War I; secretary of the CNAF until 1924; secretary of the International Council of Socialist Women; councilwoman in Brussels.

5. Denise De Weerdt and Carla Galle, SV. *100 jaar socialistische vrouwenbeweging* (Brussels, 1985), pp. 7-19, 27; Denise De Weerdt, *En de vrouwen? Vrouw, vrouwenbeweging en feminisme in België 1930-1960* (Gent, 1980), pp. 88-101; R. Christens and A. De Decker, *Vormingswerk in vrouwenhanden*, dl. 2 (Leuven, 1988).

6. Els Witte, "Tussen experiment en correctief. De Belgische gemeentelijke kieswetgeving in relatie tot het nationale kiesstelsel," in *De gemeenteraadsverkiezingen en hun impact op de Belgische politiek*, Handelingen, 16th International Colloquium, 1992 (Brussels, 1994), pp. 13-72.

7. Y.D., "Quelques mots sur la loi du 20 juillet 1932," *La Famille prévoyante* 14 (July 1935): 25.

8. The average number of children per 100 married couples was 263 in 1910, 231 in 1920, 196 in 1930, 170 in 1947. *Recensement général de la population de l'industrie et du commerce*, 7 (Brussels, 1947): 54.

9. Phillip Van Praag, *Het bevolkingsvraagstuk in België. Ontwikkeling van standpunten en opvattingen, 1900-1977* (Antwerp, 1979), pp. 23-25.

10. Denise De Weerdt, "Een kind groeit op in de stad. Een sociaal portret," in *Interbellum in Gent 1919-1939* (Gent, 1995), pp. 9-37.

11. Marie Spaak, "Proposition de loi modifiant la loi du 5 septembre 1919 instituant l'Oeuvre nationale de l' Enfance. Exposé des motifs," *La Famille prévoyante* 13 (February 1934): 9-11.

12. "La protection de la femme," *Bull. de la Prévoyance et des Assurances sociales* (November 1923): 6-7; "Voor de vrouwen", *Vooruit* (14 December 1928): 1; "De vrouwen en de sociale verzekering," *Vooruit* (2 February 1930): 6.

13. Les Femmes Prévoyantes Socialistes, *Pour la mère au foyer. Pour de nombreuses familles moyennes* (Brussels, 1947), p. 29.

14. "Les allocations familiales," *La Famille prévoyante* (September 1936): 3.

15. Ron J. Lesthaeghe, *Decline of Belgian Fertility, 1800-1970* (Ph.D. diss., University of Michigan, 1966), pp. 139-140, 223, 230; Micheline Scheys, ed. *Abortus* (Brussels, 1993), pp. 27, 104, 179; Chris Vandenbroeke, "De dualiteit tussen normerend en werkelijk gedrag," in *De Massa in verleiding. De jaren '30 in België* (Brussels, 1994), p. 133.

16. "Voor de vrouwen," *Vooruit*, September 1925.

17. Lily Braun, *De vrouwenkwestie*, 2nd ed. (Rotterdam, n.d.), 194. This translation was available in the socialist library in Gent and advertised in the periodical of the Workers' Education Center.

18. Denise De Weerdt, *De vrouwen van de Eerste Wereldoorlog* (Gent, 1993), pp. 239-41.

19. Rachel Dehuveyne, "Slachtoffers van den huisarbeid," *Vooruit* (22 May 1920): 4; Grietje, "Vrouw en huis," *Vooruit* (10 April 1921): 4.

20. Marie Spaak, "La femme et la politique," in *Avant l'action féminine* (Brussels, 1923), pp. 5-6.

21. "De Vrouwenweek in de Arbeidershogeschool," *Ontwikkeling en ontspanning. Maandblad van de CAO* III, 3 (1923): 433; Spaak, "La femme," p. 6.

22. "De tien geboden van de man," *Vooruit* (30 August 1923); Yvonne De Man, "Socialisme in het gezin," *Opgang* 1, 9 (15 June 1930): 231-32; Isabelle Blume, "La démocratie conjugale," *La Vie ouvrière* (November 1930, March 1931).

23. V. Totomianz, *La femme et la coopération* (Bruxelles, 1926), p. 30.

24. Alice Heyman, "Vrouwenbeweging in Vlaanderen," *Ontwikkeling en ontspanning* 4 (1919): 51.

25. "Kongres van de Centrale voor arbeidersopvoeding," *Ontwikkeling en ontspanning* 11 (1923): 364-65.

26. "Sociale vrouwenweek," *Vooruit* (5 September 1923): 4; "De vrouwenweek," *Vooruit* (25 September 1923): 4.

27. Isabelle Blume, *Dix femmes célèbres* (Brussels, 1923); also in Flemish.

28. Peter Scholliers, *Arm en rijk aan tafel* (Berchem, 1993), pp. 100-108.

29. "'t Geval la Garçonne," *Vooruit* (5 September 1923): 1.

30. *Vooruit*, review of ads published in 1923. Also based on interviews by the author with elderly socialist women.

31. *Vooruit* (16 February 1921): 4.

32. Denise De Weerdt, *De dochters van Marianne: 75 jaar SVV* (Antwerp-Baarn, 1997), pp. 153-157, and,"Een kind groeit op in de stad," pp. 9-43.

33. *Algemene Raad der BWP. Congresverslagen 1933* (Brussels, 1934), pp. 138-139; Arthur Wauters, "De Alcohol," in *BWP. 57e Congres, 5, 6, 7 November 1938* (Brussel, s.d..), p. 50.

34. Isidore Maus, *L' Enquête de la Société des Nations sur la traite des femmes et des enfants* (Brussels, s.d.), p. 32; *Een wetsvoorstel strekkende tot afschaffing van de officieele reglementeering van de prostitutie* (Brussels, s.d.), p. 88.

35. Based on the statistics in Fernand Pontanus, *Etude comparative des recensements de la population active 1910, 1930, 1947* (Brussels, 1959).

36. Mieke Claeys-Van Haegendoren, *25 Jaar Belgisch Socialisme* (Antwerp, 1967); see also Janet Polasky, *The Democratic Socialism of Emile Vandervelde. Between Reform and Revolution* (Oxford, 1995).

37. F.D.S., "Internationale anti-oorlogsdag," *Vooruit* 10 (22-23 September 1923); Alice Heyman, *Vooruit* 10 (22-23 September 1924).

38. Isabelle Blume, *Entretiens*, pp. 59-111.

39. Tania Eeckhout, "De hulp aan Republikeins Spanje uitgaande van de BWP afdeling Gent-Eeklo, meer specifiek de opvang der Spaanse kinderen (1936-1939)," *Revue belge d'histoire contemporaine* 18 (1987, 1-2): 243-74; Dorothy Legaretta, "Hospitality to the Basque Refugee Children in Belgium," *RBHC* 18 (1987, 1-2): 275-88; Emilia Labajos-Perez and Fernando Vitoria-Garcia, *Los Ninos. Histoire des enfants de la Guerre Civile Espagnolle réfugiés en Belgique (1936-1939)* (Gand, 1994), p. 155.

40. Isabelle Blume, *Entretiens*, p. 40.

Part III

POLITICAL FRACTURES

Introduction

Mary Gibson

In interwar France, Spain, and Italy, political upheavals absorbed the energies of parties of the Left and diverted attention from the "woman question." In Italy, Mussolini came to power in 1922 and began a successful campaign to intimidate and outlaw both the socialist and communist parties. To avoid a similar fate, parties of the Left in France and Spain merged with republicans to form Popular Front governments, an effort that failed to stop the outbreak of civil war in Spain. Yet to group these three countries under the rubric of "political fractures" is not wholly satisfying, since other nations – most notably Germany and Austria – also did not escape political discontinuities. An alternative label, "Mediterranean Socialism," is no more appropriate, as it fits France uneasily and suggests no defining characteristics other than geography. France, Spain, and Italy have enough in common, however, to justify treating them as a block when examining the experiences of women on the Left.

Perhaps the most striking similarity among the socialist and communist parties of France, Spain, and Italy was their exceedingly small female membership. While women comprised up to 40 percent of party membership in northern countries, they never exceeded 6 percent in southern Europe. Instead, women tended to organize at the workplace, where they made up at least 15 percent of trade union membership in Italy and France. Women's preference for joining unions highlights the failure of the male leadership of parties of the Left to address gender issues. Unions in Spain and Italy were also more willing than parties to organize in rural areas where much of the female workforce was concentrated. Despite these strategies, roughly half of all female wage earners remained outside unions in the three countries. Yet Mediterranean women were neither passive nor resigned, as traditional stereotypes would have it, but often outnumbered men in participation in both agricultural and industrial strikes. Such demonstrations – whether for higher wages, lower prices, or peace – were often spontaneous and involved large numbers of women organized in neither unions nor parties. The pattern of women's political activity, therefore, resembled a series of concentric circles, with party membership constituting the smallest ring surrounded by a larger one of union membership and finally an outer circle of participants in strikes and protests.

Why was female membership so low in parties of the Left in France, Spain, and Italy? It is perhaps not coincidental that in the same countries suffrage came late to women. Neither French nor Italian women received the right to vote in national elections during the interwar period, while Spanish women obtained suffrage only in 1931, later than in most of northern and central Europe. Clearly socialist and communist men did not make female suffrage a political priority, even when they supported it in theory. This gap between theory and practice was most apparent in France, where the Popular Front of Léon Blum failed to secure the vote for women in 1936. Indifference to female suffrage formed part of a larger pattern of general neglect of the woman question, bordering on contempt for women themselves within parties of the Mediterranean Left. Although the communist parties were more vocal than the socialists in proclaiming the importance of organizing women, in fact little money and effort was expended in such an effort by either camp. In all parties, any effort by women to form their own autonomous sections was prohibited by male directorates intent on keeping power centralized.

Men in all three countries excused their ambivalence toward women's suffrage by invoking the power of the Catholic Church. Socialist and communist men feared that priests would sway even their own wives and mothers to vote for conservative or confessional parties. In response, French and Italian women both pointed to Austria, a Catholic country in which female suffrage had not weakened the Left. But the specter of the Catholic Church hampered the efforts of women to enter political life, especially as their own organizations competed with well-organized and well-financed religious youth groups for girls, women's auxiliaries, and female unions. In Spain, socialist women embroidered their appeals for membership with religious imagery as a strategy for wooing new recruits, since proper female role models continued to be inextricably tied to Catholic values. The political and cultural weight of the Church also discouraged open discussions of birth control and abortion, leaving Mediterranean women cut off from lively discussions of sexuality taking place in northern Europe. While the falling birthrate in France and Italy proved that women in those countries were consciously limiting the size of their families, they carried the psychological weight of doing so secretly, against the strictures of religious exhortations and criminal law.

Ironically, the Catholic idealization of maternity as women's mission was reinforced by a similar message from eugenicists on the Left. Especially in Spain and Italy, biological determinism dominated the discourse of many socialist physicians, including gynecologists, obstetricians, and pediatricians. Useful for combating the spiritual tradition of the Church, biological determinism nevertheless reduced women to their reproductive function in the social Darwinist struggle for existence. With science complementing religion in prescribing motherhood as the natural female state, it is not surprising that women's demands for the right to work and equal pay did not become priorities in the platforms of either the socialist or communist parties. While biological determinism was less hegemonic in French scientific circles, the national obsession with depopulation similarly pressured women to remain home and bear children. Maternalism militated against demands for sexual equality but at the same time contributed to the strengthening of protective legislation for mothers, one of the few areas of legal reform for women between the wars.

Generalizations about the Left are perhaps unfair, when in fact the communist parties seemed markedly more open to the woman question than the socialists. From their founding, the communists publicly proclaimed the importance of organizing women and appointed a high-ranking coordinator of women's affairs at each national party headquarters. In the 1920s, communist leaders not only included women's right to work and equal pay in party platforms, but also publicly supported more radical proposals like the legalization of abortion and the socialization of housework. Such advanced opinions on gender issues, however, represented for the most part a mere copy of Soviet propaganda rather than the result of genuine debate between the sexes within each national party. At least the Soviet model of the 1920s, with its proclamations of sexual equality, opened spaces for women's activism, and several women did indeed reach high levels of power within the communist parties of southern Europe. Yet male commitment to gender equality was shallow, as shown for example by the willingness of the French communists in 1936 to jettison any special programs for women in order to placate their partners in the Popular Front.

Even before the rise of fascism, parties of the Left in France, Spain, and Italy lagged far behind their northern and central European counterparts in incorporating women into their membership and women's issues into practical policy. By the late 1930s, under the threat of dictatorship and war, any pretense of addressing the woman question vanished. Whether in power as part of the Popular Front or driven underground by Mussolini, socialist and communist men belittled women's concerns as parochial and divisive. For the communists, the dissolution of any specific policy for women closely followed a major shift in the Soviet Union under Stalin, symbolized by his recriminalization of abortion. The more radical demands of the 1920s for sexual equality were forgotten as maternity became the single model for all women, including those of the Left.

Despite the disappearance of any debate over the woman question in the 1930s, increasing numbers of women became active in socialist and communist causes. They threw themselves into the fight against fascism both at home and abroad. Women predominated among volunteers for the International Red Aid, which assisted prisoners of fascism, and in organizations that adopted babies orphaned in the Spanish Civil War. Strike activity increased among women workers, encouraged by the international women's movement for peace. During war, women not only performed domestic tasks for Republican soldiers in Spain and later for partisans in Italy and France, but many took on the more "masculine" roles of spies, couriers, and even combatants. Many of these women did not belong officially to any party, again illustrating that membership figures underestimated the wide allegiance of women to socialist and communist values.

Women in France, Spain, and Italy negotiated complex relationships with parties of the Left during the interwar period. On the one hand, they joined socialist and communist parties in small numbers and found their demands for the vote, the right to work, and equal wages largely ignored by their male colleagues. They were more successful at gaining improvements in protective legislation, partly because such reforms were consonant with the eulogizing of motherhood across the political spectrum, including the politically powerful Catholic Church. Yet, women did organize within parties, each of which boasted strong and articulate female leaders and writers, like María Cambrils and Dolores Ibárruri (*La Pasionaria*) in Spain, Suzanne Buisson and Jeannette Vermeersch in France, and Anna Kuliscioff and Camilla Ravera in Italy. Moreover, large numbers of women without party cards proved their allegiance to the Left by joining trade unions and fomenting a series of strikes and demonstrations that accelerated throughout the period. Because of their active involvement in the Resistance, France and Italy could no longer withhold the vote from women after 1945. In Spain, both women and men had to await the death of Franco for the reestablishment of universal suffrage.

French, Spanish, Italian Women:
Work, Gender Roles, Struggles in Times of National Turmoil

"Images of Women's Sphere: Separate or Equal?"

Vision of Women as Confined to the Domestic Sphere: Poster of Conservative Middle-class French Feminists
Source: Poster: Henri Lebasque, Bibliothèque de Musée Social, Paris

femmes de Cécile Brunschwig réclame alors de voter, contre « l'alcool, le taudis », mais aussi contre « la guerre » (affiche de Chavannaz).

Affiche de Lebasque pour l'emprunt de 1920.

French Communist Poster: Woman, the Sickle, Demands Equal Powers with Man, the Hammer, to Make the Revolution
Source: Poster: Gil Baer, La Voix des femmes, 1923

"Women Demand the Right to Vote: from Symbol to Action"

Young French Working Women Claiming
Their Right to Vote with Notice of Large
Public Meeting
Source: Bibliothèque Musée Social

Louise Weiss and Suffrage Activists in
Demonstration at French Chamber of
Deputies, 1936
Source: Bibliothèque Marguerite
Durand, Paris

ELECTIONS LÉGISLATIVES DU 26 AVRIL 1936
Comité National des Femmes contre la guerre et le fascisme — 1, Cité Paradis, Paris-X'

Les Femmes Françaises veulent voter

parce que l'avenir de leur pays
les intéresse et particulière-
ment celui de leurs enfants
qu'elles veulent voir vivre,
libres, heureux, en paix.

LA FRANCE EST UN PAYS RICHE
OU IL EST POSSIBLE D'ORGANISER
LE BONHEUR DE TOUS

Mais il faut une bonne
gérance des affaires du
pays, à la Chambre et
au Sénat de véritables
représentants du peuple
et non pas des délégués
des puissances finan-
cières, des gros indus-
triels et des hobereaux.

Voilà ce que nous, Femmes, supplions les électeurs de comprendre

Femmes, mères, jeunes filles, adhérez au Comité National des Femmes contre la guerre et contre le fascisme
Lisez FEMMES, revue illustrée, le N°1 fr — 1, Cité Paradis, C.C.P. 1818.06 Madame Duchene, Paris

Appeal for Women's Vote by the French National Committee of Women against
War and Fascism, 1935
Source: Bibliothèque Marguerite Durand, Paris

"Women Brought into the World of Work in the Era of World War

As Metal Workers in the Italian Defense
Industry
Source: Illustrazione Italiana, 1917:
General Research Division, New York
Public Library (GRD/NYPL)

In the Service Sector of Italian
Urban Transportation
Source: Illustrazione Italiana,
1917: GRD/NYPL

Mass Demonstration of Spanish Women Workers during Barcelona Textile Strike
Source: La Actualidad, 1913: Nash Collection

"Women Workers as Actors and Leaders During Strike"

French Female and Male Workers Celebrate during Occupation of the Factories in 1936
Source: Bibliothèque Musée Social

Shop Steward Rose Zehner Addressing Workers at the Citroën Plant in Paris during Strikes of 1936
Source: Bibliothèque Musée Social

"Women Demand and Take Direct Action"

Louise Weiss and Female Suffragists "Breaking the Chains of Women's Bondage,"
Bastille, Paris 1935
Source: Bibliothèque Musée Social

Spanish Women's Demonstration Demanding a "United Anti-fascist Front of All
Catalan Women"
Source: Poster 1937: Center of International Historical Studies, University of
Barcelona (CEHI/UB)

"Women in Extremis: as Participants in Armed Struggles"

Anarchist/Socialist Poster under the Slogan "They Will Not Pass" Portrays a Revolutionary Woman (Miliciana) Defending the Republic
Source: Poster 1936: CEHI/UB

Armed Italian Women Partisans Show Their Strength, End of World War II
Source: Estride come donna (Milan, 1983), 233.

Chapter 7

French Women in the Crossfire of Class, Sex, Maternity, and Citizenship

Helmut Gruber

In studying the relationship of the French Socialist party (SFIO) to working-class women and its positions on women's place in society in general one enters a minefield of contradictions running the gamut from the opportunism of electoral politics to the paternalistic manipulations implicit in technocratic visions. Why was the SFIO almost at the bottom of socialist parties in industrial Europe in its ability to attract women to its ranks and to give assistance and direction to women's quest for citizenship and gender dignity and equality? How can we explain the failure of the great expectations of prewar feminists that the march of women toward equality would be realized in the following two decades? What accounted for the absence of that spirit in which the Declaration of the Rights of Man was written and by which universal manhood suffrage was created in 1848 when that same equality was demanded by the other half of humanity? Although a higher percentage of French women were in the labor force than in most other industrial countries, why was only a small number organized? To what extent can we attribute the largely unchanged condition of women in France in the interwar period to the patent ignorance of both socialist and feminist leaders about the everyday life, needs, and demands of ordinary women and their priorities for change and action that should have been on the agendas for reform? Finally, and most tellingly, the coming of the popular front created a climate of anticipation for the improvement of the quality of life, for the further march of socialism from its political base to new social and economic frontiers. Why were women largely denied a full share in these hopes and yet made to bear an equal share of the defeats? My goal is to attempt an answer to these troubling and complicated questions by avoiding apparent black and white images in favor of nuanced explanations from perspectives that are less than obvious. In so doing, I will view the situation in France in the comparative context on which this book is based, thereby rejecting attempts to regard the condition and activity of French women as exempt from comparisons with other national experiences.[1]

Socialist Women: Neither Comrades nor Sisters

At the highpoint in 1938 women constituted 3 percent (9,500) of SFIO membership – so few that the party secretariat refused to record it in its periodic reports to the Labor and Socialist International. Women were well represented in most other socialist parties at their heights: 39 percent in Denmark; 34 percent in Austria; 33 percent in Holland; 23 percent in Germany; 16 percent in Norway; 14 percent in Sweden; and 10 percent in England. Low representation in France was matched in Belgium (3 percent), Italy (2 percent), and Spain (6.24 percent), with fascism playing a determining role in the latter two.

The SFIO's inability to create a strong women's movement goes back to the prewar efforts of working-class and feminist women to find a common ground for organization and action. A decisive split along class lines, characterized by the insistence on the primacy of either gender or class, was carried forward into the 1920s and could not be bridged even during the crisis-ridden 1930s, when unity of the essentially male, left-of-center, political parties was the order of the day. The tendency among male socialist spokesmen then and even among some historians now has been to blame female SFIO members and women per se – the victims of male prejudice – for their own marginalization and powerlessness.[2] If not the women themselves, who was to blame? Let us look more closely at both the prewar and postwar attempts of women to enter the ranks of socialism and the obstacles faced and compromises made along the way.

Before the creation of the SFIO in 1905, the Groupe Féministe Socialiste (GFS) organized working-class women independent of, but in sympathy with, the varied socialist currents at the time. After the GFS was denied affiliated status by the SFIO, it changed its name to Groupe des Femmes Socialistes (GDFS), but its members could join the party only as individuals. Even though this women's auxiliary remained minuscule in size, a fierce controversy arose among its most prominent members over the primacy of class or gender and the possibility of solidarity between working-class women and bourgeois feminists. Powerful differences in the women's movement along class lines were already apparent at the International Congress on the Condition and Rights of Women in 1900 where the atmosphere was hostile to workers.[3] Though Elizabeth Renaud and Hélène Brion championed female solidarity against Suzanne Lacore and Louise Saumoneau who denounced feminism as bourgeois, both feminists and socialist women were predominantly drawn from the bourgeoisie; working-class women were under represented in both.[4]

In the early postwar years the GDFS, purged of its feminist sympathizers, led a marginal existence: it had at most between 100 and 200 members nationally; these were enrolled in the SFIO as individuals; Saumoneau was elected to the party executive (CAP) but not as a representative of women; she also controlled the party newspaper *La femme socialiste*, through which her narrow views on the relationship of women to the SFIO became paramount. The SFIO was the only party to admit women as members, but it showed little interest in developing active female participation or in even expanding the tiny group stemming from the GDFS.[5]

What the status of women socialists should be and how more women were to be brought into the party was opened to full discussion at the SFIO congress at Bordeaux in June 1930. Several positions were presented in the pages of *La vie socialiste* in the preceding month. A suggestion that women be allowed to join the GDFS without becoming party members – as a way of participating in specific women's issues through which they would be prepared for party membership[6] – was rejected outright by Suzanne Collette. If the GDFS were to be an organization open to nonparty women, she insisted, the party would simply ignore them. Instead, she proposed adopting the Austrian Socialist party statutes, whereby every party section would have a women's commission, with an elected central women's council to be represented in the party's executive and directing bureau. In a reply, Germaine Picard-Moch rejected a women's group open to nonparty members because they would devolve into feminist organizations. She compared the handful of French women in the SFIO with the high percentage of women in virtually all other European socialist parties and concluded that changing the SFIO statutes would have no influence on increasing female membership. The latter will change only when men stop saying that women have no interest in politics and take up their recruitment in a serious way.

The issue of women's role in the party created a virtual explosion at the Bordeaux congress in June. Never before had the "woman question" taken up such a large part of the agenda, with impassioned exchanges by a variety of female speakers demonstrating both capability and commitment, and with the male delegates accused of indifference, ignorance, and blatant hostility.[7] Saumoneau, speaking for the GDFS, rejected all attempts to create a women's organization of mere sympathizers in the party. If a women's organization was to be created, and she personally was opposed, then it should only accept party members but solely on a voluntary basis. Furthermore, direct representation in the executive or bureau was unnecessary, since women already had access to them as party members. Collette accused the GDFS of supporting the inconsequential status of women in the SFIO and thus sabotaging the recruitment of women into the party. She further rejected making membership in a women's organization voluntary for female party members, because such a group needed party status to be represented at International Conferences of Women.

The argument about the nature of the women's group, which apparently was to be consigned to the margin of the party by the men, seems almost trivial in retrospect. The vehemence of the discussion suggests a hidden agenda, one that had not been annulled by the war years: the relation of class and gender. Collette exploded in a final burst of frustration and anger with the leaders of the GDFS: "Saumoneau and Suzanne Buisson accuse me of being a feminist and think that feminism is opposed to socialism … but socialist theoreticians are feminists … Bebel and the SPD 1928 Report …. We need a socialist feminist program, but the party has done nothing to counter women's isolation and to educate them."

Germaine Picard-Moch, one of the few non-Parisians in the GDFS and SFIO (Federation of the Drome), refused to consider the present impasse as simply a quarrel among women. She minced no words in accusing the male delegates: of not having taken the women's issue seriously during the vital discussion; of having left their seats during it in order to smoke in the corridors or visit the museums of Bordeaux; of having created an atmosphere of male indifference and even hostility to the idea that women might have demands of their own. The virtual nonexistence of women in the GDFS and SFIO, in comparison to the significant presence of women in most other socialist parties, she charged, must be blamed on the men. They salve their conscience by calling women apolitical and resist giving women the vote for fear that the left would lose in elections. Harangues, no matter how impressive at the moment, fail to change the ingrained habits of organizations for deflecting troublesome questions or challenges. The Congress appointed a commission of 18, equally divided between the women and men, with the major party leaders among the latter. The outcome was a foregone conclusion.

Aftershocks of the woman question at the congress appeared in the party press in the ensuing two years, but the muddled thinking of delegates did not tend to become clearer or less contradictory. The responsibility of male socialists for the small number of women in the party and for their segregation moved in and out of focus: socialist men obstructed the recruitment of women into the party by their own petty bourgeois attitudes toward their wives;[8] the SFIO has always practiced sexual equality;[9] sexual equality has always existed in the party but some mechanism – perhaps a group of nonparty sympathizers – is needed to discuss purely women's issues.[10] This is but a small sample of published complaints mixed with affirmations of party loyalty that see-sawed without getting anywhere. A real critique of the gender-hostile conditions in the SFIO that underlay the woman problem was offered by Suzanne Collette and Suzanne Lacore,[11] who suggested that misogynism in the party forced female leaders into a straightjacket of male behavior in order to function at all; that a masculine psychology and culture predominated in all local sections making female party members feel unwelcome and, therefore, made special groups necessary in which women could feel comfortable; and that for the entire party to be concerned with women's issues was not a matter of bourgeois feminism but of the gender equality to which the SFIO had so long laid claims.[12]

The decision of the women's commission created at the 1930 congress was made public at the congress of 1932.[13] The proposal outlined by Saumoneau for the GDFS was followed to the letter: no unorganized women, no obligation to join, no representation on the executive. The name was changed to *Comité national des femmes socialistes* (CNFS), with Buisson replacing Saumoneau as secretary. The latter had resigned her position on the executive, but she retained control of the two group publications, *La Femme Socialiste* and *Propagande et Documentation*, and continued as a destructive power behind the scenes. Henceforth, the CNFS graced party congresses with elaborate agendas for political, economic, and social demands on behalf of women in a ritual that became accepted without receiving much attention from the delegates. Clearly its only function was to recruit women into the party, but recruitment efforts were poorly rewarded. Female membership made only marginal gains and never reached more than 3+ percent (9,500) even during the popular front when the SFIO doubled its membership. This group of pioneers was forced to brave the inhospitable male ambiance of the party on the local level: customs and rituals of conviviality and forceful expressions of male bonding such as competition and verbal/physical familiarity and aggression. Female comrades were reduced to silence under these circumstances; respectable women, who might have been expected to join the party, refused to expose themselves to such an atmosphere.

Women remained an insignificant presence in the SFIO, where they were discouraged from reaching out to the mass of unorganized women or to feminists at the very time when the party was making cross-class alliances with the radicals in the popular front coalition. In examining the reports of international conferences of socialist women one is struck by the nearly total absence of a French presence. On a crucial vote in 1928 recognizing women's right to abortion and family planning, for instance, the French delegation never appeared. That fact was explained in a letter by Suzanne Buisson to the Secretariat before the next conference in 1931. The SFIO considered putting family planning on the agenda of the Vienna conference as premature, she declared, because "our party has always avoided tendentious subjects which might disturb its propaganda … [also] because the party considers this problem to be a matter of private morality unsuitable for public action."[14] Even when delegates from the CNFS were present, they had little to report or engaged in bombastic announcements. In reporting on the appointment of three women sub-ministers by Blum, they posed the question: "Can anyone still say that the French socialists are opposed to women's rights?"[15]

One can understand and even sympathize with the French delegates' desire to count for something in these international assemblies of women reporting on the varied accomplishments of women in their countries. But it seems a pity that so little about these gains by socialist women elsewhere was ever reported back to women in France, such as the fact that the first socialist government in Denmark between 1924 and 1926 appointed the socialist historian Nina Gang full minister of education. Furthermore, given the fear among radicals and socialists in France that women voters would fall prey to their priests, a report by the Austrian women about how educational and political propaganda had within seven years produced a parity of male and female voters for socialism in Vienna would have been a powerful instrument in the drive for female suffrage.[16] This neglect can in part be explained by the fact that *Propagande et Documentation*, which reported on the International, was controlled by Saumoneau and later Buisson, who considered their male role playing as necessary for recognition in the party.

Only some aspects of the role of women in French socialism have been touched upon. The explanation for why there was a "woman question" must be sought in the party as a whole, which means among the men.

SFIO: Underdevelopment as Context

The editorial of *Le Populaire* for 12 July 1937 trumpeted: "… socialism is the hope of the world of women." It echoed once more the progressive/tolerant position of the SFIO on the woman question, which was adopted as a statute at the 1929 party congress in a "dedication to sexual equality and to the fight for the political rights of women" and could be traced back to socialist commitments before the turn of the century.[17] When the SFIO became the dominant partner in the popular front coalition in 1936, women were mentioned once in its official program and then only concerning their right to work.[18] In comparing the bombast and programmatic genuflections with the political reality of SFIO behavior, one is led to conclude that the party's leaders and rank and file shared the ubiquitous male prejudices of the times. To speak about moral failings in the case of such a deeply embedded psychological phenomenon is almost beside the point. In a flash of insight Pierre Bourdieu has suggested that male dominance in society is exerted mainly through "symbolic violence" embodied in the masculine vision of female essence – an optic shared by women themselves.[19] This central aspect of gender relations, however, tells little about why women were kept at such a distance and were so neglected by the SFIO. We must look at the character of the party itself in relation to other parties more hospitable to women as members if not full partners.

Compared to the broad organizational network of mass socialist parties of Northern and Central Europe, the SFIO was a bare-bones organization. Considering the underlying goal of the party of extending political rights to the economic and social sphere, it remained underdeveloped in the interwar period. In scanning the party programs of two decades one is struck by the absence of a distinctly socialist orientation or program dealing with worker housing, health, education; worker leisure and life in the private sphere in general; or the transformation of workers and worker families into more complete human beings than capitalism allowed. By comparison, a number of parties – the German, Austrian, and Scandinavian – had extensive programs and actual projects in all of these social and cultural domains, and they projected the development of a new socialist humanity prepared in part before the demise of capitalism by reforms fought for and won by the existing parties. By contrast, the indifference and inactivity of the SFIO on concrete worker problems (housing, for instance) is staggering. Vienna, Berlin, Frankfurt, London, and Stockholm made considerable progress in removing slums and creating a substantial number of quality worker domiciles.[20] In Paris and even more so in the provinces the condition of worker housing remained deplorable if not inhuman.[21]

Though various attempts were made during Léon Blum's first ministry to initiate a broad-based popular social/cultural program, the SFIO did not play a leading role in its conception. It was the project of the coalition popular front government, which from the outset was severely limited by Blum's transfer of funds for such activities to the defense budget.[22] The tendency then and even now has been to exaggerate what actually was accomplished mainly by stressing initiatives without considering the small numbers served or involved.[23] That contradiction is demonstrated by the sports program of the popular front, to deal with the desperate shortage of municipal and school sports facilities, which remained largely unrealized because of inadequate funding.[24]

The SFIO was not an ingathering party intent on recruiting new members. It was an electoral machine able to produce thirteen times as many votes as party members until the great influx during the 1936 strike wave and subsequent nine months of popular front reform. Until 1935 the old party consisted of an overwhelming proportion of white-collar and public employees.[25] The party ranks swelled from 110,000 in 1934 to 286,604 in 1937, with the new recruits mostly production workers and shop assistants – those who generally had no prior experience with trade unions or political activity. They tended to gravitate to the left wing of the party (Zyromsky and Pivert) and to put pressure on the Blum ministry to use other than purely parliamentary means to carry out reforms.[26]

The SFIO's one attempt to attract sympathizers who were not party members was the creation of the organization *les Amicales socialistes*, which aimed at stabilizing the masses at the workplace, at combating the PCF, and recruiting members.[27] The socialists' foray into the workplace, despite certain frictions with the trade unions, met with an enthusiastic response in the Paris region. Within a month of initiation, the *amicales* there numbered 80,000, but their initial attraction to the SFIO was quickly dissipated. There was continuous tension between the party executive, which refused to allow the *amicales* any initiatives, and the militants at the workplace who demanded freedom of action. The SFIO expected the *amicales* to defend the popular front policies, despite the widespread discontent with many of them. Wedded to a tradition of clientism and paternalism, the SFIO leadership was unable to respond to the unpredictable demands of a mass movement. Within the context of the SFIO's relation to women's issues, one should note that the party broke its own rules in this outreach experiment. It created an organization of nonmember sympathizers, which was precisely what had been rejected for women in the early 1930s and thereafter.

The absence of a specifically socialist social and cultural program may also be explained by the fact that the SFIO clung to its amalgam of outworn prewar theories (Guesdist, Jauressian, etc.), which was translated into an extreme *attentiste* practice.[28] At the heart was a denial that any significant reform of the economic, social, and cultural existence of workers would be possible under capitalism, and an affirmation of the exclusive transformational power of socialism. Despite the continuation of radical rhetoric in party programs and publications, the SFIO relied on parliamentary maneuvers, upheld democratic and republican values, and shunned all activities which might lead to hazardous mass mobilization.

How was the woman question related to this fundamental aspect of SFIO underdevelopment? It was treated very much like all others that went beyond the most narrow political goals. It, too, was relegated to the future and was viewed from that special male perspective shared by both men and women in the party, except that the former never lost sight of the power they might lose if women received even only partial equality. As we shall see later in the discussion of welfare, socialist men were no different from Frenchmen in general in accepting state intervention in addressing problems in women's private sphere so long as power relations were not threatened.

Léon Blum set the tone and the narrow limits within which his ministry functioned. Publicly he always appeared to champion the cause of women's rights. His appointment of three female subministers – Suzanne Lacore for education, Cécile Brunschvicg for welfare, and Irène Joliot-Curie for scientific research – was a masterstroke of presenting the symbolic for the real. Privately Blum admitted that these women were not expected to do very much beyond being a public presence.[29] Joliot-Curie was hardly given a proper office and resigned in early August without having done anything. From the outset she had considered her talents misused and had accepted the appointment in loyalty to the popular front and women's cause.[30]

Before we leave the subject of the general context for the party's relationship to the woman question, let us look at one or two examples of its implications. In the 1930s many newspapers and periodicals added a woman's page or pages of some sort, and *Le Populaire* was no exception. Its Sunday edition included generally facing pages titled "La femme – la militante." The latter rubric included controversial topics (equal pay for equal work; fascism and child bearing) on occasion but generally hewed closer to traditional subjects associated with women: hygiene in the home, children, public health, recipes, household tips, food prices. But the printed text was allotted a very small space. From two-thirds to three-quarters of the section was devoted to fashion of a kind truly amazing for the national daily of the Socialist party: haute couture-style photographs of expensive looking garments (velours, silks, furs, fancy hats) more appropriate in upper class fashion magazines. These were supplemented by advertisements for clothes and household consumer items. What could the editors of *Le Populaire* have had in mind? Whom were they addressing: their members, voters, white-collar employees living on small tight budgets? The relegation of women to the trivial was also practiced in organizations not directly subordinate to the SFIO. The socialist consumers' society linked masculinity to productive public activities and to the management of the cooperative movement, while making consumption the only task of women.[31]

Trade Unions and the Role of Women

Were the trade unions (principally the *Confédération Générale du Travail* [CGT]) more encouraging to women in recognizing their equal right to work, in drawing them into their ranks as equals, and in addressing the specific demands of female workers? If one makes a distinction between official declarations and practical experience, as we have done for the SFIO, the answer is, with certain significant exceptions, not much more encouraging.

Throughout the interwar period women comprised between 39 and 36 percent of the labor force (Paris somewhat higher still), with some 20 percent married and 27 to 30 percent industrial workers. CGT membership hovered around 500,000 before 1936, increased to 4.7 million after unification with the CGTU and the strike wave of 1936, and declined precipitously after 1938. At no time did women's membership reach 20 percent of the CGT total or equal the size of the female workforce.[32] The disparity between active women workers and trade union members was typical for the other ten countries in this volume. Throughout the period women trade unionist were under represented at the local and national level. The few prominent leaders (Jeanne Chevenard, Germaine Fouchère, and Louise Chambelland) exhorted working women to join unions because only through them could their grievances and demands be met.[33] Their appeals found little response in the ranks of the unorganized, for whom their gender-limiting socialization was a barrier to entering the uninviting masculine world of union locals.

Did the discussions about women workers and resolutions adopted on the subject at national CGT congresses define the limits of theory and practice? A review of CGT congress protocols during the 1930s suggests that despite the tedious and almost ritual presentation of standard demands there was much more real difference in the presentations of women delegates than could be found in SFIO congresses.[34] Resolutions called for a living wage for all and equal pay for equal work; strict enforcement of protective legislation; maternity leaves; recognition of motherhood as a social function; provisions for the children of two working parents; and the creation of worker housing with modern facilities, among others. These routine demands were presented in a dynamic context, however. At the 1929 congress Chevenard went out of her way to draw attention to the triple burden of work, housework, and child rearing which women had to bear. At the same meeting Coulmy, representative of the more militant clothing workers' union, minced no words about accusation from men that activist women were feminists. We cannot be otherwise than feminists since we are women, she asserted and challenged her male comrades to help spread feminist oriented membership propaganda in the ranks of unaffiliated women. At the 1931 congress Chevenard responded to the earlier feminist challenge by attacking the Open Door group, which rejected protective legislation as detrimental to women's occupational opportunities, as speaking exclusively from a bourgeois perspective. A defense of Open Door by a postal service delegate drew the discussion-ending ripost from Léon Jouhaux, head of the CGT, that total gender equality was impossible, because there were jobs and conditions from which women had to be protected.[35]

Although the CGT did not take an official position against women working, it agreed tacitly with the stand taken by many of its component sections that men should earn a family wage and that women should have children, raise and educate them, and make their husbands' domestic life a happy contrast to the exploitation they had to face at the workplace.[36] This very narrow official view of gender roles continued throughout the interwar period despite the growth and transformation of the CGT during the popular front. A front page editorial of *La vie ouvrière* of 13 May 1937 proudly proclaimed: "In each proletarian home this journal has its place: with it the *chef de famille*, the mother and infant always feel more united, stronger, and happier." At the same time (20 May) the editors rhetorically questioned the introduction of a woman's page ("Who looks to find beauty tips or kitchen recipes in a trade union magazine?") and concluded that it was justified in recognition of women's responsibility to make home agreeable to all.

The strikes of 1936 were neither initiated nor participated in by the majority of CGT members who were government employees. They were largely the spontaneous outbursts of unorganized workers, who streamed into the CGT vastly increasing its size and transforming its composition. But women did not gain directly from the weakened and defensive position of the *patronat*. When the collective bargaining agreements were reached in June 1936 women's wages were set at 13 to 15 percent below men's. No one mentioned "equal pay for equal work!"[37] Even if in the general practical gains of the strikes – the two week vacations and shorter work week – women benefitted less than men because of their fragmented employment and domestic responsibilities.[38] But, by actively participating in the strike actions women workers gained experience in organization, some control over the machines they used, a sense of female solidarity, and some dignity from public recognition of their role.[39] Yet, the strikes were not a turning point in female integration into trade unions where male power prevailed and women were tolerated on unequal terms at best or more generally regarded as not fulfilling their traditional female roles.[40]

But women workers in and out of unions were not simply victims. Throughout the interwar period they also demonstrated the ability to learn quickly the traditional techniques of collective action, to assert themselves on behalf of their specific demands, to take the risk of exclusion or unemployment, and to step before the public with pride as female proletarians. Gender wage inequalities among postal workers led to work stoppages by women workers in 1926 and 1927, which culminated in their massive demonstration in front of the central post office in Paris during which thirty-seven women were arrested.[41] Direct and concerted action proved successful, because the postal administration ordered the integration of male and female clerks in administrative positions and authorized equal salaries for equal work. Militancy was, of course, not always rewarded with success. A bitter seven-month long strike of women textile workers in the department of the Nord failed to bring the owners to the point of negotiation.

By 1935 the effects of the depression in France were at a high point, with substantial male unemployment and a greater dependence on women's wages. In June of that year some 4,000 *midinettes* (garment seamstresses) went on strike. One of them gave an angry interview to the press objecting to the impression of frivolity that photos had created and called for publication of the striking workers' demands. These she summed up poignantly: "We are not dogs; we have our dignity. Long enough we have been paid with smiles and pleasantries. Now we demand bread and an honest life."[42] Male garment workers refused to join the *midinettes*, who did not know in the heat of action that their union had already settled on the same terms as the last contract. At the end of the year 6,000 unemployed women workers demonstrated in front of the Hotel de Ville in Paris, demanding the creation of jobs by the municipal authorities.[43] Until the strike wave in the following year it was the clearest demonstration that women could organize and on a scale far greater than any feminist gathering at that time. As we shall see in the discussion of suffrage mobilization, there was neither the will nor the means within the working-class movement to turn these workplace initiatives into a more general struggle for women's rights.

The extent and limits of participation by women in two quite different trade unions, those of teachers and clothing workers is revealing. Members of the teachers' union, given the higher level of education required (école normale), were seldom of proletarian origin.[44] Trade union membership among female teachers was high (about one-third), but two-thirds of female union secretaries were single, indicating that household and child rearing tasks were not shared even if both spouses were union members. Equal pay for equal hours for all teachers was put into practice in 1927; equal maxima followed in 1932. Neither gain had to be fought for by the women; they were donations from above. By contrast, women clothing workers were proletarian, underprivileged, with a high rate of militancy and low rate of union membership – about 14 percent. The garment union engaged in the clearest example of gender concern (addressed to the men no less) in a declaration at its 1937 congress.[45] In addition to equal wages, it concluded, the union should strive to assist its women members to attain rights and social independence equal to those of men. The shop floor and meeting hall reality gave little evidence of these high motives. For men the image of the worker/mother remained traditional; women's work outside the home was considered a necessary evil, and the home was their primary terrain and responsibility. Though the women's equally militant participation in the 1936 strikes was appreciated and remarked, it led to no great changes in practice except in small plants with only female workers, where women began to play a major role. Despite a considerable number of misconceptions about each other, working-class women and middle-class feminists had many common aims that should have allowed them to join for united actions. But no leadership emerged, either among the SFIO and CGT or among men or women, to bridge the two factions even on issues such as women's suffrage, which might have become the stepping stone to a far larger movement for women's rights.

French Women Must Vote!

As the world moved ineluctably toward war in 1939, the women of France found themselves in a unique but hardly enviable position. Aside from their sisters in Bulgaria and Switzerland, virtually alone in the developed world, they were denied the right to vote on any level. One is hard put to find a ready explanation for this astonishing reality, but one cannot avoid the problem. The ballot was an important instrument in women's struggle for greater equality in nearly every other country. The still fashionable evasion of the suffrage issue by some historians of French feminism (allegedly French feminists used "maternity" pragmatically as a means to attain larger ends) is no longer worthy of debate.[46]

Various reasons have been given for French difference on this vital aspect of women's power. International comparisons and particularly the Anglo-Saxon model were declared to be inapplicable, because French women did not consider voting to be central to their interests.[47] Others found explanations in the peculiarities of the French nation: It was Catholic, it was Latin, it was subject to Roman law that made the family rather than the individual primary; and its women, unlike those in other countries, had no prior experience in national political movements.[48] No detailed riposte needs to be given to these thin arguments: To be sure, voting was not considered primary either by middle-class feminists or women socialists who concentrated on reform of the civil code and the class struggle respectively. But one must ask why French politically conscious women, unlike those in other countries, failed to see that the ballot was the key to their goals. As for the suggestion that an explanation can be found in the national peculiarities of the French, comparisons become vital:[49] other Catholic states, Austria, Ireland, and Poland, for example, had given women the vote; Italy and Spain are also Latin nations; Austria, Germany, Poland, and Belgium are subject to Roman law; and did French women really gain no experience in the events of 1848, the Commune, the Dreyfus Affair, and the Great War?

The roots of the tradition and attitudes that shaped resistance to universal suffrage may well lie in French republicanism. Sian Reynolds suggests that women were denied the vote after 1848 because men began to question how they would use it, a question which had not been posed in deciding on male suffrage then or thereafter.[50] Women were simply suspected of undermining the Republic by letting their votes be determined by the priests. The language of republicanism, it seems, was used to twist an argument about rights into one about uses in order to continue to exclude women from the Republic itself. Pierre Rosanvallon, one of the staunchest proponents of French particularism, offers support for this theoretical orientation.[51] In France, he argues, the right to vote derives from the principle of the political equality of individuals, and women were denied this right because they are not regarded as true, discrete individuals. Because men feared radical individualism, he continues, they clung to the idea of marriage and the family, where women lose their individual character in favor of the husband who represents the couple. The old French fear of pluralism, he concludes, is paralleled by the fear that a wife could have an opinion different from that of her husband.

In the actual arenas in which the demand for women's suffrage was debated, contested, and ultimately defeated, women's suffrage bills were passed time after time by overwhelming majorities in the Chamber only to be postponed and ultimately rejected by the Senate. So far as the SFIO and women's suffrage was concerned, there can be little doubt that, though Bracke was allowed to introduce heroic bills for that cause in the Chamber, it was Léon Blum who determined and directed the party's position behind the scenes.[52] Blum had little to say about the ballot as a means of attaining women's agendas or rights, although he took full credit for the SFIO as being woman's constant champion. From 1927 until the end of the 1930s he referred to the need to organize campaigns for women's suffrage, but at no time did the SFIO actually organize such a campaign on the national or local level. Instead, Blum held women themselves responsible for not having acted in their own behalf, not having mobilized or seized the initiative, as if the party had no role to play in leading the politically inexperienced.[53] In a tabloid article of 1937 he proudly announced that "by taking two women into the government the SFIO has virtually realized the equality of the sexes,"[54] expressing a contempt for his female readers' ability to distinguish political sham from their own experience.

After Hitler's rise to power, the SFIO and other working-class organizations became even more cautious on women's suffrage, which in practice meant a greater contradiction between appearance of support and the reality of sabotage. Examples of this duplicity are legion, but a few will suffice:[55] in December 1933 only five of the nine-man SFIO group in the Senate voted for women's suffrage; leading Socialists such as F.O. Frossard, Vincent Auriol, and Sixte-Quenin revived fears of priests controlling women's vote and helped to reduce support for it at the party congress in 1935; in February of the same year SFIO Chamber delegates voted eighteen to fourteen against the urgency of acting on women's vote in municipal elections; reminded of its constant commitment to women's suffrage after the Blum government assumed office, Séverac, acting as spokesman, explained that until the socialists were in a majority they could only support the principle; when a bill demanding full female suffrage was introduced for the eighth time during the first session of the popular front Chamber, it passed unanimously by 409 to 0 votes, but the entire Blum cabinet was among the ninety-four deputies who abstained; when Mme. Chevenard, head of CGT propaganda and Mme. Delabit, secretary of the tobacco workers, were invited to a broad spectrum of women's suffrage organization meeting in April 1937, the CGT leadership vetoed their attendance.

How did various groups of women react to this alternation between neglect and opposition? Virtually all of the leading women socialists – Suzanne Buisson, Marthe Louis-Levy, Germaine Picard-Moch, Andrée Marty-Capgras – denounced male socialist opponents of women's suffrage, but none was prepared to challenge Blum or the rest of the SFIO leadership about the party's failure to organize real campaigns or to use organized public pressure against the Senate during the popular front. The tiny women's group in the SFIO clung to its insistence on class exclusiveness at the very time when a rallying of women across class lines (the precedents in most other countries being common knowledge) was fundamental to the attainment of suffrage and women's larger agenda. Moreover, in entering first the pact of unity in 1934 and then the popular front with Radicals the SFIO had engaged in the kind of cross-class compromise for politically strategic reasons that the women were expected to and did deny themselves. Their early isolation as an auxiliary on the fringes of the party and their subsequent fear of being considered less than comrades by the men for making gender-based demands help to explain their persistent refusal to work for a broad suffrage movement.

And the feminists? There can be no denying that their principal mainstream suffrage organization would have made united action impossible for the most compromise-minded socialist women. The membership of the Union française pour le suffrage des femmes (UFSF) was bourgeois; its leadership, Cécile Brunschvicg, Germaine Malaterre-Sellier, Marcelle Kraemer-Bach, consisted of highly visible and active members of the Radical party;[56] and its main activity consisted of attempting to influence Radical party politicians, who listened politely and did nothing. The UFSF like other feminist organizations grew in membership during the interwar period, but without crossing the class barrier.[57] As we shall see later, the focus of most feminist associations lay elsewhere – in motherhood and its protection and in the civil legal status of women.[58]

A very small number of women skirted the barriers of class and party in attempting to move beyond meetings and resolutions toward the kind of direct actions, that mainstream feminists had always rejected as inappropriate for women and socialist women had scorned as bourgeois techniques.[59] In the mid-1920s the independent suffragist Martha Bray emerged as head of the tiny Women's Action League for Women's Suffrage. Socialist in orientation, it attempted to reach working-class housewives and working women in markets and fairs. Between 1926 and 1929 the group attempted some street demonstrations blocked by the police.[60] Far more significant were the attempts by Maria Verone to bring about united actions by socialist women and mainstream feminists.[61] A skillful lawyer, Verone was also head of the French League for the Rights of Women (LFDF), for whom the vote was the cornerstone of women's struggle, where contacts between the two sides were to be established. She had become estranged from the SFIO by the machinations of Saumoneau but remained loyal to traditional socialist aspirations. Verone and the LFDF attempted direct action on 6 November 1928 by assembling on the street, bearing suffragist posters and emblems, in preparation for entering the opening session of the Senate.[62] The police dispersed the women on grounds of a threat to public safety and arrested twenty-eight of them for a few hours. Verone, undaunted, went to court against the police, but her file became inexplicably lost.

Louise Weiss was the most talented woman to appear in the cause for women's suffrage. A successful journalist and long-time editor of the political review *Nouvelle Europe*, she was asked in 1934 by some UFSF leaders about means of invigorating both the organization and the suffrage campaign which were in the doldrums.[63] Weiss quite bluntly pointed to the apparent tie between the Radical party and the UFSF (politically neutral according to its statutes), which Brunschvicg had created and through which the organization was constrained from action of any kind. A first step toward a change, Weiss proposed, would be for Brunschvicg to resign from the Radical party or from the UFSF. The expected impasse in the UFSF led Weiss to form a new organization, La Femme Nouvelle, in a grand splash of publicity on 5-7 October 1934, at offices on the Champs-Elysées, with the press in attendance. This was but one of the many events organized by Weiss with the calculated purpose of bringing suffrage before a large French public, which had until then paid scant attention to women's claims and aims:[64] she used the air services provided by three famous aviatrixes to bring the suffrage message to different parts of the country; she stood for election (self-declared) in Montmartre in May 1935 and again in the Latin Quarter in April 1936; she brought a group of women wearing chains, including the popular film actress Françoise Rosay, to the Bastille in May 1935 to publicly break these chains of their imprisonment; and on 1 June 1936 for the opening session of the popular front Chamber, members of La Nouvelle Femme showered the deputies with leaflets bearing the slogan: "La Française doit voter!" Perhaps most clever of all was her advertised appearance at the Salon des arts ménagers in 1934 to cook a meal before an audience, which was encouraged to join La Femme Nouvelle and to demand the vote and, at the same time assured that there was no conflict between demanding rights and some aspects of tradition.[65]

For virtually all of these events Weiss arranged press, photographic, and film coverage in what was surely the first publicity blitz in France. It led the "thinking woman's" weekly Minerva to claim with a certain amount of bravado that after three months of activity Weiss had succeeded in creating unity with her slogan. It would be difficult to deny Weiss's creative use of the media to give the public a sense of the issue of suffrage, not to recognize the possible sense of importance these activities gave to women outside any formal organization, and to overlook the natural self-promotion of a public figure. Weiss was not simply a grandstander; she pioneered a technique that could have been used effectively against all the Radical and other enemies of women's suffrage in the Senate. In a speech in March 1932 Senator Raymond Duplantier, a Radical lawyer from Vienne, lambasted women as incapable of anything but household drudgery and maintained that they had no business in the male domain of public life.[66] Weiss toured Vienne with an official transcript of Duplantier's diatribe, reading it aloud in a variety of public settings from local town halls to cinemas and small factories, with a straw poll on women's suffrage every step of the way. In the fall election the Senator was decisively defeated. Weiss could bring suffrage to the public's attention; neither she nor the socialists or the feminists were able to mount a national campaign at the grass roots to benefit from the public's and, especially, women's growing awareness.

One last question about the failure of French women to attain suffrage at any level needs to be asked: Where were the men – the SFIO spokesmen, the few liberals among the Radical deputies and senators, the mayors who had supported Weiss's quest for municipal suffrage for women by two-thirds in 1935? All of the above were guarding the political advantage of their party, group and, by no means least, themselves. To increase the electorate meant to surrender seats and places, and women voters were no exception to this threat. In practice neither Radicals nor Socialists had any intention of letting women (then or later) run in their safe districts reserved for insiders and not outsiders.

Ordinary Frenchwomen were not in a position to appreciate the potential benefits to be derived from their ability to vote. Nor were the disparate groups of suffragists capable of educating and rallying those in whose name they acted. To understand the apparently impassable barriers to activating ordinary French women, one must know a little more about the conditions and restraints of their lives.

The Everyday Life of Women

Who drew up the agendas of French women's complaints, most pressing needs, and more distant wants? There is every indication that there was little or no knowledge of worker everyday life among those who drew up the agendas and made the decisions. To some degree the problem is common to all of the eleven countries being compared here, but the situation was somewhat more grave in France, where tradition insured that women as subjects rather than objects remained invisible.

In February 1927 an article in an obscure journal of leftist public school teachers led to a spectacular court case that highlighted the struggle between the upholders of traditional female roles and their opponents. The trial involved a breach of the restrictive civil code statute of 1923 outlawing the demand or publicity for contraceptives.[67] We shall return later to the question of birth control posed by Henriette Alquier, the young secretary of the Hérault chapter, who signed the article. What interests us here is her wholesale condemnation of the conditions of working-class life: housing, health and hygiene, education, housework, the private sphere – with women as the principal victims of these deplorable conditions. It will be fruitful to follow her trajectory though our findings are certainly more differentiated.

All sources and commentators seem to agree that more than half of the worker housing in the department of the Seine was poor with some fifth of it in real slums.[68] This was particularly true of the *îlots insalubres* (insalubrious islands,)[69] but only to a slightly lesser degree also of many of the *hotel garnis* (apartment hotels), on which single men, young couples, and foreign workers were dependent for lodging. The in/out migration of these was startling with 2.5 million making changes in 1929 and 2.8 million in 1936, suggesting that the number of tenants living there sometime in their lives would be markedly greater than those living there at a particular moment.[70] The housing crisis, which dated from well before the turn of the century, was aggravated by the fact that decent housing became increasingly important in the more regular lifestyle of workers after the war. Tenants' organizations were extremely active in pressuring landlords to make repairs and improvements and in enjoining the government to continue the protection of rent control. Women played a major role in this struggle organizationally and through grass-roots actions.[71]

With the move of new and some traditional industry from the Paris periphery to the suburbs, workers, seeking to reduce travel time, arrived in large numbers in squatter settlements.[72] In the early 1920s these proto towns resembled the worst slums in the city with a total absence of basic infrastructure and threats to public health. Only by the end of the decade was the rampant exploitation of speculators selling unimproved lots curtailed as the public authorities took charge. All in all, throughout the interwar period, the housing crisis in greater Paris was nearly catastrophic and considerably worse than in other major European cities, where slum clearance and substantial public housing projects were undertaken (Vienna, Berlin, Frankfurt, London, to name but a few).

As mentioned earlier, the 61,500 domiciles built under public auspices (HBM) in the Seine department had little effect on the housing needs of the population and particularly workers. The typical size of an HBM apartment, consisting of two rooms and a kitchen, was thirty-five square meters, or eight and three-quarters square meters per person in a family of four.[73] Nonetheless, given their improvement over the rest of the available habitations, competition for them was fierce, with the method for selecting tenants not exactly evenhanded. An ambitious building program triumphally announced in 1928 (loi Loucheur) projected 260,000 new domiciles in five years and ended as an empty promise with the onset of the Depression. The only innovative housing programs were the garden city projects created under the guidance of Henri Sellier as director of the departmental HBM and office of social hygiene.[74] The garden city of Suresnes, where Sellier was mayor, was conceived in 1921 to provide 8,000 to 10,000 domiciles accommodating a spectrum of residents from worker to engineer. By 1939, 2,735 housing units had been built with a host of communal features: kindergartens and elementary schools with gymnasia and swimming pools; an infant hygiene center; a psycho technical laboratory (to classify children rationally); a hotel for singles with a restaurant; eighty units for the temporary homeless; a leisure center with auditorium for 800; and more. The major practical problem was the relatively high rent for workers; the fundamental problem from a socialist perspective was the technocratic-eugenic concept of the whole.

The variety of housing resorted to by working-class women was considerable: from squatters' settlements, rooming houses, and dormitories sleeping twenty, to the seventeen insalubrious islands, numerous apartment hotels and worker tenements, to HBM public housing and the garden cities. Only a tiny minority had hopes of or access to the last; the majority lived in domiciles lacking indoor water, heat, electricity, daylight and ventilation, and they shared slovenly sanitary facilities. Beyond these bare facts we know next to nothing about the life cycle and rhythm of women's lives spent in what, together with their workplace, was the principal environment in and through which changes and improvements in their condition would have to take place. The domestic life of women was not recorded by the SFIO, the CGT, or any official agency. Specific information about housing structure exists but none about the content. The worker home and its mistress, much heralded by maternalists of all stripes, came before the public only when some sensational event cast a brief light on them, when well-meaning or simply ignorant and arrogant reformers decided that the time had come to turn their lives upside down to make them better, or when the public authorities were forced to intervene or at least record conditions affecting health and safety.

That the health of the worker family was threatened by the absence of hygiene is evident from the reports of teachers about the cleanliness of schoolchildren and from the high death rate from tuberculosis and pulmonary disease among 1 to 5-year-old children.[75] Problems in the domestic sphere were laid at the feet of the housewife, who frequently was also a worker in or outside the home. The solution, proposed by Suzanne Buisson for instance, was rationalization of the domicile by the use of electricity to operate energy-saving machines, which would give the woman of the house more time to spend on her own needs and on the emotional welfare of her family.[76] Buisson was addressing working-class women about whose actual lives she appeared to know next to nothing. Most worker dwellings did not have electricity and those that did had primitive wiring that could not support appliances.[77] It is difficult to imagine where and how they actually washed their clothes and how often. The absence of communal facilities and the expense of using professional laundresses suggests that clothes, aside from undergarments, were washed very infrequently, providing grist to the mill of visiting social workers. But neither socialist nor feminist, male or female, seemed to have thought of finding solutions to this problem beyond the rationalization few could afford.

We also have some glimpses of working-class women at the workplace, which was the other principal locale of their daily lives.[78] Why did women work for wages? Mainly because male wages were insufficient to support a family, especially if there were children, but also because it brought them into the larger world beyond the home. Factory, office, and sales jobs were considered superior to artisan work that demanded long preparation and a restricted sociability. The work pattern of women who had children was interrupted for periods of time, but since one-quarter of all women had no children by the end of the 1930s, they continued to be part of the labor market. Nearly half the female factory workers in the Seine department worked in plants of one hundred or more, as *ouvrières spécialisées*, a misnomer for the unskilled assembly-line work they performed. Office work became increasingly electrified and Taylorized and, by 1928, 70 percent was carried on by women. This feminization was based on the belief that simple, automatic, and monotonous work could best be done by women who lacked expertise. Until the strike wave of 1936, sales work, particularly in the large department stores, was embedded in nineteenth-century paternalism. For the women sales clerks who played an active role in the strikes, the trade union became the protector of their interests even if they were non members. The forty-hour week became official in 1936 but was generally observed in the breach. Until then hours were longer, meals often taken at the workstation amid the dirt and noise. Few women who worked outside the home were free at the end of the workday; household chores if not child rearing often made a woman's day almost twice as long as a man's. Even though women earned considerably less than men for comparable work, their supplemental income was essential to the worker family budget.

The male leadership of trade unions was willing to let demands for equal pay, protective legislation enforcement, paid maternity leaves, and the like be adopted at annual meetings. But they were not prepared to recognize or admit that working women's main burden was their double or triple responsibility, the amelioration of which would have required a reordering of tasks and obligations within the worker family.

A few examples from women's private sphere should give some texture to the problems in women's environments sketched above. Although prenuptial and free unions continued, the number of marriages increased as the working-class family became stabilized, with increasing demands for proper housing. Marriages were contracted with little ceremony; in the Seine department 56 percent of them were purely civil in the late 1930s.[79] That was in keeping with the generally low church attendance among workers. The reform of the Civil Code, to which mainstream feminists devoted most of their efforts, was of virtually no importance to working-class women.[80] They worked and belonged to trade unions without their husband's permission; wages went into a common pot, with men receiving generally agreed upon pocket money; and there was no property to divide, protect, or pass on to heirs.

The horizons of working-class girls remained very limited: elementary school science textbooks for girls stressed home economics and child care (*puériculture*); morals texts, oblivious to women in the labor force, pictured women's destiny as home and motherhood; career choices proposed for boys outnumbered those for girls by more than four to one, with the latter limited to farmers, dressmakers, laundresses, sales clerks, and servants.[81] Although an increasing number of working-class girls received the elementary school (CEP) diploma, which was the prerequisite to further education and more challenging and better paying jobs, few families could afford to support a nonworking girl for two to three years of additional schooling.[82] What about the much discussed and celebrated new woman of the 1920s, the flapper with bobbed hair, a sexless silhouette, and smoking cigarettes?[83] Whether or not this touted image of sexual liberation and female equality fed the fantasy life of working-class girls is difficult to say. Emulation of the flappers generally went no further than bobbed hair and shorter hemlines (corsets had never been a fundamental garment in their milieu).

The purpose of these snapshots of everyday life has been to allow the central problems of working-class women that should have been the starting point of any agenda for reform to reveal themselves. As we shall see later in the discussion of welfare measures, better housing was a prerequisite for virtually any improvement in the quality of life. Health, hygiene, nutrition, child care, and family harmony all required a proper setting to be implemented. In addition, some modification of gender inequality experienced by working women had to be initiated beyond various welfare initiatives. Neither socialists, nor trade unionists, nor feminists could muster their own forces or make alliances for specific purposes to initiate the necessary changes in the national culture mired in an outdated and prejudicial image of women. An active and massive mobilization for women's suffrage would have been an effective way of challenging the power structure (the Senate, for instance), which stood in the way of all change. In the absence of leadership from these groups, the basic problems in 1939 remained what they had been twenty years earlier, with one exception. Without organization or direct communication and in opposition to threats and feeble bribes French women of all classes, but especially those who had the largest families in the past, made the one-child family the national model. This was a tough battle in the trenches of population politics.

Pro-natalism, Maternity, Eugenics, and Birth Control

The issues discussed here clearly resonated in the entire female population and offered the greatest potential basis for leadership by socialists, feminists, and progressives of every stripe in promoting a greater sense of liberty and dignity among a wide spectrum of women cutting across class lines. But, though neither the SFIO nor CGT rose to the challenge, socialist officials at the local level, individual socialists, and prominent professionals who, identified with socialism without belonging to the party, supported women's right to control their bodies. These diverse currents failed to combine into a national campaign for liberalization of abortion and birth control, as they had in Germany, Austria, Holland, and Britain.

As Hervé Le Bras has argued in a recent tour de force,[84] France has suffered from an obsession with demography, which has been used by both social scientists and the political class to explain all the problems and shortcomings of French society. In the interwar years population decline compared to other European countries – especially Britain and Germany – was treated as a national catastrophe. Obvious indicators, such as childless couples, which in 1936 amounted to 22.8 percent for France and 32.6 percent for the department of the Seine,[85] appeared to suggest a unique decline but the reality of comparative statistics demonstrated that French population declined less between 1920 and 1935 than that of most European countries including Britain and Germany.[86] Such evidence was vitiated by the powerful litany of France's wartime casualties with which various pro-natalist societies bombarded the public through the media.[87]

During the 1920s a host of repopulation leagues and alliances counted nearly half the deputies of the Chamber among their members and were championed by many prominent politicians, statesmen, industrialists, and generals.[88] The movement was bracketed by the elite Alliance for the Increase of Population with 40,000 members and the popular National Association of Large Families with many times that number. The principal aim of all of these organizations was to substantially increase the population by making maternity the primary life-goal of women, whose "production" would be appreciated by a grateful nation (medals for mothers). Newspapers supported this crusade with startling projections of the near future in which two French soldiers would face five Prussian ones, and postcards picturing healthy babies were sent to honeymooners reminding them of their duty. That the general public was well aware of the controversy surrounding a low birthrate, but not necessarily the repopulationists' message, can be seen from the fact that in the first national opinion poll taken on the subject only a negligible 4 percent of the sample failed to respond.[89] Until the onset of the Depression in France the repopulationists were a formidable force for restricting the identity of women to maternity, employing an armory of techniques to attain their ends.

The positive reinforcement for maternity was a piecemeal and contradictory family policy, which was "from the outset a conservative crusade –

its articulation, for the most part, confined to a landscape dominated by nationalists, pro-natalists, and social Catholics."[90] The view of mainstream feminists that the unconditional acceptance of maternity as women's defining role was the only means by which women could achieve their agenda has most recently been disinterred by the argument that "prewar France had a welfare state in the making and a welfare state, in matters of family policy, growing more, rather than less, ambitious in the scope of its activities."[91] Such views are hardly original; the leading maternalist Cécile Brunschvicg had claimed in 1933 that France led the world in family protection.[92] Startlingly new is the reexamination of interwar family policy from the perspective of the self-interest of employers, who sponsored reforms in order to control wages, to fight unionization, to exercise workplace discipline, and to invade the workers' homes.[93]

Let us look more closely at some specific provisions of this family/welfare policy, at the population which they served, and at the means by which they were delivered.[94] Factory nursing rooms introduced during the war to accommodate women with infants provided two 30-minute periods per day when mother and infant were expected to perform. They, as well as factory-based *crèches* (day care facilities) were unpopular with women and did not survive the early 1920s. Family child support given for one, two, three and more children, with a substantial increase beginning with the third, provided only about 20 percent of the actual cost of each additional child for a family. Guaranteed maternity leaves without penalty paid mothers about one-tenth of their normal wages as compensation (in Austria women workers received four weeks pre-delivery and six weeks postpartum leave at 60 to 70 percent of wages plus free medical care throughout). There were only 360 community crèches with 12,000 places in all of France by 1940; in Paris in 1937 there were 1,706 places with only 35 percent of these in working-class arrondissements. Given the increasing popular awareness of family economics, it is hardly surprising that family size did not increase because of child support offered as pro-natalists had hoped. Nursing at the workplace according to Taylorist schedules was a ludicrous idea as were crèches at the plant, since women workers wanted to separate work from private life. Postpartum leaves may have been mandatory, but few women, whose full wages were needed at home, could afford to subsist on the reduced compensation. Postal workers, civil servants, better-paid white-collar workers, and schoolteachers could avail themselves of the small number of crèches available as well as enjoy the benefits of maternity leaves at regular pay.

The various female agents carrying out such welfare measures – visiting nurses assigned to monitor the child care provided by those receiving family assistance; social workers, who were the intermediary between the medical establishment and lower class mothers in maternity hospitals and wards; factory superintendents, who were charged with overseeing women workers on the shop floor and through home visits; and the polyvalent social agents of the garden cities, who structured and supervised the full gamut of community services – all had the common mission of supervising, controlling, and disciplining women. There is some doubt about the extent to which these administrators actually contributed to the "welfare" of the women in their charge. Social workers at the few modern maternity hospitals such as *Maternité Baudelocque*, which provided assembly-line deliveries and postpartum regimentation, "looked down on the lower class mothers treated there as ignorant, stupid, selfish, and irresponsible."[95] Visiting nurses were often overwhelmed by the deplorably unsanitary and unhealthy living conditions of their clients for which they had no practical materials or equipment with which to intercede – conditions in which preaching hygiene would have been ludicrous.[96] The factory superintendents' efforts to inculcate a classless common interest of workers and management among politically inexperienced women came up against the class reality of worker families and, after the strikes of 1936, against a new spirit of collective action and strength.[97] The views of industrialists and other pro-natalists diverged to the extent that the former associated maternity with greater productivity and labor peace whereas the latter considered maternity as a moral force in national revival.

In their attempt to project a new symbolic Marianne, whose maternity would save France from degeneration, pro-natalists did not rely on the incentives of family policy alone. In two important revisions of the Penal Code in 1920 and 1923 (known as the "law of abomination"), passed by overwhelming majorities in the Chamber and largely ignored in the press (including *Le Populaire*), all attempts to interfere with birth from conception to delivery were to be severely punished.[98] Prison sentences and fines were to be imposed for soliciting, carrying out, and assisting in abortion, successful or not, and the publicity for as well as sale of all contraceptive devices was to be equally punished. Prison terms were actually shortened and the crimes reduced from felonies to misdemeanors in order to take cases out of the hands of juries, which had generally refused to convict their own, and to put them under the control of judges expected to be merciless in doing their duty. The outlawing not only of abortion but also of all contraception was aimed directly at controlling female sexuality. If anything, men were favored by this restrictive legislation, which excluded condoms from the declared forbidden devices.[99]

During the next decade and a half it became clear that neither welfare incentives nor the threat of prison could stem the tide of abortions, which most authorities numbered as equal to live births. Nor were judges any more inclined to put women who had gone through the travail of abortion into prison than juries had been. None of the women charged and convicted in the department of the Seine between 1923 and 1938 actually went to prison. Judges gave them a suspended sentence and put them on probation for five years.[100] The small number of women who came before the courts suggest that denunciations (perhaps to settle quarrels or for other personal motives) were rare and that gender solidarity enhanced at the workplace and in communal spaces occupied by women was very strong. However, the benign application of the law by no means freed women from the shadow it cast over sexual relations and family life. Mainstream feminist leaders supported the "law of abomination" on the grounds that women who acted against their defining maternal natures should pay for their transgressions.[101]

A new Marianne did emerge in interwar France, but she was exactly the countermodel envisaged by the pro-natalists – not the ample breeders dedicated to revising the population deficit of their country but actors with a native wisdom who restricted their progeny in keeping with economic realities necessary for survival or an enhanced lifestyle for their families. One can only surmise how women accomplished this feat. Condoms were readily available, legal, and inexpensive; diaphragms were hardly known below the middle class except for some illegal nascent birth control clinics (to be discussed later).[102] The main form of birth control continued to be coitus interruptus backed up by abortions. The former depended on the cooperation of the male partner but even then was far from safe; the latter gave women the final control, though men undoubtedly often participated in the decision and assisted in arranging for the procedure. Periodic abstinence was also resorted to, but it as well as coitus interruptus put both partners under considerable emotional stress – an impoverishment of sexuality.[103]

Where did the socialists stand on the repopulationists' attempt to restrict women's identity to maternity and to a narrowly defined sexuality through a legal reign of terror? Although August Bebel's *Die Frau und der Sozialismus*, which clearly differentiated between satisfaction of the sexual instinct and procreation, had been translated into French in 1891, not a single important socialist prewar leader had accepted its neo-Malthusian conclusions.[104] The SFIO's official position then and in the interwar period was that procreation and sexuality were a strictly private affair. The same argument was advanced by the British Labour party and the German SPD. In practice, on rare occasions, the SFIO did take a stand.[105] It joined in the campaign of support for the schoolteacher Henriette Alquier charged under the law of 1920 for propagating birth control, leading to her acquittal in 1926. It gave tacit support to its deputy Sixte-Quenin, who in a Chamber speech in 1928 demanded abrogation of the entire 1920 law. It gave even more concrete support to Sixte-Quenin's renewed campaign in 1933 to expunge Article 3 of that law, which forbade publicity about contraception, on the grounds that it constrained the republican exercise of liberty of opinion. The SFIO joined the substantial Chamber majority in the vote to abolish the article, but the Senate refused even to take up the issue. And Blum as prime minister in August 1936 made a strong statement to the Chamber about the heavy burden on families that experienced unwanted pregnancies.

We should also consider the meaning and impact of two works of literature, considered to be progressive in the cause of women, written by two prominent socialists: Léon Blum's *Du marriage*, published during his literary days in 1907 and reprinted in 1937, and Victor Margueritte's best-seller *La garçonne* of 1922. Blum proposed that women be given the same opportunity for sexual experimentation before marriage as men so as to become sexual subjects as well as objects. Blum was silent about two important questions raised by this plea for an equality of bodies. Are women to be granted other equality as well? And, most important, how will women exercising their power to experiment sexually with various partners be protected from unwanted pregnancies?[106] Despite the press reaction and later international acclaim of *La garçonne* as a provocative plea for the sexual liberation of women, the book is a morality tale in thin disguise.[107]

Du marriage let loose an avalanche of anti-Semitism directed at the despoilers of French morality;[108] but no one criticized the real flaws from a woman's perspective. *La garçonne*, which sold one million copies by 1929, led to an outpouring of hateful critiques and attacks on the author.[109] Considering that there were many more sexually explicit novels in circulation, the hostile reception no doubt stemmed from the fact that the fallen woman was of bourgeois rather than the expected lower-class origins. Though the substance of both books may have trickled down to the general public through coverage in the popular press, their direct reading audience was essentially bourgeois. Despite their notoriety, neither work really took up the issues which most concerned the large majority of women, though as titillation they may have accustomed the general public to taboo subjects.[110]

Socialists and socialist sympathizers played an important role in a series of organizations, publications, and social experiments all of which combined a primary interest in sexuality with eugenics and neo-Malthusianism. These activities coincided with the rapid decline of pro-natalist influence in the Chamber and general public with the onset of the Depression, which made the old natalist argument for large populations redundant.[111] In 1931 the Association for the Study of Sexuality was created by a small but powerful group dedicated to combatting the repressive conditions which had prevented the open study and public discussion of sexuality, abortion, contraception, and women's rights.[112] Its honorary president was Justin Godard, senator and former Minister of Public Health; the prominent venereologist Edouard Toulouse was president; the two vice-presidents were Maria Vérone, a famous lawyer and head of the French League for the Rights of Women and Henri Sellier, mayor of the progressive Parisian suburb of Suresnes; the secretary general was Jean Dalsace, a prominent gynecologist and champion of family planning; the secretary was the sex reformer Berty Albrecht. Distinguished members included: Victor Basch, professor at the Sorbonne and head of the French League for the Rights of Man, the prominent feminist lawyer Yvonne Netter, the social hygienist Sicard de Plauzoles, as well as city councillors, senators and deputies, physicians of the medical faculty, and officials from public health and mental hygiene.

Diverse individuals were allied with this core group, from the author of progressive pot boilers Victor Margueritte to the famous physicist and peace activist Paul Langevin. In 1933 Berty Albrecht, who had close ties to English political and neo-Malthusian radicals, founded the journal *Le problème sexuel* as a complement to the Association's work. Though the latter originally claimed to be devoted to research and information, it revealed itself to be much more action-focused during the next few years. It spearheaded a campaign to make premarital health examinations mandatory, propagandized for the repeal of the "law of abomination," and, most daringly, demanded the creation of prenuptial clinics to give advice on contraception and to perform abortions, with the need for the latter to be determined by medical societies.[113] Albrecht's journal, whose board drew from the same cast of characters, only produced six numbers in three years. Sold by subscription at a substantial price it was intended for an elite audience. It dealt with sexuality, abortion, birth control, and eugenics in theoretical terms, but carefully avoided any discussion of the ongoing situation in France that might have been of interest to popular readers. Most interesting, because by contrast it exposed the bigotry in France on these issues, was the report by a Polish physician about the founding and operation of the first birth control clinic in his country.[114]

A number of conclusions suggest themselves about the powerful directorates of the Association and journal: the majority associated with them were within the orbit of traditional French socialism but were not welcome to give advice on party policies to leaders of the SFIO; the prominent standing of so many of them served to protect them singly and collectively from prosecution under the 1920s law and, in effect, made that law ridiculous in practice (but not symbolically); they represented a special heterogeneous elite without ties to parties, unions, and ongoing politics which, though prepared to act for specific and limited purposes, had no intention of proselytizing the public or of mobilizing it to carry out any of its aims. Despite their commitment to contraception to end clandestine abortions, consultation clinics where medical abortions could be performed, sex education for the young, and healthy progeny, maternity remained the leitmotif defining women's calling and destiny. All other roles and definitions of women appeared to be secondary and received less attention. But even maternity was not to be controlled by the women themselves. They were to be freed from the clutches of the church and pro-natalists and put under the guidance of eugenically inspired and medically based authorities.[115]

Edouard Toulouse, founder of the first psychiatric hospital Henri Rousselle, where he created a prenuptial clinic (which may have engaged in family planning), well illustrates this latent paternalism. In 1918 he argued that motherhood was both duty and fulfillment for women; in 1921, however, he announced that French women were akin to slaves and called for their equality; in 1931 he doubted that complete sexual freedom could be given to women considering their physiological role and proposed the control of sexuality by experts. In 1933 he proposed that a monopoly of abortion practice be created in institutions of the state.[116]

The most daring and significant socialist intervention in the cause of planned motherhood was carried out in the Parisian suburb of Suresnes, where Mayor Henri Sellier, a dedicated neo-Malthusian, eugenicist, and social planner, built a garden city as a total environment based on social hygiene. Appointed Minister of Public Health by Blum in June 1936, he immediately undertook to inform the public about the need to confront abortion by creating special health facilities for women.[117] Sellier and the gynecologist Jean Dalsace, active in the Association for the Study of Sexuality, agreed to collaborate in establishing a prenuptial clinic in the garden city of Suresnes.[118] Dalsace, greatly influenced by Abraham Stone, the director of the Margaret Sanger clinic in New York, had been carrying out a one man crusade against unwanted pregnancy much earlier both as chief of laboratories at the hospital Saint-Antoine and in his private practice, by distributing diaphragms to his patients and as a lecturer on birth control before select audiences.[119]

The clinic was actually put in service at the end of December 1936 as part of the comprehensive medical facility of the garden city.[120] Early in December Dalsace appears to have presented a detailed plan of the needs and functions of the projected prenuptial clinic to the secretary of the Suresnes city hall M. Louis Boulonnois.[121] The plans were designed to improve the quality of births, to fight sterility, and to fight the plague of clandestine abortions. Sex education was to be provided to physicians, social workers, and the general public. The only material required, which was not routinely available in gynecological services, was occlusive diaphragms dispensed free for those not able to pay. The clinic, which remained in service until 1939, was open each Saturday afternoon; Dalsace took a small honorarium for his services so that no charge of clandestinity could be raised against him. It was a remarkable accomplishment, protected to be sure by Sellier, who was a force to be reckoned with whether as minister or only as mayor, but daring all the same. At the same time one must not lose sight of the fact that this clinic was part of the social hygiene and social engineering environment he attempted to create in Suresnes. There was no room for initiatives from below in the corporatist socialism he and his advisors aimed to establish.[122]

Were there other such illegal clinics nestled in socialist enclaves? I have suspicions but little hard evidence that in other Parisian suburbs such as Pantin, Vitry-sur-Seine, and especially Courbevoie, all with socialist mayors and with polyvalent medical facilities that included prenuptial clinics, family planning of some kind was practiced.[123] To these one should also add the socialist fortresses of Saint Etienne and Villeurbane, where accomplished socialist mayors, who openly denounced the "law of abomination," attempted to create comprehensive worker environments with an emphasis on social hygiene and health.

We cannot leave these truly heroic attempts by socialist physicians, mayors, councillors, and neo-Malthusians to initiate family planning facilities without remarking how very limited these attempts were and how far removed from support by women socialists, feminists, and public authorities compared to the situation in most other countries. A quick glance reveals the existence of numerous well-established and officially recognized sexual consultation and family planning clinics in Denmark, Norway, Sweden, Holland, Belgium, Germany, England and Catalonia; readily accessible and reasonably priced birth control publications available in all of these plus Austria and even Italy until 1926. In many of these countries birth control clinics were considered part of mothers' protection. In France, maternalist welfare measures were aimed at enhancing an unlimited maternity.

Perspectives

In reviewing the relationship between the French working-class movement and women in the interwar years one is almost forced to conclude that neither party nor trade union made any real effort to advance the position of women. When viewed in a comparative context, the underdevelopment of the movement becomes painfully clear: its feeble membership (except during crisis); its increasing distance from the industrial proletariat; its inability to attract or mobilize the unorganized and unwillingness to use the full armory of political actions against the Senate during the popular front; and the absence of any real socialist vision, any concrete program for improving the economic and social conditions of the majority of French. As we have seen, organized women were hobbled and victimized by these circumstances and were forced to play the game of class exclusiveness which kept them apart from the majority of women. The sad truth about women by 1939 was that they remained almost as isolated and unorganized as they had been two decades earlier, a situation to which the mainstream feminist organizations, with their own class-biased reliance on maternalism, contributed.

Latter-day students of socialism and women are hard put to explain why citizenship was for so long fiercely defended as a male preserve. Can one explain this national conservatism that runs across class lines as a consequence of the very events and instruments that have defined France's day in the sun?: the great revolution per se and its Rights of Man; the Napoleonic Code's delineation of civil rights; and universal manhood suffrage, extended in 1848 to an ignorant, priest-ridden (precisely what women were later accused of) rural population incapable of struggling for suffrage by itself. The end of World War I led to momentous restructuring in many European countries in which women gained the vote. In France, not victory but the losses were made emblematic in the postwar decades, with the "blue horizon" Chamber of veterans initiating a period of intransigent misogynism. The consequent denial of women's suffrage (engineered by the Radicals in the Senate, but with tacit support by SFIO leaders as well), became the central means of excluding French women from citizenship. This exclusion became part of the model by which the male-defined Republic represented itself to the outside world: as a system which had nothing to learn from others but rather which others ought to emulate.

Such an overview unfairly overlooks sporadic outbursts of grass-roots action by ordinary women seeking a redress of specific grievances. More ambitious and long range were the creative initiatives to improve the condition of women by socialist mayors and deputies and by a broad array of men and women in the liberal professions identified with the working-class movement. In these programs and projects the distance between reformers/leaders and the majority of ordinary women is sharply illuminated: the intended liberating actions were most often based on preconceptions about gender inequality; viewed from below, from the lifestyles of working-class women, their agenda of needs was very different from the reformers' priorities. This distance between leaders of elite groups and their potential following helps to explain why their initiatives did not become a catalyst for a national movement. Even had it been otherwise, the narrow-mindedness and immobilism of working-class organizations would have been a major obstacle.

Perhaps this is too gloomy a picture; perhaps the hesitant, partial, and largely ineffectual starts of socialists and feminists were only the birth pains of the full citizenship and excellent welfare system enjoyed by Frenchwomen today? It is impossible to deny any filiation between interwar suffragism and the final granting of the vote to women by DeGaulle in 1944. But this vote was not gained by women's own struggle, by their mobilization of public sentiment, either earlier or later. I find it difficult to view the role of "maternity" as a watershed of the contemporary welfare system. The term was clearly magical: it led men to rhapsodize about this exalted state; it prompted female socialist leaders to make inane comments about model mothers "who loved to darn socks" (Suzanne Lacore, 1932); and it convinced mainstream feminists to regard the "equality of difference" as the key to Frenchwomen's liberation. But the family policy inspired by the pro-natalists had the object of increasing the population by assisting women in the "fulfillment of their destiny" while restricting their aspirations and lives. As we have seen, both the quality and quantity of relief programs were very limited and their implementation often at odds with the recipients. Maternity, which blinded feminists and beguiled even socialists and progressive eugenicists, promoted an *inequality* of difference and acted as an obstacle to reforms more central to the lives of most women, who had had quite enough of motherhood. Those who equated maternity with a welfare system then and now failed to comprehend that the very best welfare system, aimed at reducing the responsibilities of home and child care, is also a means of making a traditional female obligation more palatable. Such systems, generally designed by men, who despite universal suffrage still dominate the political order, have the effect of maintaining the existing gender imbalance.

Nevertheless, using the yardstick of changes in "power relations" suggested by Louise Tilly,[124] one may conclude that the situation of French women at the end of the 1930s was far from hopeless. By means of their own initiatives and while facing great obstacles they had gained considerable control over their childbearing, allowing their families to survive and even to upgrade their lifestyles. That mastery was the precondition for the growth of women's selfhood, expressed in the desire for an identity, freed from male fantasies of coquetry, seductiveness, and maternity, for which neither socialism nor feminism had pointed the way. *La lutte continue!*

Notes

1. For the *sui generis* conception of French feminism as "familial" or "relational" and insistence that it cannot be evaluated by the standards of a comparative model, see Karen Offen, "Depopulation, Nationalism, and Feminism in Fin-de-Siècle France," *American Historical Review* 89, 3 (June 1984). For a rejection of this narrow perspective, see Claire Goldberg Moses, "Debating the Present, Writing the Past: 'Feminism' in French History and Historiography," *Radical History Review* 52 (winter 1992).
2. See Charles Sowerwine, *Sisters or Citizens?: Women and Socialism in France since 1876* (Cambridge, Mass., 1984).
3. See Emary Aronson, "In a Class by Themselves: The Social Basis of the Women's Socialist Movement in France and England, 1899-1914" (Ph.D. diss., University of Chicago, 1993), pp. 180-88.
4. See Laurence Klejman and Florence Rochefort, *L'Egalité en Marche* (Paris, 1989), chaps. 5-7 and Marilyn Boxer, "Socialism Faces Feminism: The Failure of Synthesis in France, 1879-1914," in *Socialist Women: European Socialist Feminism in the 19th and Early 20th Centuries*, eds. Marilyn Boxer and Jean H. Quataert (New York, 1978).
5. See Suzanne Collette, "Le Parti socialiste et l'organisation des femmes: A Propos de la révision des statuts," *La vie socialiste*, 1 June 1929; Berthe Fouchère, "La femme et le socialisme," *La Bataille Socialiste*, December-February 1929, pp. 40-43.
6. For the following, see Henry Hauk, "Organisation des femmes – réorganisation de la propagande," *La vie socialiste*, 10 May 1930, pp. 9-11; "A propos de l'organisation des femmes," *La vie socialiste*, 17 May 1930, pp. 7-9; and Germaine Picard-Moch, "Le recrutement des femmes socialistes est un problème masculin," *La vie socialiste*, 31 May 1930, pp. 8-9.
7. For the following, see SFIO, *Compte rendu: XXVII congrès (Bordeaux)*, 9-11 June 1930 (Paris, 1930), pp. 161-207.
8. Marthe Louis-Levy, "A propos du Rayon 'Femmes'," *La Bataille Socialiste*, June/July 1930, p. 7.
9. Germaine Picard-Moch, "La question féminine dans le mouvement socialiste," *La Nouvelle Revue Socialiste* 32 (15 July-15 August 1930). This article certainly shows a strange turnabout considering her attack on male indifference and hostility during the 1930 congress.
10. Marthe Louis-Levy, "Les femmes dans le parti: Projets d'organisation," *La Bataille Socialiste*, October 1930, pp. 9-11. For the old saw about French indiscipline to explain the dearth of women in the party, see Berthe Fouchère, "Difficultés de la propaganda socialiste chez les femmes," *La Nouvelle Revue Socialiste*, September-October 1930, pp. 530-33.
11. See Suzanne Collette, "A propos de l'organisation des femmes: Réponse à Marthe Louis-Levy," *La Bataille Socialiste*, February 1931, pp. 10-11, and the intervention of Lacore in SFIO, *Compte rendu: XXVIII congrès (Tours)*, 24-27 May 1931 (Paris, 1931), pp. 216-30.
12. Thérèse Bonnier-Renaudel complained about the infighting among women socialist leaders in "Chez les femmes socialistes," *La Vie Socialiste*, 27 July 1931, p. 10. To give such charges any importance would be to fall into the trap of blaming the socialist women for having created their own situation.
13. SFIO, *Compte rendu: XXIX congrès (Paris)*, 29 May-1 June 1932 (Paris, 1932), pp. 107-109, 266-67.

14. See *Third International Conference of Socialist Women of the LSI, Brussels, August 3-4, 1928*, International Institute for Social History Archive (IISGA), C. 129/28; and "Suzanne Buisson to Secretariat," IISGA, SAI 4343.

15. IISGA, *Frauenbeilage der Internationalen Informationen*, June 1936, pp. 251-52.

16. Ibid., May 1927, pp. 228-29.

17. SFIO, *Compte rendu: XXVI Congrès (Nancy)*, 9-12 June 1929 (Paris, 1929): 386-87.

18. "Le programme du rassemblement populaire," *Le Populaire*, 11 January 1936.

19. See "Remarques sur L'Histoire des Femmes," in *Femmes et histoire: colloque, Sorbonne, November 13-14, 1992*, eds. Georges Duby and Michelle Perrot (Paris, 1993), pp. 63-66.

20. See, for instance, Adelheid von Saldern, *Häuserleben: Zur Geschichte städtischen Arbeiterwohnens vom Kaiserreich bis heute* (Bonn, 1995); John Burnett, *A Social History of Housing, 1815-1985* (London, 1986); and Helmut Weihsmann, *Das Rote Wien: Sozialdemokratische Architektur und Kommunalpolitik 1919-1934* (Vienna, 1985).

21. Estimates vary, but nearly 20 percent of Parisian workers' domiciles were classified as slums. Altogether 87,797 public housing units were built between the wars, only 61,000 were considered affordable by workers. See *Annuaire statistique de la Ville de Paris* (1935-1937). The best analysis of the housing crisis can be found in Françoise Cribier, "Le logement d'une génération de jeunes Parisiens à l'époque du front populaire," in *Villes ouvrières*, eds. Suzanne Magi and Christian Topolov (Paris, 1988), pp. 112-19.

22. See Robert Frankenstein, *Le Prix du réarmement français 1935-1939* (Paris, 1982), pp. 82 and 303.

23. See Marc Boyer, "1935 et les vacances des Français" and the other articles on the local situation in *Le Mouvement Social* 150 (January-March, 1990).

24. See Richard Holt, *Sport and Society in Modern France* (London, 1981), pp. 201-208.

25. That social concentration was also reflected in the delegation of socialist deputies, among whom members of the working class virtually disappeared. See Alfred Wahl, "Les députés SFIO de 1924 à 1940: Essai de sociologie," *Le Mouvement Social* 106 (January-March, 1979) and Tony Judt, *Marxism and the French Left: Studies on Labour and Politics in France 1830-1981* (Oxford, 1989), pp. 130-33, 136-42.

26. See Helmut Gruber, *Léon Blum, French Socialism, and the Popular Front: A Case of Internal Contradictions* (Ithaca, N.Y., 1986), pp. 5-7, 10-14, 36-38, 44-49.

27. The *amicales* attracted a cross section of the population: blue-collar workers, employees in insurance companies and banks, shop assistants, functionaries, and civil servants. See Jean-Pierre Rioux, "Les socialistes dans l'entreprise au temps du front populaire: quelques remarques sur les amicales socialistes (1936-1939)," *Le Mouvement Social* 106 (January-March, 1979); Donald N. Baker, "The Socialists and the Workers of Paris: The Amicales Socialistes, 1936-40," *International Review of Social History* 24 (1979); and Frank Georgi, "Les Amicales socialistes d'entreprise en province: le cas de la Fédération du Nord (1936-1939)," *Le Mouvement Social* 153 (October-December, 1990).

28. The most penetrating, concise analysis of the origins and later development of French socialist theory is still George Lichtheim, *Marxism in Modern France* (New York, 1966), pp. 17-46.

29. In a private letter Blum assured Lacore that she would not have to bother her head about figures, laws, and bureaucratic complications. See Suzanne Lacore,

"Comment Léon Blum me fit Ministre de l'enfance," *Le Vétéran Socialiste* 18 (March 1960).

30. Birgit Buddel-Asmus, "Politische Kultur und Engagement von Frauen im Frankreich der Zwischenkriegszeit am Beispiel der drei Frauen in der ersten Volksfrontregierung," Hausarbeit, University of Bremen, 1993.

31. See Ellen Furlough, *Consumer Cooperation in France: The Politics of Consumption 1834-1930* (Ithaca, N.Y., 1993), p. 223.

32. See Madeleine Roberioux, "Le mouvement syndical et les femmes jusqu'au front populaire," *Le Féminisme et ses enjeux* (Paris, 1988), pp. 70-82; Judt, *Marxism and the French Left*, pp. 155-58.

33. For instance, Germaine Fouchère, *La travail des femmes* (Paris, 1934); C.G.T. Fédération des Syndicats d'Employées, *La femme au travail ou au foyer* (Rennes, 1938); and the speeches of Chavenard at virtually every CGT national congress after 1929.

34. See C.G.T., *Congrès Confédéral de Paris: Compte rendu sténographié des débats* (17-20 September 1929): 264-71; (15-18 September 1931): 479-82; (1933): 307-09; and (24-27 September 1935): 269-73.

35. For the majority of shop floor women workers a reduction of daily hardships was clearly more important than keeping the full variety of employment opportunities open. In Sweden and Norway protective legislation was supported by the male-dominated unions but opposed by the women themselves. See Ulla Wikander, Alice Kessler-Harris, and Jane Lewis (eds.), *Protecting Women: Labor Legislation in Europe, the United States, and Australia, 1880-1995* (Champaign, Ill., 1995).

36. See Jean-Louis Robert, "La CGT et la famille ouvrière, 1914- 1918: Première approche," *Le Mouvement Social* 116 (July-September 1981): 58-59.

37. Apparently, equal pay was considered too radical by the CGT leadership, and female trade union leaders were too timid and inexperienced to ask for it. See Sian Reynolds, "Women, Men, and the 1936 Strikes in France," in *The French and Spanish Popular Fronts: Comparative Perspectives*, eds. Martin S. Alexander and Helen Graham (Cambridge, Mass., 1989), p. 197.

38. See Annie Fourcaut, *Femmes à l'usine: Ouvrières et surintendantes dans les entreprises françaises de l'entre-deux-guerres* (Paris, 1982), p. 237. Since paid vacations were granted only after a year's employment by the same firm, women, whose work was often interrupted or who were fired in the 12th month, were less assured of this benefit.

39. See Catherine Rhein, "Jeunes femmes au travail dans le Paris de l'entre-deux guerres" (Ph.D. diss., University of Paris VII, 1977); Monique Couteaux, "Les femmes et les grèves de 1936: L'Exemple des grands magasins" (M.A. thesis, University of Paris VII, 1975); Reynolds, "Women, Men, 1936 Strikes," 189-97; Marie-Hélène Zylberberg-Hocquard, *Femmes et féminisme dans le mouvement ouvrier français* (Paris, 1981).

40. See Paulette Birgi, "Femmes salariées et grèves des mois de mai-juin 1936 en France" (M.A. thesis, University of Paris, 1969); and Suzanne Lacore [one of Blum's three subministers], *Femmes socialistes* (Paris, 1932).

41. See Theresa McBride, "French Women and Trade Unionism: The First Hundred Years," in *The World of Women's Trade Unionism: Comparative Historical Essays*, ed. Norbert C. Soldon (Westport, Conn., 1985), pp. 35-46.

42. Quoted in Huguette Bouchardeau, *Pas d'histoire, les femmes ... 50 ans d'histoire des femmes, 1918-1968* (Paris, 1977), pp. 170-71, from articles in *L'Oeuvre* and *La Française*.

43. McBride, "French Women Trade Unionism," p. 46.

44. For the following, see Anne-Marie Sohn, "Exemplarité et limites de la participation féminine à la vie syndicale: Les Institutrices de la CGTU," *Revue d'Histoire moderne et contemporaine* (July-September, 1977): 394-405 and Marlène Cacouault, "Diplôme et célibat: Les femmes professeurs de lycée entre les deux guerres," in *Madame ou mademoiselle?: Itinéraires de la solitude féminine XVIII-XX siècle* (Paris, 1984), pp. 177-91.

45. See Françoise Blum, "Féminisme et syndicalisme: Les femmes dans la fédération de l'habillement, 1914-1935" (M.A. thesis, University of Paris I, 1978) and Agnès Denis Morillon, "Les femmes et le syndicalisme dans la fédération CGT de l'habillement, 1936-1946" (M.A. thesis, University of Paris I, 1981).

46. See, for instance, Karen Offen, "Women and the Politics of Motherhood in France 1920-1940," *Working Paper* 87/293, Florence, European University Institute, 1987; and Anna Cova, "French Feminism and Maternity: Theories and Policies 1890-1918," in *Maternity and Gender Politics: Women and the Rise of European Welfare States 1880-1950*, eds. Gisela Bock and Pat Thane (London, 1991).

47. See Paul E.A. Smith, "Women's Political and Civil Rights in France, 1918-1940" (Ph.D. diss., Oxford University, 1991), pp. 1-10.

48. See Steven C. Hause and Anne R. Kenney, *Women's Suffrage and Social Politics in the French Third Republic* (Princeton, N.J., 1984), pp. 253-61.

49. That France had anything to learn from other countries was explicitly denied in the Senate's report on female suffrage of 1919 and became the basis for the Senate's rejection of the Chamber's integral suffrage bill in 1922.

50. "Marianne's Citizens? Women, the Republic, and Universal Suffrage in France," in *Women, State and Revolution: Essays in Power and Gender in Europe since 1789*, ed. Sian Reynolds (Brighton, 1986), pp. 104-20.

51. "L'Histoire du vote des femmes: Réflexion sur la spécificité française," in Duby and Perrot (eds.), *Femmes et histoire*, pp. 81-86.

52. For instance, see Bracke, "Le vote des femmes," *Le populaire*, 17 February 1935, where one finds the statements "women are half of humanity," "only the party of the proletariat supports political rights of both sexes," and "sexual equality is basic to the proletariat," among others.

53. See Léon Blum, "Le suffrage des femmes," *Le populaire*, 24 December 1927. In 1933 Blum claimed, "Women would have the vote already if they really wanted it." Quoted in Marthe Louis-Levy, *L'Emancipation politique des femmes* (Paris, 1933), p. 34.

54. *Le matin*, 23 May 1937.

55. For the following, see Andrée Marty-Capgras, "Le suffrage des femmes," *La bataille socialiste* 86 (15 March 1935). Paule Gautier-Billaudel, "Le front populaire et la question féminine" (mémoire de recherche, University of Grenoble, 1986), pp. 120-27; and Smith, "Women's Political and Civil Rights," pp. 11-13, 217-18.

56. Kraemer-Bach was a member of the Radical party's executive committee and became the secretary of its bureau in 1930. See Marcelle Kraemer-Bach, *La longue route* (Paris, 1988).

57. See Christine Bard, *Les filles de Marianne: Histoire des féminismes 1914-1940* (Paris, 1995), pp. 182-83, 235-37. Bard points out (388-89) that the average age of members in feminist organizations was 46.40 years in 1920, 50.68 in 1930, and 57.30 in 1939.

58. For a good presentation of maternalist feminism, see Anna Cova, "Cécile Brunschvicg (1877-1946) et la protection de la maternité," *Colloque sur l'histoire de la sécurité sociale à Strasbourg, 1988* (Paris, 1989).

59. The classic statement for conservative feminism was made by Edmée de la
    Rochefoucault in a letter to the Senate in 1925: "We do not wish at any time to
    depart from the greatest courtesy and we desire in our acts to preserve the per-
    fect moderation appropriate to our sex." Quoted in Cox, "Mouvement suffrage
    féminin," 53.
60. Klejman and Rochefort, *Egalité en marche*, pp. 294-95.
61. For the following, see Smith, "Women's Rights in France," pp. 47, 107-09.
62. The rather terse police report includes clippings from two tabloids, *L'Ere Nouvelle*
    of 10 November and *Le quotidien*, of 11 November. Both accounts are very well
    disposed to Verone's actions and support her charges against the police. See
    Archive de la Préfecture de Police, (hereafter APP) dossier BA 1651,
    no.259.616. This was not the only favorable newspaper account of suffragist
    action, and it raises questions about whether public opinion was as massively
    opposed to women's suffrage as feminists and socialists appeared to believe.
63. For the following, see Louise Weiss, *Ce que femme veut: Souvenirs de la IIIe
    République* (Paris, 1946), and, *Mémoires d'une Européenne*, vol. 3 (Paris, 1970).
64. For the following, see APP, dossier BA 1651, no.90.772.1. Furious at Brun-
    schvicg's stalling and obstruction and her appointment due to Radical pressure
    on Blum as the third woman subminister, she and twenty other women disrupted
    Brunschvicg's speech to an international group in July 1936 (no.90.772).
65. See Ellen Furlough, "Selling the American Way in Interwar France: Prix Uniques
    and the Salons des Arts Ménagers," *Journal of Social History* 26, 3 (spring, 1993):
    509.
66. Smith, "Women's Rights in France," pp. 203-05, 211-12.
67. Henriette Alquier, "La maternité, fonction sociale," *Bulletin des groupes féministes
    de l'enseignement laïque*, supplément de *L'Ecole Emancipée* 36 (27 February 1927).
68. Rhein, "Jeunes femmes au travail," pp. 226-27, remarks that most of these lacked
    indoor running water, making personal hygiene very difficult.
69. Official resident population in these was still 145,116 in 1936 (certainly a con-
    servative estimate in view of migration) with the tuberculosis rate at 2.88 per
    100! *Annuaire Statistique*, 1935ff, pp. 528-29.
70. In 1929 there were 350,036 formal tenants; in 1936, there were 188,185. For-
    eigners comprised some 25 to 30 percent of the in/out migration. *Annuaire
    Statistique*, 1929ff, p. 296; 1935ff, p. 530.
71. See Suzanne Magri, "Consensus ou résistance populaire au réformisme social
    dans le domaine du logement?: L'exemple du mouvement des locataires
    parisiens," *Cahiers de la Recherche Architecturale* 15-17 (1985): 18-23.
72. For the following, see Françoise Soulignac, *La banlieue parisienne: Cent cinquante
    ans de transformation* (Paris, 1993); and Centre de documentation d'histoire des
    techniques, *Evolution de la géographie industrielle de Paris et sa proche banlieue au
    XIXe siècle 2* (Paris, 1976): 592-96; and Tyler Stovall, *The Rise of the Paris Red Belt*
    (Berkeley, 1990) and Annie Fourcaut, *Bobigny: banlieue rouge* (Paris, 1988).
73. *Annuaire Statistique*, 1935ff, p. 525.
74. See Katherine Burlen (ed.), *La Banlieue Oasis: Henri Sellier et les cités-jardins
    1900-1940* (Paris, 1987).
75. "Typhoid and other waterborne diseases continued to be a threat even in Paris
    into the 1930s." See Jean-Pierre Goubert, *La conquête de l'eau: L'avènement de la
    santé à l'âge industriel* (Paris, 1986), pp. 160-61, 245-56. Deaths from tuberculo-
    sis in the whole population still was 27.6 percent of mortality; for children ages 1
    to 5 it was 43 percent! *Annuaire Statistique*, 1935ff, 178, pp. 370-77.

76. Buisson was head of the SFIO's CDFS and the leading female socialist in the 1930s. See *Les répercussions du travail féminin* (Paris, 1931), pp. 4-8.
77. For the following, see Robert L. Frost, "Machine Liberation: Inventing Housewives and Home Appliances in Interwar France," *French Historical Studies* 18 (spring, 1993), and Furlough, "Selling the American Way." Only 30 percent of Parisians subscribed to electricity service in 1932. Domestic electricity consumption in France was one-seventh that of Switzerland and one-twentieth that of Norway. See J.-P. Goubert, *Du luxe au confort* (Paris, 1988), pp. 67-74.
78. For the following, see Rhein, "Jeunes femmes au travail" and Fourcaut, *Femmes à l'usine*, as well as D. Gardey, "Les femmes, le bureau et l'electricité," *Bulletin d'histoire de l'électricité*, 19-20 (June-December 1992); Louise Tilly, "Worker Families and Occupation in Industrial France," *The Tocqueville Review* 5, 2 (fall/winter 1983); Catherine Rhein, "Structures d'emploi et marchés du travail dans l'agglomération parisienne au cours de l'entre-deux-guerres," in Magri and Topolov (eds.), *Villes ouvrières*; and Daniel Bertaux and Isabelle Bertaux-Wiame, "Jungarbeit bei freier Unterkunft und Verpflegung:Bäckerlehrlinge und Hausmädchen im Frankreich der Zwischenkriegszeit," in *Mündliche Geschichte und Arbeiterbewegung* eds. Gerhard Botz and Joseph Weidenholzer (Vienna, 1984).
79. See Pierre Pierrard, *L'Eglise et les ouvrières en France (1840-1940)* (Paris, 1984), pp. 506-507.
80. See Louise A. Tilly, "Women's Collective Action and Feminism in France, 1870-1914," in *Class Conflict and Collective Action,* eds. Louise A. Tilly and Charles Tilly (New York, 1981), p. 226 and Anne-Marie Sohn, "Les roles féminins dans la vie privée: Approche méthodologique et bilan de recherches," *Revue d'histoire moderne et contemporaine* 28 (October-December 1981): 606-11.
81. For the following, see Linda L. Clark, *Schooling the Daughters of Marianne: Textbooks and the Socialization of Girls in Modern French Primary Schools* (Albany, 1984), pp. 82-99, 102-104, 108-109; John W. Shaffer, "Family, Class, and Young Women: Occupational Expectations in Nineteenth Century Paris," in Wheaton and Hareven (eds.), *Family and Sexuality*, pp. 195-96; and Matine Martin, "Femmes et société: le travail ménager 1919-1939" (Ph.D. diss., University of Paris VII, 1984), pp. 120-35.
82. Monthly wages of semi-professional jobs in 1935 Paris were high: 950 to 1,125 francs for nurses, 1,200 to 1,400 francs for social workers, 3,000 francs for executive secretaries. But sales clerks at the *prix-uniques* earned 450 to 600 francs. See Françoise Thebaud, *Quand nos grand-mères donnaient la vie: La maternité en France dans l'entre-deux-guerres* (Lyon, 1986), p. 308.
83. See Mary Louise Roberts, "Samson and Delilah Revisited: The Politics of Women's Fashion in 1920s France," *The American Historical Review* 98 (June 1993).
84. *Marianne et les lapins: L'obsession démographique* (Paris, 1991).
85. Françoise Thébaud, "Donner la vie: Histoire de la maternité en France entre des deux guerres" (Ph.D. diss., University of Paris VII, 1982), pp. 15-16.
86. Michael Teitelbaum and Jay M. Winter, *The Fear of Population Decline* (New York, 1985), pp. 158, 160. The real problem was not the birthrate but the extremely high death rate, which significantly exceeded live births throughout the interwar years and was the highest among developed countries. For France, see Colin Dyer, *Population and Society in Twentieth Century France* (New York, 1978), pp. 82-83; for Paris, see *Annuaire Statistique*, 1923-37.
87. War casualty figures were something of a red herring. Statistics for the actual number of soldiers killed vary considerable (Dyer, *Population*, pp. 40-41). Annex-

ation of Alsace- Lorraine made the loss of males in French society far less significant than pro-natalists were prepared to mention.

88. For the following, see Richard Tomlinson, "The Disappearance of France, 1896-1940: French Politics and the Birth Rate," *The Historical Journal* 28, 2 (1985): 405-07, 411-12; Marie-Monique Huss, "Pro-natalism in the Interwar Period in France," *Journal of Contemporary History* 25 (1990): 440-44, 51-52; William H. Schnei der, *Quality and Quantity: The Quest for Biological Regeneration in Twentieth-Century France* (New York, 1990), pp. 176-77, 185; and J. M. Winter, "Family, and Fertility in Twentieth-Century Europe," in *The European Experience of Declining Fertility, 1850-1970: The Quiet Revolution*, eds. John R. Gillis et al., (Cambridge, Mass., 1992), pp. 299-303.

89. Christine Peyrefitte, "Les premiers sondages d'opinion," in René Remond and Janine Bourdin (eds.), *Edouard Daladier. Chef de gouvernement* (Paris, 1977), pp. 274-75.

90. That is the conclusion reached in the excellent study of Susan Pedersen, *Family, Dependence, and the Origins of the Welfare State: Britain and France, 1914-1945* (Cambridge, Mass., 1993), pp. 421ff.

91. Philip Nord, "The Welfare State in France, 1870-1914," *French Historical Studies* 18 (spring 1994): 863ff.

92. See Anna Cova, "Cécile Brunschvicg (1877-1946) et la protection de la maternité," Colloque sur l'histoire de la sécurité sociale à Strasbourg, 1988 (Paris, 1989), p. 94.

93. See Laura Lee Downs, "Women in Industry, 1914-1939: The Employers' Perspective: A Comparative Study of the French and British Metals Industry" (Ph.D. diss., Columbia University, 1987); and Petersen, *Family, Dependence, Welfare State*, p. 288.

94. For the following, see D. V. Glass, *Population: Policies and Movements in Europe* (New York, 1967 [1940]), pp. 112-14; Downs, "Women in Industry," pp. 213-23, 342-63; Sian Reynolds, "Who Wanted the Crèches? Working Mothers and the Birth Rate in France 1900-1950," in *Continuity and Change* 5, 2 (1990): 173-97; *Annuaire Statistique* (crèches), (1923): 488-89; (1929): 478-80; (1932): 564; (1935): 628; Yvonne Knibiehler et al., *Cornettes et blouses blanches: Les infirmières dans la société française (1880-1980)* (Paris, 1984), pp. 137-62; Yvonne Kniebiehler and Catherine Fouquet, *La femme et les médecins: Analyse historique* (Paris, 1983), pp. 235-49, 269-74; and Lion Murard and Patrick Zylberman, "Robert-Henri Hazemann, Urbanist social," *URBI: Art, histoire et ethnologie des villes*, 10 (winter 1987): 68-76.

95. Knibiehler and Fouquet, *Femme et médecins*,pp. 239-49. By the end of the 1930s about 65 percent of births took place in public facilities. The overwhelming majority of these serving the popular classes (others went to private clinics) were quite horrifying in the lack of adequate hygiene in wards mixing otherwise healthy women with those suffering from tuberculosis and venereal disease. See Fred B. Burkhard, "Henriette Valet's *Madame 60 bis*: French Social Realities and Literary Politics in the 1930s," *French Historical Studies* 18 (fall 1993), about this semi-fictional best seller of 1934 that exposes the conditions in the maternity ward of the *Hotel Dieu*, one of the most prestigious older Parisian hospitals.

96. Knibiehler, *Cornettes*, pp. 153-57.

97. Downs, "Women in Industry," pp. 342-48.

98. Abortion was outlawed in most of the countries discussed in this volume, but France was virtually alone in proscribing all contraceptive devices, publicity about them, and even sex manuals that advised about spacing conceptions.

99. The reason given for this exception was that men had to be protected from vene-
    real disease. Presumably this was meant for soldiers engaging in commercial sex
    and for civilian clients (such as the politicians who framed the law?) who fre-
    quented closed houses of prostitution. Protecting women against the venereal
    disease they might receive from their legal partners seems not to have been
    considered.
100. Midwives, especially those sentenced before, were fined and imprisoned. See
    Anne-Marie Dourlen-Rollier, *La vérité sur l'avortement* (Paris, 1963), pp. 142-52.
    For similar findings in the provinces, see Mathilde Dubesset and Michelle Zan-
    carini-Fournel, *Parcours de femmes: Réalités et représentations, Saint- Etienne 1880-
    1950* (Lyons, 1993), pp. 151-52. Judges in other countries – Germany and
    Austria, for instance – also refused to send women convicted of abortion to jail
    and put them on probation instead.
101. For instance: Marguerite Pichon-Landry, Marguerite de Witte-Schlumberger,
    and Cécile Brunschvicg.
102. A pamphlet found among thousands of others was a catalog of contraceptives
    offered for sale under strict measures of anonymity and with instructions for their
    application. It offered five styles of condoms at from 39 to 75 centimes each and
    diaphragms and their accessories, pointing out that a doctor's visit would be nec-
    essary for a fitting but that this would not incriminate him before the law. See
    Institute Hygiène Genéve, *Plus d'avortements! Plus d'avaries!: Hygiène, Beauté,
    Santé* (Geneva, n.d.), 20 centimes. Also in German and Italian language versions.
    IFHS, Lambert Collection 14 AS 515/4.
103. See Wally Secombe, "Men's 'Marital Rights' and Women's 'Wifely Duties':
    Changing Conjugal Relations in the Fertility Decline," in *European Experience of
    Declining Fertility, 1850- 1970*, pp. 69-82. Condoms became popular through mass
    distribution among soldiers during World War I. Methods of abortion became
    safer, especially if practiced by a midwife or physician, who treated initiated abor-
    tions as miscarriages. See Angus McLaren, "Abortion in France: Women and the
    Regulation of Family Size 1800-1914," *French Historical Studies* 10 (spring 1978):
    473-79.
104. See Roger-H. Guerrand, *La libre maternité 1896-1969* (Tournai, 1971), p. 59. The
    CGT took a similar position. See Francis Ronsin, "La classe ouvrière et le neo-
    malthusianism: l'exemple français avant 1914," *Le Mouvement Social* 106 (Janu-
    ary-March 1979): 95-99.
105. For the following, see Francis Ronsin, *La grève des ventres: Propagande néo-
    malthusienne et baisse de la natalité française* (Paris, 1980), pp. 200-201; Sixte-
    Quenin, *Le problème de la natalité au parlement* (Paris, 1933), pp. 3-24; and
    Thébaud, "Donner la vie," pp. 114-15.
106. Guerrand, *Libre maternité*, pp. 69-70.
107. See the two significant studies of *La garçonne*: Anne-Marie Sohn, "La Garçonne
    face à l'opinion publique: type littéraire ou type social des années 20?" *Le Mou-
    vement Social* 83 (July-September 1972) and Mary Louise Roberts, "'This Civi-
    lization No Longer Has Sexes': *La garçonne* and Cultural Crisis in France after
    World War I," *Gender and History* 4 (spring, 1992).
108. See Pierre Birnbaum, *Un mythe politique: la "République juive: de Léon Blum à
    Mendès France"* (Paris, 1988), pp. 221-23.
109. *Le populaire* was among the few journals to defend Margueritte against the vicious
    personal attacks, but it carefully avoided discussing the novel itself. See Patrick
    de Villepin, *Victor Margueritte: La vie scandaleuse de l'auteur de "La Garçonne"*
    (Paris, 1991), p. 194.

110. The huge success of Margueritte's subsequent novel about abortion, *Ton corps est à toi* of 1926, as well as his later work in which birth control is discussed made a mockery of the 1920/23 law. It was only one of many examples by which Article 3 of the law was contested by individuals too prominent to bring before the courts. *La grande reforme* edited by the anarchist neo-Malthusian Eugène Humbert from 1931 to 1939 dealt with family planning, birth control, and eugenics and attracted prominent deputies, physicians, radical feminists, and sex reformers as contributors.

111. See Schneider, *Quality and Quantity*, pp. 183-86; and Tomlinson, "*Disappearance France*," pp. 411-12.

112. See Doctor Edouard Toulouse, "L'Association d'Etude Sexologiques: Déclaration et Programme," *La Prophylaxie antivéner ienne* 3 (September 1931): 597-607. The Association quickly became affiliated with the World League for Sexual Reform.

113. *Bulletin de l'Association d'études sexologiques*, 1931 to 1934.

114. *Le problème sexuel* 4 (1934).

115. The class bias of such views – that the lower orders, which bred more than the higher ones, needed to be screened before reproduction, which should be planned and limited in any case – was very explicit in the writings of some of the most important members of this directorate. See, for instance, Justin Sicard de Plauzoles, "L'Avenir et la préservation de la race: Eugénique," *Prophylaxie antivénérienne* 4 (1932): 201-203.

116. Docteur Toulouse, *La question sexuelle et la femme* (Paris, 1918), *La question sociale* (Paris, 1921), "Le tabou," *L'Oeuvre*, 22 July 1931; and "Un effort constructif," *Pamphlet*,numéro spécial (12 May 1933). All from the private archive of Dr. Jean Dalsace, Box "birth control 1932-35." I am indebted to Mme. Vellay for access to her father's papers in his medical office.

117. See Henri Sellier, *Radio address*, 6 June 1936 (typescript), Archives National (AN), private papers of Henri Sellier, temporary box 9; and "Un interview de Monsieur Henri Sellier, Ministre de la Santé Publique," *Revue Médicale "Guérir,"* 15 July 1936. I am greatly indebted to M. Guillot, conservateur at the AN, for making unclassified material available to me there as well as in the archive of the mayoralty in Suresnes.

118. Dalsace applauded Sellier for his firm stand against the "marathon of maternity" and argued for courses in sex education, the creation of special dispensaries for women like those in England and the United States, and that these provide the means for women, who for hygienic, social, economic, or moral reasons should not become pregnant, to prevent it. "Travail et natalité," *La Flèche*, 21 November 1936, Municipal Archive of Suresnes (AMS), files of Cabinet Ministériel of Henri Sellier.

119. Interview with Mme. Vellay, 3 September 1993. Also, "Conférence de M. le docteur Jean Dalsace, 'Le Birth Control,' devant le Groupe d'études philosophiques et scientifiques pour l'examen des tendances nouvelles," 15 February 1934 and Conférence de M. le docteur Jean Dalsace, 'Le problème de la natalité dirigée,' devant Les Mercredis Documentaires, 6 March 1935. Both typescripts are in the Dalsace Archive, box 1934-36, nos.59 and 67.

120. See the following exchange of letters: "M. Louis Boulonnois, Secretary General de la Mairie de Suresnes to Dr. Jean Dalsace," 18 December 1936; "M. Louis Boulonnois to Mme. Gonse Boas, Président de la Société Maternelle 'La Pouponnière," 30 December 1936; and "Mme. Gonse Boas to M. Louis Boulonnois," 31 December 1936, AMS.

121. "Consultations prénuptiales et prénatales," AMS. See also Jean Dalsace, "Quelques étapes difficiles du planning familial en France," *Planning Familial*, June 1965.

122. See Murad and Zylberman, "Hazemann Urbanist Social," pp. 71-79.

123. See G. Schreiber, "Le centre familial de santé et de médecine préventive de Courbevoie," *La presse médicale*, December 1931, AMS, file for Cabinet Ministériel, carton 2; and Annie Fourcaut (ed.), *Banlieue rouge 1920-1960: Années Thorez, années Gabin – archétype du populaire, banc d'essai des modernités* (Paris, 1992).

124. "Industrialization and Gender Equality," Center for Studies of Social Change, *New School for Social Research Working Paper*, No. 148 (1992).

Chapter 8

The French Communist Party and Women 1920-1939

From "Feminism" to Familialism

Christine Bard and *Jean-Louis Robert*
Translated by Nicole Dombrowski

Contrary to typical French political behavior, the French Communist party (PCF), from its inception in 1920, devoted a remarkable amount of attention to attracting women to its ranks. It advocated sexual equality and created several women's organizations devoted to such issues as peace, anti-fascism, and the education of young girls. It specifically denounced the exploitation of women workers, calling upon them to join the United General Confederation of Labor (CGTU). And finally, for nearly a decade the PCF fought the Law of 1920, which severely punished women caught having abortions and prohibited all advertisement and circulation of information on contraception.[1]

Had the PCF succeeded in escaping the dominant ideology of the time concerning the place of women in French society? No, not exactly. Still, in the atmosphere of the period following the war few favored women's emancipation. The PCF was, therefore, unique, especially because it employed directives, slogans, and images issued from Moscow. This particular "wind from the East" carried with it the promise of women's liberation. Lenin himself declared as much by announcing that "the moment has come when each cook must now learn to govern the state." On 10

November 1923, the French communist women's newspaper, *L'Ouvrière*
hailed Lenin's call exclaiming, "Glory to the Russian Revolution which
has liberated women!"

Despite this early solidarity, ten years later the PCF sacrificed its commitment to contraception and the freedom to have abortions on the altar
of the Popular Front. Softening its revolutionary rhetoric, the PCF insisted
upon its republican and national character. It adapted its discourse on
women to fit its new conciliatory strategy; from that moment on femininity, maternity, and respectability were lauded according to the fashion of
the day. At the National Conference of the Union of French Women held
in July of 1936, Jacques Duclos, then leader of the PCF, declared: "Yes,
comrades, women of the PCF, it is not necessary that just because you are
communists, you should no longer concern yourself with fashion, love,
and psychological problems that have interested your sisters."[2]

Paradoxically, the party that paid the most attention to its propaganda
among women and on behalf of women actually had a very small number
of women members, even though the engagement of its female militants
tended to hide that reality. The problem stemmed partly from the fact that
the party was a sort of foreign transplant into French culture, but in addition, by joining the Popular Front, the PCF entered an arena of electoral
politics from which women were excluded. Its rank and file, especially
during the 1930s, reflected the cultural characteristics of a working class
in which sexual hierarchy was a reality. At the time of its second birth, as
a mass political party with nearly 300,000 members, the PCF mirrored a
political and social reality in which feminism no longer had a place.[3]

Women's Place in the Party

In 1907, the International Socialist Conference of Stuttgart established
the line of conduct for socialist women, forbidding them to collaborate
with the so-called bourgeois feminists. A few French socialist women
such as Madeleine Pelletier, Hélène Brion, and Marthe Bigot resisted this
prohibition with grave consequences and tried to maintain a radical feminism on the extreme left, which expressed itself after 1917 through *La
Voix des femmes* (the Voice of Women). They joined the PCF majority at
the Congress of Tours in December 1920, at least symbolically because of
their pacifist convictions during the war years. But they numbered no
more than a handful; only a dozen women were present among the 370
participants. Among them, seven (out of 160) voted for the communist
motion of Cachin-Frossard and two (out of 80) followed the Longuet-
Faure socialist line. They were enthusiastic but also vigilant members of
the PCF, as can be seen in the newspaper published by Hélène Brion, *La*

lutte féministe (The Feminist Struggle) which was critical of the party despite its change of title to *La Lutte féministe pour le communisme* (The Feminist Struggle for Communism); and in the account published by Pelletier in 1922 titled, *My Adventurous Trip to Soviet Russia*, which drew up a balance sheet of the Russian experiments that was more than mixed.

In contrast to another communist intellectual, Magdeleine Paz, who published her narrative account in 1923 entitled, *It's the Final Struggle!*, Séverine, a famous journalist and member of the Central Committee of the League of the Rights of Man, also stoked the feminist fires in the PCF, which included militants of very diverse backgrounds. At the time of the party's organization, Séverine turned in her party card, refusing to conform to the directive which forbade membership in the League of the Rights of Man and in the Free Masons. She did not leave alone, although other feminists stayed, defending their ideas, particularly in *L'Ouvrière*, whose "petit bourgeois" character was soon denounced by the PCF leadership. The second wave of departures took place between 1924 and 1927 after which the party did not include a single woman engaged elsewhere in a feminist association. This was the end of a period of bitter failure for the first generation of militants, the so-called "migrants." Jacqueline Tardivel identifies two other generations: the "loyalists," who worked energetically when the party was at its lowest ebb between 1927 and 1933, and the "heirs," who participated in the renaissance of the party during the Popular Front era.

The change in membership numbers confirms the accuracy of this chronology. In 1924 there were 2,600 female members (3 or 4 percent), in 1926, 964 members (1.7 percent), and in 1929, only 200 members (0.6 percent). The party did not keep track of their membership numbers during the 1930s, but one can assume a significant increase during the period of the Popular Front. In any case, it consistently stagnated at a particularly low level,[4] whereas the Socialist party (SFIO) already had 1,500 female members in 1914 and claimed 2,800 women members (3 percent) in 1932. Therefore, one can almost talk about an over-representation of women during national congresses of the PCF: 15 delegates (6 percent) in 1925, 30 delegates (8.6 percent) in 1926, and 23 delegates (2.7 percent) in 1936. The Central Committee declined from 15 percent women in 1920 to 6 percent in 1922 – a decline that ended in a complete absence in the 1930s. Finally, in street protests, which were often rough, women never exceeded more than 15 percent according to photographs.[5]

One can give many explanations for the small number of women communists. The political engagement of women was minimal in part due to their official exclusion from political life. Because of the lack of time and money, and because of health problems, activism was a luxury for working women whom the party hoped to recruit. The trade unions never ceased to complain about their relative absence. (There were only 15 percent women among the union members in France in 1919.)[6] Finally, the political culture of France favored the "enlightened minorities," and for men as well as women, political engagement was exceptional. But the comparison to the SFIO invites one to consider the specific reasons for the low membership in the PCF. Were they ideological? In 1925, 24 women signed the "Letter of 250," which denounced the leadership of the PCF. Did bolshevization, which was accompanied by an exclusion of feminists, discourage the membership of women, more than of men? Between 1927 and 1933, were the sectarian methods and practices of violent opposition frowned upon more by women than men? One might well suspect this and also consider the reluctance of most women to engage in militant practices – such as the obligation to join a factory cell – that would have been acceptable to only a few exceptional women.

However, the party did not lack strong female personalities who were in the limelight. In the early years of the party these women were generally teachers or journalists and only very rarely workers. They had a rich past as militant feminists, union members, and pacifists. Louise Bodin (1877 to 1929), a journalist and writer, came from a bourgeois milieu (she was the wife of a professor of medicine), then joined the Central Committee in 1921 and directed the Ille-et-Vilaine Federation.[7] She left the party in 1927. Lucie Colliard (1877 to 1961), a pacifist teacher who had faced charges before the War Council in 1918, became a functionary in 1921 and entered the International Secretariat of Women Communists. As a member of the left faction, she initiated the party's propaganda for women. She entered into active opposition in 1926 and left the party shortly thereafter. Alice Brisset (1894 to 1974) was a worker and the secretary of the Seine-et-Oise Federation (1923). These first female dissidents found themselves face to face with Suzanne Girault (1882-1973) who led the party with Albert Treint between 1923 and 1925: "the captain" and "the amazon," who together took charge of the bolshevization of the party that resulted in some very heavy losses. Suzanne Girault, who had lived for twenty years in Russia working for the Checka, was famous for her authoritarian methods as leader of the Seine Federation. She was finally removed by Stalin in 1926 but remained at the head of the Women's Commission, which she ran with an iron hand.

After the teachers came the workers. Alice Brisset was the first female worker elected to the Central Committee, in 1926 when she was thirty-two. Martha Desrumeaux (1897 to 1982), who began working at the age of nine and became a popular figure in the Textile Federation of the North, sat on the Central Committee and in the Polit-Bureau from 1929 to 1937. The "red virgin," it was said, distinguished herself during strikes through her physical courage, verbal violence, and leadership capacity. Desrumeaux masterminded one of the major strikes of the interwar period, that of "ten pennies," against the cutting of wages initiated by the Textile Consortium of Roubaix-Tourcoing. Another famous figure was Jeannette Vermeersch, born in 1910, a worker from the North who joined the Communist Youth and the CGTU at the age of seventeen. In 1934 she became the companion of Maurice Thorez (Secretary of the Polit-Bureau from 1930 on and General Secretary in 1936) and was closely associated with the cult that surrounded him.[8]

During this second period (1927 to 1933), the wives of leaders, such as Marie-Thérèse Gourdeaux, joined the leadership. Gourdeaux was a postal worker who in 1926 was elected to the Central Committee, of which her husband was a member. This new, much younger generation of militant members encountered problems at first in getting published in the party press.[9] Recruitment from labor unions was stronger thanks to the CGTU, an excellent breeding ground. Between 1934 and 1939, its sphere of influence expanded thanks to its massive organizations of women. The Central Committee no longer included a single woman, but communist women leaders were at the head of the World Committee of Women against War and Fascism (Bernadette Cattanéo and Maria Rabaté) and of the Union of Young Women of France (Claudine Chomat, Danièle Casanova, and Jeannette Vermeersch) all of them companions of party leaders.

The memoirs of Charles Tillon, *They Sang Red*, pays hommage to a number of female trade unionists, as always devoted and untiringly modest – feminine qualities that were merely part of the reality, because the predominant image of the female communist was that of the militant woman. Belonging to a stigmatized opposition party, she faced dismissal, removal, arrest, prison, and altercations with the police. Her baptism by fire often occurred during strikes, when militant leadership was crucial. They learned the craft thanks to training made available by the party, which allowed them to surmount the cultural disadvantages stemming from their working-class background. The political militant, unlike the union activist, was the spouse of a militant, or more often the companion of a militant outside the conventions of marriage. Endogamy was extremely strong. Was this the necessary prerequisite for being a communist twenty-four hours a day? Engagement was total; it set the rhythm of private life and shaped one's affective life. Women activists knew how to avoid being left behind the stove and were able to entrust their children from the age of six to PCF groups of pioneers (scouts).

The case of Bernadette Cattanéo, born in 1899, could be considered representative. Raised in a poor peasant family from Brittany, orphaned by her father's death when she was five, she attended elementary school until age twelve. Cattanéo considered herself to have a solid standard education and attributed her awakening to the social question to her socialist and anti-clerical teacher. She read and appreciated Diderot, Rousseau, Hugo, and Sand, and, much later, she studied Marx's *Capital*, not without difficulty. After leaving Brittany in 1919, she found a job with a Parisian clothing manufacturer. She joined the party in 1923 at the same time as her companion. One year later she became a member of the Commission on Women: "I had developed the habit of public speaking and I became a good agitator."[10] She was recruited as a party functionary after being fired from her job, and entrusted her two children to her mother, who "despite her ignorance ... understood the importance of the party and was very sympathetic."

Cattanéo's exercise of writing a "biography" is of course a highly controlled and self-controlled exercise, underscoring the importance that the Comintern attributed to the domestic life of militants. Whatever the intent, her sincerity was apparent, and she never questioned her own abilities. However, she took no pride in her exceptional career as a militant. She displayed her humility when she admitted to having received a private reprimand from the party for having participated in the disbanding of the Union of Women against Poverty and War: "I must say that I was convinced that the party was aware and in agreement, otherwise I would never have taken on such a responsibility, and I would have asked for discussion beforehand. But I relied on the comrade in charge of party women, comrade Cilly Vassar, believing that everything was clear. But the party was right to be strict."

Female militants seemed to distance themselves from the traditional female role by recognizing the party as the supreme authority, which weakened the authority of the father, husband, and companion, unless they themselves were figures of authority in the party. In principle, women lived as comrades of their companions. In its resolution on women the Congress of Marseilles in 1921 recommended that a wife accompany her husband if he was a militant, persuade him if he was politically indifferent, and demand the right to be an activist on her own if necessary. The most flagrant anti-conformism manifested itself among teachers, who remained the most open to feminism within the party. One teacher, Maria Rabate, publicized her refusal of marriage and dressed in a provocative style, draped in a black cape lined with red. Communist youth groups also attracted girls who were very liberated in daily life; they walked around with red scarves, a bit like tomboys. This was not the typical girl of the period."[11]

Although women militants lacked contemporary role models, there were historical ones like the famous Communard Louise Michel, whose memory the party celebrated.[12] As testimony of her admiration for Louise Michel, the young activist Waicziarg, the only woman elected to the first

National Committee of the Communist Youth, chose the pseudonym of Rosa Michel, also commemorating Rosa Luxemburg who had just been murdered.[13] The school teacher Jeanne Labourbe, secretary of the French Communist Group of Moscow, executed in Odessa in 1919 by French soldiers, presented a model of heroism that was quickly forgotten.[14] No French woman had the stature of Clara Zetkin, who represented the executive of the Comintern during the Congress of Tours, where she was hailed as the, "noble, great, and glorious woman,"[15] or of Alexandra Kollontai, master theoretician of the most feminist communists from the beginning of the 1920s. The Comintern seemed to take great care of its gendered image and thus offered French women a possible source of inspiration. For example, at the time of the first National Youth Conference, held in Paris in 1925, in addition to the young widow of Andre Sabatier, a militant assassinated a few days earlier at Suresnes, two delegates from the Russian Youth, Petroff and "the comrade Nadia" were seated on the tribune. The Romanian Anna Pauker was among various Comintern delegates participating in the PCF's leadership school.

Although few in number, female PCF members were, more than in any other political party, militants. Their consistent activism compensated for their small numbers. This might explain why, during the 1930s, the PCF appeared "happier than the SFIO when it came to the question of mobilizing women." This is the opinion of the historian Charles Sowerwine, who argued that for socialist women to put up with smoky section meetings where men were preoccupied above all with electoral campaigns "bordered on heroism."[16] Jacqueline Tardivel, studying the living conditions of communist propagandists, noted that the most surprising aspect was not the paucity of numbers but that there were any women at all in the PCF.[17]

Propaganda

From 1920 on, the party decided to give special attention to the most disinherited part of the proletariat – female workers. PCF founders announced that a special kind of propaganda addressed to proletarian women must be undertaken using the most appropriate methods, "to help exploited women understand that only socialism will liberate them by realizing their economic enfranchisement; in order to group them, organize them, and politically educate them."[18] Before the split in the SFIO, the group of socialist women, like the youth, were organized at the last minute[19] and were treated like "poor relations."[20] The young Communist party, desiring to break with the past, sought not to repeat past errors – all the more so since "feminism" for the communists was a distinct attribute that allowed them to highlight the hypocrisy of the socialists vis-a-vis women, in particular regarding the right to vote.

A Women's Secretariat was constituted and accepted by the party "under the pressure of the Executive Committee of the Comintern, itself alarmed by communist female militants," wrote Lucie Colliard on 7 October 1921. "The program is far-reaching, but our courage is without limits." The Congress of Marseille decided upon the organization of conferences and the installation of structures for women in factories and in local federations, but the decision had no practical results. The party only succeeded in creating a female bi-weekly in November 1922. In the editorial of the first issue, L.O. Frossard declared: "The International prescribed that we create an organ of communist propaganda for women." Six months later, only half of the 3,000 copies of *L'Ouvrière* had been distributed. There were so many difficulties that the publication was interrupted several times. During the next five years, *L'Ouvrière* attempted to mobilize working women. Although feminism inspired the first years of publication, its evolution followed upon the heels of the party's changes of course.

After 1924, the promotion of real workers to leadership positions and the absolute priority given to class struggle for a short time gave a new tone to the periodical; nonetheless, it ceased publication in 1927. To appeal to working women via a newspaper was not enough. Female militants deplored the fact that women read very little. Speeches and slogans did have an important role, especially during strikes, on May Day, or during International Woman's Week around 8 March. In 1926 the party counted on twenty-eight female agitators able to speak for five minutes, on twenty-nine who could carry on for ten minutes, and on nine who could surpass this speaking time. The meetings could attract hundreds of women in Paris, where the number of members was higher, but in the provinces such meetings were not always successful. That was the case in 1927, in the mines of Pas-de-Calais, where only fifteen working women attended a meeting organized by Anne Lobel, who decried the indifference of women "at the time when the working class found itself in a critical situation."[21]

Certainly it was the low point of party activity, but one has to recognize that the recruitment of women was laborious work. Female passivity? Male indifference? Both probably accounted for this situation. In 1932 Michelle Gay spoke out in *Les Cahiers du bolchévisme*: "How many examples could one cite of our militants who refuse to organize women, who prevent their very own wives from joining our ranks, who ridicule the work of women in the party? How many times after scraping away the surface of a militant communist man does one find the presence of a petit-bourgeois?"[22] Despite the propaganda efforts of the Central Secretariat of

Women, in 1926 the party admitted that only one percent of its members were women, of which a very small number were workers.[23] The absence of the three men who represented the Polit-Bureau, the Organizational Bureau, and the Communist Youth at meetings of the Women's Secretariat was typical of male disinterest in women's affairs. In 1926, the Secretariat requested a third permanent member in vain. Its activity continued to decline, and it was finally eliminated in 1936. The PCF having become a major party, explained Martha Desrumeaux, the woman question no longer deserved separate attention.[24] In any case, one must recognize that PCF propaganda directed at women was always somewhat irregular and weak. For example, on the occasion of International Women's Day, the woman question was hardly mentioned in L'Humanité.[25]

Sister Organizations

These types of recruitment problems explain the birth of women's associations controlled by the party, which hoped to recruit future members. Implicitly, a division of labor among militants followed typical gender conventions: the party at the center of a constellation of organizations was perceived as masculine, the satellite organizations as feminine. Reserved for women were humanitarian causes and pacifism. The original women's auxiliary organizations, such as the Committee of Mothers and Widows and the Group of Friends of L'Ouvrière remained in an embryonic form. Female activists invested themselves more willingly in aid committees, such as the Committee of Assistance to the Russian People created in 1921, which appealed to the generosity of French mothers. Numerous others were active around the French Rescue Committee for Russian Famine Victims. Militants of great importance like Germaine Willard and Marie Lahy-Hollebecque joined the International Red Rescue, founded in 1922 and presided over by a Russian, Hélène Stassova.[26] Women were present, when the organization was recognized at the celebration of its tenth anniversary, but in a subordinate position. In 1926, only 14 percent of its executive commission was female.[27] In 1927 the Fraternal Union of Women against Imperialist War was created, directed by Antoinette Gilles (1893 to 1939), a bank employee and member of the party since 1925.

The Union was officially devoid of any political character but it did not fool anyone; its slogans as well as its practices echoed those of the party. Nonetheless, it had seventy-four sections and 1,500 members by 1930. It disappeared in 1934 to make way for the World Committee of Women against War and Fascism, directed by Gabrielle Duchene, a feminist with a rich activist past, seconded by Bernadette Cattanéo. Solidarity with Victims of Fascism was organized. The press of International Red Rescue published *Women under Fascist Terror, Women on the Front of Solidarity and Combat*, with a list of the victims made public at a big meeting at the *Mutualité* meeting hall in Paris. Thereafter, intellectuals joined the World Committee: Irène Joliot-Curie, winner of the Nobel Prize in Chemistry in 1935 and appointed Under-Secretary of State for Scientific Research in 1936. Also attracted were: Andrée Viollis, coeditor of the weekly publication, *Vendredi*, her journalist daughter Simone Téry, and the physicist, Luce Langevin.

Concerning French communist participation in the Spanish Civil War, the International Brigades presented an exclusively and arrogantly masculine image. In fact, the Brigades depended on a significant participation by women, of course subject to the traditional gender division of activist work. One party sympathizer, Madeleine Braun (1907 to 1980) was General Secretary of the International Committee for the Coordination of Information for the Aid of the Republic of Spain between 1936 and 1937. Marguerite de Saint-Prix, an experienced activist working with the pacifist minority during the Great War, presided over the French Section of the Committee of International Aide to Women and Children of the Spanish Republic. In addition, some French women doctors, nurses, and secretaries, left for Spain.[28] The review *Women in World Action* encouraged women's engagement by lauding the courage of the women who served in the Spanish Republican militia and engaged in combat. The charismatic, Dolores Ibarruri was very visible in the feminine antifascist propaganda.

Finally, there was renewed enthusiasm for the Communist Youth whose numbers increased considerably from 4,000 in 1934 to 30,000 one year later.[29] In 1935, the presence of girls was not negligible since they numbered seventy-three (16.5 percent) out of 442 delegates to the Congress of Marseille. But at the Office of the National Federation of Communist Youth, there was only one woman, Danièle Casanova,[30] surrounded by twelve men (the percentage of women fell to 8 percent). The party thus decided to put in place, as it had for the students and rural youth, an organization specifically attractive to female youth. The first Congress of the Union of Young Girls of France, which took place on 26 December 1936, brought together 600 delegates, representing 9,643 members. In addition to circulating the monthly publication *Young Girls of France*, militants developed a network of a thousand young girls' clubs throughout France and recruited nearly 20,000 members by 1939. They sent get-well packages to sanitariums, knitted pullovers for the elderly and the unemployed, and participated in relief efforts for Spain.

Sexual segregation was a telling characteristic marking the desire to build a supportive female mass organization. Danièle Casanova explained its mission at the first congress:

At the beginning, some of us asked ourselves if we hadn't turned our backs on our principles by wanting to organize girls separately. Let us just frankly admit that a co-ed organization would not have given us a large enough recruitment. The parents and the young girls themselves were opposed to these methods of organization. On the other hand, we know from experience that a co-ed organization would not, at the present time and in the society in which we live, allow us to address and resolve in a desirable way, the particular problems which are of interest to young girls. But that is not all. Since the founding of our organization, we have discovered new and courageous militants. Our work is of interest to them. They have taken their task to heart and for the first time we can say, young girls are participating in large numbers in the political life of the Federation of Communist Youth in France. Tomorrow they will be able militants, having been well educated in our best sources of Marxist-Leninist doctrine.[31]

This optimism was certainly justified and confirmed in reports made by other organizations – the Christian Unions for example[32] – on the positive effects of sexual segregation on membership recruitment. Undeniably, the separation of the two sexes reassured parents. Probably, it suited the young girls as well who did not necessarily see the attraction of being a minority in very masculine groups and who appreciated an atmosphere favorable to the complicity and camaraderie between women.

Brothers, Sisters, Comrades

How does the word "*camarade*" (comrade) which is without a doubt the most typical word in the communist vocabulary, agree with the feminine? The female "comrade" made its appearance in 1920. The term "citoyenne," or female citizen, which had been used to precede the name of militants, fell into disuse. This happened at the same time that its universalist and even nationalist connotations, with its assortment of historical reminiscences (the citizens of 1789), its suffragist implications, as well as its association with the smaller fatherland represented by the party and the larger fatherland of the proletariat were also disappearing. "Comrade," to the contrary, sounded "Russian," even though etymologically it was Spanish and Italian before being adopted by the French. In Spanish, *camara* (literally "bedroom" in French) came from *camarada*, or soldiers' barracks, whereas *camerata* in Italian designates a companion in arms.[33] It was at the price of a sort of masculinization of the word that the female militant would become *un camarade* (a masculine comrade) in a virile and military community.

This "cross-gendering" remains rare. The militants were more often considered by the men as "female comrades," an expression which evidently emphasized the difference in gender and imposed a certain distance. In 1937, *La Vie ouvrière* called these newcomers "the charming female comrades." Considering the operetta connotations of the latter term, Jacqueline Tardivel observed that "one might conclude that the introduction of an androgynous revolutionary world had failed."[34] It wasn't easy for the militants of the first generation to feel at ease with this word. "Comrade" was, for example, often associated with the more affectionate word "sister." Lucie Colliard, during the 1925 strike of women sardine plant workers in Douarnenez, described herself as "ill at ease with this 'comrade,' more bolshevik than Breton," and "she used it in her own way by softening it with sentimental adjectives like: 'my good comrade' or 'my poor comrade.'" The victorious outcome of the strike gave the word a class content: "Yes, my comrades, organize yourselves!" or, in conclusion, "female comrade workers."[35]

The use of the word by women to designate men posed fewer problems and sometimes even allowed for the expression of understated sarcasm, criticizing men's lack of real camaraderie and their absence of solidarity with women. Relationships of camaraderie, that is to say fraternal ones between male and female militants, were what the party wished. Due to the constraints of the French language, relations between women were also spoken of as "fraternal" (as in the title of the Fraternal Union of Women against War and Poverty). The term *sororité* is a feminist neologism coined in the 1970s. The historian Lynn Hunt demonstrated how the "fraternity" so present in the representations and the symbolism of the French Revolution has been used to kill the Father, but also to exclude women from an ideal community of men.[36] The PCF's idea of the family may have in a certain unconscious manner reproduced this scheme without being so extreme, since the father figure is present. The French communists had their father, Joseph Stalin, "the little father of the people," and the son, Maurice Thorez, "the son of the people." The 1920s for the PCF corresponded to the most brutal phase in the destruction of the family during the French Revolution, a period which also excluded women. The party of the 1930s, reintegrated into national life, reestablished a concern for women on the condition that they stayed in their place as sisters, wives, and mothers, thus evoking the period of the Directory, which rehabilitated family morality.

Despite all difficulties, female militants adopted camaraderie and "fraternity." As a minority they displayed a tendency to stick together and developed a kind of friendly bond somewhat out of the ordinary.

Communist Contribution to the Emancipation of Women and its Limitations

The PCF defended the equality between the sexes, with particular attention to the exploitation of working women. The majority of feminists, despite their ideological disagreement with the PCF, recognized this position while underscoring the party's limits and doubting the sincerity of its program. The political parties, like the trade unions, disliked the existence of an autonomous feminist movement, which avoided political polemics in order to remain neutral. This opposition was longstanding. New during the interwar period was the usefulness of feminist themes for the political recruitment of women; the PCF declared itself an ardent defender of the vote for women, an objective that was not necessarily central to an anticapitalist perspective. In practice, the party adapted the majority of feminist claims to its own program. The contradictions, however, remained apparent between the virile and martial style of communist militancy and the feminist positions of the party.[37]

Soviet Model or National Model?

These "feminist" positions owe much to the Soviet model. It is, outside the scope of this chapter to study the experience of women in the USSR. Rather, we will trace the transmission of the principal representations of Soviet women into France. The problem is complex, since the sources which transmitted these images were very diverse. Male and female communists did not only read the newspapers and pamphlets of the party; they also had access to a number of books and pamphlets, most often travel memoirs, which still need to be studied. All the same, since we are interested in the most authoritative official discourse, it is acceptable to select one homogenous source, in this case, *L'Humanité*. In order to obtain a body of information that can be compared over time and supplies enough data, this communist daily is worth systematic study for the periods surrounding the International Women's Day, around 8 March.

As with all images, and particularly those in the radical press, it is difficult to distinguish between the results obtained and the immediate and long range strategy of the source. For example, the value placed on women's work during the watershed of the 1930s is only one element of a plan of action that, above all, tried to demonstrate the success of the Five Year Plan and Soviet workers' determination to achieve it. Therefore, one has difficulty finding permanent features beyond the already prevalent discourse on the USSR as the "country of women's liberation." The Soviet female image reached its high point of exposure in the period from 1927 to 1935, which provides the main body of references. In the previous period, the woman question was raised at the time of the International Women's Day but rarely through the Soviet model. In the later period, the woman question was rarely addressed and the 8th of March was hardly ever the object of attention in *L'Humanité*. The documents that address the question are of a different nature: diverse articles, official texts, photos; but also numerous letters supposedly spontaneously penned by Soviet "working women." We have not tried to make fine distinctions between these sources here because we are most interested in the total system of representation.

What then are the essential aspects of this "luminary example of the Russia of Soviets" (as proclaimed by the PCF Central Committee of 6 March 1927)? First is the important place of Russian women (above all, working women) in the Russian Revolution – their decisive role at the time of the February Revolution and their contribution to the construction of socialism. The discourse here is very coded and functionalist. Its aim is to convince male French communists of the importance of women in the revolutionary process, persuading them of the need for propaganda directed towards women. In a 1935 example, an article is accompanied by photos of revolutionary heroines Clara Zetkin, Martha Desrumeaux, La Pasionaria, Inès Armand, Rosa Luxemburg, and Jeanne Labourbe. Significantly, the women presented as models were fighters with the attributes of determination, willpower, and physical strength. These characteristics were customarily attributed to men, most notably in representations of the working-class movement. In 1927, *L'Humanité* referred to "tough women of the people" present at meetings. In 1929, it underscored women's participation in street fighting resulting from class-against-class tactics.

A beautiful caricature, "The middle class and women," appeared on 8 March 1925 in three vignettes: "Prayer" contrasted the middle class in the guise of a gorged, fat man with a thin, fragile, impoverished woman; "Reform" showed a woman begging; "Class Struggle" transformed "Reform" into a dignified, muscular working woman dominating her boss. These images of female laborers were of course associated with those of their male companions in the struggle of their class which must first be united for a common objective, the revolution. They also suggest a possible transformation within the French working-class movement. Nevertheless, these representations probably had a limited meaning despite the actual participation of women workers in strikes and despite their dynamism.

The discourse about the liberation of Soviet women is perhaps more important. It is complex and filled with multiple meanings. One simple argument automatically made revolution the necessary precondition sufficient for the liberation of women. In this case, the line of argument is limited and the assertion is enough. ("Only a proletarian government like the one in Russia will give to women as well as men ...." Losowsky, 8 March 1928.) Others followed the theme of maternity "as social function" recognized and not separated from women's work. This theme was illustrated by the descriptions of pregnancy shelters, maternity clinics, and day care centers (photo of the Illitch crèche, 10 March 1931). Women's suffrage was de-emphasized, which was understandable for a movement rather contemptuous of this right. Women's access to education was mentioned more frequently.

But the most prevalent issue was equality, presented in a manner more or less progressive, as much by the authors of the articles (such as Marcel Cachin, which demonstrated a serious engagement of his newspaper – and of his personal feeling) as much as in letters attributed to Soviet workers. Many of the printed testimonies emphasized meaningful participation by women in political life, such as in the Soviets (seen at electoral meetings or the general assemblies of the Kolkhoz; photographed during a meeting of a workers' club at their factory; exercising power as underlined by a headline, "Power to Women," inscribed in large capital letters 6 March 1929).

Articles also probed the sphere of private and familial life. The liberation of the Soviet woman was seen as the liberation from her domination by man. In one letter (10 March 1931), a woman worker speaking for herself mentioned that the Russian woman was no longer "the maid" of Russian man or his possession: "In the old days a woman in the home was regarded as an object or even worse as a maid; now, under Soviet power, women are the equal of men." She gave the concrete example of her divorce, which permitted her to obtain one third of her former husband's pay for the care of their children and the equal division of benefits. Two articles by Marcel Cachin, written in 1934 and 1935, constituted the pinnacle of this image of the USSR. Evoking 1917, he stated that the equality of man and woman was a central aspect of the Russian Revolution: "Such a deep revolution has not happened for centuries." This idea, that the revolution did not reach its deeper meaning without the liberation of women, was already formulated from the beginning of the 1920s in an important unsigned lead story on 6 March 1923: "If the revolution abandoned women and children to themselves, the revolution … would very well be only a political revolution; it would not, it could not be, that which it aspired to be: a radical break with all the institutions and behaviors of the past, a profound social revolution."

As such, the Bolshevik Revolution suppressed "the injustices and the inequalities imposed by the bourgeoisie and the stupefying traditions of the clergy." Woman had become equal to man not only in rights, but also in work (salary), education, and culture. This image of the woman worker occupying all the functions generally reserved for men, and positively presented, was all the more important because it was present during all stages of change in the USSR. One finds these images in abundance in photos of Soviet women workers or peasants. Even at the

end of the 1930s, a time of return to family and maternal values, an article by Odette Blanc, ("In the Country of Krupskaia: Nothing is More
Beautiful than Women's Share," 3 March 1939) introduced women
train conductors, judges, managers, doctors, parachutists, and a young
ship captain, naturally "the only one in the world." The contradiction is
striking between these images and those that return to the most traditional femininity in *Regards*, an illustrated popular weekly of the PCF,
during the 1930s.

More fundamentally, noted Cachin, "the Soviets have not removed
women from the factory in order to put them back in the home. This is
the conception of fascism and 'social fascism' according to which women
must take care of cooking and housework and are to be supported by their
companion. But this is not the communist view!" A woman in the USSR
was neither "housewife nor courtesan" but rather a "worker, producer,
scholar, manager of an industrial or rural enterprise, architect, artist, engineer, collective farm worker! …" which opened the door for true love and
the free choice of a partner. "This radical transformation of the situation
of women," in the USSR was for Cachin, the "greatest claim to fame" of
the country of socialism. Elsewhere Cachin claimed that the French
housewife was "fatally oppressed," whereas in the USSR the growing
number of its cooperative restaurants, day care centers, etc., had abolished prostitution and "marital slavery." He had already said it at a vast
meeting on 7 March 1925: "Women must not suffer under two bosses: her
employer and her husband."

This position posed the problem of grafting this Soviet model onto
French society and culture. Without going into all the aspects of the labor
movement, most studies (since that of Madeleine Guilbert)[38] agree, that
the French labor movement, and more particularly its trade union wing,
showed an extreme reticence toward women's emancipation. Declarations violently protesting women's work for a variety of reasons – from
"feminine nature," as it was conceived of by Proudhon, to the under-
handed competition that led to the lowering of wages – were innumerable
and dominated the trade union landscape until the First World War.
Although the Socialist party theoretically declared itself in favor of the
vote for women, it took little action on the issue. Many of its members
viewed it as solely a bourgeois demand. This body of male sentiment and
doctrine was little affected by the war, a complicated moment of progres-
sions and regressions. One could put forward the hypothesis that the system of representation of the Soviet woman that we have described
corresponded to a form of transplant or a tentative grafting of the Soviet
model. The rapidity with which the system of representation of the Soviet
model collapsed in 1936 leads one to think that the transplant did not
take, or took very poorly.

The Party of Working Women

The CGTU, which accepted PCF leadership of the whole labor movement, is a good place to observe communist practices regarding the work
and struggle of working women.[39] Was this a reflection of the "transplant"
of the Soviet model that we have mentioned, or the increased desire to
take into account the difficulties of the most exploited categories of the
proletariat, women, youth, immigrants? In either case, the CGTU gave
increased attention to the demands of working women. By 1927 the
CGTU was moving toward the defense of the "right to work for everyone," and during the Depression declared itself against the return of
women to the home (Congress of 1933). Despite the acceptance then of
the inescapability of women's entry into production, such entry had not
always been considered in a positive way, as was demonstrated by the
Congress of 1925. The CGTU defended equal pay (its congresses recommended that wage demands take this request into account), the strict
observance of the eight hour day, paid vacations, and the protection of
jobs during the period of pregnancy and early motherhood. The PCF and
the CGTU supported women's strikes, highlighting the model strike of
the Breton women sardine workers of Douarnenez in 1925.

As soon as one descends to the local level or the work level, the
CGTU's actions are less positive. The communist influence was strong in
feminized sectors like clothing. *L'Humanité* wrote at length about of the
Parisian salesgirls' strikes of 1923 and 1934. Organizations such as the
Communist Youth of the Seine and the Seine-et-Oise intervened in
1923. One of their tracts denounced "the bourgeois conception that your
salary doesn't need to be high, since women cannot hope to live without
the support of a man."[40] In the metal industry, on the other hand, several
notices appeared in *La Vie ouvrière*, expressing reservations over women's
permanent presence in the workforce. But case studies are rare, and it
remains difficult to give a rigorous verdict on the attitude of the majority
of communist activists or CGTU members.

The progressive decline of feminist influence was confirmed within
the CGTU as well as within the PCF. The year 1932 marks the disappearance of feminist groups in secular education, a group of elementary
school teachers that defended intransigent feminist positions within the
CGTU (suffrage, coeducation, contraception).[41] All the more remarkably, the CGT, reunified in 1936 (socialist and communist), maintained
its defense of women's right to work during the Popular Front era. Certainly proposed quotas limiting women's work were unrealistic in a country where women represented more than a third of all wage earners.
Nonetheless, the slogan "return to the home" was part of a tempting
demagoguery, to which the CGT with its strong communist component,

refused to yield. Difficult to understand is this continued support of women's work at the very moment when the influence of organized feminism was weak. Although the sincerity of the CGT cannot be dismissed – the strikes of 1936 having had a remarkable mix of the sexes – it is also possible to consider the addition of women's right to work to the program of the Popular Front as a "gift," which compensated for its neglect of women's right to vote.

A Party of Suffragists

In parliament, in the municipalities, and in its own press and meetings, the PCF supported the vote for women. By regularly running women candidates in elections, it even adopted a suffragist strategy of running feminist candidates, which was obviously doomed to failure but which allowed it to attract the attention of public opinion and the government. In 1925, the party ran several candidates, ten of whom were elected as city councillors and held on to their positions until the invalidation of their election. In 1928, again, "as a means of signaling their intention to fight for the rights and emancipation of women, the PCF presented the candidacy of their comrade Madeleine Charpentier, a union member in the fur industry of the 10th municipal district."[42] But there were reservations about this tactic in the party. Criticizing the prosuffrage position of her comrade Marthe Bigot, Rosa Michel warned that "the emancipation of women cannot be the work of a paper weapon."[43] At each legislative election, the party program demanded civil and civic equality for women. Over the years criticism of suffragist organizations hardened; they were accused of maintaining and consolidating the bourgeois regime.[44] But from 1934 on, the PCF adopted a conciliatory attitude and sought unity among women's groups. Within the framework of antifascist mobilization, in which the party played a major role, women's right to the vote reappeared in the slogans for the defense of liberty, democracy, and peace.

The communist deputies contrary to their socialist colleagues, constantly defended the political equality of the sexes.[45] In all elections they voted as a bloc in favor of it. They opposed the proposals for the family vote put forward by the right, but in 1925 accepted a proposal that limited women's right to vote to municipal and county (cantonal) elections. Three different times – 1924, 1927, 1928 – in the name of communist deputies, Marcel Cachin introduced bills for full female suffrage. Never again did the communist deputies introduce such a bill, nor did they agree sign bills or resolutions originating from other groups, demanding that the government put pressure on the Senate (which consistently blocked women's suffrage). The PCF came out of isolation on 6 June 1936, when Thorez and Cogniot agreed to sign the Socialist Scapini's proposal in favor of women's vote. Here we observe a confirmation of three distinct phases that marked the evolution of the party.

Despite an open affirmation of suffrage, the communist deputies took little part in the discussions. Was their motivation insufficient, or was it a means of expressing opposition to the endless speeches by the opponents of reform? When the communist deputy, Garchery, intervened in the debate in 1925, he announced that he would be brief "in order to get positive results."[46] In his spiritless speech he affirmed that his party was not afraid of the electoral consequences of the women's vote. This was, he claimed, contrary to other parliamentarians of the left who often declared themselves favorable, at least in principle, but who were hostile to its immediate adoption. He even judged that women's suffrage "would become an instrument capable of efficaciously contributing to the process of emancipating the proletariat." He seized the opportunity to remind everyone that the "feverish pace of capitalist production" forced women to work in order to compensate for the inadequacy of men's salaries. He sympathetically evoked the positive effects that the "feminine instinct" could have: common sense, clear sightedness, and the ability to take care of questions concerning maternity, childhood, public health, higher prices, social work, working conditions and salaries, and problems of housing. Thus, his lines of argument were as particularist and differentiating as those that dominated all the suffragist speeches, regardless of their political orientation. The PCF synthesis thus advanced three broad arguments in favor of the vote: it supported the principle of universal civic rights, but attempted to demonstrate their social utility, while adding the party's specific spin by underscoring its role in the class struggle.

Apart from the sincerity of its convictions, the party may have had other motivations. It would be astonishing that the PCF, which remained 98 to 99 percent male, did not experience the reluctance and the motives of opposition of other parties on the left. Did the PCF understand that the women's vote had become a popular cause in public opinion? To defend it was also a way of insisting on a significant failure of the Third Republic, of emphasizing the hypocrisy of the socialists, and of denouncing the parliamentary behavior of a "rotten" system.

From Supporting Abortion to Praising Large Families

In the early 1920s the PCF adopted an avant-garde position close to that of the radical feminists and neo-Malthusians on the subject of contraception and abortion. By the end of the Great War pro-natalism had become a largely shared obsession and an important element of the Republican consensus from the extreme right to the Radical party. It was through repression (of abortions, abortionists, and neo-Malthusians) that the "blue horizon" Chamber of Deputies – denounced as "the national-capitalist quagmire,"[47] attacked the problem. Family allowances were created twelve years later. The majority of reform feminists approved of this pro-natalist policy, making the attitude of the communists all the more remarkable.[48]

L'Ouvrière of 10 April 1924 proclaimed:

> the state does not have the right to refuse women, who do not have the means to raise a child, access to an abortion under the best conditions, which means practiced in hospitals using the most modern methods of science so long as it does not assure the mother, by means of a basic allowance, the economic independence which would permit her to dedicate herself to her maternal task.

Physician Madeleine Pelletier, who in 1913 had published the first feminist plea in favor of the right to abortion, and who also practiced secret abortions in her medical office, collaborated with the newspaper.[49] The party did not entrust any responsibility to this brilliant activist, however undisciplined, but it did give her a voice. The support of the communists was constant during the trial of Henriette Alquier, an elementary school teacher, activist of the Feminist Group for Secular Education and member of the party, charged with having signed a 1927 report favorable to birth control, "Maternity as a Social Function," in the trade union paper *The Emancipated School*.

At the beginning of the 1930s, the fight against the anti-abortion Law of 1920 was vigorously resumed. While the neo-Malthusians reorganized themselves at the same time as the League for the Rights of Man mobilized itself, communist and socialist deputies introduced several bills. Berty Albrecht, one of the rare women to commit herself to the fight for birth control, then came closer to the PCF. There she encountered doctor Jean Dalsace, a Parisian gynecologist and ardent defender of the cause of birth control.

Nevertheless, after 1935 the position of the PCF began to change. It no longer "accused the bourgeoisie of preaching fertility but of doing it without providing the necessary support."[50] In the 31 October 1935 issue of *L'Humanité*, Paul Vaillant-Couturier noted the negative effects of decreased births. At the approach of the election of 1936, the PCF experienced this turnabout at the moment when the USSR underwent an identical change (prohibition of abortion in April 1936 following Stalin's speech denouncing "abortion which kills"). The issue was no longer a question of fighting against the villainous law of 1920 that the Radicals and certain socialists had voted for. Maurice Thorez henceforth supported population increases, demanding, for example, a wage supplement for fathers of large families. Finished were the diatribes against the state that was supposed to keep its nose out of the bedroom; finished too were criticisms of the ineffective repression incapable of stopping back-alley abortions, of which the most destitute women were the first victims. Forgotten was Lenin, who had considered the freedom of abortion and contraception on a par with other democratic freedoms (in "The Working Class and Neo-Malthusianism," 1913).

This reversal had lasting consequences: prudishness and pro-family values remained astonishingly vigorous in the PCF up until the end of the 1970s. But it also had complex causes. Electoral politics of a party that henceforth had the will and the means of integrating itself into national political life is one explanation, which is equally appropriate for the socialists. The demographic question played a key role in the Republican consensus, and as always, in the patriotic mobilization in view of a possible threat to the nation. It was on the basis of this large political consensus that the Radicals developed the Family Code that went into effect in 1939. The opening of the Moscow archives and the work in progress on the Comintern will doubtless confirm that the revival of the PCF corresponded to the new orientation advocated by Stalin. Finally, the new family policy of the PCF followed the fashion of the times and probably coincided with a prevalent desire within the working class of the 1930s. The economic and social crisis seems to have provoked a return to family values, as demonstrated by the success of sympathy for the campaigns demanding the return of the mother to the home, lead by the Catholic clergy and associations.

Certainly in practice, French men and women were convinced Malthusians. However, in the collective imagination, the more or less mythical figure of the mother-housewife occupied a privileged place. In the 1930s anxiety resulting from unemployment finally led the labor movement to take up once more "the praise of the housewife," a masculine discourse popular in the nineteenth century.[51] Neo-Malthusianism, whose success among the working class was intimately linked to anarchist influences, was finally rejected.

In a more general manner, the question of sexuality, was above all reduced to modes of alienation put in place by the bourgeois class, which used it to divert workers' attention away from real problems. According to this line of communist thought, the struggle for the improvement of material conditions of existence required a certain negation of sexuality. Denounced as a bourgeois vice in capitalist countries, sexuality, despite everything, was imbued with positive values in socialist countries. In this vein, the critical PCF journal *Regards* printed two very similar photos of women wearing bikinis. One photo showed bikinis worn by "the whores of luxury who tan their buttocks on the beach," while the other emphasized the athletic shape of the basketball playing working woman.[52] However, bourgeois prudishness was also stigmatized, even if less systematically so than bourgeois debauchery. Both indicated that capitalist sexuality was fundamentally unwholesome. Denunciations of the hypocrisy of the dominant morality, often to defend women who were its victims through prostitution or harassed as the "boss' lay," were common even though such defenses might use the ridiculous notion of virtue.

Going over the list of proscribed sexual conduct, the historian François Delpla sketched an outline of the agreed-upon sexual behavior: legitimate sexuality was above all that of a couple, but not necessarily a married one. This relationship was based on reciprocal love and established a home. The division of roles including sexually seductive play was conventional. This couple was always heterosexual. The PCF denounced male and female homosexuality, about which it expressed disgust and condescension, and gave the party press an opportunity to expose the behavior of the upper bourgeoisie but also to project a virile image of communist man. Until the change of course in 1934, *Regards* remained open to a less conformist vision of sexuality as exemplified by the pleas of Daniel Guérin (who still hid his homosexuality) for proletarian nudity; the advertisements for *The Sexual Revolution of Wilhelm Reich*; or the discussion of the German refugee sexologist Magnus Hirschfeld. Anticlericalism, anti-militarism, and antifascism were used to demonstrate that the frustration of sexual needs had ideological purposes. While the Popular Front was being constituted, *Regards* dropped its haughtiness about "love that masked the real problems" and moved closer to popular tastes, as evidenced in the evolution of its criticisms of American films or the growing number of less rigid articles regarding female coquetry. Communist originality declined until the war, while a rather consensual vision of femininity and of family values took over.

From Marthe Bigot to Jeannette Vermeersch

In the middle of the 1930s, the PCF adopted a very conformist vision of feminine identity. Pacifism, which had a predilection for the image of motherhood, reinforced the stereotypes by insisting on the preconceived idea that all women as mothers were natural pacifists. In 1937 Cilly Vassart praised female uniqueness: "It would be a mistake to ask them [women] to put up political posters or to do work that is too difficult for them …. Let's not forget that communist women are women like all others, with the same charm and physical weaknesses of their sex, and that they are overloaded with housework."[53] *Regards* translated this change through images that conveyed the conventional representations of elegance *à la française*. The celebration of the Festival of Joan of Arc further confirmed this desire to give a national character to the party. One could multiply the examples of this 1936 turn in policy. In *L'Humanité* of 12 March 1936, Martha Desrumeaux wrote that women "want their husband and their sons returning from work to a home with the necessities for happiness." Also in 1936, the paper's "Woman's" page became "The Woman and Child" page. Two noteworthy photos appeared in the 6 March 1937 issue – one of the mother of Dimitrov, one of the sister of Lenin!

One can measure the distance traveled since Marthe Bigot denounced the burden of maternal chores and housework and called for a new society "reconstructed in light of a socialist organization of housework" by examining a pamphlet entitled, *The Servitude of Women*, published by *L'Humanité* in 1924. This first generation of female activists marked by a radical feminism would continue to play a political role on the extreme left, in the factional Trotskyist ranks that did not experience this maternalist and pro-family turnabout.[54] In any case, this retreat was a success from the point of view of the PCF, probably because it corresponded to its new aspirations and its new membership (male and female), drawn from a working class attached to family values and to a traditional gender code. This was already the case, certainly less clearly, during the preceding years.[55] The ephemeral encounter between feminism – including its most subversive dimension, that of sexual liberation – and communism is all the more astonishing. One could offer several explanations. Some of these stemmed from the internal history of the party, in which on the one hand an atmosphere of freedom still lingered around internal debates and, on the other, a strong desire to break with reformism and the parliamentary system was growing. Feminist voices could thus make themselves heard. This encounter had been prepared before and during World War I, when pacifism brought together men and women who shared the same revolutionary hopes.[56] Finally, although the Comintern blessed this encounter, its bolshevization of the PCF resulted in the split between communism and feminism.

Conclusion

In France where the progressive parties have laid claim to the universality of rights since 1789, male suffrage was precociously obtained in 1848, that of women, late in 1944. This advent of a truly universal suffrage was the result of a struggle led by feminists in which the communists had a role. It was in fact Fernand Grenier, a delegate of the PCF to the Consultative Assembly in Algiers who, in 1944, broke the Radical party's final resistance to female enfranchisement.[57] Thereafter, the PCF, reinforced by the Resistance, became the mass party it had dreamed of becoming during the first twenty years of its existence; it has maintained the best representation of female elected officials up to the present. While the level of women's activity in France is one of the highest in Europe,[58] the PCF has also taken up the question of the social citizenship of women. It has maintained, on the other hand, conservative positions on the family and sexuality.

The attitude of the Communist party toward women resulted from multiple causes: a dominant masculine tradition within the French labor movement; a minor but enduring presence of feminism within French socialism; a complex trick of mirrors with the image of the Soviet women; and, of course, the absolute primacy given to revolutionary and political requirements. All of this led to an astonishing feminism within the PCF in its first guise, at the beginning of the 1920s. This was followed by the sectarian pretension to exercise a monopoly of the liberation of working women, and by a break with the feminist groups of the party in its second guise. Finally, at the time of the Popular Front, the party held out its hand to feminists, while at the same time implementing a pro-natalist, moralist, and pro-family reversal. This liquidation of the feminist orientation would have lasting consequences on the political orientation of the party but not on recruitment, because "red women" were well represented during the Resistance and after the Liberation.[59] Militancy of the whole family remained the rule, and the sexual division of activist work would have its hours of glory in the 1950s and 1960s.[60] Perhaps most striking is the identical positions taken by Communists and Catholics when the issue came down to the emancipation of women.[61]

Notes

1. This question has been understudied. A few articles treat the matter, notably one by Jean-Louis Robert, "Le PCF et la question féminine," a report presented at the Conference of Linz, 1978, published in *Bulletin du Centre de recherche et d'histoire des mouvements sociaux et du syndicalisme* 3 (1978). See also Jacqueline Tardivel, "Des pacifistes aux résistantes, les militantes communistes en France dans l'entre-deux-guerres" (Ph.D. diss., University of Paris 7, 1993). *Le Dictionnaire biographique du mouvement ouvrier français (DBMOF)*, written under the direction of Jean Maitron and Claude Pennetier, is the richest source of information. The relationship between feminism and communism is one aspect of the work of Christine Bard, *Les Filles de Marianne: Histoire des féminismes 1914-1940* (Paris, 1995).

2. Tardivel, "Des pacifistes aux résistantes," p. 58.

3. In 1934 the PCF had 42,500 members; by the end of 1935 it had 87,000, 235,000 in 1936, 302,000 in 1937, and 319,000 in 1938. From 1936 on, its adherents outnumbered those of the SFIO, according to Jean-Paul Brunet, *Histoire du PCF* (Paris, 1982), p. 52.

4. Tardivel, "Des pacifistes aux résistantes," p. 58.

5. This is the opinion of Danièle Tartakowsky in "Les Manifestations de rue en France" (Ph.D. diss., University of Paris I, 1994).

6. Madeleine Rebérioux, "Le mouvement syndical et les femmes jusqu'au Front Populaire," *Le Féminisme et ses enjeux* (Paris, 1988), p. 70.

7. See her biography by Colette Cosnier, *La Bolchevique aux bijoux* (Paris, 1988).

8. Jeannette Vermeersch met Maurice Thorez in Moscow. Married, he separated from his wife and lived with his new companion from 1934 on. They had one child out of wedlock and only married after World War II.

9. As an example, there was no text written by a woman in the entire collection established by Nicole Racine and Louis Bodin. See *Le PCF entre les deux guerres* (Paris, 1972). It is true that texts by women were fewer, but they did exist, even during the low tide at the end of the 1920s. Marguerite Faussecave, member of the Central Committee from 1920 to 1923, published *La Femme dans la société capitaliste* (Paris, 1926). She was excluded in 1928 and became a Trotskyist. One year before being elected to the Central Committee, she published *Debout les femmes. A bas la guerre* (Paris, 1925). The militant women of the first generation had easier access to publishing than their succeeding ones.

10. This quote from Bernadette Cattanéo and the following ones are taken from two manuscript autobiographies: one of five pages is dated 1931 the other of seventeen pages is dated 1937. Written for the Third International, they are preserved in the Moscow Archives. We thank Claude Pennetier for having directed us to them.

11. Colette Jobard, interview with Jacques Varin, 3 January 1975. Cited in *Jeunes comme JC* (Paris, 1975), p. 239.

12. A battalion of the International Brigades in Spain was named for her.

13. "As far as my pseudonym is concerned, it might appear very pretentious today. But in my juvenile enthusiasm of an eighteen-year-old, I at first took as my patron, Louise Michel, the heroine of the Commune, for whom I had great admiration. Later on, at the time of the first talk I gave in my cell (which was called the local group of Fontenay-sous-Bois), I was asked to talk about Rosa Luxemburg, who had been murdered in Germany. From that day on, I decided that my

two patrons were Rosa Luxemburg and Louise Michel." (Interview with Rosa Michel, 7 January 1975, *Jeunes comme JC*, p. 77).

14. During the 1920s, a group of pioneers (scouts) had the name, Children of Jeanne Labourbe.
15. Gilbert Badia, *Clara Zetkin: féministe sans frontières* (Paris, 1993), p. 218.
16. Charles Sowerwine, *Les Femmes et le socialisme* (Paris, 1978), pp. 237-38.
17. Tardivel, "Des Pacifistes aux résistantes," p. 197.
18. Jean Charles, et al., *Le Congrès de Tours* (Paris, 1980), p. 135.
19. While the International of Socialist Youth was founded in 1907 at Stuttgart, the National Federation of Socialist Youth was not created until 1913.
20. Speech made by the young Vandomme at the Congress of 1920, quoted in Charles, *Congrès de Tours*, p. 640.
21. The police report on this meeting is quoted by Tardivel, "Des pacifistes aux résistantes," p. 104.
22. 1 March 1932, cited in Tardivel, "Des pacifistes aux résistantes," p. 423.
23. Tartakowsky, "Le PCF et les femmes," *Cahiers de l'Institut Maurice Thorez*, 14 July 1975.
24. Tardivel, "Des pacifistes aux résistantes," p. 90.
25. For the years 1922, 1924, 1926, 1927, 1930, 1932, 1933, 1936, 1937, and 1938.
26. This tradition was continued with the Popular Rescue Mission of France, founded in 1938.
27. Tardivel, "Des pacifistes aux résistantes," p. 39.
28. In the *DBMOF* Tardivel enumerates twenty-three notices of French women who departed for Spain.
29. See the perceptive article by Susan B. Whitney, "Embracing the Status Quo: French Communists, Young Women and the Popular Front," *Journal of Social History* 30, 1 (fall 1996).
30. Danielle Casanova, born in Corsica in 1909 joined the Communist Youth in 1928 when she was a student of dental surgery in Paris. She created a women's committee in October 1940, was arrested in 1942, and died at Auschwitz in 1943. The PCF celebrated her as a great heroine of the Resistance.
31. Varin, *Jeunes comme JC*, p. 238.
32. Christine Bard. "L'Apôtre sociale et l'ange du foyer. Les femmes et la CFTC à travers *Le Nord-Social* (1920-1936)," *Le Mouvement social* 165 (October 1993): 23-41.
33. Tardivel should be commended for undertaking the linguistic research we are relying upon here.
34. Tardivel, "Des pacifistes aux résistantes," p. 439.
35. Ibid., p. 438.
36. Lynn Hunt, *The Family Romance of the French Revolution* (Berkeley, 1992).
37. Eric Weitz underscores the point in "The Heroic Man and the Ever-Changing Woman: Gender and Politics in European Communism, 1917-1950," in *Gender and the Reconstruction of European Working-Class History*, eds. Laura Frader and Sonya Rose (Ithaca, N.Y., 1995).
38. Madeleine Guilbert, *Les Femmes et l'organisation syndicale avant 1914* (Paris, 1966). See also Marie-Hélène Zylberberg- Hocquard, *Féminisme et syndicalisme en France* (Paris, 1978).
39. The following draws upon the work of Françoise Blum, "Féminisme et syndicalisme. Les femmes dans la Fédération de l'Habillement 1914-1935." (M.A. thesis, University of Paris I, 1978).
40. Ibid., Annex IV.

41. See Anne-Marie Sohn, "Exemplarité et limites de la participation féminine à la vie syndicale: les institutrices de la CGTU," *Revue d'histoire moderne et contemporaine*, XXIV (July-September, 1977): 391-414.
42. Leaflet of Madeleine Charpentier, *DBMOF* 22: 140.
43. *L'Ouvrière*, 25 March 1922.
44. *L'Ouvrière*, 14 April 1923.
45. Christine Bard, "Proletarians of the Proletariat: Women's Citizenship in France," *International Labor and Working-Class History* 48 (Fall 1995): 49-67.
46. Quoted by Christine Vérot in "La Question du vote des femmes devant le parlement entre les deux guerres." (M.A. thesis, University of Lille III, 1987), p. 93.
47. *L'Ouvrière*, 13 December 1923.
48. See Bard, "Marianne and the mother rabbits: feminism and natality under the Third Republic," in *Population and Social Policy in France*, eds., Maire Cross and Sheila Perry (London and Washington, 1997), pp. 34-48.
49. See Bard (ed.), *Madeleine Pelletier (1874-1939). Logique et infortunes d'un combat pour l'égalité* (Paris, 1992) and Charles Sowerwine and Claude Maignien, *Madeleine Pelletier, une féministe dans l'arène politique* (Paris, 1992).
50. François Delpla, "Les communistes français et la sexualité (1932-1938)," *Le Mouvement social* 91 (April-June, 1975): 140.
51. Michelle Perrot, "L'éloge de la ménagère dans le discours des ouvriers français du XIXe siècle," *Romantisme* 13-14 (1976): 105-121.
52. See Delpla, "Les communistes français," based on a detailed reading of *Regards* in 1933.
53. "Les femmes dans le parti communiste," *Cahiers du bolchevisme* (1937): 118-21. Quoted by Tardivel in "Des pacifistes aux résistantes," p. 114.
54. See Jean Rabaut, *Tout est possible. Les gauchistes français 1929-1944* (Paris, 1974).
55. See Jean-Louis Robert, "La CGT et la famille ouvrière 1914-1918. Première approche," *Le Mouvement social* 116 (July-September, 1981): 47-66.
56. See Christine Bard, "Diversité des parcours de féministes dans le *Dictionnaire biogaphique du mouvement ouvrier*," in *Les Dictionnaires biographiques du mouvement ouvrier: lectures, exploitations, apports à l'historiographie* (Paris, 1996).
57. See the testimony of Fernand Grenier in *C'était ainsi …* (Paris, 7th ed., 1978), p. 220; and the document reproduced in the annex, p. 279: "Comment fut acquis le vote des femmes française," drawn from a note of 1958 for the publication *d'Heures Claires* (a magazine of the Union of French Women). See also William Guéraiche, "Les femmes politiques de 1944 à 1947: quelle libération?" *Clio, Histoire, femmes et société* 1 (1995): 165-86.
58. See Anne-Marie Sohn, "Entre-deux-guerres. Les roles féminins en France et en Angleterre," *Histoire des femmes en Occident. Le XXe siècle*, eds., Georges Duby, Michelle Perrot, and Françoise Thébaud, vol. 5, (Paris, 1992), pp. 91-114.
59. Renée Rousseau, *Les Femmes rouges* (Paris, 1983).
60. Dominique Loiseau insists on the importance of the activism of "housewives" in "Femmes et militantisme: Saint-Nazaire et sa région 1930-1980" (Ph.D. diss., University of Paris 7, 1993) and idem, "Associations féminines et syndicalisme en Loire-Atlantique, des années 1930 aux années 1980," *Clio, Histoire, Femmes et Société* 3 (1996): 141-61.
61. See Sylvie Chaperon, "Le creux de la vague. Mouvements féminins et féminismes 1945-1970" (Ph.D. diss., European Institute University, Florence, 1996) on the women's movements in France from Liberation to the beginning of the 1970s.

Chapter 9

"Ideals of Redemption"
Socialism and Women on the Left in Spain

Mary Nash

I n Spain, the relationship between socialism and women unfolded within a complicated context: the labor movement was under the strong influence of radical anarchism; the Catholic Church with its social reform institutions also was a significant competitor and opponent. The Socialist party, *Partido Obrero Socialista Español* (PSOE), was founded in 1879, and the Socialist trade union, *Unión General de Trabajadores* (UGT) almost a decade later, in 1888. Together with anarchism, which had a more radical labor and revolutionary agenda, socialism shaped the socio-political scenario of the Left in Spain from the nineteenth century to the Civil War. Although a small number of socialists adhered to the Third International in the 1920s, communism did not play a significant role on the Spanish Left until the appearance of Soviet aid to the Spanish Republic during the Civil War.

A Male Scenario: Socialist Organizations

Since its creation the PSOE followed a strict labor agenda excluding feminism and paid little attention to gender issues. Until World War I the PSOE was essentially male, with a tiny female membership. Even then, only about one hundred women with traditional occupations such as dressmaking, ironing, tailoring, and laundering were among the 37,000

Notes for this chapter begin on page 375.

affiliates of the *Casa del Pueblo*, the socialist cultural center in Madrid.[1] Women socialists were negligible in both the party and trade unions. They played a very ancillary role in the official socialist movement, which neglected women's issues.

In 1923 General Primo de Rivera took over state control in a political dictatorship that lasted until 1929. During this period the collaborationist policy of the PSOE saved it from the brutal repression experienced by the anarchist movement. The fall of the dictatorship and the impact of democratization under the Second Republic established in April 1931 led to the renewed vigor of the Left. Moderate reformism, social democracy, or a combination of Jacobinism and reformism enacted by republicans and socialists have been the historical interpretations used to describe the political project of the progressive coalition government (1931 to 1933).[2] As a social-democratic party the PSOE followed a gradualist, reformist agenda that aimed to achieve a long-term policy of social transformation within the legally proclaimed democratic system. During its term of office the PSOE was committed to reformist policies that did not pursue radical changes.[3] However, by 1934 the increasing radicalization of some sectors of the socialist movement, the acceptance of revolutionary rhetoric, and the inability to overcome internal organizational rivalry seriously split the socialist movement; this later undermined its effectiveness during the Civil War.[4] By the early 1930s UGT affiliation was very high, representing around 20 to 25 percent of the active population of the working-class. In April 1931 the UGT had around 300,000 affiliates and by the fall this number had more than doubled to 654,403 members. A year later, at the UGT Congress held in October 1932, socialist syndicalism reached its peak of 1,041,539 members.[5] By then the UGT was the most powerful union, followed by the anarchist CNT which had a membership of approximately 800,000 by 1934.[6]

Socialism continued to be a male domain, since women were only a small minority of members holding party or union cards. The favorable political climate in the 1930s accounts for some increase in women's involvement with socialism. Although the UGT established lower membership fees for women in 1932,[7] female membership was just over 4 percent of UGT affiliates (with 41,948 female members at the time of its over a million membership peak in 1932).[8] A highly significant number of female unionists did not come from an urban, industrial background; the greatest increase in female membership was in the Agrarian Union (FNTT), which accounted for over a third of the overall female affiliation of the UGT in 1932. Agrarian workers represented 34 percent of female membership followed by smaller representations in the traditional trades of garment and canvas sandalmaking, leather and furs, textiles, commerce, and chemicals.[9] The female constituency of socialism was quite different from that of anarchism as it was composed mainly of women in nonindustrial occupations. By the early 1930s a slight shift in the professional profile of female members can be detected, although traditional occupations still predominated. A majority of women members of the Madrid organization gave their profession as "their labors," that is, housewives. Wives and daughters of male militants amounted to 51 percent of the total female membership. Nonetheless, there was a significant increase in the presence of new female professions in the 1930s, with 25.7 percent coming from the more modern careers of primary and secondary schoolteachers, office workers, stenographers, typists, and nurses.[10]

The Woman Question: A Socialist Agenda?

The question remains to be answered why Spanish socialism was a hostile environment to women and incapable of attracting them to the movement, and why Spanish women did not identify with the official politics of socialism. Since the beginning, the official party line neglected women and offered a reductionist view on their emancipation: the social struggle was the only agenda and socialism the universal answer for women. Any concern for women's rights tended to be voiced around work. By the early twentieth century, the denial of specific gender issues led socialist leaders, including activist women such as Virginia Gonzalez, later a cofounder of the Spanish Communist party (PCOE), to reject a feminist agenda and to propose a complementary role for working women as dependent spouses and helpers for the socialist cause.[11] Most male socialists viewed women's role as peripheral and complementary. Women were not accorded direct political or syndical agency nor did socialists officially discuss the "woman question" through the vision of feminism. How then, did women within the socialist movement organize and define their agenda? Were the official women's organizations strongholds of socialist feminism or did they abide by official policies?

A number of responses to these questions may be found in an exploration of the women's socialist organizations. The first official female socialist groups were created in 1902 by the PSOE to accommodate female membership.[12] In 1925 María Cambrils referred to the Feminist Socialist Groups (AFS) as "feminist organisms" where "all women desirous of vindicating their rights" could find a place.[13] She claimed that socialist feminism represented an expression of social confraternity. Cambrils envisaged the AFS as a strategy to achieve a state of social justice through cooperation among women[14] and believed that through the bonds of fraternity, the AFS would defend civil liberties and a socialist agenda. Working together within a clearly defined socialist political environment was seen as a feminist strategy that would empower women and thus overcome the existing status of being "a slave to men."[15] The ultimate goal of the AFS was not only to train women to be more convinced socialists but also to gain equal rights and gender parity. These challenging aims sought to create spaces that empowered women with a clearly defined feminist and socialist agenda. However, available sources on women's socialist associations tell quite a different story from the enthusiastic feminist scenario envisaged by Cambrils.

The example of the most important women's socialist organization, the Group of Feminist Socialists of Madrid (AFSM), illuminates the ancillary role prescribed for and, to a large extent, accepted by the socialist women's groups. Records of the organization do not provide a feminist reading of the goals and strategies of the AFSM in accordance with the views expressed by Cambrils.[16] In the years of its existence between 1926 and 1927, the AFSM had a total of 527 members.[17] Of these, 158 did not declare any occupation and almost half were housewives. Among those with declared professions, 62.4 percent worked in jobs in the garment sector as dressmakers, seamstresses, shirt makers, hat makers, embroiderers, ironers, tiemakers, trimmers, and laundresses. Domestic servants and teachers each accounted for 6 percent, followed by midwives with 4.5 percent. The rest came from a variety of different professions such as students, actresses, cooks, journalists, hairdressers, saleswomen, bookkeepers, and florists. Striking for a labor organization, only one member had an industrial occupation.[18]

The AFSM was not autonomous; it functioned as a mere auxiliary to the PSOE. According to its regulations AFSM members had to conform to party directives, but the right to vote at the general assemblies was limited to PSOE members. Moreover, any public contestation of the official PSOE line could lead to expulsion from the AFSM. Significantly too, men played an influential role in the development of the AFSM through the post of Assessor and Vice Assessor. They did not have a vote in its Assembly but were extremely influential in establishing the policies to be followed.[19] Few women expressed dissent either about the level of party control or male authority. One exception was Carmen Jordan who confronted Assessor Francisco Saborit about the presence of male speakers at a meeting of the AFSM. Saborit replied that if there were no male speakers the meeting would be a failure. Jordan also challenged the influence of the Socialist Youth Organization in the activities of the AFSM. However, when these differences were put to a vote, Jordan lost by twenty-six to six.[20] Jordan, a dressmaker and embroiderer, was one of the few dissenters who actively claimed women's authority and voice within the AFSM. The majority of members followed strict party discipline and the established agenda.[21]

The regulations left no doubt that the priority of the AFSM was attracting women to socialism. Members had to propagate socialist principles, read and disseminate the official socialist newspaper, *El Socialista*, and attend socialist rallies. In contrast to Cambrils' view that the AFSM represented the interests of socialist feminism, its record makes no mention of a feminist agenda. Moreover, in twenty-seven meetings of its General Assembly between 1906 and 1915, there was just a single reference to feminism raised by a male assessor, Francisco Saborit. He proposed a motion for the next PSOE Congress that the socialist press devote more attention to a "feminist class movement."[22] The goal of the AFSM was not the promotion of socialist feminism but rather of mainstream socialism, and it quite clearly acted as a vehicle to transmit a socialist agenda to women and not, as Cambrils alleged, to empower women through a socialist reading of feminism. Margarita Nelken, a fringe socialist in 1919, a prominent socialist parliamentary deputy during the Second Republic, and finally a PCE member during the Civil War, was very critical of socialist women's initiatives. She criticized the AFSM for its total lack of enterprise and complete dependency on their male companions: "Everything begins and ends in aiding a number of prisoners or carrying banners at the marches organized by their companions."[23] Indeed, throughout its long existence, the AFSM confirmed Nelken's doubts, since its activities focused primarily on solidarity campaigns for imprisoned socialists, economic aid for socialist congresses, and attendance at socialist rallies. Only a few gender-specific activities were undertaken: sporadic political training for women and promotion of the enactment of existing protective labor regulation for women workers. The AFSM was not effective in developing a feminist vision of socialism. The socialist initiative to organize women as a distinct constituency in separate organizations was not a success, since it did not lead to an increase in overall female party or union membership. By subordinating women's issues to class politics and the larger socialist struggle, it did not identify a specific women's agenda in gender or feminist terms and thus failed to create a strong female socialist constituency.

The "Ideal of Redemption": Socialist Feminism

In the 1920s a number of women developed a socialist understanding of feminism and women's needs, although their views had little resonance in official party structures. Exceptional voices representing socialism such as María Cambrils, or fringe socialists such as Margarita Nelken and the writer Carmen de Burgos, addressed feminism in popular books and writings. This, however, did not imply recognition of female authority and women's goals within socialist feminism. The problems of a silenced group finding a voice comes to the fore in the expression of socialist feminism. The lack of acknowledgment of female individuality, the implication of transgression by women wielding the pen, the complex power relations among couples, and the diverse strategies of resistance used by women writers must be addressed. As a professional writer and pioneer journalist, Carmen de Burgos, a fringe socialist who for a period of time was a member of the AFSM, managed to establish herself in the world of journalism and letters.[24] Yet she was fully aware of the difficulties involved in the acknowledgment of the legitimate authority of a female voice and used diverse strategies such as a pseudonym to differentiate between her "serious" works and other writings.[25] Although not definitively proven, it has been alleged that *Feminismo Socialista*, published by Maria Cambrils, was in fact written by her companion, the anarchist journalist J. Alarcón.[26] This allegation raises numerous problems in reading this work as an expression of the voice of socialist women.

Another example of the difficulty in establishing the legitimacy of the female socialist voice is the case of María Lejárraga. Historians and literary critics have agreed that most of the highly regarded literary works signed by Gregorio Martínez Sierra had in fact been written by his wife, María Lejárraga de Martínez Sierra.[27] She intentionally hid her female identity in the subversive act of writing and occupying a male-defined space. Yet, paradoxically, she also had a high public profile in the 1930s as one of the very few female socialist parliamentary deputies. From 1930 to 1936 she energetically devoted herself to socialist campaigning throughout Spain.[28] Again, in another major paradox, she was the acknowledged author of some significant works on women's rights,[29] yet she continued deliberately to use her husband's name as a pseudonym. In the tense atmosphere of constraints by gender codes, she used the strategy of anonymity to conserve her respectability in a society that regarded literary women to be disreputable.[30] However, she also used the legitimacy of a public male signature to espouse feminist principles.[31] She was a feminist activist and the Spanish representative on the International Women's Suffrage Association. Still, she continued to reject her public female subjectivity as a writer by maintaining her anonymity and in silence assumed the identity of the other, her long estranged husband. Her first book was published in 1898, but she waited over fifty years, until after her husband's death, to finally proclaim what she called her "motherhood" of almost eighty works attributed to her husband.[32] Despite a commitment to socialism and feminism, the force of patriarchal social control and the pressure of the symbolic violence of gender codes threatened female transgression to such an extent that energetic, convinced feminist socialists bowed to traditional gender codes or negotiated strategies for survival and dissent.

In the postwar years the term feminism became more generalized in socialist circles. In 1919 Margarita Nelken identified feminism mainly in economic terms as the means of fulfilling women's economic independence through gainful employment.[33] In 1925 María Cambrils broke with tradition by actually entitling her book *Feminismo Socialista*. Two years later, Carmen de Burgos defined feminism as a "social party that works to achieve justice that does not enslave half of humankind to the detriment of everyone" and espoused it as the defense of justice, gender equality, women's freedom, and the social good.[34] The adoption of a feminist agenda was always hesitant on the Spanish Left. The weak development of liberal feminism and suffragism in Spain influenced the development of socialist feminism. The crucial role of Catholic and confessional feminism, and the traditional identification of women's issues as Church matters, however, were even more significant constraints on its formulation.

Both socialists and anarchists tended to feel that Catholic and bourgeois women had appropriated the usages and meanings of feminism as a strategy to recruit women to a religious and class reading of female roles in society. Mainstream anarchism had traditionally rejected the specificity of female subordination and located the problem of human emancipation outside the context of gender differences. Federica Montseny,[35] the anarchist leader and revolutionary activist, later the first Spanish woman to hold ministerial office in 1936, openly rejected feminism proclaiming: "Feminism? Never! Humanism always!"[36] She identified feminism with bourgeois women but also rejected it on the grounds that there was no such thing as a woman question. For her, the heart of the matter was the enigma that men and women were for one another. She postulated the development of the full potential of the human personality by both men and women in the framework of libertarian communism.[37]

A careful distinction must be made between the heightened awareness of women's issues by a number of women writers and the absence of an official socialist feminist policy. The initial development of socialist feminism was, like other strands of Spanish feminism, a response to other definitions of feminism.[38] It responded to strong Catholic feminism and had to deal both with the pervasive influence of Church doctrine on women and the appropriation of feminism by Catholic feminists. In the presentation to her book *Feminismo Socialista*, María Cambrils openly stated her anti-clerical opposition to sectarian Catholic feminism that she characterized as "sterilized feminism, which is inspired by a phobic sectarianism that is a declared enemy of liberties, individual rights, and female civil emancipation."[39] Aware of the great impact of conservative Catholic organizations on women, Cambrils denounced Spanish women who had been captivated by the message of a sectarian religious discourse that had increased women's subjugation. Her definition of socialist feminism was clearly opposed to Catholic misogyny and dogmatic principles. It also recognized the repercussions of the Church's ongoing dedication to women's issues and organizations and to the meanings of Catholic culture in Spain. Moreover, the development of Catholic social reform in the labor movement and its constant dedication to working-class women offered a stark contrast to the lack of dedication by socialists to women's issues and was a bitter reminder of the powerful rivalry between the two in the labor movement. Cambrils openly admitted that the political force of the Church and its cultural supremacy among women were a double obstacle to the achievement of socialism in the political sphere and to the development of feminism among women.[40]

Traditional Catholic beliefs considered women's dedication to waged work as unnatural, degrading, and a deviation from women's divine destiny as mothers with a full-time dedication to the home. However, faced with the reality of women in the labor market by the 1920s, social reform Catholicism had developed a very active role in the labor movement through its dedication to working women.[41] A year before the publication of Cambrils' book the impact of Catholic syndicalism on women was already demonstrated in the creation of the National Federation of Catholic Workers (CNOC). The Catholic women's union movement focused on protective legislation for female workers, maternity insurance, regulation of home work, representation of female workers in social organizations, and professional training. The CNOC was openly confessional and espoused a defense of religion and the need to foster the religious education of working women. It also defended the existing capitalist regime, private property, and deference to authority. By 1926 approximately 35,000 women workers were represented at the CNOC Confederal Assembly and by 1931 the CNOC had representatives in 103 unions. It also ran sewing and food cooperatives, mutual benefit societies for the sick, and employment agencies. During the Second Republic the CNOC lost some members to socialist syndicalism.[42] María Cambrils and socialist leaders were right to be concerned about the rival Catholic unions and their greater attraction for women workers. In fact, not until 1932 – with the PSOE well installed in government – did female members of the socialist union reach the level of CNOC membership.

Following a longstanding tradition on the Spanish Left, a religious vocabulary and cosmology permeated Cambrils' vision of feminism. She posited a view of socialist feminism as an "ideal of redemption," a religion of love, peace, tolerance and respect, based on the values of social justice.[43] In her view religious beliefs were not an impediment to the practice of socialist feminism. Her feminist creed evoked the figure of the worker, Jesus of Nazareth: "We are, then, profoundly religious – not catholic – in our personal views."[44] She went on to invoke her sources of moral inspiration, the Bible, the Gospels, Marx's *Capital*, and Bebel's *Woman in the Past, Present, and Future*.[45] In her autobiography María Lejárraga also used religious language to conjure up her commitment to socialism.[46] Despite a religious cosmology expressed by many female socialists,[47] it is also revealing that María Cambrils severely criticized religious organizations for accentuating the ignorance and dependence of Spanish women. Like Federica Montseny, Cambrils believed that Spanish women were victims of ignorance enforced by a religious education that made them unconscious, submissive instruments of male supremacy.[48]

Class politics was also at the core of Cambrils' feminism. As a follower of Marx, she challenged capitalism and considered socialism as the means to socialize interests, work, means of production, and general wealth.[49] María Lejárraga regarded socialism mainly as a means to social justice and to overcome the endemic poverty that characterized Spain. In contrast to Cambrils' working-class reading of socialist feminism, she espoused a middle-class reading of socialism as a solution to the economic distress of middle-class families like her own, which had suffered economic deprivation. Her feminist activism was also oriented toward promoting consciousness among middle-class women. Margarita Nelken also expressed a significant interest in the economic plight of middle-class women. She identified feminism in economic terms as the agenda of middle-class and working-class women workers inspired by economic needs.[50] In the immediate postwar period she even invoked the authority of U.S. President Wilson's claim that feminism was democracy. Feminist dissidence remained isolated, because mainstream socialism did not openly raise the woman question. Few women denounced "male dictatorship" as Cambrils had, nor was the need for a specific feminist agenda based on equality and individual rights within a socialist framework often expressed.[51] The nature of socialist feminism was never clearly defined and disseminated under the banner of socialism during the Second Republic, which accounts for the continued blurring of a specific socialist feminist identity throughout the period of the Civil War.[52]

Domesticity, Gender Identity, and the New Modern Woman

Socialist women had to measure their behavior against set models of femininity and masculinity that shaped their contestation, compliance, and feminist strategies. Political conservatism, the weight of the Roman Catholic Church as a pervasive political institution, and economic underdevelopment have often been given as the main explanation for the situation of women in modern Spain.[53] The modernization of gender discourse also was a significant force in the interwar period. The conceptualization of sexual difference within cultural parameters is one of the keys to understanding the difficulties Spanish women had in contesting cultural norms and established gender identities.[54]

Sociobiological thought – expressed in the notion of the biological destiny of motherhood – continued to determine women's social commitment and role in interwar Spain. In line with the prevalent European ideology of domesticity, motherhood was evoked as the apogee of women's social destiny and self fulfillment. This model of good mothering and housewifery, based on the cultural representation of the "Angel of the Hearth," encouraged the notion that women's role in society was restricted to home and family. The continued centrality of domesticity in Left ideology also justified women's exclusion from gainful employment. In the labor movement femininity was defined exclusively through motherhood and masculinity through the male breadwinner's monopoly to paid work.[55] This led to a pervasive cross-class rejection of women's right to gainful employment while also reserving the public arena of politics as a male preserve.

The growing modernization of Spanish society in the interwar years entailed significant modifications in economic and social structures which, in turn, generated changes in the ideological discourse on women. The traditional cultural representation of women was challenged by a more modern gender discourse based on the model of the new modern woman, already in vogue in many European countries.[56] This shift modified more restrictive gender roles to the new needs of the labor market. The "new modern woman" came to represent women's emancipation in the collective imagery of Spanish society, in which modernity was associated with progressive views and values. The concept was liberating for many Spanish women, who used it in their struggle to legitimate their claims to public spaces, new experiences, and freedom.

The importance of the notion of modernity in the subjective construction of a new gender identity by women on the Left can be seen in *La Victoria*, the first novel published by anarchist leader Federica Montseny in 1925. In the subtitle she presented her book as a narrative of "the problems of a moral order that are presented to women with modern ideas." Montseny claimed that her novel was subversive because it addressed the problem of the freedom and dignity of women and thus confronted all "the millenarian prejudices of masculinity."[57] The prototype of the "modern woman" advocated by this highly individualistic anarchist was one full of confidence and awareness that the destiny of humankind depended on individual woman. Two years later the notion of the modern woman was also energetically defended by Carmen de Burgos who argued that modernity gave a decisive impulse to women's emancipation by developing the female personality and legitimating women's voice of authority, freedom and dignity.[58]

The new modern woman was not associated with the flapper, who was generally viewed with disapproval by many women on the Left. Yet, Burgos and Montseny's own unorthodox lifestyles broke with traditional canons of gender respectability; Montseny openly defended free love, and de Burgos challenged the constraints of married life, but both also reinvented their own codes of moral decency and respectability.[59] Women across the political divide of Right and Left used this new gender model as active social agents in their claim for the recognition of a work identity for women. Despite its modernizing effect, it must be stressed that the new gender model of modernity also maintained the cornerstone of traditional gender identity by redefining women in a new way, essentially as mothers and child bearers. Moreover, the modern version of gender discourse was still based on biological essentialism, which was highly effective because it was formulated by doctors who legitimated it on modern scientific and medical grounds.[60] This new social-biological discourse of domesticity continued to define women's destiny as motherhood, thus converging with traditional discourse on domesticity in its legitimation of a strict division into two spheres: the sexual division of labor; and the construction of female cultural identity through motherhood. In this way, biological motherhood embraced the notion of social motherhood with the implication of a mandatory contribution of maternal resources and services to society. This new concept of social motherhood was decisive in the legitimation of a differential notion of citizenship that produced a gendered understanding of political subjectivity and female agency, which became crucial in shaping women's experience of politics throughout this period.

Few female socialists dissented from the sociobiological view that defined women's identity through motherhood. María Cambrils was outstanding in voicing another vision of women's potential. She braved general public and medical hostility by daring to challenge Dr. Gregorio Marañón,[61] the major proponent of medical gender discourse, for disseminating pseudo-scientific opinions that reinforced the subjugation of women. Domesticity and motherhood, she argued, reinforced women's slavery.[62] This challenge to established gender discourse was highly exceptional, even on the Left.

The anarcho-feminist Lucia Sánchez Saornil was another significant dissenting female voice which also dared to repudiate Marañón's view of motherhood as the irrefutable destiny of women. She denounced this notion of destiny as representing the subjection of women to the biological process of reproduction: "To be born, to give birth, and to die."[63] The development of women's potential irrespective of the biological condition of motherhood was one of the principal goals of this feminist anarchist. The individual rights of a woman as a person were paramount in Sánchez

Saornil's view that claimed woman's identity as an individual. In more moderate, conciliatory, and highly contradictory terms De Burgos also denied that sexual difference should be of any importance in the "domains of thought, free access to employment, and equality before justice and the law."[64] At the same time she expressed her immense admiration for Marañón and gave a more favorable reading of his texts.[65] Still, both openly subversive viewpoints and moderate critiques were highly exceptional among Spanish women on the Left.

It is difficult to identify distinguishing traits of gender discourse developed with a specific socialist focus. Apparently the ideology of domesticity, representing both inter-class and cross-political gender values, was generally accepted in the Spanish labor movement. The subversive critique by a small number of women did not raise a collective response among fellow socialists, anarchists, or other feminists. The late entrance to higher education by Spanish women (1910) may account for this lack of critique. Thus, they did not have an established group of physicians or scientists who might have offered an alternative scientific view to the discriminatory gender norms espoused by male doctors. Medical authority appeared incontestible in a society that founded gender identity on nature, religion, and modern science. The neglect of feminism in the PSOE and the lack of a cohesive group of socialist feminist thinkers and politicians also helps to explain the limitations of the theoretical and practical challenges to the predominant gender discourse on the Left.

Work and Women's Collective Agency

During World War I Spain was a nonbelligerent country. The sudden increase in production, economic expansion, and enrichment of manufacturers contrasted sharply with galloping inflation, price increases, and deterioration of living conditions among the working classes.[66] These adverse circumstances provoked acute social conflict throughout Spain peaking in what has been called the "failed revolution" of the immediate postwar years.[67] In Barcelona, between 1915 and 1921 prices of the principal food requirements increased 80 percent. Difficulties in subsistence intensified social tensions with an increasing number of strikes leading in December 1916 to a general strike in Barcelona under trade union leadership, protesting against the increases of food prices, that spread throughout Spain with a political and labor agenda.[68]

International postwar instability had a variety of repercussions in Spain: The Catalan nationalist movement mobilized under the banner of the promise of Wilson's defense of self-determination;[69] the myth of the Bolshevik Revolution, which sparked numerous strikes and peasant uprisings during the period known as the Bolshevik Three Years (1918 to 1920);[70] and several experiments at collective expropriation of capitalist property in rural areas, with Bolshevik Republics proclaimed in some Andalusian villages.[71] Although these protests were led mainly by anarchist syndicalists, socialist unions also played a part. By 1918, however, a policy shift led the PSOE leadership to abandon radical politics and opt for parliamentary action to achieve its goals.

The increased number of female wage workers spurred the participation of women in labor and social conflicts, although socialist and anarchist unions did not provide a friendly environment for them or attempt to implement gender demands such as equal wages in their everyday practice. As early as 1879 the founding program of the PSOE addressed the issue of women's waged work by demanding the prohibition of all unhygienic work and any job contrary to the "proper conduct" of women.[72] The first Conference of the PSOE in 1888 declared the principle of wage equity but, almost fifty years later, the 1932 Conference of the UGT still felt compelled to claim wage parity for women in order to end gender wage discrimination. There were clear discrepancies between official socialist statements and commonplace discrimination.[73] Women's access to paid jobs continued to be a contentious gender issue in the interwar years and even during the period of more revolutionary changes during the Civil War.[74] Despite lip service to the contrary, the persistence of discriminatory practices was openly acknowledged by prominent male socialists such as Dr. César Juarros, who denounced socialists for using such tactics to exclude married women from the labor market.[75] During the reformist period of the Second Republic (1931 to 1933) there was greater commitment to women's right to work; however, at labor conventions, sponsored by socialists, wage parity was not demanded despite the egalitarian character of the new Constitution.[76] The strong commitment to the breadwinner definition of male identity continued to prevail, despite legal changes and the stance of some socialist women such as the lawyer Matilde Huici, who claimed that gainful employment was the principal means to achieve economic independence and women's emancipation.[77]

Male monopoly of paid work was the underlying assumption within the socialist movement. Concern for the state of women workers was not necessarily voiced to solve the triple burden of paid work, housework, and childbearing, but rather to eliminate the need for women in the labor market. A very negative view of women workers prevailed, portraying them as disloyal competitors to male workers, with the implication that they were an impediment to the social struggle due to their lack of political awareness. Male workers' resistence to female waged workers was both explicit and constant.[78] One writer referred to the universal war of male against female workers.[79] Most working-class organizations assumed that female workers were responsible for lower wages and were an obstacle to the advance of the labor struggle.[80] Hostility to women workers was quite effective in dissuading them from seeking jobs. Male strategies for preventing women from holding jobs were many, but few reached the degree of provoking a strike, as happened in Barcelona in the summer of 1915. Then, workers in a number of soup factories launched a four-month strike with the explicit goal of having women occupying so-called men's jobs dismissed and of enforcing labor regulations that would impede women from holding production jobs in those factories.[81] Twenty years later, in July 1935, another such strike took place in a paper factory in Alcoy to protest a female worker being assigned a job at a specific machine.[82]

The hostility of male workers together with the pressure of the predominant discourse on domesticity created significant obstacles for women in the labor market. Despite a hostile work environment and occupational segregation, many women were gainfully employed without being recorded in official data.[83] During the interwar years women were very under represented in the labor market and, despite the growing modernization of the economy, their numbers did not increase. Between 1920 and 1940 they represented just 12 percent of the labor force, mainly in the traditional sectors of domestic and agrarian work.[84]

By the 1920s some exceptional women campaigned for women's right to work as individuals and not to serve the needs of the family economy. Margarita Nelken openly criticized working-class leaders for not mobilizing women workers to defend their rights as a means of achieving overall improvements in the condition of male and female workers. In her view the blindness of the labor movement towards women workers derived from their ignorance of the fact that the woman question was an economic problem and, hence, a social question. She claimed that feminist demands for wage parity had to be considered as a strategy to defend the global labor interests of the whole working class. Significantly, one of the main goals of her writings was not to focus public attention on the plight of industrial workers but rather on clerks and shop assistants who, she claimed, were the most exploited of working women.[85] She also championed the cause of poorer middle-class women, obliged to hide their economic needs because of social conventions, which compelled them to accept inferior working conditions. The high incidence of women in the unregulated sector of home work also drew her attention. She demanded protective legislation for women workers, a work schedule differentiated by gender, and nursery services for married workers to help them comply with their domestic duties.[86]

To some extent her views reflected the attitudes of mainstream socialism given the inevitability of women in the workforce. What distinguished her position was that she challenged the notion of the male family wage by claiming married women's economic independency through their right and duty to gainful employment. Despite such advances, gender codes defining female identity through motherhood overrode the more egalitarian approaches to women's work. Nelken, like all socialist feminists, never clearly challenged predominant gender discourse, nor did she uphold work as a basic aspect of female identity. The protective measures she demanded reflected cross-class values regarding the unchanging sexual division of labor. However, like fellow socialists such as Isabel de Palencia and most Spanish feminists at the time, she fought to gain greater social recognition for the dignity and value of the housewife.[87]

By the 1930s a number of female union leaders such as Claudina Garcia, the president of the Association of Needle Workers, reiterated the idea of women's right and duty to paid work and the need for further unionization to defend their interests.[88] Attitudinal changes and new values can also be detected in the position of a small number of socialist intellectuals, such as lawyer Luis Jímenez de Asúa, who contested the biosocial norms of domesticity by arguing that women's employment was compatible with motherhood.[89] However, even as late as the 1930s, women's right to employment was controversial among a wide range of socialists. The socialist feminist María Pi de Folch were still uneasy about women's presence in the labor market, because she believed that women's overall life conditions had deteriorated due to their double burden at home and in the workplace.[90] A number of UGT branches persisted in demanding women's exclusion from jobs, while the official newspaper *El Socialista* at times expressed the traditional arguments that female employment led to low wages, male unemployment, and a decline in the standard of living of the working class.[91] Official party and union structures were still reluctant to take on board the implementation of effective gender equity at the workplace.

Despite the prevalence of a collective imagery that described women workers as conservative and lacking in social agency, in areas of greater industrialization such as Catalonia, the Basque Country, and Valencia, women had been active participants in labor conflicts since the early twentieth century.[92] In the period from 1905 to 1921 the overall strike participation rate of female textile workers was higher than that of their male counterparts.[93] Recent research revises the traditional image of Spanish women workers as lacking in union and social consciousness and acting as an impediment to the development of labor and social struggles. It remains to be established to what extent gender informed the patterns of female mobilization in labor conflicts. The most important demand on the agenda of female labor conflicts was higher wages. In the interwar years this demand was still a top priority; wage discrimination meant that women earned under 50 percent of male workers' wages. Other common issues included problems of discipline, firing, work-rhythms, relations with superiors, and the right to organize. There were some additional gender specific issues involving the mobilization of women workers to strike against sexual harassment at the workplace.[94]

During the Second Republic, strike activity and social conflicts became very acute as the economic recession and political changes increased social tensions. Although unacknowledged as union partners, women workers participated in numerous strikes especially from 1933 to the spring of 1936, during a right wing government.[95] There is no evidence that gender-specific demands were voiced by women strikers. Their recorded demands were similar to those of male workers and related to wages and the organization of work.[96] The low level of union affiliation and, more significantly, the official socialist movement's reluctance to contest women's issues account for the lack of a specific gender dimension to labor disputes in this period.

Women mobilized in collective action as workers but also in their gender-defined role as nurturers and providers of family well-being. Female collective action was not restricted to the organized labor movement, since women mobilized conclusively around such issues as food scarcity, rising prices, and maldistribution of basic goods during World War I and its aftermath. Women resorted to direct action and attacked stores and food distribution centers in Barcelona, Malaga, Cordoba, Vigo, Madrid, and Alicante. Better documented cases of Barcelona and Malaga show how female networks were developed and permeated both the community and workplace and how women played a significant role in the leadership of the conflicts.[97] During the early 1930s the economic crisis led women to mobilize in collective action in many regions of Spain. In 1932 and again in 1934 rural women led social protests against increases in food prices.[98] Much of this social agitation took place outside the official union and party circles.

Women as Citizens

Both political and gender culture were decisive historical experiences that shaped the definition of Spanish feminism.[99] Feminist activists did not focus primarily on demands for women's suffrage and political rights. They developed a strand of social feminism whose political legitimation was founded on the acceptance of gender differences rather than the paradigm of equality. Prevalent political culture and the predominance of the discourse of domesticity that checked women's presence in the public arena led to the overall development of a feminism that had little interest in political rights and suffrage but focused on the struggle for social and civil rights for women. The discourse of gender difference prevailed, and feminist claims were articulated from a socio-familial context that acknowledged gender differences and precluded equality paradigms by definition. Education, work, dignity, and not the ballot were defined as priority feminist goals both on the Right and Left of the women's movement.

After the granting of universal male suffrage in 1891 men were considered active political subjects with the right to exercise full political citizenship. A social citizenship, founded on human reproduction but also on social motherhood, was the ground for women's gradual political integration into the public arena. This political framework legitimated women's access to some spaces within the public arena, while safeguarding others as out of bounds. Motherhood was in many ways fundamental to a political reading of differential gender citizenship.[100]

The social-democratic program proposed the transformation of the existing bourgeois state through the political action of the organized working class. However, political citizenship for women was not a central aspect of the woman question for socialists. The inauguration of the democratic regime in 1931 forced a redefinition of citizenship along the paradigm of equality and political rights.[101] The main protagonist of the parliamentary debate on female suffrage was not a socialist. She was Clara Campoamor, a lawyer, member of the Radical party, and the major figure of Spanish suffragism, who earlier had written the prologue to María Cambrils' book on socialist feminism.[102] In the hostile climate of the parliamentary debate on women's enfranchisement in the fall of 1931, she brilliantly defended the notion of political citizenship without any gender restrictions and argued for gender equality in the new constitution. By placing the legitimacy of the young democracy on the foundations of equality, Campoamor established universal political citizenship as the basic tenet of the Second Republic. She also based her arguments on feminist politics by claiming that if the constitution did not admit the principle of equal political rights, the newly established Republic would be disqualified as a democratic system and exposed as a patriarchal social order defending male interests in violation of the principle of the sovereignty of the people.[103]

Campoamor's clear espousal of equality and universal individual political rights was quite exceptional in this period characterized by the ambiguities of both Left and Right regarding female enfranchisement. Although some socialist women such as Maria Cambrils had openly defended female enfranchisement almost a decade earlier, political citizenship for women was not considered central to the woman question by the Left. Even Cambrils gave a differential reading to women's political agency when she claimed that Spanish women would play a decisive role in municipal politics as "official mothers" to abandoned children and as guardians against "pernicious social practices."[104]

Many socialists were still quite ambivalent in their attitudes towards female suffrage in 1931. The theoretical principal of equality was acknowledged, but discussions focused on the political implications of a female electorate that was defined as unprepared, uneducated, politically conservative and as putty in the hands of the clergy. Significant socialist leaders including Margarita Nelken forcibly argued against giving women the vote on the assumption that it would strengthen conservative forces.[105] Women's lack of autonomous political subjectivity was based on the dual assumption of male authority within the family – women would vote however husband or father prescribed – and on male religious authority – women would vote at the dictates of the priests. As the socialist candidate María Lejárraga warned during her electoral campaign in 1933, "The only religious duty universally understood by the devout Spanish female sex is to comply with all that priests say."[106] Her speeches reveal her continuing conviction that Spanish women were politically backward: "The great amorphous mass, women of the provincial middle class, women who work outside union organizations, peasant women, have no preparation to vote nor any idea of the meaning of voting."[107]

It goes beyond the scope of this chapter to explore the debate on female enfranchisement.[108] The point to be stressed is that there continued to be a gendered reading of political subjectivity and citizenship across a political divide of Left and Right. The argument of biological determinism was used to claim unequal capacities between men and women in parliamentary debates. One republican deputy, Dr. Novoa Santos, disqualified women as active political subjects by arguing that hysteria was an essential component of the female character and concluded that enfranchising them would mean handing over the new Republic to female hysteria. Sexual differences were invoked by Professor Manuel Ayuso of the Republican Federal party, who maintained that women should not be given the vote until the age of forty-five, because they did not achieve psychological equilibrium and mental maturity until that age, while males attained these attributes at the age of twenty-three. Biological essentialism, this time defined as the end of the female reproductive cycle, still justified the limitation of women's rights as political subjects. More progressive deputies such as the socialist Dr. César Juarros Ortega also had recourse to biosocial reasoning to justify the concession of the vote to women. Social motherhood was central to his argument, which stressed the need for women's active presence in the world of politics, since "women represented a sentiment of motherhood that man cannot even imagine. Female psychology is different from that of men."[109] Juarros Ortega justified women's right to vote on the familiar grounds of the gender discourse that Marañón had elaborated earlier: men and women were complementary, and women's experience of motherhood defined a differential political agency.[110]

María Léjarraga expressed a continued acquiescence to differential gender roles as she embraced the view that women were essentially housewives and mothers. She hailed the new Republic for providing women access to political posts, but she also felt that due to their nature women should occupy themselves with more practical issues and the care of humankind, leaving affairs of state to men because of their higher capacity for abstraction.[111] As a parliamentary deputy she challenged preconceived notions about the differential nurturing role of women in politics, but she also defined her own political role as that of caretaker and consoler.[112] A deep tension can be detected in her political activities that on a first reading could be described as fitting neatly into established gender codes. She blatantly used traditional stereotypes as, for instance, when she provokingly recriminated rank-and-file male militants about their masculinity when their wives did not attend her meetings: "If I were a man, the woman who loved me would go where I told her."[113] Yet there is also another reading to this compliance with gender models that can be interpreted as an effective strategy to gain access to women at public meetings. Here she appears to have intentionally had recourse to the traditional parameters of male hierarchy and authority to oblige the wives and companions of socialist militants to attend her meetings – an effective subversive strategy. Gender constraints also provided her with limited contact with women, since she focused on domestic issues in order to convince them to vote for socialist candidates. Her lack of confidence in the capacity of most Spanish women to develop autonomous political agency may account for her lack of feminist vision and traditional views in her political encounters with women throughout her electoral campaigns. Her travels in Southern Spain as a parliamentary candidate for Granada reveals the continued and uncontested exclusion of women from the public arena. As a female politician, public figure, and role model she undoubtedly challenged the boundaries that limited women to domesticity. Feminism has been defined by its capacity to openly contest women's discrimination. Perhaps it can also be defined through its ability to negotiate gender changes in society while not openly contesting the constraints of gender identities. The meanings of socialist feminism varied according to individual biographies and political circumstances. But in keeping with tradition, a feminist politics was never clearly defined by official socialism not even during the suffrage debate in parliament.

In 1931, the Socialist party voted in favor of female enfranchisement. This action cannot be attributed to a suffragist or feminist agenda but rather to democratic principles shared with its coalition partner, the Radical Republican Democrats. Apprehension about the electoral use of the vote by women characterized the early 1930s, when women in the 1933 and the 1936 electoral campaigns were addressed as mothers and spouses. For socialist men and for many women, access to political citizenship meant neither shared political power nor challenging male monopoly in the world of work and politics. Differential citizenship and social roles were still prescribed rather than equal partnership in political power and policymaking. Despite a more egalitarian political commitment to female enfranchisement, continued gender imbalance demonstrates the continuity of gendered cultural values and the validity of differential gender roles and identity politics.

Few women held positions of power in the party or union structures: No women were elected to the executive board of the PSOE in 1931 or 1932; and merely token number of socialist women were elected as parliamentary deputies in the elections prior to the Civil War (one candidate in 1931, three in 1933, and three in 1936). It is significant that the Left constantly maintained that women were to blame for the shift to the Right in the 1933 elections, even though no evidence for this allegation has ever come to light. As María Lejárraga put it, "I suppose that they, manipulated by more occult, flexible, and astute forces than ours, made us lose the elections."[114] Male unionists and party members controlled policy-making and power structures, while women were relegated to the margins. Even during the peak periods of socialist political power (1931 to 1933 and 1936 to 1937), women never acquired a high profile. With few exceptions such as Margarita Nelken, they also lacked strong individual leadership in contrast to other powerful female leaders such as the anarchist Federica Montseny and the communist Dolores Ibárruri (Passionaria). Socialist women and their organizations failed to create a socialist women's lobby and feminist agenda and thus lacked an effective collective voice to influence mainstream socialist politics or even gender-specific issues.

The Civil War (1936-1939) brought about the greatest mass political mobilization of women in Spanish history.[115] Women's fight against fascism was organized by a number of female organizations that became instrumental in promoting a women's mass movement in villages, towns, and cities, throughout unoccupied Republican Spain. Women's agency was crucial in undertaking new social, economic, and military activities in anti-fascist resistance. In the early weeks of the war some women, mainly anarchists and dissident Marxists, challenged conventional gender roles by undertaking an active part in warfare as militia women.[116] They created a groundbreaking definition of female citizenship by claiming women's right to bear arms, a role hitherto reserved for men in the exclusively male definition of citizenship in contemporary European liberal and democratic practice. The militia women fought on the fronts as well as providing necessary auxiliary services for male militiamen. At first they symbolized the good fight against fascism and were an inspiration for anti-fascist resistance and revolution. The belligerent image of the woman combatant in her blue overalls was predominant in war posters that aggressively urged men to enlist in the popular militias. This image played a key role in the symbolic representation of the bravery of the Spanish people in their fight against Franco. Yet the courage, tenacity, and dedication of the women in arms were insufficient to gain acceptance of a military role for women and failed to stave off the gradual discredit eventually heaped upon them. Women's mobilization in the anti-fascist resistance did not entitle them to assume male citizenship by carrying arms, not even in time of war, anti-fascist resistance, and revolution.[117]

Welfare and Maternity Schemes

In the course of the Second Republic, women benefitted from reforms such as maternity insurance schemes, labor legislation, education, civil marriage laws, divorce, and the abolition of regulated prostitution. Despite the reaction of feminist groups, married women were not granted equal civil rights except in Catalonia. In fact, it can be argued that many of the reforms implemented did not respond to a feminist or equality agenda but rather to socialist and republican political policies to reduce Church influence and promote the overall secularization of Spanish society.

In Spain, protective legislation for women workers and children was introduced in 1900. Socialist policies towards women waged workers had traditionally focused on the need to develop legislation geared to safeguard them as mothers or as potential mothers. Maternity protection through welfare insurance policies was the core of socialist policies in the 1930s. In contrast to the situation in many other European countries neither welfare issues nor sex reform politics became part of a cohesive socialist or even feminist agenda in this period. It would be wrong to assume that women on the Left identified gender-specific issues such as maternal welfare, abortion or birth control as being of particular relevance to their political or feminist agenda. Male leaders defined the agenda for Spanish women without considering their agency and choices. Although vocal on labor issues, socialist women did not collectively address a number of issues such as birth control, abortion, or sex reform, often identified as major components of a feminist agenda in other countries. Even more surprising in an international context, but not so considering Spanish society, was their failure to develop a women's lobby on issues regarding welfare and motherhood.

During the early reformist years of the Second Republic the political climate favored the introduction of progressive reforms in the interest of working-class women. The constitution of 1931 specifically guaranteed state protection of motherhood. The most prominent socialist trade unionist, Francisco Largo Caballero, Secretary General of the UGT, was Minister of Labor in the coalition government, and Prime Minister during the Civil War. He represented a more radical socialism and the labor interests of the UGT rather than mainstream PSOE policies. Thus, a union agenda shaped the important labor legislation he implemented between 1931 and 1933. Some have argued that his background as a union leader influenced his ministerial policy and accounts for his favoring the UGT in labor regulations over the rival anarchist union CNT.[118] Furthermore, his trade union commitment may explain both the predominant labor focus given to welfare policies and the marginalization of female agents from welfare issues.

Largo Caballero played a significant role in developing a gender dimension to labor regulations. He encouraged the development of reforms to improve the condition of female workers and defended married women's right to waged work. Working women were included in social security measures regulating pensions, accidents, and unemployment schemes. The first attempts to provide maternity insurance were under the paternalistic dictatorship of Primo de Rivera in 1929. Largo Caballero effectively implemented it by decree in May 1931.[119] Very few women were officially involved with this initiative and only one woman, the union leader Claudina García, was among the 15 members of the National Commission of Maternity Insurance.[120] As the scheme was exclusively oriented to waged workers, few feminists lobbied or attempted to shape maternal welfare policies in a collective manner. Like many social and gender issues in Spanish society, the maternity scheme became contentious. Opposition was shaped by political fractures and extreme union polarization rather than by feminist disagreement. Maternity insurance was considered a socialist initiative and rejected on these grounds by the anarchist CNT, which led the opposition.

Although maternity insurance was politicized, there was also specific resistance to the new regulation by women workers, all of whom had salary withheld to pay for the scheme. Single, widowed, and older women objected to mandatary withholding quotas. Moreover, many women workers who had contributed to the plan did not apply for the entitlements, because of the custom of women giving up their jobs on marrying, although this was no longer obligatory. Women objected to the costs of financing this scheme from their wages, arguing that maternal entitlements should be totally state or management funded. Another major objection was that it excluded domestic workers, who were the largest group of employed females. Opposition to the new scheme spread during 1931, with strikes and protests in numerous regions. By spring 1932, however, the protests had died down due to agreements with management to take on part of the workers' contribution and because anarchist opposition became focused on other issues. Women workers between sixteen and forty-nine years of age were entitled to health and medical maternal benefits, six weeks paid maternal leave, and a subsidy for breast-feeding. Between October 1931 and December 1935, 741,771 women workers benefitted from the maternity insurance,[121] that for the first time provided efficient state maternal services to working-class women.

The Gendering of Sex Reform

Gender norms proscribed women's claim to a voice in the public arena as a transgression of traditional codes of behavior. In the context of a society where the Roman Catholic Church was all pervasive as a social institution whose role was to guard traditional moral values, the stigma attached to any discussion of sexuality or reproductive issues was enormous, even for men. According to gender codes, topics such as sexuality, birth control, or abortion were taboo, and morally improper and threatened any woman's respectability. Sex reform and birth control were neither on the agenda of most Spanish feminists and socialists, nor significant issues on the Left. In the "Republic of Intellectuals (1931 to 1933)," major intellectuals held public office and played a decisive role in shaping reformist political and social policies.[122] Some were involved in the progressive eugenics movement and concerned with maternal health and social medicine. A very small minority of male professionals and intellectuals of this movement raised issues of sex reform and birth control.[123] By contrast, the anarchist sex reform movement, although a minority within mainstream anarchism, was very strong and active in the 1920s and 1930s, although there too, women were largely absent.[124] Sex reform was not an issue for official socialism, although some commitment was voiced on an individual basis by prominent leaders such as criminal lawyer Luis Jímenez de Asúa, who advocated the right to birth control but rejected the right to abortion.[125] During the Second Republic, birth control remained a highly controversial issue that even progressive eugenicists were reticent to defend.

On the publication of her book *Feminismo socialista* in 1925, María Cambrils justified her audacious discussion of matrimony and free love by the need to overcome ignorance, hypocrisy, and religious prejudice.[126] As

a socialist she demanded an end to contractual marriages based on economic interests and the subjection of women. A eugenic argument also
underpinned her contention that women should be protected from
unhealthy or much older marriage partners. While criticizing the views
on free love by anarchist sex reformers who were publishing popular journals on sex reform in Spain, she defined her socialist vision of free love as
a moral position sanctioning a free relationship without marriage but
rejecting sexual license.[127] Although she strongly criticized the Spanish
family, she avoided a discussion of sexuality, birth control, and abortion in
her consideration of free love.

Described by Havelock Ellis as the "Red Virgin," Hildegart Rodriguez
can be considered the outstanding exponent of an innovative vision of
sex reform and "conscious maternity" in the feminist and socialist movements in Spain.[128] However, her extraordinary lifestyle, youth, deviant
gender discourse on sexuality, and tragic, untimely death as well as individualistic socialism make it quite clear that she was not a spokeswoman
either for Spanish feminism or socialism. In her subversive views she
expressed a singular voice of dissonance that provides a different perception of sexual issues than can be found among other Spanish women.

Rodriguez joined the UGT in 1929, became a member of the Socialist
Youth, and eventually served as the only female on its board. By 1931, she
had become a leading representative of Left-wing radical socialist youth,
a feminist leader, and sex reformer – altogether a most unusual profile for
any young Spanish woman. Despite her initial enthusiasm, by 1932 she
grew disenchanted with the moderation of reformist socialist policies.
Her critical attitude led to her expulsion from the Socialist Youth, after
which she joined the Federal Republican party. She published very popular articles and books on sex reform that were influential in disseminating
sex education in Spain.[129] Although her writings can be considered to a
large extent undigested compilations of the ideas of international sex
reformers, she popularized the work of Mary Stopes, Margaret Sanger,
Havelock Ellis, and Magnus Hirschfeld in a fairly accessible manner.
Thus, she challenged the male professional monopoly of sex reform by
making sex education and information available to the general public. In
1932 she became General Secretary of the Spanish branch of the League
for Sexual Reform.[130]

Rodriguez's views, like those of other feminists, reveal a line of anti-
clerical argument quite similar to that of anarchist sex reformers, although
she differed in her feminist vision.[131] She advocated a new sexual ethics
that would replace the sexual double standard that demanded sexual
purity and chastity for women while it condoned extramarital relations
and male prostitution. "Both sexes, whose equality feminists claim with
respect to the law, with respect to public opinion, must also be equal with

respect to sexual conduct, with no other limitations than those which their conscience imposes."[132] Contesting established gender codes, she did not defend sexual purity but rather women's full sexual potential. She denounced traditional Church doctrine that pronounced sexuality as sinful and blamed both the sexual double standard and conventional cultural and religious values for the deprivation and sexual hunger of Spanish women. The cultural pressure of the Church, she charged, had led women to identify sexual activity with procreation, and their rejection of that goal as obscene, libidinous, and pornographic.[133]

Gender discourse in Spain had traditionally reinforced the notion of male identity through sexual virility and based male honor on the control of women's sexuality. In contrast to this sexual construction of masculinity, the key elements to femininity were purity, chastity, and a lack of sexuality. This amounted to a gender identity based on motherhood and an asexual, cultural representation of women, as the traditional "Angel of the Hearth." According to Rodriguez the sexual revolution was a necessary and crucial force of modern human civilization. Thus, she promoted sexual education and birth control as the means to achieve the development of human potential.[134] Her firm endorsement of birth control clearly deviated from conventional cultural and religious values, which repudiated its practice because it disassociated sexual activity from procreation. She understood that birth control was crucial to women's emancipation, and releasing women's sexual energy from the constraints of gender-imposed female decorum was high on her agenda. But her major effort lay in providing sexual education that would permit conscious maternity. Rodriguez considered voluntary motherhood through the practice of birth control as a means of overcoming women's biological mandate of reproduction and to converting it into an intentional and free choice.

As an active member of the progressive eugenics reform movement, it is not surprising that a eugenic discourse also permeated Rodriguez's view of birth control. Part of the civilizing force of birth control, she argued, was precisely that it prevented race degeneration by promoting the birth of healthy children in an economically viable environment.[135] Family limitation and conscious maternity were seen as the means to achieve a healthy sex life and eugenic procreation within the context of sexual revolution and women's emancipation. Although highly critical of religious ethics on sexual practice, a religious vocabulary also permeated Rodriguez's language on sex reform where birth control and sexual revolution were described as "ideals of redemption." The ambiguity of being known as the "Red Virgin" can be considered problematic in the context of her advocacy of sex reform. Yet, in the context of the religiously charged discourse in Spain, as a virgin she can also be seen as a savior, a female messiah, whose sacred mission was to redeem humankind through the "Gospel of Redemption" of sex reform. Her birth control campaigns were often formulated in this familiar religious discursive form, a practice indeed quite common among other socialist women.

Official Spanish socialism totally neglected sex reform, and when in December 1936 anarchist sex reformers obtained the legalization of a progressive public health scheme on abortion in Catalonia, neither male or female socialists or communists supported it. Even anarchist women were overcome with inhibitions and failed to support their male anarchists comrades in this measure.[136] During the Civil War, birth control and abortion were not included in the program of the women's Popular Front organization, Group of Anti-fascist Women (AMA), in which socialist women were incorporated. Nor was support forthcoming for the women's anarchist organization Free Women, although the problem of prostitution was high on its agenda.[137] In addition to her denunciation of the continued political inequality of women during the war, the socialist feminist lawyer Matilde Huici was unique in addressing the issues of sexual education, birth control, and abortion within the AMA. Despite lip service to the need of relieving women of "oppressive maternity" in the AMA program, only Huici included such issues in her reports to the organization. However, she failed to have them discussed at the second conference of the AMA in October 1937. The public avowal of feminist advocacy of birth control as a key to women's emancipation was unusual for socialist women. The incapacity to deal with changing cultural values and needs on these subjects points to a traditional, moral trend within the socialist movement, and also to its labor-oriented approach, which allowed little room for alternative cultural and social forms. It also speaks to the incapacity of socialist women to challenge social conventions by embracing such women-oriented issues.

The Blurring of Identities: War and Anti-fascism

During the Civil War, the woman question as developed by socialists was raised within joint anti-fascist initiatives with communists through the AMA and led to the blurring of a specific socialist identity on gender policies when communists took over the leadership of the united anti-fascist women's movement.[138] During the war, political polarization with open confrontation among the different tendencies on the Left and strong internal disagreements within the socialist movement between moderates and radicals affected women and gender issues.[139] The lack of consistent official PSOE policy on women, the pro-communist shift of significant socialist leaders such as Margarita Nelken, together with the drive for a trans-political unitarian women's anti-fascist movement led to a shortage of specifically socialist initiatives.

The AMA was to some degree a trans-political organization, for most of its members belonged to communist, socialist, or republican parties. But, although the rank and file was composed of women of diverse political affiliation, the AMA was the vehicle for orthodox communist mobilization of Spanish women, with the programs and policies reflecting Communist party leadership.[140] This situation led to some policy differences by a small number of prominent socialist women such as Matilde Huici, Matilde Cantos, and Matilde de la Torre.[141] Matilde Huici bitterly denounced the ongoing discrimination against women by all political parties and trade unions which continued to be a source of male privilege: "With extremely rare exceptions public offices, especially the most important, continued to be held by men; married women were ignored and hindered if they wished to do something without the consent of their husbands."[142] Legislative measures to ensure equality, Huici pointed out, such as the Decree on Civil Parity of Married Women finally promulgated in February 1937, had yet to be effectively put into practice.

The weakness of the socialist women's caucus, along with the disintegration of a cohesive women's socialist position during these years, undoubtedly weakened their situation within the AMA and prevented their influencing the direction of the movement to any ostensible degree. There was no concerted drive by socialist women to develop specific strategies and programs that responded to this conjunction of war and revolution with potential change for women. At a time when women in orthodox communist and dissident marxist parties and in the anarchist movement were developing party-specific women's organizations, the expression and activity of socialist women's groups were limited to the AMA, where their socialist specificity was blurred. The widening political rift within the Left also debilitated collective feminist actions.

Women's mobilization was geared to war needs and anti-fascist activities but within well defined gendered boundaries. Socialist women followed the official party line by rejecting the radical militia woman and female armed participation at the front. The designated gender role of anti-fascist women was as "homefront heroine," dedicated to civil resistance, survival, and voluntary relief work – a vital task in anti-fascist resistance to Franco, but still a limited role. Of course, some socialist women's organizations continued to be active during the Civil War, although the available documentation does not reveal many innovative activities specific to women. Evidence also indicates that a number of women's groups decided to disband and fuse into the local socialist groups, but it is impossible to determine whether this became a general pattern. Although the socialist press gave sporadic coverage to the activities of women's groups, and in the spring of 1937 the socialist paper *Claridad* inaugurated its first weekly women's page,[143] socialist women did not develop a strong voice on feminism or women's mobilization in the anti-fascist cause. The weakness of the socialist women's movement undoubtedly has to be understood in the immediate context of sharp political rifts within official socialism, a strong procommunist shift of many socialists particularly in the Socialist Youth and the UGT, and the difficult political developments in Republican Spain at war.[144] Moreover, the lack of a strong collective definition of socialist feminism in former decades made it difficult for the caucus of socialist women to develop an alternative political and gender option for Spanish women during the Civil War.

Notes

1. Andres, "La Casa del Pueblo de Madrid," *Acción Socialista* (10 October 1914).
2. Santos Juliá, "Objetivos políticos de la legislación laboral," in *La II República española: el primer bienio*, ed. José Luis García Delgado (Madrid, 1987), p. 28.
3. Manuel Contreras, *El PSOE en la Segunda República: Organización e ideología* (Madrid, 1981); Richard Gillespie, *Historia del Partido Socialista Obrero Español* (Madrid, 1991); Santos Juliá (ed.), *El socialismo en España* (Madrid, 1986); and Manuel Redero San Román, *Estudios de historia de la UGT* (Salamanca, 1992).
4. Helen Graham, *Socialism and War. The Spanish Socialist Party in Power and Crisis, 1936-1939* (Cambridge, Mass., 1991); Santos Juliá, *La izquierda del PSOE (1935-1936)* (Madrid, 1977), and, *Madrid 1931-1934. De la fiesta popular a la lucha de clases* (Madrid, 1984).
5. Redero San Román, *Estudios de historia*, p. 48.
6. Ibid., pp. 100-107.
7. UGT, *Actas de las sesiones del XVII Congreso de la UGT de España celebrado en Madrid los días 14 al 22 de octubre de 1932* (Madrid, 1933).
8. Maria Gloria Núñez Pérez, *Trabajadoras en la Segunda República: Un estudio sobre la actividad económica extradoméstica (1931-1936)* (Madrid, 1989), pp. 611-41; Redero San Román, *Estudios de historia*, p. 100.
9. Núñez Pérez, *Trabajadoras*, p. 614.
10. Marta Bizcarrondo, "Los orígenes del feminismo socialista en España," in *La mujer en la historia de España (siglos XVI-XX)* (Madrid, 1984), p. 158.
11. Virginia González, *A las obreras* (Madrid, n.d.), pp. 7-9.
12. María Cambrils, *Feminismo socialista* (Valencia, 1925), p. 56.
13. Ibid., p. 57.
14. Ibid., pp. 18-19.
15. Ibid., p. 19.
16. Mary Nash, *Mujer y movimiento obrero en España, 1931-1939* (Barcelona, 1981), pp. 143-46.

17. *Libro de Contaduría de la Agrupación Femenina Socialista de Madrid* and *Libro de Actas de Juntas Generales de la Agrupación Femenina Socialista de Madrid* (1906-1915), Archivo de la Guerra Civil, Salamanca.
18. Ibid.
19. *Libro de Actas.*
20. Ibid., Minutes of the Ordinary General Assembly, 9 October 1910.
21. *Libro de Contaduría.*
22. *Libro de Actas*, Minutes of the Extraordinary General Assembly, 11 June 1911.
23. Margarita Nelken, *La condición social de la mujer en España* (Madrid, 1919), p. 188.
24. Paloma Castañeda, *Carmen de Burgos: "Colombine"* (Madrid, 1994).
25. Michel Ugarte, "Carmen de Burgos ("Colombine"): Feminist avant la lettre," in *Spanish Women Writers and the Essay: Gender, Politics, and Self,* eds. Kathleen Glenn and Mercedes Mazquiaran Rodriguez (Columbia, M.O., 1998), p. 20.
26. This allegation is in a manuscript by banker Jorge Moreno, former secretary of the Socialist Association of Valencia, Archive of the Fundación Pablo Iglesias Madrid; See also, Bizcarrondo, "Los orígines," p. 157.
27. Alda Blanco, "Introduction," in María Martínez Sierra, *Una mujer por caminos de España* (Madrid, 1989); Patricia W. O'Connor, *Gregorio and María Martínez Sierra* (Boston, 1977).
28. Martínez Sierra, *Una mujer por caminos de España.*
29. María Martínez Sierra, *La mujer española ante la República* (Madrid, 1931).
30. María Martínez Sierra, *Gregorio y yo* (Mexico, 1953), p. 29.
31. Gregorio Martínez Sierra, *Feminismo, feminidad, españolismo* (Madrid, 1917), *Cartas a las mujeres de España* (Madrid, 1916), and, *La mujer moderna* (Madrid, 1920).
32. See the bibliography in Blanco, "Introduction," pp. 43-46.
33. Nelken, *La condición social.*
34. Carmen de Burgos, *La mujer moderna y sus derechos* (Valencia, 1927), pp. 9-11, 20.
35. Mary Nash, "Federica Montseny: dirigente anarquista, feminista y ministra" and Susanna Tavera García, "Federica Montseny y el feminismo: unos escritos de juventud," *Arenal. Revista de historia de las mujeres* (July-December 1994).
36. Federica Montseny, "Feminismo y Humanismo," *La Revista Blanca* 33 (1 October 1924) and *El problema de los sexos* (Toulouse, n.d.).
37. Federica Montseny, "La mujer, problema del hombre," *La Revista Blanca* 86 (15 December 1926) and 94 (15 April 1927).
38. Mary Nash, "Experiencia y aprendizaje: la formación histórica de los feminismos en España," *Historia Social* 20 (autumn 1994) and "Political culture, Catalan Nationalism and the Women's Movement in Early Twentieth Century Spain," *Women's Studies International Forum* 19 (January-April 1996).
39. Cambrils, *Feminismo socialista*, p. viii.
40. Ibid., p. 28.
41. Amelia García Checa, *Catolicisme social i trajectòria femenina (Mataró, 1910-1923)* (Barcelona, 1991).
42. Rosa M. Capel Martínez, *El trabajo y la educación de la mujer en España (1900-1930)* (Madrid, 1982), p. 244; Núñez Pérez, *Trabajadoras,* pp. 569-600.
43. María J. Lacalzada de Mateo, *Mentalidad y proyección social de Concepción Arenal* (Ferrol, 1994); Manuela Santalla López, *Concepción Arenal y el feminismo católico español* (A Coruña, 1995).
44. Cambrils, *Feminismo socialista*, p. 58.
45. Ibid.
46. Martínez Sierra, *Una mujer por caminos de España*, p. 80.

47. Ibid., pp. 91-92, 101-02.
48. Cambrils, *Feminismo socialista*, p. 54.
49. Ibid., p. 15.
50. Nelken, *La condición social*, pp. 36 and 45.
51. Cambrils, *Feminismo socialista*, p. 52.
52. Mary Nash, *Defying Male Civilization: Women in the Spanish Civil War* (Denver, 1995), pp. 63-77.
53. Pilar Folguera (ed.), *El feminismo en España: dos siglos de historia* (Madrid, 1988); Mary Nash, "Two Decades of Women's History in Spain: A Re-appraisal," in *Writing Women's History: International Perspectives*, eds. Karen Offen et al. (London, 1991); Geraldine Scanlon, *La polémica feminista en la España Contemporánea,(1868-1974)* (Madrid, 1986).
54. Mary Nash, "Maternidad, maternología y reforma eugénica en España," in *Historia de las mujeres en Occidente*, eds. Georges Duby and Michelle Perrot, vol. 5 (Madrid, 1993), and, "Identidades, representación cultural y discurso de género en la España Contemporánea," in *Cultura y culturas en la Historia*, eds. Pedro Chalmeta et al. (Salamanca, 1995).
55. Mary Nash, "Identidad de género, discurso de la domesticidad y la definición del trabajo de las mujeres en la España del siglo XIX," in *Historia de las mujeres*, vol. 4.
56. Elisenda Macià, "L'Institut de Cultura: un model de promoció cultural per a la dona catalana," and Mary Nash, "La dona moderna del segle XX: la nova dona a Catalunya," *L'Avenç* 112 (February 1988).
57. Federica Montseny, *La Victoria. Novela en la que se narran los problemas de orden moral que se le presenten a una mujer de ideas modernas* (Barcelona, 1930), p. 6.
58. De Burgos, *La mujer moderna*, p. 11.
59. Carmen Alcalde, *Federica Montseny. Palabra en rojo y negro* (Barcelona, 1983); Castañeda, *Carmen de Burgos*; Federica Montseny, *Mis primeros cuarenta años* (Barcelona, 1987).
60. Nash, "Maternidad, maternología" and "Identidades, representación cultural."
61. Cambrils, *Feminismo socialista*, p. 32.
62. Ibid., p. 19-20.
63. Lucía Sánchez Saornil, "La cuestión femenina en nuestros medios," *Solidaridad Obreran* (15 October 1935).
64. De Burgos, *La mujer moderna*, p. 34.
65. Ibid., p. 53.
66. Santiago Roldán, José Luis García Delgado, and Juan Muñoz, *La formación de la sociedad capitalista en España. 1914-1920* (Madrid, 1973).
67. Gerald H. Meaker, *La izquierda revolucionaria en España. 1914-1923* (Barcelona, 1978), p. 15.
68. José Luis Martín Ramos, "Consequències socials:" la resposta obrera," *L`Avenç* 69 (March 1984).
69. Jésus M. Rodes and Enric Ucelay Da Cal, "Nacionalisme i Internacionalisme: 'Els amics d'Europa'i 'Messidor'," *L`Avenç* 69 (March 1984).
70. Carlos Forcadell, *Parlamentarismo y bolchevización del movimiento obrero español, (1914-1918)* (Barcelona, 1978).
71. Meaker, *La izquierda revolucionaria*, p. 194.
72. Programa del PSOE en el Acta de la Sesión celebrada por el grupo madrileño el día 20 de julio de 1879," *El Socialista* (March 1910).
73. Carmen Iglesias and Antonio Elorza, *Burgueses y proletarios: Clase obrera y reforma social en la Restauración* (Barcelona, 1973), p. 163.

74. On women and work during the Civil War, see Nash, *Defying Male Civilization*, pp. 124-140.
75. César Juarros, "La mujer en la República. Conferencia del Doctor Juarros sobre el socialismo y la mujer," *Luz* (20 April 1932).
76. Mary Nash, "Política, condició socical i mobilització femenina: les dones a la Segona república i a la Guerra Civil," in *Més enllá del silenci. Les dones a la història de Catalunya*, ed. Mary Nash (Barcelona, 1988); Núñez Pérez, *Trabajadoras*, pp. 192-217.
77. Matilde Huici, "Mitin femenino socialista en el teatro María Guerrero, "*El Socialista* (15 November 1933).
78. Nash, *Mujer y movimiento obrero*, pp. 61-68, 106-109, 146-53, 181-86.
79. Nelken, *La condición social*, p. 105.
80. Capel, *El trabajo*, pp. 199-297.
81. Mary Nash, "Treball, conflictivitat social i estratègies de resistència: la dona obrera a la Catalunya contemporània," in *Més enllà del silenci*.
82. Núñez Pérez, *Trabajadoras*, p. 432.
83. Pilar Pérez-Fuentes Hernández, "El trabajo de las mujeres en la España de los siglos XIX y XX. Consideraciones metodológicas," *Arenal. Revista de Historia de las mujeres* 2 (July-December 1995).
84. Data reproduced from Pérez, *Trabajadoras*, pp. 109 and 133.
85. Nelken, *La condición social*, pp. 71-75.
86. Margarita Nelken, *La mujer ante las Cortes Constituyentes* (Madrid, 1931), pp. 37-65.
87. Nash, "Experiencia y aprendizaje" and "Political culture."
88. Claudina García, "El derecho al trabajo y el seguro de maternidad," *El Socialista* (4 May 1932).
89. Luis Jiménez de Asúa, *Al servicio de la nueva generación* (Madrid, 1934).
90. María Pi de Folch, "Horitzons socials femenins," *Justícia Social* (10 February 1934) and *Una visió femenina del moment present* (Barcelona, 1932), p. 11.
91. "Situación aflictiva: El paro en la industria mundial," *El Socialista* (30 July 1931).
92. Alvaro Soto Carmona, "La participación de la mujer en la conflictividad laboral (1905-1921)," in *Ordenamiento jurídico y realidad social de las mujeres*, ed. Maria Carmen García-Nieto Paris (Madrid, 1986).
93. Soto Carmona, "La participación"; Albert Balcells, *Trabajo industrial y organización obrera en la Catalunya Contemporánea (1900-1936)* (Barcelona, 1974), pp. 27-30.
94. Soto Carmona, "La participación."
95. Pérez Núñez, *Trabajadoras*, p. 431.
96. Ibid., p.432.
97. Lester Golden. "Les dones com avantguarda: Els rembomboris del pà del gener de 1918," *L'Avenç* 44 (December 1981); Temma Kaplan, "Female Consciousness and Collective Action: The Case of Barcelona, 1910-1918," *Signs: Journal of Women in Culture and Society* 7 (spring 1982); Maria Dolores Ramos, "Realidad social y conciencia de la realidad de la mujer: obreras malagueñas frente a la crisis de subsistencias (1918)," in García-Nieto Paris *Ordenamiento jurídico*.
98. Pérez Núñez, *Trabajadoras*, p. 446.
99. Nash, "Experiencia y aprendizaje" and "Political Culture."
100. Mary Nash, "Género y ciudadanía," in *Política en la Segunda República*, ed. Santos Juliá, *Ayer* 20 (1995).
101. Nash, "Género y ciudadanía."
102. Cambrils, *Feminismo socialista*, pp. ix-xii.

103. Clara Campoamor, *Mi pecado mortal: El voto femenino y yo* (Barcelona, 1981), p. 61; Concha Fagoaga and Paloma Saavedra, *Clara Campoamor. La sufragista española* (Madrid, 1981).

104. Cambrils, *Feminismo socialista*, p. 25.

105. Nelken, *La mujer ante las Cortes.*

106. Martínez Sierra, *Una mujer por caminos de España*, p. 125.

107. Ibid., p. 124.

108. Rosa M. Capel, *El sufragio femenino en la Segunda República española* (Madrid, 1992); Concha Fagoaga, *La voz y el voto de las mujeres. 1877-1931* (Barcelona, 1985); María Gloria Núñez Pérez, *Madrid. 1931. Mujeres entre la permanencia y el cambio* (Madrid, 1993); Scanlon, *La polémica feminista.*

109. Cited in Campoamor, *Mi pecado mortal*, p. 116.

110. Nash, "Género y ciudadanía."

111. María Martínez Sierra, "Pensando. Realidad," *Mundo Femenino* 95 (December 1933).

112. Martínez Sierra, *Una mujer por caminos de España*, pp. 173-83, 220.

113. Ibid., p. 152.

114. Ibid., p. 127.

115. Martha A. Ackelsberg, *Free Women of Spain. Anarchism and the Struggle for the Emancipation of Women* (Bloomington, Ind., 1991); Carmen Alcalde, *La mujer en la guerra civil española* (Madrid, 1976); Shirley Mangini, *Memories of Resistance. Women's Voices from the Spanish Civil War* (New Haven, Conn., 1995); Mary Nash, *Mujeres Libres: España 1936-1939* (Barcelona, 1976), and, *Mujer y movimiento obrero: Las mujeres en la Guerra Civil* (Madrid, 1989), and, *Defying Male Civilization. Women in the Spanish Civil War.*

116. Mary Nash, "Milicianas and Homefront Heroines: Images of Women in War and revolution 1936-1939," *History of European Ideas* 11 (1989), "Women in War: Milicianas and Armed Combat in Revolutionary Spain, 1936-1939," *The International History Review* 2 (May 1993), and, *Defying Male Civilization*, pp. 48-62, 101-19.

117. Ibid.

118. Juliá, "Objetivos políticos," pp. 28, 34-39.

119. Josefina Cuesta Bustillo, *Hacia los seguros sociales obligatorios: La crisis de la Restauración* (Madrid, 1988); Mercedes Samaniego Bonet, *La unificación de los seguros sociales a debate. La Segunda República* (Madrid, 1988).

120. Samaniego Bonet, *La unificación de los seguros sociales*, p. 163.

121. Pérez, *Trabajadoras*, pp. 268-70.

122. Paul Aubert, "Los intelectuales en el poder (1931-1933): del constitucionalismo a la Constitución," in *La II República española*, pp. 169-231; Manuel Tuñón de Lara, "La política cultural del primer bienio republicano: 1931-1933," García Delgado, *La II República española*, p. 267.

123. Mary Nash, "Social Eugenics and Nationalist Race Hygiene in Early Twentieth Century Spain," *History of European Ideas* 15 (1992): 4-6.

124. Mary Nash, "El neomaltusianismo anarquista y los conocimientos populares sobre el control de la natalidad," in *Presencia y protagonismo: aspectos de la historia de la mujer*, ed. Mary Nash (Barcelona, 1984), "Reforma sessuale e nuova morale nell'anarchismo spagnolo," in *Spagna anni Trenta. Società, cultura, istituzione*, eds. Giuliana Di Febo and Claudio Natoli (Milan, 1993), and, "La reforma sexual en el anarquismo español," in *El anarquismo español y sus tradiciones culturales*, eds. Bert Hofmann et al. (Frankfurt, 1995).

125. Luis Jímenez de Asúa, *Libertad de amar y derecho a morir. Ensayos de un criminal-ista sobre eugenesia, eutanasia, endocrinología* (Santander, 1929), pp. 101-103.
126. Cambrils, *Feminismo socialista*, p. 109.
127. Ibid., pp. 118-21.
128. Mary Nash, "A disreputable sex reformer: Hildegart, the Red Virgin," in *Wayward Girls and Wicked Women. In Memoriam of Angela Carter*, eds. Aránzasu Usan-dizaga and Elizabeth Russell (Barcelona, 1995).
129. Hildegart Rodríguez, *El problema sexual tratado por una mujer española* (Madrid, 1931), and, *La rebeldía sexual de la juventud* (Madrid, 1931, 1977).
130. Raquel Alvarez Pelaez and Rafael Huertas García-Alejo, *¿Criminales o locos?. Dos peritajes psiquiátricos del Dr. Gonzalo R. Lafora* (Madrid, 1987); Eduardo de Guzmán, *Aurora de Sangre: Vida y muerte de Hildegart* (Madrid, 1972).
131. Nash, "Riforma sessuale e 'nuova morale' nell'anarchismo spagnolo."
132. Hildegart, *La rebeldía sexual de la juventud*, p. 57.
133. Ibid., p. 195.
134. Ibid., p. 151.
135. Ibid., p. 208.
136. Mary Nash, "Marginality and Social Change: Legal Abortion in Catalonia during the Spanish Civil War," in *Marginated Groups in Spanish and Portuguese History* (Minneapolis, 1989), and, "Género, cambio social y la problemática del aborto," *Historia Social 2* (autumn 1988), and, *Defying Male Civilization*, pp. 165-76.
137. Ibid., pp. 146-64.
138. Ibid., pp. 63-100.
139. Graham, *Socialism and War*.
140. Nash, *Mujer y movimiento obrero*, pp. 243-76, and *Defying Male Civilization*, pp. 63-97.
141. Carmen Calderón, *Matilde de la Torre y su época* (Santander, 1984).
142. Matilde Huici, "Los derechos civiles de la mujer y su ejercicio," *Mujeres* (Octo-ber 1937).
143. "Para nuestras lectoras," *Claridad* (24 April 1937).
144. Santos Juliá (ed.), *Socialismo y Guerra Civil* (Madrid, 1987).

Chapter 10

Women and the Left in the Shadow of Fascism in Interwar Italy

Mary Gibson

The "woman question" did not become central to the policies of either the Italian Socialist party (PSI) or the Italian Communist party (PCI) during the interwar period. Neither party made women's issues like equal wages for equal work, the vote, and assistance to families central to their platforms. Although both parties boasted a group of intelligent and energetic female members of national prominence, few women held positions of power within the two party hierarchies. Women made up a tiny minority of members holding party cards. Yet it would be unfair to discount the contributions of Italian women to the history of the Left between the two world wars. They belonged to trade unions in much larger numbers than to the party, and an untold number supported the two parties as "sympathizers" or wives of members. The dedication of large numbers of women to socialist and communist ideals was most apparent in their participation in waves of strikes, even when outlawed during fascism, and their courageous activities during the Resistance.

The failure of the PSI and the PCI to integrate seriously the woman question into their policies was partially the result of the early, rapid, and successful fascist rise to power beginning with the March on Rome in 1922. For both the political development of the Left and the lives of Italian women, the consolidation of Benito Mussolini's dictatorship by 1926 constituted a momentous watershed in Italian history. After years of violent harassment by fascist squads, the PSI and PCI were outlawed in

1926. Subsequently, members of either party involved in clandestine activity were subject to trial and certain punishment by the Special Tribunal for the Defense of the State, a military court erected specifically to prosecute opponents of fascism. As for women, Mussolini used his famous Ascension Day Speech of 1927 to prescribe their role in his fascist state, exhorting them to devote themselves to maternity and bear as many children as possible to strengthen the race. To encourage high natality, a series of laws limited women's participation in education and the workforce and rewarded mothers of large families. While some bourgeois feminist organizations were tolerated as long as they devoted themselves to charity rather than politics, the major organizational structures for working-class women, the General Confederation of Labor (CGL) and the parties, were outlawed by 1927.

This essay, therefore, focuses on the period before 1926 in tracing the relation of the "woman question" to both the PSI and the PCI.[1] A focus on only one party would be incomplete and distorted, since both parties played important and unique roles in the history of twentieth-century Italy. The socialist party had a long and venerable history by the end of World War I, growing steadily in membership and parliamentary power after its birth in 1892. At its peak in 1919, the PSI received 22 percent of the vote for the Chamber of Deputies, deriving part of its popularity from its courageous opposition to the war, in contrast to most other European socialist parties that abandoned internationalism for war credits. PSI membership also formed the backbone of the CGL, founded in 1906 as the largest national union in Italy. Socialist membership and glory foundered not only with the secession of its left-wing in 1921 to form the PCI, but also with the expulsion in 1922 of the right-wing reformists, who founded the splinter Unitary Socialist Party (PSU). When outlawed in 1926, the directorate of the PSI transferred its headquarters to Paris and many leaders went into exile abroad. Those remaining in Italy tried to organize clandestine opposition to the regime, but sweeping arrests by the fascist police led to the virtual dissolution of the socialist party within the Italian peninsula by the 1930s.

The PCI was a small party in its early years, holding only 3 percent of the seats in the Chamber of Deputies after the last really free elections of interwar Italy in 1921. Yet it maintained an active underground organization in Italy, even after its headquarters were removed to Paris in 1926. It strengthened its ties with the CGL, officially disbanded in 1927 but clandestinely working on shop floors to prevent the enrollment of workers in the new fascist unions. Some leaders went into exile, often in the Soviet Union, and many others underwent long periods of imprisonment in Italy. Although Antonio Gramsci, a founder of the PCI and a brilliant Marxist thinker, died in prison, most other communist exiles and inmates survived to become the backbone of the Italian Resistance after 1943 and subsequently the leaders of a postwar party that significantly outdistanced the old PSI in numbers and popularity.

Women's Legal and Social Position

Although World War I brought important changes in women's legal and social status, Italy trailed behind most other Western European nations in progress toward sexual equality even before the setback of fascism. Most importantly, women did not receive the vote after World War I. Female suffrage was not a new issue in Italy, as almost fifteen bills had been introduced into Parliament since 1863 to extend at least the local "administrative" vote, or both the administrative and the national "political" vote, to women.[2] Such efforts were for the most part doomed until suffrage was finally enlarged to include all men in 1913. By the end of the war, women had proven both their ability to work as they replaced men in factories and offices and, in the case of many bourgeois women, their patriotism in volunteer efforts to help the troops. No major party could now officially oppose votes for women.

Why did a bill for female suffrage not succeed in the Italian parliament? Part of the responsibility lay with the male leaders of all parties, who devoted more energy and passion to other issues in the immediate years after World War I. Such a charge can be made even against the PSI, although in 1913 its parliamentary delegation had tried to amend the law on universal manhood suffrage to include women. But in fact opinion among socialist men was divided, many fearing that women would be influenced by priests to vote for the conservative Right. This fear deepened with the founding of the Popular party, the first Catholic political party in Italy, immediately after the war. Not only were socialist men ambivalent about female suffrage, but also younger women, many of whom later joined the PCI, belittled the vote as an old-fashioned and bourgeois strategy compared to revolution on the Russian model. Their reverence for the Soviet Union was consistent with party policy, as the PSI joined the Third International and retained its membership even after the formation of the PCI in 1921.

Despite such reservations, the vote was considered a foregone conclusion in the pages of the women's journal of the PSI, *The Defense of Women Workers*. On 1 June 1919, the *Defense* published a calendar of dates when other countries had recently awarded women the vote in recognition of their service during the war.[3] In September, the Chamber approved legislation giving both administrative and political suffrage to women, but the Senate, by failing to act before the end of the legislative session, effectively vetoed the bill. Prominent socialist women, like Clelia Montagnana, lamented the silence of socialist deputies about the issue, warning that both the Popular party and bourgeois feminists were attracting future female support by keeping the issue alive.[4] But serious debate did not again revive in the PSI until 1923, on the occasion of the introduction of a fascist bill proposing only administrative suffrage for women. Socialist deputies like Constantino Lazzari opposed the fascist proposal as "not being a law of progress and civilization, but a law of privilege invented to impede real and proper female suffrage," because it limited the vote to women with an elementary education, those paying at least forty lira in communal taxes, war widows, and mothers of sons killed in the war.[5]

By the time the fascist bill came to a vote in May 1925, the PSI had withdrawn from parliament in protest over the assassination of their deputy, Giacomo Matteotti, by fascist thugs the previous year. The deputies of the PCI, however, had returned to parliament and took up the socialist mantle of opposing the fascist proposal in the name of universal female suffrage. In earlier years, women as well as men in the PCI had been lukewarm to the issue of votes for women, following the Comintern's analysis that only revolution, and not social-democratic gradualism, would bring a new society of sexual equality. For example, in 1921 the communist activist Felicità Ferrero argued that female suffrage had not bettered the lives of lower-class women in Weimar Germany, whereas "for women workers in Russia, the communist revolution had resolved the problems of the family, maternity, and real independence."[6]

After the appointment of Mussolini as prime minister in 1922, however, the PCI began to evaluate more positively the vote as a weapon against the Right. In the debate over the fascist bill, the communist deputy Ruggero Grieco led a ringing denunciation of the hypocrisy of the bourgeois parties who claimed to speak for women but privately denigrated them as "beautiful and stupid animals."[7] He and his party supported suffrage not for the restricted groups of "ladies" enumerated in the bill, but for all women, especially factory workers, peasants, and "that vast number of women who do exhausting housework [which is] the most barbarous and difficult of work."[8] But the Communist party had waited too long to endorse female suffrage. Italy's rump parliament passed only the restrictive fascist bill which itself became void when Mussolini abolished local elections in 1926.

Despite the failure to receive the vote, Italian women did improve their legal position after World War I. The Sacchi law of 1919 abolished the doctrine of "marital authorization" (*autorizzazione maritale*) from the Civil Code.[9] According to this doctrine, married women had to seek their husband's permission for property transactions such as taking out mortgages, bequeathing gifts, or opening bank accounts. But working-class women owned little property, so that the PSI did not show much interest in the issue.[10] A second doctrine embedded in the Civil Code, of potentially more significance for lower-class women, was that of "paternal power" (*patria podestà*). This doctrine made men the legal head of household, with the authority to choose the place of residence of the family, manage its financial affairs, and guide the upbringing of children.[11] This legal subordination of wives to husbands was not abolished during the interwar period but continued until the reform of family law in the 1970s.

The absence of divorce also limited married women's autonomy between the wars. The Civil Code allowed only legal separation of spouses, and this on patently unequal grounds: a man had to prove simple adultery on the part of his wife, while a woman had to show that her husband was maintaining a concubine in the family house or in a scandalously public manner.[12] Although the PSI leadership considered bad marriages to be mainly a problem of the decadent bourgeoisie, it sponsored a divorce bill in 1920 as it had several times before the war. Initially, the socialist divorce bill elicited enthusiasm from a broad coalition of bourgeois feminists and socialist women, who together founded a "National Committee for Divorce." But over the next few years, middle-class resolve crumbled in the face of not only the usual Catholic outcry but also the growing reactionary climate. Denounced as "bolshevist" and corruptly foreign, divorce began to lose support among middle-class feminists and had not passed parliament by 1922 when the fascist takeover assured its death. Divorce did not become legal until 1970.

Unlike divorce, birth control and abortion received little public debate after the war, even among bourgeois feminists and socialist women.[13] Not only did the cultural influence of the Catholic Church make such topics taboo, but both groups feared being denigrated as proponents of free love. That Italians were increasingly using contraception, probably withdrawal, is clear from the declining birthrate, which dropped from thirty-eight per thousand in the 1880s to thirty-three by the turn of the century to twenty-nine after the war.[14] Even after fascist legislation made the dissemination of information about contraception illegal in 1926, Italian birthrates continued to decline, reaching twenty-three per thousand on the eve of World War II.[15]

Although criminalized under the Zanardelli penal code of 1889, the practice of abortion also contributed to lower birthrates.[16] It does not seem to have been vigorously prosecuted and punishment was often reduced drastically, when the motive for abortion was "to save the honor of the mother, wife, daughter, adopted daughter, or sister."[17] The PSI ignored the issue of abortion, aside from generally promising that the future revolution would eliminate the economic reasons for limiting families. In its early years the PCI was more courageous, at least in the figure of Camilla Ravera, who followed the lead of the Bolsheviks in defending the right of overworked and underpaid women to limit the size of their families.[18] Her voice remained rather lonely on this issue, especially as the cultural atmosphere in Italy became less sympathetic to women's rights by the mid-1920s. In the Rocco Criminal Code of 1930, the fascists increased penalties against abortion and redefined it as "a crime against the race," since it interfered with Mussolini's eugenic campaign for demographic growth.[19] Despite his loud denunciation of abortion, women increasingly sought this method of family limitation during the interwar period.[20]

Work and Unions

Women's participation in the workforce declined in interwar Italy. According to census figures, this decline constituted part of a general downward trend that started in 1881 and lasted until World War II. While women made up 37.6 percent of all employed persons in 1881, this percentage dropped to 31.2 in 1911, 28.6 in 1921, and 22.6 in 1931.[21] Like many other Western nations, the rate of women working outside the home followed a U-curve, hitting its lowest point in the interwar period and then rising continuously in the postwar period. These figures do not reveal the rise in female employment during World War I, since Italian censuses have always been conducted at the beginning of each decade. Fascist policies, as will be discussed below, discouraged women's work outside the home and partially account for the decline in female participation in the workforce. But other long-term factors would have produced a similar if less pronounced curve, even in the absence of fascism.

One such factor was the replacement of light manufacturing, which employed large numbers of women, with heavy manufacturing as the bulwark of the Italian industrial economy in the early decades of the twentieth century. Because of this structural change, greater reductions of female employment occurred in industry than in agriculture or services. While 45.1 percent of all industrial workers were women in 1881, the rate dropped to 27.2 percent in 1921 and 24.2 percent in 1931.[22] The textile industry accounted for many of these lost jobs as it continued a decline begun in the late nineteenth century. Always the largest industrial employer of women, textiles had a workforce that was 77 percent female in 1931.[23] This sector, however, was reducing production and laying off workers for most of the 1920s and 1930s.

In addition to industry, agriculture also saw a significant decline in female workers. Women had always participated in farmwork, whether their families owned land, sharecropped, or rented the land of others.

Many were also day laborers, most notably the rice weeders (*mondine* or *mondariso*) who provided seasonal labor in northern Italy. For six weeks in early summer, up to 100,000 women stood over twelve hours each day in stagnant water up to their knees while they weeded the budding rice fields.[24] Despite the growing number of rice weeders, the percentage of women in the overall agricultural workforce declined from 35.9 percent in 1881 to 30.2 percent in 1921 to 19 percent in 1931. Outside of industry and agriculture, the employment pattern for women was mixed. Domestic service, one of the largest urban employers of women, declined as technological advances made housework less burdensome and as the economic dislocations of the interwar period reduced the number of bourgeois families able to afford servants. On the other hand, the employment of women as teachers, secretaries, and salesclerks rose. These latter jobs were open only to women with some education, mostly those in the middle and lower-middle classes. Thus, the multiplication of these white-collar jobs benefitted lower-class women little, and their numbers were too small to counterbalance the drastic declines in other sectors.

World War I temporarily reversed the downward trend in women's wage work. In the province of Milan, for example, the female share of the workforce rose from 34 to 37 percent between 1914 and 1918.[25] The increase was even more dramatic in the industrial sector, as the number of female factory workers jumped from 27,106 to 42,937 in the same period.[26] With their increased involvement in the workforce, women showed a burst of enthusiasm for joining unions. Union membership grew astronomically during and immediately after the war. By 1920, the socialist CGL boasted 1,930,000 members while the Catholic Confederazione italiana del lavoro (CIL) counted almost as many.[27] Of the total, perhaps 15 percent were women.[28] What is striking about Italy's pattern of unionization is that agricultural workers made up about 50 percent of the CGL and 80 percent of the CIL.[29] Unlike most other European nations, Italy had a long tradition of organizing in the countryside, especially in the fertile Po valley. Unions within the CGL that had a large share of female membership shared in the general upward trend. For example, the Textile Federation jumped in size from fewer than 8,000 in 1914 to 35,000 in 1918, 80,000 in 1919 and 130,000 in 1920.[30] Membership in the Federterra, the union of agricultural workers, declined during the war but climbed sharply from 86,470 to 300,000 in 1919 to over 800,000 in 1920.[31] Over a tenth of the membership in 1920 was made up of female rice weeders, the most feminized sector of agriculture."[32]

After 1921 with the rise of fascism and the violence of the squads against workers and offices of the CGL, union membership dropped precipitously. The Textile Federation and Federterra participated in this decline, losing 75 to 80 percent of their members by 1923.[33] The fascist unions claimed to have attracted many of these workers, reporting a membership of 1,764,423 in 1924.[34] Yet individual shop floors reported many fewer members of fascist unions; most workers tended to drop out of organizations and remain apolitical. The CGL officially moved its headquarters to Paris in 1927, after the Vidoni Pact outlawed all nonfascist unions as representatives of the working class in labor negotiations. Units of the CGL continued to work clandestinely, however, within factories and usually in alliance with the PCI.

Whether unionized or not, women participated in the waves of protests and strikes that characterized Italy both during and immediately after World War I.[35] The refusal of the PSI to vote for war credits in Parliament was quite popular with working-class women, and female participation in antiwar demonstrations was widespread even in the South. Strikes for better wages and conditions, although illegal, accompanied the flood of women into wartime factories. While women's wages did rise during the war, they lagged behind both growth in productivity and prices. They also remained significantly lower – usually 50 percent lower – than those of men working the same jobs.

Socialist women took the lead of calling for "equal wages for equal work" (a uguale lavoro uguale salario) during the war, even at the risk of being charged with promoting the petty interests of women at a time when men were being killed on the battlefield. In a pamphlet of 1917, Cristina Bacci enunciated a theme that would be taken up by the Defense, that women needed equal wages not only to earn a decent living but also to become psychologically independent. Admitting that the desire for the latter was still unconscious in many women, Bacci nevertheless foresaw that equal wages would potentially allow women "to be self sufficient, to become masters of themselves, to liberate themselves from the protection and support of men ... to take part in a new, shining, and whirling life and to feel in themselves a sparkle, a force, their own will ...."[36] She admitted that many men, even in the PSI, resisted equal wages for women, asking themselves if "I, the man, the strong one, the lion, the king of the universe, must have my work judged just like my woman?"[37] But Bacci was optimistic that these "atavistic prejudices" would disappear once equal wages made women more productive workers and better companions in the struggle against capitalism.[38] After 1921, communist women also pointed out the injustice of gender disparity in pay, noting that shops did not charge lower prices to women. They blamed both employers and working-class men for disparaging the skills and the needs of women.[39]

Despite the lukewarm support from most male colleagues in the party, women did leverage their important role in "industrial mobilization" into better working conditions during the war. In "male" occupations like metallurgy, chemicals, and mining, women's wages at least doubled between 1914 and 1918.[40] Buoyed by a sense of power from the war years, women continued to try to wrest further concessions during the "red two years" (*biennio rosso*) of 1918 to 1920. Textile workers won not only increased pay, but a minimum wage applicable to all factories in certain northern regions.[41] Women began to vote for, and even serve on, factory councils that represented workers' interests on shop floors.[42] By 1920, women workers began to look toward new goals like overtime pay and paid vacations.[43]

By the end of the "red two years," however, women workers could hope for few further improvements and began to focus most of their organizational energies on defending their recent gains. With demobilization, veterans rallied public support to pressure women out of their relatively well-paid jobs in industry and offices. A series of articles in the *Defense* lamented this public campaign, based on false charges that women were inferior workers. As one writer argued, "the modern technology of work is an awesome equalizer," as had been proven by the rapid transformation of women during the war from dressmakers and housewives to chemical and steel workers.[44] Another writer reminded men that capitalism was their real enemy: "Get rid of women? No, veterans: get rid of wealth! This must be your cry!"[45] Communist women came to similar conclusions, as is evident from the "Women's Tribune," a column in Gramsci's paper, *L'Ordine nuovo* (The New Order). Although sympathetic to men who were expected, in the present social order, to support their families, one article condemned the widespread practice of invading factories and offices and throwing women out of their jobs. Warning men that such behavior would satisfy "only their petty egotism of sex and class," it counseled them rather to organize for revolution and a rational society with work for all.[46] According to the "Tribune," women needed to defend their jobs, "not only in the name of their own independence, but also from the necessity to keep themselves in bread, a necessity that first pushed them into factories and offices."[47]

While both the PSI and the PCI leadership officially supported the right to work of women, in reality they did little to oppose the strong forces threatening it. Opposition came not just from working-class men, mostly veterans, who demanded jobs after demobilization, but also employers and ultimately the fascists. Once the war was ended, employers were generally quick to fire large numbers of women from formerly male jobs, while by 1920 fascist squads had become more vicious than the veterans' groups in invading the workplace and harassing female workers. Women were especially loathe to lose their jobs at a time when the cost of living was rising exponentially. In Milan, for example, the price of items in a typical working-class budget rose 650 percent between 1914 and

1926.[48] The *Defense* lamented the high cost of living and routinely printed lists of current prices of necessities as they rose. In such a situation where many women could not feed their children, the Russian slogan of "peace and bread" was particularly appealing.

Women who successfully held on to their jobs faced employers who were emboldened by the March on Rome to roll back recent working-class gains. After 1922, management in industry after industry broke recently negotiated contracts by lowering wages, increasing hours, and reintroducing piecework. Rationalization of the work process along the lines of Taylorism or the Bedaux system was also popular, although in Italy higher productivity came less from the introduction of sophisticated machinery than from simple speed-ups of the assembly line.[49] Letters from female workers to both socialist and communist papers described the widespread suffering caused by fascist economic policies. In 1924, a "spinner" wrote that after enduring three years of unemployment, her new job offered only one-third of her former wages.[50] In 1929, another textile worker reported that her employer had downgraded the classification of many female jobs, declaring them unskilled and therefore worthy of lower remuneration.[51] Periods of apprenticeship had also been extended to five years, with apprentices getting only half the standard wage. Receiving little protection from fascist unions, women were forced to accept these conditions, since the regime's economic policy kept men's wages too low to support their families.

The only improvement in working conditions for women between the wars came from the expansion of protective legislation under fascism. In 1919, Italy's first "Law for the Protection of the Work of Women and Children" remained on the books; it had been passed in 1902 and been amended in 1907 and 1910. Also called the "Carcano law," this initial legislation limited the workday of adult women in industry to twelve hours, including two hours for meals and rest; guaranteed a one-month, unpaid maternity leave after childbirth; and recognized the right of mothers to breast-feed after returning to work. An addendum of 1910 established a Maternity Fund, which paid women a modest sum at the time of birth or miscarriage. Both laws applied only to women employed in factories or workshops with at least five employees, and it excluded homework, domestic service, white-collar work, and agriculture. The PSI was a strong advocate of protective legislation for women, having designed its own, more progressive bill as early as 1897. The socialists proposed a ban on work at night or in dangerous environments for adult as well as minor women; a maternity leave of two months with half-pay; and the eight-hour day.[52]

In some ways, the fascist dictatorship succeeded where the liberal state had failed in implementing some of the more radical proposals of socialist women. But Mussolini's interest in strengthening protective legislation came not from a concern with the rights of working women or with the burdens of motherhood, but from his obsession with demographic growth. His more generous measures, therefore, were addressed almost exclusively to mothers, rather than to women in general. For example, maternity leave was extended to two and one-half months; nursing mothers were guaranteed two breaks during the workday; and companies employing more than fifty women had to institute a special room for nursing. Pregnant women could not be fired and they received unemployment benefits, in addition to the traditional stipend from the Maternity Fund, during maternity leave.

That Mussolini little intended to improve the lives of female workers in general is clear from the limited nature of protections for the majority of women who were not young mothers. Fascism did extend the reach of protective legislation to include white-collar as well as industrial workers. But it continued to exclude agricultural and home work, two sectors with long hours and grueling conditions. Even in the protected sectors, the legal workday could extend to eleven hours, much longer than the eight-hour day sought by socialist women even before the war.[53] The pattern of fascist policy becomes clearer when protective legislation is considered together with a series of repressive laws against female labor. Beginning in 1923, the state began to bar women from certain positions in the schools, public administration, and finally even private enterprise as white-collar workers. The clear message was for women to return to the home, both to boost the birthrate and ease male unemployment. But fascists made no attempt to prevent women working in the home; on the contrary they encouraged it by the low wages paid to men and the failure to extend protective measures to agricultural or domestic work. In fact the Italian economy, and the survival of many families, depended on the unregulated, exploitative, and often illegal labor of unorganized female home workers.

The Italian Socialist Party

Anna Kuliscioff was one of the founders of the PSI, and women participated in the party from its early years.[54] This section will look at the role of women in the PSI, beginning at the grassroots level and moving toward the top ranks of the party. The exact number of female members is difficult to ascertain, since the organizational structure for women changed periodically. In 1916, the party directorate sanctioned the founding of autonomous female "groups" (*gruppi*), similar to the youth groups, to attract the growing numbers of women in wartime factories. But in 1919, this policy was reversed, and women were ordered back into the regular mixed sections (*sezioni*) to work alongside males. Yet official party policy had only tenuous links with reality, since many women had formed groups before 1916 and remained in these formations after 1919. Other women never left the mixed sections during the war. Further complicating the picture was the existence of a small number of all-female sections, that is, regular local party organizations that sent delegates to party congresses. These female sections were usually in large cities, alongside several sections of men, or in textile towns where the workforce was predominantly female. Also confusing was the approval by the party of female "educational" or "cultural" groups after 1919; these groups differed from the former "autonomous" groups in being organized, theoretically, within each "mixed" section.

Such a variety of groupings makes the numbers gathered irregularly by the party on female membership invariably incomplete. According to official party figures, during the war the number of female autonomous groups increased from eight in 1914 with a total membership of 248 to twenty-seven in 1919 with a membership of 934.[55] This latter figure represented little more than 1 percent of those holding party cards in 1919.[56] But these numbers underestimated the total female membership, since many women remained in mixed sections. The official count also seems even to have missed some groups, since the *Defense* received fifty-seven responses when it asked its readership to identify existing groups in 1919.[57] These figures do show, however, the growing attraction of the PSI for women who wanted an end to the war and to obtain better working conditions. As with union membership, party adherence among women continued to rise in 1920, when the first National Female Conference of Socialist Women was held in Milan. The delegates claimed to represent 115 groups with a total membership of 3,695 women; again, this number left out women in those mixed sections that had never organized an internal educational group.[58] Even so, female membership probably still made up no more than 2 percent of the total.

These membership statistics underestimate, however, socialist sympathies among women. As shown by the electoral strength of the PSI, many Italians considered themselves socialists without holding party cards. This was especially true of women, who often could not afford party dues or did not have time to attend political meetings. Even among women active in their sections, many believed that it was sufficient for their husbands to join the party. Women and their families were involved in official socialist holidays like 1 May as well as private rituals such as socialist weddings, baptisms, and funerals. In many regions, the local party also organized "family clubs," with libraries, lectures, sports, and other activities open to women and children. Rather than joining the party, women tended to become union members, perhaps reflecting their anxiety about daily economic needs. Despite periodic grumbling by the PSI that women were short-sighted in limiting their membership to labor organizations, it devoted few resources to attracting women.

Socialist women were split over the issue of party organization, and their debate dominated many of the pages of the *Defense*. The strongest support for separate female groups came from the province of Piedmont which, because it included the industrial center of Turin and extensive rice cultivation, boasted a large number of organized women. Piedmontese women did not oppose equality between the sexes but believed that "it is not yet possible to put this into practice."[59] Even though they worked in fields and factories, women did not yet understand the need to fight for their rights. Thus, the party should organize female educational groups, on the model of the youth groups, that would include sympathizers or women not yet holding party cards and would prepare them for full party membership.

The Piedmontese group received bitter criticism of its position from several angles. Some letters to the *Defense* claimed that separate female groups implied the inferiority of women. As one correspondent asked, why was it that "at the moment in which the economies of entire nations have continued to function because of the really heroic efforts of women, women are proclaimed to be inferior?"[60] Women should not be isolated, she insisted, because "women boast equal powers of judgment as men."[61] In a subsequent issue, another writer agreed, pointing out that "in fact, only one difference exists between male and female workers: when the former returns to the house he finds everything taken care of and he therefore *relaxes*; while the latter has to do all of the domestic chores and therefore *works*. And yet she is the famous weaker sex ...."[62] Other contributors condemned any policy of dividing the sexes as a bourgeois or religious error, typical of "priests."[63] Women would learn more quickly how to become good socialists by having men close to them as models.

The National Congress of the PSI in 1919, held at Bologna, hosted a short auxiliary women's conference that ratified the second position, as requested by the directorate. All women were ordered to join mixed sections. Party leaders did approve female educational groups, but only if formed within regular sections and composed of members holding party cards. While many socialist women defended mixed sections on the principle of sexual equality, male leaders of the PSI had more practical motives. The directorate seemed to fear any autonomous action or even debate on the part of socialist women. This had not always been true, as Kuliscioff had obtained the approval of the party in 1912 to organize the National Union of Socialist Women. The National Union coordinated local groups of women and gathered support for issues like female suffrage. During the war, however, it came under severe attack by the overwhelmingly male directorate and never regained its legitimacy.

With the National Union in disintegration, women began to look to the *Defense* for central coordination. But the *Defense* had also lost the confidence of the directorate, and editorial control had been handed over to a male director. Socialist women, led by Clelia Montagnana, finally got up the courage to criticize this arrangement at the end of 1919. They charged that the *Defense* lacked any coherent editorial line, especially one that was "frankly female."[64] It was crucial, in anticipation of the passage of female suffrage, that the *Defense* become more aggressive in recruiting women to the socialist cause. The party directorate unexpectedly gave in to female pressure. It appointed two female editors, Enrica Viola Agostini and Maria Zanini Coppini, at the beginning of 1920.

The organized power of women in the PSI in interwar Italy peaked in 1920. Having replaced the Female Union as a national coordinating committee, the editors of the *Defense* began to call for a congress of socialist women. This congress would meet independently of the yearly party congresses and be organized by women. In this way, the problems of the Bologna conference of 1919 could be avoided: too little publicity, too few female delegates, and too little time for debate on women's issues.[65] After approval by the party executive, the women's congress was planned for the autumn, with all sections encouraged to send a female delegate. Five major issues were identified for debate: the socialist press; propaganda and education; culture; suffrage; and the constitution of a national coordinating committee for socialist women (to replace the Female Union).[66]

According to the *Defense*, "the National Congress of women on 28 November [1920] was the largest and most important event in the history of the Italian socialist women's movement."[67] In triumphant tones, the journal reported that 150 sections or female groups had sent delegates to the Congress in Milan, representing twenty-six provinces and a total of several thousand women in the PSI.[68] Although scarce funding prevented the congress from running more than one day, each report was debated and put to a vote. Despite the continuing preference of some delegates for autonomous women's groups, the Congress reconfirmed the Bologna policy of requiring all women to join mixed sections and to form educational groups only within the sections. But the Congress provided a clear mandate for strengthening women's voices within the party by recommending that the editors of the *Defense* be paid, that female congresses take place yearly, and that the party directorate approve and fund a National Executive Committee to coordinate local educational groups.

The *Defense* was overly optimistic, however, in labeling the Congress of 1920 as "the first step" toward female empowerment in the PSI. Women did meet again the next year, but the conference was demoted to an auxiliary panel at the regular party congress. The gathering was therefore small, since few sections elected female delegates, and most of the women attending the congress were wives of male members and lacked party cards. In such circumstances, the *Defense* pronounced the socialist women's movement to be in "a state of inaction."[69] By 1923, the *Defense* itself was in decline, appearing only sporadically and having again fallen into male hands.[70] When the women's federation of Milan regained editorship, they wrested a promise of funding from the party executive, but publication remained irregular. Only in 1925 did the directorate finally approve the formation of a National Female Federation with its own central committee at party headquarters. But rather than a genuine effort to support socialist women, this policy showed the desperation of the PSI to rally support in the last few months before complete repression by Mussolini.

Why did socialist women fail to build on the Congress of 1920 to regenerate an active and powerful movement in the PSI? They blamed their lack of success on socialist men, and a chorus of lament over male indifference runs through the issues of the *Defense*. At the local level, men failed to encourage the formation of female educational groups, send female delegates to party congresses, or even welcome women as members of mixed sections. The *Defense* charged that "the woman question is slighted to an unbelievable extent by our male companions in the Sections, who show a lack of awareness that is a real crime in light of the ideas that they claim to profess."[71] Female membership in the PSI was low partially because women were hesitant or embarrassed to enroll in regular sections, where men often greeted them with ridicule and irony. Replicating the power relations in the family, the mixed sections held little attraction for many working women. The party directorate was no better; as Carlotta Clerici complained in her report to the 1920 Congress, the party had taken no official position on many of the issues most dear to women, such as equal wages for equal work, the protection of homework, the legalization of paternity suits, and increased assistance for mothers.[72] While the party gave lip service to increasing propaganda and educational efforts among women, it committed almost no economic resources to enforcing the policy.

The decline in the socialist women's movement after 1920 also coincided with the escalation of attacks on all leftist institutions, and parliamentary government itself, by fascist squads. In such a state of emergency, the woman question assumed a low priority in a party consumed by organizing its own political and even physical defense. As early as 1921, the *Defense* lamented that fascist attacks had wiped out female groups in Reggio Emilia, previously the most active center of socialist women along with Piedmont.[73] Violent repression caused the suspension of the *Defense* in 1923 and, by 1925, only a few issues escaped the government censor,

who indicted the journal for printing "tendentious assertions and arguments meant to incite class hatred as well as to inflame minds in a way
that might endanger public order."[74] For the last years of its life, the
Defense had to be smuggled into regions where local fascist strongmen
had anticipated national policy by suppressing free speech. The female
editors proudly pointed to a large readership as late as 1923, even "where
secrecy and a thousand stratagems are needed to distribute our *Defense*."[75]
But they admitted to few subscribers in some cities like Rome and Turin
and blamed this situation on "the lack of good faith on the part of our
male companions who show acute laziness if not criminal indifference."[76]
They contrasted the "idiotic skepticism" of the PSI toward female participation with the socialist parties of England and Germany which took
seriously the "woman question."[77] Outside of the female organizations of
the PSI, only a few women played an important role in developing general
party policy. At the Bologna Congress of 1919, for example, only eleven
of almost 1,000 delegates from local sections were women. Of these, three
represented exclusively female sections (although illegal by party policy)
and eight represented mixed sections.[78]

Proceedings of the postwar congresses of the PSI show that women
made no major speeches and rarely participated in debate over leading
issues such as the appropriate stance toward the Russian revolution, the
Third International, and, after 1921, to the PCI. The successive splits in
the PSI weakened the small cadre of women who participated in party
politics at the national level. Many of the younger women transferred
their allegiance to the PCI in 1921 and others, like Kuliscioff, followed the
expelled reformists into the PSU. Thus, the group of women available to
publish the *Defense* or organize a new national coordinating committee
dwindled with each passing year.

Despite the lack of broad female representation at party congresses,
quite a few individual women enjoyed strong reputations among both
women and men in the PSI. Unfortunately for the revival of the women's
movement, most of the "historic" female socialists were quite old by the
end of the war, and several died during the early 1920s, like Linda Malnati, Clerici and Maria Goia. Three women stood above all others in
their access to power within the highest echelons of the PSI in the early
twentieth century. Kuliscioff, sixty-four years old at the end of World War
I, was the most revered woman in the party. Although one of the founders
of the PSI and co-editor with Turati of its intellectual journal, *Critica
sociale*, she was never made a member of the party directorate.[79] Her
power to shape policy was indirect, through her friendships, correspon-
dence, and frequent conversations with leaders of the reformist faction.
She led the campaign for passage of protective legislation in 1902, provoked an open and well-publicized dispute with Turati in support of

female suffrage in 1910, and founded the *Defense* and National Union in 1912. By the end of the war, however, she was quite sick and intervened infrequently in party affairs.

Only two women, Argentina Altobelli and Angelica Balabanoff, ever served in the party directorate before the fascist suppression of 1926. Altobelli rose in the party hierarchy not from any activity in the women's movement, but from her position as the secretary of Federterra. As one of the few female leaders of a major union, she was inducted into the directorate of the PSI in 1908. While most of her professional energies continued to be devoted to the cause of agricultural workers through the early 1920s, she did not hesitate to support campaigns by her female colleagues for the vote, divorce, and equality between the sexes.[80]

Balabanoff was less supportive of such women's rights than Altobelli, counseling the subordination of female needs to the cause of revolution. Yet she dedicated some of her vast energies to women, founding a journal in 1906 called *Su, compagne* (*Upward, Women Comrades*) and helping to found the Female Socialist Union in 1912. But her principal mission for the party was quite different: she served as liaison of the PSI to the Second and Third Internationals.[81] A member of the directorate from 1912 to 1917, Balabanoff was active in the Zimmerwald movement for an end to the war, where she formed ties with socialists of many nations. Russian by birth and knowledgeable about international politics, she was then sent to Moscow to represent the PSI in the Comintern. After the war, she collaborated periodically with the *Defense*, offering several articles on women in other nations.

What was the relationship between these prominent socialist women and leaders of the bourgeois feminist movement? Although agreeing on many issues, these two groups became increasingly estranged in the postwar period. Such a distance had not always existed between the two pillars of the Italian women's movement: many individual socialists, like Malnati and Clerici, had worked closely with middle-class women in the prewar Pro-Suffrage organization and at the first National Italian Women's Congress of 1908.[82] Cooperation began to break down after 1910, when some middle-class feminists began moving to the right, first supporting the colonial war with Libya and later intervention into World War I. Pressure also came from the dominant maximalist wing of the PSI, which ordered Clerici and Malnati to give up their membership in the interclass Pro-Suffrage organization.[83] By the end of the war the break seemed complete, with bourgeois organizations trying to placate nationalist and later fascist critics while socialist women reemphasized the importance of class as they looked to the Russian revolution.

Contributors to the *Defense* exhibited ambivalence as well as disdain for middle-class feminists. After the war, the journal continued to report on international feminist meetings dealing with issues like suffrage and peace, mostly of interest to older socialist women who had a long experience of participating in such events and had even called themselves feminist before the war.[84] But for the most part, the *Defense* had little appreciation for what it called "extreme feminism which seems more against men than for women."[85] It warned working women against the lure of the bourgeois leagues, interested only in superficial legal reforms. It also ridiculed the new nationalist women's groups, composed of "an *elite* … who go around in fur coats, who wear silk garments *dessous*, who perfume themselves with *rose sans fin*, who have at least one lover and such a serious, deep, and broad culture that they have learned perfectly the steps of the *fox-trot*."[86] In expectation of imminent female suffrage, the *Difesa* sought to entice working women to cast their vote for the PSI rather than bourgeois or religious parties. Even pacifism, the backbone of PSI policy during the war, was denounced as "a typically bourgeois activity" which might not always be in the proletariat's class interest.[87] Yet many socialist women continued to adhere to peace as a universal principle, and the editors of the *Difesa* inserted a query about the position of the party directorate on pacifism.[88] That the editors had to resort to a public appeal to prod male leaders to pay attention to a lively debate among women shows a pathetic lack of private interchange between the sexes in the PSI.

The Italian Communist Party

Like the PSI, the PCI did not keep exact records on the breakdown of its membership by sex after its formation in 1921. In any case, it is extremely difficult to calculate mass participation at the local level once party activities were pushed into semiclandestinity by the violence of fascist squads in 1923 and finally outlawed in 1926. Statistics indicate that women formed a relatively small percentage of party membership. At the Congress of Livorno, four hundred women left the PSI for the PCI, but female membership seems to have dropped to little more than a hundred in the next few years. In 1925, the PCI reported to the Women's Secretariat of the Third International that 300 women held Italian party cards.[89] Thus, from 1921 to 1925, female membership constituted between 1 and 2 percent of the total, since party size declined in 1923 but rose again in 1925.[90] The failure of the PCI to attract a growing number of women after its establishment reflected not only periods of disattention to women but also the general crisis of all leftist parties in a climate of fear and repression. Like the socialists, however, the PCI boasted a large number of female sympathizers who may not have held party cards but participated in labor sabotage, shop-floor strikes, and later the armed Resistance against fascism.

From the beginning, the PCI insisted that women not form their own sections, as had happened periodically in the PSI, but join mixed sections with men. Yet the party recommended special measures for its female members, "in consideration of the arrested spiritual development of women, of their backward habits and of the special position that they often hold because of their domestic duties."[91] Debate ensued between two leading communist women over the form that these measures should take. Teresa Noce argued for optimal integration of men and women in order to emphasize the class nature of communist ideology, while Ravera preferred female groups, as long as they remained subordinate to the sections and party discipline.[92] The party did approve the formation of groups for female recruitment within the sections although, as in the PSI, the interest of the Central Committee in women's issues waxed and waned over the years. Yet most male leaders, including Gramsci and Palmiro Togliatti, did seem to genuinely realize the importance of organizing women, perhaps because of the well-publicized role of Russian women in the October Revolution. They therefore approved the formation of a Female Secretariat, giving communist women a central coordinating committee lacking to socialist women after the war.

The PCI, like the PSI, enjoyed high levels of female activism in the North while little to none in the central and southern regions. Communist women were concentrated for the most part in Piedmont, having followed Gramsci and his "new order" movement out of the PSI in 1921. The defection to the PCI was especially high in Turin, where the PSI estimated that it lost 80 percent of its female members.[93] As women of PSI had the *Defense*, communist women also expressed their views in print, first in *The Female Tribune* and later in *The Female Comrade*, a journal established by the party in 1922. Although its editor was always a male deputy, ostensibly because he had parliamentary immunity from arrest, the *Comrade* seemed to have been genuinely controlled by women. It met with early success; during its first three months of publication, the list of subscribers jumped from 500 to 1,200 and the number of copies sold from 5,000 to 7,200.[94] But it began to appear irregularly by 1923 because of fascist violence and was published only sporadically, often on International Women's Day, after it went underground in 1926. Like the *Defense* for the socialists, the *Tribune* and *Comrade* offer perhaps the best guide to the thinking of prominent communist women. Part of each issue was devoted to general news about the PCI, foreign affairs, and the Soviet Union, since it was thought that many women did not read daily newspapers or regular publications of the party. But the novelty of the *Tribune* and *Comrade* were the articles on women's issues, often unsigned but representing the views of the major collaborators like Ravera, Rita Montagnana, and Ferrero. As noted above, the communist publications were similar to the *Defense* in their concern with unemployment among women and equal pay while they differed from the socialist publication in almost ignoring the vote. Other issues prominent in the *Tribune* and *Comade* were the family, education, and resistance to fascism.

A clear theme running through the publications of communist women was the need for valorizing motherhood. They blamed capitalists for hypocritically praising women as "angel[s] of the family" while destroying the proletarian family through "a whirlpool of industrial development."[95] Working women left their houses each morning only "to be swallowed up by the factory which, like a monstrous beast, opens its avid throat but is never satiated with human flesh."[96] Yet less clarity existed on how to save the family from disintegration. Ravera, in an article entitled "Our Feminism," emphasized the need for longer maternity leaves "since nursing and raising a baby, besides satisfying the natural maternal instinct, constitutes productive and useful work for the human family."[97] Such maternity leaves should last about a year, after which mothers would have the right to return to their jobs and thus retain their economic independence. Other writers seemed to condemn all wage labor for mothers, arguing that it weakened their health and took them away from their children.[98]

Agreement did exist, however, that a communist revolution would validate maternity as liberalism could not. No specific plans were proposed, but Russia always provided a model for the future. In 1921, Elena Blonina reported that the Soviet government was taking over the burdens of housework and child rearing so that future parents would experience few economic worries.[99] Eight years later, the *Comrade* printed a list of the advantages enjoyed by Russian mothers side-by-side with a list of what Italian women wanted and lacked under fascism. According to this article, women in Russia enjoyed equal pay, long maternity leaves with job protection, free maternity care, nurseries in factories, and free abortion. Italian women wanted all of these, although the last was phrased more moderately as "the liberty to have or not have children."[100] Communist women's allusions to abortion, although usually indirect, distinguished them from their socialist counterparts as did their enthusiasm for public kitchens and other government services to lift the burden of housework.

Communist women showed a concern for devising a new type of education in anticipation of a revolution in the family. Such an education would come not from the present public schools, but from "communist children's groups." These groups would combat bourgeois prejudices and train children from their earliest years to become good proletarians.[101] Thus trained, the children would bring a needed "fresh breeze of revolutionary thought and sentiment" back to their schools and even their families, especially unpolitical mothers.[102] After the consolidation of power by Mussolini, the *Comrade* promised that communist families would forbid their children to join the new fascist youth groups and wear the black shirt. Opposed to the militarization of youth, one writer declared that "We refuse to give our children to fascism."[103]

Finally, a theme that ran through the later (clandestine) issues of *Comrade* was a call to arms to fight fascism. Even before Mussolini's consolidation of power, the journal bemoaned the outdated spirit of pacifism among many communist women, pointing out that the violence of the bourgeoisie had to be met in kind. By 1929, one article commanded women to be ready to "take up a gun" if the fascists began a second capitalist war. The phrase referred to a famous anti-war song of 1917 whose lyrics were: "Take the gun and throw it on the ground/We want peace, we want peace and never war." Denigrating this type of pacifism – typical of a socialist policy that had failed to stop World War I or the rise of fascism – the author advised women not to throw the gun on the ground. She boasted that proletarian women, unlike petit-bourgeois ladies, were not the "weaker sex" and did not have "a holy fear at the sight of blood." [104] That communist leaders had to exhort so strongly women to armed struggle shows how deeply the tradition of pacifism was rooted in Italian women of the Left after the horrors of the first World War.

Communist women held their first and only national conference of the interwar period in March 1922. Like most of the conferences of women in the PSI, the gathering of communist women ran parallel to a general party congress and therefore was plagued by certain problems. The number of women in attendance was disappointing, since few sections had sent female representatives to the party congress. According to accounts of the meeting, men dominated the discussion, including Gramsci who presided over the proceedings. While the presence of Gramsci boosted the importance of the conference, the dominance of male speakers may account for the emphasis on organizational strategy rather than issues of more substance like equal pay, right to work, and maternity benefits in the final resolution.[105] The resolution called for active recruitment among factory workers, peasants, housewives, and petit-bourgeois "intellectuals" (teachers, clerical workers), with most energy going toward the first category.

Despite their small numbers, women were visible from the beginning as leaders in the general party. The most powerful woman was Ravera, promoted from editor of the *Tribune* and *Comrade* to membership in the Central Committee in 1923 and the Directorate in 1926. Other women active in the early years of the party and often delegates to national and regional congresses were Rita Maierotti, Ferrero, Caterina Piccolato, Noce, and Rita Montagnana, sister of the socialist stalwart Clelia. The strength of the communist women's movement lay particularly in its youth, as Ravera was only thirty-four when she entered the central committee and Ferrero, Piccolato, Noce, and Montagnana at least ten years younger. While still lacking a strong theoretical background, these younger women offered the PCI unlimited reservoirs of energy and an image – in contrast to the PSI – as the party of the future.

Two reports to the Comintern give us a glimpse of party policy toward women in its last days of legality. Again the emphasis was on organization, but with recommendations for ameliorating the plight of female workers in both urban and rural areas. The demands for women included equal pay for equal work in city and countryside; a workday of six hours for factory workers and eight hours for peasants; prohibition of dangerous or unhealthy work; longer maternity leaves with salary; and professional training under the auspices of unions.[106] The party was less specific in its proposals for working-class housewives, although it realized that they tended to be "ignorant of the reasons for struggle, overwhelmed by poverty, frightened of dangers and tired of sacrifices" and therefore ripe for cooptation by fascism.[107] It proposed simply educational groups aimed at housewives. White-collar workers were not even mentioned, since by 1925 the lower-middle class had become a pillar of fascism.

Prison, Exile, and Resistance

After the banning of the PSI and the PCI in 1926, the lives of socialist and communist women changed radically. Of course most women, like men, simply cut all ties with any party that would bring them under suspicion with fascist thugs and police. This can be seen from the plummeting rates of membership in both parties, from as early as 1923. Others continued underground activities, even at the risk of arrest. Such activities included printing and distributing antifascist propaganda, attending secret party meetings, and organizing on factory floors. The PCI also organized a network of mutual assistance called "Red Aid" (*Soccorso rosso*). Based heavily on the efforts of women, Red Aid sent food and books to political prisoners while trying to take care of their families.

Even after strikes were outlawed, women continued to protest their increasingly abysmal working conditions. Such labor resistance would have been impossible without the cooperation of many women not holding party cards, showing the large number of sympathizers around the PSI and especially the PCI. Women were prominent in the chronology of labor unrest under fascism: strikes occurred among textile workers, rice weeders, cigar makers, and sardine packers in 1927; textile workers and rice weeders in 1929; textile workers and button makers and rice weeders in 1931; textile workers in 1933 and again in 1934, accompanied by a huge protest of 20,000 rice weeders.[108] Women also participated actively in a series of antiwar demonstrations, first organized by the PCI in 1929 and occurring periodically in response to the Nazi seizure of power in Germany, the colonial war in Ethiopia, and the fascist support of Franco during the Spanish Civil War. Labor resistance accelerated again after 1943, with a strike at the Fiat plant in Turin on 5 March followed by an anti-war demonstration by thousands of women to mark International Women's Day three days later.[109] Protest and sabotage continued on shop floors until the end of the war. Involvement in clandestine activities often led to arrest. Ferrero, for example, was entrapped by a fascist decoy pretending to need help from the Red Aid.[110]

The crackdown on political opposition was so sweeping that by the 1930s the PSI had almost disappeared within Italy and the PCI was severely weakened, with many of its leaders in jail. While most political prisoners were men, the Special Tribunal sentenced 124 women to a total of 675 years in prison.[111] Others were tried and convicted in regular courts while about 175 were sent by police to *confino*, a type of internal exile. Perhaps a total of 500 women were punished for political crimes under fascism.

As the writings of female prisoners attest, confinement was more difficult for women than for men. Men were guarded by civilian personnel, while women, according to Ferrero, were under the control of "nuns who were almost always zealous, ideologically motivated, often fanatical, omnipresent and all powerful …. To save money, these sisters exploited the work of the inmates to take care of their clothing: to sew, mend, and iron it."[112] The pressure on female inmates to attend religious services was strong, and even a few political prisoners of the Left gave in to the temptation to try to find solace in the Catholic religion of their childhood. One of these was Ferrero herself, who later underwent unrelenting interrogation and demands for self-denunciation by her communist comrades suspicious of her loyalty.

One reason that a few inmates like Ferrero turned to religion against the tenets of their Marxism was the extreme isolation experienced by political women in prison. Male socialists and communists were interned in such great numbers that they could bolster each others' spirits. For men, prison became a "university" where they could read and discuss politics and philosophy, thus keeping their minds active and prepared for taking power after the fall of fascism. Women, on the other hands, were interned in smaller numbers and sometimes isolated from each other. Their cell-mates were mainly prostitutes, who were illiterate, apolitical, and sometimes spoke such a heavy dialect that communication became difficult. Even when political women could congregate, they often lacked appropriate readings since the Red Aid tended to ignore female prisons when shipping care packages of books.

Confino was equally lonely, although usually more active than prison. A uniquely Italian institution, *confino* allowed police to send suspicious persons to small towns in the South or on the islands. Prisoners rented rooms in their assigned village and were free to walk around and even work. For example, the socialist Lina Merlin continued her profession of teaching while in *confino* in the Sardinian towns of Orune and Nuoro. Prevented from employment in the local schools since she had refused to sign the loyalty oath required by the fascist government, she instead prepared young teachers for their promotional exams. Merlin reported that these "willing and intelligent teachers … thanked God for having inspired Mussolini to send me to their village," since she was better educated than anyone else in the vicinity.[113] Typically, local townspeople refused to despise the prisoners in their midst as antifascist traitors, but instead showed deference to their higher social standing and rejoiced at the skills they brought to neglected rural areas. But life for Merlin was nevertheless boring, as she was not allowed to read newspapers, and even her copy of a novel by Tolstoy was confiscated because he was Russian!

Other women of the Left went into exile, either alone or with their husbands and companions. Most lived in Paris, where both the PSI and the PCI transferred their headquarters in 1926, although smaller groups gathered in Switzerland for easier access to Italy. Communist women sometimes spent periods in Moscow. Noce's life in exile was more active than that of most women, but illustrates the range of activities pursued by leftist women outside of Italy.[114] Young, working-class, and poorly educated, she was sent to schools first in Switzerland, run by the PCI, and later in Moscow under the aegis of the Comintern. She then served the party both in Paris, preparing propaganda including clandestine issues of the *Comrade*, and in Moscow in the labor office of the Comintern. What perhaps most distinguished her among other women in exile were her courageous secret missions into northern Italy to organize labor resistance, particularly among women working in textile factories or in rice fields. She could also be found in Spain during the Civil War, writing publicity for the International Brigades. Noce accomplished this astounding amount of antifascist work not as a single woman, but as the wife of a prominent communist leader, Luigi Longo, and the mother of two children. In her memoir, *Rivoluzionaria professionale* (A professional woman revolutionary), she conveys the exhaustion of finding safe havens for her children and the anguish of leaving them, sometimes for long periods. Many women in exile shared similar burdens of child care while trying to match their male comrades in political work.

A few words must be said about the participation of women in the Resistance, although it occurred after the interwar period that defines this essay. Beginning in 1943, the Resistance involved women in all antifascist parties, although the bulk were communist and socialist. While official statistics counted 125,000 women in the ranks of the Resistance, other estimates run as high as two million.[115] Such a wide variation in estimates comes partly from the clandestine nature of the Resistance. Women fought not only alongside men in mixed units but also founded their own organization, the Women's Defense Groups (*Gruppi di difesa della donna*). It is also clear that many unorganized women lent support to the Resistance, for example housewives who fed and sheltered partisans or runaway soldiers. Women carried out a wide variety of tasks including the dissemination of antifascist propaganda, organization of strikes and sabotage of production, assistance to families of partisans and political prisoners, domestic tasks in the mountains for male fighters, and even armed combat itself. The most well-known female figure of the Resistance was the *staffetta*, who carried secret information across enemy lines. Women made especially suitable couriers, since they could play on female stereotypes (innocent mother or flirtatious young girl) to slip by fascist police. That women undertook dangerous missions is clear from the punishment they received when caught: according to official figures on the Resistance, 2,750 women were killed in armed combat or shot by the enemy; 3,000 were deported to concentration camps; and 4,500 others arrested and tortured.[116] The innumerable rapes went unreported.[117]

Conclusion

Italy offers an unusual periodization in the history of the relation of socialism to women in the twentieth century. While World War I brought modifications to both terms – "socialism" and "women" – the consolidation of the fascist dictatorship in 1926 constituted an even more important watershed in the development of the PSI and the PCI as well as the lives of women. Since its founding, the socialist party had ignored the woman question, and this changed little after the war. Despite support of suffrage and divorce by several parliamentary deputies, the PSI directorate paid little attention to women's issues and discouraged women from organizing autonomously. The founding of the communist party in 1921 was a bit more propitious for women, as male leaders immediately approved the formation of a Female Secretariat and began to promote one woman, Ravera, to important positions of power. But the PCI was no more successful than the PSI in increasing female membership above 2 percent of the total in the interwar period, indicating a similar failure to take the woman question seriously.

The behavior of women on the Left also displayed continuities from the prewar period through the early 1920s. Rather than taking out party cards, women tended to join unions. Yet even rates of union membership under-estimate the political consciousness of Italian women, large numbers of whom participated in labor agitation even if officially unaffiliated with a party or union. Often discounted by male leadership, women nevertheless organized waves of strikes and antiwar demonstrations before, during, and after World War I. This pattern continued after the advent of fascism, although most women, like men, seemed to accept the new regime. Only further research can establish whether this tradition of labor militancy among women translated into other less visible methods of resisting the fascist regime during the so-called years of consensus in the 1930s.

The postwar women's movement was born even before the end of World War II with the establishment of the Union of Italian Women (UDI) and its journal, *Noi Donne* (We Women) in 1944.[118] Like the Women's Defense Groups, UDI sought to unite all antifascist women, although its membership came most heavily from the PCI and the PSI. UDI grew in strength after the war and represented the voice of Italian women during the 1950s and 1960s. At the end of the war, women finally received the vote in recognition of their contributions to the Resistance and as a confirmation of new democratic principles. Some women who had suffered imprisonment and exile under fascism went on to hold important positions in the new Republic: for example, Ravera, Noce, Rita Montagnana, and Merlin were elected to Parliament. Many inequalities remained in work and family, however, and these were not overturned until the stalwarts of UDI were joined by the younger feminists of the "second wave" in the late 1960s and 1970s.

Notes

1. A PSC-CUNY Grant supported the research for this essay. The American Coun-cil of Learned Societies provided funding for travel to Paris for a meeting of the authors of this volume.
2. Mariapia Bigaran, "Progetti e dibattiti parlamentari sul suffragio femminile," *Riv-ista di storia contemporanea* 14 (January 1985): 50-82.
3. "I progressi del voto alle donne durante la guerra," *La difesa delle lavoratrici*, (1 June 1919): 1.
4. Clelia Montagnana, "Per il suffragio femminile," *Difesa* (4 July 1920): 1.
5. Constantino Lazzari, "Il privilegio dell'elettorato femminile," *Difesa* (15 Decem-ber 1923): 2.
6. Felicità Ferrero, "Le teorie riformiste e l'emancipazione femminile," "La Tribuna delle Donne," *L'ordine nuovo* (29 September 1921): 4.

7. Parlamento, Camera dei Deputati, *Discussioni*, Legis. 27, 1924-1927 (15 May 1925): 3622.
8. Parlamento, *Discussioni* (15 May 1925): 3620-3621.
9. Embodied in Articles 134-37 of the Civil Code of 1865.
10. The *Difesa* did reprint part of the parliamentary debate on the Sacchi bill but did not bother to comment. See the issue of 10 March 1919.
11. Articles 131 and 222-239 of the Civil Code of 1865.
12. Article 150 of the Civil Code of 1865. The grounds for separation were obviously modeled on the Napoleonic Code.
13. On bourgeois feminists, see Rosanna De Longis, "'In difesa della donna e della razza" and on socialist women, see Susanna Bucci, "La guerra tra il pane e l'amore," both in *Nuova Donnawomanfemme* 19-20 (winter-spring 1982): 149-77 and 178-89, respectively.
14. Agopik Manoukian, "La rappresentazione statistica dei vincoli familiari," in *I vincoli familiari in Italia: Dal secolo XI al secolo XX*, ed., A. Manoukian (Bologna, 1983), p. 446.
15. Denise Destragiache, "Un aspect de la politique démographique de l'Italie fasciste: La répression de l'avortement," *Melanges de l'École Francaise de Rome* (1980): 694. Fascism first prohibited the circulation of information about birth control in Articles 112 and 113 the Public Security Law of 1926.
16. Articles 381-85 of the Italian Criminal Code of 1889.
17. Article 385, Ibid.
18. Even communist women were indirect in their support of abortion, as the *Tribune* simply reprinted a French article rather than voicing its own analysis of the issue. See "Il mestiere della maternità," *Tribuna, L'Ordine* (10 March 1921): 4.
19. Articles 545-555 of the Rocco Criminal Code of 1930.
20. Two excellent articles that document the frequency of abortion during fascism are Destragiache, "Un aspect," and Luisa Passerini, "Donne operaie e aborto nella Torino fascista, *Italia Contemporanea* (September 1983): 83-109.
21. Pierfrancesco Bandettini, "The Employment of Women in Italy 1881-1951," *Comparative Studies in Society and History* (April 1960): 374. No census was take in 1941. The percentage of the workforce that was female in 1951 had risen slightly to 25.1.
22. Bandettini, "The Employment," p. 374.
23. Bruna Bianchi, "I tessili: lavoro, salute, conflitti" in *L'Internazionale operaia e socialista tra le due guerre*, ed. Enzo Collotti (Milan, 1985), p. 974.
24. See Elda Gentili Zappi, *If Eight Hours Seem too Few: Mobilization of Women Workers in the Italian Rice Fields* (Albany, N.Y., 1991).
25. "La donna nell'industria milanese," *Difesa* (28 July 1918): 4.
26. "La donna nell'industria," p. 4.
27. Paolo Spriano, "Sindacati e lotte operaie," in *La crisi italiana del primo dopoguerra*, ed. Giovanni Sabbatucci (Bari, 1976), p. 217. The CGL had increased from only 250,000 at the end of World War I.
28. This estimate of 15 percent is based on Italy's report to the International Workers Congress of 1921 held in Vienna as reported in "A Vienna si sono discussi i problemi della donna operaia: Un Congresso vuoto ed inconcludente," *Difesa* (22 September 1923): 3.
29. Spriano, "Sindacati," p. 217.
30. *Storia del movimento sindacale italiana*, ed. Sergio Zaninelli, vol. 2 (Milan, 1971): 363 for statistics on 1914, 1918, and 1919. The *Difesa* reported the membership of the Textile Federation as 100,000 in 1919 and 130,000 in 1920. See "La pro-

paganda nelle masse lavoratrici femminili," *Difesa* (7 December 1919): 2 and "Il primo passo," *Difesa* (12 December 1920):1.

31. Renato Zangheri (ed.), *Lotte agrarie in Italia* (Milan, 1960), p. 370.
32. "Argentina Altobelli," in *Il movimento operaio italiano: Dizionario biografico*, eds. Franco Andreucci and Tommaso Detti, vol. 1 (Rome, 1978), p. 51.
33. Bureau International du Travail, *Annuaire International du Travail*, pt. 3 (Geneva, 1925), p. 110.
34. Ibid., p. 108.
35. Several interesting articles on women's protest during World War I can be found in *Le donne delle campagne italiane del Novecento*, ed. Paola Corti [Istituto 'Alcide Cervi,' *Annali*, 13] (Bologna, 1991).
36. Cristina Bacci, *A uguale lavoro uguale salario* (Milan, 1917), pp. 7-8.
37. Ibid., p. 8.
38. Ibid., p. 19.
39. "Il sotto-salariato femminile," *Tribuna, L'Ordine* (24 February 1921): 3.
40. Camilla Ravera, *Breve storia del movimento femminile in Italia* (Rome, 1978), p. 86.
41. "Attività della Federazione Arti Tessili," *Difesa* (20 January 1918): 4.
42. Maria Coppini-Zanini, "Per il voto alla donna: Una incoraggiante e sintemico esperimento," *Difesa* (31 December 1918): 4.
43. *Storia del movimento sindacale*, vol 2, p. 388.
44. Gianni Cesira, "Ma che cosa pretendono?" *Difesa* (24 March 1918): 3.
45. Un impiegato, "Smobilitare la donna?" *Difesa* (16 November 1919): 3
46. "La concorrenza femminile nel lavoro," *Tribuna, L'ordine* (26 May 1921): 3.
47. "La rivoluzione sociale e le donne," *Tribuna, L'ordine* (2 June 1921): 3.
48. Alberto De Bernardi, *Operai e Nazione: Sindacati, operai e stato nell'Italia fascista* (Milan, 1993), p. 128.
49. See Perry R. Willson, *The Clockwork Factory: Women and Work in Fascist Italy* (Oxford, 1993) and Chiara Saraceno "La famiglia operaia sotto il fascismo" in *L'Internazionale operaia*, pp. 189-230.
50. "Palestra delle lettrici," *Difesa* (1 September 1924): 4.
51. Carla (operaia tessile), "I contratti di lavoro fascisti permettono e favoriscono lo sfruttamento fino all fame delle lavoratrici," *Compagna* (8 March 1930).
52. See Maria Vittoria Ballestrero and Oriella Antozzi, "I socialisti e la legislazione sul lavoro delle donne e dei fanciulli," *Movimento operaio e socialista* 20 (October-December 1974): 285-314.
53. See the articles by Annarita Buttafuoco and Chiara Saraceno in *Maternity and Gender Policies*, eds. Gisela Bock and Pat Thane (New York, 1991) as well as Victoria De Grazia, *How Fascism Ruled Women* (Berkeley, 1992), pp. 178-79
54. Franca Pieroni Bortolotti wrote the pioneering work on socialist women entitled *Socialismo e questione femminile in Italia, 1892-1922* (Milan, 1974); a subsequent volume traced the "woman question" until 1926. See her *Femminismo e partiti politici in Italia, 1919-1926* (Rome, 1978).
55. Maurizio Ridolfi, *Il PSI e la nascita del partito di massa, 1892-1922* (Rome and Bari, 1992), p. 35.
56. Total membership in the PSI was 41,876 in 1915; 29,144 in 1916; 26,834 in 1917; 24,359 in 1918; 83,422 in 1919; and 208,974 in 1920. See Renzo Martinelli, *Il Partito comunista italiano, 1921-1926* (Rome, 1977), p. 30.
57. "Le sezioni femminili," *Difesa* (19 January 1919).
58. Evia, "I gruppi e il movimento socialista femminile," in *Almanacco socialista italiano, 1921* (Milan, 1921), p. 395.

59. "Appello del Comitato Regionale femminile piemontese," *Difesa* (28 July 1918): 2.
60. Zitellona, "Un problema e un errore: Uomini e donne nel partito socialista," *Difesa* (1 September 1918): 1.
61. Zitellona, "Un problema," p. 1.
62. Ada Pandolfi, "Donne e uomini nel Partito Socialista," *Difesa* (29 September 1918): 3.
63. Pierina Ronchi, "Non divisi ma uniti," *Difesa* (13 October 1918): 1; Cecilia Baggi, "Donne e uomini nel Partito Socialista," *Difesa* (29 September 1918): 3.
64. [Clelia Montagnana], "Ed il nostro giornale?" *Difesa* (7 December 1919): 2.
65. Clelia Montagnana, "Prepariamoci al Congresso femminile," *Difesa* (4 April 1920): 1.
66. "Convegno femminile socialista nazionale," *Difesa* (16 May 1920): 1.
67. "Il primo passo," *Difesa* (12 December 1920): 1.
68. The vagueness of the phrase "parecchie migliaia" [several thousand] women illustrates the inability of even the *Difesa* to identify the exact number of female members of the PSI. "Il primo passo", *Difesa* (12 December 1920): 1.
69. "Relazione sul movimento femminile: Il nostro Convegno" *Difesa* (13 October 1921): 1.
70. "La Direzione del Partito per la propaganda femminile," *Difesa* (25 June 1923): 1.
71. "La Direzione del Partito per 'La Difesa delle Lavoratrici,'" *Difesa* (1 June 1924): 2.
72. Carlotta Clerici, "Conclusioni sul comma 'Organizzazione socialista femminile,'" *Difesa* (21 November 1920): 1.
73. "Relazione sul movimento femminile: Il nostro Convegno," *Difesa* (13 October 1921): 1.
74. Angelica Balabanoff, "La 'Difesa' e morta ... evviva la 'Difesa,'" *Difesa* (25 June 1923): 2; quote from the Prefect of Milan reprinted in the 19 March 1925 issue of the *Difesa*.
75. Noi, "Per la propaganda femminile: Constatazioni," *Difesa* (15 October 1923): 1.
76. Ibid.
77. Ibid.
78. PSI, *Resoconto stenografico del XVI Congresso Nazionale del PSI (Bologna, 5-6-7-8 ottobre 1919)* (Rome, 1920), pp. 342-82.
79. Like other prominent women, she was appointed to the executive committee of her local party section, in her case Milan. For accounts of Kuliscioff's personal and political life, see Claire LaVigna, *Anna Kuliscioff: From Russian Populism to Italian Socialism* (New York, 1991); Beverly Tanner Springer, "Anna Kuliscioff: Russian Revolutionist, Italian Feminist," in *European Women on the Left*, eds. Jane Slaughter and Robert Kern (Westport, Conn., 1981), pp. 13-27; Maria Casalini, *La signora del socialismo italiano: Vita di Anna Kuliscioff* (Rome, 1987); and Marina Addis Saba, *Anna Kuliscioff* (Milan, 1993).
80. "Altobelli," in *Il movimento*,vol. 1, eds. Andreucci and Detti, pp. 49-51.
81. On Balabanoff, see Jane Slaughter, "Humanism versus Socialism in the Feminist Movement: The Life of Angelica Balabanoff" in *European Women*, pp. 179-94. Balabanoff's autobiography has been translated as *My Life as a Rebel* (Bloomington, Ind., 1938), but contains few references to the woman question.
82. The best account of relations between bourgeois and socialist feminists before World War I is Annarita Buttafuoco, "Il movimento di emancipazione femminile," in *L'Italia di Giolitti* [*Storia della società italiana*, pt. 5, vol. 20] (Milan, 1981), pp. 145-88.

83. "Clerici," in *Il movimento*,vol. 2, eds. Andreucci and Detti, p. 55.
84. "Il Congresso Femminile Internazionale di Zurigo," *Difesa* (1 June 1919): 1; Giudetta Brambilla, "Impressioni di un Congresso," *Difesa* (25 June 1923): 3.
85. "Femminismo e socialismo," *Difesa* (1 May 1918): 2.
86. L'ammonitore, "Il blocco delle gentildonne," *Difesa* (7 December 1919): 1. The article refers specifically to the "Pro fatherland" organization presided over by Teresa Labriola, a famous former bourgeois feminist and one of the first women in Italy to earn a law degree.
87. Evia, "Il pacifismo e le pacifiste," *Difesa* (6 July 1919): 1.
88. [Note from the Editors], *Difesa* (6 July 1919): 1.
89. Nadia Spano and Fiamma Camarlinghi, *La questione femminile nella politica del PCI, 1921-1963* (Rome, 1972), p. 17. While Spano and Camarlinghi's text remains a classic, Patrizia Gabrielli is carrying out the most exciting new research on women in the early PCI. See her articles, "Le origini del movimento femminile comunista in Italia, 1921-1925," *Critica marxista* 27 (September- October 1989): 103-31; and "La solidarietà tra pratica politica e vita quotidiana nell'esperienza delle donne comuniste," *Rivista di storia contemporanea* 22 (January 1993): 34-56.
90. Total membership in the PCI was 24,568 in 1922; 8,696 in 1923; 17,373 in 1924; 24,837 in 1925; and 15,285 in 1926. See Martinelli, *Il Partito*, pp. 196, 213, 284.
91. "Le donne e l'Internazionale communista," in *Tribuna, L'ordine* (10 February 1921): 3.
92. See Patrizia Gabrielli, "Camilla e Teresa: Un conflitto clandestino," *Nuova Donnawomanfemme* 26-27(April-September 1995): 18-30.
93. "Alla 'Difesa delle Lavoratrici,'" *Tribuna, L'Ordine* (14 July 1921): 4.
94. Spano and Camerlinghi, *La questione*, p. 36.
95. Pina Belloni, "La donna lavoratrice e la famiglia," *Compagna* (2 April 1922): 2.
96. Belloni, "La donna lavoratrice," 2.
97. "Il nostro femminismo," in *Tribuna, L'Ordine* (10 March 1921): 4.
98. Belloni, "La donna lavoratrice," p. 2.
99. Elena Blonina, "L'operaia nella Russia dei Soviet," in *Tribuna, L'Ordine* (14 July 1921): 4.
100. [No title], *Compagna* (1 August 1929): 4.
101. "Gruppi infantili comunisti," in *Tribuna, L'Ordine* (31 March 1921): 3.
102. "I gruppi infanti comunisti," *Compagna* (2 April 1922): 2.
103. "Rifuitiamoci di dare i nostri figli al fascismo," *Compagna* (September-October 1930): 2.
104. Wanda, "Prendi il fucile!" *Compagna* (1 August 1929): 2.
105. The minutes of the First Conference of Communist Women have been lost, but the final resolution is contained in Spano and Camarlinghi, *La questione*, pp. 31-33. *Compagna* reported part of the debate in "La prima Conferenza Nazionale delle donne communiste" (2 April 1922): 2.
106. Spano and Camarlinghi, *La questione*, pp. 48-50.
107. Ibid., p. 49.
108. Alessandra De Perini, "Alcune ipotesi sul rapporto tra le donne e le organizzazioni storiche del movimento operaio," in *Dentro lo specchio*, ed. Franca Bimbi (Milan, 1977), pp. 252-53; Spano and Camarlinghi, *La questione*, pp. 57-63.
109. De Perini, "Alcune ipotesi," p. 255.
110. Felicità Ferrero, *Un nocciolo di verità* (Milan, 1978), p. 61.
111. John Cammett, "Communist Women and the Fascist Experience," in *European Women*, p. 167; on the experience of female political prisoners, see also Laura Mariani, *Quelle dell'idea: Storie di detenute politiche, 1927-1948* (Bari, 1982).

112. Ferrero, *Un nocciolo*, p. 64.
113. Lina Merlin, *La mia vita*, ed. Elena Marinucci (Florence, 1989), p. 43.
114. See the memoir by Teresa Noce entitled *Rivoluzionaria professionale* (Milan, 1974).
115. Lydia Franceschi et al., *L'altra metà della resistenza* (Milan, 1978), p. 17.
116. Ibid., p. 29.
117. On women's experiences in World War II and the Resistance, see Anna Bravo and Anna Maria Bruzzone (eds.), *In guerra senza armi: Storie di donne, 1940-1945* (Bari, 1995), Anna Teresa Iaccheo, *Donne armate: Resistenza e terrorismo: Testimoni dalla Storia* (Milan, 1994), and B. Giudetti Serra, *Compagne* (Turin, 1977).
118. As early as 1937, an association of Italian women emigrées in Paris had formed an association of the same name and issued a journal called *Noi Donne*. The GDD also issued periodic journals named *Noi Donne*. Thus, by 1944, UDI and *Noi Donne* were names already carrying historic connotations. See Maria Michetti, Margherita Repetto, and Luciana Viviani, *Udi: Laboratorio di politica delle donne* (Rome, 1984), p. 5.

Part IV

PRELUDE TO WELFARE STATES

Introduction

Ida Blom

The Scandinavian countries of Denmark, Norway, and Sweden are often seen as models of welfare states. They are often grouped together as a unity having common characteristics. More often than not, Sweden is regarded as representative of the group, and to some extent that interpretation is correct. Small, culturally homogeneous societies with a pronounced egalitarian social structure, the Scandinavian countries share a more or less common history. While during the interwar period many European countries experienced social and political polarizations that endangered – and in Italy, Germany, Austria, and Spain toppled – democracy, Scandinavian political parties demonstrated an ability to form coalitions and stabilize democratic institutions. This situation is perceived as the foundation for present-day Scandinavian welfare states and of recent egalitarian gender relations.[1]

A bird's-eye view of the socialist movements substantiates this conclusion. Taking Denmark and Sweden as examples, it can be maintained that Scandinavian social-democratic parties at an early stage were reconciled to a basic national political system. Already in the 1920s they formed either coalition or minority governments; in the 1930s at the latest they transformed themselves from class parties to "people's parties," entering into red/green coalitions with peasant parties to counteract economic crises and to protect democracy. According to this interpretation of Scandinavian history, one would expect that the development of socialism and gender relations within the socialist movements of the three countries would be very similar during the interwar period. As the following three chapters will demonstrate, this was not the case.

A closer look reveals very important differences between the three socialist movements, Norway in many ways proving to be the exception.

Notes for this chapter begin on page 420.

In Denmark and Sweden social democrats cooperated with the liberals in the prolonged struggle for parliamentary government during the late nineteenth and early twentieth century. Another common effort gained full suffrage rights for men. Danish and Swedish social democrats consequently were, until 1915 and 1920 respectively, involved in establishing national democratic institutions. Developments in Norway were quite different. A parliamentary system already existed in 1884, three years before the Social Democratic party was formed, and only a short period of political contests was needed to bring about general male suffrage (1898). In Norway, unlike Denmark and Sweden, social democrats and liberals never joined forces in fighting to obtain democracy. Add to this that, despite a growing number of socialist voters, the Norwegian electoral system until 1919 effectively barred socialists from parliament. Consequently, they had less reason to believe in parliamentary and ministerial socialism than their comrades in Denmark and Sweden, who quickly gained parliamentary representation.

Divergent histories are part of the explanation for why Norwegian socialists persisted in revolutionary ideologies and practices, even in the interwar period, to a degree unknown in Denmark and Sweden. In joining the Communist International (Comintern), even if only for a short span of time, Norwegian social democrats publicized the revolutionary class character of their party throughout the 1920s and early-1930s. When the first Norwegian socialist government was formed in 1928, widespread resistance within the party led to an open confrontation with the capitalist establishment, and the socialist government was ousted after two weeks. In Denmark and Sweden social democrats formed either coalition or minority governments throughout the 1920s. Although disappointed by cooperation with the Liberals and fearful of losing votes to the Communists, the Swedish Socialists temporarily turned ideologically to the left. After a massive electoral defeat in 1928, they mitigated their class politics and developed the vision of "the people's home." In Denmark, cooperation across class barriers was long the rule and social democrats increasingly perceived their party as a "people's party." In 1934, as Hilda Romer points out, the party program featured the electoral slogan, "Denmark for the people."

In all three countries the red/green alliances (1933 in Denmark and Sweden; 1935 in Norway) were responses to the Great Depression as well as affirmations of democracy in the face of threats to it elsewhere in Europe. The predominance of small, independent, and democratically minded farmers within the rural segment of society facilitated these coalitions. So did the fear of seeing fascist tendencies spread among small conservative groups. But all the same, the actual events were the result of widely differing trajectories. For Denmark and Sweden they may be understood as a logical consequence of earlier cooperation. For Norway the red/green alliance of 1935 was much more of an about-face. A severe electoral defeat for the revolutionary program of the Norwegian Labor party in 1930 paved the way for renewed emphasis on the parliamentary road to power and resulted in a social-democratic landslide in the 1933 election. Another labor electoral victory in 1936 confirmed the popularity of the new course. As in Denmark and Sweden, the road was cleared for successive social-democratic governments and for the development of the future Scandinavian welfare states.

Where does the woman question find its place in the context of the working-class movement?

The following three chapters convincingly demonstrate that the general policy followed by the Scandinavian social-democratic parties resulted in a distinct difference between the strategies followed by Danish and Swedish women and Norwegian women. In Norway, class solidarity eclipsed gender cooperation. The strict adherence to class solidarity and a refusal to cooperate along gender lines continued throughout the interwar period. Not even the parliamentary alliance of the Norwegian Labor party and the Peasant party in 1935 changed this position. Neither did the rise of academically educated young women to the leadership of the social-democratic women's movement. Only on a few important questions, and then on a person-to-person basis, was gender given a cautious priority over class.

The attitude toward separate women's organizations within the three social-democratic parties equally indicated important differences in the way the woman question was addressed. Again, the situation in Denmark and Sweden differs from Norway. Whereas, Norwegian socialist women were welcomed in their special organizations within the party as early as 1901, a separate women's organization was never really admitted to the Danish party. In Sweden, the women's clubs of the 1890s only united in a national federation in 1920. In the 1930s, though, while cooperating in the modern project of economics and "social esthetics," Swedish women were well represented in the social democratic arena. However, their large number in influential positions may, as indicated in Renée Frangeur's chapter, be explained at least in part by family and friendship ties. One might also speculate whether Swedish socialists were more open to intellectual women than was the case with their counterparts in the other two countries. In Norway, at least, the deprecatory attitude to women intellectuals, found within a trend-setting group of socialists, may have created a barrier that was hard to overcome.

There seems to have been an obvious connection between the form of organization and the tendency toward cooperation across class barriers. Although Danish and Swedish social democrats were advocating a policy of cooperation, they may still have feared the bourgeois influence of women's rights feminists. The mutually supportive atmosphere between leading socialist women and bourgeois women's rights organizations may have strengthened the opposition of men to a separate women's organization within the social-democratic parties. Hilda Romer suggests that this male opposition was supported by rank-and-file Danish socialist women who feared that a separate organization might act as a Trojan horse for bourgeois feminism. In Norway, on the other hand, the clear class position of socialist women and their consistent refusal to cooperate with bourgeois women guaranteed that a separate women's organization would remain loyal to the socialist course.

A different pace of industrialization and urbanization may also have had some effect on the question of gender relations within Scandinavian social democracies. Although Sweden lagged behind Denmark on the issue of women's suffrage, the two countries shared a long period of change from rural to industrial economies. In Norway, this development started later and was much quicker. Also, industrialization in Norway did not necessarily equal urbanization since, due to the preponderance of water-generated power plants, important sectors of the growing industrial enterprises were located in rural settings. Thus, the bonds between rural and urban life and rural and urban attitudes toward gender relations may have been a good deal stronger in Norway than in Denmark or Sweden. This may be part of the explanation for the very low rate of participation of married women in the Norwegian labor force as compared to the other two countries. Gender relations in the peasant family burdened married women with heavy workloads as they participated in providing for the family and household. But, contrary to women working in urban settings, the peasant's wife performed all her work in or very near the family home.

Although married, urban working-class wives continued the rural tradition of coproviders, they may have experienced the conflict between woman's domestic responsibilities and paid work outside the home more sharply because rural traditions were closer in time. This may have added to the tenacity with which social-democratic women in Norway followed their male comrades in combating "the double wage." In Sweden, by contrast, in the light of modern economic theory, women's – even married women's – work was considered essential in overcoming the economic crisis. In that case the interests of the women's movements and social-democratic policies coincided.

Despite very clear differences between the Scandinavian social-democratic parties, however, the pursuit of social policies in the 1930s united them in attempts to combat class inequalities. Since the late eighteenth century, they advocated tax-financed public responsibility for needy groups.[2] Conquering political power at the municipal level, social-democratic parties started from the early nineteenth century to construct so-called welfare municipalities with social policies such as old age and mothers' pensions. Women's local initiatives added to political pressure for national welfare measures. Municipal socialism paved the way for welfare policies at the national level.[3] In the 1930s national insurance schemes regarding sickness, unemployment, and old age were enacted or enlarged. Social policies witnessed the breakthrough of the principle of universality, a central concept guiding the later emergence of Scandinavian welfare states. Through this the stigmatizing perception of public assistance as poor relief was gradually transformed into citizen rights and public responsibilities. Universal welfare measures, financed through taxation, were intended not just to provide a safety net for the poorest, but also as a redistribution of resources to create an egalitarian society. These ideas formed the basis for the Scandinavian model of the welfare state that emerged after World War II.

But social-democratic visions of equality during the interwar period and for a long time thereafter continued to build on the gendered division of labor and responsibilities existing in the family setting. Welfare initiatives took for granted that the care of children and of the sick and elderly was mostly a private enterprise, shouldered mainly by women within the family. Thus, although protection of working mothers demanded they be allowed to withdraw from the workforce for a period around childbirth, paid leaves of absence were not legislated in Sweden until 1930. However, a cunning change of strategies, most pronounced in Sweden but also practiced in the other two Scandinavian countries, put the reduction of the birthrate high on women's agenda and made it an instrument for a wide range of social policy initiatives. Social-democratic women were active agents in shaping many of these policies, such as the mother's wage in Norway and the extensive social measures in Sweden. In all three countries fierce battles were fought to legalize information on family planning. In Denmark and Sweden, abortion based on restricted criteria was legalized, allowing for the termination of unwanted pregnancies. This did not happen in Norway until 1960.

The predominance of complementary understandings of gender continued to make the male full-time wage earner the model for social rights, to the detriment of women who were not taken care of by a male provider. These conceptions of gender relations also stamped most of the social-democratic constructions of welfare states after 1945. It was not until the advent of the new women's movements of the 1960s and 1970s that serious steps were taken to consider the inequalities based on gender in welfare state provisions.

Notes

1. For a discussion of similarities and differences between the Nordic social democracies (including Finland) in the interwar period, see Justein Ryssevik, "Party v. Parliament: Contrasting configurations of Electoral and Ministerial Socialism in Scandinavia"; Lauri Karvonen, "'A Nation of Workers and Peasants': Ideology and Compromise in the Interwar Years"; Bo Rothstein, "Social Classes and Political Institutions: The Roots of Swedish Corporatism"; and Jan Sundberg, "Participation in Local Government: A Source of Social-Democratic Deradicalization in Scandinavia?"; all in Lauri Karvonen and Jan Sunderberg (eds.), *Social Democracy in Transition in Northern, Southern, and Eastern Europe* (Aldershot, 1991), pp. 15-138. See also Lauri Karvonen and Per Selle, "Introduction," in *Women in Nordic Policies: Closing the Gap* (Aldershot, 1995).

2. A comprehensive literature discusses the concept of the Scandinavian model of welfare states. See, especially, G. Esping-Andersen and W. Korpi, "From Poor Relief to Institutional Welfare States: The Development of Scandinavian Social Policy," in R. Erikson et al. (eds.), *The Scandinavian Model: Welfare States and Welfare Research* (New York, 1987), and G. Esping-Andersen, *The Three Worlds of Welfare Capitalism* (Princeton, N.J., 1990). See also Birthe Siim, "Women and the Welfare State: Between Private and Public Dependence. A Comparative Approach to Care Work in Denmark and Britain," in Clare Ungerson (ed.), *Gender and Caring* (New York, 1990); "Welfare State, Gender Politics and Equality Policies: Women's Citizenship in the Scandinavian Welfare States," in Elizabeth Mechan and Selma Sevenjhuisen (eds.), *Equality Politics and Gender* (London, 1991); and Arnlaug Leira, "The 'Woman-Friendly' Welfare State?: The Case of Norway and Sweden," in Jan Lewis (ed.), *Women and Social Policies in Europe: Work, Family and the State* (Aldershot, 1993), pp. 49-71.

3. Anne-Hild Nagel (ed.), *Velferdskommunen* (Oslo, 1996).

Swedish, Norwegian, and Danish Women:
Citizenship, Maternity, Selfhood – a Contradiction?

"Youth, the Pride of the Ineluctable Socialist Future"

Danish Socialist Female Youth in Holiday Garb Demonstrating for Peace, 1918
Source: Danish Workers' Movement Archive & Library (DWMAL), Copenhagen

Young Danish Female Socialists in Action through Sports, 1931
Source: DWMAL

"Conflicting Ideals: Housewife, Mother, New Woman"

One Million Swedish Housewives Demand Higher Wages and Jobs
Source: Morgonbris, July 1936: Swedish Labor Movement Archives & Library (SLMAL), Stockholm

Norwegian Workers Party: a Well-run Home and Healthy Children Are Woman's Foremost Responsibility
Source: Arbeidermagasinet, 1935: Norwegian Labor Movement Archives & Library (NLMAL), Oslo

Image of the New Swedish Woman: Working, Married, Mother, 1934
Source: Morgonbris, 1934: SLMAL

"Women Stand up for Their Rights in the World of Work Outside the Home"

Swedish Domestic Workers Demand Respect and the Eight-Hour Day, 1938
Source: SLMAL

Danish Female Metal Workers on Strike, 1930
Source: DWMAL

"From Projections of Revolution to Practical Politics"

Norwegian Socialist Banner of 1918: Women and Men as Comrades Fight for a Better World
Source: NLMAL

Swedish Election Poster, 1936: "We Women Vote Socialist; We Build the Future" *Source:* Morgonbris, Sept. 1936: SLMAL

Chapter 11

Social Democrats and the Woman Question in Sweden
A History of Contradiction

Renée Frangeur

In 1910, the Social Democratic women's club in Norrkoping, a textile town in the south of Sweden, prepared a resolution for the International Social Democratic Women's Conference to be held in Copenhagen later that year. It read:

> All women's organizations, working for socialism and striving towards freedom, equality, and brotherhood, must be prepared, in a spirit of solidarity not sexual antagonism, to pin the label of scab on any man who abandons a woman and the child he has fathered.

This was the second time that the Swedish delegation had attempted to get the party to endorse their view that working men's failure to take responsibility for their pregnant women comrades was as much a betrayal of working-class solidarity as crossing the picket line. Elma Danielsson, from the women's club in Malmo, had proposed a similar resolution at the Social Democratic party conference in 1905. As it turned out, social democratic women leaders were no more inclined than the men to support what they regarded as a nonpolitical and potentially divisive issue. The 1910 conference secretary, Clara Zetkin from the German party, asked the Norrkoping women to withdraw their "anti-socialist" resolution. Although they decided not to do so, the conference never had an opportunity to discuss it, because it was neither translated nor included in the printed list of resolutions.[1]

This small incident in the history of Swedish social democracy and the women's movement conveniently introduces the three main themes of this chapter. First, like socialist women in most of Europe, those in interwar Sweden had to struggle to find an accepted, let alone an equal, place with men in the Social Democratic party organization. Secondly, the fate of the Norrkoping women's resolution was representative of social Democratic women's struggle to persuade the party leadership that women's concerns, particularly the plight of unmarried mothers and married women's right to work, were valid political issues that deserved party support. Third, the incident points to the disagreements among Social Democratic women, as well as with the men, over the question of women's place in the party and which reforms were appropriate for their party to adopt.

The idea that gives unity to the three themes is contradiction – between the socialists' rhetoric of comradeship and their assumption of gender separation and female inferiority; between Social Democratic work and welfare policies and the realities of working women's lives; and between class politics and feminist values. These contradictions persisted even after the significant policy reversal on the woman question that occurred in the mid-1930s when the Social Democrats became the ruling party under the leadership of Per Albin Hansson. The party's state-sponsored social welfare program called "The People's Home" provided comprehensive and universal services from which Swedish women derived enormous benefit as mothers, wage workers, and wives, but it still affirmed their separate and largely maternal responsibilities, not their equality.

A Traditional Male-Dominated Class Party

The Swedish Social Democratic party (SAP) was founded in 1889 to serve the interests of skilled male workers in regard to wages, hours of work, and industrial safety. It was closely linked to the powerful Trade Union Confederation established ten years later. In this overwhelmingly male environment, women and their concerns were secondary, and party policy towards them was shaped more by traditional ideas about women's place in the working-class family than by the lived and changing circumstances of their lives.

Large-scale industrialization came late to Sweden. It was only at the end of the nineteenth century that the iron and steel and timber industries entered the age of monopoly capitalism. Perhaps for this reason, organized workers retained work and family values originally associated with the guilds. The idea of the family wage, earned by the male bread-winner, persisted long after it had ceased to be economically feasible for anyone except the aristocracy of skilled workers. Many married working-class women had to do paid work to support their families, either because they were the sole breadwinners or to compensate for their husbands' low wages and irregular employment. In addition, Sweden had a compara-tively large surplus of women in the population from 1850 to 1920, mainly due to emigration of young men from rural areas. As a result, the number of unmarried mothers was high – about 20 percent of all births in the cities and 11 percent in the country. To provide for their children, these mothers had to work outside the home as housemaids, textile oper-atives, or brewery workers.

Given such conditions, the issues that mattered most to Sweden's working-class women from the turn of the century were the conflict between child rearing and paid work, women's low wages, the lack of maternity provision, and the need for information about birth control. But they were not the issues that the Social Democratic party chose to address. The only women-related industrial issue that appeared on the party agenda before 1921 was protective legislation, and this was in response to the Second International's endorsement at the Bern Con-vention in 1906. The Parliamentary party supported legislation forbidding night shifts for women in 1909 despite the overwhelming opposition of its own women members and of the middle-class Women's Movement.[2] The party's record on suffrage was similarly weak. Most members understood universal suffrage to mean universal male suffrage, arguing that women's claims for the right to vote would divide the socialist movement. Some expressed doubts as to whether women had the necessary political matu-rity to vote in their own interests – which was, of course, for the Social Democrats.[3] As a result, while universal manhood suffrage became law in 1909, women had to wait until 1919, making Sweden the last of the Nordic countries to grant women their political rights.

Early Organization of Social Democratic Women

In the late nineteenth century, the prospects for women who joined the Social Democratic party seemed promising. The need to build up the membership encouraged local parties to recruit women, and in 1894, the party congress recommended setting up separate women's clubs and trade unions. In these early days, traditional views about distinct gender spheres prevailed over fears of dividing the party along gender lines. The Women's Trade Union (*Kvinnornas fackförbund*), which lasted from 1902 to 1909 was successful in recruiting both home and industrial workers, especially the thousands of dressmakers and seamstresses. Its publication, *Morning Breeze*, became the Social Democratic women's paper and is still published. But the Women's Trade Union did not last. Once the better-financed Tailors' Union opened its doors to women members, the WTU could not compete and its numbers fell. Whatever benefits women workers gained from integration into the men's union, the dissolution of their own trade union meant much smaller female representation in the Trade Union Confederation and at Social Democratic party conferences. In 1920, although women made up 19.6 percent of the industrial and craft workforce, they constituted only 11.7 percent of trade union members.[4]

Wage-earning women's issues also took second place in the party's women's clubs, since club members tended to be housewives more concerned with political solutions to problems of maternity and child care. Nevertheless, the legacy of the WTU was not entirely forgotten. A working committee of the Social Democratic women's conference took over *Morning Breeze* and members addressed some of wage-earning women's concerns. In 1907, for example, they demanded equal pay for men and women, instead of the family wage for men, and refused to approve the prohibition of night work for women in industry, despite pressure from party leaders. But by 1917, the primary focus of articles in *Morning Breeze* was not paid work but motherhood. Contributors rejected the Marxist view, as Engels and Bebel expressed it, that women's emancipation must come through wage labor. One argued that Swedish working-class women had not "voluntarily entered the labor market ..." and that for most of them such work was a much-regretted necessity.[5] What they demanded instead was maternity insurance so that women could care for their children at home. In a society in which more than 50 percent of women up to age thirty-nine were unmarried, maternity might be considered a minority interest, but given the number of unmarried mothers, the issue effectively linked younger wage-earning women with housewives.[6]

One of the most ardent Social Democratic advocates of motherhood as the essence of femininity, and wage-work as its greatest threat, was Ellen Key. Well into the 1920s, her vision of women's roles in the party and in society both attracted and repelled her female comrades. Many could not accept her extreme view of gender difference, which went beyond the conventional "men for the world, and women for the home" to insist upon male rationality and female emotions as the fundamental determinants of appropriate gender roles. She outraged equal rights feminists, but her emphasis on motherhood's social value and her insistence on state responsibility for the care of mothers and their babies, struck a responsive chord among many working-class mothers.

The Suffrage Struggle

Voting rights for women was a divisive issue among Swedish Social Democratic women for most of the prewar period. The division was clear as early as the 1905 party congress, when two of the seven women representatives on the executive, Anna Sterky and Elma Danielsson, both widows of leaders of the working-class movement, voted with the male majority to postpone any declaration of support for women's franchise until all adult men could vote.[7] While the other five women opposed the party's decision, the debate revealed the tension between class and gender loyalty. Left adrift by their party, Social Democratic women suffragists developed their own strategy for the struggle. They recommended that their members stay away from middle-class feminist organizations that were ready to sacrifice working-class women's right to vote for the sake of a limited female suffrage, and asked them to work instead within their own clubs. Should individuals still prefer to join the middle-class feminists, they were expected to oppose all franchise measures that excluded working-class women.

As it did in Britain, the Swedish campaign for women's suffrage became a class issue. In 1908, Swedish women secured the municipal franchise only if they paid local property taxes and had an income, individually or with their husbands, of at least five hundred crowns.[8] Few working-class women could meet these requirements, and if the national franchise was to be based on the same limitations, they would still not be able to vote. For this reason, most Social Democratic women suffragists refused to support anything less than universal adult suffrage. Middle-class suffragists, on the other hand, argued that the vote on the same limited terms as men then held it was more attainable and would secure the principle of women's right to vote. It would then be much easier to win the inclusive measure. The class divide seemed unbridgeable until 1911 when persistent Right-wing opposition to extending the vote to women on any terms persuaded middle-class feminists that their only chance of success was to ally themselves with the parties on the Left. After the war, socialist and feminist supporters of women's right to vote conducted a joint campaign for universal adult suffrage with mass public meetings and street marches. At last, in May, 1919, they were able to celebrate their success together in a "women's civil rights banquet."

The suffrage victory had no long-term impact on either cross-class gender cooperation between Social Democratic women and feminists or cross-gender disagreement within the Social Democratic party. Tensions persisted in both relationships throughout the 1920s, but the more troubling area of struggle for Social Democratic women was in their own party, where their efforts to persuade the male leadership to allow them a recognized place and a voice in policy making caused dissent among themselves.

The Social Democratic Women's Federation (SSKF)

The suffrage issue was not the only point of disagreement among Swedish Social Democratic women in the period from 1908 to 1920. For years, at party congresses, they debated whether or not to form a separate women's federation, without reaching a consensus. The party executive and the Trade Union Board opposed a separate women's organization on the grounds that it would create a "party within the party." The advocates of a separate organization, notably Anna Sterky and Ruth Gustafson, argued that Social Democratic women already had their own women's clubs, women's committee, annual women's congresses and publication, *Morning Breeze*, but they had to run them without adequate funds or staff. Separatists advocated giving constitutional sanction to this existing structure. The separatists finally won the day in 1920, soon after Swedish women gained the right to vote. No doubt, party leaders were eager to woo the new women voters and saw the advantages of a Women's Federation in attracting women members. In this regard, they showed more flexibility on the woman question than did their Danish comrades.

Social Democratic women did not at first propose that the new Federation should concentrate solely on women's issues or take on distinctly female political responsibilities. They emphasized their solidarity with the men, and their shared commitment to the class struggle, and made every effort to recruit women to the party. The Federation's official mandate was to "investigate, and work for the solution of those political and social questions which especially affect the interest of women, their children and homes," but members did not discuss precisely what those questions were, or whether party men would be obliged to give them equal weight in policy making. Overall, Federation members remained ambivalent on issues of gender politics at least until the 1930s. Recent research suggests their ongoing and unresolved conflict over the place of women and women's concerns in a workers' party.[9]

Despite this early confusion, the Federation offered women socialists some definite advantages. As an affiliated organization, it had a formal contract with the party executive that defined its rights within the party. When club women complained that their local parties consistently neglected the recruitment and organization of women, the Federation took their complaints to the party executive and the representatives of the local districts concerned. The executive responded by ordering the local party organizations to change their ways and support the women's clubs, both financially and in their political work.[10] Of course, a few lines on paper did not change centuries of patriarchy. Women went on accusing their male comrades of lack of support, and the men, in their turn, blamed women for party losses at municipal and national elections. Party women found it hard to respond to this accusation because, although they knew they were not responsible, voting declined among working-class women as early as the beginning of the 1920s. Women least likely to vote were domestic servants and unmarried agricultural or industrial workers. Only 58 percent of working-class women voted, on average, as compared to 70 to 80 percent of women from the middle and upper classes.[11] Since the vast majority of the population consisted of the industrial working class and smallholders, with the middle and upper classes counting for only about 12 percent, the female working-class vote, or lack of it, had a significant impact on election results.

Ironically, male criticism of the Women's Federation for failing to mobilize working-class women, helped resolve socialist women's ambivalence about their place in the party. Women saw with increasing clarity that despite the "women comrades" rhetoric and the board responsibilities assigned to the Federation in the party constitution, the male party leadership had a very narrow view of their job as members. Like many of their European counterparts, the men expected party women to deliver the female vote and do little else. At the Women's Congress in 1928, women retaliated with criticisms of their own. The chairwoman asked why it was that women, who made up half or more of the population, were so poorly represented among the Social Democratic representatives at both the municipal and parliamentary levels.[12] Increasingly, Social Democratic women demanded an equal place in the party, as candidates for office, and as policy makers.

These gender tensions resulted in the reorganization of the Women's Federation. The Federation's leaders argued that women's separation, instead of giving them a louder voice in the party, had effectively marginalized them. At the same time, they recognized that integration, instead of improving the situation, might make women invisible and subordinate their concerns to male interests. In negotiations with the party executive in 1927, they called for the Federation to be dissolved as an independent affiliate but asked to keep the women's clubs. The party chairman, Per Albin Hansson, tried to persuade them that the women's clubs should disband too, "so women could belong to the party in the same way as men did."[13] Gustav Moller, the party secretary, agreed. He advocated eliminating all the organizations and programs specific to women, and replacing them with a women's organizer, chosen by and responsible to, the executive committee. As compensation for the loss of the Federation, another male committee member put forward the idea of a special lower membership fee for Social Democratic wives. Women's Federation leaders had their doubts about the "wives' fee," fearing that the special rate would appear discriminatory to single members or those unrelated to party men. The following year, 1928, they placed this concern and the various proposals for reorganization before the Women's Congress.

The congress debate on women's future place in the party surprised the leadership. A majority of the women's clubs' delegates argued strongly for keeping the Federation as well as the clubs. Their concession to the need for some reorganization was to agree to the creation of a women's secretary, appointed by the party executive. The members of the party executive approved the compromise. From their point of view, a women's secretary working directly under the party secretary, was the first step towards strengthening the party's influence over the Federation. But, as Gunnel Karlsson has argued, the Women's Federation was the real winner in this modest reorganization. It continued its work without changes except for the additional advantage of having one of its own "sister comrades" at the top of the party hierarchy. In theory, Swedish Social Democratic women had the best of both worlds after 1929 – integration into the mainstream party at an executive level, which gave them official status and economic support, and segregation on their own terms in the Federation and the clubs.

The first woman secretary and organizer, appointed in 1929, was Hulda Flood. She put energy and enthusiasm into her new job, traveling all over the country, starting new clubs and encouraging those already in existence. Her agitation brought steady growth in the number of Federation women. She was not afraid to criticize her male comrades in the local parties or in the upper echelons of the party. She liked to point out that although they were very eager for her to sign up women members, they did not show any inclination to recruit their own wives and daughters.[14] Flood was an open supporter of feminism. When the middle-class feminists tried to form a women's party in 1927, she commended their efforts in an article in Morning-Breeze, calling on her party to find "room for the rebels" in its ranks and mocking her male comrades for being afraid of bourgeois women.[15]

Although her career was exceptional, it shows the complicated balancing act between wage work, party work, wife, and motherhood, that political activism demanded from a proletarian woman. Hulda came from a working-class family and in 1899, when she was thirteen years of age, she began a six-year stint as a housemaid. She then became a seamstress, continuing in the job after the marriage. She joined a Social Democratic women's club and a temperance group in her early twenties, and combined her widening political responsibilities with employment and marriage, and later on, widowhood. When she became the party's woman organizer in 1929, she had already made her way up the Federation ladder from assistant clerk to secretary. In a period with few labor-saving devices, her "triple burden" was characteristic not only of political activists but of growing numbers of married working women.

Class and Gender Politics in the 1920s

The Swedish economy in the 1920s brought conflicting pressures to bear on working-class women. On the one hand, high levels of unemployment, close to 25 percent, created – as elsewhere in Europe – a demand that married women stay out of the labor market. At the same time, the need to feed the family and pay the rent, with husbands and fathers out of work, forced married women to find paid work. In this decade, Swedish women were also experiencing all the disruption of a modernizing society. While the popular press urged them to stay within the traditional confines of the home and the farm, and to allow their husbands and fathers to be family wage earners, employers in the emerging service sector of the economy sought their services as shop assistants, clerks, typists, and waitresses. Just as the new women's magazines and a host of sociologists reminded them that their true vocation was in the female sphere, serving their husbands and raising their children, the postwar Liberal government passed legislation granting them equal rights as marriage partners and equal access to jobs at equal pay in the civil service. It was in this contradictory and unsettling environment that Social Democrats, both men and women, attempted to find a solution to the woman question.

The popular backlash against married women in the labor force was directed at the public sector. The Consumer Organization introduced a clause into their collective contracts of 1927 making it obligatory for women secretaries and shop assistants to resign on demand.[16] Public-sector trade unions tried to enforce the earlier marriage ban, allowing married women to be hired only for temporary jobs – in the post office during the Christmas season, for example. In the private sector, married women textile workers, assumed to be second earners who could be supported by their husbands, found they were the first to be dismissed in periods of economic downturn. The old union law, "last in, first out," did not apply to married women. In at least one case, in the working-class city of Malmo, the Social Democrats who controlled city government jumped on the bandwagon. In 1926, they introduced a ban on married women working as municipal employees, whether as clerks or attendants at the local public baths.[17]

The attack on married women's right to work coincided with changes in the female labor market. Between 1870 and 1920 Swedish women increased their participation in the workforce from 28.5 percent to 29.8 percent. Female workers made particularly strong gains in the public sector, moving from 6.1 percent in 1870 to 18.5 percent in 1920. Women also increased their numbers in the industries that had traditionally employed them, such as textiles, clothing, leather, tobacco, and bookbinding, but in overall industrial employment they lost ground as men dominated the newer metal, engineering, paper, chemical, and printing industries. The largest growth sector for women in this period was in the service industries, where they worked as clerks, shop assistants, and waitresses. More and more married women sought employment in these jobs until by the end of the 1930s, roughly 40 percent of all married women were in the workforce. This number included thousands of smallholders' wives who labored for up to 1,700 hours a year, in the fields and on the farms, tending the cows, pigs, and hens. Their work created little interest because they had done it for centuries. In a relatively poor country with thousands of small family farms, Swedish married women were used to working for a living.[18]

Despite this economic structure, the value system that prevailed in the 1920s continued to be that of the middle class where most wives stayed at home. Members of the labor aristocracy adopted this model because it fit the patriarchal ideal of the family wage. Skilled workers held positions of power in the working-class movement, and they used their influence to argue that wives should leave wage earning to their husbands. Separate spheres had indeed "filtered down." The frescos in the entrance to the Trade Union House in Stockholm are a visual reminder of its influence. The painter Olle Hjortzberg portrayed his working-class hero in 1927 as a blacksmith – young, blond, muscular, and gazing straight ahead into the future. The working-class heroine was not a comrade worker but a mother with two small children, a naked boy and his demurely dressed sister, shyly clinging to her mother's skirts.

To add to the confusion of the 1920s for Swedish women, this vigorous reassertion of separate spheres emerged shortly after postwar legislation that had overthrown women's legal restrictions within marriage and affirmed their equal rights as workers. In 1919, progressive liberals and socialists together with middle-class feminists succeeded in securing a new marriage law to replace the medieval concept of "master of the household." Instead of being classed with the children as her husbands's dependent, a wife was now legally an adult with the same rights and responsibilities in relation to her children and the household economy as he had. The International Congress of Women (ICW) declared the Swedish marriage law the most advanced among the member nations. A second law, the State Qualification Law, which proved more controversial, guaranteed an equal right to work for men and women in the public sector, including post office clerks, telegraph operators, school teachers, doctors, and so on. The law took six years to implement, and in that period, exceptions were added. The highest salary in each category was reserved for men because of their "greater needs" and a "compulsory clause" could force a mother of a child under fifteen to take an indefinite leave, if the authorities decided that motherhood was affecting her ability to carry on the job. (The Social Democratic government eliminated these exceptions in the 1930s.)

The provisions of the State Qualification Law that provoked the most debate and division among Social Democrats, and between Social Democrats and feminists, were those related to married women's right to work. In the parliamentary debate of 1925, when the law was finally expected to pass, a group of young Social Democratic members of parliament asked for a new commission to reexamine the issue of married women's right to work in the public sector. They argued that the high level of unemployment necessitated revisions in the law that would encourage the married woman to stay at home, rather than going out to work merely to provide herself and her family with "little luxuries." Middle-class feminists, they said, had failed to understand that paid labor was not liberating for married working-class women, who much preferred to be at home. They ended by stating, "The ability of a man to provide for his family ought to be a necessary precondition of any marriage." The parliamentary debate began a national argument over the morality of two wage packets in some families where there was one in others.

Despite a strong minority of supporters, this effort to change the State Qualification Law on the issue of married women's right to work failed. Women of Left and Right political persuasions argued against the change, because it was a violation of the principle of equal rights, and would therefore threaten women's position, not just in the labor market, but as citizens. Most parliamentary members agreed that it was bad policy to amend a law so soon after its passage. However, the group of male Social Democrats, now led by Elof Lindberg, the chief editor of a workers' paper in northern Sweden, returned to the fight in the parliamentary sessions of 1926 and 1927 with new and more extreme arguments. They used expressions such as "a woman cannot serve two masters," and "Parents should think carefully before allowing their daughters too much education," which infuriated feminists and women in their own party.[19] A more compelling argument was their appeal to class solidarity. The proletarian family should have only one wage to conform to the "one for all and all for one" principle. The middle-class professional family might have two incomes, but the working-class ought not to emulate this selfish individualism. Whether they won support through their anti-feminist or class statements is unclear, but they were only three votes away from victory in 1926.

Growing support for amendment galvanized the opposition. Women trade union members in Stockholm organized a protest meeting and sent a resolution stating their objections to any interference in married women's right to work. At a second public meeting held there on 8 March 1926, leading feminists joined Social Democratic women as they had done in the suffrage fight to denounce the male Social Democrats. After angry speeches, the meeting passed a resolution: "The participants at this meeting, who fulfill their obligations to the state as taxpayers, workers, and family breadwinners, demand the human right to apply for and accept, any work for which they are qualified."[20] Inside Parliament, Liberal members accused the young Social Democrats of adopting the same Right-wing arguments that Conservatives had used to oppose women's right to vote. Social Democratic leaders, Per Albin Hansson and Mauritz Vastberg, defended married women's right to work, on the grounds of their equal civil rights. Hansson accused the young men of "reactionary intent" and drew a parallel between their position and the views propounded by the Nazis in Germany. Once again the motion to deny married women's right to work was lost.

Although the number of women likely to be directly affected by the proposed changes in the State Qualification Law was small, since only about one thousand married women worked at the national state level and of those only 6.2 percent were married to other state employees, the principle of married women's right to work became the central focus of the struggle for women's rights in the Social Democratic party, in the trade unions, and in the feminist movement. Broadly speaking, it divided one group of prominent, progressive women – radical liberals from the Women's League, feminists, Social Democratic and trade union leaders – from a less cohesive group of rank-and-file Social Democratic and trade union women who expressed much greater ambivalence on the subject.

The progressives argued for married women's right to work on the principle of equal right and some out of a concern that a marriage ban would lead women into "free" sexual unions. Hulda Flood poured scorn on women who thought of marriage as a way of providing themselves with financial support and maintenance, while Signe Vessman, Federation chairwoman, criticized her own party for taking its stand against married women and against the policy agreed at the Second Workers' International Conference in 1925. Eva Wigforss, a schoolteacher and the wife of the Minister of Finance, Ernst Wigforss, made the more sophisticated economic argument that gainfully employed married women created new jobs through higher consumption and by employing servants in their households. "Stay-at-home wives" on the other hand, while they did not compete for jobs with "telegraphists, postmasters, or heads of department," certainly did take a living away from "seamstresses, children's nurses, housemaids, bakers, and all sorts of craftsmen."[21]

The second and probably the larger group, mostly working-class club women, showed much greater reluctance to condemn the Social Democratic members of Parliament who wanted to restrict married women's right to work. Their motivation seems to have been a desire to show class loyalty. Those who wrote letters to the editor of *Morning Breeze*, even if they did not want married women to lose their jobs, wanted to find solutions to the employment problem that would give priority to male breadwinners. Some argued that well-paid (presumably middle-class) women should withdraw from the labor market in the interests of family breadwinners and single women. One women's club wrote to express the belief that women ought "by nature" to be at home with their children, while men had a natural claim to be wage-earners. The disagreement between the two groups made it impossible for the Social Democratic Women's Federation to take a united stand on the issue of married women's right to work in the 1920s. On the surface the dispute was about gender or class priorities, but it went deeper into attitudes towards motherhood and femininity, and these were at the heart of the other women's issue that created divisions within the Social Democratic party – maternity.

Gender and Sexual Politics in the 1920s

For most of the interwar period, the Federation placed the protection of mothers in the workplace and at home, high on its political agenda. Married and unmarried women agreed on this issue, and common resolutions were taken about free childbirth clinics, maternity insurance, and the "population issue," which meant information about sexual problems and birth control. Liberal feminists also worked closely with social democratic women on this campaign. Ada Nilsson, a Liberal women's physician, for example, had started a private advice clinic for parents in the apartment building where the Liberal women's newspaper was published. Social Democratic women were enthusiastic about the project and advertised it in *Morning-Breeze*. Nilsson hoped that city government would take over the clinic when she was no longer able to run it, but it was ten years before birth control advice clinics received official support and spread through the country. The Social Democratic Women's Congress gave Nilsson an award in 1928 for her pioneer work.

In interwar Sweden, as elsewhere in Europe, there was a movement away from Victorian sexual mores in favor of freer relations between the sexes and an acceptance of women's sexuality. Freud and the war played a part in the movement that movies, novels, and magazines popularized in the form of the "new woman."[22] Yet the law was slow to respond to the change in sexual attitudes and this disparity created social problems. Both abortion and advertising or selling contraceptives were punishable by fines and imprisonment. In the 1920s, the number of illegitimate births rose to 20 percent of the total birthrate, a figure that was among the highest in the world, according to one child care officer writing in *Morning-Breeze*.[23] Single mothers faced so many problems in trying to raise and support their children that many gave them up for adoption. Pregnant women in industry were legally obliged to stop working for six weeks without pay at the time of the birth. They had to pay the midwife and the birthing clinic. Jobs were hard to come by for single mothers, even as housemaids, because of the stigma still attached to sexual immorality and illegitimacy.

Social democratic women first took up the cause of unmarried mothers in the prewar decade. At their 1907 Congress, they demanded maternity insurance and criticized the social pressure on single mothers to give their children away to "keep their reputations." But no government attempted any maternity reform until 1931. Until then the only recourse for a single mother was to swear an oath, giving the name of the father and making him financially responsible for his child. After 1917, a child welfare officer could help the mother, but in reality few single mothers took advantage of these options. Most were uneducated, working on the family farm, still living with their parents, or serving as housemaids. Their suspicion of outsiders deterred them from contacting the welfare officer, and although in some cases an employer seduced the woman, for the most part, the fathers of their babies were from their own social class and without resources.[24]

In 1926, the Liberal government formed a national committee with four members, of whom two were prominent Liberal feminists, Kerstin Hesselgren and Ada Nilsson, to draft a maternity benefit law. Hesselgren was a good choice. Educated in Britain, she became the first woman factory inspector in Sweden and was therefore much more aware than most Social Democratic men of the circumstances in which women lived and worked. Social Democratic and Liberal women alike praised the recommendations of the committee. It proposed a small maternity benefit for most mothers paid in the form of health insurance, plus repayment of two-thirds of salary lost during the six weeks of maternity leave required for women in industry. It drew a clear line between maternity benefit and poor relief and requested state-supported mother and child care clinics. The Maternity Benefit Law of 1931 only partially implemented these recommendations, reducing to a minimum the repayment of lost income.

On the issue of unmarried mothers, Social Democratic women had contradictory opinions. While they fully supported maternity reform and rejected bourgeois morality, they had their own line of moral condemnation of their fallen sisters. Some writers in *Morning-Breeze* accused them of being irresponsible for getting pregnant in the first place, and considered them morally reprehensible for giving up their children. Others emphasized that fathers must be made to recognize and pay for their children and that illegitimate children should have the same right to inherit from their fathers as those who were born inside marriage. Many eulogized motherhood as the most important event in a woman's life, "the highest mission ... to bear the humanity of the future," and expressed anxiety that free abortion and the legalization of contraceptives would make women vulnerable to sexual exploitation.[25] Others argued that birth control and abortion were the necessary price to pay for sexual emancipation and voluntary motherhood. Despite the range of these opinions, they shared a primary focus on the mother who was assumed to bear the greater part of responsibility for her child.

Ellen Key was, without doubt, the source of inspiration for the idealization of motherhood that is so apparent in the 1920s contributions to *Morning-Breeze*. In 1925, the journal celebrated her seventy-fifth birthday with songs and articles. The clubs staged specially written plays to dramatize her ideas about women, home, and motherhood. She was variously referred to as, "the preacher of the deepest values of life" and "the great moral genius." Her face appeared frequently on the front page of *Morning Breeze*. When she died the following year, Hulda Flood represented the Social Democratic Women's Federation at her funeral. Key's idea of social motherhood – that women should apply their special biological capacity for nurturing to the social problems of the modern world – became a significant strand in Swedish social democracy. But it increased the division between the progressive leadership, often allied with liberal feminists, and local club women. The latter responded with pride and enthusiasm to Key's affirmation of their social value as actual or potential wives and mothers, while progressives argued that by equating women with their biological function of motherhood, Key was ensuring their dependence on men, and denying them an opportunity to develop other interests and skills. Reconciliation came in the 1930s, when their party gave a measure of support to both points of view.

The "People's Home": Social Welfare Policies in the 1930s

The 1928 general election was a wake-up call to Swedish Social Democrats who lost seats to both Conservatives and Communists. Party leader Per Albin Hansson heard the call, then step by step transformed the SAP from a Marxist Socialist party to a reforming "people's party." Social

Democratic instability in the 1920s had had a lot to do with factionalism. The Trade Union Board under Communist influence, allied with Left-wing members in the party – including the men who campaigned against married women's right to work – to challenge executive committee decisions on a number of issues, including major strikes. After the 1928 election defeat, Per Albin Hanssen mobilized the party majority against the Left and ordered an end to factionalism. His personal strength and the electoral good sense of his reform initiatives convinced the Trade Union Board to accept his leadership and integrate the unions more closely with the party.[26]

In 1932, Hansson became Social Democratic prime-minister with a social reform program designed to meet the needs not just of the industrial working-class but of the mass of the people, including smallholders, the lower middle-class, and women. He called this program "The People's Home," and it became the model for the modern European welfare state. He appealed to the party's women members to bring their special powers to the task of building a more just and well-organized society: "We have now gone so far as to furnish the great People's Home. Now it is a matter of creating comfort and well-being, making it bright and happy and free. Women will be ideal for this work, and need only bring their enthusiasm."[27] He labeled party men who tried to limit women's participation in the project "non-democrats." However, Per Albin Hanssen emphasized that he was not a feminist. His views on the woman question appear to have been similar to those of Ellen Key, especially her idea of social motherhood. His call for women's help in "decorating" the People's Home was essentially a bid for their votes.

Swedish Social Democrats, like their comrades in Norway, were able to introduce the welfare state in the mid-1930s because they applied Keynsian economics to the unemployment crisis of 1931. Ernst Wigforss, minister of finance, became a convert to the new economics under the influence of the Swedish economist, Gunnar Myrdal. Myrdal argued that instead of attempting to save money, the state ought to create new jobs, paid with cash wages, which would then increase consumption and revive industry. Under Wigforss's direction, the Social Democrats produced a program of modest state intervention that would supplement but not replace traditional mutual aid societies with state subsidies for the sick and the unemployed.[28] A well-timed alliance with the Smallholder party enabled the Social Democrats to win support for their unemployment program in return for subsidies to the farmers. The electorate endorsed the program in the 1936 election, and the two parties formalized their cooperation in a coalition government led by Hansson. This was the government that gave Sweden an extensive welfare state, with pensions, social security, secondary education, subsidized housing, state loans for newly married couples to buy their first home, and expanded maternal and child welfare.

Most historians have had nothing but praise for the Swedish welfare state, reflecting the overall enthusiasm with which people from all social classes and reform organizations received it at the time. Although the protection of labor was central to his idea of social justice, Hansson listened to different points of view and came up with a program that was to be universally applied. For example, by the end of the 1930s, 90 percent of all mothers took advantage of maternity insurance and assistance. They and not their husbands were the direct recipients of the cash benefits. Private philanthropic initiatives in child welfare and postpartum maternity care were drawn under the state umbrella. Historians argue that this early model of the welfare state created a popular perception of government as a bulwark of democracy and civil rights, not a "big brother" invading the private sphere. It gave the (male) working class a direct and participatory interest in government. But questions remain about the welfare state and women. How much did women's own efforts, as members of the party or as feminists, ensure that the welfare state met women's needs? What influence did changes in popular cultural images of women, labeled "the new woman," have on socialist policy makers?

The Women's Movement and the New Woman

The 1930s was a period of growth and achievement for organized women in Sweden. The older, mostly middle-class feminist organizations, which included the Frederika Bremer Federation (FBF) and the more radical Swedish Women's Federation of the Left (SKV) were joined by the new Professional Women's Federation (YKR) and the Swedish branch of the Open Door International. Professional women, from teachers to clerks and telegraph operators, formed unions in this period, and, not wanting to be left out, so did housewives. Social Democratic women experienced dynamic growth, with membership increasing from 8,200 in 1930 to 28,000 at the end of 1939. The party as a whole, including collective membership through trade unions, counted 30,000 women, or 12 percent of total membership, in 1929, and 82,300, or 19 percent, in 1938.[29]

Although women's influence in the male political arena did not grow in proportion to their numbers, women made every effort to show that they took their citizenship seriously and fully intended to share with men the responsibilities that it implied. They developed strategies identified with late nineteenth-century popular movements, "protesting, lobbying, and struggling for their rights in the state."[30] Organized women were united in condemning the "masculine culture" that denied women's right or ability to participate in political life, as reactionary or fascist. Changes in popular cultural images of women in the 1930s furthered their cause. By adopting their own versions of the new woman image, they identified feminist and socialist reform programs with modernity and progressive politics.

The Swedish women's movement was unique among the European counties covered in this volume, in the skill with which it linked the cause of women's emancipation to developments in the arts and popular culture. An early example was the response to "social aesthetics," a new art/science that applied modern functional design and technology to such areas of everyday life as living and working spaces, health and recreation. The concept became so popular in Sweden that reformers of various kinds began to apply the tests of rationality and efficiency to social institutions. Organized women were among them, arguing the necessity of rationalizing a woman's environment in the home and the workplace, and, by extension, her relations with men and with her children.

The Stockholm exhibition of 1930 marked the beginning of the movement to create a modern, healthy, and rational life through well-designed apartments and homes. It was a showcase for Swedish design in architecture and furniture and had four million visitors at a time when the country's entire population was only about six million! Social Democrats could claim a major share of the credit for the exhibition, since the architects were socialists and the Myrdals, as well as Ernst Wigforss, contributed their ideas and organizing skills. But it was Social Democratic women who gained the most political mileage from it. They used the exhibition to draw party and national attention to their long-standing demands for better-designed and cheaper working-class housing, simplified housework, and experiments in collective housekeeping and child care. They pointed out how irrational and inefficient it was for women to carry the "triple burden" of housework, wage work, and child care, and hoped that the exhibition would encourage the government to follow the example of Red Vienna and provide working women with municipal washhouses, nursery schools, and communal kitchens.[31]

Taking advantage of the popularity of the exhibition, *Morning Breeze* launched a women's housing program. The aim was to draw attention to the problem of overcrowded housing in the cities, where most working-class families were living in one room with a small kitchen and shared toilet, and in rural areas, where housing for agricultural workers and their families was often dilapidated and unsanitary. Physicians, architects, and journalists contributed their ideas of rational and healthy housing, while one of the exhibition architects designed a model apartment for young, single workers with one room, a kitchen, sleeping nook, and bathroom. In the early 1930s, *Morning Breeze* promoted collective kitchens and child care arrangements as the best solution for working wives and mothers, but these met with generally unenthusiastic responses from contributors and were dropped.

Morning Breeze clearly reflects the fact that the editors intended to educate their readers in social aesthetics and introduce them to the image of the socialist new woman. The paper portrayed her as an alert, healthy, working-class comrade, sometimes a professional woman, sometimes a "modern" socialist housewife, or both, according to her life-stage.[32] She understood modern technology and the consumer market, which helped her protect her family in hard economic times. To help its readers approach this ideal, the paper sent two hundred housewives on study-visits to ASEA, one of the largest factories in the country, to see women at work in a modern, technological environment. It conducted market surveys and gave ten of its twenty-five pages over to detailed descriptions of consumer goods rated the "most useful and most beautiful."

The ideal socialist woman was a consumer, but no longer only a stay-at-home wife. *Morning Breeze* reflected the opinion of its new working-class editor, Kaj Andersson, who believed with the Myrdals and Wigforss that "We cannot put the clock back and confine women to the home. We do not wish it because we believe that a comrade marriage in which the wife is economically independent is a happier marriage."[33] Ellen Key's image of the socialist woman as eternal mother disappeared. The idea of women's emancipation through wage labor, associated with Engels, Bebel, and Kollontai, had triumphed. The illustration of the family that appeared on the cover of a special edition of *Morning Breeze* in 1934 showed the professional wife in the foreground, her husband and child at the back. Feminist and professional women's organizations, even the Housewives' Union (SHR), endorsed this superwoman who combined employment with family responsibilities. She was the heroine of contemporary novels and the subject of admiration and advice in women's magazines. She appeared in advertisements for a myriad of products from stockings to canned soup. The fashion industry designed her wardrobe – a tweed skirt, sweater, and beret set at a jaunty angle.

The new woman appeared all over Europe in the 1930s, but in Sweden, Social-Democratic women had been active in creating her image and incorporating it into socialist ideology and policy. In this sense, they were in marked contrast to Social Democratic women in Red Vienna where male party leaders defined the desirable characteristics of the socialist new woman and imposed her upon the women from above. Swedish women showed a similar aptitude for making a cause their own in the case of population politics, a major political issue of the decade, which Social Democratic women adopted as a way of getting women's family needs placed at the top of their party's agenda.

Social Democratic Women and the Population Problem

In December 1934, Alva and Gunnar Myrdal published a book entitled *The Population Crisis*, which sounded the alarm about the declining birthrate in Sweden. They pointed out that live births had dropped from twenty-seven per thousand inhabitants in 1900 to only fourteen per thousand in 1933, which gave Sweden the lowest birth rate in Europe.[34] They warned that Sweden would be a country of old people in the near future if the rate did not rise. In the past, the solution to the population problem had been a selective breeding policy, encouraging birth control for the poor to improve the quality of the race. Instead of this negative population policy, the Myrdals proposed a progressive one in which adequate social welfare provisions would encourage couples to have children. This was a timely publication since conservative neo-Malthusian solutions became hard to justify in the light of Nazi racial eugenics. It also had important implications for the woman question because it endorsed not only health care provisions for mothers and babies, state-funded child care and free school lunches, but also family planning, women's right to control their own bodies, and married women's right to work, on the grounds that these, too, contributed to the well-being of the family.

Not surprisingly, various women's groups rushed to express their support for *The Population Crisis*. *Morning Breeze* published an article by Alva Myrdal that called for sex education for everyone, not just married couples, and referred to religious hypocrisy on sexual matters. "Every new born child has the right to be welcomed," she argued. The *Housewives Review* devoted an entire issue to the Myrdals' book, expressing their preference for kindergartens, collective child care, and playgrounds over monetary compensation for poor families, and supporting the right of married women to work.[35]

Women's organizations saw that the publicity given to the population crisis by the Myrdals' book could transform popular ideals about women's social value and increase their power and responsibility. However, they were aware that pro-natalism might reinforce the arguments against married women's right to work. With considerable skill, they deflected such attempts by arguing that if society wanted to increase the birthrate, it would have to allow married women to contribute to the financial support of the family. Ada Nilsson, the close friend of the Soviet communist, Alexandra Kollontai, warned that if society provoked a conflict between work and marriage, then society would get fewer children.[36] The argument had its effect. According to Gunnar Myrdal, even private employers who were committed to dismissing women workers when they married or became pregnant were beginning to realize their responsibility for the declining standard of living in the families thus deprived of a wage earner.

The Myrdals' book on the population crisis had an immediate impact on the Social Democratic government. It set up a Population Commission of forty-six politicians and experts to study the problem and designated ten women to attend. The chairman, who was from the Peasant party, appointed a subcommittee to consider maternity benefits for working mothers and investigate the thorny subject of married women's work. Concerned about the conservative slant of the subcommittee's members, Ernst Wigforss, the finance minister, decided to create a separate committee to study married women's work. He chose Kerstin Hesselgren, the Liberal feminist, as the chair, Alva Myrdal as secretary, one woman from the Textile Workers' Board, the chairwoman of the organization Women in State Employment, and a female economist from Open Door International. Then he added two male opponents of married women's right to work. The result was an unusual committee for the time; women outnumbered men, five to two, and the female majority strongly supported married women's work. Wigforss asked them to look at every aspect of the subject and to cooperate with the Population Commission's subcommittee. He gave them the benefit of his prestige and his powerful position in the party, and thus prevented the issue from being subordinated to the population problem.

The Depression of the early 1930s had revived the contentious question of whether married women should be allowed to continue working when many male providers were unemployed. By 1934, nine bills prohibiting the employment of married women in the public sector had been introduced into Parliament. Socialist and feminist women's groups responded by organizing public support against the legislation. The culmination of their campaign came in October 1933 when Social Democratic women organized the largest women's assembly of the year – seventeen hundred women drawn from twenty organizations, including all the political parties except the Communists and Conservatives, trade unions, liberal feminists, professional women, and housewives. The assembly was called "Women Face-to-Face with the World Crisis." Kerstin Hesselgren, in the chair, reminded the participants that women were just as much the victims of dictatorship and unemployment as men. To protect themselves, they must stick together and fight back. Several speakers referred to the recent Nazi policy restricting married women's right to work as a warning against allowing a similar law to be passed in Sweden. The assembly adopted a resolution declaring that women's right to professional training and work was integral to their full and equal civil rights.[37]

This was the context in which Wigforss's committee and the subcommittee of the Population Commission pursued their investigations into the question of maternity benefits and married women's right to work. The commissioners were thorough; they looked at the entire female labor

market, questioned employers, and trade unionists and held public meetings. In 1938, they produced their reports. A consistent, if not surprising,
finding was that the vast majority of employers in the textile, shoe, and
clothing industries, which had significant numbers of women workers,
considered female employees, whether married or unmarried, indispens-
able to the manufacture of their products and therefore to their profits.
The government followed up the reports with a bill that prohibited the
dismissal of women on the grounds of their being engaged, married, pregnant, or recently delivered. The bill gave women workers the right to
three months of maternity leave without penalty of job loss. After a long
debate in which the financial benefits of women workers weighed heavily
in the bill's favor, the Swedish Parliament passed the bill into law. It had
taken five years to achieve.[38]

On the issue of maternity benefits, the legislative outcome was equally
positive. All mothers were entitled to free health care during pregnancy
and delivery, and three months of paid maternity leave if they worked in
the public sector. Maternity insurance benefits were increased. Single
mothers could get a maintenance advance to help them support their
children while the state pursued fathers who were in arrears with their
payments. Mothers with special needs received maternity relief, and
allowances were paid for orphaned children. In 1938, the advertising and
selling of contraceptives finally became legal. Abortion was allowed for
ethical, medical, and eugenic reasons, but not on request. Finally, Swedish
women working for the state, as teachers or in any other capacity, were to
receive wages and benefits equal to those of men in the same jobs.

Conclusion

Judged by their achievements in civil rights and social welfare programs,
Sweden's Social Democratic women were among the most successful in
Europe at combining their socialism with a specific focus on the needs of
women. Some of the reasons for their success are clear. First, compared to
most other European countries, women's organizations in Sweden were
more inclusive and cooperative. Liberal and radical feminists, women from
all the political parties, professional women and housewives, women in
trade unions, and a host of groups working on particular issues, were organized and active. In the 1930s, their numbers increased and so did their
activism. Social Democratic women worked closely with all the branches
of the Swedish women's movement with little of the class antagonism that
prevented cooperation in other countries. Leading women moved com-
fortably between and among the various organizations, all of which had
similar goals and agendas. They all wanted to open the doors that had kept

women out of political parties, large sections of the labor market, state and local government. They all took part in the protracted struggle to secure married women's right to work and to protect mothers, both married and unmarried. They worked together on reform commissions and committees and engaged in public debate at mass meetings in Stockholm and other towns and cities. Although cross-class cooperation was less likely among local Social Democratic club women, especially in class segregated industrial towns or rural areas, this did not impede the national leadership.

A second reason for Swedish women's success was their extraordinary ability to link their cause to popular cultural or political developments. They took advantage of the social aesthetics movement to draw attention to the poor living conditions among the working class, and to push for a wide range of reforms from sanitation to child care. They converted the new woman image from that of consumer and heroine of popular novels into a comrade-worker and equal partner in the struggle for socialism. They even adapted their own ideal of socialist womanhood from social mother, so dear to Ellen Key, to the Myrdals' independent woman, who managed to combine wage work and domestic responsibilities – with a little help from the modern, collectivist state.

Third, Social Democratic women had the benefit of male support among the leaders of their party. Both Ernst Wigforss, the finance minister and Gustav Moller, the minister of internal affairs, were married to leading feminists who held responsible jobs in their own right. They were distinguished from most other politicians of the Left in Sweden, and elsewhere, by their willingness to listen to what women said they wanted, and to act upon it. They worked to ensure that the Welfare State legislation recognized women's distinct needs and provided for them, rather than treating them merely as workingmen's wives. Without their support, Social Democratic women's own efforts, no matter how persistent or extensive, would have gone unheeded.

Yet, despite these successes, the theme of contradiction is still apt for the Swedish Social Democratic response to the woman question. Although Wigforss and Moller were powerful men, they could not offset the pervasive masculine culture in the party and in the country. Even after the party gave full legal recognition to the Women's Federation in 1936, women's representation in Parliament scarcely reached double figures. After 1936, there were ten women members in the Second Chamber, five more than in 1932, eight of them socialist. In city councils, women's representation in the best year, 1938, was 8.4 percent, in county councils 3.9 percent, and on local councils 2.9 percent.[39]

The welfare state may have improved women's health and well-being and insured them against a descent into poverty, but it did little to change the relations between the sexes. In general, the majority of men continued to be the family wage earners and the majority of married women to be housewives. Separate spheres survived the increase in the number of married women in the workforce and allowed men to retain their financial and political power. Not until the 1960s and 1970s did economic changes and the extension of the public sector make it possible for the majority of women to combine work and child rearing, but when this happened, the ideas and debates of the 1930s provided a model for their new roles.

Notes

1. Birgitta Johansson, *Arbetarkvinnor och barntillsyn I Norrköping* [Working-class Women and Child-Care in Norrkoping] (University of Linkoping, 1983), p. 55.
2. The debate over protective legislation in Sweden is discussed by Lynn Karlsson in "The Beginning of the Masculine Renaissance: the Debate on the 1909 Prohibition against Women's Night Work in Sweden," Alice Kessler-Harris, Jane Lewis and Ulla Wikander, (eds.), *Protecting Women: Labor Legislation in Europe, the United States, and Australia, 1880-1920* (Urbana and Chicago, 1995), pp. 235-67.
3. Christina Carlsson Wetterberg, "Likhet och Sarart. Den Tidiga Arbetarrorelsens Kvinnopolitik,"[Equality and its Peculiarities. The Woman Question in the Early Labor Movement] *Arbetarhistoria* (Arbetarrorelsens Arkiv och Bibliotek 51, March, 1989), p. 48.
4. Gunnar Qvist, *Statistik och Politik. Landsorganisationen och Kvinnorna pa Arbetsmarknaden* [Statistics and Policy. Trade Unions and Women Workers] (Stockholm, 1974), pp. 38 and 56.
5. Renée Frangeur-Sonden, Marianne Linner, "Kvinnans Frigorelse. Argument I ett Antal Kvinnotidskrifter 1909-1917" [Women's Emancipation: Arguments from Women's Journals] Gunnar Qvist (ed.), *Kvinnomystik och Kvinnopolitik* (Goteborg, 1974), p. 152.
6. Qvist, *Statistik och Politik*, p. 18.
7. Hulda Flood, *Den Socialdemokratiska Kvinnororelsen I Sverige*, (Stockholm, 1960. First ed. 1930), pp. 55-57, 75.
8. Gosta Bagge, Erik Lundberg, Ingvar Svennilsson (ed.), *Wages in Sweden* (Stockholm, 1933). The average income for a skilled male industrial worker was 1,460 crowns a year in 1906.
9. Gunnel Karlsson, "Fran Broderskap till Systerskap. Det Socialdemokratiska Kvinnoforbundets kamp for Inflytandeoch makt I SAP" [From Brotherhood to Sisterhood: the Fight for Influence and Power in the Federation], (Ph.D. diss., University of Gothenburg, 1996), pp. 75-81.
10. Ibid., p. 83.
11. *Morning Breeze* (June 1927): 1, and (February 1930): 12. James Rossel, *Kvinnorna och Kvinororelsen I Sverige, 1850-1950*, YSF: Skriftserie 2 (Stockholm, 1950): 89
12. Women made up only 1.5 percent of Social Democratic party representatives in Parliament and the municipal councils in 1929.

13. Karlsson, "Fran Broderskap till Systerskap," p. 88.
14. *Morning Breeze* (December 1929):17.
15. Ibid., (May 1927): 18.
16. Kommittearkiv 580, *Anteckningar till SOU* 38:47, vol. 7: Ja till avsked, Riksarkivet (The National Archives, Stockholm).
17. Stadsfullmaktigegruppens protokoll 15:e December, 1926. Tjanste-och avloningsreglemente for Malmo Stads tjansteman, antaget av stadsfullmaktige 17:e December, paragraphs: 6,9. (The Archives of the Labor Movement, Malmo).
18. Qvist, "Statiskik och Politik," p. 44; Anita Nyberg, *Tekniken – Kvinnornas Befriare? Hushallsteknik, Kopevaror, Gifta Kvinnorss Hushallsarbetstid och Förvärvsdeltagande 1930-1980* [Technology: the Key to Women's Liberation?], (Ph.D. diss., University of Linkoping, 1989), p. 164.
19. *Andrakammarprotokoll* 24 (1927): 38-60.
20. *Morning Breeze* (March 1926): 5.
21. Ibid.(September 1925): 1-3. The headline on the front page read: "Who are Married Women Workers Competing With?"
22. Yvonne Hirdman, "Det glada tjugotalet och den svara karleken," in *Den Socialistiska hemmafrun och andra kvinnohistorier* (Stockholm, 1992), p. 169.
23. *Statistisk Arsbok for Sverige, 1933:* 45; *Morning-Breeze* (November 1925): 3-4.
24. Alva and Gunner Myrdal wrote about single mothers in, *Kris I befolkningsfragan* (Stockholm, 1935, 4th.ed.), p. 111. *Herta* (June 1937), p. 150 and (July 1937), p. 183, "Report on the Condition of Single Mothers and their Children."
25. *Morning Breeze* (December 1926): 14, quoted the British Labour activist, Emily Lutyens who visited Stockholm in 1926.
26. Bengt Schullerqvist, *Fran kosackval till kohandel. SAP's vag till makten* (Ph.D. diss., Uppsala University, 1992), pp. 287-93.
27. *Morning Breeze* (December 1927) and (March 1929).
28. Birger Simonson, "Mutual Benefit Societies in Sweden – Sickness and Burial Funds and Unemployment Relief Funds" *International Conference on the History of Mutual Benefit Societies* (Paris, 1992).
29. Hulda Flood, *Den Socialdemokratisk Kvinnororelsen I Sverige*, p. 322; Gunnel Karlsson, *Fran Broderskap till Systerskap*, p. 9.
30. *The Professional Woman* (February, 1938): 6 (the author was probably the association's chair, Alva Myrdal).
31. *Morning Breeze* (July 1930): 2-3.
32. Yvonne Hirdman referred to "the socialist housewife" in "*Den socialistiska hemmafrun och andra kvinnohistorier* (The Socialist Housewife and Other Stories), pp. 36-111. However, in my opinion, both Hirdman and Gunnel Karlsson exaggerate the importance of this ideal and neglect the parallel model of the professional worker. My research suggests that *Morning Breeze* and the *Housewives Journal* included both ideals of the new woman in the 1930s.
33. *Morning Breeze* (January 1933): 10. The author was Eva Wigforss.
34. Ann-Sofie Kalvemark (now Ohlander), *More Children of Better Quality? Aspects of Swedish Population Policy in the Nineteen-Thirties* (Uppsala, 1980), pp. 38-9.
35. *Medlemsbladet* (Member's paper), May 1935.
36. Ada Nilsson, *The Epoch* (August 1934): 1, 3.
37. *Morning Breeze* (February 1934): 22.
38. *Andrakammarprotokoll* (March-May 1939): 53 (Reports of the Proceedings of the Second Chamber).
39. Gunnel Karlsson, *Fran Broderskap till Systerskap*, p. 130.

Chapter 12

A Double Responsibility
Women, Men, and Socialism in Norway

Ida Blom

In December 1918, Christian Holtermann Knudsen, one of the most important founders of the Norwegian labor movement, greeted women of the Norwegian Labor Party (NLP) in their journal *The Woman (Kvinden)* with the following words:

> Woman decides the direction and the speed of development in society .... Woman has a double responsibility: She may foster a generation to which she has given values for life and which knows when to act; and she may herself actively contribute to forming a society that makes life worthwhile for everyone. Let us hope she will know her responsibilities.[1]

This appeal indicates that gender mattered in Norway during the interwar period. But how? Were socialist women willing and able to assume the double responsibility of raising future generations and participating actively in party politics? What were the relations between women and men within the working-class movement during the interwar period? These questions will be addressed in this chapter after a brief glance at the gendered history of the Norwegian labor movement.

Setting the Stage: Prewar and Postwar Continuities

The NLP was founded in 1887.[2] In 1901, when women won limited suffrage in municipal elections, the socialist women's associations within the

Notes for this chapter begin on page 474.

party joined a number of women's trade unions to form the NLP Women's Association. Eight years later, this association started publishing its own journal, *The Woman*.[3]

The years preceding World War I had changed women's position in society in important ways. Although between a fifth and a quarter of the population still worked in agriculture, forestry, and fishing, since the 1880s industrialization and urbanization opened new economic possibilities, which were also explored by women, mostly unmarried. During the growth of voluntary organizations and democratization marking the advent of modern society, many of the goals of first wave feminism were realized. Women gained access to all forms of education, up to and including university level. The process of nation-building expressed in Norway's break from political union with Sweden in 1905 furthered women's struggle for full political citizenship. By 1913 women had achieved the vote on the same conditions as men.[4] Political parties began to vie for their votes, and a lively struggle ensued between socialists and liberal and conservative parties to win new voters for their programs. Pronounced class conflicts throughout the interwar period made this contest much fiercer.

Since the 1880s most working women had joined male unions but had little impact on their policies. Others had formed all-female unions at the instigation of male coworkers who feared the competition of unorganized female labor.[5] Still others formed their union in opposition to male colleagues, who tried to oust them from their trade. But servant girls, the biggest group of women working for wages, only sporadically managed to organize, and only for short periods.[6]

The heterogeneous labor movement was kept together by sharp opposition to the bourgeois parties. Consequently, labor women kept the bourgeois women's movement at arm's length. As in most other industrializing countries, a fierce struggle over special protection for women workers between 1901 and 1915 cemented class conflicts among politically active women.[7] In contrast to Denmark and Sweden, Norwegian social democrats did not succeed in legalizing specific restrictions on night work for women.[8] By the end of World War I, despite working-class solidarity, women's role within the movement remained uncertain. Labor party discussions confirmed the dual view of women's role expressed by Holterman Knudsen in 1918.[9] The importance of organizing and educating women for the fight against capitalism was stressed time and time again. Still women's primary responsibility to the family, housework, and child care was seen as the very essence of femininity. Femininity was characterized by allowing for the equality of men and women but also by stressing the differences between the sexes. Thus, Norwegian socialists shared the generally contradictory view of women in the working-class movement: as equals and as mothers. No one questioned a man's responsibility for providing for his wife and children, but leadership within the labor movement was also assumed to belong to men. These perceived core qualities of masculinity were undisputed.

Between the wars, working-class families continued efforts to free women and children from the onerous responsibility of contributing to the family income. A solution was sought in higher wages for the male providers, the so-called family wage. The period from 1920 to 1940 saw overall marked improvements in working-class standards of living. Reduction of wages was paralleled by declines in the cost of living, resulting in better real wages for those who had an income.[10] A sharp fall in marital fertility in working-class families reduced social differences and made wages go further.[11] Fewer people lived in overcrowded houses;[12] average life expectancy increased.

The working class, however, did not experience the interwar years as a period of universal improvement. The early 1920s saw a radical, if temporary, reduction in real wages and the onset of massive unemployment, which grew to 35 percent during the Great Depression and fell only in 1939 to around 20 percent.[13] The numerous families hit by unemployment did not share in the generally rising standard of living, and the percentage of heads of families forced to fall back on poor relief decreased very little even after 1935.[14]

The everyday life of working-class families was marked by these contradictory circumstances. Children's work in factories, outlawed in 1892, disappeared in the face of new technologies and adult unemployment. But children still earned pocket money by running errands, looking after smaller children, and helping out with housework, with girls paid lower wages than boys.[15] At the age of fourteen to fifteen, boys and some girls started working full-time, but possibilities were more limited for girls than for boys. Girls and young women worked in factories producing food, beverages, and tobacco products, as well as in the textile industries. Gradually, the growing sector of retail businesses, restaurants, hotels, and other community and social services absorbed working-class women with little education, although domestic service remained the largest of all female occupations.

The census as for 1920 and 1930 list 2 to 3 percent of married women as gainfully employed.[16] Careful studies of working-class communities, however, reveal as many as 16 to 17 percent of married women economically active in 1930.[17] Still, marriage remained the expected livelihood for women, and the working class was no exception. The housewife shouldered the important responsibility of making a husband's earnings go as far as possible, economizing strictly on food, clothes, and other expenses. In precarious situations, wives took on paid work outside the home, such as washing, cooking, or sewing for other families. In many ways a "traditional" responsibility meant that working-class housewives modernized more quickly than their middle-class sisters. At the end of the 1920s they were more likely, for example, to rely on ready-made products, pioneering the role of consumer.[18] The consumer economy demanded knowledge of prices and qualities of goods to be purchased. Moreover, the drive for cleanliness, well-prepared and nutritious food and, gradually, the use of new household technology, emphasized the need to educate and train women to become good housewives.[19]

If a husband was not able to provide for his family and was forced to accept his wife as a co-provider, he failed to conform to widely accepted ideals of masculinity. The struggle for social respectability might therefore have strengthened ideals of the male provider and the dependant housewife. These complementary but hierarchical understandings of gender colored the political priorities of the two sexes as well as power relations between them and influenced the arenas open to women and men of the movement. Women's responsibility for fostering the new generations was seen as belonging mainly to "the small home," the private sphere. But the small home remained dependent on the bigger home, on structural and political changes in the male-dominated public sphere. Women's responsibilities in the public arena were highlighted particularly at election time.[20]

Throughout the interwar period *The Woman* issued appeals to working-class women to fight for certain items on the agenda of the NLP: provisions for better child care, assistance to mothers, the sick, and disabled, and aid for the older generation. Housing programs, free school supplies, better wages for male workers, and support for strikers were seen as policies to protect the family against the inroads of capitalist exploitation. The struggle against alcoholism, ostracism of strikebreakers, and support for conscientious objectors were all meant to strengthen working class morale and were seen as depending to a high degree on women's actions.[21] But although social policies were important for the NLP, the 1920s especially were dominated by internal frictions over strategies.

From Revolutionary Flirtations to Government Responsibility

The socialist parties won between 30 and 40 percent of votes during elections in the interwar period, but for a good part of the 1920s the political wing of the labor movement was split. A brief flirtation of the radical wing of the NLP with revolution led to its membership in the Communist International (Comintern) in 1919.[22] This split the NLP, with a minority forming the Social Democratic party committed to parliamentary politics. The NLP was finally reconstituted in 1927 after the radicals had been expelled from the Comintern for lack of revolutionary fervor.

Electoral successes in 1927 led to the formation of the first Labor Government in 1928 – a minority government toppled after two weeks by the Liberal party. A strong program of social policies contributed to a landslide for the NLP in the 1933 election, paving the way for the second Labor Government in 1935. This was also a minority coalition, which lasted until the German occupation of 1940.

The socialist movement had turned full circle. A short revolutionary period, starting in 1918, was already weakened in 1923. The amalgamation of the reformist Social Democrats and the NLP in 1927, the Labor Government the following year, and the importance given to parliamentary reform policies from 1932 on, were all steps towards the formation of a durable social-democratic minority government in 1935.

The Role of Women within the Party

How did women react to these important developments within the NLP? What opportunities did they have to influence decisions?

Numerically, women were a clear minority within the party, ranging between 14 and 16 percent of party members throughout the interwar period.[23] Starting in the mid-1920s two women, elected by the Women's Secretariat, had seats on the central committee of the NLP. To parallel this concession, two men were elected by the NLP to permanent seats in the Women's Secretariat. In municipal councils women comprised 1 percent of all members in 1919 and still only 3 percent in 1938. The parliament was also an almost totally masculine assembly. Only the NLP and the Conservative party had female deputies elected in the interwar period. In 1921 one, in 1927 two, and in 1936 one woman were elected to represent the NLP, amounting to 2 percent, 3 percent, and 1 percent of labor deputies.[24] No doubt socialists as well as other political groups regarded politics as an almost exclusively masculine arena.

Male domination of the socialist movement made it difficult for women to oppose policies if they disagreed or to set priorities that ran counter to those of the male hierarchy. But did they disagree with men within the movement? If so, on which questions? How did they react to or influence general developments in party politics?

The journal *The Woman*, after 1923 *The Working Class Woman (Arbeider-kvinnen)*, and the socialist press as a whole made it possible for women to follow general debates within the movement. Informative articles appeared regularly, and discussions of political priorities were animated.

However, gender seems to have mattered little, if at all, to the major political problems debated.

The reorganization of the radicalized NLP in 1923 in compliance with Comintern demands for structural centralization weakened the independence of its Women's Association. At the national level, the association was replaced by a Women's Secretariat, consisting of five women and two men, nominated by the central committee of the party; its secretary was given a permanent seat on the National Council of the NLP. Special women's conferences were to be held in conjunction with national party congresses, among other things to suggest candidates for the Women's Secretariat, who would, however, be nominated by the central committee of the party. This change clearly ended the independent nature of the Women's Association within the NLP and was a step towards integrating women into the general party structure.[25]

The responsibility of the Women's Secretariat, in cooperation with the party leadership, was to assist local women's associations in their work, to lead political agitation and organization among women, to provide copy for special women's columns to be introduced in all socialist newspapers, and to edit the socialist women's journal, *The Working Class Woman.*

During the NLP's radical phase as member of the purportedly revolutionary Comintern (1919 to 1927) the main purpose of appealing to working-class women had also been to mobilize them for the party and not to initiate or promote women's policies. Hertha Sturm, secretary of the International Women's Secretariat, explicitly declared that there was no such thing as specific women's problems. Echoing these thoughts, Rachel Grepp, from 1923 on co-editor of the *Working Class Woman* (and widow of Kyrre Grepp, leader of the NLP from 1918 to 1922), maintained that cooperation between women and men was needed to support the united proletarian front. But the critical formulations that characterized some appeals to working-class women left the impression of a leadership – including women – somewhat frustrated with what they saw as the passive female masses, also a major complaint in other countries.[26]

The organizational changes of 1923 did not, however, take place without opposition. There was a long discussion of the decision to admit men into the leadership of the Women's Secretariat.[27] Even stronger was the opposition to dissolving the local women's associations and creating women's committees at all levels within the party. One of the objectives of this move was to weaken the influence of housewives who played active roles within the women's associations and to create common meeting places for all women party members whether married or single, wage earners or housewives. At the International Communist Women's Conferences in 1923, Clara Zetkin and Hertha Sturm, leader and secretary of its Secretariat, criticized Norwegian women for not wanting to dissolve the local women's associations and refusing to integrate individual members into the party. By explaining that the women's associations were in fact doing the same jobs as men in the party – agitating, informing, recruiting, and reaching out to the masses of working-class women – the Norwegians were allowed, for the time being, to maintain the traditional local women's associations.[28] Few local women's associations were, in fact, ever dissolved, and *Working Class Woman* continued to reflect the interests of its primarily working-class housewife readership. Attitudes and routines among grass-roots members remained unaltered; party leadership continued to be predominantly male with a small sprinkling of leading women.

Despite organizational changes, continuity characterized the socialist women's movement throughout the interwar period. Sigrid Syvertsen, leader of the NLP Women's Secretariat (1923 to 1939) and its secretary Thina Thorleifsen (1923 to 1953), both had leading positions within the women's association before 1923. Syvertsen had been active in the typographers' union and was one of the NLP councillors on the Oslo municipal board from 1919 to 1959. Thorleifsen had worked as a domestic servant and actively promoted a servants' trade union. She was a member of the central committee of the NLP from 1919 to 1959, and active in the abstinence movement. Rachel Grepp, another outstanding member of the Secretariat from 1923 to 1945, was on the editorial committee and international correspondent for *The Woman/The Working Class Woman*.[29]

During the conflict over women's associations, communist women loyally dissolved their branches and joined the party individually. But no sooner had this happened than they reversed course in 1924 and started creating so-called Housewives Organizations.[30] These declared themselves to be nonpolitical in the sense that they were not linked to any party. One of their main purposes was to educate housewives for active participation in the class struggle as a counterweight against the strong middle-class housewives association, which in the interwar period became one of the largest women's organizations in the country. The Housewives Organizations of the left were strongest in industrial areas. Their activities were clearly political: lobbying political authorities on housing problems, unemployment, control of food prices, and the legalization of abortion. In the 1930s, the Housewives Organizations numbered about forty, and in 1937 The Norwegian Association of Housewives Organizations was established.

Surprisingly socialist women's organizations affiliated with the NLP as well as sympathetic to the Communist party devoted much attention to housewives. Probably, this was the result of current perceptions of femininity and masculinity, an observation supported by the fact that more than 40 percent of all women over fifteen years of age accepted classification as housewives by the census. In sharp contrast to other Scandinavian countries, only 2 to 3 percent of Norwegian married women appeared to be economically active.[31]

Both NLP and communist women were loyal to party leaders, even when it came to healing ideological rifts in 1927. Nevertheless, they found their own ways to circumvent the effects of organizational changes. Indeed, changes at the local level were never forced on them, which may explain the low level of protests. The same loyalty characterized women's attitudes to the main trends of party politics in the 1920s and 1930s. The political turbulence that characterized the period up to the 1933 election had reached a climax in 1931, when police and soldiers were mobilized against workers, reinforced strict class and party loyalty. The revolutionary potential of the NLP expressed itself in repeated unauthorized strikes, in violation of laws protecting strikebreakers, and not least in the boycotting of conscription into the armed forces. All these confrontations promoted class solidarity and dampened gender conflicts within the labor movement. Moreover, since women had gained the vote in 1913, there was a general belief, within both middle-class and proletarian quarters, that a separate women's movement was no longer necessary. A climate of overwhelming class solidarity characterized the period between the two world wars, especially prior to 1935.

Even though there were few women in influential political positions, women's networks – both working-class and middle-class – were important in mobilizing the electorate and in putting certain political questions on the agenda at both the municipal and parliamentary level. What were these questions, and how did they correspond to the general political goals of the labor movement?

Fewer Children

One of the most striking changes affecting everyday life in the interwar period was the decline in marital fertility. Since the turn of the century household production had been replaced by industrial means. Such modernizing trends presupposed schooling and some sort of higher education as a means of competing in the labor market, and they thus made the raising of children more costly. Increasingly children were regarded as less necessary, perhaps even as a burden. Not surprisingly, family limitation started in the urban middle classes and quickly spread to other social groups. The twenty years between 1920 and 1940 saw a drastic reduction of the number of children born, including to working-class couples.

Surveys as late as the 1940s and 1950s indicate that much of this reduction was reached by "natural methods" such as withdrawal and sexual abstinence. However, the fall in fertility was also accompanied by vehement discussions about contraception and abortion.[32] From the very beginning, Norwegian socialists were split on the question of birth control. For revolutionary socialists, family planning could be seen as yet another device to delay the overthrow of capitalist society by making working-class families believe the neo-Malthusian maxim that they could improve their standard of living if they had fewer children. The reformist branch of the Norwegian labor movement, however, considered family planning one of many weapons in the hands of workers themselves for attaining a better future. From this perspective fewer children would enhance the family budget, reduce the triple burden of working mothers, and even improve the chances for children's education. Although some socialists actively promoted knowledge about contraception from the beginning, the party as such avoided this controversial theme. The women's associations mentioned it occasionally and never directly opposed it.

This situation changed drastically in the interwar period. In 1915 and 1918, local labor women's associations welcomed the liberal feminist lecturer Katti Anker Møller, who strongly advocated dissemination of information on contraception as the most important measure to assist care-worn mothers. Married to a liberal country gentleman, Møller pioneered a number of important measures to benefit working-class mothers in particular. Her progressive ideas made her a close ally of socialist women, whose confidence she had won during their long common struggle for the Castberg Children's Laws (1901 to 1915).[33] These laws gave children born out of wedlock paternal inheritance rights and the right to use the father's family name. More importantly, they created guidelines for municipal councils to assist single mothers financially during the months surrounding the birth of a baby without involving poor relief. Møller's plans for assisting mothers with many children were popularized by leaflets containing information on contraception and public mothers' wages, printed at the expense of the Oslo NLP and distributed through local women's associations. "The mothers' class war" and "the mothers' wages dispute," as she phrased it, were to end women's economic dependence on husbands. Møller wanted the state to pay all mothers for bringing up their children, and recommended that mothers reduce the number of children born to render "the goods" more sought for and consequently better paid. Her phraseology was well tuned to the revolutionary language of the labor movement:

> Socialist ideology … must be widened to encompass socialization also of child care and child nourishment, so that all children as far as possible will get the same good treatment. Socialization must therefore comprise the work of mothers, our production, the breeding of children and the work involved in taking

care of the new generation …. I would think these claims correspond to Karl Marx' view of the state and to what August Bebel expected from women. This way of understanding socialism also in our field, is … the effort that women must make as their mission in the construction of the socialist state.[34]

After a visit to London to study the Marie Stopes birth control clinic, Møller undertook to copy this British initiative. Contact with Thina Thorleifsen, the leader of the Oslo Labor Women's Organization, resulted, after consultation with the newly elected party secretary, Martin Tranmœl, in acceptance of the project. Despite the difficult negotiations and the NLP split in 1923, a Mothers' Clinic that provided contraceptive advice, was opened in Oslo in April 1924, led by a board consisting of two women from each of the three socialist parties. The will to cooperate in this matter must have been strong.

The Oslo Labor Party provided financial assistance. Interestingly, its records never mentioned the clinic, whereas the *Working Class Woman* advertised the services of the clinic in every issue. Family planning clearly was seen as a woman's responsibility. It took about ten years to establish the clinic on a solidly basis, but by then it was supported by the municipality and by the regional Health Insurance Service.

In the 1930s the passive good will of the labor movement changed to active assistance. The Workers Educational Association distributed booklets on family planning, and socialist physicians actively promoted contraception. One of them, Karl Evang, soon to become the head of the National Health Office, edited a much disputed but widely circulated journal on family planning and sexual problems. Other political organizations gradually became more friendly to family planning. By 1937 Mothers' Clinics providing information on birth control spread to fourteen other cities. In 1939, Karl Evang was instrumental in having Parliament grant national economic support for the socialist Mothers' Clinics.

This development was not without setbacks. Opposition was strong from men and women with religious and conservative beliefs and also from many doctors, especially of the older generation. Socialist men also sometimes added to the problems in creating such clinics. When one was established in Stavanger in 1927, the local head of the medical services demanded that a doctor be among the personnel of the clinic. A decision to contribute the money needed for a doctor's salary was defeated in the municipal council because socialist deputies were absent; they had preferred taking part in a demonstration against unemployment. Thus, gendered priorities pursued by members of the labor movement contributed to blocking the Stavanger clinic.

By the mid-1930s the debate changed character.[35] Partly inspired by the Swedish discussion and especially by Gunnar and Alma Myrdal's book *Crises in the Population Question*, published in 1934, the fall in marital fertility was now used as an argument for social policies, and questions of contraception were more or less shelved. The pro-natalist character of social policies, however, never became as pronounced in Norway as in Sweden.[36]

A further reason for this shift was the active campaign to legalize abortion, another important initiative spearheaded by socialist and some radical liberal women. Since 1917, repeated attempts by socialist women to demand decriminalization of abortion had failed either because of lukewarm support from leaders of the NLP's Women's Association or from local male socialists. Opposition to legalizing abortion by changing Section 245 of the criminal code was also strong within the labor movement. Since the 1920s were replete with divisive political problems, socialists felt justified in avoiding the question of abortion. Priority was given to promoting contraception, a difficult campaign requiring concentrated efforts during most of the 1920s. Not until 1930 was legalization of abortion again on the agenda, and this time the initiative came from powerful and probably somewhat unexpected circles.

The Norwegian Surgeons' Association in 1929 discussed how to deal with the increasing number of illegal abortions brought to their attention. A sharp increase between 1920 and 1933 from 1.2 to 3.9 abortions for every 1,000 women aged twenty to forty-nine was a drastic indication of the problem. The increase was a good deal higher for married than for unmarried women, substantially weakening the interpretation of abortion as the result of extramarital sexual relations. At the national convention of physicians in 1930, a committee, on which the daughter of Katti Anker Møller, Dr. Tove Mohr, had a seat, proposed legalizing abortions performed for medical, humanitarian, and social reasons. But there was no agreement as to how to define these criteria for legal abortion.

This medical convention started a nationwide discussion of possible changes in Section 245 of the Penal Code. As in so many other countries, age and religion were important in determining people's attitudes. Although there certainly was no agreement among socialists, they were more likely than others to support the demand for legalizing abortion. A proposal was circulated in 1934 to legalize abortions performed by physicians for medical reason during the first trimester and with the consent of the woman. It provoked a flood of protests, especially from clerical and other religious circles. Many women's organizations protested, among them the two biggest, the Housewives Organization (different from the communist Housewives Association), and the Norwegian Women's Sanitary Organization – both nonsocialist. Many protests were based on the fear of "giving any woman the right so to speak to kill unnumbered unborn babies, of allowing state-supported killing of babies in public hospitals and paid by public finances," as well as of a strong increase in "flighty relations."[37]

Supporting resolutions above all came from women of the labor movement. They argued for instance that

> Feticide [i.e., abortion] will be performed by the woman herself or by ignorant quacks with the danger for the life and safety of the woman inherent in these ignorant encroachments. Feticide cannot be fought by criminalization, only by creating conditions for mother and child that are safe enough for the need for abortion to disappear.[38]

In the spring of 1935 a nationwide campaign resulted in 130 resolutions from local labor Women's Associations and five from communist Housewives Associations. The Oslo Liberal Women and the Club for Economically Active Women also sent supporting resolutions.

Eugenic arguments were central to family planning proposals. Socialists like Martin Tranmœl and Karl Evang in the 1930s also supported the view that only healthy people who were genetically fit should have children. When a law on sterilization was accepted by the Parliament in 1934, no socialists protested.[39] Contemporary discussions continued to focus on abortion. The socialist government, which assumed power in 1935, immediately set about reviewing and extending social policies, such as health insurance, disability pensions, and old-age pensions. But the proposal to legalize abortion was never submitted to Parliament, not even a more moderate version put forward in 1938. The strong opposition in 1934/35 seems to have deterred the socialist minority government from action. Socialists themselves were divided on the issue. There are also indications that the recriminalization of abortion by the Soviet Union in 1936 carried some weight.

Determination of the importance of the abortion question in the overall change of the labor movement in 1935 from an opposition to a government party is difficult. The fact that the small Communist party persistently worked to decriminalize abortion, suggests that the generally more moderate political stance of NLP also made for less willingness to change Section 245. In contrast to Sweden and Denmark, legalization was not achieved until the law was changed by a labor government in 1960 and took effect in 1964.

Social Policies – Women's Policies?

During the interwar period socialist women discussed housing policies, better educational opportunities for working-class children, higher wages for providers, and other social policy measures. Their priorities, however, seemed to be measures to assist mothers. The mothers' clinics did not limit their activities to giving advice on family planning. They also offered information and advice on the best care of infants and children.

One of the best known social innovations, "Mothers' Pension," was started on a municipal level in Oslo in 1920 by a local circle of labor women. They suggested a municipal pension for all single mothers to allow them to give their small children better care. The leaders of the Labor Party's Women's Association forwarded this proposal for further discussion, but again showed more moderate ambitions by limiting the pensions to "worthy" single mothers, (i.e., widows). Nonetheless, the social-democratic majority in the Oslo City Council managed to secure a municipal pension for all needy single mothers, even those who were unwed. This was a very radical initiative; most other municipalities that instituted mothers' pension schemes during the interwar years limited support to widows or poor married mothers.[40] Conditions for eligibility to mothers' pensions were as strict as for many other social support measures: women had to prove that they had lived in Oslo for at least fifteen years so that there was no possibility of moving there just to receive assistance. Nevertheless, the Oslo mothers' pension scheme certainly was a pioneering initiative. The national government only adopted a similar provision in the 1960s.[41]

Many working-class homes were poorly suited to offer women adequate lying-in care. The earliest maternity wards, however, were set up primarily to train midwives and attracted the poorest, often unmarried mothers. Poor women were offered free maternity assistance in exchange for serving as training subjects for midwifery students. Better-off women who could afford to pay for maternity services mostly gave birth in their homes or were cared for in special wards. Again Oslo pioneered a maternalist measure: beginning in 1917 socialist women, in cooperation with Katti Anker Møller, managed to gain municipal assistance for a number of lying-in homes where mothers were offered a period of rest and good medical care. The interwar years saw a proliferation of small municipal lying-in homes, more friendly and homelike for women in labor than hospital wards.[42]

These initiatives reflect the gendered division of labor in the socialist movement. Women's uppermost interests seem to have been to create better conditions for motherhood. This was also the most important argument for demanding child allowances, another central question initiated by women of the NLP. In 1923, social-democratic women in Oslo appointed a women's committee to study the possibility of establishing a national "mothers' wage." The idea originated with Katti Anker Møller, who for some years had campaigned for such a plan.[43] Remuneration for the work mothers did when producing the new generations was, in her view, the responsibility of society. Paying all mothers for their important contribution to the common good, she argued, would also be a means of liberating wives from dependence on husbands' income. This proposal met with strong criticism, even from some working-class women, but it won the support of the Labor Party's Women's Association. At the elections in 1930, the question of "mothers' wage" was included in the NLP program.

By 1925, the question had also received attention from the Norwegian Women's Council, the national branch of the International Council of Women. It appointed a committee to work out a proposal for family wages built on the principle, established in 1913, of additional wages for civil servants with children. In 1928 it recommended a basic wage for persons without children and an allowance for each child regardless of the sex of the wage earner. The labor victory in the 1933 election stimulated interest in the question, and a parliamentary committee was established in 1934 charged with considering the matter. Vehement discussions followed the committee's positive recommendation in 1937, but no action was taken before 1940. In 1946, however, in the euphoria of political cooperation across party lines following the war, the law on child allowances was enacted. With minor exceptions, it adhered to the principles suggested by the parliamentary committee in 1937.

This law was the first step towards a welfare state, building on the principle of universality, (i.e., giving all citizens the same right, regardless of income). What was started by working-class women and their allies in the early 1920s led to an important step in the construction of the welfare state. But why did it take so long – from the early 1920s to the post World War II era – to implement child allowances?

That social program involved many conflicting interests. Socialist and bourgeois women did not agree on how the proposal should be implemented. Liberal and conservative women were inspired by the French system of *allocation familiales* and preferred regular wages to cover only the needs of one individual, man or woman, with allowances given in relation to the number of children for whom the individual wage earner provided. This system would abolish the tradition that male wages provided for the needs of a whole family, whether the individual male wage earner had a family to support or not. This tradition, it was argued, was responsible for women's low wages, because women, providers or provided for, were regarded as economically dependent on a man's wage. Consequently, if wages for men who were not providers were reduced and wages for providers, male or female, were upgraded, public finances would not be burdened with the reform. Both women and men of the NLP wanted a "mothers' wage" financed through the tax system. This implied that all mothers should be paid a certain amount of money for each child.

Another central difference was that many working-class and middle-class women saw the mothers' wage as a means of freeing mothers from work outside the home, making it possible for them to concentrate on the welfare of their children. By contrast, some of the most active liberal women saw "a family wage" as a means for mothers to pay for child care, making it possible for married women to work outside the home. This perspective formed part of the ideas that in the late 1930s led to a rebirth of the liberal feminist movement.[44]

Within the NLP, however, gender differences also came to the fore, especially on whether the benefit should be paid to women or men. In the 1930s the male members of the Mothers' Wage Committee did not want mothers' work to provide the central motivation for what they preferred to call "child allowances," nor did they want the money to be paid to mothers. The female members of the committee made a concession by accepting the term child allowances instead of mothers' wage, but they advocated highlighting mothers' vital contribution to the survival of future generations. They insisted that the money be paid to mothers to assure that it was properly used for the benefit of the children and not wasted on husbands' pub allowances. In the end this version prevailed.

A final interesting conflict should be noted. A group of young economists stressed the possibilities of influencing the labor market by gearing child allowances to national production. Assistance could be rendered not in cash, but through services such as free school meals, cheap clothing, and better housing for children. These ideas were partly derived from Swedish social policies initiated by Gunnar and Alva Myrdal. Part of the reason for supporting the Swedish alternative was lack of confidence in women's capacity for "the rational use of income." Ella Anker, sister of Katti Anker Møller, sharply criticized Alva Myrdal for suspecting that women would use the money for "silk-stockings and lipstick" instead of better child care and for preferring public institutional child care to the private care by mothers in the home.[45]

Although gender to some extent explains attitudes and actions on these controversies, women behaved primarily as comrades and loyal working-class party members when promoting their political interests. They in no way challenged perceptions of femininity and masculinity. Rather, they reinforced the conventional view of women as mothers and wives and men as providers and active politicians. The conflict over women's paid work outside the home illustrates this supportive role, but it also signals changes in gender relations within the labor movement in the late 1930s.

Women as Workers

Trade unions grew in importance up to the crisis years in the early 1920s. The split of the political arm of the movement did not affect them, but

economic crises reduced membership until the late 1920s, after which
both trade unions and the NLP attracted a growing number of members.
Throughout, women increased their share of union membership, growing
from 6 percent in 1920, to 11 percent in 1930 and 16 percent in 1936.
Nonetheless, the unions continued to be dominated by men. Even the
women-dominated unions mostly had male leaders; only 2 to 3 percent of
elected delegates to trade union congresses were women; and there was
no special women's institution within the unions until 1940.[46]

Unfortunately, sources documenting women's activities in trade unions
during this period are scanty, and no systematic studies of this subject
have been undertaken, except for the few and futile attempts to organize
female servants.[47] Even during the 1930s, when the National Association
of Trade Unions showed some interest in organizing domestic servants,
the idea was met with resistance from the trade unions involved. They
feared that supporting female servants, who lagged far behind other workers in wages, working hours, holidays, and other benefits, would imperil
their own position. Until 1948, all attempts to legally regulate servant's
work also failed. By then, however, female servants had become a small
group among economically active women.

Throughout the interwar period the view of women as primarily
housewives and mothers stamped the politics of the labor movement.
Only one important issue to some extent challenged this perception of
gender and created a gender conflict within the socialist movement – the
controversy over married women's right to be gainfully employed.[48]

The Trade Union Congress of 1925 clearly and expressly opposed the
gainful employment of both wife and husband if this was not necessary
"for the existence of the family." Union leaders believed that especially, in
times of high unemployment, priority in employment belonged to male
providers and to unmarried women; married women were to be provided
for by their husbands. Until 1932 and 1933, the NLP's Women's Secretariat agreed. By then, new arguments in favor of married women's rights
to gainful employment were advanced by younger women within the
socialist movement. Johanne Reutz, educated as an economist and a
trade union activist, pointed out that the number of married women gainfully employed was so low that making them redundant would have no
impact on unemployment figures,[49] and that they mostly worked in jobs
(in health services and domestic work) that would not be taken over by
men. In a counterattack against male conservatism at the Socialist
Women's Conference of 1933 Reutz described restrictions on married
women's right to paid work as harmful to individual families and as expressions of fascist policies.

But the party leadership refused to change its policies. In 1935, the
principle of the right to work was accepted but with the exception that if

one spouse worked full time the other should not be gainfully employed. Despite the gender neutral formulation, this would hardly bar men from gainful employment. Women of the labor movement were still divided on the issue, although by now half of the members of the Women's Secretariat were of the opinion that married women should have the right to work for wages. At the National Congress of Labor Women in 1936 a small majority opposed the restrictions on married women's rights. They were led by a small group of younger academically educated women, among them the economists Reutz and Åse Lionœs, and physician Tove Mohr. Significantly Sigrid Syvertsen, long-time head of the Women's Secretariat and co-editor of *Working Class Woman* until 1936, now changed her opinion and joined the younger generation. These younger women considered women's equal rights to paid work as self-evident. They argued that restrictions of these rights might delay marriages, and that women's economic independence was not only a socialist goal but could also be regarded as a weapon in the fight for a socialist society.

Such equal rights arguments, however, played only a minor role in the discussion. In 1936, calling restrictions on women's rights an expression of fascism no doubt was effective. But even more weight was given to trade union arguments about the danger of perpetuating low wages within women-dominated industries if married women were replaced by younger unmarried and untrained female workers. The Congress majority also argued that the labor movement might be split if women were driven to join the Liberal party, which had all along defended married women's right to waged work. The Trade Union Congress now also changed its position. In 1936 it joined the International Federation of Trade Unions, where married women's right to gainful employment was an accepted principle. Yet the most influential social-democratic newspaper still continued to give priority to men's right to work and to appeal to the solidarity of working-class women in a period of economic crisis. At the same time, the small communist press as well as the bourgeois papers consistently defended married women's rights to waged work.

Finally, in 1937, the executive of the NLP declared that defending everybody's right to paid work had always been a socialist principle; that only the economic crisis had made it necessary to exempt married women; and that a decline in unemployment made this exception redundant. The NLP's changed position, then, was a consequence of changed economic circumstances and not a change of principles. In practice the conflict continued, with married women being frequently laid off, even within the Cooperative Associations. One of these incidents resulted in a law suit that took the question all the way to the Supreme Court, which in 1939 ruled that married women's right to work had to be legally accepted. The German occupation in April 1940 brought a final spasm to the conflict. Foreseeing a new increase in unemployment, the National Board of Trade Unions reopened the question of barring married women from paid work. As no unemployment crises materialized, this did not become necessary.

This long conflict clearly reveals the persistent attitude that married women should work only in their homes. Within the socialist movement, as in most of society, femininity and masculinity continued to be understood as dichotomous qualities, and clearly gendered activities and responsibilities were perceived as the normal situation. During the 1930s a new generation of better educated women introduced the principle of gender equality within and outside the labor movement. However, this understanding of gender was not widespread until the new women's movement emerged in the early 1970s.

The Labor Movement as Counterculture

Adherence to the labor movement was not only a question of political preference. The socialists also attempted to combat bourgeois values by creating a counterculture, which would permeate the lives of all individuals from cradle to grave. The means was organization of children, youth, and women around special interests such as sports and film. Such activities created a sense of solidarity, togetherness, and the anticipatory atmosphere of a new and better society. The cultural impact of socialism was strengthened through well-organized mass meetings and demonstrations, that made lavish use of banners and songs. No one has as yet attempted a systematic analysis of the gendered nature of these activities; even a brief study offers insights suggesting a coherent picture of how gender was understood within the labor movement.

A growing awareness of the importance of childhood, and of the development of class consciousness from an early age, led to discussions of the possibility of organizing children's groups within the labor movement as early as 1906 and again in 1915. Not until the early 1920s, however, were concrete steps taken.[50] Inspired by a youth congress in Moscow, young men and women of the NLP together pioneered the Children's Movement. In 1921, with 6,000 members, organized in fifty-one groups, it was said to be smaller in size only to those of Austria and Germany. The political split in 1923 weakened the Children's Movement, which was reorganized only in 1933. The intention then was to counteract the bourgeois scout movement and to mobilize children between the age of seven and fifteen for socialism.

Activities were meant to educate children to become good socialists and to understand what their parents were fighting for. Play, folk dancing, and outdoor activities were used as means to shape strong and healthy working-class children. In the 1930s, summer camps in tents became a main feature of the movement. To encourage personal hygiene, children were admonished to wash properly and to avoid spitting, precautions in the fight against the much feared tuberculosis.

A closer look at the journals published by the NLP Children's Movement reveals the same gendered orientation as in the rest of the labor movement. Some of the children's groups were divided according to sex. Boys were seen as future socialist leaders, as for example in this presentation of a boys' orchestra in 1922: "… a group of boys who will become the vanguard of future struggles … who will blow the trumpets in the battle for our ideas. They will … blow the fanfares of victory when the time comes."[51]

There was little explicit mention of girls or women. In a series of "portraits" of important socialists published in the movement's journal, only a few women were portrayed. Information on politics was to be given in the form, "Father tells about solidarity" or "Father tells about Spain." When the importance of trade unionism was explained, it was depicted as fathers' domain. Nine out of ten depictions of the importance of "all that has been produced by work" and of front-page illustrations were pictures of working men. Only once was women's work, represented by a seamstress, used as a front-page illustration. Mothers were rarely mentioned, and then only as an angry disciplining figure, the providers of a helpful hand for a small girl, or as plaintively waiting for a drunken husband.[52] Many more examples of gendered messages could be given, but these should suffice to indicate the problems of integrating the understanding of girls (and women), different from men yet equally important, within the NLP's Children's Movement.

The NLP Youth Organization, started in 1903, followed the general trend of gender preference.[53] It was charged with recruiting members for the party and was to voice the special interests of young people of both sexes. During the interwar period it by and large followed the splits and reunifications within the main party. The leaders were men, a good number of whom later became important in the party.

Other significant examples of cultural expressions of interwar socialism were The Workers' Sports Organization, established in 1924, and the Workers' Film Group, started in 1928. Workers' Sports was created to challenge bourgeois sports organizations, which had been mobilized as strikebreakers in the early 1920s. Contrary to bourgeois sports, which cultivated elite and competitive forms, the goal of Workers' Sports was collective achievement in mass sports such as gymnastics. In competitive sports, women had traditionally been marginalized as not fit for hard physical competition. Most women seemed to have accepted this view and preferred mass sports, especially the popular "housewives gymnastics" where large groups of women performed together. This was also the case within the Workers' Sports Organization. The desire to offer alternative activities for unemployed youth probably also accounts for the rather masculine profile of Workers' Sports Organizations.[54] The Workers' Film Group was started in 1928 by young male amateurs, some of whom later became very able filmmakers. Most of the films are now lost, but contemporary descriptions give some indication of the contents. They were propaganda films aimed at winning elections and they mainly pictured problems connected with the male labor market and the politics of the bourgeois parties. The world of working-class women was patently absent. The few references to women typically refer to the girlfriend of the young working-class hero, or the farmer's daughter, awarded as a prize to the young cropper after many social problems had been solved. In these films women were marginal to the world of work and politics.[55]

Only in one organization were women expressly not welcome – an elitist students' organization centered on the journal *Dawn*, (Mot Dag) soon to become the foremost critical intellectual journal. In 1925, Dawn left the NLP and, apart from a short adherence to the Communist party, remained unaffiliated with any political party until it dissolved in 1936. Nevertheless, it was very important to the radical wing of the NLP. Although women had had access to the university since 1884, they were still a small minority among students. The combination of strict discipline, compulsory attendance at meetings, and the expectation of a high intellectual level among Dawn members all worked to exclude women. Dawn's somewhat despotic leader, Erling Falk, simply stated that "the weight of their [women's] brains is less [than men's]." Even marriage was regarded as a breach of loyalty to Dawn. However, when two prominent men, who were already married, wanted to join the organization, their wives were admitted to the meetings. This was not considered "dangerous ... so long as they [their wives] behaved modestly."[56]

Despite opposition, more women joined Dawn. Falk now required that he be kept informed of "which woman belonged to which man," in order to prevent promiscuity. Despite vehement protests from some of the women who wanted to remain within the main organization, they were soon relegated as a special section of Dawn. Around 1930, however, one woman became a member of the Dawn's leadership. Falk continued to find women a problem; his contempt for them was pronounced in what was said to be one of his favorite expressions: "these cackling geese." One of the "cackling geese," Kirsten Moe Hansteen, in 1945 became a member of government, representing the Communist party; another, Nina Haslund Gleditch, organized international aid for Spanish children and acted as secretary to the Foreign Department of the Norwegian exiled government during World War II.[57]

The Threat of Nazism and Fascism

In general, socialist women followed the predominant socialist attitudes to political developments in Europe. The Russian revolution was greeted as "a glimpse of light."[58] Admiration for the Soviet Union and abhorrence of the Nazi and fascist regimes was partly explained by the fate of women under the latter. Alexandra Kollontai, among the most prominent Bolsheviks – commissar for social policies after 1917, Soviet ambassador to Norway in 1927 and to Sweden in the 1930s – was viewed as the symbol of the important possibilities offered to women in the Soviet Union. Many of the articles on the U.S.S.R. in *Working Class Woman* stressed positive changes for women. True, there were difficulties in building a socialist society, but improvements were considered more important: better wages, better employment opportunities, and better education. Even the Soviet restrictions on abortion adopted in 1936 were defended on the grounds that assistance to pregnant women and mothers was now sufficient and that day care centers were being built at an astonishing rate. Although there still was room for improvement, dire want and poverty no longer required abortion as an option. Restrictions on abortion were also seen as a protection of women against sexual exploitation. A number of articles in 1938 and 1939 praised the wonderful conditions for children, the marvelous school system, and other improvements of importance especially to women.[59] *Working Class Woman* offered no criticism of the Soviet Union before 1939.

But admiration for the "first socialist state" was brought to an abrupt end with the Finnish-Soviet war of 1939. All sympathy now was directed towards the Finnish working class. Immediate action was taken to send assistance in the form of doctors, nurses, medicine, clothes, all provided by extremely successful fund-raising campaigns in which labor women participated. Fearing a general European war, the journal of the NLP's Women's Secretariat consistently admonished women to knit gloves and socks for Finnish and Norwegian soldiers. The Defense Department paid for the wool. Different patterns for Finland and Norway were published in the journal, and so many women responded that in the spring of 1940, it was impossible to provide enough wool.[60] The end of the Soviet-Finnish war in the spring of 1940 only brought scorn for the "so-called socialist state." The Soviet Union had demonstrated that all socialist principles of people's freedom and self-determination had been abandoned and thus had behaved exactly like the capitalist states.[61] Well over twenty years of admiration disappeared in a very short time.

Fascist Italy was hardly mentioned, while outspoken abhorrence characterized attitudes toward Nazi Germany and Fascist Spain. The "enslavement of women" was mentioned in every article on these regimes. German women were asked to consider if they had been strong enough in their defense of freedom. The barbaric conditions for German women were used to warn about what might happen in Norway if the NLP did not win the 1936 election, because only democratic nations would defend women's rights.[62] Spanish women, on the other hand, were seen as heroes, defending socialism and freedom against fascism. Nazi Germany was criticized for mobilizing women in the defense industries and pressing them to take over men's jobs, while, understandably but a little ironically, when in 1938 Spanish women did the same thing, they were seen as playing an important role in a worthy cause.[63] The main contribution to the socialist side in the Spanish Civil War was fund-raising for medical and sanitary aid and especially for building children's homes. This activity continued until the outbreak of World War II.[64]

Conclusion : Class Solidarity and Gender Differences

Some have maintained that the core of working-class culture has been the concept of solidarity,[65] not with strong leaders, but with the weakest members of society. Solidarity was said to have kept the labor movement together through all disputes of the interwar period and have permeated working-class culture in all of its manifestations. In this light, gender differences are easily seen to be of minor importance, an attitude that has been amply demonstrated in this chapter. The main purpose, for women and men alike, was the fight against capitalism and for a socialist society. Demands for the election of women to municipal and parliamentary offices were often met with the argument that the best representatives were wanted, regardless of their sex. This was repeated again and again in *Working Class Woman*: "Women and men, in loyal faithful union, will make the Labor party the weapon that will give victory to the working class."[66]

But unequal gender differentiations were rampant. Women were considered primarily as crucial voters and as recruiters of other women to the party. At elections, they were summoned to agitate and vote for the NLP, to support men who were fighting for a better world, and to fight themselves "not from their situation as women, but as … socialists."[67] The fact that very few women ever won seats in municipal and parliamentary elections was often explained as their own fault: Since they had the vote and were a majority of the voters, they had the power to be elected.[68] The problem, it was said, was that too many women still adhered to "the old prejudice that they should not meddle in politics."[69] Another difficulty women had to overcome was their lack of self-confidence. They tried too hard to think and act as men, "as coldblooded rational beings," as Fernanda Nissen, a socialist activist, claimed in 1919.[70] That went against the norms of "feminine character" and, therefore, women blamed themselves for their subordination within the party.

Women's most important talents were deemed to be taking care of the home and family. Their journal was full of information on better housekeeping, cleaning, cooking, child care, sewing and knitting.[71] A good home was seen as an invaluable support for a hard-working and politically active husband, and every husband was expected to do his best to support his wife "to the degree it was physically and economically possible."[72] On the one hand, taking part in public activities was recommended only for women who had the energy to do so after having done their best in the home. "Those who think that the home demands everything" should regard that as their most important task.[73] The attitude toward married women's paid work perfectly reflected such beliefs. Not until the late 1930s did a new generation of socialist women, committed to combining work and family, more consistently advocate women's responsibility in public life.

On the other hand, women's labor in the family was said to give them a special understanding for social policies. Again and again, women were reminded that society was a "big home," where they could apply the talents they had developed in "the small home." Women were admonished to work for the best housing policy, the best education policies, the best care for children, mothers, the handicapped, and elderly. The social welfare arena was seen as appealing especially to women and as an important justification for asking them to vote for labor.

Shouldering this double responsibility was an onerous task. Most socialist women were either unwilling or unable to support the double burden of work and politics, and most gave all of their efforts to the homes. They made an extremely important contribution to improving family health standards by cooking nourishing food and provided clean and warm clothes and clean homes. They also improved the family economy by careful consumer habits and cunning administration of their husbands' wages and, if need be, by paid work.

That did not mean that women regarded their responsibilities in active party politics as unimportant. They were hurt when poor results for the NLP at the 1918 election were partly blamed on them. "If something wrong happens, women are always blamed; men are blameless," lamented their journal in January 1919. Men did not want to assist women, it charged, did not trust them, feared them as competitors, and did not want to lose their privileges. Such outspoken criticism of male comrades was very rare, but the conclusion mitigated the impression of a gender conflict: women should consider their faults and learn from their mistakes. The time had come for women and men to cooperate.[74] There were no demands that men change their attitudes.

As opposed to the double responsibility expected of women, there was nothing ambiguous about the role ascribed to men. They were perceived as undisputed heads of families, providers, and leaders. The socialist press, be it children's magazines, women's journals or other media, time and again carried portraits of socialist leaders, all of them men. No one criticized the visual exclusion of women, no one pointed to the effect this might have on men's and women's self-perception. Despite problems with practicing such ideals of masculinity, especially in periods of unemployment, no one questioned them and no one seriously challenged male supremacy.

Such polarized understandings of gender created a power hierarchy, allocating to men the public, open, and institutionalized power channels, to women the private and hidden means of influencing men. These ideas were by no means confined to the socialist movement,[75] but they may have been strengthened there by the need for solidarity between women and men in the fight against capitalism. Vigilance against the threat of splitting forces within the socialist movement, so harmful in the early 1920s, remained of the utmost importance all through the interwar years. Feminism, understood as solidarity among women across class boundaries, was clearly perceived as one such threat. From 1918 to 1940 warnings against cooperation with bourgeois women were uttered repeatedly, and in the 1930s parallel membership in socialist and bourgeois women's organizations was explicitly banned.[76]

The overall position of the NLP as an opposition party until 1935, and after that as the base of a fragile minority government, also fostered class solidarity and dampened criticism of male comrades. A crisis atmosphere in the latter part of the 1930s grew out of the threat of international Nazism and fascism and the collapse of the much treasured Soviet ideal. Solidarity was as important as ever. But small signs of a stronger opposition to male hierarchies and a more open support for women's activities in the public sphere came to the fore in discussions of married women's right to gainful employment. With a younger generation of better educated women within the NLP, new approaches were slowly gaining ground. The German occupation in April 1940 disrupted these new trends, and it took the 1950s and most of the 1960s to revert to more clearly feminist politics within the NLP.

Notes

1. *Kvinden*, December 1918. Holterman Knudsen was editor of the movement's main journal, leader of the NLP from 1889 and a labor member of Parliament at repeated intervals.
2. For a general overview of Norwegian history, without a gender perspective, see Rolf Danielsen et al. (eds.), *Norway: A History from the Vikings to Our Own Times* (Oslo, 1995).
3. Vera Espeland Ertresvaag, "Arbeiderkvinnenes faglige og politiske organisering 1889-1901," in *Kvinner selv … Sju bidrag til norsk kvinnehistorie*, eds. Ida Blom and Gro Hagemann (Oslo, 1980, 1st ed. 1977), pp. 47-70, and Ingrid Andersgaard, "Settersker og typografer – splittelse mellom menn og kvinner," in Blom and Hagemann, *Kvinner selv*, pp. 22-46.
4. Ida Blom, "The Struggle for Women's Suffrage in Norway, 1885-1913," *Scandinavian Journal of History* 4 (1980): 3-22.
5. Ertresvaag, "Arbeiderkvinnenes faglige."
6. Linda Kvinge, "Hushjelpene i norske byer 1930-1948" (M.A. thesis, University of Bergen, 1983).
7. Gro Hagemann, "Protection or Equality? Debates on Protective Legislation in Norway," Lynn Karlsson, "The Beginning of a "Masculine Renaissance": The Debate on the 1909 Prohibition against Women's Night Work in Sweden," and Anna-Birte Ravn, "Lagging Far Behind All Civilized Nations:" Debate over Protective Labor Legislation for Women in Denmark, 1899-1913," in *Protecting Women: Labor Legislation in Europe, the United States, and Australia, 1880 – 1920*, eds. Ulla Wikander et al. (Chicago, 1995), pp. 210-89.
8. Kirsten Flatøy, "Utviklingslinjer innen Arbeiderpartiets Kvindeforbund fra 1901 til 1914," in Blom and Hagemann, *Kvinner selv*, pp. 71-94; Gro Hagemann, "Særvern av kvinner-arbeidervern eller diskriminering?" in Blom and Hagemann, *Kvinner selv*, pp. 95-121; Blom, "Struggle for Women's Suffrage," pp. 3-22.
9. Ertresvaag, "Arbeiderkvinnenes faglige," Flatøy, "Utviklingslinjer," and Hagemann, "Særvern av."
10. Per Maurseth, "Gjennom kriser til makt (1920-1935)," in *Arbeiderbevegelsens historie i Norge*, vol. 3, eds. Arne Kokkvoll et al., (Oslo 1983), p. 336.
11. Ida Blom, *Barnebegrensning – synd eller sunn fornuft?* (Bergen 1980), pp. 23-37.
12. There was a reduction from 21 percent to 15 percent of the urban population living in overpopulated houses during the decade 1920 to 1930. Maurseth, *Gjennom kriser*, p. 338.
13. Ibid., p. 338.
14. *Historisk statistikk* 1968, diagram 68, p. 567.
15. Ingeborg Fløystad, "Vi lærte tidlig å arbeide!" *Forskningsnytt* 4 (1979): 20-31.
16. Olav Ljones, *Female Labour Activity in Norway*, Central Bureau of Statistics of Norway (Oslo, 1979), pp. 135-36.
17. Anna Jorunn Avdem and Kari Melby, *Oppe føst og sist i seng. Husarbeid i Norge fra 1850 til dag* (Oslo, 1985), p. 147.
18. Knut Kjeldstadli, "Et splittet samfunn 1905-35," in *Norges historie*, vol. X, eds. Knut Helle et al. (Oslo, 1994),pp. 135-36.
19. Avdem and Melby, *Oppe først*, pp. 127-54. Ida Blom, "Nødvendig arbeid – skiftende definisjoner og praktiske konsekvenser," in Ida Blom, *Det er forskjell på folk – nå som før. Om kjønn og andre former for sosial differensiering* (Oslo, 1994), pp. 117-42.
20. See for instance Gunnar Ousland, *Kvinden* (November 1919): 84-85.

21. See, for instance, ibid. (October 1918), (October and November 1919); also *Arbeider-kvinnen* (June 1924) extensively on women and the fight against strike breakers, on support for striking husbands, (October 1924), (December 1924), on fund-raising to support conscienscious objectors, (November 1928).

22. For an overall history of the period, see Kjeldstadli, "Et splittet folk," and Edvard Bull, "Klassenkamp og fellesskap 1920-1945," in *Norges historie*, ed. Knut Mykland (Oslo, 1979).

23. Tore Pryser, "Klassen og nasionen (1935-1946)," in *Arbeiderbevegelsens historie i Norge*, vol. IV, eds. Arne Kokkvoll et al. (Oslo, 1988), pp. 64 and 125.

24. Torild Skard (ed.), *"Kvinnekupp" i kommunene* (Oslo, 1979), 133, and, *Utvalgt til stortinget* (Oslo, 1980), p. 18. The Conservative party had one woman elected in 1921, two in 1930, one in 1933.

25. Pryser, *Klassen og*, pp. 130-36.

26. See for instance Rachel Grepp in *Arbeider-kvinden*, (January and February 1923).

27. Ibid., (March 1923).

28. Ibid., (spring 1923).

29. Biographical articles in Sigrid Syvertsen and Thina Thorleifsen, *Kvinner i strid* (Oslo, 1960) and in *Pax leksikon* (Oslo, 1979-1981).

30. Harriet Clayhills. *Kjerringer mot strømmen. Arbeiderhusmødrenes organisering og kamp i 20- og 30-åra* (Oslo, 1978), pp. 24-43. Although few sources are left of these organizations, Clayhills has combined the written material with interviews to give an enthusiastic account of the communist Housewives Organizations.

31. Ljones, *Female Labour*, pp. 23 and 27. Census reports ranged people according to what they themselves indicated to be their main source of livelihood. Kari Skrede, "Gifte kviner i arbeidslivet," in *Det norske samfunn*, eds. Lars Allden et al. (Oslo, 1986), pp. 145-68.

32. Where no other information is given, the following builds on Ida Blom, *Barnebegrensning – synd eller sunn fornuft?* (Bergen, 1980), pp. 155-251. For an analysis of the regional differences, motivations, and means in Norwegian family planning, see Sølvi Sogner et al., *Fra stua full til tobarns kull* (Oslo, 1984).

33. Katti Anker Møller never joined the NLP, but her policies were very close to those of the socialist women's movement. She was, however, sometimes criticized by socialist women for provoking discord between socialist women and men. Her sister, Ella Anker, and her daughter, Tove Mohr, were active members of the NLP. Blom, "Voluntary Motherhood," pp. 21-39.

34. *Kvinden* (September 1919).

35. Alva and Gunnar Myrdal, *Kris i befolkningsfrågan* (Stockholm, 1934).

36. See Renée Frangeur's chapter on Sweden in this volume and Ann-Sofie Kälvemark, *More Children of Better Quality? Aspects of Swedish Population Policy in the 1930's* (Uppsala, 1980).

37. Blom, *Barnebegrensning*, pp. 232-33.

38. Quoted in Blom, *Barnebegrensning*, p. 235. The original letters are preserved in the archives of the Department of Justice, Oslo.

39. Synnøve Didriksen, "Steriliseringsloven av 1934-et ledd i norsk befolkningspolitikk" (M.A. thesis, Bergen, 1995).

40. Øyvind Bjørnson and Inger Elisabeth Haavet, *Langsomt ble landet et velferdssamfunn. Trygdens historie 1894-1994* (Oslo, 1994), chaps. 6, esp. pp. 120-22.

41. Ida Blom, "Widowhood: From the Poor Law Society to the Welfare Society: The Case of Norway, 1875-1964," *Journal of Women's History* (fall 1992).

42. Ida Blom, *"Den haarde Dyst" – Fødsler og fødselshjelp gjennom 150 år* (Oslo, 1988), pp. 158-79.

43. For detailed discussions of this theme, see Bjørnson and Haavet, *Langsomt ble*, pp. 203-27; Anne-Lise Seip and Hilde Ibsen, "Family welfare, which policy ? Norway's road to child allowance" in *Maternity and Gender Policies*, pp. 40-60; Blom, "Voluntary Motherhood," pp. 21-39.

44. Elisabeth Lønnå, Stolthet og Kuinnekamp (Oslo 1996), chaps. 7-9 and Ida Blom, "Margarete Bonnevie – skisse av et liv," in *Portretter fra norsk historie*, eds. Jorunn Bjørgum et al. (Oslo 1993), pp. 161-84.

45. Bjørnson and Haavet, *Langsomt ble*, p. 219.

46. Maurseth, *Gjennom kriser*, pp. 51 and 56; Pryser, *Klassen og*, p. 125.

47. Pryser, *Klassen og*, pp. 136-41; Linda Kvinge, "Hushjelpene i norske byer 1930-1948" (M.A. thesis, University of Bergen, 1983).

48. For a full account of this question, see Elisabeth Lønnå, "LO, DNA og striden om gifte kvinner i arbeidslivet" in Blom and Hagemann, pp. 151-76 and Pryser, *Klassen og*, pp. 130-36.

49. Tore Pryser, "Johanne Reutz – fra arbeiderbevegelsen til fredsbevegelsen," in *Portretter fra norsk historie*, eds. Jorunn Bjørgum et al. (Oslo, 1993), pp. 185-202.

50. Magnus Bratten, *Den unge slekt – Med Fram-kamerater gjennom 25 år* (Oslo, 1960), pp. 19-72.

51. *Barnebladet* (October-November 1933); *Fram-kameraten* 4 and 5 (1938); *Aarsberetning* (1922); *De kommunistiske barnelag i Kristiania* (brochure in the archives of the Labor Movement, Oslo): 5-7, 24.

52. *Fram-kameraten* (November, 1934); (January 1935); (May, 1936); (May, 1937); (January, 1938); *Barnebladet* 2 (1932).

53. Article on the NLP Youth Organization in *Pax-leksikon* (Oslo 1978).

54. Article on The Workers' Sports Organization (AIF) in ibid; Marie Herigstad Strømman, "Kjønn og organisert idrett i Norge c. 1860-1970. Noen hovedlinjer" (M.A. thesis, University of Bergen, 1994).

55. Bjørn Sørenssen, "Arbeiderfilmen i Norge 1928-1940," *Tidskrift for arbeiderbevegelsens historie* 1 (1982): 105-30.

56. Trygve Bull, *Mot dag og Erling Falk* (Oslo, 1955), pp. 261-70.

57. Biographical articles in *Pax leksikon*.

58. *Kvinden* (January, 1918).

59. Ibid.; *Arbeider-kvinnen* (September, 1923 and February, 1924); Max Hodan in ibid. (1937); also nos. 9-10 (1938) and no. 1 (1939).

60. Ibid., no.10 (1939) and nos. 2 and 3 (1940).

61. Ibid., nos. 3 and 4 (1940).

62. Ibid., (October, 1936).

63. Ibid., (October, 1936) and (June, 1938).

64. Ibid., (December, 1936); nos. 7, 9, 11, 12 (1937); nos. 2, 6 (1938); no. 2 (1939).

65. Arne Kokkvoll, "Hovedtrekk i arbeiderbevegelsens kulturstrev," *Tidskrift for arbeiderbevegelsens historie*, 1982:1, 5-32.

66. *Arbeider-kvinnen* (December, 1923). See also Martha Tynœs, *Kvinnen* (July, 1918), and *Arbeider-kvinnen* (February, 1937).

67. *Arbeider-kvinnen* (February, 1938). See also *Kvinden* (May- July, 1918).

68. Sigrid Syvertsen in *Arbeider-kvinnen* (February, 1937).

69. Ibid., (November, 1923).

70. *Kvinden*, (August, 1919).

71. *The Worker's Magazine*, a popular entertainment monthly, gives the same impression, although it offered advice to women in a special column, under the heading "The Sewing Club Chatterbox." See *Arbeidermagasinet* 2-5 (1930).

72. "Tillidsmandens hustru," *Arbeider-kvinnen* (September, 1923); Eugene Olaussen in ibid. (June, 1928).

73. Fernanda Nissen in *Kvinden* (August, 1919).

74. Anna Nœss in ibid. (July, 1919).

75. The Liberal party voiced exactly the same perception of gender. Ida Blom, "En liten ondskap?" in *Venstres hundre år*, eds. Ottar Grepstad and Jostein Nerbøvik (Oslo, 1984), pp. 45-61.

76. Martha Tynœs in *Kvinden* (July, 1918) and Aase Lionœs in *Arbeider-kvinnen*, 1940:1.

Chapter 13

Socialist Feminists and Feminist Socialists in Denmark 1920-1940

Hilda Romer Christensen

I always say that Social Democratic men have been very reactionary. But I under-stand why. Because all these men, who had seen their mothers standing worn out at the wash-tub, had only one thought: my wife ought not to work. On the face of it, it was a noble ideal, but it did not further the emancipation of women.[1,2]

This was how Nina Andersen, one of the few prominent female Social Democratic politicians of the interwar period, summarized the pre-vailing attitude of the men in her party towards women's emancipation. Her judgment was sound even if her explanation did not go far enough. Danish Social Democratic leaders, like their trade union comrades, were willing to accept women into their ranks but were opposed to any sepa-rate organization or distinct women's agenda. As Andersen implies, they held the conventional view that women's place was in the home, and they had no intention of sharing political power with them. At the same time, they feared the divisive impact of gender-based factionalism in the party. Throughout the period, they insisted that women fit into existing party structures and accept existing (male) party leadership. But Danish Social Democratic women, like so many of their comrades in other parts of Europe, refused to abide by these limitations. With remarkable tenac-ity, they struggled for female autonomy inside the party and for reforms to secure the well-being and equality of Danish women.

This pattern of gender relations was established early in the party's history. Two years before its formal foundation in 1878, the party had launched the Gimle program, which in tone and content strongly favored gender equality. The program addressed "men and women (male and female citizens)" and referred to "the equality of all human beings in spite of gender difference." It explicitly supported women's suffrage and in this sense was more progressive than its German model, the Gotha Program. Yet, during the next three decades, the party's political practice departed significantly from the inclusive rhetoric of the Gimle program. Working women found they had to fight male workers for the right to work and unionize. On the issue of women's suffrage, the Social Democrats adhered to the Gimle promise when they joined the liberal parties as sponsors of the key measure in the Danish parliament, but their main objective was to broaden the democratic base, not to emancipate women. Party leaders consistently refused to allow socialist women to have their own suffrage organization. When Social Democratic women ignored this prohibition and formed the Social Democratic Women's Suffrage Association in 1907, the party refused to recognize the new association as an affiliate.

In the prewar decade, Danish Social Democratic women leaders began their struggle to build a distinct women's organization, an initiative that was to be the central issue in the gender battles of the interwar years. In Copenhagen in 1908, they established the Social Democratic Women's Association, (SDWA) as an offshoot of the suffrage group. Socialist women in Aarhus and Aalborg soon followed their example. Some of these early women's groups survived into the 1920s and provided the foundation for the next organizing effort. Party leaders again refused to allow these early, independent associations membership or branch status. They published a statement in 1908 declaring that there could be only one workers' movement, and therefore there was "no space for a specific women's movement or a separate women's party among working women."[3] As an inducement to women to accept their terms, and recognizing that women were paid less than men, they reduced their membership fees. Whether by intention or not, the gesture merely confirmed women's second-class membership status.

In the prewar suffrage campaign another pattern emerged that was to shape the relationship between Danish socialists and women's issues in the interwar decades. To secure the female vote, Social Democratic women had worked in close cooperation with organized Danish feminists, most of whom were middle-class liberals. Such cooperation was not unusual; Swedish, Norwegian, Dutch, and British socialist women did much the same in the prewar decades. What distinguished Danish Social-Democratic women was their resumption of the alliance in the 1930s. It could be argued that this cross-class cooperation was in keeping with the mainstream party's move toward a politics of class compromise and consensus. Also, only a minority of Social Democratic women, most of them middle-class and feminist in outlook, formed these organizational ties to the women's movement. Nonetheless, the move has to be seen as a response to years of frustration with the male leadership's continued resistance to women's organization and female-specific reforms.

Two developments of the interwar years sustained the uneasy gender relations among Social Democrats and the ties between socialism and feminism in Denmark. First, the Danish Social Democratic Party made a major political shift in this period. The reformist line already introduced in the prewar years was made into a moderate reform strategy. After 1920, it became democratic and centrist with the idea of attracting middle-class support. Such an ideological switch inevitably created confusion over class and party loyalties. Left-wing socialists, including many working women, felt betrayed. Social Democratic leaders were more concerned than ever about party fragmentation and more resistant to women's autonomy. In this unsympathetic environment, women leaders had to adjust their strategies and programs to meet the needs of a diverse female constituency.

The second distinctive change was an acceleration of urbanization and industrial growth that disrupted the traditional gender relations of an essentially agricultural society. Danish women were often the first to leave their farms in the 1920s and go to the towns to work as servants or in the new textile, leather, and shoe industries. With more women engaged in manufacture and living away from home, men felt they had reason to fear female competition in the labor market and a loss of patriarchal authority. As Danish working-class women became less homogeneous, they had difficulty in articulating a common agenda. The needs and interests of urban working women and their families differed in important areas from those of farm families. Social Democratic women were divided over how best to respond to these changes, especially during the Depression and with little or no support from their party. The cultural changes associated with the "new woman" only added fuel to the gender tension and internal divisions among Social Democrats and women reformers.

Denmark's distinctive struggles should not obscure the commonalities of its experience with that of other northwestern European nations. Women in Denmark won the municipal vote in 1908 and the parliamentary vote in 1915 encouraged by the suffrage success of women in Finland and Norway a few years before. They struggled with some of the same organizational problems as women socialists in many other countries. Were they better off as socialists and reformers working inside male-controlled parties or on their own? Should class loyalty take precedence over their special needs as women when the two were in conflict?

Their reform agendas contained many of the same demands as socialist women almost everywhere in this period – birth control, safe and healthy motherhood, the care and education of young children. They did not escape the economic and social problems generated by the Depression nor those raised by an emerging mass culture with its new images of women. Finally, although their national circumstances differed, they were engaged in the same ambiguous struggle with their male comrades for partnership on the one hand and separate space for a distinctly female contribution on the other.

Social Democratic Politics and Women in Denmark

In the immediate postwar years, Danish Social Democratic women avoided the contentious issue of separate organization and focused their efforts on proving their commitment to socialism within the party structure. An incident following the women's suffrage grant in 1915 is evidence of this desire for socialist comradeship. While prominent women's associations joined in a victory parade before King Christian X, socialist women stayed away, preferring to celebrate with members of their party. From that year until the late 1920s, Social Democratic women were active in a wide range of political and social causes from municipal socialism to international peace, without the support of a strong women's organization inside or outside the party.

The Danish labor movement was at its most militant in the postwar period. Revolutions in Russia and Germany galvanized Danish workers, and they embarked on a wave of strikes and street protests. Socialist militancy found practical expression in a dozen or more "red towns," which served as models of municipal socialism. These were towns where elected Social Democratic councils experimented with the principles of universal social welfare and redistributive taxation to improve working-class health and living standards. They modernized or rebuilt schools and hospitals and made them free and open to all, regardless of income. They built tax subsidized housing, libraries, parks, and other civic amenities. Although Danish municipal socialism did not have the same comprehensive quality as that in red Vienna or some Norwegian towns, it demonstrated all the leading principles that were embodied in the Danish Welfare State after 1945.[4]

A few of the elected Social Democratic councillors in the "red towns" were women, and a handful of them went on to win election to the Danish parliament. These pioneers gained their early political experience in the female trade unions founded before the war when male-controlled unions refused to represent women workers. Most had been active in the suffrage struggle and had ties with middle-class feminist organizations. As soon as they were legally able to do so, they ran for political office. Henriette Crone is a good example. From 1906 to 1933, she was the president of the female printers' union. She was elected a member of the Copenhagen City Council in 1909, one of the first women representatives. From 1920 to 1933, she was a member of the Second Chamber of the Danish Parliament and a prominent member of the party executive. She was a keen participant in international socialist organizations and during the 1920s, represented Denmark on several international boards.

Andrea Brochman was another member of this remarkable first generation. She became a member of the Copenhagen City council in 1917 after many years presiding over the Women Tailors' Union, which sponsored a number of social democratic women leaders in these years. She had been a founding member of the Social Democratic Women's Association in Copenhagen in 1908 and retained an honorary membership in the Danish Women's Society, the largest feminist organization. Elected a member of the Second Chamber in 1926, she served until 1940.[5]

In the postwar years, radical men and women found common ground in their demands for international peace and cooperation and better working and living conditions for the working class. Issues tended to be divided along traditional gender lines, but there was a prevailing sense of shared goals. With women's support, male workers fought successfully for the eight-hour day and wage increases. Women had men's support in their campaign for sufficient and affordable food. In 1918, a crowd of women led by a new radical group, the Working Women's Housewives' Guild, demonstrated in front of Parliament demanding fair prices, household necessities, and "bread and butter."[6] The rank and file of both sexes vehemently opposed any continuation of the wartime truce with the bourgeois parties, and leadership efforts to centralize and bureaucratize the trade unions.

By the end of 1920, the postwar boom had turned into a recession and hopes for a socialist transformation faded. The mood of working people became defensive as they faced rising unemployment and wage and benefit cuts. In 1921, a fourth of the industrial work force, 40,000 workers, was out of work. Militant socialists in "Red towns" lost popular support. Social Democratic party leaders, never enthusiastic revolutionaries, were able to argue that the party's future would now depend upon electoral success and that to achieve it, they would have to appeal to a broader section of the population than the relatively small, industrial working class. They had in mind the lower middle class of small holders, shopkeepers, and white-collar workers. The revised party platforms of 1923 and 1934 confirmed this shift from a class party to a people's party with a repudiation of class struggle and revolution. Instead of trying to destroy capitalism, the party would regulate it; in place of social transformation, the party promised modest reform initiatives. After their first brief period in office between 1924 and 1926, they formed a coalition in 1929 with the small Social-Liberal party (*Det radikale Venstre*) which lasted until 1940.

The political shift had some initial benefits for the women's cause. More middle-class women were attracted to the party and the 1924 social democratic government had the distinction of being the first in Europe (outside the Soviet Union) to have a woman in a ministerial position. Historian Nina Bang became Minister of Education, and although she had little sympathy with feminism or party women's desire for autonomy, she was symbolic of women's arrival in national politics. Their party's move towards a centrist, liberal position also encouraged social democratic women to expect an extension of women's civil and economic equality. In the aftermath of the war, the Social-Liberal government had made Denmark the first European country to give women civil servants equal pay with men. A follow-up law in 1921 guaranteed their equal access to all jobs in the public sector.[7] Finally, in 1925, the Social Democratic government passed a marriage law that gave wives equal rights with their husbands to property and earned income, equal responsibility for debt, and easier access to divorce. For a decade or more, women from the feminist Danish Women's Society had lobbied for changes in women's legal status in marriage. The law, which was a result of this in cooperation with the efforts of the Commission on Family Law, was carried and supported by the Social Democrats.[8]

However, the Social Democratic party quickly showed that it had no intention of changing its policy towards women members. The new organizational structure made no provision for women's separate associations or their welfare reform interests. A good indication of the male leadership's attitude was the Workers' Education Association (WEA), which was founded in 1924 to prepare socialists for their new responsibilities in local and national government. The WEA assumed that all socialists were male and offered no classes for women or courses in subjects of concern to them. The message was clear. Social democratic party machinery was made by and for men and would remain so regardless of any changes in political orientation. Danish social democratic women were disappointed but undeterred. In the late 1920s, they resumed the struggle to build their own organizations inside and outside the party.

The Social Democratic Women's Clubs

The renewed effort to create a special field of activity for women in the Social Democratic party began in 1927. The idea was to form women's clubs in association with local party branches. The driving force behind the women's clubs was Sylvia Pio, and her inspiration was Austria where the socialists supported women's groups and incorporated women's welfare issues into the party program. Pio brought the experience of a long and varied political career to her task. She was the daughter of the socialist pioneer Louis Pio, who emigrated to the United States in the 1870s. She had joined the Communist party for a short time in the early 1920s before finding her political home among the Social Democrats. In the first draft of the women's clubs' by-laws of 1929, she defined their goals as recruiting women and educating them in socialist theory and practice. The clubs would provide support to the constituency parties and cooperate with the WEA. She hoped that the clubs would give working-class women an opportunity to learn practical political skills such as how to set up a women's club, elect a chairperson, run meetings, and speak in public. She suggested that they might hold discussions on topics such as the psychology of love, pregnancy and child-rearing, the laws relating to marriage, modern housing, and community laundries. Although Sylvia Pio's ideas implied that the women's clubs would be, at least in part, a support system for the male-controlled party branches, she also proposed to set up a coordinating committee comprising a chairwoman, a member of the party executive, and delegates elected by the clubs, which would have the independent authority to decide on club programs and women's contribution to party policy.

In keeping with its established practice, the male leadership was initially hesitant and then hostile to Pio's project. Time and again, they found reasons to oppose the establishment of a woman's club. In one working-class constituency in Copenhagen, when women declared their intention of forming a club in 1928, male opposition was so vehement that the women had to back down. To overcome this opposition, social democratic women in Copenhagen tried a new strategy. In the next municipal election campaign, they demonstrated their solidarity with the party by working hard to get out the women voters. They offered to take care of the children while mothers went to the polls, and they called on unmarried women to remind them of their civic responsibility. This effort was to no avail; the male leadership reiterated its opposition to any separate women's organization, arguing that women could get their political education alongside men in the existing party structure. Nor did Pio's proposal for a coordinating committee get off the ground. When social democratic women in Copenhagen began to organize it in 1929, city party leaders declared that without official sanction from local and national party officials, the committee was illegal.

Determined to break down the party's resistance or to find ways around it, a core of activists in Copenhagen proceeded to set up, on an informal basis, the women's clubs coordinating committee that male party leaders had refused to sanction. Calling themselves the Women's Clubs' Network (WCN), they provided a vital center of communication for the fifteen beleaguered women's clubs that had successfully ignored leadership opposition.[9] They also kept in touch with the surviving sections of the prewar independent Social Democratic Women's Association. Acting on Pio's proposals, the WCN outlined a common agenda for party women, organizing sub-committees to discuss the social reforms they wanted the party to adopt. These included support for birth control clinics, holidays for housewives, and protection of women and children against sexual offenders. At the same time, they lobbied the national government to make old-age pensions the same for women as men and to change the electoral law so that women would have a realistic chance of being elected to the *Folketinget*, the first chamber of Parliament. Between 1918 and 1940, socialist women held only one seat in this chamber and between one and two in the *Landstinget*, the less powerful second chamber.[10]

With remarkable consistency, male leaders refused to give official status to the WCN or support its activities. Ironically, it was the feminist movement that indirectly forced them to pay more attention to their women members. In 1931, the Danish Women's Society (DWS) asked social democratic women to join them in a campaign to promote women in politics. They proposed setting up cross-party women's committees in the constituencies. When social democratic women began accepting the invitation, the party issued a strong warning against any cooperation with the DWS. Worried that the feminists might lure their women members and supporters away, however, the party hurried to offset its injunction with more positive action. Leaders encouraged the WEA to offer a series of lectures to women on subjects of specific interest to them. In light of this show of goodwill and their own organizing efforts, party women's hopes ran high for real progress at the 1931 Party Congress. Once again, they were disappointed. The long-awaited official endorsement of the Women's Clubs was only a grudging acceptance of their existence. Even this was so hedged about with warnings against any autonomous action as to make the concession empty and demeaning. Male leaders reminded the members of the fifteen clubs already in existence that they were not to organize any meetings or take any initiatives which were not sanctioned by (male) party officials.

The New Woman and Danish Social Democratic Youth

The tension between men and women in the interwar Social Democratic Party was over the gender distribution of power in a traditionally male area of responsibility. Similar tensions developed in all the Euro-pean countries where women had won the right to enter the male polit-ical domain following the grant of suffrage. Yet the political change was only part of a broader cultural movement, associated with the growth of consumerism and the mass media, which added to the confusion over appropriate gender roles. A range of influences, from sex reformers and social scientists to mass marketers and feminists, all contributed to the reshaping of women's image and public identity which became known as the "new woman".

As it was in France and Belgium, Victor Margueritte's book *La Garçonne* was the seminal work in identifying for Danes, the characteristics of the "new woman." The short-haired, cigarette-smoking garçonne, with her bright red lips and nails, her straight dress, silk stockings on highly visible legs, and fox fur slung nonchalantly around her neck, was a provocative and very disturbing female image. As well as evoking fears of social disin-tegration and decadence, she created anxiety about the blurring of sex and class differences. A secretary from the Young Women's Christian Association (YWCA) expressed a common reaction when she wrote: "It is striking how young, slim females with their bobbed hair and modern suits look like boys." She then pointed to the feminine appearance of men in frock coats, colored socks, rings, and bracelets and commented: "When men are not masculine any longer, and women not feminine, one is anxious about the future."

No one in the 1920s and 1930s could have been unaware of this media-driven, cultural phenomenon, but in the Danish Social Democra-tic party, the impact was greatest among the young members of the Youth Association (SDYA), founded in 1920. Social Democratic Party leaders generally ignored the subject, but the SDYA made an effort to tame the new woman and turn her into a good socialist comrade. The task of mak-ing free and equal comrades out of the young male and female members was not an easy one. Women were a permanent minority in the move-ment (never more than 25 percent of total membership throughout the period). At Nina Andersen's suggestion, the SDYA introduced special sections and sewing clubs at the end of the 1920s to attract more young women. Some male youth leaders expressed reservations about this gen-der separation, arguing that it was more progressive to have mixed gen-der meetings, and where this was the case, the men invariably dominated and women were intimidated into silence.

The SDYA took a lot of its ideas from its German counterpart. The two groups corresponded and leaders met each other at international conferences. In what was called the "cultural period" of the late 1920s, they emphasized the teaching of socialist values in a cultural context. They condemned "trashy" activities such as beer drinking and card playing, that had been common to most male socialist gatherings and wanted to replace them with expressions of "red culture" such as mandolin bands (as opposed to bourgeois brass bands) and socialist songs.

The adaptation of the new woman became part of this new socialist culture, and it initially took the form of a rejection of bourgeois "depravity" in favor of socialist comradeship and a puritanical sexual morality. Youth leaders denounced dancing, popular literature, and the custom of using socialist meetings as a hunting ground for romance. Their slogan might well have been "a clean mind in a clean body," the former requiring the banning of pornographic literature and the latter, healthy outdoor exercise. In 1936 to 1937 they joined a united front with bourgeois and confessional youth groups who all aspired to elevate young people's reading matter.[11]

In view of their rejection of the dangerous sexuality associated with the new woman, it is not surprising to find that the SDYA had a mixed reaction to the encouragement given by K.K. Steincke, a prominent Social Democrat, to the idea of comrade-unions. Steincke urged young men and women to live together without legal obligations until they had children. He agreed with sex reformers and eugenicists that medical examinations and sex counseling should be obligatory preconditions for these comrade unions, and he was convinced that such nonbinding arrangements would cut the divorce rate.[12] The Youth Association members seem to have found it safer to ignore the suggestion. Caja Rude, one of the few women who discussed the issue, argued that women needed the legal bonds of marriage to ensure the man's commitment to provide financial support. She also questioned the priority given to eroticism in the comrade-union, because it threatened the instinct of motherhood.[13]

This glimpse of opinions within the youth movement and the party shows the confusion and varied reactions that the new woman raised among socialists. The ideal of the liberated female comrade living in a free and equal association with her male counterpart was difficult to reconcile with the older socialist ideal of the married working-class housewife, dependent on her husband's support and content to make him a comfortable home and raise good socialist children. There was, however, never much doubt that the latter vision would prevail among the majority of Danish social democrats, women as well as men. Nonetheless, fears of the former remained, adding to the sense of confusion over gender roles in the party.

Women in the Labor Force – Organization and Agendas

The new woman culture was by no means the most critical cause of gender tension in the interwar Danish Social Democratic party. More dis-

ruptive were the evident changes taking place in women's social and economic roles. Although Denmark remained an agricultural country
throughout the interwar years, for the first time in its history, more than
half the population lived in towns – 65 percent by the end of the 1930s.
Women were often the pioneers in the move from the countryside, as
they tried to find jobs in domestic service and manufacturing. Many Danish towns and cities had a female surplus, so that in a sense, they were
female metropolises. Although men retained their dominance in all the
major industries and in political life, they may well have felt that these
social changes affected their patriarchal authority in the home.

The movement of women into the industrial labor market, in a
period of economic upheaval and unemployment, was easily seen by
men as a threat to their jobs, wages, and authority. Since the beginning
of Danish industrialization the number of wage-earning women made
up a considerable part, which rose steadily throughout the interwar
decades. Although the overall increase was only 3 percent – women
were 38.5 percent of the total labor force in 1920 and 41.2 percent in
1940 – there were significant changes in the structure of the female
labor force. Women increased their participation in manufacturing
industries by 20 percent. They were heavily represented in the new textile, leather, and shoe industries, which survived the Depression of the
1930s better than most because they had state protection through
import control. By 1940, there were 100,000 women in the industrial
labor force as compared to 60,000 in 1925. Despite this overall growth,
women represented only about 16 percent of all workers in manufacturing industry in 1930.[14]

Another significant structural change affecting traditional gender
roles was the growth of married women's employment outside the home.
Their numbers more than doubled, from approximately 45,000 in 1921
to over 90,000 in 1940. Of these, close to half were middle-class, 16 percent of all married women as opposed to 18 percent from the working
class. Middle-class married women often found secretarial or administrative work in a branch of the civil service or in the liberal professions.
By 1940 over 5 percent of the total female workforce were occupied in
schools and hospitals, post and telegraph offices, and the expanding
social services.[15]

The growing ranks of women in the workforce raised the issue of
women's access to another conventionally male institution – trade
unions. That many were eager to join is clear from the high percentage,
65 percent, of union members among those employed in registered industries, which were the larger, male-dominated trades represented on the
national Trade Union Council.[16] But the majority of women worked in
unregistered, nonunionized trades, in small workshops, laundries, domes-

tic service, on the farms, or as part-time and seasonal workers. They were unskilled, working alone or in small groups for thousands of employers, and their hold on the job market was tenuous. The female Union of Unskilled Women Workers (UUWW), formed in 1901, made gallant efforts to organize and represent these workers throughout the interwar period. Because of their weak bargaining position, the union's leaders, most of them social democratic women, invariably adopted a defensive strategy, struggling to hold the line on wages and working conditions. They relied on the Trade Union Council's collective bargaining and often found they had no choice but to accept salary cuts when the Council's bargaining failed. The general union of unskilled male workers, their counterpart, fought much more tenaciously for higher wages and with greater success. The UUWW did not demand equal pay and probably would not have achieved it if they had. In 1935, women's wages were still less than two-thirds of those earned by men.[17]

In 1925, a small group of radical women workers in the iron industry, disappointed with what they saw as the weak and conciliatory stance of the UUWW's social democratic leaders, formed the Working Women's Association (WWA). They published a journal edited by Marie Nielsen, a radical socialist. One of Nielsen's comments shows the militancy of the WWA compared with the older organization: "What sense does it make to be always following in the footsteps of the men's unions … when we are paid less than two-thirds of men's wages and still do work in the factories that is just as difficult and demanding as the work they do?"[18] The WWA supported a strike of women workers in the iron industry in 1930. The strike radicalized the rhetoric, and leaders demanded equal pay for equal work, a seven hour workday, with rests every hour for those on the assembly lines, and maternity leave.[19]

The Working Women's Association remained a much smaller organization in terms of membership than the Union of Unskilled Working Women. While the Union had 11,000 members in the 1920s, the WWA could boast a mere 400. But its influence far outweighed its size. It was more uncompromising than the UUWW in demanding radical reforms that would improve the lives of working-class women in the home as well as in the labor force. It conducted campaigns for sexual counseling, birth control, and abortion, which attracted both young wage-earning women and married women at home. The program was not dissimilar to that pursued by the social democratic women's clubs in the 1930s, but while the latter were seeking to find policies acceptable to a broader constituency of women, including the middle class, the WWA continued to identify itself as a radical working-class women's organization and lobbied vigorously for reforms strictly in their interests.

The Debate over Protective Legislation

The WWA swam against the tide of the mainstream social democratic women's movement in another area. It supported some measures of protective legislation for women workers, which several other female unions and social democratic women, did not. The issue was a contentious one throughout the interwar period. Danish socialists endorsed the international resolutions on sex-based protective labor legislation and the prohibition of night work for women passed at Bern in 1906 and at the International Labor Organization (ILO) meeting in 1919. Yet Denmark was one of the few countries represented at these conventions, which failed to follow up their initial endorsement with legislation. In part, this was due to the political upheavals in the Social Democratic party, and its limited access to political power in the 1920s, but strong opposition from the middle-class feminist movement and certain of the women's trade unions also weakened support for the measure.

The women's unions who joined the feminists in opposing sex-based protective legislation were those like the printers, whose members were in direct competition with men in the same industry. Prohibition of night work for women would only weaken their position and lead to a loss of jobs. Instead of discriminatory legislation, they argued for better pay, safer working conditions, and strong unions for men as well as women. The preference for equality over special treatment was a powerful current among Danish female union leaders in the 1920s. The Danish historian Anna-Birte Ravn has recently pointed out that "women workers, despite the obvious gender difference, were not seen as having special interests that distinguished them from men in the workplace." The use of the equal rights argument in the debate over protective legislation was part of a broader tradition in Denmark that rejected advocacy of women's special needs.[20]

The subject of heated debate among social democratic and trade union women in the 1920s, protective legislation gave way to the struggle over married women's right to work in the 1930s. When a bill prohibiting night work for women was finally introduced in 1938 in response to the findings of a parliamentary committee, it failed to pass. In their opposition to the bill, organized women found themselves uncomfortably allied with employers and patriotic Danes who objected to bowing to international pressure. No doubt the limited numbers of women workers involved (only about 3,500 to 4,000 women worked at night, including both full-time and part-time) contributed to the different history of sex-based protective legislation in Denmark compared to that in more heavily industrialized countries.[21]

Socialist Feminists or Feminist Socialists?

Social democratic women's struggle to organize their own women's clubs changed direction in the 1930s. In part, this was because the second generation of party women was rather different from the first. The pioneers had generally come from the working-class. The second generation included more women from the middle class and their origins were more diverse. Some were feminists from the Danish Women's Society, and some were teachers or office workers with no previous political experience. There were several reasons for this change. On the one hand, it reflected the broader recruitment policies of the party which were in full swing by the 1930s. On the other, worsening social conditions during the Depression years and the growth of state welfare convinced many socially conscious middle-class women that the Social Democrats were the most likely to promote the interests of poor women and their children.

In the interwar period, Denmark was still an agricultural country supplying the larger industrial nations, Britain and Germany in particular, with dairy and grain products. As a result, it was severely damaged by the collapse of the American stock market in 1929. By 1932, the unemployment rate was 33 percent for men and 20 percent for women where it stayed for the rest of the decade. The Social Democratic/Social Liberal government turned to Keynesian economics to meet the crisis, adopting a planned economy involving state intervention and public investment. In 1933 the Social Democrats formed a major political compromise, the "Kanslergade-compromise," with the Social-Liberals and the Liberal Agrarian party, that offered state subsidies and tax relief to hard-pressed farmers and passed a comprehensive social security measure. Based on the principle of national entitlement rather than local charity, the Social Reform Act guaranteed old-age, accident and disability pensions, health insurance, unemployment benefits, and child care subsidies. It also introduced a public works program for the unemployed and subsidized public housing.[22] The act made Denmark the most generous of all the Scandinavian countries in tax-funded allowances.[23] Danish women certainly benefitted from the Social Reform act, but their benefits and pensions were consistently less than men's and the reforms that feminists and Social Democratic women wanted in the areas of health and child care received only limited attention and inadequate funding.[24]

Many of the middle-class women who joined the Social Democratic party in the early 1930s did so in the expectation of persuading the party to increase state protection for those whom they saw as the worst victims of the depression – working and lower-middle-class women and their children. When they experienced party leaders' resistance to their women-centered reforms, and hostility to their separate organization, they turned to organized feminists. The socialist-feminist alliance they forged was unique in Europe. Not only was there a cross membership between the leading feminist society and social democratic women, but representatives from each organization came to hold high office in the other. For example, Edel Saunte, a prominent social democrat and lawyer, won election as chair of the Danish Women's Society in 1936. Much to the surprise of female party members, male leaders gave the election their blessing, seeing it as a means to increase support among middle-class women. The irony of the party opposing independent activity among its own women members but supporting those who held high office in a middle-class and feminist organization did not escape rank-and-file party women. They were quick to argue that they ought to have an association of their own where they could discuss their interests without being forced to do so with bourgeois women.[25]

For women leaders and many middle-class party women the feminist movement became a substitute for a strong and independent social democratic women's organization. They were more attracted to the feminist agenda than the postwar generation had been. They wanted to extend the Social Democratic party program to include the demands and needs of working women, but they also aimed at creating a more socially oriented feminism. In other words, they wanted to make socialism more feminist and feminism more socialist, and they were convinced that there was enough political common ground between the two to make it work. Social democratic and social liberal women agreed on such vital issues as married women's right to work and the need for reform in the area of birth control. They came to feel that their different political affiliations were of less importance than their shared experience of belonging to a small band of elite women who were politically active at the national level.

Working-class rank-and-file women were outside this charmed circle and continued to look upon feminists as 'bourgeois.' Not even Nina Andersen, then one of the most prominent social democratic women, could overcome their suspicions. An enthusiastic proponent of the alliance, she tried to build closer cooperation between the Union of Unskilled Women Workers and the feminists, but at the meeting she arranged between them, the chairwoman of the union, Fanny Jensen, sat stone-faced and made it clear that "she simply did not want to co-operate."[26] For Jensen and other union-based social democratic women, class differences had not become a thing of the past. They retained the traditional socialist view of a society divided by class into "them" and "us" and they could see no reason to make allies out of bourgeois feminists merely because they agreed with them on the issues of married women's right to work and reproductive rights.

The 1930s alliance between the elite group of social democratic women and the Danish Women's Society (DWS), while it alienated the more class-conscious urban working-class women, brought some significant advantages. It gave socialist women a louder political voice and a larger female constituency. Because it was independent of any party, the DWS had developed its own network of political connections and was an effective lobbyist, (e.g., in the defense of married women's right to work). Politically, however, the alliance pushed social democratic women onto a narrow centrist ledge between right and left-wing women's organizations. The social disruption and class tension associated with the Depression encouraged both lower-middle-class liberals and conservatives, and left-radicals to organize women's groups, and these cut away at the alliance's cross-class feminist membership and agenda.

On one hand, liberal and conservative lower-middle-class women joined the housewives' guilds, where they were offered validation for women's traditional roles and condemnation of birth control, abortion, and married women's work outside the home. At the other extreme, the Working Women's Association (WWA) introduced their radical agenda. They demanded gender equality in civil rights, the labor market, and the home as an integrated part of a socialist ideology. The WWA enjoyed some initial success, its numbers grew and its policy of petitioning local and central authorities in the interest of women workers brought some positive results. In the early 1930s, however, the WWA lost momentum and membership due to their loss of independence. From a broad based left-winged association, the WWA developed into a close affiliate of the Communist Party, which after 1933 did not support independent women's associations.[27]

Social democratic women had to find a middle path between the housewives' guilds and the WWA. They chose to reject socialist radicalism and offer an alternative to the guilds by maintaining their alliance with social liberal feminists. In electoral terms, the choice proved to be sound. The Social Democratic/Social Liberal strategy of class compromise combined with a policy of state intervention in the economy was a success with the electorate, even though it sacrificed workers' standard of living and left them to cope with high unemployment. The SDP received 46 percent of the vote in 1935, and in that year it endorsed the women's clubs. At long last, the party consulted with the Women's Clubs Network (WCN) and established a coordinating committee between the party and the women's clubs. It was based in Copenhagen only and it was to have five members appointed by the party executive, five chairmen from the local constituencies, and five women from the women's clubs.

The concession still fell short of women's demands. Party leaders would not agree to a nationwide extension of the women's clubs, nor would they allocate any resources for travel or recruitment. They rejected a series of WCN proposals citing bureaucratic obstacles or giving no reason whatsoever. For example, in 1936, they refused to provide a list of women's groups outside Copenhagen that might be interested in joining the club network; in 1937, they turned down a request for a second Danish representative on the women's committee of the Socialist International and for a social democratic women's journal similar to the Swedish *Morgonbris*.[28]

With considerable imagination, leading women chose a new form of self-assertion. They published a satirical newspaper in 1936 called *The Woman and the Home* and used it to attack male attitudes. In one article, a social democratic woman interviewed another as if she were a political candidate. She asked: "Do you wish to abolish men?" "Yes, absolutely," was the reply, "because in any well-ordered and profitable society, one has to use the cheapest means of production and men are too expensive. They require higher pensions in case of disability or old age and they also eat more than women. Even for reproductive purposes, we could certainly manage with fewer than we have now." In another imaginary interview, a female party member questioned the chairman of an urban working-class constituency containing a number of high-rise apartment buildings. "Is the participation of women members valuable in your constituency?" she asks. "Not at all," replies the chairman, "women have been useful only because they were good at climbing stairs to get out the vote. Now that elevators are being installed in these buildings, women will slowly be squeezed out of political life."[29] With this ironic acknowledgment of the sorry state of gender relations in their party, social democratic women leaders turned their attention to the critical issues raised by the economic crisis of the 1930s – protecting married women's right to work and "voluntary motherhood" through birth control.

The Fight for Married Women's Right to Work

In Denmark as in many other European states, mass unemployment brought on by the Depression triggered an attack on married women's right to hold jobs while male "family providers" were out of work. The public debate became so heated that organized women called it a smear campaign against all married women workers without regard to their circumstances. Dismissals of married women in the civil service, teaching, and the private sector were common, and much to the astonishment and anger of socialist women, several social democratic municipal authorities followed the trend. In Aarhus, for example, the municipal council decided in 1932 to discharge women employees as soon as they married. The council also passed a resolution stating that it would no longer employ married couples and in 1933 fired six cleaning women working at the local schools who were married to other public servants. It stated that it would replace them with widows who would otherwise be dependent on social security and a burden on local tax payers. When the Union of Unskilled Women Workers took the Aarhus Council to the court of arbitration, they lost their case.[30]

Social democratic women vehemently protested against using marriage as a reason for firing women. They appealed to the male leadership to denounce the practice, arguing that otherwise their female constituents would label the Social Democratic party anti-women. The appeal to electoral interest was effective. In 1933, the party executive announced that any restriction on married women's right to work was inconsistent with socialist values. In 1934, they warned local authorities against further discriminatory actions that would give credibility to the impression that "our party is against women with gainful employment and their right to equal opportunity in the labor market."[31]

Social democratic women did not leave the matter there. Nina Andersen took the opportunity to point out that the campaign against married women's work might easily develop into a threat to all women's right to work in paid employment outside the home. In an influential article from 1934, she stressed the potential of women's paid work to emancipate men as well as women and help win the fight for socialism:

> Today's workers ought to learn that a woman's employment in an integrated, unionized work-place can rescue her from disgraceful working conditions … and adapt her to stand side by side with men in the fight for the transformation of society, for the emancipation of work.[32]

Nina Andersen was a member of the Danish Women's Society and another feminist group, the Open Door which lobbied for equal pay and the complete equality of women with men in access to all forms of employment. Social liberal and social democratic women members worked together to register discrimination and act against it locally and nationally.

The inclusion of married women's right to work in the Social Democratic statements was a victory for leading socialist women and their feminist allies. The party refused to endorse their additional demands for equal pay and access to all jobs, on the assumption that under normal circumstances, a woman's career was marriage, her work temporary.

Reforms Related to Sexuality and Reproduction

Birth control and abortion became major issues for Danish women reformers, socialist and feminist, during the Depression when it was evident that unemployment and immiseration were driving more women to seek illegal abortions and to ask for information about effective birth control. Socialist and feminist women's groups had already laid the foundation for reforms in these areas in the 1920s. In 1924, the Association for Sex Education was founded. Thit Jensen was its most prominent leader, and she campaigned across the country for "voluntary motherhood."

Among organized socialists, The Working Women's Association was the first to assert that birth control and abortion were essential to any socialist reform program. From the mid-1920s, they arranged meetings in a number of different cities to discuss sex education and birth control with working-class women. In 1929, the association petitioned the government to provide compulsory sex education in schools, allow legal advertising of birth control devices, and give its support to voluntary motherhood. Inspired by the Norwegian example, the association initiated a plan to set up sex counseling clinics in the local sick-benefit societies.

Not surprisingly, the government and the local authorities refused to have anything to do with these programs. So the WWA went its own way. The leaders joined forces with the famous doctor and sex-reform advocate, Jonathan Leunbach and the Danish section of the League for Sexual Reform to establish a sex counseling clinic in Copenhagen in 1932. The following year, they opened a second clinic in Esbjerg. In 1933, the Communist party introduced a bill on the association's behalf, containing the same measures for which they had petitioned the government in 1929 – sex education, birth control, and voluntary motherhood, but the bill was never discussed.[33]

Social democratic women began their campaigning in the early 1930s, following the WWA example and holding a series of local meetings which were well attended. As social conditions worsened in the Depression, the efforts finally achieved a response from the government, which appointed a *Pregnancy Commission* in 1932 to investigate pregnancy termination in abortion. The Commission's report in 1936 raised the hopes of socialist women reformers. It argued that abortions were not manifestations of moral depravity or a lack of social responsibility but acts of desperation arising from material circumstances and fear. The report also criticized the gap between the existing law on abortion and its enforcement. The few cases of illegal abortion that came to trial invariably resulted in acquittals. A majority of the commissioners recommended that abortion should be given in any case where there was a strong social indicator, which amounted to abortion on demand. They also recommended sex counseling services for women in general. The one social democratic woman on the Commission, Alvilda Andersen from the Union of Unskilled Women Workers, was among the majority supporting these changes in public policy on abortion.[34]

Unfortunately, when new legislation appeared, it fell far short of the recommendations in the majority report. Legislators, including the social democratic Minister of Justice, K.K. Steincke, substituted a medical reason for a social indicator and made no changes in the penalties for illegal abortion. The only reform measure that survived was the provision of sex counseling clinics. One reason for this outcome was the strong opposition to the proposed changes in abortion law from various religious groups. Another was the differences of opinion among social democrats, including women. Nina Anderson supported K.K. Steincke and warned against allowing liberal access to abortion. Explaining her reason for this position, she said, "Men are likely to abuse women if they know they have easy access to abortion."[35]

Anxiety about the falling birthrate was a third reason for the unwillingness of the Danish parliament to encourage the use of birth control or liberalize the abortion laws. The *Population Commission,* appointed by the social democratic minister K.K. Steincke in 1935, drew government and popular attention to the problem of declining births and suggested that women be encouraged to have more children and that the state play a role in ensuring their health and well-being. The Population Commission recommended some of the reforms suggested by Swedish sociologists Alva and Gunnar Myrdal in their extraordinarily influential study, *Crisis of Population* published in 1936. They included sex counseling, extended maternity leave, more kindergartens and state-subsidized housing. Overall the intent of the reforms was more qualitative than quantitative. Instead of offering cash incentives that rewarded couples for the number of children they produced, the emphasis was on improving the environment surrounding childbirth and family life.

Two successful programs resulted from the government's pro-natalism. The former private institution called Mother's Help was made into a nationwide network of state funded social institutions, which was to provide support for mothers – single and married, during and after pregnancy. The institutions were headed by professional women, who – through a committee had the power to advise abortion within the framework of the law. The second interactive was the institution of local health visitors who would check on new mothers, weigh babies, and give advice through the first year of the child's life.

The sex counseling clinics, which had won social democratic and government approval, never materialized. Instead, Mother's Help clinics were later allowed to offer sex counseling, but only to pregnant women – single or married. The government rejected the Communist party's bill for mothers' pensions, a predictable fate. The Social Reform of 1933 which mandated free midwifery services and a six week maternity leave for working women, went only part way towards meeting the International Labor Organization's 1919 recommendations. But the social welfare initiatives of the 1930s, aimed primarily at low income working-class women, were expanded after World War II to become part of the universal tax-funded welfare state.

Grass-Roots Politics: The Women's Clubs

The women's clubs for which social democratic women fought so long and hard spread out from Copenhagen to most of the larger Danish towns and cities in the 1930s. They generally attracted a membership of working-class housewives with their leaders drawn from the professional middle class. Wage-earning women with an interest in socialist politics were more likely to be active in trade unions. An anniversary pamphlet published in 1939 summarized the goals that women's clubs had pursued throughout the decade. "The aim of the women's clubs is to bring women together, educate them in the ideas of social democracy, and motivate them to become party activists."[36]

A look at the activities of one particular women's club in Copenhagen shows how seriously it took its responsibility for educating both members and women voters. The program for the early 1930s included study circles and lecture series with prominent speakers sometimes addressing large meetings which several clubs attended. The discussion subjects were political and serious-minded, clearly aimed at teaching women socialist history, culture, and ethics. The 1930 program titles were "The History of Social Democracy," "The Case for Disarmament," "The Working-Class Wife and Birth Control," and "Bringing up Socialist Children." Some clubs ran study circles in which the members were expected to prepare for their discussions by reading a text before the group met. In 1931, the subject in one such circle was "The Social Position of Women" using Bebel's *Women and Socialism*.[37]

One of the women's clubs in a Copenhagen constituency was responsible for a social reform measure of considerable and long-term significance. Under the leadership of progressive reformers outside the Social Democratic party and one of its own members, Viola Norlov, the club developed a new program for the education of the preschool child. They shaped their ideas on pedagogy for the young in their meetings and study groups. As social democrats, they wanted to offer a secular and socialist alternative to the prevailing Church-controlled parish kindergartens. Their efforts culminated in the formation in 1939 of the Association of Free Kindergartens which made state-subsidized education for the young children available at a national scale after 1945.[38]

By the mid-1930s, the women's clubs in Copenhagen clearly showed the influence of the party's emphasis on democratic principles and class conciliation. The Social Reform Act of 1933 stimulated discussion of the role of the state and the social welfare needs of the people. Instead of discussions on how to bring up socialist children, a common topic in the later period was "School Reform and Education in Democracy." Instead of teaching their members the principles of socialism, the clubs gave them lessons in citizenship. The rise of fascism in Germany served to reinforce the message of one prominent social democratic woman, Margrethe Host, that uneducated voters were a threat to democracy because they had no defense against emotional manipulation by demagogues. If enlightened women were essential to the preservation of democracy, then the women's clubs could claim that their activities represented the contribution of social democratic women to the fight against fascism.

In the provinces, the women's clubs had different interests and activities from those in Copenhagen. They were less likely to engage in theoretical discussions or have political lectures from visiting speakers. A local chairwoman in Roskilde spoke with some misgivings about the local club's first year:

> There was a surprisingly large attendance at two of the meetings and they were the ones devoted to home economics. Most of our members are married working-class women and they want to talk about issues relating to their homes and children … I personally dislike the idea of our women's club becoming a socialist housewife's guild! But we have attracted several new members with topics of this kind and next winter, the executive committee members have organized a knitting evening, where an expert will teach knitting stitches! What comes next, I wonder, cooking lessons?[39]

Towards the end of the 1930s, leading women on the coordinating committee began to recognize the importance of domestic issues and the need for the party to acknowledge the housewife's role in society. Nina Andersen, who had been one of the most eloquent advocates of women's emancipation through paid employment in the late 1920s, declared in 1937 that "… we ought not to forget that many women want us to fight for their right to work in the home and only there." Perhaps her change of heart had something to do with the housewives' guilds that were attracting thousands of women in these years but she must have known that a majority of social democratic women were housewives and mothers like those in Roskilde and deserved to have their concerns represented in the party. She and others encouraged the introduction of nutrition and domestic science as topics for study circles, although these official presentations tended to be based on science, not the housewife's experience. Typically a male physician, armed with slides or a film, visited the women's clubs to lecture on the latest scientific prescriptions for a sanitary environment and a healthy diet.

Social democratic women had come a long way from their postwar socialist militancy and even from their feminist program of support for married women's right to work and reproductive freedom. The concern with domesticity emphasized the role of the man as family breadwinner and the "respectable, small working-class home" which male party members had long held as the ideal. Women in the party now came to see that the stay-at-home housewife represented progress because her presence in the home meant better care for children. In addition, a return to the home seemed to be an immediate solution to working women's impossible double burden of wage work and family responsibility. But unlike their conservative and liberal sisters, social democratic women did not place the housewife on a pedestal. They continued to support the rights and interests of women who worked outside the home for wages, whether married or not.

Male social democrats, especially party leaders, were in the habit of deriding women's clubs as nothing more than chatting over coffee or playing charades. They gave scant recognition to the fact that the SDWC mobilized women often regarded as impossible to organize, many of them with limited education and even more limited material resources. They raised their political consciousness, educated them in areas both practical and theoretical, and gave them political skills. The outcome of this process is hard to calculate, but there is no doubt that educated citizens – especially women – become educators in their turn, and this intangible must be put on the scales to balance the charges of political ineffectiveness levied against the women's clubs.

Conclusions

In comparison with other Scandinavian countries, the Danish Social Democratic party was the most resistant to separate organization for its women members and the least supportive of a political program in the specific interest of women constituents. Although the party, alone or in coalition governments, passed legislation that increased women's civil rights and social welfare, the benefit to women was either an unintended consequence or a concession to electoral pressures. The Social Reform bill came into the first category, and women's legal rights in marriage in the second.

The evidence suggests two possible reasons for the Danish party's troubled gender relations. First, the increase in women's participation in what were considered to be male areas of responsibility – politics, of course, but also industrial labor and independent urban living – appeared to threaten patriarchal authority, despite the relatively small numbers of women involved. The popular image of the new woman added to this general anxiety over women's place, since Danish social democrats were unsuccessful in transforming her into a comrade-woman. Second, the Social Democratic party's shift to the political center alienated the left, women as well as men, and absorbed the party's energies in fighting elections, and building coalitions. Such a difficult environment made the leaders determined to prevent party splits, especially along gender lines.

Yet Denmark belongs with its Scandinavian neighbors to those countries where the social democrats made considerable progress towards a welfare state in the 1930s. The spur was the Depression which prompted the party in coalition with the Liberals to pass the Social Reform Act. This legislation provided for a full range of tax-funded and universal social welfare services, from child care subsidies to old age pensions and unemployment benefits. At the end of the 1930s, the Population Commission Report affirmed the state's responsibility for the welfare of mothers and children. Organized women of the left as well as feminists had lobbied for many of these reforms, but they found that the programs that were fully funded and implemented were those that supported the rights and needs of men, as wage earners and heads of families. Those of specific benefit to women, birth control and access to abortion, for example, were omitted.

Deprived of power in their political party, Danish social democratic women fought hard for autonomous women's clubs. After years of struggle, they achieved them, and the clubs did valuable work in educating groups of Danish working-class women in citizenship, and "progressive" ideas of child rearing, household management, and health. But they did little to improve women's standing in the party or to gain party support for their women-centered agenda. Frustration and class differences divided social democratic women. Those with middle-class backgrounds allied themselves with middle-class feminists in the Danish Women's Society. The alliance changed them both. Social democratic women abandoned a class-based approach in favor of reforms for all women, and feminists met them halfway by adopting a practical program of social reform. But the alliance cost social democratic women the support of many women in trade unions and in the radical working-class Working Women's Association, for whom class differences still mattered. Although all the women's organizations had similar programs, the division weakened their chances for serious consideration from the dominant male leaders.

The Danish case seems to support the argument that so-called strong states and labor movements leave less space and give less power to organized women than so-called weak ones. When the Danish state accepted the responsibility of caring for women and children, the poor, the sick, and the elderly, in one sense, they preempted organized women's reform efforts. Women had to accept the state's idea of what was good for them and their families, and overall, despite its progressive direction, it was a male vision.

Notes

1. Intervies with Nina Andersen, in Beth Helle Lauridsen, :De politiske Kvindegrupper i Socialdemokratiet fra 1929-58." (MA thesis, Copenhagen University 1985), 1.
2. Niels Ole Finnemann: *I Broderskabets Aand. Den socialdemokratiske arbejderbevaegelses idehistorie 1871-1977* (Gyldendal 1985).
3. Drude Dahlerup, "Kvinders organisering I det danske Socialdemokrati 1908-69. For og imod en selvstaendig socialistisk kvindebevaegelse." *Meddelelser om forskning I Arbejderbevaegelsens historie* 13 (1979): 9.
4. E. Wiinblad og Alsing Andersen, *Det danske Socialdemokratis Historie. 50 Aars Jubilaeum* (Copenhagen, 1921), p. 142. Soren Kolstrup, *Velfaerdsstatens rodder – fra kommunesocialisme til folkepension* (Copenhagen, 1996).
5. National Biography of Danish Women (*Dansk Kvindebiografisk Leksikon*) was the source for all the biographies of Danish women used.
6. Inge Lise Jensen, Karin Steen Moller, Karen Marie Sanden, "De organiserede ufaglaerte kvinders vilkar I perioden 1918-25 – pa godt og ondt" (M.A. thesis, Aarhus Universitet, 1979), pp. 50-51. The guild of working-class housewives joined the mainstream guild of housewives in Copenhagen in 1920.
7. Svend Aage Hansen, Ingrid Henriksen. *Dansk Socialhistorie 1914-39. Sociale brydninger*, (Copenhagen 1984), p. 354.
8. Aagot Lading, *Dansk Kvindesamfunds Arbejde gennem 25 Aar* (Copenhagen, 1939), pp. 66-93; and Hanne Rimmen Nielsen, "Den kvindelige karriere I 1920 erne," in *Nar baner brydes*, eds. Adda Hilden og Jytte Larsen (Copenhagen, 1994), pp. 41-43.
9. Sylvia Pio to Nina Andersen, April 1929, in "Koncept," April 1929 (SD Collection). The letter reported on women's work in Nørrebro, a strong working-class constituency in Copenhagen. "Udtalelse vedtaget af Formandsmodet 23.9. 1930," letter from the party to members in Copenhagen 2 October 1930 and "Partikongressens Beslutning om Kvinderne og Partiarbejdet," 1931, SD Collection.
10. Drude Dahlerup, "Kvinders Organisering," p. 18; Social democratic women's representation in the Danish parliament was consistently below the female average, which was between 2 and 3 percent. The middle-class parties had the highest representation. Social democratic women's representation on municipal councils was also low and declined from 3.6 percent in 1909 to 1.6 percent in 1925.
11. Hilda Romer Christensen, "Kammerat Tinka, Kvindeideologi" I DSU 1920-1940 belyst ved Nina Andersen politiske agitation og Caja Rudes "Kammerat Tinka," *Aarbog for Arbejderbevaegelsens Historie* (1986): 109-45; Christensen, *Mellem Backfische og paene piger,* p. 234.
12. K.K. Steincke wrote an enthusiastic preface to the translation of Ben Lindsey, *Kammerataegteskabet, med forord af K.K.Steincke* (Copenhagen, 1928).
13. Hilda Romer, "Mellem opbrud og tradition, DSU og 'den ny kvinde' I Mellemkrigstiden," in *Arbejderkvinder I Bevaegelse*, ed. Anette Eklund Hansen (Copenhagen, 1992), pp. 64-65.
14. Kirsten Geertsen, *Arbejderkvinder i Danmark. Vilkår og kamp 24-1939* (Copenhagen, 1982), pp. 47-51. The percentages of women workers relates to all women between fifteen and seventy years of age. The total number of workers in industry and trade in Denmark during the interwar period was as follows: 1925, approximately 270,000; 1935, 318,000; 1940, 477,000.
15. Hansen and Henriksen, *Dansk Socialhistorie,* p. 345.

16. Kirsten Geertsen, *Arbejderkvinder i Danmask. Vilkår og kamp 24-1939*, (Copenhagen 1982), p. 79.
17. Hansen and Henriksen, *Dansk Socialhistorie*, p. 353.
18. Geertsen, *Arbejderkvinder*, p. 84.
19. Hanne Caspersen, "Arbejderkvindernes Oplysningsforening 1925-1934" in *Aarbog for Arbejderbevaegelsens Historie* (Copenhagen, 1978), p. 115.
20. Anna-Birte Ravn, "Lagging Far Behind All Civilized Nations: the Debate over Protective Legislation for Women in Denmark 1899-1913" in *Protecting Women: Labor Legislation in Europe, the US and Australia, 1880-1920*, eds. Ulla Wikander, Alice Kessler-Harris, and Jane Lewis, (Chicago, 1995), p. 226.
21. Geertsen, *Arbejderkvinder*, pp. 159-160.
22. Hansen and Henriksen, *Dansk Socialhistorie*, pp. 281, 392-97.
23. In Denmark, the state funded 56 percent of the social budget in 1933 as compared to 51 percent in Norway and only 28 percent in Sweden. Staffan Marklund, *Klass, stat och socialpolitik* (Lund, 1982), p. 102.
24. Lading, *Dansk Kvindesamfunds Arbejde*, p. 92; Geertsen, *Arbejderkvinder*, pp. 278-80; Kolstrup, *Velfaerdsstatens rodder*, pp. 304-5.
25. Notes from meetings held at the Social Democratic party office on 20 February 1936 (SD Collections).
26. Fanny Jensen became a government minister with special responsibility for women's issues in 1947 to 1950.
27. Caspersen, "Arbejderkvindernes," pp. 141-42. In 1934, the WWA abandoned its name and joined the Communist Anti-Fascist Frontier, which meant that it lost its identity as a working women's organization.
28. Social Democratic women made requests for their own journal to the party leadership in 1929, 1935, and again in 1938 to 1939, but they did not get their own publication until 1947.
29. Lauridsen, "De Politiske Kvindegruppern, p. 76.
30. Geertsen, *Arbejderkvinder i Danmark*, pp. 141-45.
31. The SD party executive circulated the memorandum again in 1934 with an additional note to underline the party's non-discriminatory principles. See *Kommunale Meddelelser, Udquivet af Socialdemokratisk Forbund* (February 1934).
32. Nina Andersen, "Kvindens ret til arbejde" in *Socialisten. Socialdemokratisk Tidsskrift* (publ. by The Social Democratic Party-constituencies, discussion-clubs and the WEA).
33. Geertsen, *Arbejderkvinder i Danmark*, pp. 294-301.
34. The Council of Medico-Legal Experts requested the Pregnancy Commission and the Ministry of Justice appointed the members. There were eight women and ten men. Among them was a Conservative woman physician who approved the report and a Liberal woman who was the lone dissenter.
35. Interview with Nina Andersen, in Lauridsen, "De Politiske Kvindegrupper" (enclosures), p. 14.
36. Margrethe Host, *10 Aars Kvindeudvalgsarbejde* (Copenhagen, 1940), p. 7.
37. All information on the club's activities comes from *Beretning om Kvindeudvalgsarbejdet i Kobenhavn og Omegn*, 1934ff. For the period before 1934, scattered handwritten reports from some of the clubs provided information.
38. Annette Borchorst, "Moderskab og bornepasning i 1930 erne," in *Tidens Kvinder. Om Kvinder i Mellemkrigstiden*, eds. Hilda Romer Christensen and Hanne Rimmen Nielsen (Aarhus, 1985), pp. 36-58.
39. Letter from Gudrun Kristoffersen, teacher at a municipal school in Roskilde to a fellow party member, 7 October 1934, (SD Collection).

Part V

REFLECTIONS

Chapter 14

Women, Citizenship, and Power

Louise A. Tilly

In their introduction to this volume, co-editors Helmut Gruber and Pamela Graves ask the question "Why did the ballot fail to endow women with full citizenship, not to speak of gender equality?" The question resounds throughout their ensuing examination of the national histories of women and socialism/socialism and women in Western Europe in the 1920s and 1930s. They and their co-authors provide much empirical historical evidence about the political, economic, and ideological components of an answer to this question. I believe that major changes in gender relations were blocked by powerful constraining economic and social structures arising in the late nineteenth century, developments in which socialist and working men played a role.

A theoretical framework will be useful in addressing the question. R. W. Connell's 1987 study, *Gender and Power: Society, the Person, and Sexual Politics,* lays out an exceptionally comprehensive theoretical approach for evaluating the dimensions of inequality. His framework both separates out the critical structures (labor, power, and "cathexis," as elaborated below), and argues that they are neither a system, nor independent of each other, but integrally intertwined, a "unity – always imperfect and under construction – of historical composition … at the level of a whole society. [This process of composition] produces the gender order."[1] What are these critical structures then? For Connell, a structure is not simply a pattern, but refers to "the intractability of the social world: limits on freedom; the constraints on social organization." Connell's concept is similar to what Nancy Folbre calls the "structures of collective con-

Notes for this chapter begin on page 515.

straints," which she sees as necessarily "qualified by the form of group [gender, race, class, ethnicity, sexual orientation] membership it is based on."[2] This qualification is important, because it conceives of the person being constrained as a member of an identifiable group, the conditions of which can be empirically traced, thus becoming accessible to historical analysis. Women are a gendered group, but for all women, as for all human beings, gender is cross-cut by other group identities.

Both Folbre and Connell see structures of constraint as located in multiple systems of power relations, but Folbre has a more developed concept of the collective "groupness" of individuals (she also further emphasizes collective action), while Connell focuses more on tracing individual psychological interaction, and on psychoanalysis as a tool to further understanding. Again, both insist on the importance of individuals as agents. Indeed, Connell derives his dualist account of structure from Anthony Giddens' "theory of structuration" which links structure and action (or human practice), each one presupposing the other, since "structure is always emergent from practice and is constituted by it."[3] Connell, with whom I disagree about this, nevertheless rejects the Giddens version as too inflexible, tending to preclude historical change in structural forms. Although Connell has a point that different structural forms may be dominant at one or another historical moment, I agree with Giddens that under certain conditions, structures may be a powerful obstacle to individual and collective agency. Oppression is real, and resistance or collective action often fail to produce far-reaching change. Moreover, historical change is path-dependent, that is, what happens at one point in time may block alternatives at a later point in time, or, alternatively, may open the way to unintended change. Folbre illustrates such path dependency when she reminds her readers that "traditional inequalities based on gender and age are reproduced and internalized within modern institutions such as ... the mother-headed family, and the welfare state."[4]

Connell discusses three structures of power/constraint: "labor," which includes the division of labor in household/family, labor market segregation, discrimination in employers' treatment of workers, and inequality of wages; "power," which addresses state and economic hierarchies that control and coerce, social controls (including sexual regulation), and interfamilial authority; and "cathexis", having to do

> "with the patterning of object-choice, desire and desirability ... the production of heterosexuality and homosexuality and the relationship between them: with the social structured antagonisms of gender ...; with trust and distrust, jealousy and solidarity in marriages and other relationships; and with the emotional relationships involved in rearing children" (i.e., interpersonal or social psychological relations).[5]

The characteristics of the first two of these intertwining structures (labor and power) intersect the arenas of action, which other schemes for classifying gender inequality take as their units. Thus, for Connell, labor is performed and power is exercised in *both* public and private arenas; his concept of structures likewise combines production and power relations in both arenas. Even cathexis, which seems to be a relationship occurring primarily in the private arena, has a social dimension in the structured gender antagonisms that may be expressed in the public arena in political preferences, hiring decisions, and legislation, and exclusions such as entry into full citizenship.

The Historical Context Analyzed

In Europe, there had long been a division of labor by gender within rural and urban households, but it was relatively flexible in these family economies, combining reproduction and agricultural or small-scale manufacturing production, because of high mortality. Mature men and women, children, and the elderly were economic producers in family economies in small or large ways. In the late eighteenth century and the first half of the nineteenth, the capitalist industrial revolution in the manufacture of textiles led to an increased scale of production and eventually mechanization and concentration. This industry, along with larger scale food processing and garment production and nonrevolutionized domestic service offered wage jobs for women and young people primarily. As the capitalist market economy grew in scale and specialization, however, women found wage work only in certain segregated sectors. Although poorly paid with limited or interrupted work periods, familial and other social gender constraints on single women probably loosened somewhat in this period; married women, however, continued to bear the primary burden of nonmarket production (bearing and raising children, feeding workers, and caring for their families' material needs).

In the late nineteenth century a second surge of industrialization involved the development and growing importance of new industries (chemical processes, including the production of dyes, new textile fibers like rayon, rubber, and the distillation of coal to produce coke; vehicle construction like bicycles and eventually automobiles, and the machines required in those processes; electrical engines and other products using electricity led to a further increased scale of production. These heavy industries mainly hired men as workers, in contrast to the earlier industrializing sectors, which became much less important in West European economies. Trade unions in heavy industry and elsewhere supported state policies such as protective legislation (sponsored by employers who greatly preferred male workers), which promoted mother-centered family households in this period. New job opportunities opened up for young and unmarried women as the bureaucratic administrative function in government and business expanded. Mass production was accompanied by larger commercial establishments and mass distribution. Large stores displaced small family businesses and employed armies of salesclerks. Although the proportion of women wage workers continued to expand, their jobs were primarily in the female occupations, less remunerative, and clearly differentiated in function and opportunities from male jobs.

This schematic view works best as a description of the northwestern European countries and Germany at the end of the nineteenth century. Austria and the Mediterranean and Scandinavian peripheries continued to be more rural, with a greater continued importance of agriculture. Nevertheless, the peripheral states were affected by expanding capitalist markets and the specialization in manufacturing in northwest Europe and Germany. Scandinavian countries were increasingly drawn into European markets to sell their agricultural products and raw materials, while Austria, Italy, and Spain industrialized regionally and themselves began to sell textiles and machines in national and international markets. New provisions for social welfare were passed in all these states at least locally and in some cases nationally well before World War I.

A second major transformation of the fin-de-siècle period was social: the weakening of fathers' power over children. Formerly, in family economies, children had either contributed to the production of subsistence and sometimes marketed products or, if involved in the labor market, had to a large degree owed their earnings to their parents for their share of household services and goods. The reduction of paternal control was an outcome of the spread of exclusionary child labor laws and compulsory public schooling, which severely limited children's access to wages. The consequent increased freedom of older children to leave the household once they were wage workers themselves led to the increasing relative cost of child rearing. Parents could no longer count on children defraying the cost of their upbringing through their wage labor. This was an important contributing factor to the general fertility decline, which gathered force in the period in all the European countries considered here (i.e., fertility fell in both central, northwest, and peripheral regions, hence was not directly or tightly linked to industrialization per se). A reduction in paternal responsibility ensued, which made mothers and children more vulnerable to poverty, as well as a reduction of adult children's responsibility for their aged parents, which made the elderly more vulnerable to poverty.[6]

The intersection of the growth of capitalist markets and fertility decline with its concomitant reduction in the interfamilial reciprocal responsibilities, ideally typical of the family economy, raised questions about parental responsibility for the training and education of their children for adult life and the need to socialize responsibility for vulnerable groups. In the late nineteenth century, publicly supported education became obligatory and at least partially subsidized by state funds in most countries. Under the pressure of collective action from workers, sometimes to forestall such collective action, states began to further expand into the socioeconomic arena with unemployment schemes and pension plans for the elderly no longer able to work. By the early twentieth century, some European states offered assistance for mothers (occasionally including working mothers) and widows who were raising children, sometimes under pressure of collective action by feminist or religious groups.

This expansion of state activity beyond its earlier limited functions – the control of public order, administration of justice, preparation for or conduct of wars (the latter tended to be rather localized and small-scale in nineteenth century Europe), and raising funds through taxation to pay for these activities – lay behind the expansion of women's employment in state bureaucracies. The limited function state of the early nineteenth century had virtually excluded women as functionaries as well as citizens. Expanding state activities and the bureaucracies that made them possible incorporated women as workers in lower level clerical positions and also in new social welfare activities – as factory and school inspectors, teachers, and social workers. Nevertheless, as in industry, women's job possibilities were segregated in terms of rank and remuneration and by sector of activity.

European economic and political developments in the nineteenth century had produced a transformed world by the early twentieth century. In this world, there was a much bigger gap than in preindustrial times between the household economy, now more likely to be urban but still small-scale and largely nonmonetized, and the wider large-scale economy, with the most valued industrial jobs monopolized by men and a growing service sector directed by men in which women found work especially in the lower echelons. Nonmarket workers in social reproduction were primarily women. Family size had declined in step with fertility, and both the elderly and lone mothers and children had become more vulnerable to poverty. States had incorporated new social functions including public education and welfare, in which the activities that women were once again involved in represented the lower ranks of the workforce and volunteer positions. Despite sweeping transformations in both public and private arenas, gender inequality had been re-embedded in new institutional forms shaping economic and political power relations as well as interpersonal ones.

Michelle Perrot's preface describes well the optimistic mood of socialists and suffragists, two of the major social movements of the prewar period: of the countries considered here, Norway passed women's suffrage in national elections first, in 1912, and in others, women's suffrage campaigns seemed to be close to success. Socialist votes peaked in Europe in the period before 1914, and the possibility of those parties gaining greater power looked promising.

World War I was a brutal interlude of death and destruction. In the early postwar period, women's suffrage was achieved on a national level in Austria, Britain, Denmark, Germany, the Netherlands, and Sweden; Belgium legislated female suffrage in local elections and paradoxically women were permitted to stand for election to parliament (which several did, and were elected) although unable to vote themselves. In France, Italy, and Spain efforts to pass women suffrage failed, despite substantial sentiment of support. The Russian Revolution and the Bolshevik victory resulted in the split of Western European Socialists and the emergence of new Communist parties. The postwar treaties of peace imposed a heavy financial burden and political humiliation on Germany as the guilty party, and did nothing to ease the burden of debt to the United States that the Allies had taken on. Economic recession hit nearly every country simultaneously with demobilization. This quick end to optimism was to some degree reversed in the late 1920s, but the onset of the Depression and spread of fascism in the 1930s renewed the gloom and concern as Europe slid toward war.

Commonalities and Contrasts

Connell and Folbre theorize that the transformative effects of changes in material life may be attenuated by new institutional changes that permit values and preferences to continue unchanged or only superficially modified. Even before the hopeful intimations of progress in gender relations expressed in the first decade of the twentieth century, a more rigid gender segregation of jobs had been established in Europe's newer industries and services in place of the relatively flexible household division of labor of family economies. The proportion of male workers who were wage-earning proletarians had greatly increased, and a new form of class organization, labor unions, sought wages for men that permitted them to support a family, thus prejudicing the potential wage level of all women workers, whether members of a family or not. The changes in women's rights in marriage (other than that to control their own earnings) that had been legislated under pressure from propertied women had done little to help working-class women. And despite overall declining fertility, some wage-earning men saw little reason to accept their wives' possible desire for fewer children.

The pro-natalist politics of some groups grew ever more insistent with wartime population losses, which weighed heavily in Belgian and French politics in particular. Postwar recessions slowed economic recovery or progress. Communist and Socialist parties competed against each other for votes, and the prewar political opposition to labor unions was resumed.

Although local or particularist socialist experiments like Red Vienna and the German communists' progressive views on women's sexual autonomy and political equality showed great promise, the first was isolated in a conservative state, and both were snuffed out when the Nazis came to power in Germany in 1933 and after Dollfuss' coup d'état of 1934. Italy in 1922, then Germany, Austria, and Spain under Fascist control in the 1930s rapidly liquidated Socialist and Communist parties and initiatives.

As this volume's authors clearly demonstrate, in no European country were women's interests or needs high on socialist political agendas from 1920 to 1939. Socialists in Belgium, France, Italy, and Spain were reluctant to support women's suffrage out of fear of their potential pro-Catholic votes. Liberal parties in these states usually concurred; hence suffrage was achieved only after World War II. In countries with limited or full women's suffrage, only token women candidates were run by Socialist parties in national elections. Some of them in Britain, Belgium, and Sweden were active advocates for women when elected to parliament, but others, as in Germany, were effectively silenced by party discipline. Nowhere were enough women elected to public office to form a bloc, as women, promoting a woman's agenda. (Given cross-cutting identities, however, we should no more assume a common women's public interest than we do men's, whose gender identities are divided along lines of class, age, ethnicity, and race – at minimum.)

Overall, organized women, Socialist or not, tended to support maternal and infant health programs, assistance for vulnerable single mothers and children and elderly widows, and birth control, but usually only discreetly (sometimes under the guise of programs for maternal health and welfare). Where these programs were instituted, socialist women, as in Britain and Belgium, worked on them locally, while socialist or liberal men were responsible for those that were passed at the national level (or even at the level of a major urban center like Vienna) and directed centrally. Labor unions fighting for political power, as in Britain where the Labour party was the creature of the trade unions, opposed some social legislation, such as mother's pensions and family allowances, because they feared these would lead to reductions in male workers' collectively bargained wage. Most women who continued to be active in Socialist parties eventually abandoned female cross-party coalition action about social goals and subordinated their own agendas to their parties, especially with the growing fascist threat of the 1930s.

Returning to the question that prompted this reflection posed by Gruber and Graves, the achievement of suffrage merely gave women in most European countries one ballot each, as it did to men. The ballot has not been a key to full citizenship or equality for all men, but some men have had more power in the public arena than others. *No* women have had as much power as those men, nor can they be seen as equal to most men. The reason? Male power has successfully institutionalized and rein-stitutionalized itself despite enormous economic and political changes. In the 1920s and 1930s, socialist men were beneficiaries of quasi-public institutions like unions and parties that could sideline women's agendas or concerns, or address such programs in a manner suiting men as the current power holders.

Men were the current power holders in families as well, supported by state policies that depended on family organization to encourage reproduc-tion, preferably leading to increased population. This is not a new insight but it is forcefully brought forward in this overview of a period in which the European economy, political stability, reproduction, and the male power that was intertwined institutionally in all of these seemed at risk.

Sweden is known to have been the one country that embarked on a remarkably extensive Socialist-sponsored social welfare program (not incidentally under the slogan of the "People's Home") between the wars. Why? One common answer is that it had a relatively homogeneous pop-ulation and a long history of popular movements for social change. Equally important was the fact that it had not suffered population loss and economic destruction in World War I and was not threatened directly by Soviet or German aggression. In short, it was shielded from some of the events that blocked socialist attention to women's agenda. Of course, this does not explain the differences between Sweden and the other Scandinavian countries. Another explanation for the Swedish wel-fare program is the social democrats' concern with national population decline. Nor was Sweden a paradise for working women: even today occupational segregation by sex in Sweden is on the high end for Euro-pean countries! The institutional structures of constraint that all the authors of this volume so clearly show as operating in the period between the wars were decisive everywhere in denying women full citizenship.

Notes

1. R.W. Connell, *Gender and Power: Society, the Person, and Sexual Politics* (Stanford, 1987).
2. Connell, Gender and Power, p. 92; Nancy Folbre, *Who Pays for the Kids? Gender and the Structures of Constraint* (London, 1994), p. 53.
3. Connell, p. 94, discussing Anthony Giddens, *Central Problems in Social Theory* (London, 1979). Philip Abrams, *Historical Sociology* (Ithaca, N.Y., 1982) sees the dualism of structuration as useful to historians who are writing about change, as does Christopher Lloyd, *The Structures of History* (Oxford, 1993).
4. Folbre, *Who Pays for the Kids?*, p. 125.
5. Connell, *Gender and Power*, p. 97.
6. The analysis offered here is loosely related to that offered by Folbre, *Who Pays for the Kids?*, pp. 91-92.

Chapter 15

From Welfare Politics to Welfare States
Women and the Socialist Question

Geoff Eley

Gender, Citizenship, and Democracy

Once we move away from the older organizational or biographical approaches to the history of women in the socialist tradition, the boundaries of the topic begin to blur. How do we distinguish between this particular relationship (women and socialism/socialism and women) and the history of women in general? How do we contextualize the history of socialist women within the broader circumstances of women without writing a general women's history? And conversely, how do we address the general issues of socialism's gender politics without sacrificing the sense of the socialist movement's specificities to the more general arguments about sexuality, the family, labor markets, the labor process, the politics of welfare, and the character of the gender regimes all of these things entail? This is a particular version of a broader social historian's dilemma, one might argue, which goes back to the 1960s and early 1970s and the turn from labor history (as the study of parties and trade unions) to the history of the working class (as the study of class formation, social conditions, social practices, popular culture, and everyday life). The dilemma can harbor a double danger – in which on the one hand the history of ordinary people becomes claimed as the site of the real action, as the source of authenticity and the place of "resistance," in a potentially over-politicized understanding of the everyday; and on the other hand the specifically political agencies of the movement (the party, the trade unions, and the larger repertoire of organized social and cultural activities) can recede from significance. Though these worries properly exercised the workshop to which the essays in this book were first presented, the finished essays admirably resolve them in the richness of their individual accounts. In various ways, they manage to keep moving *out* from the specific histories of the various national movements into the wider contexts where the movements' politics can be relativized and properly understood; and then *back again* to the ways in which new features of the movements' practice were being produced. This movement back and forth between the histories of socialism and women's history in the fullest sense is one of the strengths of the collective discussion from which this volume proceeds.

Another set of questions concerns the specificities of the period dealt with by these essays. What are the distinctive features of the relationship between women and socialism in this particular period of the history of the tradition? How did Socialist and Communist parties construct this relationship differently in the interwar years from the time before 1914 or from the one that came later during and after the World War II? What pressures did the overall contexts of the state and the economy exert on the socialist tradition with respect to women, and how did those pressures both produce creativity and movement, and yet structure and constrain the latitude for innovation? Indeed, what are the appropriate boundaries for the "interwar period" per se, given the variations of national history involved? Are they imposed by the outbreak of World War II in 1939, or by the occupation of Western Europe by the Nazi armies during 1940, or should they be measured by the international threat of fascism dramatized by the Spanish Civil War in 1936, or perhaps by the earlier victories of fascism over democracy in 1933 and 1934? How do we deal with Italy, where conditions for the democratic exercise of citizenship capacities were swept away violently by the success of the Fascists at the very start of our period, between 1920 and 1922? Does it make sense to include Italy at all in this comparative framework, as opposed to Czechoslovakia (for instance), where the continuities with other Central European socialisms were very strong, where the largest Communist party outside the Soviet Union in the 1920s provides an excellent opportunity for considering socialism's gendered histories, and where democratic conditions lasted until 1938? What establishes the appropriate comparative context for the thematics of this book?

In developing an answer to this question, it makes sense arguably, to begin with the juridical infrastructure of women's political agency, namely female citizenship in the right to vote, and to do this on a comparative European scale. In this respect, the beginning of our period is clear enough, for the end of World War I saw the first decisive breakthrough to female enfranchisement. Before 1914 women were voting citizens in only Finland (1906) and Norway (1913), but by 1918 they were participants in the general European democratization, from Bolshevik Russia (in the Soviet Constitutions of 1918 and 1923) to Republican Ireland (in the Constitution of 1922). Surveying Europe as a whole, we can find the following pattern:

1) The new states formed from the East-Central European "national revolutions" of 1918, where women received the vote as part of the general republican constitution-making, in Austria, Germany, Czechoslovakia, Hungary, and Poland.
2) Established liberal constitutional states, where the postwar impetus for reform also produced votes for women, mainly in Northwestern Protestant Europe – in Denmark and Iceland (1915), Sweden (1918), Britain (1918), Luxemburg(1919), and the Netherlands (1920) – but also in Ireland (1922).
3) Europe's Southern periphery, where the democratization had clearer gendered limits, from Spain and Portugal to Romania, Bulgaria, Yugoslavia, Albania, and Greece.
4) States which experienced extensive reform during 1918 to 1919, but where major political conflicts took place precisely around the defeat of women's enfranchisement, in Italy, Switzerland, Belgium, and France.

If we then turn to the juridical situation at the end of the interwar period – that is, on the eve of World War II, just before the Third Reich's military success abruptly suspended normal political life for the societies considered in this book – the situation looked extraordinarily bleak. By 1939 and 1940, the ideals of the emancipation of women had become stymied where they had not been violently rolled back, whether in relation to the suffrage, women's civil rights under the law, or the broader progress of women towards acknowledged and instituted forms of equality with men. Where fascism had not effected counter-revolutionary gender settlements directly inside particular societies (Germany, Austria, Italy, Spain), it swept the democratic framework of any emergent alternatives away by the expansionist juggernaut of its military machine, leaving only Britain, Switzerland, and Sweden with sovereignties intact. Even before 1939, the combination of the social catastrophe of the Depression with the permanent pressure of an international crisis had immensely complicated the optimistic projections of women's citizenship accompanying the end of World War I.

On the other hand, from a vantage point in 1945, the situation had changed again. If 1918 had brought women the vote in Northwestern and

Central Europe, 1945 extended it to the Southwestern Catholic arc of Italy, France, and Belgium, as well as restoring universal suffrage where fascism had taken it away.[1] Allowing for the more complicated situation in Eastern Europe, now only Portugal, Spain, Greece, and Switzerland held out for an exclusively male polity. In other words, the question of women's citizenship or political agency – I am deliberately avoiding the term "equality" here – has to be related in the first instance to these rhythms of democratization in the juridical and constitutional sense, because they established the dynamic and changing overall context in which the complex field of relations between "women" and "socialism" could materialize and from which everything else had to begin. For all the convergences and correspondences we can find across the contrasting political regimes of Fascist Italy, Nazi Germany, National Government Britain, Republican France, Social Democratic Sweden, and so on, in areas like social policy and conceptions of child raising and the family, or the organization of labor markets, or the public representations of sexual difference, the degrees and forms of nationally instituted democracy and its absence remained a crucial determinant of whatever quality of public political identity women were able to claim.

There are two further points to be made about this gendered setting of democratization. First, whatever the detailed complexities and contradictions in the relationship of women to socialism, it is a salient fact of twentieth-century political history that female enfranchisement followed the fortunes of the Left. When socialist projects captured the popular imagination, in times of massive public mobilization organized by Socialists and Communists, widespread industrial militancy and extra-parliamentary activism, extensive legislative innovation, and radical structural reform, with utopian hopes for a better world, the space was also open for expanding women's participation (namely, in 1918 to 1923, and again during 1943 to 1947). Conversely, when socialism was on the retreat, under fascism, in the period of National Government and Depression in Britain, in the aftermath of the French Popular Front, or in Western Europe as a whole during the Cold War, women's political interests were constricted more easily around a limiting and conservative social agenda. Likewise, by subsuming women's identities inside the family, the welfare state measures, and social policy legislation of the post-1945 settlement may have proven notoriously conservative on the gender-political front, but where the Left was strong and guided by a clear strategic vision, as in Sweden during the later 1930s, or in Italy during the period of anti-fascist coalition in 1943 to 1947, the conduct of reform worked more strongly with the grain of women's emancipation. In other words, the presence of Socialists or Communists in government certainly did not *guarantee* any advance for women's democratic citizenship, witness the French Popular

Front of 1936 to 1937, or for that matter the British Labour Government after 1945. Nor did the strongest advocacy of women's political claims necessarily come from Socialist or Communist Parties themselves, as the French feminists could bitterly attest, whether (like Madeleine Pelletier) they were formally Socialists or (like Louise Weiss) they were not. But *without* the Left's political upswing, the expansion of women's citizenship was unlikely even to begin.

But secondly, though foundational, democratic political rights were only part of the story. Thus, while the French Committee of National Liberation included women's suffrage in its crucial Proclamation of 21 April 1944, which became the basis for the Fourth Republic's 1946 Constitution, the Free French women's committees created two years before had been concerned almost exclusively with the family. Women might be welcomed into the circle of national citizens, that is, but in public discourse they were addressed primarily as mothers. In other words, in establishing women's political equality, which notionally meant "a civil status identical with that of men" (as Louise Weiss put it), these measures simultaneously reasserted the social basis of female difference.[2] In judging the relationship between socialism and women, this doubled perspective has to stay constantly in one's head. Though the socialist tradition consistently upheld an ideal of women's emancipation, and explicitly linked the franchise to a broader program of economic reform, in a combination of women's productive employment and socialized services, in practice socialists equally consistently assimilated women's interests to the ideology of the male breadwinner and the family wage, within a model of the male headed household and the respectable working-class family. Because socialists participated in this way in gendered languages that remained hegemonic, they were capable of both advocating the advancement of women, while simultaneously enjoining the continuing forms of women's subordination. How exactly this field of difficulty became negotiated out, in the varying national contexts of interwar social and political history, in the conflicting practice of Socialists and Communists, and in relation to the subsequent trajectories of the 1940s and 1950s, is the unifying problematic and special interest of these essays.

Communism and Women

The place of women in Communism between the wars was heavily structured by events in the Soviet Union, both via the power of the Soviet example and through the influence of the Comintern. In theory, the Bolshevik Revolution had removed all impediments to female emancipation, admitting women to full and equal citizenship in the Soviet State, overhauling the law on property, labor, and the family, and treating women as equal participants in the new political community of labor. With the accompanying projections of social collectivism – the intended replacement of the child raising, child care, and social-reproductive functions of the family with the collective provision of services, through the centralized facilities of model housing developments, public laundries, dining-rooms, nurseries, and so on – Soviet Communism seemed to be offering a radical model of gender equality and sexual freedom. Yet during the 1920s, in that familiar simultaneity of radical programs and social conservatism, borne by the recalcitrance of the given attitudes, the constraints of inadequate resources, and the rhythms and continuities of an intractable everyday, a more conventional gender regime soon became renormalized, which redomesticated women's identities, and reinscribed motherhood as women's primary social responsibility. Even during the Revolution's earlier and most radical phase, Alexandra Kollontai had distinguished between the public sphere of men ("building soviet apparatuses of government, production, regulation; … creating the Red Army") and the sphere of everyday life that was left for women ("setting up dining halls, communal houses, social education, protection of motherhood").[3] This logic was clear in the activities of Zhenotdel (the Women's Department of the Central Committee Secretariat of the Soviet Communist Party, set up in November 1918), which soon exchanged its feminist ambitions for the re-establishment of a conventional female sphere – the socialization of housework and child care, and the provision of social services. Even in these limited terms the Women's Department was seen by the Soviet leadership as a troublesome special interest, and in 1930 it was closed down.

Between 1917 and 1930 in the Soviet Union, there were 301 party resolutions and decrees on the subject of "women," and during the next 30 years there were only 3.[4] This pattern of initial recognition and encroaching neglect was repeated in the Comintern. A first international conference of Communist women met during the second Comintern Congress between 30 June and 2 August 1920, and produced an International Women's Secretariat, initially with two sections in Moscow and Berlin, later unified under the leadership of Klara Zetkin in November 1922. This Secretariat was necessarily dependent on the vitality of the national parties for its effectiveness, but Soviet insistence on a single model of women's agitation, and Soviet dominance of the Comintern Executive caused friction from the beginning. Thus, Soviet support for the idea of women's "delegates" attached to party cells as a kind of political apprenticeship clashed with the German Communists' preferences for non-party organizations that would allow better access to non-Communist women on a wider front. This conflict proceeded year by year till the Comintern

Executive abolished the Secretariat in April 1926 and replaced it with a new women's department directly responsible to itself.[5]

How this scenario played itself out in the individual Communist parties varied. In smaller parties, or in countries where the party was banned or repressed, the question of a strategy for women barely arose, because the priorities were elsewhere. Sometimes a radical opening became abruptly closed off. In Italy, the socialist tradition had always seen the "woman question" (questione femminile) in strictly "workerist" (operaista) terms, ruling everything else, from women's suffrage to social policies, dogmatically out of order. After the split in 1921, the new Communist Party then immediately made the questione femminile a leading cause, treating women's political rights as an essential part of the missing democratic revolution the Left was now to make good. Overall, the Communists maintained the focus on women as workers, seeing them otherwise as a potential source of conservatism against the militancy of working-class men. Mary Gibson describes the constraints on the PCI's ability to break out of a tightly circumscribed political situation very well. In the foundation years Antonio Gramsci was already broadening the vision, forcing discussion onto the ground of culture, where the non-economic issues of family, schooling, and religion could be raised. From 1921 he persuaded Camilla Revera to address these questions in l'Ordine Nuovo as a regular feature – "problems of contraception, abortion, the burden of housework, ... the commercial nature of marriage ... the most radical aspects of the Soviet experience ... the implications of socialism for the transformation of the traditional family."[6] But this initiative was violently terminated by the Fascists, who after 1922 smashed the labor movement, dismantled democracy, and reinstated the most reactionary of gender regimes against women.

For a small Communist party like the British, with only 3,000 to 5,000 members in the early 1920s, any extensive agitation to mobilize women as women was out of the question. Organizing among factory women (for instance, in textiles in Lancashire and Yorkshire, or the jute industry in Dundee) was already beyond its resources. Moreover, the areas of the party's emerging industrial strength – mining in Scotland, South Wales, and the North, or engineering in South Yorkshire and greater Manchester – were precisely the areas of skilled masculinity in the labor movement most exclusionary against women, and this reemphasized the separateness of spheres. Party women were also themselves resistant to the idea of specifically women's agitation. When politically active women were recruited into the party – young women from socialist families, individual worker militants, teachers, and other educated women radicalized by the First World War and its aftermath – they entered the mainstream of party work rather than being shunted off into some siding of special women's activity (as they saw it). The general mood was quite hostile to the notion of separate women's sections, stressing instead an ideal of emancipated and egalitarian comradeship.[7] For female activists, the party's attraction was precisely that it ignored conventional gender roles and offered an escape from the conservatism of society. As one women Communist, a clerical worker mainly active in the Young Communist League in central London, remembered: "All I can say is that we felt ourselves to be emancipated, that we went about with the boys on an equal footing. We insisted on paying for ourselves. We weren't going to be treated like other girls, being expected to be made a fuss of, and so on."[8]

This experience worked for women with some economic independence, whether coming from wage-work, family background, and a profession, or from full-time employment in the party itself. By contrast with these "cadres," for whom the party was a support for equality, which "they took … to mean emancipation from anything designated 'women's work,'" the ordinary female "supporters" were connected to the party mainly through their husbands: they "tended to be married to party activists and have several children. They were home centered and placed their domestic responsibilities before their political involvement." In fact, relieving their husbands of domestic duties was itself considered "party work." It was here that the Women's Sections found their function, usually with afternoon meetings in homes, ensuring that party wives remained supportive of their husbands' political activity, giving them some chance for political discussion, and overcoming their isolation as housewives to this extent. Of course, this also institutionalized the wider society's sexual division of labor inside the party itself, and drew the women supporters into party life largely through servicing activity – as "a sort of housewife to the party," as one Communist husband disarmingly put it. In the 1920s, the CPGB never escaped this dilemma: women were hard to organize because they were removed from the public sphere as wives and mothers, or (with some exceptions) were working in contexts resistant to trade unionism; yet when they were recruited into the party's orbit (with the exception of the category of the "cadres" mentioned above), they assumed the old familiar role – making the tea, organizing the social, sometimes developing a speciality in welfare or education, but generally confining themselves to these "women's" concerns.[9]

Some of this came from the smallness of the British party. Diversifying its strategy to recruit outside the conventionally recognized core of the working class would have stretched its resources very thinly. It also meant that female cadres were drawn immediately into the same organizational priorities, leaving little intermediate space between such full-time officialdom and the more marginally involved women supporters where a more creative gender politics might have developed. As Kay Beauchamp, a CPGB organizer in London in the 1920s, explained it:

> You see, it was a small party then. The women who had any ability at all were seized on. Within six months of joining the party I was secretary of the biggest organization in London, St. Pancras .... Those of us who were active in that way, I suppose, didn't feel any need for any special women's activity, except as a means of winning other women, and you hadn't got time to do much of that because you were so busy on other things.[10]

There was also serious ideological resistance in the party to taking non-economic forms of oppression seriously. This was clear from an early crisis over birth control in summer 1922, after which the leading advocates of women's reproductive rights, Stella Browne and the Pauls (Maurice Eden and Cedar), either left the party or withdrew into less prominent roles. As Bruley points out, feminists radicalized during the suffrage campaigning before 1914 were a significant group in the foundation of the British CP, and the party missed a valuable chance to build on this relationship. That it let this opportunity pass reflected both the gender blindness of the socialist tradition and the limiting effects of the tightened discipline the Comintern was imposing on national Communisms by 1922 to 1924.[11]

This British experience typified most of the new Communist parties in the 1920s. Initial assembly points for diverse radicalisms frustrated with the available Left parties, which might include feminists and sexual radicals, the new parties provided a brief context in which experimental and heterogeneous ideas could flourish, before "discipline" took over and a more orthodox frame of revolutionary politics became restored. It was the smaller parties more marginal to their national labor movements that showed this pattern most strongly, and there seemed least room for any feminist politics of gender where Communists failed to carry a mass social democratic membership with them in the course of the split. At the Fourth Comintern Congress in December 1922, the International Women's Secretariat reported a women's membership of only 2 percent in France, 1.5 percent in Italy, 6 percent in Belgium. To a get a better sense of Communist politics on the gender front, therefore, it's important to look at the larger parties, which took a larger body of the existing labor movements with them in the splitting of 1917 to 1921, and which showed a larger proportion of women in the membership. In 1922 these included Germany (12 percent of overall membership), Norway (15 percent), and Czechoslovakia (20 percent).

In many ways the KPD displayed a predictable outlook for the time in gender terms – the insistence on the primacy of the class struggle in production, for both the party's general strategy and the specific mobilization of women; the belief that women's emancipation was an economic question linked to productive employment in industry, with the associated socialization of child care, housework, and other domestic services; the hostility to reformist politics short of these goals, whether the SPD's stress on the welfare state, or the more individualistic emancipation espoused by the so-called bourgeois women's movement; and so on. But as it consolidated its politics during the 1920s, the KPD also took these perspectives to an extreme, demanding that all women's activity be focused on the factory, denying the validity of women's separate concerns, and attributing to women a specific psychology (including even the most "proletarian" women, such as the women textile workers), whose "petty-bourgeois backwardness" could only be overcome by an undeviating stress on the necessity of the class struggle and the unity of the working class. For instance, true proletarian consciousness, Ruth Fischer claimed, could never be generated within the four walls of the household, so that working-class housewives could never escape their backward mentality until shown the "hard reality" of working for wages in industry.[12] But at the same time, the KPD was a large and extremely unruly party, whose membership experienced wild and unpredictable fluctuations: 66,373 in July 1920, rising to a notional 450,000 after the unification with the USPD majority in October; down to 157,168 paid-up members in summer 1921; back to 255,863 in October 1922; 294,230 in September 1923, plummeting to 121,394 in April 1924; 112,511 in the second half of 1929, rising to 176,000 in December 1931, and 287,180 by March 1932. These see-sawing membership figures give a better clue to the experience of being a German Communist than the now stereotypical representations of the party. In much of the literature the KPD is a by-word for stolid and unimaginative Stalinist orthodoxy. But almost despite itself, it provided a home for politics that frequently belied this description.

In the first place, a large party like the KPD had a range of contacts with women that were simply not available to a small sectarian cadre party like the CPGB in the 1920s. Aside from its efforts among women as wage workers in industry (the true female proletarians, according to its strict understanding), in the early 1920s the KPD had three main fields of activity among working-class women: 1) consumer cooperatives, seen not just as a practical benefit for overburdened and individualized working-class households, but also as a school of the class struggle comparable in principle to the trade unions; 2) anti-inflation actions and the wider protest activity against shortages and prices; and 3) general educational work among workers' wives. For our purposes, the second of these provides the best illustration. Beginning as spontaneous protests by housewives and the young, initially at the end of 1919 and again in summer 1920, repeated in the winter of 1921 to 1922, before reaching a climax in the second half of 1922, with a major coda in the summer of 1923, such actions frequently produced negotiated settings of fair prices with shopkeepers and the local authorities, but often also escalated into full-scale riots, with looting of food, shoes, and clothing, and violent confrontations with the police. From the outset the KPD was concerned to shape and discipline this activity. At first, this took the form of political injunctions: while understandable, "robbing the property-owner is not the abolition of property," and instead of looting, working-class housewives should concentrate on working for a revolutionary movement to expropriate the bourgeoisie.[13] But by fall 1922 "control committees" were being formed based on the works councils to monitor prices, but with an unclear and uncertain relationship to the women's direct actions that originally posed the issue.

In fact, such committees had diverse origins – elected from city-wide mass meetings of works councils, initiated by local trade unions, elected from mass meetings of the major companies, or formed from informal assemblies of workers and housewives. In Berlin on 30 August 1922, a spontaneous meeting of working-class women passed a resolution of protest against food prices and formed an eight-person control committee, which then liaised with the city-wide works council committee. In Düsseldorf, on the other hand, the KPD initiated a common action with the USPD and SPD, which foundered on the obstruction of the SPD executive, and which took no apparent account of any specifically women's activity at all. By November 1922, KPD strategy was proceeding independently of the many food protests which again erupted ("the desperation of emaciated sections of the people," as *Rote Fahne* described them).[14] The party sought to harness women's resentment to the given structure of the works councils, thereby subsuming the issue in the larger course of the class struggle, and guaranteeing the primacy of the (male) worker in production. The climax came in a national congress of works council on 24 November 1922, attended by only 16 housewives and 16 working women among the 840 delegates: it established a representative regional and local structure of *factory-based* control committees charged with coordinating local protests and supervising prices, and to which workers, renters, pensioners, unemployed women, small farmers, war victims, and youth could rally under "proletarian" leadership. But this essentially coopted a vigorous grassroots activity of women into an increasingly bureaucratized revolutionary posture, neglected an opportunity to work creatively within an independently-initiated and distinctively women's movement, and converted the latter into an auxiliary support for the familiar factory-oriented strategy. Instead of fashioning a framework for longer-term politicization, participatory democracy, and sexual egalitarianism on the basis of women's specific experiences, this process was reduced by the KPD into a formulaic episode of class-political militancy, in a grander struggle to be decided elsewhere.[15]

Nonetheless, the food protests did indicate an important intersection between Communist politics and wider women's activity, and in the early 1920s there was still a big gap between the KPD's shifting national politics and the actions of Communists on the ground. Occasionally, dissenting voices could be heard against the dogma of the emancipatory necessity of wage labor. One activist, Emilie Ehm, saw wage work as less of a help than a hindrance for consciousness raising, because the double burden (wage labor *and* housework) simply heightened women's exploitation: "Lack of time, lack of physical strength, of energy, is the stamp that marks the slow development of the entire proletarian women's movement," she said; and if the Communists wanted to help women under capitalism, they should demand greater state support for families. Some of the KPD's positions, however well-grounded in the technical categories of Marxist economics, were poorly fitted to appeal to hard-pressed working-class mothers: in one course for female cadres, the class understandably bridled at the argument that housework was "unproductive." Finally, one series of women's discussion evenings in Berlin-Neukölln in 1922 vigorously rejected the exclusive primacy of the factory struggle, advancing instead a battery of demands relating to women's immediate needs: cooperative households to ease women's domestic burden (as opposed to the official KPD policy of factory canteens, municipal provision, and nationalization of services); the *"real* eight-hour day" (that is, in the home as well as in the factory); wages for housework; free choice of profession for women (as opposed to current assumptions about women's work); and genuine sexual freedom (not just abortion reform, civil marriage, and so on).[16]

It required some effort on the part of the KPD leadership to discipline this local radicalism into manageable conformity with an official line. This was easier to handle in the much smaller British party because dissenters had an easier option of taking their radicalism elsewhere, but in the local areas where the CPGB did achieve a mass appeal, a similar independence can be seen.[17] In the German case, the KPD's revolutionary militancy and large size made it the obvious refuge for radical spirits impatient with the gradualism of the SPD and angry with all the compromising this involved; and this was no less true of radical women than of radical men. Moreover, among the German parties the KPD *was* committed to the strongest program of women's liberation across all the normal criteria, including not only the freeing of women from the home via the right to work and the socialization of domestic labor, and complete civil and professional equality, but also a strongly developed program of reproductive freedom, especially birth control and access to abortion, as

Atina Grossmann's chapter makes clear. Thus, the German Communists might undercut their own appeal on the gender front by the relentlessness of their stress on the factories and a purely "proletarian" strategy, and the KPD's official outlook certainly reflected assumptions about the secondary status of "women's issues" and the "backwardness" of women if left to themselves that were hardly conducive to women's equal participation in the movement. But they nonetheless provided a context in which women's political militancy could be articulated during the Weimar Republic.

Social Democracy and the Gendering of Citizenship

If Communists tended to espouse a militant economism, subsuming women's issues in a politics of the class struggle in industry, linked to the socialization of reproduction after the revolution, Social Democrats put their energies into the welfare state and addressed women mainly through the family. Of course, neither of these summary descriptions tells the whole story. Membership of a Communist party could give individual women a rare possibility of egalitarian comradeship – providing she followed the party's particular strategy of women's emancipation, and was economically independent (and had no children). Similarly, social democratic parties provided some opportunity for women's activity in the established realm of women's expertise – as in the appointment of Marie Juchacz (1879 to 1956) to be head of the SPD's newly created Workers' Welfare Bureau (the *Arbeiterwohlfahrt*) on 13 December 1919, or of Susan Lawrence (1871 to 1947) as Parliamentary Secretary in the Ministry of Health in the British Labour Government of 1929 to 1931. Moreover, mass parties of the Left could never maintain complete conformity. In particular areas of party life, in the branches and localities, in the more "marginal" cultural fields of action, radicalism and creativity could always reappear, eluding the frame and breaking the rules. But for the mainstream of social democratic politics in the early twentieth century, women's issues belonged securely within the family's emerging social-policy domain.

One of the effects of World War I in the combatant countries was a new prominence of the state in domestic life: if husbands, fathers, and male "breadwinners" were absent, then the resulting new "presence" needed careful government attention. The most obvious intervention was help for soldiers' wives, and as the war dragged on the numbers of recipients and the scale of expenditure became enormous. Similarly, the dislocation of conventional family relations by the war and the *de facto* furtherance of women's independence – the "unhusbanding of women," in a phrase of the time – had the effect of sucking public policy increasingly into the "generative and socializing realm of family reproduction" in order to compensate for the fact that the men were gone.[18] The absence of men at the front created a disturbing sense of moral endangerment. It not only placed women in new roles as heads of households and breadwinners. It also conjured up huge anxieties around women's independence, their lack of restraint, and the "abnormal excitement" that allegedly came from the removal of the husband's or father's moral authority. Drinking, loose living, and neglect of children engendered a range of social ills, it was thought, from crime, "race suicide," improvidence, and "feeble-mindedness," to "reckless procreation" and "immorality and faithlessness ... to their absent husbands."[19] The further connection, from unhusbanding and immorality to militancy and trouble-making, was then easily made.

The turn to domestic surveillance of women and families by both police and social workers – as important to the maintenance of the home front as the state's vigilance against trade-union militants and left-wing agitators – was the universal consequence among World War I's combatant governments. The disbursement of welfare observed the same disciplinary precepts. In Britain, the payment of soldiers' allowances was monitored for the domestic regularity and sexual chastity of their wives, first through the volunteer casework of the Soldiers' and Sailors' Families Association (SSFA), and then under the direct control of the state (a Statutory Committee of military, political, and philanthropic representatives created in 1915, passing into the new Ministry of Pensions a year later).[20] As Pedersen argues, at a time of unprecedented female independence, these measures carefully constructed both women's entitlements and women's agency as a dependency on men. At a time when women were being exhorted to patriotic sacrifice, and massive new social expenditures devoted to this end, they were kept strictly to their social and legal identity as dependent wife. In effect, a conception of social citizenship was taking shape in which "motherhood" became the ideological complement to "soldiering." If recognition of women's wartime contribution could be mediated through their husbands in this way, the potential effects of their becoming independent workers and household managers might be successfully contained.

Social Democrats were completely complicit in this process. For one thing, they found this recognition of public responsibility very attractive. The payment of soldiers' allowances established the principle of the state's obligation to its (male) citizenry and enabled a language of social citizenship, of social rights attaching to social functions (like soldiering or working) to emerge; at the same time, the charities, the private apparatus of middle-class moral reform, were finally levered out of the picture, to be replaced by a system of state-provided welfare, which socialists could at some point in the future (after winning the expected electoral majority) hope to control. In Britain, it was easy enough for the Labour party to see the Ministry of Pensions, where the trade-union parliamentarian George Barnes was already in charge, as a building-block for the future welfare state. In Germany, the SPD was less successful in establishing an exclusive principle of public control: as in Britain, the labor movement's strength in local government guaranteed *de facto* influence over social services delivery after the democratization of 1918, but the religiously organized private charities also secured a central place for themselves in the confusing tangle of laws and jurisdictions that made up the Weimar Republic's welfare sector. But in neither case were women's rights given autonomous recognition. When the benefits system for women was extended after the war – as in Britain with benefits for unemployed workers' dependents in 1921, and widows' pensions in 1925 and 1929 (where out-of-work soldiers and war widows had provided the precedents) – it happened in virtue again of women's dependent status. In this way, soldiers' allowances had provided the opportunity for valuable welfare-state innovation. But they did so by admitting women only as the secondary beneficiaries of their husbands' rights.

For the reformist wing of the European labor movements, these developments seemed good cause for congratulation: they made social needs the public responsibility of the national state rather than leaving them to the moralizing of middle-class charitable visitors; they constructed the welfare of families as a class demand, for which the labor movement became the legitimate voice; and they implied a strong theory of entitlement, in which a series of social rights became attached to the conception of citizenship. In all of these ways, lines descended to the full post-1945 development of the Western European welfare states. But at the same time, the effacement of working-class women as democratic agents with rights independent of their marital relationships to men was also consistent with deeply conservative assumptions about women's proper place. This was instantly visible in the revolutionary turbulence of 1917 to 1923, when Social Democrats in Germany and Austria anxiously reassured their new democratic public of their moral reliability, a question posed all the more urgently by the enfranchisement of women and their appearance for the first time as voting political subjects. The SPD denied that it was interested in free love, that it would introduce a "whore economy," or that it planned to remove children from their mothers to the charge of the state. These were "fairy stories" spread by priests and demagogues.[21]

Instead, the SPD offered itself as the protector of the working-class family. The party was formally committed to civil equalities and equal pay for women, of course. But the main weight of SPD practice in relation to women – in common with other social democratic parties – was focused on the family: a social-policy support system for families-in-need through benefits, home visiting, and advice centers, backed by maternal and child protection, and laws on contraception and abortion, ideally coordinated through unitary "family care agencies" at the level of the city; trade union demands for adequate housing and a "living" or "family" wage; and an ethical commitment to partnership in marriage and democratic child raising. In effect, this was the "social worker's eye-view" of working-class daily life, and it was no accident that it coincided both with the SPD's long-awaited inheritance of local government in newly democratized urban Germany and with the arrival of a new professional cadre of socialist doctors, teachers, and social workers in public life, which placed the reformist and "responsible" social democratic wing of the labor movement in an increasingly didactic, patronizing, and administrative relationship to the mass of the working-class poor. Increasingly, this social democratic practice distinguished between a respectable part of the working class, which had its domestic affairs in order, and the rough and disorderly poor, who for a variety of reasons needed help. As a result, working-class family life appeared in social democratic discourse either as the solid fundament of socialist culture or as the pathology that needed cure. The social democratic image of the family was an ideal in which the rough culture of the poor was to be recast. In this respect, it was mainly the skilled, regularly employed, and trade-unionized sections of the working class that already displayed the orderly living that social democratic ideology desired.

But in either case – the respectable working class who embodied the ideal, or the rough working class whose reformation it required – the image of the family had little emancipatory promise for women as later twentieth-century feminism would come to understand it. Women – as mothers and social workers – were to be the agency of family moralization, not the independent political subjects whom dismantling the conventional family could empower and free. Whether it was through the budding welfare-statism of SPD city administrations, or the related projects of housing reform and the campaigns for the rationalization of housework (and the analogous experiences in Red Vienna and municipal socialism in Britain), socialist social policy defined a dependent and secondary place for women, which was firmly bounded by the home. As with the Communist Parties, contrary possibilities could certainly be found. But most of the socialist creativity in the domestic sphere concerned the young – the various free school experiments, the "child republics," the youth movement, and so on – in ways that left the sex-gender distinctions in the family intact. Critiques of the latter – as in one speech by a Leipzig woman delegate to the SPD's Heidelberg Congress in 1925, which

attacked SPD men for failing "to introduce socialism into their own families" – were very rare.[22]

This validation of motherhood within a practical separate-spheres ideology was institutionalized around the role of women inside the SPD,
which after the opening of female membership in 1908 became almost
exclusively focused on welfare.[23] Together with the wartime splitting of
German socialism, this produced a new generation of female leaders (of
85 women at the SPD women's conference of June 1919, 58 were active
only since 1914, and most of the rest since 1908), who by contrast with
the Klara Zetkins and Luise Zietzs in the 1890s and 1900s now gravitated
naturally towards a specialism in social welfare, invariably graduating
through work in municipal welfare offices or the party's child labor
committees before 1914.[24] Women's contribution to the party was now
articulated as "practical activity in the service of socialism," a service
embodied in the launching of the Workers' Welfare Bureau at the instigation of Marie Juchacz in December 1919. A conservative understanding of women's capacities was at the heart of this outlook: "women are
the born protectors of humanity and, therefore, social work corresponds
so well with their nature."[25] In the process, the conception of women's
emancipation was also being changed. Before 1914, the SPD's view was
held firmly to the tradition established by the founders – Marx, Engels,
Bebel – with its stress on the oppressiveness of private property organized
through the family and the liberating necessity of women's productive
labor. Now, Juchacz and other spokespersons stressed women's reproductive contribution to the nation: as mothers of future generations, women
should be a priority of national policy, not least because of their contribution to national defense in the war. In this way the SPD became incorporated rather strongly, by comparison with their Communist rivals, into
the prevailing maternalist consensus.

In this the SPD was quite typical of the socialist parties of the old
North-Central European social democratic core – Germany and Austria,
the Czech lands, the Low Countries, and Scandinavia. At the same time,
the lines were accentuated by the extremism of the split in German
socialism, which faced the SPD with a large and more radical Communist
party to its left, where more militant spirits could gather. If we turn to a
reformist party that lacked this mass competition, like the British Labour
party, we find an outlook less wholly dominated by the politics of social
work. There was a similar tendency to shunt women into areas like education, health, and social services (and for Labour women to be self-
selecting in these roles). By the practice of trade-union bloc voting, the
annual Labour Party Conference was also structurally rigged against key
feminist issues being raised and carried: this was the fate of the birth control issue in the 1920s; and it was also the fate of the comparable worth

strategies proposed by the 1930 equal pay report, rejected by Conference in favor of the traditional line of "equal pay for equal work," which would directly benefit women much less. But Labour's first woman cabinet minister, Margaret Bondfield (1873 to 1953) in 1929, was Minister of Labour not of some narrower welfare area, and other leading women MPs, such as Susan Lawrence and Ellen Wilkinson (1891 to 1947), made a point of speaking for the labor movement as a whole, without distinction of gender, much as Rosa Luxemburg and other women socialists had done in the European movement before the First World War. The party's women's sections in practice addressed a full range of feminist concerns. They

> encompassed believers both in equality and in the essential difference between the sexes and many who blended both beliefs. They contributed both to the further promotion of equal rights feminism *and* were early proponents of the new feminism which sought to change society to reflect women's experience rather than just to open up opportunities previously claimed by men.[26]

They insisted characteristically that "sex" issues were really "class" issues. In fact, what most separated Labour women from feminists in women-only organizations (notwithstanding overlaps of membership) was the feeling that the latter were middle-class individualists insensitive to the specific circumstances of the industrial working class.

From this point of view, Labour party thinking had more in common over the longer term with the "new feminist" campaigning of Eleanor Rathbone (1872 to 1946) for a "national endowment for motherhood" than with the demands of the "equality feminists," with their critique of the entire system of gender discrimination.[27] Feminist maternalism – the motherhood-as-citizenship argument – amounted to a wager on the patriotic debt of World War I. Female mobilization on the home front, the rhetorics of patriotism and sacrifice, the visible experience of women's independent agency, and the related social policy initiatives provided a language of political validation that seemed capable of securing women's citizenship in the nation. In the prevailing atmosphere, maternalism – the construction of sexual difference into a political program – seemed to offer a political space for distinctive feminist intervention with some chance of success. Given the resistance of the male-dominated political process to admitting women on equal terms, this had the advantage of taking men at their word – there *were* irreducible differences based in biology – while fashioning the argument for women's special nature into an instrument of female empowerment rather than oppression. Motherhood was to become a recognized public value. It, rather than the fruitless quest for external employment and equal pay, would be the basis of women's independence, because once the state had "endowed" women's role in the family through a system of direct payments, all the arguments

for the male breadwinner norm (the need for men to support a family on
the strength of their own wage), and the present mechanism of women's
subordination, would begin to fall away. The war economy had suffi-
ciently destabilized the naturalness of existing gender norms to create the
sense that this might work. As Pedersen says, "'Endowment of motherhood' activists hoped to take advantage of fluid circumstances. Their
campaign was an attempt to build, on the shifting sands of difference-
based definitions, the feminist castle of a 'separate but equal' state".[28]

The problem was that the ground of maternalism was already aggressively occupied. From the beginning of women's mobilization during
World War I, policy-makers of all kinds – in government, business, the
parties, trade unions, the churches, the press – had seen motherhood as a
key term of postwar renormalization. Here maternalism was the medium
of restabilization, of reestablishing women's place in the home – not as the
foundation of female emancipation as Rathbone wished, but as the basis
for gender restoration. By equating motherhood with citizenship, new
feminists like Rathbone positioned the debate about women's emancipation on precisely the ground conservatives preferred. At one level, maternalism was the only game in town, and to be effective feminists also
tended to join in, appropriating the terms for their own agenda of practical reforms, rather than trying to question the consensus. But in a case
such as Britain, where the Labour party was so heavily dominated by the
trade-union big battalions, and the movement's culture so deeply in thrall
to masculinist working-class traditions, the endowment for motherhood
could only proceed by leaving the lineaments of patriarchy intact.

The best counter-example – where a much stronger socialist movement could integrate maternalist measures inside a larger vision of
reform, mobilizing its own expertise and dominating the operative social-
policy languages in the national public sphere – was Sweden. For maternalism could either disable women politically, by fixing them in the
domestic role; or it could empower them by constructing particular sites
of activity and validating women's participation. By contrast with Britain,
in Sweden the foregrounding of motherhood was not accompanied by an
attack against married women's work in the 1930s, and on the contrary
the Social Democrats consistently beat such proposals back. At the same
time, Swedish women's groups coalesced around "a host of issues, such as
paid vacations for housewives, decriminalizing contraceptives, increased
political representation of women, support for single mothers … , and
mothers' right to work," producing exceptional unity across party and
class lines, exemplified in the "Call to Swedish Women" issued by twenty-
five women's groups in 1936.[29] Crucially, the trade unions raised no opposition to the women's demands, partly because in the highly segregated
Swedish labor market women's competition posed no threat. Moreover,

the notion of the "People's Home" captured the high moral ground of the national interest for the Left in the 1930s, enabling feminist social policy experts like Alva Myrdal to bend population policy discourse for their own purposes, by hitching it to the demand for women's rights: "for women the idea of a People's Home provided ideological space for a range of policy initiatives around everyday life and social reproduction: housing policies, maternal health and welfare, and fertility."[30] The key Parliamentary Commissions on Married Women's Work and Population Policy between 1935 and 1938, which laid down progressive policies in both these areas, were decisively influenced by the new cohort of Social Democratic feminist women.

Anti-Fascism, Democratic Patriotism, and the Welfare State

Under the impact of fascism – between the Popular Front and the Cold War – the experience of women tells a familiar story. On the one hand, the Popular Fronts in France and Spain seemed to bring women into the public sphere, whether through the franchise of the Spanish Republic and the Republican cause in the Civil War, or through the French strike wave of June 1936. World War II then mobilized the rhetorics of patriotic service across Europe as a whole, organized around women's employment for the war economy in Britain, and the dangers and sacrifices of the Resistance in Nazi-occupied Europe. Wartime conditions necessarily suspended the established gender regimes, massively disrupting family life, confusing the boundaries of private and public, bringing women into normally male-defined spaces, and generally destabilizing the normativities of being a woman or a man. Yet on the other hand, after 1945 major continuities with prewar gender regimes were strongly reinstated. Although the importance of women's gains in the postwar settlement should never be underplayed (whether via the franchise or the welfare state), the place the settlement made for women was not new: Rather than full participation in democratic citizenship, *motherhood* and *domesticity* were again the mobilizing themes.

In Spain, the Popular Front immediately improved women's legal status and access to divorce, for example, including civil marriage and even voluntary abortion in Catalonia (where anarchist reformers ran the Ministry of Health and Social Assistance). Republican mobilization for war necessarily recruited women into industry and public services, including transportation (especially important for women's visibility in the cities), as well as the new collectives in agriculture, and initially women were also in the militias. But the PSOE had the usual deficit on the gender front, as Mary Nash compellingly shows, neither organizing women into party and unions (in 1932 the UGT had only 4.3 percent female membership, over a third of whom were in agriculture), nor validating their identities at work. Even female suffrage met with Socialist disdain, on the old anti-clerical grounds that women were voting fodder for the Right. Instead, women were addressed as mothers and wives, in elections and the priorities of Socialist legislation. Once the popular upsurge in 1936 was normalized into the disciplined anti-fascism advocated by the PCE, women were also repositioned into the conventional auxiliary roles (running field kitchens, washing and sewing for the troops, staffing hospitals, organizing refugees, and sustaining morale on the home front, as well as filling the vacated male jobs). The *Agrupacion de Mujeres Antifascistas* (AMA, launched in 1933, with 50,000 members in 255 locals by July 1936) was formally committed to a strong program of female emancipation (to "take the Spanish woman out of the ignorance in which the patriarchal Spanish society had held her subjugated for centuries"), but in practice concentrated wholly on such conventional modes of female address.[31] Likewise, while the anarchist *Mujeres Libres* (a coalescence of groups in Barcelona and Madrid in summer 1936) had a more developed autonomous program, committed to liberating women from their "triple enslavement to ignorance, as women, and as producers," it also ran up against the entrenched sexism of the CNT, and was still marginalized at the latter's congress of October 1938.[32] In any case, if women's organizations had at least opened a space for future work, such possibilities were brutally suspended by the Nationalist victory in the Civil War, which returned women to an unrelenting subordination for the next few decades.

The same pattern occurred in France. If women joined the 1936 strike wave, their agency was still contained by the practices of male militancy, whether in the shop floor committees or the public languages of the trade unions and the SFIO and PCF.[33] Of course, "universal suffrage," the pride of French republicanism, still denied the vote to women, and as in Spain Socialists invoked the specter of a female clericalist majority, paying lip service to democratic principle while acquiescing happily enough in the parliamentary denial of the franchise: Blum and others could hypocritically support female suffrage in the Chamber in July 1936 (where it passed by 488 to 1) in the secure knowledge that the Senate would ultimately vote it down. The broader juridical terms of citizenship served French women no better: the reformed Civil Code of 18 February 1938 removed some legal disabilities but simultaneously instated the husband as *chef de la famille*. The Resistance, and the heightened rhetorics of democratic patriotism, finally forced the issue. While the Radicals managed to keep female suffrage out of the CNR Charter of 15 March 1944, the decision of the Algiers assembly on 21 April 1944 was clear – "Women will vote and be eligible in the same way as men" (Article 17) –

and in 1945 the vote was won. In the wider field of public policy, on the other hand, women's place stayed the same. Socialists and Communists mouthed the old nostrums (productive employment as a condition of emancipation), while their trade unions perpetuated the gendered repertoire of female exclusion, family wage, and unequal pay. Women workers made few gains from the 1936 strikes (pay differentials were untouched, and female unemployment actually peaked in 1939); and in the postwar social reforms the interwar family policy consensus was simply redeployed. In the 1936 strikes, Duclos had called on "the women of France to unite for the protection of their homes" and the "future of the race," while CGT leaders applauded women strikers for "defending [our] bread, the home, the survival of our children."[34] In this sense, anti-fascist radicalism stopped at the doors of the family, and even took a conservative turn. In the later memories of working-class women, "the crisis, the recession, unemployment, newspapers, trade unions, and politics were all domains or concepts reserved for men."[35]

If we turn to the other large Catholic country of the South, Italy, where (like France and Spain) the Communist Party was also strong, we find a similar pattern. Here the Resistance had even organized women into a mass movement, the Italian Women's Organization (*Unione Donne Italiane*, UDI), which emerged from the earlier Defense Groups in September 1944. With its own journal *Noi Donne*, some 3,500 local circles, and a membership of a million by 1954, the UDI was a classic vehicle of the Togliattian alliance strategy, formally independent of the PCI, and focused on the mobilization of non-Communist and particularly Catholic women. With the Cold War, this ecumenical function became much harder to discharge (the new Christian Democrat auxiliary, the *Centro di Iniziativa Femminile*, CIF, inevitably syphoned off Catholic women), and the UDI became largely a major flanking organization of the PCI. But while Togliatti's goal of a broadly based emancipatory movement was genuine, the party's gender politics were at best unsure. Leading Communist women tended to see UDI activity as implicitly second-rank, "a form of exile from the real business of the party."[36] Moreover, the alliance strategy inscribed a particular logic of women's politics, de-emphasizing issues that might give offense (like contraception, abortion, divorce), and pushing the UDI towards the familiar ground: motherhood, child raising, family.

Italian Communists addressed the "social function" of housework and maternity in two ways: by pressing for maximum social security under the welfare state (including family allowances, in many ways the emblematic "women's gain" of the postwar settlements in Europe); and by the classic socialist route of universal technology and collectivized services – "popular housing with communal kitchens, laundries, and baths, along with the sports fields, common meeting rooms, and day care centers" that defined "the Communist model of the ideal workers' community."[37] As such, PCI policy descended directly from Red Vienna and other municipal socialisms of the prewar era. The result was an ambiguous project, which certainly broke women from the exclusive circuitry of *casa e chiesa* (home and church) and gave them public roles, but without challenging the gendered relations of families, or indeed the subordinate status of the "women's sphere" in general. Women were addressed in ultimately conservative ways:

> appeals were made to the maternal spirit of women, to their pacific spirit, to their attachment to the family, all of which were posed as "natural" characteristics of the female soul, in this way falling, more or less unconsciously, into an exaltation of the feminine role as understood in the most traditional sense.[38]

For its second Congress in 1947, the UDI chose the slogan, "For a happy family, for peace, and for work."[39]

In practice, this produced an amalgam of fixity and empowerment, old and new. While the PCI recorded high levels of female membership, for instance, reaching 25.9 percent in 1959, this was unreflected in the party's national leadership, where some 5 to 6 percent of the Central Committee and the *Direzione* were women between 1945 and the 1960s, apart from 1956 to 1962, when there were none. Communist difficulties were clearest in a city like Turin, a major bastion, but with the powerful masculinist culture of its workerist traditions. On the one hand, the CGIL unions lobbied to keep the UDI safely away from their own domain, confining its energies to the typical "women's issues." On the other hand, when the UDI embarked on its campaigns of the 1950s for equality at work, the Communist unions were too weakened by the Cold War repression to offer effective help, while the demand for regulating domestic industry was simply ignored. The archetypal "workers' city" was an extreme case of the general syndrome in this respect. One UDI circle described its aim in 1954 as "women's emancipation, which must be the human and political motif which animates all our activity." But the context remained discrete, uncoupled from the main party life. The circle met every two weeks in the house of the mother of one of the activists:

> On 8 March (Women's Day), the local girls' choir and ballet gave a performance and the trousseaus of the members who were to be married that year were put on display. Other activities included petitions for public housing and for peace, the selling of the journal *Noi Donne*, assistance to older and sick women during the winter months, solidarity with women workers sacked at the local shoe factory, the organization of a children's camp by the sea, bus trips to local museums.[40]

As in the 1920s, therefore, when the first wave of female enfranchisement did disappointingly little to dislodge the given structures of politics, women's recognition as voting citizens after 1945 failed to unlock an established gender regime. Once again the dialectic of equality and difference supervened: even as women exercised their new political rights, the postwar social legislation tracked them out of the public domain. The main logic of postwar social reform fixed women firmly in the familial sphere of the home. "During marriage most women will not be gainfully employed," Beveridge had declared flatly, and European welfare legislation constitutively privileged the male "breadwinner" in his delivery of the "family wage."[41] This inability of the Left to escape the prevailing maternalist frame after 1945, I would argue, prefigured a more general loss of vitality. For it marked the outer limits of the popular democratic expansiveness which the remarkably successful anti-fascist politics of the 1940s claimed to connote. Where Communists reached out to progressives and non-proletarian social groups with great flexibility and often much success, women tended to be addressed very conventionally, while social democrats cleaved even closer to the conservatively gendered terrain. In principle, and according to its own lights, the socialist tradition had always promised a very far-reaching liberation of women, and could do so persuasively in the context of an overall transformative societal project. But, individual exceptions notwithstanding, combinations of sexism, misogyny, the separation of spheres, and simple indifference on the part of heavily masculine movements remained the main story.

The gap between the forms of women's recognition – as citizen participants in the democratic nation – and the place accorded them in the postwar settlement, even in the strong Scandinavian example, is crucial to the overall thematics of this volume. On the one hand, it's clear that in World War II the barriers to women became reduced. In 1938 Florence Keyworth, then a respectable working-class teenager in flight from her parents' nonconformist religion, had been rebuffed from the Young Communist League by its exclusively masculine culture of trade-union militancy; but four years later, toughened via the League of Nations Union and the Left Book Club, and sustained by the wartime expansion of women's public roles, she joined the CP with two women friends, becoming a journalist on the *Daily Worker* in 1945.[42] In Nazi-occupied Europe, women's Resistance activity could also be strong: thus in Italy an estimated 70,000 women joined the Defense Groups, and 35,000 fought with the partisans.[43] In this context, the PCI moved away from its exclusive focus on working women, stressing the origins of women's oppression in the family and civil society as well as the economy, and allowing women a stronger place in the rhetorics (written and visual) of anti-fascist liberation.[44]

Yet on the other hand, as we've seen, by 1950 the separation of spheres was restored. In Britain during the war, women's politics were already being focused mainly on social services, particularly the provision of day nurseries, nursery schools, and municipal restaurants for the working mother, and after 1945 defending these gains against closure was also the key aim. Moreover, as Florence Keyworth says, the hierarchy of value had not changed: "many Communist women (I was one) decided we were not interested in 'women's work' which we despised." Above all, the labor movement's masculinity remained a default characteristic: in Yorkshire, the CPGB subsisted in the occupational cultures of the Engineering and Mining Unions, from which women were excluded; and at a week-long party school in Rotherham in 1944, Keyworth was the only woman in a class with seventeen men.[45] The high unemployment of the Depression had already marginalized women as workers, but after 1945 full employment added its own new twist: women's politics were now almost wholly subsumed by the family form, whether through the breadwinner rhetorics and the family wage, restrictive trade-union practices for married women, or the prevailing welfare-state paradigm. As far as any feminist construction of women's interests was concerned, therefore, after 1945 social democratic parties were starting to lose their status as a magnet for general progressive aspirations.

This is the important general point. The key strength of the Communist parties in the era of anti-fascism, and *mutatis mutandis* of the social democratic parties in Britain, the Low Countries, and Scandinavia during the same time, was their appeal to general progressive sentiment, and their ability to rally a general coalition of democracy and reform, which outgrew the normal limits of a labor party based on the working class. The Left emerged from the Liberation – sometimes as a coalition of Communists and Socialists, sometimes extending to Christian Democracy, and occasionally (as in Britain) as a single dominant party – exercising moral leadership in the nation, refashioning the people-nation in a democratic image, and ordering a varied repertoire of progressive causes around the central Keynesian-welfare-statist or state-socialist projects, or *hegemonizing* them, to use Gramsci's term. In this respect, the maternalist normalizing of politics in relation to women amounts to an enormous failure. The politics of anti-fascism, otherwise so creative in transcending vanguardism and the Left's class-political ghetto, settled all too easily into conservative political repetitions of existing working-class attitudes when it came to women. In this respect, the patriotic dimensions of the wartime consensus, which privileged older notations of gender (men soldiering, women keeping the home fires burning), played a key role. As in World War I, women were wrenched out of domesticity by wartime mobilizations, brought into employment and other public roles, and called upon for a commitment to the collective good. This process was motivated implicitly by a promise of citizenship, of equality in the nation at the war's end. Yet by 1950, women were back in the old subordinate place.

Conclusion: Maternalism's Limits

The 1940s and 1950s were an intermediate time for women, suspended between the novelty of juridically equal citizenship and the normalizing of a subordinated domesticity, in a gender regime of public and private, which for women entailed the opposite of emancipated personhood. In both its positive and its disabling characteristics, this situation had been fashioned by socialist parties. Here the maternalist framing for so much of the welfare-state legislation, especially in its strongest pro-natalist versions, including the classic social democratic valuing of the working-class child, was key, because even the most radical approaches worked with a distinction between housewife-mothers (the "real" mothers working-class women should have the right to become) and women who worked (younger women, childless women, women able to purchase child care). In fact, such approaches made their priority the enabling of lower-paid workers to stay at home, as opposed to middle-class career women or better-paid female workers, who could afford to buy child care services; and this same outlook further solidified the popular identification of "feminism" with single or childless professional women. In this way and many others, the social democratic achievement of the welfare state – and the languages of social citizenship as they emerged from the postwar settlement in Western Europe – constructed a domesticated and dependent place for women.

This was not a necessary outcome. In theory, the structural requirements of the postwar capitalist recovery (the expanding labor market and the availability of female labor) and related innovations from the war (nursery provision for mothers mobilized for industry) might have sustained an alternative development. But in the end, the ideal of the full-time housewife-mother, supplied with social services, free milk and orange juice, and educated into technical competence, dividing responsibilities with the husband-breadwinner bringing home the wage, carried the day. The elaboration of powerful specialized and common-sense knowledges concerning the needs of children and mothering by John Bowlby and others, via theories of maternal deprivation, and attachment and loss, helped secure this consensus.[46] The continuing trend towards increased participation of women in the economy, via employment, higher education, and consumer spending, which over the longer term redefined women's relation to the public world, was thereby obscured. Even the most politically conscious of left-wing women found it hard to escape.

The exclusion of radical possibilities, amidst so much conformity around the family during the later 1940s and early 1950s, was also an effect of the Cold War. The mobilizing of patriotic sentiments for the struggle against Communism after 1947, in distorted continuity with the anti-fascist solidarities of World War II, inevitably found the rhetorics of family and home attractive, suturing an idealized domesticity to the threatened security of the nation and its way of life, only recently salvaged from the ravages of the fascists. If women were positioned as mothers in this discursive economy, men were not only constructed as fathers, but more powerfully as the bearers of public responsibility, in a rigidly elaborated system of gender differences. Of course, there are other ways of telling the story of the interwar years in relation to the post-1945 histories of gender, and in this respect the future explosion of radical possibilities in the 1960s and after, when women's circumstances received a decisively different political articulation, are sharply illuminated by the discussions of sex reform in the socialist movements of the 1920s by Grossmann, Nash, and other contributors to this book. If we consider the areas of sexuality and recreation, in the emergent consumer economies and mass entertainment cultures of the interwar years, in which young people and the "new woman" in particular found new forms of subjectivity, the relationship between "women" and "socialism" may be differently addressed, even if the forms of political realization became largely suppressed.[47] More to the point, perhaps, when the contemporary women's movements of Europe emerged during the 1970s the socialist parties had virtually little to say. It was here, in the fracturing of socialism's relationship to feminism, that the maternalist normalizations discussed above had their long-term negative effect.

In this sense, sexualities, as well as gender relations more broadly, remained the uncharted territories of socialist politics in the mid-twentieth century, despite the radical potentials glimpsed in the 1920s. They were the unreflected ground of a conservatism that became more visible and limiting in the next broad phase of the Left's history, after 1968. When the organ of populist Labour identification, the *Daily Mirror,* urged British women to "Vote for Him," meaning their soldier husbands, in the 1945 election, it not only sold the promise of female citizenship blatantly short, but also bespoke an entire universe of gendered social and political assumptions. After the interlude of independence in World War II, of self-confident entry into the nation's public goods, the normalizing of postwar life into structures of domesticity was bound to be experienced by many women as a contraction:

> Come 1945: a letter in the post one Friday morning: "This nursery shuts today (for good) at 6 p.m. Please remove all your belongings with your child this

evening." And I was a single parent; no more nurseries. The Government needed jobs for the returning heroes; women had to make their homes and beautify them with feminine charm (up the birthrate). Came Macmillan and we'd never had it so good. Came Bowlby who told us that it was all our fault if anything went wrong with our children's lives if we left them for any time at all. Came demand feeding, babies inseparable from mothers on slings around our backs and fronts; came television, washing machines, and durable goods to make us feel wanted in the home. Came Do It Yourself. Came Guilt – never think of yourself as a person, never have sex outside marriage, never never never leave your child, be content with Uncle Government's lovely domestic hardware; never breathe a word of the orgiastic nights on the gun site (or the warmth of the all-women's residential Nissan huts and officers' buildings, not a man for miles).

Just remember, everything is always your fault. You don't have rights. The children have rights. The children are always right. You are always wrong. Just get on and do the washing and bake a cake. Don't speak. Be silent. You are no one (except a machine to spend money).[48]

Notes

1. The democratic gains of 1945 from the aspect of women's suffrage should not be underestimated, given the fragility of the gender egalitarianism inscribed in the post-1918 settlement. Not only were women never enfranchised in Italy, France, and Belgium, but elsewhere the political equality of women only lasted for fifteen to twenty years before being taken away. Only in Britain and Scandinavia was there some minimal continuity of female suffrage, extending back to World War I.
2. See Joan Wallach Scott, *Only Paradoxes to Offer: French Feminists and the Rights of Man* (Cambridge, Mass., 1996), p. 161.
3. Gail Warshofsky Lapidus, *Women in Soviet Society: Equality, Development, and Social Change* (Berkeley and Los Angeles, 1978), p. 66.
4. Ibid., p. 72.
5. In the Soviet model, women's delegates were elected in the factories and the villages to form assemblies that were then apprenticed to state, party, or trade union agencies to facilitate women's administrative training and political education.
6. Judith Adler Hellman, *Journeys among Women: Feminism in Five Italian Cities* (New York, 1987), pp. 31-32.
7. In the words of one woman Communist, recruited in Glasgow as a student before marrying a party official in London in 1922: "No, it [the Tottenham branch] didn't have a Women's Section. As a matter of fact Women's Sections were rather frowned on at that time, because people thought that women and men should work ... in equality, no difference." See Sue Bruley, *Leninism, Stalinism, and the Women's Movement in Britain, 1920-1939* (New York, 1986), p. 116.

8. Ibid., p. 118.
9. Ibid., pp. 122-25, 118.
10. Ibid., p. 136.
11. For the role of feminists in the CP's foundation, see ibid., pp. 63-64. See also Sheila Rowbotham, *A New World for Women: Stella Browne – Socialist Feminist* (London, 1977).
12. Silvia Kontos, *Die Partei kämpft wie ein Mann. Frauenpolitik der KPD in der Weimarer Republik* (Frankfurt, 1979), p. 134.
13. Ibid., p. 210 (*Rote Fahne*, 27 November 1921).
14. Ibid., p. 219. The typical pattern was to call a public meeting of women, which then marched to city offices to present demands for concrete measures against price rises or shortages. A women's control committee would be formed, or else women would be delegated to the existing committee.
15. Ibid., pp. 222-23.
16. Ibid., pp. 145-49.
17. See here Stuart Macintyre, *Little Moscows: Communism and Working-Class Militancy in Inter-War Britain* (London, 1980).
18. Ute Daniel, *Arbeiterfrauen in der Kriegsgesellschaft. Beruf, Familie und Politik im Ersten Weltkrieg* (Göttingen, 1989), p. 152.
19. Susan Pedersen, "Gender, Welfare, and Citizenship in Britain during the Great War," *American Historical Review* 95 (1990): 996, 998.
20. Ibid.: 991-1000. See also Lucy Bland, "In the Name of Protection: The Policing of Women in the First World War," in *Women-in-Law: Explorations in Law, Family, and Sexuality*, eds. Julia Brophy and Carol Smart (London, 1985), pp. 23-49.
21. See especially David Crew, "German Socialism, the State, and Family Policy, 1918-1933," *Continuity and Change* 1 (1986): 235-63.
22. Dietmar Klenkes, *Die SPD-Linke in der Weimarer Republik. Eine Untersuchung zu den regionalen organisatorischen Grundlagen und zur politischen Praxis und Theoriebildung des linken Flügels der SPD in den Jahren 1922-1932*, vol. 2 (Münster, 1983), p. 853. See also Mary Nolan, "'Housework Made Easy': The Taylorized Housewife in Weimar Germany's Rationalized Economy," *Feminist Studies* 16 (1990): 549-78; Helmut Gruber, "Sexuality in 'Red Vienna': Socialist party Conceptions and Programs and Working-Class Life, 1920-1934," *International Labor and Working-Class History* 31 (1987): 37-68.
23. In 1908 national legislation in Germany allowed women to join and form political organizations properly for the first time.
24. Jean H. Quataert, *Reluctant Feminists in German Social Democracy, 1885-1917* (Princeton, 1979), p. 222. Seven of the SPD's nineteen female parliamentarians in January 1919 had followed this route before 1914. Quataert characterizes them collectively as a "second-generation female leadership" typified by Marie Juchacz. Eleven of the nineteen were born in 1875 or after.
25. Ibid., p. 223, quoting the proceedings of the 1921 SPD women's conference in Görlitz.
26. Pat Thane, "The Women of the British Labour Party and Feminism, 1906-1945," in *British Feminism in the Twentieth Century*, ed. Harold L. Smith (Aldershot, 1990), p. 136.
27. "Most women," argued Rathbone, "were and would continue to be primarily wives and mothers. The problem was not their role, but the fact that their work – unlike that of bus drivers or businessmen – was undervalued and unpaid. True equality meant freeing these women from economic dependence on their husbands by granting equal honor and financial support to their work in

'women's sphere.' This could not be done through 'old feminist' campaigns for equal pay and open access to men's jobs; labor market reforms would not answer the needs of the unwaged. Only State intervention could do so; welfare programs could circumvent the labor market to provide the independent support for mothers." This is Susan Pedersen's paraphrase of Rathbone's argument in her Presidential Address to the National Union of Societies for Equal Citizenship, 11 March 1925, "The Old and the New Feminism." See Pedersen, "The Failure of Feminism in the Making of the British Welfare State," *Radical History Review* 43 (1989): 86.

28. Ibid., p. 104.
29. Barbara Hobson, "Feminist Strategies and Gendered Discourses in Welfare States: Married Women's Right to Work in the United States and Sweden," in *Mothers of a New World. Maternalist Policies and the Origins of Welfare States*, eds. Seth Koven and Sonya Michel (New York, 1993), p. 403. The Social Democratic Women's Union boosted its membership from 7,302 to 26,882 during 1930 to 1940. The National Association of Housemothers, on the conservative end of this coalition, grew from 10,000 to 23,550.
30. Ibid., p. 412.
31. Martha A. Ackelsberg, "Women and the Politics of the Spanish Popular Front: Political Mobilization or Social Revolution?," *International Labor and Working-Class History* 30 (fall 1986): 8.
32. Martha A. Ackelsberg, *Free Women of Spain. Anarchism and the Struggle for the Emancipation of Women* (Bloomington, Ind., 1991), p. 1.
33. See Sian Reynolds, "Women, Men, and the 1936 Strikes in France," in *The French and Spanish Popular Fronts. Comparative Perspectives*, eds. Martin S. Alexander and Helen Graham (Cambridge, Mass., 1989), pp. 185-200.
34. Ibid., p. 199.
35. Catherine Rhein, "Jeunes femmes au travail dans le Paris de l'entre-deux-guerres" (Ph.D. Diss., University of Paris VII, 1977), cited by Reynolds, "Women, Men, and the 1936 Strikes," p. 199.
36. Hellman, *Journeys Among Women*, p. 35.
37. Ibid., p. 39.
38. Mariester Negro, "Il PCI e la Questione Femminile," (M.A. thesis, University of Turin, 1977), p. 434, quoted by Hellman, *Journeys Among Women*, p. 40.
39. Paul Ginsborg, *A History of Contemporary Italy. Society and Politics 1943-1988* (London, 1990), p. 85.
40. Ibid., p. 196.
41. See Lynne Segal, "'The Most Important Thing of All – Rethinking the Family: An Overview," in *What Is To Be Done About the Family?*, ed. Segal (Harmondsworth, 1983), p. 19.
42. Florence Keyworth, "Invisible Struggles: The Politics of Aging," in *Feminism, Culture, and Politics*, eds. Rosalind Brunt and Caroline Rowan (London, 1982), pp. 137-38, 135.
43. Anna Maria Bruzzone, "Women in the Italian Resistance," in *Our Common History. The Transformation of Europe*, ed. Paul Thompson (London, 1982), p. 282. An estimated 623 women were executed or died in the field, while 7,403 were arrested or deported to Germany.
44. See especially Eric D. Weitz, "The Heroic Man and the Ever-Changing Woman: Gender and Politics in European Communism, 1917-1950," in *Gender and Class in Modern Europe*, eds. Laura L. Frader and Sonya O. Rose (Ithaca, N.Y. and London, 1996), pp. 311-52. Weitz finds much greater flexibility in the PCI than in

the PCF and KPD on the gender front, and uses visual representations (especially posters) to make his point.

45. Keyworth, "Invisible Struggles," p. 139.

46. For a complex discussion of this ideological context, see especially the writings of Denise Riley, "The Free Mothers: Pronatalism and Working Mothers in Industry at the End of the Last War in Britain," *History Workshop Journal* 11 (spring 1981): 59-118; and *War in the Nursery. Theories of the Child and the Mother* (London, 1983); also Nikolas Rose, *Governing the Soul. The Shaping of the Private Self* (London, 1989), pp. 151-77.

47. See above all, Atina Grossmann, *Reforming Sex: The German Movement for Birth Control and Abortion Reform 1920-1950* (New York, 1995); Jill Julius Matthews, "They Had Such a Lot of Fun: The Women's League of Health and Beauty between the Wars," *History Workshop Journal* 30 (autumn 1990): 22-54; Sally Alexander, "Becoming a Woman in London in the 1920s and '30s," in *Becoming a Woman and Other Essays in 19th and 20th Century Feminist History* (New York, 1995), pp. 203-24.

48. Pauline Long, "Speaking Out on Age," *Spare Rib* 82 (May 1979), quoted by Gail Braybon and Penny Summerfield, *Out of the Cage. Women's Experiences in Two World Wars* (London, 1987), p. 280.

List of Contributors

❧

Christine Bard is Maître de conference at the Université d'Angers. She has published *Les filles de Marianne: Histoire des féminismes entre deux guerres* (Paris, 1994), has edited *Madeleine Pelletier*, (Paris, 1993), and has written articles on feminism, welfare, and citizenship.

Ida Blom is Professor of Women's History, University of Bergen. Her publications include *Cappelens kvinnehistorie* (Cross-Cultural Women's History), 3 vols. (Oslo, 1992 to 1993)and *Den haarde Dyst* (Birth Practices & Help in Norway) (Oslo, 1988). She has written numerous articles on women, maternity, and gender in Scandinavian and English language journals. Member, Norwegian National Commission for UNESCO, 1983 to 1992; Member, advisor board of *Gender*, *L'Homme*, *Nora*; President, International Federation for Research in Women's History.

Hilda Romer Christensen is Associate Research Professor, Department of Sociology, University of Copenhagen. She has published: *Among Flappers & Respectable Girls: Gender & Culture in the Danish YWCA* (Aarhus, 1993); *Women Power and Health* (Aarhus, 1991); "The Social-Democratic Youth Movement & the 'New Woman' in the Interwar Period," in *Arbejderkvinder I Bevaagelse* (Copenhagen, 1992); "Kammerat Tinka," *Aarbog for Arbejderbe vaegelsens Historie* (Gender Ideology within Danish Social-democratic Youth) (1986). She is also Coordinator of Women's & Gender Studies, Denmark.

Denise De Weerdt is Chief Librarian (emeritus), Royal Library, Brussels, and Collaborator, Archive and Museum of the Socialist Workers' Movement, Gent. Her publications include: (ed.) *"We are the New Generation: Socialists and Sexuality"* (East Flanders, 1998); *Socialisme en* *socialistische arbeidersbeweging in Belgie* (Gent, 1988); "100 jaar Internationale Vrouwenraad en feminisme in Belgie," *Stem der Vrouw* 73 (1988).

Geoff Eley is Professor of History, University of Michigan, and Member, Executive Comm. of the Council for European Studies. He has edited *Society, Culture, and the State in Germany, 1870-1930* (New York, 1996) and published *Wilhelminismus, Nationalismus, Faschismus: Zur historischen Kontinuität in Deutschland* (Münster, 1991; "Labor History, Social History, *Alltagsgeschichte*: Experience Culture, and the Politics of the Everyday," *The Journal of Modern History* 61, 2 (1989); and numerous journal articles on Germany, fascism, labor.

Renée Frangeur is Assistant, Department of History, University of Gotenburg; and Teacher of Women's Studies in folk high schools. She has published *Pro and Contra Exclusion of Married Women from the Labor Market: A Struggle in Interwar Sweden* (in press); articles in *Historisk tidskrift* (1995), *Arbetarhistoria* (1996-7); and co-authored *Women and the Practice of Teaching* (1993).

Mary Gibson is Professor of History, John Jay College/CUNY and Deputy Exec. Ph.D. Program in Criminal Justice, CUNY. Her publications include: *Prostitution and the State in Italy* (New Brunswick, N.J., 1986, Italian ed. 1995); "On the Insensitivity of Women: Science and the Woman Question in Liberal Italy," *Journal of Women's History* 2, 2 (1990); "Female Sexuality in Renaissance, Early Modern, and Modern Italy," in Bargot Badran and Midge Quandt (eds.), *Sex, History, and Culture* (Binghamton, N.Y., 1990); numerous conference papers.

Pamela Graves is Assistant Professor of History, Eastern Michigan University. She has published *Labour Women: Women in British Working-Class Politics, 1918-1939* (New York, 1993). Her current research focuses on the impact of World War I on working-class women in organized labor politics.

Atina Grossmann is Associate Professor of History, The Cooper Union. Her publications include: *Reforming Sex: The German Movement for Birth Control and Abortion Reform 1920-1950* (New York, 1995); "Zum Mythos der 'neuen Frau': Thesen zur Ursache und Bedeutung des Klischees," *Fräulein vom Amt* (Frankfurt/Main, in press); "Feminist Debates about Women and National Socialism," *Gender and History* 3 (autumn 1991); numerous conference papers.

Helmut Gruber is Charles S. Baylis Professor of History emeritus, Polytechnic University, New York. He has published *Red Vienna: Experiment in Working-Class Culture, 1919-1934* (New York, 1991); *Léon Blum, French Socialism, and the Popular Front: A Case of Internal Contradictions* (Ithaca, N.Y., 1986); numerous articles and conference papers on the European working class, Socialist parties, and internationals. He is co-editor of the *International Labor & Working-Class History, 1983-present*; chair, Columbia University Seminar in History of the Working Class, 1976 to 1988; member of Executive Comm., International Conference of Historians of the Labor Movement, Vienna, 1981-90; organizer (with Patrick Fridenson) of international colloquia on "Working Class & Sociability" (1985) & "Working Class & Mass Culture" (1988) at the Maison des sciences de l'homme, Paris.

Ulla Jansz is Assistant Professor of Feminist History, University of Utrecht. Publications include: "Women or Workers?: The 1889 Labor Law & the Debate on Protective Legislation in the Netherlands," in *Protecting Women: Labor Legislation in Europe, the United States, and Australia, 1880-1920*, edited by Ulla Wikander et al. (Chicago, 1995); "Sex & the Social Question in Political History: The Labor Law of 1889," *Op het strijdtoneel van der politiek* (Nijmegen, 1991); *Thoughts about Sex in the First Feminist Wave* (Amsterdam, 1990). Her current research focuses on gender and the origins of the modern Dutch welfare state.

Mary Nash is Professor of Contemporary History, University of Barcelona, and co-editor of *Arenal*. She has published *Defining Male Civilization: Women in the Spanish Civil War* (Denver, Colo., 1995); *Experiencias Desiguales: Conflictos sociales y respuestas colectival* (Madrid, 1994); "Marginality & Social Change: Legal Abortion in Catalonia during the Spanish Civil War," *Marginated Groups in Spanish & Portuguese History* (Minneapolis, Minn., 1989); "Social Eugenics & Nationalist Race Hygiene in Early 20th Century Spain," *History of European Ideas* 15, 4-6 (1992). Her current research focuses on gender, multiculturalism, identity politics, and citizenship in Spain.

Michelle Perrot is Professor of History, University of Paris VII, emeritus. Publications include: *Histoire des femmes en occident*, 5 vols. (edited with Georges Duby) (Paris, 1992); (ed.) *History of Private Life in the 19th Century*, vol. 4 (Cambridge, Mass., 1990); (ed.) *Writing Women's History* (Oxford, 1992); *Femmes publiques* (Paris, 1997); (ed.) *Femmes et histoire* (Paris, 1993); numerous books, articles, and conference papers on nineteenth-century France, focusing on women, prisons, the family, gender, feminist theory and work in particular. In addition, she is the doyenne and moving spirit of women's studies in France.

Jean-Louis Robert is Professor of History, University of Orleans, and member, editorial board of *Le Mouvement Social*. He has published *Nous crions grâce* (Paris, 1990); *Le Congrès de Tours* (Paris, 1990); and numerous articles and conference papers on French labor, and Socialist and Communist parties.

Adelheid von Saldern is Professor of History, University of Hannover. Publications include: (ed.) *Amerikanisierung: Traum und Alptraum im Deutchland des 20. Jahrhunderts* (Stuttgart, 1996); *Häuserleben: Zur Geschichte städtischen Arbeiterwohnens vom Kaiserreich bis heute* (Bonn, 1995); *Neues Wohnen in Hannover: Wohnungspolitik und Wohnkultur im Hannover der Weimarer Republik* (Hannover, 1993); *Auf den Wege zum Arbeiterreformismus: Parteialltag in sozialdemokratischer Provinz* (Frankfurt, 1984); numerous articles and conference papers on: workers' domestic culture and housing; workers' subcultures; popular and mass culture; the role of women.

Louise A. Tilly is Michael E. Gellert Professor of History and Sociology at the Graduate Faculty, New School for Social Research, New York. She edited with Jytte Klaussen, *European Integration in Social & Historical Perspective* (London, 1997); *Politics and Class in Milan, 1881-1901* (Oxford, 1992); edited with John Gillis and David Levine, *The European Experience of Fertility Decline: The Quiet Revolution* (London, 1992); edited with Patricia Gurin, *Women, Politics, and Change* (New York, 1990). Other activities include: President, American Historical Association, 1993-94; co-editor, *International Labor & Working-Class History*, 1994-; organizer with Patrick Fridenson of International Colloquia on "Tradition & the Working Class" and "Citizenship & Workers" at the Maison des sciences de l'homme, Paris: 1991 and 1994; on "Migration and the Working Class" at the Institute for Social History in Amersterdam: 1997.

Index

Name Index

Subject Index

Subject Index by Country

Austria

Belgium

Britain

The Netherlands